Praise for *Endzone*

"This is an obvious must-read for University of Michigan fans but is also recommended to anyone interested in college sports, university administration, and organizational leadership."   —*Library Journal*

"John Bacon is deservedly regarded as the poet laureate of Michigan football, but his writing is essential to anyone who wants to understand how a big-time college sport works and why it is stuck in hearts even when it makes us crazy."   —Joe Drape, author of *New York Times* bestseller *Our Boys: A Perfect Season on the Plains with the Smith Center Redmen*

"I did not skip from the beginning to the end. I kept reading, saying to myself, 'I just want to see where this is going.' Soon I realized I was going on the whole trip, so interesting was the narrative about Dave Brandon, so deep and thorough was the research, so fascinating were the roles the two student government leaders played, so compelling was the story of the punter who lost his way before finding himself with, almost ironically, Brandon's compassionate support. To sum it up: *Endzone* is plain excellent."
                    —Phil Hersh, award-winning Olympic and college sports reporter

"No person is more qualified to tell the story of the milestones and missteps in Michigan's football programs than John Bacon, who has the sources, relationships, and storytelling mastery to pull back the curtain at an institution where the curtain is thick. *Endzone* provides a fascinating view into a powerful and successful program that, for a while, lost its way."
                    —Joe Schad, ESPN college football insider

"John Bacon has fast become the preeminent documentarian of all things Michigan football and this is just the latest in a long line of must-read material."   —Rich Eisen, lead host of the NFL Network and author of *Total Access*

"Jim Harbaugh always has been one of the most intriguing figures in all of football, the NFL or college. *Endzone* brings them together, helping to understand what motivated Harbaugh to leave the successful San Francisco 49ers for the struggling Michigan Wolverines, and why Michigan fans have received him as their savior."   —Adam Schefter, ESPN NFL insider

"More than just the story of how Jim Harbaugh came home to Ann Arbor, *Endzone* takes readers deep inside one of college football's most storied programs at a critical moment of uncertainty and tumult. Bacon's incisive reporting reveals details even die-hard fans couldn't know about what went wrong with Michigan football and who emerged to fix it."

—Stephen Henderson, *Detroit Free Press* columnist and editorial page editor, Pulitzer Prize winner for commentary, and U-M class of '92

"You should read it. If you are a Michigan fan, you should read it. If you are a rival fan, you should read it. If you are part of any organization that has customers and/or employees, you should read it. If you are a fan of a college football team you should read it, then try to get your athletic director to read it.

The lasting lesson of *Endzone* is that one man can't do anything, but many can. It teaches that loyalty out of love is greater than loyalty out of fear and that either is a weak substitute for morality. It teaches that candor is virtue, that authenticity is recognizable, and that a person or a program's aspirations are every bit as important as their accomplishments."

—Seth Fisher, MGoBlog

ENDZONE

ALSO BY JOHN U. BACON

Three and Out
Fourth and Long
Bo's Lasting Lessons
America's Corner Store
Blue Ice
Cirque Du Soleil: The Spark

ENDZONE

THE RISE, FALL, AND RETURN OF
MICHIGAN FOOTBALL

JOHN U. BACON

ST. MARTIN'S GRIFFIN ⚞ NEW YORK

www.stmartins.com

Designed by Steven Seighman

Library of Congress Control Number: 2015950616

ISBN 978-1-250-07897-1 (hardcover)
ISBN 978-1-4668-9154-8 (e-book)
ISBN 978-1-250-07932-9 (trade paperback)

Our books may be purchased in bulk for promotional, educational, or business use. Please contact your local bookseller or the Macmillan Corporate and Premium Sales Department at 1-800-221-7945, extension 5442, or by e-mail at MacmillanSpecial Markets@macmillan.com.

First St. Martin's Griffin Edition: October 2016

10 9 8 7 6 5 4 3 2

For Christie

When people tell me I've outkicked my coverage,
and they always do, they have no idea how far.

With admiration, gratitude, and love—always.

CONTENTS

PART VI: 2014
THE FALL

PART VII: 2014
THE RETURN

XII • CONTENTS

PREFACE

The jet cut through the clouds and eased onto the airstrip at Detroit Metro Airport, just a few miles from where Charles Lindbergh once tested World War II bombers.

This plane's mission wasn't nearly so serious, of course. But the joy it gave to the people below seemed to exceed just about everything since V-J Day.

The jet's cargo happened to be one James Joseph Harbaugh. He's just a football coach, but that day he had done what so many experts said he would never do, right up until the minute he did it: leave the bright lights, big cities, and even bigger money of the NFL for the cornfields and college towns of the Big Ten. This decision—so mystifying to NFL reporters—explains why the masses might have been forgiven if they mistook Harbaugh for their savior.

But why did Harbaugh make that decision—and how did he even get the chance?

Most reporters kept saying there was no way Jim Harbaugh would ever bypass the NFL for Ann Arbor. It turns out their doubts were well founded—but not for the reasons they offered. The odds against Harbaugh's return really were astronomical—but when a stunning series of departmental mistakes inspired a grassroots effort for reform, bold leaders stepped in to remove each obstacle, one by one. That it all happened just in time for Michigan to offer Harbaugh the chance to come home completed a chain of events that would have been impossible for anyone to predict even six months earlier.

That chain actually reaches back more than a century.

The University of Michigan was founded in 1817, and a band of students formed the school's first football team in 1879. The two have been inextricably linked ever since.

The university boasts world-renowned professors, researchers, and alumni—500,000 strong, more than any university in the world—with an endowment fast approaching $10 billion, and a QS Ranking as the nation's top public university.

That university also claims the iconic banner, the band, and the Big House—the biggest stadium in North America—not to mention "The Victors," the winged helmet, and the most wins in college football.

Arguably the nation's greatest public university and its greatest college football program can both be found on the same campus in Ann Arbor, Michigan.

Michigan students, lettermen, alumni, faculty, and fans take a great deal of pride in that unique combination—and they watch the source of their pride very closely. They believe it's not just Michigan's victories that matter—on and off the field—but the values behind them that are so important, values that place a premium on community, achievement, and integrity.

When they feel those values are threatened, they rise to defend them.

When dawn broke on Friday, November 17, 2006, the Michigan Wolverines stood atop the college football world.

They had notched the most wins in the sport's history (871), the highest winning percentage (.735), the most conference titles (43) in the sport's oldest, most storied league, the biggest stadium (107,501), the largest crowds—exceeding 100,000 for 251 straight games, going back to 1975—the biggest revenues and, many believed, the most respect.

That morning, the Wolverines stood at 11–0, and were ranked second in the nation. A win over top-ranked Ohio State the next day, in the first "Game of the Century," would give them a shot at a twelfth national title, which would provide a fine springboard for the complete renovation of the stadium, ensuring the Big House would remain the nation's biggest and most profitable, for years to come.

Retired coach Bo Schembechler, the program's patriarch, gave the team a vintage speech Thursday night. But he did not spend much time on that weekend's game, or the stakes involved. Instead, he talked to them about what it means to be a Michigan Man, and how becoming one was the ultimate goal of everyone in that room.

In Ann Arbor, life couldn't get much better.

The next morning, Friday, November 17, 2006, Bo Schembechler died from heart failure. For Michigan fans, the bad news has lasted almost a decade.

The next day, Michigan lost a nail-biter, 42–39, to Ohio State—then dropped the next three straight, including the 2007 season opener against Appalachian State, still considered the greatest upset in the history of college football.

When head coach Lloyd Carr retired after that season, Michigan hired Rich Rodriguez, whose troubled three-year run produced a 15–22 record and a fractured fan base. In 2011, little-known Brady Hoke replaced Rodriguez and enjoyed a honeymoon season when the Wolverines beat the Buckeyes for the first time in eight years, and won a BCS bowl for the first time in twelve, to finish 11–2. But the next three seasons, the program slid steadily downhill, culminating in a 5–7 record in 2014, and Hoke's dismissal.

Since the day Schembechler died eight years earlier to Hoke's firing on December 2, 2014, mighty Michigan had gone 55–48 overall, and 24–33 in the Big Ten—not the kind of numbers that had made Michigan the envy of its peers. Once the pride of a powerful conference, the Wolverines had become also-rans in an often overlooked league.

When the football program collapsed into almost unrecognizable mediocrity, its fall pulled the university itself into conflict, controversy, and crisis.

What went so wrong, so fast?

The losses, fans could see. But most of the problems that led to those losses were invisible to the public—as were their solutions, and the people who conceived them.

On January 5, 2010, University of Michigan's president, Mary Sue Coleman, announced she had hired former Michigan football player, university Regent, and Domino's Pizza CEO Dave Brandon, ahead of three experienced athletic directors with strong Michigan ties, to become Michigan's eleventh athletic director. She introduced him as the "ideal candidate."

Brandon put his guiding principle, "If it ain't broke, break it!" to work as soon as he took office, transforming Michigan's rock-solid 135-year-old operation into a dazzling money machine, pushing revenues roughly 50 percent higher in just a few years, up to $150 million.

But Brandon also replaced loyal, experienced employees who had built great relationships with the students, the lettermen, the fans, and the media, with outsiders who quickly alienated all those groups. Just four years into Brandon's tenure, the money started drying up, the fans stopped filling the Big House, and just about everyone was bailing on Brandon's vision. In October of 2014, the students held a campus rally outside the home of recently hired President Mark Schlissel to demand he fire Dave Brandon.

It was not simply the 2014 team's 2–3 record to that point that had them upset, or they would have been asking for Hoke to be fired, not Brandon. It went deeper than that: They no longer had confidence the athletic director represented the values of the university they loved.

In different ways and at different times, the many constituents of Michigan football reached the same conclusion: This is not Michigan.

Something had to give. But could anyone make the needed changes fast enough to prevent a truly disastrous 2015 season, on and off the field, and avoid missing out on Michigan's slim chance to hire Jim Harbaugh?

Why Michigan pined for Jim Harbaugh is simple: He had been raised in the Michigan tradition, he'd embodied those values while quarterbacking the Wolverines to a Big Ten title, and he had since become the hottest coach in the country, leading the San Francisco 49ers to three straight NFC title games.

But why Harbaugh wanted to return to his beleaguered alma mater was harder to see—and most observers dismissed even the possibility that Harbaugh would consider leaving the NFL to captain Michigan's sinking ship. If Harbaugh wasn't going to stay in San Francisco, surely he would accept the riches of another major-market NFL team looking to land the nation's most wanted coach.

But if you knew Jim Harbaugh, and the hold Michigan had always had on him, the idea of turning down the big time for small town Ann Arbor wasn't so far-fetched. Countless people, both inside the university and out, worked to fix what had been broken, to make that marriage irresistible to both parties.

If Harbaugh had gone to New York, Chicago, or Oakland, he'd still have been a great coach—and he probably would have been fired one day. But his boosters made it clear that if he returned to Michigan, he'd be greeted as a savior.

For all college football's commercial trappings—including NFL-style coaching salaries—its fans still believe their favorite sport is less a business than a religion. This is why Penn State, Ohio State, and Michigan draw almost twice as many fans as the NFL teams do in their states. That religious fervor is what draws college football fans to the game, year after year.

But the question remained: Was that spirit strong enough to pull the Michigan family back together and call its native son back home when the chance arose—or would they miss their opportunity and suffer through another cycle of mediocre Michigan football, one that would test the patience of even the most ardent Michigan fan?

This is the story of how Michigan fixed itself.

PART I: 1879–2007

THE RISE

CHAPTER 1

THE ABSORBING INTEREST

If Dave Brandon had been named the athletic director of a school whose football program had recently joined the NCAA's top division, like the universities of Buffalo, Connecticut, or Central Florida, he would have had no tradition to contend with, and no loyalists to object if he did. But he was taking over the University of Michigan's athletic department, with a rich history going back to 1879—and a faithful following that knew that history, and cared deeply about it.

It's as difficult to separate Michigan football from the university as it is to separate the university from Ann Arbor, and Ann Arbor from the Midwest.

The Midwest is so flat you can see three state capitals just by standing on a park bench. But the area comes with a set of beliefs recognizable to anyone who grew up here, moved here, or even visited the Great Lakes states. Chief among them is community, which developed not as some quaint trait, but to ensure survival. Hard work and teamwork are encouraged. Boasting is not. The stoic toughness of farmers and factory workers is the norm; the flash of the Fab Five, the exception.

The University of Michigan was founded in Detroit in 1817, 20 years before Michigan became a state. That simple fact came with a crucial consequence: Because the university's charter predates the state constitution, the University of Michigan has enjoyed more autonomy than any other state university, by design—although that autonomy has been threatened recently from an unexpected source.

In January of 1824, two men with checkered pasts, John Allen and Elisha Rumsey, bought 640 acres of land for $1.25 each and called the area "Annarbour," in honor of their wives' common names and as a means to market its bountiful trees.

"Our water is of the purest limestone," Allen wrote in a sales pitch, "the face of the country moderately uneven, our river the most beautiful I have beheld, and abounding with the most valuable fish, [and the] climate is as pleasant as 'tis possible to be."

I was born and raised in Ann Arbor, and I love it dearly, but I have to tell you that last one is a whopper. Ann Arbor is home to bitterly cold winters, surprisingly humid summers, and springs filled with so much rain, muck, and sometimes snow we occasionally skip that season altogether.

But falls in Ann Arbor are glorious—and that's what this town was made for. In 1837, Ann Arbor convinced the state legislature to relocate the state university from Detroit with a promise of forty free acres, land that today is called the "Diag." By the Civil War, the University of Michigan had attracted some 1,500 students, surpassing Harvard as the nation's largest university.

When you recruit thousands of single young men and women to a beautiful campus with little adult supervision, what could go wrong?

Just about everything, starting with drinking. As early as 1863, university president Henry Tappan urged residents to "root out the evil influences" of alcohol. Six years after the Civil War, President Erastus Otis Haven said Ann Arbor was "disgraced all over the country" as a "place of revelry and intoxication."

The second most-popular student vice that drove presidents crazy was violence, in the form of football—a game that requires a lot of land, and a lot of young men willing to crash into each other for a couple of hours. Where better to find those two ingredients than a college campus?

Given the amazing profits universities can make today from their football teams, it's worth noting that the game was invented by college students, for students. For decades, no one bothered calling it "college football," because there was no other kind.

The game spread from the Northeast, crossing the Alleghenies for the first time on May 30, 1879, when a band of Michigan students hopped on a train bound for Chicago to play the "Purple Stockings" from Wisconsin's Racine College and beat them, 1–0. Racine closed its doors eight years later, while the Wolverines soon became one of the nation's most popular attractions, worthy of the nation's largest stadium and an estimated 2.9 million fans around the world. I have traveled to forty countries on six continents, and in every single one of them I have heard someone shout, "Go Blue!"

Michigan's football team thrilled the students, the alumni, and the newly created sporting press. But it was not so enthusiastically received by James B. Angell, Michigan's longest-serving (1871–1909) and most influential president, who transformed Michigan into an internationally respected research university. He was alarmed by the popularity of the sport, and the unethical conduct of the teams, which would pull in just about any ringer they could—student or not—just about any way they could.

In December 1893, Michigan created a faculty-run "Board in Control of Athletics," which elevated the squad from a student-run renegade outfit to an officially sanctioned varsity team. This Board in Control effectively ran Michigan athletics for more than a century, until 2002. A few years later, after Minnesota, Wisconsin, Northwestern, Illinois, Purdue and the University of Chicago all followed suit, they formed what we now call the Big Ten conference. It was no accident the presidents first named their new league "The Intercollegiate Conference of Faculty Representatives."

Those two bodies, the Big Ten and Michigan's Faculty Board in Control of College Athletics, were largely responsible for both institutions earning reputations for being among the cleanest in the country for more than a century.

Still, it was not enough for President Angell. The creation of the Big Ten, he noted, only raised the stakes, putting rivalries and titles on the line every weekend.

"The absorbing interest and excitement of the students," he wrote, "not to speak of the public—in the preparation for the intercollegiate games make a damaging invasion into the proper work of the university for the first ten or twelve weeks of the academic year. This is not true of the players alone, but of the main body of students, who think and talk of little else but the game."

If football distracted the students from their studies, it surely helped the university in ways President Angell would never have dreamed of—or admitted. Football may be irrelevant to the academic mission of a major university, but it can help the community connect and prosper. From Michigan's inception in 1817 to 1960, state taxpayers could be counted on to pick up at least 70 percent of the budget. But if you were a farmer in Fennville, Michigan, or a factory worker in Flint, why would you care about the flagship university in Ann Arbor? For many Michiganders, the best reason then and now were the football, basketball and hockey teams. That's why Michigan athletic director Dave Brandon often referred to the Big House as the "front porch of the university." In fact, fully a quarter of those who visit the Big House have never taken a class at Michigan, and only a sixth of Michigan's 2.9 million fans earned a degree there.

Over the past five decades, the state has whittled down the percentage it provides of the university's budget from 70 percent to 4 percent—from most of it, to almost none of it. To avoid falling from its perch, Michigan has relied more heavily on research grants and private donations. The university now employs some 500 people in development, a hundred more than the entire College of Engineering has tenured professors.

I once told Jerry May, Michigan's director of development currently in charge of Michigan's $4 billion campaign, that he must have seen every Michigan home football game.

"No," he said, then added with a wink, "I haven't seen any of them. But I've been to them all."

By which he meant, the director of development attends every home game, but his back is turned to the field so he can talk with donors. Most major donors come to at least one game every fall to reconnect with old friends and the university itself, which makes football Saturdays some of the busiest days of the year for the development officers.

Football, even at a world-class research institution like the University of Michigan, still matters.

How it is run matters greatly, too, though the influence is often indirect. Unlike Harvard alums, who don't seem to care too much if the Crimson falls to the Elis, most Michigan alums care passionately about each and every game. Unlike fans of the football factories, where the "how" is less important than the "how many," the vast majority of Michigan's alums care just as much that the department be run the right way, too. Better to finish second with honor than first without.

When the Fab Five's Chris Webber had to admit, under oath, that he had taken some $280,000 from a booster, the Fab Five's two NCAA finalist banners came down, and few Michigan alums have argued for their return.

These two competing and often conflicting demands, you could argue, have long made Michigan's athletic department the nation's most demanding and difficult to lead.

CHAPTER 2

THE FIRST MICHIGAN MEN

In its 135-year history, Michigan football has produced 128 All-Americans, six Hall of Fame coaches, and three larger-than-life athletic directors. But the most important person in the history of the program might have been someone who never played a down or called a play, someone most Michigan fans have never heard of: Charles Baird, Michigan's first athletic director.

He was also the first public example of the Michigan Man—a term that requires some explaining.

Sportswriter John Kryk has discovered "Michigan Man" used in newspapers dating back to the 1890s, and it has popped up just about every decade since. But the traits now associated with the term were formed long before the term itself.

The coach Baird hired, Fielding Yost, stamped the term forever in one of his final speeches, as we'll see. But the phrase really took off in the popular press in 1989, when Michigan athletic director Bo Schembechler announced he was firing basketball coach Bill Frieder on the eve of the NCAA tournament because Frieder had signed a secret deal to coach Arizona State the next season. Schembechler famously barked: "A *Michigan Man* will coach Michigan!"

Anyone coaching at Michigan had better be completely committed to Michigan.

After that, the phrase was used more often to beat somebody over the head than to underscore the values it's supposed to represent, and Michigan's critics often use it as a mocking insult. Since half the students and varsity athletes on campus are women, the term clearly needs an update.

Despite the temptation to chuck the well-worn "Michigan Man" phrase forever, there's still something to it. Everyone knows the values it's supposed to stand for: honor, sacrifice, pride in your school, and humility in yourself. A true Michigan Man is expected to be more devoted to his alma mater than to money—and proves it by turning down bigger salaries to go elsewhere, and giving back generously to ensure his alma mater remains "Leaders and Best."

But ultimately, you have to resort to Supreme Court Justice Potter Stewart's description of pornography: "I know it when I see it."

Michigan fans know it when they see it, too. The football stars might be Big Men on Campus, but they're not supposed to act like it—in college or afterward. Despite Michigan's reputation for arrogance, I've rarely seen it among the lettermen. Almost all of them become the kind of adults you'd want to hire, to work for, to be your neighbor or your brother-in-law. The Michigan Man makes no claims to being a saint, but you want him in your corner.

A simple example: A few years after graduating, Scott Smykowski, a backup player under Schembechler, discovered he needed a bone marrow transplant, but his health insurance wouldn't cover all his expenses. That's all Schembechler needed to know to rally the Michigan Men from coast to coast. And that's all they needed to hear to raise $150,000 in just a few weeks—even though most of them had never played with Smykowski or even met him. That's what being a Michigan Man meant to them.

Despite the best efforts to kill it, the ideal of the Michigan Man is still alive, and helps explain a lot of what makes Michigan special, from the past to the present.

Baird might have been the first known specimen of the breed.

Charles Baird arrived at Michigan in 1890 to study literature, but Baird's passion was football. In 1893 and 1894, he was elected team manager, a job that entailed scheduling games, selling tickets, and keeping the books—not to mention promoting the team and raising the revenues to keep it running. Baird did just about everything that the athletic department today hires more than 300 people to do.

When Baird moved to Chicago, the students who replaced him turned the surplus he'd left them into a $3,000 deficit. In 1898, the team tried to bring Baird back by creating a position called, in various publications, "graduate manager" or "superintendent" of athletics, and promised him "complete control of all branches of athletics at Michigan." The players' pitch worked—and that is how Baird became the University of Michigan's first athletic director.

The Wolverines went undefeated that year, finishing with a thrilling 12–11 victory over archrival Chicago to earn Michigan's first Big Ten football title.

That game inspired a music student named Louis Elbel to write "The Victors," and the money started pouring into the program. The university was apparently so pleased with Baird's work it created the title of "director of outdoor athletics" for him, with a salary of $2,000—more than a full professor earned at the time.

Baird was more than a mere business manager, however. He perfected what might be the most important innovation in college sports: the fiscally independent athletic department. Without that, it's likely none of the virtues or vices we know so well today would ever have come into being.

When Michigan's peers followed Baird's lead, the Big Ten schools had the money to hire better coaches and build bigger stadiums, which shifted the locus of the game from the East to the "West." But like the great athletic directors who followed, Baird knew all the business savvy in the world can't save you if you hire a weak coach—or fail to support him.

The next year, 1899, the Wolverines finished 8–2, good for third place. When head coach Gustave Ferbert and two of his former players bolted for the Klondike gold rush, Baird hired former Princeton star Langdon "Biff" Lea to coach the 1900 squad, but his Wolverines finished 7–2–1, losing once again to the hated Chicago Maroons. It will come as no surprise to modern Michigan fans that their forefathers didn't think two-loss seasons were good enough for the Wolverines.

I've said it before, and I'll say it again: Some Michigan fans aren't happy unless they're not happy—and it started more than a century ago.

Throughout Michigan's history, whenever the Wolverines have hit a rough patch, the right man has almost always come along to save the day. Charles Baird hired a man who would become one of the greatest coaches in the history of the game, an eccentric, energetic, egotistical young man whose passion for self-promotion was exceeded only by his passion for the game he loved—and eventually, the university that gave him his chance.

Born in the foothills of West Virginia in 1871, Fielding Yost earned a law degree, then set out to see the country by coaching football. Each year, from 1897 to 1900, Yost took a new job, beat the school's main rival, won their league championship, received glowing reviews, then packed up for his next job—from Oberlin to Nebraska to Kansas to Stanford. But by December of 1900, Yost was out of a job again.

When Baird learned Yost was available, he wrote to him immediately. "Our people are greatly roused up over the defeats of the past two years," Baird wrote, "and a great effort will be made."

Those were the words Yost longed to hear: Somebody out there was serious about football. Baird fulfilled his promise with free room and board, plus a $2,300 salary, for just three months' work. He then happily let Yost, not himself, take the spotlight, which is why almost every Michigan fan has heard of Fielding Yost, and almost none have heard of his boss—and that's the way both men wanted it. Someone once asked Ring Lardner, the legendary sports reporter, if he had ever talked to Fielding Yost. "No," Lardner replied, "My father taught me never to interrupt."

Yost's ego aside, he understood a simple rule: if you want good publicity, you better talk with the people who provide it. Yost started grabbing headlines the day he arrived in Ann Arbor, predicting, "Michigan isn't going to lose a game." Then he backed it up for 56 consecutive contests, going undefeated from 1901 through 1904, winning national titles every year—the first team other than Harvard, Yale, Princeton, and Penn to win even one. Yost's teams crushed opponents with scores like 119–0, 128–0, and 130–0. Yost offered no mercy, and only an uninformed opponent would have expected any.

In the first of those seasons, 1901, the Wolverines outscored opponents 550–0, which inspired the "Point-a-Minute" nickname. Michigan kept up that incredible pace through 1905, when the average score of a Michigan game during Yost's first five years was 50–1.

According to Yost biographer John Behee, "No other coach and no other football team ever so dominated their era as Fielding H. Yost and the Michigan teams for 1901–05."

Given the parity of the modern game, no other coach ever will.

When Yost started at Michigan, he didn't pretend to follow the loose off-field guidelines—although few of his peers did. But on the field Yost's teams played scrupulously. His former employers at Nebraska and Kansas, respectively, wrote that Yost "teaches only straight-forward, legitimate football," and "He insists on *clean* football." Compared to his coaching peers, Yost stood out as an intelligent, well-educated, and well-spoken man who didn't drink, smoke, or swear.

Yost thereby added two elements to the Michigan Man model: playing straight and acting the part. He added a third when he returned to West Virginia for the 1902 off-season and witnessed the coal-mining boom. "If I had been here in the state the last two years I would have made a fortune," he wrote Baird. "So many opportunities gone by. I ought to quit the football business for good but it seems I cannot bear to give it up." He had more passion for the game than for profits.

But as good a coach as Yost had been at his four previous stops, he didn't set the football world on fire until Baird was his boss. This points to an important precedent: when both the athletic director and the coach are Michigan Men—native or naturalized—the clock ticks reliably. But when one isn't, it introduces a flaw in the machine that you might not notice at first, when it's just a few seconds late, or even a few minutes, but over time the error is glaring.

Baird's impressive work didn't go unnoticed. In 1903, Boston Red Sox owner Henry Killilea—a fellow Michigan grad—offered Baird a sizeable raise to run his baseball team. Michigan's panicked alumni did their best to increase Baird's salary, while the students signed petitions to show Killilea how badly they wanted Baird to stay.

Big money once again made a very strong argument for one of Michigan's leaders to leave. And for the second time, big money lost to Michigan. Baird stayed.

Five years later, in 1908, Baird declared, "Michigan today has the finest athletic grounds in the United States." Believing his work was complete, he became a successful banker in Kansas City. But in 1936, at age 66, Baird proved the pull of Michigan was greater than money again, when he gave $70,000 to the university to commission the third-largest carillon in the world. It was so big, the university decided to build a suitable structure to house it. And that's how Burton Tower, Michigan's most iconic structure, came to be.

Baird was not only Michigan's first athletic director, he was its most important, creating the manual for all who followed: work with the Faculty Board in Control; give the students affordable tickets, and pack the place; keep the revenues in-house, and use the money to build great facilities; hire proven coaches, and get out of their way; and finally, and most important, understand you're not merely running a business, but a religion, one whose values go deeper than dollars—which Baird proved with his final gift.

Those athletic directors who followed Baird's example did exceedingly well. And those who didn't, did not.

In 1905, the Big Ten began to require coaches to be full-time faculty members. Yost urged Michigan's Faculty Board in Control of Intercollegiate Athletics to pull the Wolverines out of the Big Ten in 1907—which they did, for a decade. But the decision had an unintended side effect, forcing Michigan to replace its main rivals, Chicago and Minnesota, with Ohio State and Michigan State, both of which were not yet in the Big Ten. But the rivalries didn't catch on for decades, which proved real rivalries can't simply be manufactured, and shouldn't be taken for granted—a lesson that would be tested a century later.

The decisions to leave the Big Ten, and to return in 1917, were both made by the Faculty Board in Control of Intercollegiate Athletics—a body Yost worked with well when he served as Michigan's athletic director from 1921 to 1941.

"From Yost to Crisler to me, we had a Faculty Board in Control," athletic director Don Canham (1968–88) told me, "and the presidents we served under believed that faculty control was the way to control athletics. Yost had support from the Board for the same reason I did: He never took stupid things to them [for approval]."

The mere presence of the Faculty Board deterred Yost from enacting his worst ideas.

"We've got the first field house ever built on a campus," Canham said. "We've got the first intramural building. We've got the largest stadium in the country. That was no accident. That was Fielding Yost." And, necessarily, it was the Faculty Board, too.

If Yost was no better than his peers at following eligibility rules when he first arrived in Ann Arbor, by the time he returned to the Big Ten in 1917, he had become a stickler. In the 1920s, he showed the rest of the country how to use the forward pass, and when he stepped down in 1927, his program had produced a staggering 68 head college coaches, but Yost had also established Michigan's reputation.

In 1929, Big Ten Commissioner Major John L. Griffith was moved to write Yost, "You have built the finest athletic plant in the world. . . . I always come away from Michigan with the feeling that you . . . have built your own ideals into Michigan's athletics and that everything is on a sane and sound basis. I hardly ever make a talk when I do not mention the things that you are doing. Our colleges and universities may well look to Michigan as an ideal."

When it all works, that's what it looks like.

Yost's ego was almost superhuman, but so was his charm; his ambition was grand, but so was his vision; his stubbornness was remarkable, but so was his ability to change.

Yost's most prominent quality, however, had no counter force: his love for "Meeshegan," as he called it, and all it could be. That love drove everything Yost did.

Twenty years ago, when I was writing a book section on Fielding Yost, I came across John Behee's book, published locally in 1971. That's where I learned about Yost's retirement ceremony, "A Toast to Yost from Coast to Coast," broadcast by NBC radio.

When Yost's friends had finished their speeches, Yost said, "My heart is so full at this moment and I am so overcome by the rush of memories that I fear I could say little more. But do let me reiterate . . . the Spirit of Michigan. It is based upon a deathless loyalty to Michigan and all her ways; an enthusiasm that makes it second nature for Michigan Men to spread the gospel of their university to the world's distant outposts; a conviction that nowhere is there a better university, in any way, than this Michigan of ours."

I've used this simple statement in articles, books, and speeches many times since, and I've been struck by how Yost's words resonate with people whose grandparents weren't even born when he said it—which Yost would surely interpret as proof that he was right all along.

In 1938, Michigan had to find another coach. But, not trusting the 67-year-old Yost with the mission, law professor Ralph Aigler, chairman of the Faculty Board in Control of Intercollegiate Athletics, took control of the search behind Yost's back. While Yost sought Navy coach Tom Hamilton, Aigler secretly courted a reluctant Fritz Crisler, who had already led Princeton to national titles in 1933 and 1935. Aigler was going for the very best coach available— and to almost everyone's surprise, he got his man.

Don Lund recalled Crisler telling the team, "There's no rule saying you can't block as hard as you want, tackle as much as you like. But remember that you're Michigan Men—none of the extras."

Crisler's famed "Mad Magicians" won a national title in 1947 with their creative play-making, which set up Crisler's successor, Bennie Oosterbaan, to win another national title the next year. Crisler was a first-rate coach, and one of the game's leaders.

Crisler created Michigan's trademark winged helmet, tear-away jerseys, and the two-point conversion. But his greatest invention was the platoon system, the game's most important innovation since the forward pass, which separated players into offensive and defensive specialists. He also forged the Rose Bowl pact between the Pac-10 and Big 10 that ran from 1948 to 1998, and he served for more than two decades on the NCAA rules committee, including two terms as its chairman.

"Crisler's contributions to the University of Michigan and to intercollegiate athletics were monumental," said Canham, who would follow him. "He was simply the most respected and admired man in intercollegiate athletics during his time."

During Crisler's tenure as Michigan's athletic director, from 1942 to 1968, the Wolverines won 18 national titles in a variety of sports. But over Crisler's last 18 years as AD, the football team won exactly one Big Ten title, Michigan's facilities were falling apart—literally—and the department was bleeding red ink.

"Crisler couldn't read a balance sheet," Canham said.

By 1968, Michigan was getting slow, tired, and overrun by the upstart NFL. Once again, Michigan needed someone to save it from irrelevance.

Yost and Crisler were not angels, with flaws as big as their strengths. They didn't even trust each other. But they had more traits in common than not— chief among them their profound belief in the spirit of Michigan.

"Tradition is something you can't borrow," Crisler said, echoing Yost's famous speech. "You cannot go down and buy it at the corner store, but it's there to sustain you when you need it the most. I have watched countless Michigan football coaches, countless Michigan players call upon it time and time again. There is nothing like it. I hope it never dies."

CHAPTER 3

THE CANHAM MODEL

In 1968, the Faculty Board in Control named Don Canham Michigan's next athletic director.

"I was not a popular choice to succeed Crisler," Canham wrote later. "I think the average Michigan alumnus was saying something to the effect of, 'Who the hell is this track coach to take Fritz Crisler's place?'"

It was a fair question, but there were good answers. Don Canham grew up in Oak Park, Illinois, where he was an average high-jumper, until he learned the new "Western Roll" technique for clearing the bar. He quickly mastered it, made Michigan's team, and won the NCAA title in 1940.

In 1942, when Michigan's track team boarded a train in Champaign, Illinois, to return from the Big Ten meet, Fielding Yost was holding court. A young high-jumper named Don Canham was the only one willing to stay up the entire night, listening to Yost tell him how he'd built Michigan's athletic empire, and what it meant to be a Michigan Man.

Canham learned the lessons well. He added his own innovations, too, particularly in marketing Michigan athletics. He sent four-color brochures directly to prospective ticket buyers, a practice considered as scandalous in Canham's day as selling tickets to an intercollegiate football contest was in Baird's. Canham then sold everything from coffee mugs to toilet seats, and went so far as to copyright the "Block M" and even the name "Michigan."

But it's a misconception that Canham tried to sell everything in sight. He brought three key insights to his mission that are often overlooked, which perpetuated the success he'd inherited from Baird, Yost, and Crisler.

First, Canham never promised victory in his ads, and rarely even mentioned the team itself. If you can't control it, he figured, you can't sell it. Instead, Canham cleverly promoted the beauty of the fall colors, the pleasure of tailgating with your friends, and the joy of the marching band. Canham was consciously targeting not the man of the house, but the woman.

Canham's widow, Peg, served 30 years as his secretary at Canham's company, School-Tech, which made equipment for coaches and teams and made Canham a millionaire. "He got the idea of marketing to moms from a woman he knew," she told me, "who told him she had the kids all week, and when the weekend comes, the father better be ready to spend some time with them! So *she* decides what they do on the weekend. If Don could make a pitch to get her some time off, and keep dad happy, Don would have the whole family. He listened, and he found she was right. It worked."

Canham sent his brochures to people who had just bought new cars, figuring they wanted to show them off. What better way to do that than at a Michigan football tailgate?

Canham proved the power of this approach on September 29, 1979, when he invited Slippery Rock and Shippensburg State to play a game in Ann Arbor. The contest drew 61,143 fans—more than Michigan's team drew that same weekend in Berkeley, California—and was covered by ABC's *Wide World of Sports*. Canham had so effectively sold Michigan fans on the game day experience over the results—even over the team itself—that he could re-create the spectacle with two Division II teams from Pennsylvania.

Second, to create the illusion of a hot ticket in the early days, Canham packed the stadium by selling two-dollar tickets to students, inviting Boy Scout troops and Little League football players in uniform free of charge, and sponsoring a high-school band day, in which three-dozen bands would fill the field during halftime and an otherwise vacant section during the game. By November 8, 1975, Canham could charge everyone full price and still get a sellout—and Michigan kept it up years after he retired.

Once again, Canham was ahead of his time.

Canham's third stroke of genius I learned in the late nineties when we were talking one day in his School-Tech office, just down State Street from campus. Canham asked me, "What's everyone's favorite restaurant?" I was stumped. He said, "The one with the line out the door. No one wants to walk into a restaurant that's empty." The waiting line had value in itself—and was more valuable than the money Canham could have gained from raising ticket prices to exploit the demand, as a Marketing 101 teacher would tell him to do.

"Canham was a genius at this," former associate athletic director for ticketing Marty Bodnar told me. "He worked the 'Scarcity Principle' like no one else. Once you've sold it out, they're not gonna let go of those tickets. 'Oh,

God, I'll never get back in!' You should have heard the phone calls we'd get when people feared they'd missed the deadline to renew!"

Canham also brought a vital intangible to his position—one he shared with Baird, Yost, and Crisler: He never appeared to be in it solely for the money, because he wasn't. Canham's buildings were solid, understated, and far from opulent. His salary was relatively modest—under $100,000 for most of his tenure. So were his staff's, including his coaches'—often to their chagrin. There was a logic behind this, too: If the salaries were too high, Canham reasoned, you'd attract people who were more interested in money than in Michigan—and they would leave as soon as someone offered them more.

Perhaps most important, there were many things Canham wouldn't do for money. He supported on principle a lot of ideas that would cost college athletic programs revenue, like freshman ineligibility. He opposed the Big Ten basketball tournament, the BCS, the college football playoff, and even night games—because they either negatively affected the student-athletes or Ann Arbor, and Canham cared a great deal about both. Canham never sold his soul—or Michigan's—to TV.

Schembechler often said, "Toe meets leather at 1:05. If you want to televise it, fine. If you don't, that's fine too." Canham backed him. For years, TV was dying for a night game at the Big House, and would have paid handsomely for it. Canham wasn't. So, they compromised—and didn't have one.

Canham got a lot of credit for his marketing, but not enough for his savvy hiring. He had the uncanny ability to pluck talented young coaches from the mid-majors. This increased the coaches' devotion to Michigan, and decreased the amount of money Canham had to pay to get them there.

When Canham hired Schembechler in December of 1968, the reaction was, "Bo *who?*"

Canham realized Schembechler's employer, Miami University, could have thrown more money at Schembechler. But, he said, "they couldn't compete with Yost's hole in the ground or with the prestige of Michigan."

The ethos of the Michigan Man was so well established, even by 1968, that it was an unspoken selling point—one so powerful that Schembechler accepted the job in Ann Arbor, and returned to Oxford, Ohio, before he realized he had never asked Canham what his salary would be.

When he sheepishly called back, Canham asked Schembechler what he was making at Miami. Schembechler said $19,000, though he'd been promised a raise to $20,000 the next year. Okay, Canham said, we'll pay you $21,000. And that concluded a "negotiation" where both parties were clearly more interested in working with each other at Michigan than making top dollar.

When Schembechler and his assistants arrived in Ann Arbor, they had to dress in the second-floor locker room of Yost Field House, sit in rusty folding chairs, and hang their clothes on nails in the wall.

"My coaches were complaining, 'We had better stuff at Miami,'" Schembechler recalled. "I said, 'No, we didn't. See this chair? *Fielding Yost* sat in this chair. See this spike? *Fielding Yost* hung his hat on this spike. And you're telling me we had better stuff at Miami?! No, men, we didn't. We have *tradition* here, *Michigan* tradition, and *that's* something no one else has!'"

And thus, the loyalty oaths of Yost and Crisler had been recast by their latest reincarnation: Bo Schembechler.

Schembechler never introduced any eye-popping innovations like Yost's forward pass or Crisler's platoon system, and he never won a national title. But he burnished Michigan's reputation for excellence, winning 13 Big Ten titles in 21 years, while doing it the right way. He proved to be the modern embodiment of the Michigan Man.

In 1982, Schembechler declined Texas A&M's offer of $3 million for 10 years, which would have quadrupled his salary, and made him the highest paid coach in the country. He explained, "Frankly, I've come to the conclusion that there are things more important in this world than money. For that reason, I've decided to stay at Michigan."

Canham knew Schembechler was the star, and that suited him fine. During games, Canham would steer clear of the locker room and sidelines, and instead cruised the press box, chatting with his many friends in the media.

Probably no athletic director enjoyed better media relations than Don Canham did, for a simple reason: It was important to him. He had a strict policy of always returning phone calls from every media member—national or local—and never gave them "No comment." When I asked him why, he said, "First, you guys have a job to do, so I need to help. Second, you say, 'No comment,' and you look guilty—fairly or not."

Canham went so far as to create a Michigan Media Hall of Fame with photos of his favorite columnists, reporters, and sportscasters, which covers the first wall you see off the elevator in the stadium's new press box. He also hired two strong public relations professionals, Will Perry and Bruce Madej—both former journalists—and let them do their jobs.

One day in Canham's office, he told me one of the simplest, smartest things I've ever heard, his guiding principle for crisis management: "Never turn a one-day story into a two-day story."

I've repeated this countless times, because it explains what went wrong in just about any PR crisis you can name. But the advice must be harder than it looks, because so few ever seem to follow it.

Canham had a few days he could have done without, like everyone else, but no one remembers his because he followed his own advice.

But perhaps Canham's best idea for media relations was hosting his famous Friday night parties out at his School-Tech office. On any given Friday night, the guest list could include Keith Jackson, Frank Deford, or Tim Russert—who was a big Notre Dame fan—or even Notre Dame president Father Ted Hesburgh himself. Michigan All-American Ron Kramer would bartend, with Jim Brandstatter filling in.

"They loved that party," Peg Canham recalls. "And those parties made a difference."

During one of our last conversations, about a year before Canham passed away in 2005, I asked him out of the blue what Michigan athletics would be like for the next 50 years.

He pondered the question for a moment or two, then finally said, "It will probably be successful. But it absolutely will be different—and, on most days, nowhere near as much fun as we had."

CHAPTER 4

STUMBLING ON STAGE

From the inception of the University of Michigan's athletic department in 1898 to Canham's resignation in 1988—nine full decades—Michigan needed only five athletic directors to lead arguably the nation's leading athletic department.

Proof of the latter came in the form of Frank Deford's 1975 feature spread in *Sports Illustrated* explaining how Canham filled the Big House, which prompted Canham to create an annual conference to show hundreds of athletic departments how to run their programs the Michigan way.

When Canham stepped down in 1988, the founding fathers of Michigan athletics proved hard to replace. You needed someone who understood Michigan tradition, but could adapt it to the modern world.

Michigan wanted Bo Schembechler to replace Canham, but there was a catch: Schembechler was still the football coach, and few believed anyone could do both jobs well. To solve this problem, Michigan appointed the university's director of business operations, Jack Weidenbach—a well regarded, capable man—to help Schembechler with the administrative duties.

Predictably, the public was absorbed by Schembechler's appointment to AD, but Canham focused on the potential promotion to athletic director of his old friend, Jack Weidenbach, and warned him about it: "Jack, there is no way you're qualified for the job as athletic director at this school or any other school at this level. This is not some backwater high school situation. Someone must be kidding."

Schembechler's reign as athletic director proved far shorter than expected. When the Big Ten presidents admitted Penn State in 1990, without informing their athletic directors, "I knew right then and there that the old days were over, when an athletic director was expected to run his department," Schembechler told me. "That did it for me. I knew I was out that day."

"It didn't change until Bo left," Canham told me, "and then it changed almost overnight."

This was the first of many breaks with the past within Michigan's athletic department that ultimately led to the unforgettable fall of 2014. Disasters don't start when the flood begins. They start years earlier, when the engineers perform careless inspections of the dams, the corroding infrastructure is ignored, and the levees' weak points go unaddressed year after year. When the sun is out and the clouds are far away, no one notices the safeguards falling away, one by one. But when the weather turns treacherous, only then does the public discover the protections they assumed were always there to save them have been compromised—and by then it's too late.

When that happens—from the Johnstown flood to Hurricane Katrina— most people blame the storm. Were it not for an act of God, everybody would be fine. But those very same storms would be little remembered if the experts had not failed to protect them, years before the storms showed up.

Michigan's problems didn't start when the 2014 Wolverines lost to Notre Dame 31–0, or Shane Morris got hit against Minnesota. They started in 1990, when the sun was out, and no one was paying attention to the protections being removed that had so often sheltered the program in a storm. Few would realize it until it was too late.

Michigan did indeed hire Weidenbach to replace Schembechler as the full-time athletic director. When he stepped down in 1994, the University named the athletic administration building Weidenbach Hall. He was followed by a man from development named Joe Roberson, who had led the "Campaign for Michigan," then held the AD post for three years. In 1997, Tom Goss, a football player under Bump Elliott and a favorite of Canham's, left the business world to run the department, and developer Bill Martin took the post in 2000. The same department that needed only five directors for its first 90 years had to hire five more athletic directors in the next 12 years.

All of them were genuinely decent men who had been great successes in their fields, usually on campus or in business. But three of them hadn't sought the job, two were hired as interim directors, and after Schembechler, none of them had worked an hour in an athletic department before becoming the director.

In the process, the limitations of the Michigan Man model were exposed. Those attributes were essential to leaving a lasting legacy, but they weren't enough to cover a lack of experience. Michigan suffered more scandals in the nineties alone—with 28 separate headline-grabbing stories in the Detroit papers' front pages—than Michigan had incurred in the previous nine decades combined.

The first major crisis hit on a Friday night in the spring of 1995, when head football coach Gary Moeller went out for dinner with his wife, Ann, became intoxicated, and spent the night in jail, all completely out of character. That might have blown over, until someone recorded his tirades from his cell and gave the tape to ESPN, which played it for several days.

Athletic director Joe Roberson called longtime sports information director Bruce Madej, who tried to reach Schembechler, but he was deep-sea fishing in Mexico, so Madej could only leave a message. Four days into the ordeal, Madej returned home after midnight. As he sat down, he noticed a yellow note on the floor under his seat: a message taken by his teenage son, Mike, from Bo Schembechler. Madej dashed upstairs to wake his son and ask when Schembechler had called. Half-awake, his son said, "Two days ago," not realizing the import of the message, since Schembechler called often. Madej called Schembechler instantly but he was already flying back to Michigan.

When Schembechler returned, it was too late. Moeller had stepped down. Furious, Schembechler stormed into Schembechler Hall and demanded to see Madej. After a shouting match, in which Madej—supported by Schembechler's secretary, Lynn Koch—explained that his son was just a kid, Bo finally realized Madej was right, and collapsed in his chair, defeated. There was nothing he could do.

This marked the first time in decades that Michigan's boringly stable program had been publicly embarrassed.

Nine days later, Roberson named Lloyd Carr Michigan's interim head coach, but specified in his public statement that Carr would not be a candidate for the permanent position, which they expected to fill prior to the 1995 season. Because it was May, they figured they had time to run a national search. But three months later, heading into the 1995 season, Carr was still running the team. Canham, who had recommended Carr to become Wisconsin's head coach back in 1990, recalled in his book, "In a remarkable performance in a terrible situation, [Carr] proved far more competent than anyone, including me, had imagined. After four games it was obvious this guy was a coach. . . . In addition, Carr said all the right things at every press conference and handled every emergency with dignity."

Ten games into the 1995 season, with the Wolverines holding an 8–2 record and a number 12 ranking, Roberson named Carr the permanent head coach. Two years later, Michigan won its first national title in 50 years, and Carr was named National Coach of the Year. Michigan's football crisis had worked out far better than anyone could have hoped.

Not so basketball. A few years after the Fab Five made it to the 1992 and 1993 NCAA finals, it was discovered Chris Webber and others had received hundreds of thousands of dollars from a booster. After a lengthy investigation, in 2002 Michigan self-imposed four years of probation, a postseason ban, and vacated 113 wins, all records, and every NCAA, NIT, and Big Ten banner Michigan had won during that era. The NCAA would end up doubling the length of the probation and postseason ban.

The power shift occuring that decade not only favored presidents over athletic directors—which only made sense—but campus bureaucrats over former coaches or even experienced athletic administrators, which is debatable.

"They say it's more important nowadays to have a business background than an athletic one," Canham told me for a story in 1999. "I disagree. You have to have an athletic background first, or you don't know what's going on. When I was hiring a football coach, I knew exactly what I wanted, and knew Bo was it in the first fifteen minutes of our interview.

"And that's my point. The administrators have never been in the trenches, and don't know what to look for."

Canham's views are shared by Bump Elliott, an All-American player on Crisler's "Mad Magicians," a former Michigan coach, and finally Iowa's athletic director, who ushered in a golden era for Iowa athletics. "It's become more of a business situation than it used to be, but the biggest thing is still to help your coach succeed," says Elliot. "If your [football] coach doesn't win, it doesn't matter how good a businessman you are."

Even the shift to presidents nationwide had its downsides. "The problem is," Canham said, "they confused presidential *control* for presidential *management*. What would a bureaucrat know about that?"

It was the presidents, reasserting control across the country, who approved conference basketball tournaments, conference football title games, the BCS bowl system, and the twelfth regular-season football game. All those changes expanded schedules and increased revenues, while not giving the athletes anything in return for their extra work.

"It's all being driven by money," the normally soft-spoken Weidenbach told me, when these changes occurred. "I can think of no other reason. And if it is the only reason, we are short-changing the student-athlete—and I think it's wrong. It's hard enough to be a student-athlete already. Bo was against it, I was against it—but nobody asked us."

When Michigan athletics entered its second century in the Big Ten, its vaunted tradition, autonomy, and reputation were all in jeopardy.

CHAPTER 5

ALL THE EGGS IN ONE BASKET

In 1996, the Regents hired a new president, Lee Bollinger, who had no interest in being a caretaker president. Soon after taking office, he broke ground for a state-of-the-art life-sciences building, and took on a case brought in 1997 by two students who had not been accepted to Michigan and sued the university for discrimination. Bollinger decided to make Michigan a national test case for Affirmative Action.

That meant he'd be working closely with the Board of Regents, including one of the newest members, Dave Brandon, who won election in 1998.

Who is Dave Brandon?

Annette Howe worked for Brandon for more than 12 years at Domino's and Michigan as his administrative assistant, and is very highly regarded by everyone I know in the department. She and Brandon, she wrote, "communicated almost every day. The position I held was very unique because even though it was business, in the life of an athletic director, CEO, or any top level executive, there is no clear line between your business life and personal life. Business and personal just merge together and it becomes their life." It's fair to say Annette Howe probably knows Dave Brandon better than anyone outside his family. (Brandon declined my interview request.)

"Dave treated me as if I were an important part of his family. Dave never treated me like I was 'just an assistant.' He also had a special way of treating me like I was an important part of his leadership team. I still have a very special relationship with Dave and his wife, Jan, and all of their grown children and their spouses."

To know him, she said, you have to understand where he came from.

Dave Brandon was the second of Barbara and Phil Brandon's three children, born on May 15, 1952, in Dearborn, Michigan.

"His beginnings were very humble," Howe says. "His family owned a chicken farm [in South Lyon]. I have often listened to Dave tell the story about how his high-school football coach contacted his father to ask him to let his son play football. But his father said no, because he needed Dave, his older sister Phylis and younger brother Bill to work at his family egg business."

But eventually, Howe writes, "His father made the difficult decision to close the family business and give Dave the opportunity to play high-school football, basketball, and baseball."

"When you see Dave with his siblings, it's striking," one of Brandon's former employees says. "They're all normal height and normal looking, and then there's Dave, this dashing guy who towers over them. It's like *Sesame Street*: one of these things is not like the other. And that's Dave. It just kind of seemed like Dave was their big chance, and they did everything they could to put their eggs in his basket, and take care of it."

Their bet paid off when Dave earned nine varsity letters and became an All-State quarterback his senior year, 1969. Bo Schembechler soon started recruiting him and scheduled Brandon's official for January 1970.

Before Brandon made the 15-minute trip to Ann Arbor, however, Schembechler suffered a heart attack on December 31, 1969—the day before Michigan's Rose Bowl game against USC. When it was time for Brandon's visit, Schembechler was still in his home at 870 Arlington, recovering.

In late 2006, shortly after Schembechler passed away, I asked his former assistants, players, and friends to send me their memories for the final section of *Bo's Lasting Lessons*, which Bo and I had been working on together. Brandon sent me this:

"I stood at the foot of his bed while Bo laid there in his pajamas and robe passionately explaining the importance of the Michigan Football tradition. He explained that those who were tough enough to stay would be champions. He told me how committed he was to running a program that played by the rules. He explained how he would make no promises to any player about starting, playing time, or the position they would play on the field. Everything would be earned by performance on the practice field."

After just twelve months on the job, Schembechler could define with complete confidence what a Michigan Man looked like, acted like, coached like and played like. Like Michigan's previous converts, Yost and Crisler, Schembechler learned the hymnal quickly, and sang it with conviction.

"The amazing thing about this experience," Brandon continued, "was the fact that it only took me about 30 seconds to forget I was standing in the bedroom of a guy who just had suffered a heart attack! He was as intense, committed, enthusiastic, and passionate in that circumstance as he proved to be at every meeting, practice, and game I participated in over the succeeding four years as one of his players. I knew immediately that I wanted to prove to this guy I was tough enough to stay . . . and be a champion."

The good news for Brandon: This was the era of unlimited scholarships, and Michigan gave out as many as anyone, always more than 100. But that was also the bad news: Every August, 140 serious players showed up in Ann Arbor to compete for those jobs. Just months after Brandon's greatest triumph, he was headed for his greatest disappointment.

In the summer of 2000, I started gathering material for *Bo's Lasting Lessons*, and sought out two of Schembechler's most successful alums: Jim Hackett, then the CEO of Steelcase, and Dave Brandon, who was in his second year as CEO of Domino's Pizza. Brandon probably didn't know me from Adam, but he was nice enough to give me an hour of his time, probably because the interview was about Schembechler, a lifelong mentor. Brandon didn't spend our time telling me about his biggest victories, either, but his most painful defeat.

Brandon had the good timing to join Bo's 1971–73 squads, which won 30 games, lost only 2, and tied 1, with all three setbacks occurring in the last game of the season against Ohio State or at the Rose Bowl. Dave was a junior on Michigan's 1972 team, which ran the table, outscoring opponents in Yost-like fashion, 253–43, until the Buckeyes upset them, 14–11, in Columbus.

"That team was one of my best," Schembechler said, "but it was still a challenge keeping everyone happy and involved, even when you're winning big every Saturday."

Schembechler always tried to bring the All-Americans down to earth, and keep the benchwarmers' morale up. But when the coaches moved Brandon from quarterback to defensive end and then to kicker, rarely brought him on away trips, and put him in a grand total of one game in three years, even the promise of a varsity letter wasn't enough to keep Brandon's spirits from slipping.

At a Monday practice in the middle of that 1972 season, Schembechler decided to work with all the guys who didn't get into that Saturday's game by making up a scrimmage they called the Toilet Bowl. They were just getting started when one of the assistants told Brandon which team he would be playing on.

"Well," Schembechler told me, "Brandon apparently responded with something less than *complete enthusiasm*. This happened on the opposite sideline from me, but the coach told me about this situation right away, because he knew I'd want to know. The second I hear this, I'm rushing across the field and in Brandon's face, yelling and screaming, probably less than a minute after he mumbled his protest to the assistant. Boy, was Brandon surprised!

"'I hear you'd rather not partake in our little scrimmage,' I said. He was too stunned to respond. 'Well, I can solve your problem. Son, you're going straight into that locker room, you're cleaning your locker out, and you're going home. You're done playing football for Michigan. This is an honor you clearly don't deserve.'"

"Now, I've gotta tell you: In my mind, Brandon was only suspended. I knew he'd be back, because there was just too much character in that guy to end his career like that. That man was not a quitter. And I knew that because I knew Brandon.

"But in his mind, he's been kicked off. He's done. And he's got to drag his sorry butt back into that locker room, and think about what he just did. Dave sits there in his empty stall for what he's convinced is the last time, completely crushed. He's got to think about what he's going to tell his girlfriend, his dad, and his kids someday: that he had a chance to play for the greatest university in the country and he blew it simply because he didn't appreciate it. If you ask him about this today, he'll tell you he was about to cry at that moment—and this is a tough guy!—and I guarantee you, he didn't get a second of sleep that night."

The next day, Brandon called to make an appointment to see Schembechler first thing in the morning, just like Schembechler thought he would.

"He's scared, he's nervous, he's troubled—and he looks like hell," Schembechler recalled. "He apologizes for his conduct, and promises he'll never be so stupid again. Of course, I take him back. I *wanted* him on that team. But you can bet we never heard Dave Brandon complain about any scrimmages after that!"

But even after Brandon became a successful executive, that incident still bothered him. He told me it was embarrassing and humiliating, something he had a hard time forgiving himself for. He even asked Schembechler, years later, "How could I be so selfish, so negative, so weak?"

It's not hard to appreciate how much that must have stung. Brandon's family had sacrificed for his big chance, he was their Great Hope, and he'd been kicked off one of the greatest teams in Michigan history for whining about a Monday scrimmage. It's also not hard to see how a man that driven could use that incident for motivation the rest of his life.

After Brandon became athletic director in 2010, just a few minutes into his speeches he often displayed a disarming candor when he joked that he had already been speaking longer than he had actually played at Michigan. In hindsight, he added, getting kicked off the team "was the best thing that ever happened to me. I was the hotshot kid coming out of high school with nine varsity letters, and I learned that didn't count for very much.

"I left the program feeling a lot like a failure."

Brandon was far from alone in that, of course. On a team that attracted countless all-state phenoms, where even the backup player could get to the NFL, hundreds of Michigan football players have left campus disappointed in themselves.

But even in that context, it was unusual to earn a full scholarship, then get moved from quarterback to defensive end to kicker, and get into only one game. Combined with the weight of his family's dreams, Brandon's setback probably cut a little deeper than most. He clearly felt diminished by it—and more determined to make a mark on the world big enough to eclipse that failure. This helps explain not only Brandon's incredible work ethic, but his desire years later to take a severe pay cut to return as Michigan's athletic director.

But in responding this way, Brandon might have missed the bigger point of Schembechler's favorite mantra: "The Team, the Team, the Team." Other Michigan players whose football careers hadn't panned out seemed to get over it faster. They've been able to enjoy their football reunions, where they know their contributions are respected, and they'll be treated as equals by their friends.

Not Brandon. I have talked with many of his former teammates, who either don't remember him, or recall him as a "malcontent," the term that pops up most frequently.

"Like anyone else, Dave wanted to play," said one of the team's stars, echoing his teammates' comments. "You don't get that far without being competitive. Guys who don't play can get frustrated—and that was him. He wasn't a happy camper. Some guys who quit had better attitudes. He could be his own worst enemy.

"'The Team, the Team, the Team'? He didn't live that lesson. At least not then. I've only talked with him a few times since."

Having spent his Michigan career on a team crowned with laurels, Brandon seems to have left it not with a sense of shared achievement, but a burning desire for personal redemption.

Brandon graduated in 1974 from the School of Education with a degree in secondary education and a certificate to teach. But instead of pursuing a career in teaching or coaching, as he had planned, he got his first job at Procter & Gamble in Cincinnati, where Schembechler had put in a good word with friends at the company.

At Procter & Gamble, Brandon became close friends with former team-mate Larry Johnson, who married Diane Valassis. Her father created Valassis Communications, a Michigan-based marketing company that sends out millions of postcards every week stamped with coupons and other promotions, but is probably better known for the "Have you seen me?" photos of missing children on the front. When Johnson decided to leave Procter & Gamble to work in the family business, Brandon joined him in 1979, at age 27. Ten years later, Brandon rose to CEO, and in 1992, launched the company's Initial Public Offering at $11.34 a share. He led the company to the Fortune 500, and also to the list of *Fortune* magazine's 100 best places to work in 1997, 1998, and 1999.

But long after Brandon had become a multimillionaire, he still had never told anyone outside his family that he'd once been kicked off the Michigan football team, however briefly. Finally, 17 years later, in 1989, at the first re-union Schembechler had for all the men who'd played and coached for him, Brandon was sitting with his football classmates, when he decided he was far enough removed to confess his sins. After Brandon spilled his guts, they all laughed—which stunned Brandon, until he learned why: One by one, they went around the table, and confessed that they'd been kicked off the team at one time or another, too.

"That same night," Schembechler recalled, "when it was time for introductions, Brandon gets up—and I've quoted this statement a hundred times—and he tells his old teammates: 'I didn't get in many games. I wasn't an All-American like a lot of you guys, or even an All-Big Ten player. Hell, some weeks I wasn't even on the All-Scout Team! But in the long run, I became an All-American in business.'

"They all cheered. People, believe me when I tell you, *that* is what we were trying to teach when I was head coach."

For a man aching to be admired by his teammates, that must have felt cathartic. But Brandon's burning desire to prove himself was far from quenched. His love for his alma mater was just as strong.

"Dave always told the story about giving back to the University of Michigan because of everything he received," Annette Howe told me. "Even more important than his scholarship, Dave was always grateful and praised the University of Michigan hospital for saving his twin sons at birth," on Valentine's Day, 1980. One of the twins was taking blood from the other in the womb, causing the first to build up an excess of red blood cells, and the other to become anemic—and come out purple.

"That's not something you forget," Brandon told the *Michigan Daily*. He never did, giving $4 million to the university in September of 2006, half of which was earmarked for the hospital's new neonatal intensive care unit.

"Dave openly talks about his battle with prostate cancer," Howe says, "and how he searched all over the country for the best medical care, and he ended up back at the University of Michigan."

In 1998, Brandon decided to run for one of the two seats on the university's Board of Regents that come up for statewide election every two years. Because the terms run eight years, the eight-person board enjoys unusual stability, but the system also creates intense competition for a down-ticket office. Once Brandon decided to run, he told his old coach-turned-friend, Bo Schembechler.

"Now, Bo is about as apolitical as you can get," Brandon told me in our 2000 interview. "It's not his thing. But I called and said, 'I just wanted you to know that I've decided to run.' His immediate response was, 'Well, that's the best damn idea I've heard in a long time! Tell me, what can I do to help?' I said, 'Are you sure?' because I really don't think Bo has much stomach for this stuff. It's not his business. He said, 'Just tell me what I can do.'

"Well, what he did was speak and sign little plastic footballs with 'Brandon for Regent' printed on them, for three hours in Grand Rapids—750 little footballs! And they moved 'em all. The audience would've gobbled up hundreds more if we had 'em. On one of them the pen slipped or something, so he chucked it to the side. At the end of the night, it was the only one left. So when we were done, he wrote something else on the other side, and handed it to me: 'To Dave: Win or Die!'

"I won the [Republican] nomination the next day in a landslide. At the nominating convention that day, I read the football to them, 'Win or Die!' and said, 'Thanks for helping me win!' The alternative wasn't too appealing.

"I called Bo up, told him I won the nomination, and thanked him. He said, 'You haven't won anything yet. You've got to win the general election! What can I do to help?'

"We had some money for radio ads, and we asked Bo to do some for us. He wouldn't take a dime. In the ads he said he'd coached me, he knew me, and I had his highest recommendation for the job. Now, I did a lot of work to get elected, but I *know* that for a lot of people in this state, 'If Bo said this guy would be a good Regent, that's good enough for me.' I got the most votes of the four candidates [Brandon actually finished second, behind Kathy White, by 26,334 votes]. The point is, he was still helping me out, doing whatever he could for me, many years after I first met him in his bathrobe, fresh from heart surgery. What can I say about the guy?

"I still have that little plastic football in my trophy case."

Brandon quickly earned a reputation among his fellow Regents for playing well with others, including his Democratic colleagues.

"We always worked at being collegial with each other," three-term Democratic Regent Larry Deitch told me. "We didn't always agree, but it was always clear to me that Dave and I shared the view that bipartisan agreement, to the extent possible, was good for the university.

"We might have had different visions for Michigan on certain issues, but there's no doubt about it, Dave loves Michigan and he made significant contributions as a Regent, and generous financial contributions as an alumnus."

This brings us back to President Bollinger's Affirmative Action lawsuits. Not surprisingly, the five Democratic Regents enthusiastically backed Bollinger's effort to defend Michigan's Affirmative Action admissions program, while the three Republicans did not. The two cases earned a spot on *60 Minutes* and went all the way to the Supreme Court, where Michigan received a split decision: It could not use race in a formula, as the Court ruled it had in undergraduate admissions, but it could take race into consideration, as it had for law school admissions.

What the Democratic Regents remember, however, was the Republicans' restraint, including Brandon's.

"Dave always articulated what I would call the 'principled basis' against Affirmative Action," Deitch recalls, "that it is not color-blind, and it raises the question of who chooses the 'winners' and 'losers'? But he never engaged in demagoguery over it. Not once.

"He was content to let the courts decide the outcome. But the cheap political trick would have been to demagogue the issue, get a lot of national attention for it—and I think he probably could have—and he didn't do it. He knew that would be damaging to Michigan. I think that's very much to his credit."

Kathy White, a fellow Democratic Regent, concurs that the Republican Regents "could have demonized us, the whole mission, and I'm sure the national media would have picked up on it—but they didn't do it. They refused to gain cheap political points by grandstanding."

As a result, the Regents demonstrated they could disagree without being disagreeable, which spared the university an ugly public fight.

CHAPTER 6

THE MAIZE HALO

In 1997, after four years on the job, 61-year-old athletic director Joe Roberson stepped down. Near the end of his run, Roberson told the *Flint Journal*, "I'd be lying to you if I said I hadn't been under a lot of stress lately. In fact, it's been very stressful for the past four years. I never could have predicted any of this happening."

He would not be the last Michigan athletic director to say that.

When president Bollinger replaced Roberson with Tom Goss on September 8, 1997, he seemed to have gotten the best of both worlds: a former All-Big Ten lineman who had also served as a vice president at Faygo Beverages and ShasCo, Inc., the makers of Shasta soda. When a Michigan wrestler, Jeff Reese, died trying to cut weight before a match, Goss showed exactly what a Michigan athletic director could do with a national platform. After requesting a report on Reese's death, and its causes, Goss decided that Michigan would no longer put its student athletes in such obvious danger.

Goss, his wrestling coach, and other experts came up with sensible reforms to end the long-standing practice of extreme weight cutting, then told the Big Ten and the NCAA that Michigan would only wrestle under those rules, and would only wrestle against other teams that abided by them, too. Such a stand might have gotten another program blackballed from the wrestling community. But when it came from the Michigan athletic director, it proved to be the lever needed to reform the sport at every level, with the Big Ten adopting Michigan's reforms, followed by the NCAA, and the high schools—a sequence of events that Yost, Crisler, or Canham would have readily recognized as Michigan's influence at its best. Those rules are still in effect today.

But Goss's problems began after firing basketball coach Steve Fisher, and elevating Fisher's assistant, Brian Ellerbe, to the permanent position in 1998.

The next year, despite taking in record revenues, Goss had to admit the department had run a $2.1 million deficit. But a formal audit in September revealed the deficit was $750,000 more than that, pushing it close to $3 million. Reports submitted by the university to the federal government, which went public in December, revealed that the deficit was actually $3.9 million.

But no mistake damaged President Bollinger's reputation locally more than one of his own making: the Maize Halo. When an architectural firm presented a popular plan to encase the Michigan Stadium in brown brick, President Bollinger didn't let the Regents vote on it. Instead, he awarded the commission to a Philadelphia firm, Venturi, Scott Brown & Associates, which has won numerous national awards, and worked on the Bollingers' home in New Hampshire.

But the VSBA architects had never worked on a stadium before. They also had little notion of the traditions they were tampering with, and no idea how fiercely Michigan fans clung to them. They proved it when they added a yellow-and-white-striped aluminum "halo" around the entire structure, which made the stadium look like a circus tent, and then attached refrigerator-magnet-style letters on the halo to spell "Hail to the Victors" and "The Conquering Heroes."

The halo generated hundreds of hostile letters, the most the *Ann Arbor News* had ever received on any issue, from the day it went up to the day it came down. Donations to the athletic department fell by 15 percent, or about $500,000 at the time. It's instructive to note that Michigan fans understand immediately when a foreign antigen is introduced—and they reject it just as quickly. Bollinger countered by claiming the design was "genius," and that those who disagreed didn't know much about architecture. Michigan fans responded that Bollinger didn't know much about Michigan tradition.

Although Bollinger spearheaded the construction of the halo, Goss took the fall for it like a good soldier. In 1999, Bollinger announced he was letting Goss go, but refused to explain why.

Bollinger emerged with his career ambitions intact.

On a Thursday night in March of 1999, President Bollinger called his old friend Bill Martin, who had grown up in Detroit, lost his mother when he was twelve, lived by himself in high school, and started his construction, development, and management company in the 1960s with a student loan he took out when he was enrolled in Michigan's business school. He grew the company into the second-largest property owner in Washtenaw County, behind only the university itself.

Marketing, however, was never Martin's thing. When he went on vacation one time, he asked his lawyer to come up with a name for his company, and that's how First Martin Corporation got its identity.

In 1995, Martin gathered a few business leaders to open Ann Arbor's first local bank. They didn't spend too much time brainstorming before naming it Bank of Ann Arbor. But twenty years later, the local bank they started with one location, 14 employees and $6 million now has seven locations, 176 employees, and ranks second out of 24 banks in the county for market share, behind only Chase.

If Martin isn't too big on marketing businesses, he's very good at building them.

On that March night in 1999, with Michigan's basketball team under investigation and the department drowning in $3.9 million of debt, Bollinger asked Martin to "go down there and see what you can do" for six months, while Bollinger started looking for a full-time replacement. Martin asked Bollinger if he could think about it overnight, then called his best friend, presidential pollster Bob Teeter, who had run George H. W. Bush's 1992 campaign—that rare politico who was deeply respected by people on both sides of the aisle.

Martin recalled Teeter telling him, "This is a no-win situation, but you'll do it no matter what I tell you, so I might as well tell you how to do it right."

Teeter's advice: Get the department's 225 employees together in one room, "tell 'em who you are, what you're going to do, and if anyone has a problem, tell 'em to bring it to you."

Martin called Bollinger to accept, on two conditions: One, the Maize Halo had to come down, and two, he be paid only a dollar a year until Bollinger found a permanent athletic director.

Bollinger agreed to both conditions.

"I never had a contract," Martin says. "And I never did get that buck!"

CHAPTER 7

REBUILDING THE BIG HOUSE

After Bollinger narrowly missed out on becoming Harvard's president, Columbia University hired him for their top post in 2002. But on Bollinger's very last day in office, he made a seemingly insignificant, largely ignored decision, but one that would have dramatic consequences years later: He reduced the Faculty Board in Control of Intercollegiate Athletics—which first convened in 1893, five years before Charles Baird created the athletic department itself—to an advisory board. In other words, the Faculty Board members could tell the athletic director what they thought, but the athletic director wouldn't have to listen. The motive was simple: reduce the conflicts and inefficiencies that occasionally arose when the athletic director answered to both the Faculty Board and the president, and allow him to balance the budget and get the stadium renovated faster by giving him only one master. Although the Regents were pleased Martin was staying, they could see down the road that, if Michigan happened to have a maverick athletic director and a president who lacked the resolve to restrain him, there would be almost nothing stopping the athletic director from doing whatever he wanted.

"Some of the Regents urged President Bollinger to hold off [on reducing the Board in Control to an advisory board], so the next president could make that decision," recalls Percy Bates, an education professor who served as Faculty Athletic Representative and a member of the Board in Control for 22 years. "They asked him, 'Why are you doing this? You're leaving!' But Bollinger insisted."

But another safeguard had been removed. Most Big Ten universities followed suit.

After Bollinger left for Columbia with some acrimony in his wake, one candidate emerged as the favorite to replace him: University of Iowa president Mary Sue Coleman.

A chemist who earned her degrees from Grinnell College and the University of North Carolina before logging almost two decades as a biochemist at the University of Kentucky, Coleman was named president of the University of Iowa in 1995. When Michigan's Regents interviewed her, they found a woman who wore simple dresses, and was not too proud to pick them up the at the Iowa City airport in her own Buick. Where Bollinger wore suits tailored in London and Paris and made no secret of his Ivy League ambitions, Coleman made it just as clear that, if hired, Michigan would be the last stop of her career—a destination, not a stepping-stone.

"When you looked at Mary Sue Coleman, she seemed like the right person at the right time," Deitch recalls of the downhome, straight-shooting, and "relentlessly pleasant" Coleman.

Like most presidents, Coleman enjoyed a honeymoon with the board that hired her. But contrary to popular opinion, the Regents are adamant that Dave Brandon did not have any special role in her hiring. True, the Regents once used Brandon's corporate jet from Domino's Pizza—where he was named CEO in 1999—to fly to Iowa City to offer Coleman the job, but it's hard to believe one free flight would carry much influence. Further, the Regents approved Coleman by a vote of 8–0.

"I was the chair of the committee," Deitch says. "It was a fully collaborative effort. We sorted through a great pool of candidates, until we achieved unanimity. In no way did Dave deliver the deciding vote.

"But I would say that she quickly came to respect Dave a lot, and like him a lot, and I think he was somebody that had a lot of influence with her."

In 2000, when Martin became Michigan's fifth athletic director in 12 years, he did exactly as his friend Bob Teeter advised, and addressed his new staff directly. The department's objectives, he told them "are to graduate our student-athletes, make sure everyone is representing the University in a highly ethical manner, run winning programs—because that's part of our DNA—and pay our own way."

"How you do that," he said later, paraphrasing the philosophy that Michigan's athletic department had followed since Charles Baird created it, "is pay all your bills, invest in first-class facilities and coaches, endow scholarships, have a little reserve to protect the future, and never be a financial burden on the institution, so the cash can flow uphill" to the university's central administration, where the money goes to support the academic mission of the university.

Martin—who couldn't play high-school sports because he was working thirty hours a week to pay his bills—did the job so well that Michigan's coaches circulated a petition asking Martin to stay, and sent it to Bollinger's office.

Both parties agreed. If Martin had known what he was in for, he might have asked for more than a buck. The department he inherited suffered from red ink, neglected buildings, and a growing basketball scandal. Likewise, when Martin added United States Olympic Committee president to his duties in 2002, the beleaguered outfit had all those problems, plus steroids. By 2004, both institutions were clean and thriving.

Four years into Martin's administration, Michigan had finally gotten through the NCAA's endless investigation into its basketball program. The team was off probation, out of trouble, and about to raise its 2004 National Invitational Tournament banner. The department had already turned the $3.9 million deficit Martin had inherited into a $5.5 million surplus, and he would grow that dramatically. He and his staff had put ambitious renovations for old facilities and plans for new ones—14 total, for Michigan's then-26 varsity teams—in the pipeline. Most Michigan teams were very successful, especially football, hockey, and softball, on and off the field. In the 2003–04 Directors' Cup, awarded to the school with the most successful athletic program, Michigan finished second only to Stanford, which was in the midst of its run of 21 consecutive titles, which continues to this day. During Martin's ten-year run as Michigan's athletic director, the Wolverines would finish in the top six for the Directors' Cup every year but one. Michigan's negative headlines had stopped, and the school's reputation had been restored.

Most important, Michigan had demonstrated the ability to recognize when it had veered off course, and then self-correct, led by a man who understood the values that drove the department.

Martin was an unlikely candidate to lead those resurrections—or to do anything else he's accomplished. He's a multi-millionaire businessman whose high-school teacher once told him, "You'll never amount to anything"; a world-renowned sailor who tipped over his first boat when he was eight; an acclaimed athletic director who never earned a varsity letter; and the esteemed president of the USOC, who had never attended an Olympics. Bill Martin always wanted to create a successful business, and he has—but he seemed to do his best work on jobs for which he hadn't applied, wasn't trained, and didn't get paid.

Getting the Wolverines back to where they had been in the 1980s was one thing. Moving the department forward would be another—although having the Faculty Board reduced to advisory status sped things up. In 2004, Martin knew the department needed more money to update the facilities, but he had to decide whether to follow Michigan's peers, who were raising money through transfer fees, personal seat donations (PSDs), and priority points systems, which rewarded donations. In fairness to Martin, since 1974, Michigan had finished first in attendance every year but one, 1997, but remained the nation's only program in the top 20 for attendance that didn't charge a seat license, and one of the few that didn't charge a transfer fee or reward donations through priority points. It was behind the times—and leaving money on the table because of it.

This presented Martin with the classic arms-race dilemma: start running and keep up, or drop out and get passed by? Michigan fans didn't want to get charged more than any other fans, but they weren't too fond of seeing their teams left behind, either. Martin decided to add these revenue programs, but very gradually, and only after communicating to thousands of Michigan fans how they worked and why they were needed.

Marty Bodnar, Michigan's former associate athletic director for ticketing, remembers the planning meetings that went into those rollouts. "Before this policy change," he explains, "you could transfer your tickets to your spouse, but not to your kids or to anyone else. I knew from daily conversations with these ticket holders that they would love the opportunity to give these tickets to their kids or nephews or whoever.

"So, two years before we started the PSD, probably in '03 or '04, we set eight seats as the maximum for any ticket holders, to give more people on the waiting list access to tickets. Out of 24,000 season ticket holders, only about 300 had nine or more—one had 80!—so it wasn't that hard to do. Whether they had 10 tickets or 100, they could transfer to anyone they wanted to, for $500 per season ticket, tax deductible. Sure enough, they jumped at the chance. Someone transferred their tickets to their four-month-old baby. I called all 300 or so big account holders personally to explain the policy, and I only had two angry phone calls.

"We made $7 million from the transfers alone, and almost everyone was happy about it."

They used a similar procedure to introduce the personal seat donations (PSDs), a fee most top programs were charging their fans just to reserve the right to buy the tickets. It's considered a donation—which is a stretch, since all fans apparently decide to "donate" exactly the same amount, or lose their tickets. But that allows fans to claim it as a gift to a state university, and a tax deduction. So far, the IRS has gone along with it.

"We were sitting there in May of 2005, trying to decide where to price the PSD," Bodnar recalls. "It was about a week after Michigan State announced $500 for a PSD to reserve a ticket at midfield. So we ran the math, and found that $500 for a PSD at midfield would generate sufficient revenue to meet the financial challenges that we were facing. Then we built out from there: $375 for the next group of sections, then $250, and $125 in the corner, and zero in the endzone. If someone didn't want to pay the PSD, they could move to the endzone, and about 3 or 4 percent of our ticket holders did that."

But instead of simply jamming the policy down the fans' throats, the department conducted a survey of the fans and held "town hall meetings" in Ann Arbor, Detroit, Flint, Grand Rapids, and countless alumni clubs with hundreds of students, alumni, fans, and longtime season-ticket holders.

"We gave them all kinds of notice about the PSD," Bodnar recalls. "Over a two-year period, we sent out six letters to explain it to season-ticket holders. And we always said, 'Hey, if you have any questions, just call us up,' and we gave out our numbers. We actually got some interesting feedback, to tweak things here and there, and we did. But the town hall meetings confirmed that the fans would be okay with it. We're asking for more money, but they understood why, they understood how we were going to do it, and they knew we're giving something in return, the ability to transfer to the younger generation."

With each new policy, the department found very little resistence from the fans, who knew their tickets were underpriced due to the long wait list, and the scalpers who eagerly bought their tickets for more than face value. They also knew Michigan was behind its peers in pursuing these policies, and that the department probably could have asked for a lot more and gotten it. The fans weren't begging to pay more, of course, but they went away feeling like they were being asked to contribute more to a worthy cause, instead of having their goodwill exploited for a few more bucks to pay for some extravagance.

In 2005, Martin instituted Michigan's new Priority Points system, modeled on the best plans around the country. But again, the department refrained from moving their fans' seats, this time according to their donations. They knew their fans felt a great connection with the people in their sections, people they often had known for decades. Despite seeing each other only on football Saturdays, their relationships often generated invitations to graduations and weddings.

As Martin learned, "Michigan Stadium on a football Saturday is truly a collection of neighborhoods. These are families who've known each other for generations, through Michigan football—and they do not want to leave their neighborhoods! That kind of loyalty, that kind of connection, you don't want to break the chain. Keeping them is one thing. Getting them back would be another."

While Martin's new policies certainly marked a break with the past, their easy reception by Michigan's fans proved once again it's not just what you do, it's how you do it. The proof was the wait list—the last of the policy changes.

"We had about 10,000 people on the wait list," Bodnar recalls. "We started charging ten bucks to stay on it, just to make sure you're serious. There's no point having a wait list of people who don't really want tickets. Well, after all these changes, almost everybody paid the ten bucks to stay on the list.

"But, as part of the Priority Points system, if you donated $2,000, $5,000, or whatever, you'd get off the wait list, and get tickets. Limited supply. Before the Points program, everyone had to have a conversation with me to move their seats toward midfield. There were no hard and fast rules, so I got a ton of calls—and I had to make a lot of tough decisions. But after we put the Priority Points system in, calls were cut in half. We desperately needed that program!"

The rollout of these new policies was careful and successful, and it underscored with Bodnar some basic truths about Michigan ticket holders: "You hear their stories and read their e-mails, and you realize pretty quick: They all had such a strong emotional tie to Michigan. Generation to generation to generation, people who've gone to every game, home or away, going back to the 1960s or farther.

"One of the great things is Michigan tradition, and it's the emotional pull. This showed me it's family, it's generational."

Martin then took on the biggest, most ambitious and difficult project: renovating Michigan Stadium, which needed expanded aisles, concourses, and bathrooms, just to comply with legal standards.

"Now, what to do about it all?" Martin said. "We figured, if we were going to open this up, we might as well get as much done as we could. There didn't seem any point in going halfway, and leaving it for another athletic director down the road to fix."

If they simply renovated the existing bowl, they calculated they would need to raise ticket prices for everyone by about 30 percent, and the Big House would no longer have room for 100,000 seats—two prospects they knew would not appeal to most Michigan fans. So they decided to go all out and update the stadium so thoroughly it wouldn't require any major changes for decades—and that meant adding stadium suites. By 2006, six other Big Ten schools already had skyboxes, and two more were planned. By 2010, the only other Big Ten schools without skyboxes would be Indiana and Northwestern—not exactly Michigan football's peers. Again, Martin faced the same dilemma: join the arms race, or join the bottom division.

To keep resistance to a minimum, Martin, his right-hand man, Mike Stevenson—the department's unsung hero—and his staff came up with a classic brick design that fit the rest of the athletic campus. There would be no Maize Halo this time. Martin also made sure the plan would have something for everyone, no matter where they sat, including wider aisles, better bathrooms, and better acoustics, to address the common complaint that the Big House was too quiet.

Just as important, Charles Baird's vision for a fiscally self-sufficient department would be bolstered. The plan would not require a dime from the university's general fund, nor a student surcharge, which is how most schools pay for their athletic programs.

The department also made an implicit promise in its pitch: The skyboxes would keep ticket prices down for the average fan, serving as a progressive tax on the wealthiest Michigan boosters, who would effectively be subsidizing the football program, tickets for the average fan, and the non-revenue sports— exactly what Yost intended when he finished Michigan Stadium in 1927. In effect, 5,000 premium ticket holders—in the suites and the indoor and outdoor club seats—were paying to upgrade the stadium for the other 100,000 fans.

Unlike its peers, however, Michigan predictably faced resistance from fans and Regents alike. But after a lot of presentations, debates, and wrangling, Martin eventually got the plan approved by a 5–3 vote of the Regents, with Dave Brandon leading the charge. Before opening day, 2010, the renovations were finished on time and under budget, all 5,000 premium seats had sold out, and the plan was, ultimately, embraced by the vast majority of fans.

Life was pretty good for Michigan athletics, and its director.

Just about every morning, he woke up at 5:30 in the house he and Sally bought in 1972 for $41,000 ("It works for us"), put on a pair of khaki pants and a button-down shirt, stopped by First Martin's four-room "World Headquarters" at 6 a.m. for coffee and a paper ("I'm still too cheap to buy my own"), then drove to his office at Weidenbach Hall a half hour later. For lunch, he ordered his usual turkey salad from a place just a block up State Street, Pizza Bob's. Success hadn't changed Martin much.

Martin's great strengths were handling budgets and buildings, but he had to go outside his comfort zone to hire new coaches. Nonetheless, when he hired Tommy Amaker to lead the men's basketball team in 2001, almost everyone hailed it as a great selection. But the team didn't get good enough, fast enough, so Martin had to make a change. When Amaker left for Harvard in 2007, however, there is little question Amaker had left Michigan's program better than he'd found it.

Martin discovered John Beilein when he was flipping channels one night and came across one of Beilein's games at West Virginia. "The announcers were going on about how creative he was on offense," Martin recalls. "And he had a player named Pittsnoggle, a big man who could hit the three. How can you forget a name like that? I started following John, and looking into his background. Everyone I talked to liked him, and respected him. When we had to make a change, I knew he was the guy I wanted."

Martin gave Beilein the support he needed, including patience, and a totally remodeled Crisler Center, complete with a new practice facility. When Beilein's teams missed the NCAA tournament in 2008 and 2010, some Michigan fans—incredibly—were demanding Martin fire Beilein. Martin didn't flinch. Fans were soon rewarded with two Big Ten titles, five NCAA berths, and a return to the NCAA finals in 2013, Michigan's first since the Fab Five got there 20 years earlier. They also have one of Michigan's most popular coaches.

Eight months after hiring Beilein, Martin would have to hire a head football coach. In just about every way imaginable, that would prove much trickier.

CHAPTER 8

THE PRODIGAL SON

Before Martin could start weighing the candidates, however, one of them was already making national news—news that would affect the coaching search, and the two searches that would soon follow.

When Jack Harbaugh coached defensive backs for Bo Schembechler in the seventies, his sons John and Jim would come to practice when they could and horse around, and serve as the unofficial ball boys when they could. Jim later became the favorite babysitter of Schembechler's youngest son, Shemy.

In 1980, Jack left Michigan to coach Stanford's defense. Jim transferred to Palo Alto High, where he starred at quarterback, but only Wisconsin—then a Big Ten bottom dweller—offered Harbaugh a scholarship, until Schembechler called. Jim's mom, Jackie, called Schembechler to be certain Schembechler was not simply doing the family a favor. Schembechler assured her his interest was sincere, then proved it two years later when he started Harbaugh as a red-shirt sophomore in 1984. Harbaugh surpassed all the big-name recruits in the Big Ten to become the league's MVP in 1986.

Harbaugh enjoyed a fourteen-year career in the NFL before retiring in 2001. The next year he applied to become Michigan's quarterback coach, but when Lloyd Carr picked Scott Loeffler, who already had four years of experience, Harbaugh accepted Al Davis's offer to coach the Oakland Raiders' quarterbacks. Two years later, in 2004, the University of San Diego—a I-AA Jesuit school that did not offer athletic scholarships, but wanted to leverage football to attract more male students to a student body that was roughly two-thirds women—offered Harbaugh the head coaching position at $80,000 a year.

"Al Davis begged him, *begged* him, not to do it," says Todd Anson, a friend of Harbaugh's who has occasionally served him as a lawyer and adviser. "He told Jim, 'In three to five years you'll be an NFL head coach.' But Jim wanted to be a head coach *now*."

Soon after Harbaugh took the USD job, he got a call from Schembechler, who asked only two questions: "Are you gonna have a tight end?"

"Yes," Harbaugh said.

"Are you gonna have a fullback?"

"Yes."

"Fine. You'll do great!"

Schembechler was right. Harbaugh had a tight end. He had a fullback. And in just his second season, the Toreros captured their first league title since the program started in 1956. They went 11–1 that year, and again the next, in 2006, to claim the team's second league title.

Between Harbaugh's second and third seasons at USD, Anson received an invitation from the University of Michigan to the President Ford/Bo Schembechler golf outing in Palm Springs, California. Anson knew Harbaugh still dreamed of coaching Michigan—a dream Anson, who'd gone to law school in Ann Arbor, shared. So, when Anson got the invitation, he called Harbaugh.

"When was the last time you saw Bo?"

"Two years ago, at the 2004 reunion."

"You're coming with us," Anson said.

Harbaugh's schedule didn't allow him to stay for golf, but he drove two and a half hours from San Diego to Palm Springs just to visit with Schembechler for an hour, before he drove back. The mutual affection between them was obvious. At one point Schembechler asked Harbaugh, "How many years did you play in the NFL?"

Jim proudly answered, "Fourteen," knowing it was by far the most of any Michigan quarterback. He knew Schembechler knew it, too.

"Hot damn!" Schembechler said. "Isn't that something!"

That was the last time Jim Harbaugh saw Bo Schembechler.

Near the end of Harbaugh's second 11–1 campaign at the University of San Diego, Bo Schembechler died on Friday, November 17, 2006.

"I never met Bo," Jim's wife Sarah told me, "but Jim used to have these CDs of Bo's team meetings, which he listens to all the time when he's driving."

Jim met Sarah in 2006, his third season coaching San Diego. That first season together, Sarah went along for a road game. Since she was on her own, she asked if she could sit in the locker room for the pregame speech. Jim agreed, but asked her to hide in the back of the locker room so no one would know she was there.

"Now, you have to realize," she said, "I only know Jim outside of football. I've only seen his softer side. So when he starts his speech, he morphs into this person I've never seen before! He's yelling and screaming. *What* is he *doing?* I think, 'Maybe it's a joke?'"

After the game, Sarah asked him, "'*What* was *that?!*' He just kind of laughed. He didn't do it because I was there. He did it because that's who is he is when he's coaching. That's *him!*"

A year later, the two were driving together when Sarah heard one of Schembechler's locker room speeches come through Jim's car speakers. "Oh my god!" she said. "You're mimicking this man! You're playing Bo!' He just laughed. Guilty!"

When Jim's father, Jack, called to tell him Schembechler had died, Sarah understood Jim's reaction.

"I had never seen my husband break down before. But when he heard Bo died, I've never seen him react to anything like that—and I don't think I ever will again until maybe his parents die. You see that, you knew what Bo must have meant to him."

Jim and Sarah Harbaugh joined hundreds of his teammates at Schembechler's service. "I learned a lot about Bo that week," she said. "He was like a second father to Jim, and his teammates. I can see why everyone reveres him."

That trip marked Sarah Harbaugh's first visit to Ann Arbor. Her second would not come until late December 2014.

A month after Schembechler died, I called Harbaugh in his new Stanford office to ask if he might provide a recollection for the book Schembechler and I had been working on. He had just taken over Stanford, but he took the time to send a few stories, including these lines:

"No matter what he had to say to you," Harbaugh wrote, "it always felt great to be noticed by Bo."

He recalled Schembechler calling him into his office the Monday after Harbaugh's clutch performance in a 27–17 victory over Ohio State in 1985, one of the finest games Schembechler had ever seen a Michigan quarterback play.

"Then he leaned back in his chair and looked up at the ceiling," Harbaugh recalled. "'What it must feel like to have a son play the way you did! To stand in that pocket with the safety bearing down on you, unblocked, and hit Jon Kolesar on the post to seal the victory. UNBLOCKED!' He then let loose his familiar chuckle. 'I'm proud of you, Jim.'

"I felt as loved and appreciated as I have ever felt, like I was one of Bo's sons. In reality I was one of Bo's thousands of sons."

The last team Schembechler watched, the 2006 Wolverines, was one of Michigan's best, winning its first 11 games before he passed away, then losing an "instant classic" to Ohio State, 42–39, the next day. The Wolverines still earned a trip to face USC in the Rose Bowl, just a few weeks after Stanford announced Harbaugh would be the Cardinal's new head coach.

Harbaugh traveled from Palo Alto to Pasadena to see his old Michigan friends at the Rose Bowl, show his support for his alma mater, and take in the New Year's Day game. At a Michigan pep rally on the Santa Monica Pier, Todd Anson, Bill Martin, and Jim Harbaugh got to know each other better. Martin told Harbaugh he still needed an opponent for the rededication game of the Big House in 2010, and invited Harbaugh to bring the Cardinal.

Stanford had just finished the 2006 season at 1–11, and hadn't had a winning record since Tyrone Willingham left for Notre Dame in 2001, two head coaches ago. Michigan, meanwhile, had recently been ranked second behind only Ohio State, and would be ranked fifth going into the 2007 season—reason enough, perhaps, for Harbaugh to decline. But the real reason was far more personal.

"Now, playing Michigan made a lot of sense, on a lot of levels," Harbaugh told me. "And Stanford had played Michigan a lot in the past. But when I started visualizing what it would be like to coach on the other side—the 'wrong' side!—and to coach *against* Michigan, I thought, 'I don't know if I want to do that. I don't know if I *could* do that!'

"So, we didn't do that!"

Five months later, in May of 2007, Harbaugh had settled in as Stanford's head coach, and was immediately impressed by the academic success of his players, five of whom were engineering majors, and 20 more enrolled in Science, Technology and Engineering. In an interview with Glenn Dickey of the *San Francisco Examiner*, Harbaugh made what seemed to be a casual observation.

"College football needs Stanford," Harbaugh said. "We're looking not for student-athletes, but scholar-athletes. No other school can carry this banner. The Ivy League schools don't have enough weight. Other schools which have good academic reputations have ways to get borderline athletes in and keep them in."

Then Dickey asked Harbaugh, who had earned Academic All-Big Ten honors, about his alma mater.

"Michigan is a good school, and I got a good education there," Harbaugh said. "But the athletic department has ways to get borderline guys in and, when they're in, they steer them to courses in sports communications. They're adulated when they're playing, but when they get out, the people who adulated them won't hire them."

Harbaugh's comments got back to *Ann Arbor News* sports columnist Jim Carty, who wrote, "With fewer than 100 words, Harbaugh made himself a major topic of conversation on Web sites devoted to Michigan's sports programs and drew the attention and concern of school officials.

"No one so closely associated with the football program has ever suggested Michigan was actively cutting corners academically to succeed in football.

"Given Harbaugh's history—his dad was a Bo Schembechler assistant, and he led the Wolverines to the Big Ten title and the Rose Bowl in 1986—it was hard not to wonder if he hadn't been misquoted or joking."

It was Carty's job to find out, so he called Harbaugh's PR person at Stanford to ask to talk with the head coach. Harbaugh called back almost immediately, and they talked for 10 or 15 minutes.

"It was typical Harbaugh," Carty told me recently, "based on my other interactions with him. He asked what I needed, and then gave me what I needed by directly answering my questions, then asked if I needed anything else, and we were done."

To Carty's surprise, "Harbaugh not only stood by his comments," Carty wrote, "he expanded on them. When asked to defend his claim that Michigan pushes athletes into easy majors, he paused for a second, and then dropped a bombshell.

"'I would use myself as an example,' Harbaugh said. 'I came in there, wanted to be a history major, and I was told early on in my freshman year that I shouldn't be. That it takes too much time. Too much reading. That I shouldn't be a history major and play football.

"'As great as the institution is at Michigan, I think it should be held to a higher standard,' Harbaugh said. 'I don't think it should cut corners that dramatically for football and basketball players. I love the university. I got a tremendous education there. I think it should be held to a higher standard.

"'I think it should hold itself to a higher standard.'"

In 2015, Carty told me, "The only thing I can add, is that there was a general attitude of 'Seriously? Am I saying anything that controversial here? Who are we kidding? You know how they do things, right? Am I saying anything crazy?' No, he wasn't."

Loyalty to Michigan has never been blind—and indeed, it cannot be, or

Michigan will lose its way, like any successful institution. Harbaugh had seen how Stanford handled its players academically, and saw how the players themselves met their academic obligations, and he was understandably impressed. One of his first reactions, as a dyed-in-the-wool Michigan Man, was to wonder why Michigan had not met the same standards when he played.

Taken alone, this is exactly the reaction a Michigan Man is supposed to have when he discovers another university might be doing something better: Why can't Michigan do that?

Harbaugh ran into trouble, however, on two fronts: one, failing to place his comments in context, by noting that Michigan was ahead of all but a few of its football peers academically; and two, saying it publicly to a reporter, and not privately to someone at Michigan who might be able to give him a good answer, do something about it, or both.

On the context question, when Harbaugh said, "the [Michigan] athletic department has ways to get borderline guys in," he of course was right. To its credit, Michigan has never denied giving student-athletes preference in admissions—just as it does for children of alumni, kids from Alaska, and underrepresented minorities.

Every school has done this—including Harvard and Yale, Williams and Wesleyan, and even Stanford—since the dawn of college athletics, and still does. The question is how far a school will dip its standards to get a talented athlete. The answer for Michigan: not nearly as far as most of its peers. That's why Michigan football players, at the time Harbaugh made his comments, ranked third in graduation rate among Big Ten teams, behind only Penn State and Northwestern.

Likewise, Michigan's Bachelor of General Studies degree—which has often been criticized as a loophole for athletes—is not some backdoor program, but is as good as you make it, like most undergraduate programs at large state universities. It has almost all the same requirements as a traditional BA or BS, with two differences: the BGS major does not have to focus on a particular field, nor take four semesters of foreign language.

Michigan's Bachelor of General Studies alums include Steve Nissen, the chair of the Cleveland Clinic's Cardiology Department; Rick Snyder, the former chairman of Gateway Computers, and now the governor of the State of Michigan; and Jim Hackett, the CEO of Steelcase Furniture, who also played football for Schembechler.

As for getting talked out of his history major, Harbaugh obviously had no reason to make that up, but it's worth noting that two of Harbaugh's predecessors as Michigan's starting quarterback, Tom Slade and Rich Hewlett, became Schembechler's dentist and lawyer, respectively. One of Harbaugh's teammates, Stefan Humphries—who would play five years in the NFL before becoming a doctor and joining the faculty of the Mayo Clinic—achieved such a sterling transcript in engineering at Michigan, while playing offensive guard, that *Sports Illustrated* printed it in a feature story on the lineman.

Unlike the University of North Carolina—a world-class teaching and research university that was recently exposed for providing bogus courses, grades, and even majors for thousands of students—Michigan was still a national leader academically, athletically, and ethically.

But it's worth repeating that nothing Harbaugh said was false, or even a cheap shot—and if Michigan couldn't handle the truth, its alumni could hardly call themselves the Leaders and Best with a straight face. If Harbaugh's critics believe he should have provided more context, it's fair to point out most of them ignored the context of his comments, too. He was the Stanford head coach, who said repeatedly Michigan was a "great institution" where he received a "tremendous education."

After the story hit the newsstands, Michigan's leaders had the chance to open a dialogue with the former Michigan quarterback, provide a broader perspective, defend its program where appropriate, and make whatever improvements were needed. Instead, no one from Michigan called Harbaugh to discuss his comments; no one explained its program to the public, or looked into Harbaugh's claims.

But Jim Carty did. "When Jim Harbaugh, a man who played here and makes his living in college football, is willing to burn down one of the most important bridges in his life to make the point Michigan can do a better job balancing football with academics, it's impossible not to ask whether he might be right."

And when Carty did so during the paper's six-month investigation into Harbaugh's claims, no one at Michigan agreed to sit down with him or his editor. (President Coleman's office did offer to answer questions by e-mail, which the paper declined—perhaps a mistake on both sides.) What followed instead was the least productive exchange possible for both sides, with players and coaches taking ad hominem attacks at the former Michigan captain, while ignoring his actual points.

Coach Carr called Harbaugh's comments "elitist," "arrogant," and "self-serving." At the Big Ten Media Days, Michigan's all-time leading rusher Mike Hart went farther. "That's a guy I have no respect for," Hart said. "You graduate from the University of Michigan, and you're going to talk about your school like that, a great university like we have? . . . He's not a Michigan Man. I wish he'd never played here."

But those shots missed the mark. While a Michigan Man might attempt to address his concerns privately before airing them publicly, the same could be said in return. Apparently, neither Hart nor Carr tried to contact Harbaugh privately before making their public criticisms. Further, if a Michigan Man is "elitist" and "arrogant" because he believes his school should aspire to be the very best both academically and athletically, then every Michigan alum would qualify.

The only charge Harbaugh's critics made that stuck was "self-serving," insofar as Harbaugh was the head coach of Stanford, not Michigan. But even if Harbaugh was selling himself in his new role as Stanford's head coach, he was raising the right question for Michigan to answer. The proof is the contrapositive: Imagine how it would have played if Harbaugh had said he had been talked out of becoming a history major—and that's exactly what Michigan football should have done then, and should be doing now?

And that's about how Harbaugh replied when columnist Pat Forde followed up for his reaction. The responses from Coach Carr, Mike Hart, and others, Harbaugh said, "seemed very orchestrated and organized, especially coming two months after my comments were made. I'm not going to allow those comments to define who I am. Mike Hart and Jamie Morris are not the makers of the Michigan Man list. I put in the blood, sweat, and tears to prove I belong on that list.

"My motivation was positive. I see how it's done now at Stanford, and I see no reason to believe it can't be the same there. I have a great love for Michigan and what it's done for me. Bo Schembechler was like a second father. Michigan is a great school and always has been, and I don't see why they can't hold themselves to a higher standard."

If there was a flaw in Harbaugh's logic, no one pointed it out.

If Michigan's president, athletic director, and head coach had reached out to Harbaugh, all parties would probably have delivered revised public statements soon thereafter, followed by a stirring defense of Michigan as it was, and a promise to make it even better. Such an exchange would have given the nation the lasting impression that this was a university that had its act together.

Instead, at the end of this churlish give-and-take, it was hard to say anyone had come out ahead—with the possible exception of Michigan's rivals.

CHAPTER 9

SEARCHING OUTSIDE THE FAMILY

After the 2007 Wolverines were upset by Appalachian State in the season opener, then blown out by Oregon at home the next weekend, they clawed their way back by winning their next eight games, before ending the regular season with losses to Wisconsin and Ohio State. Two days later, on November 19, 2007, Lloyd Carr announced he would be stepping down as Michigan's head coach after the team's Capital One Bowl matchup against Florida.

Emboldened by his successful search for a basketball coach, Bill Martin embarked on the quest to find a new football coach. But football and basketball at Michigan are not the same, especially when Martin knew Michigan would have to go outside the current football coaching staff for the first time since 1968, and only the fourth time since 1879. (Of course, the first three—Yost, Crisler, and Schembechler—worked out pretty well.)

"The first hurdle is that we didn't have an obvious successor," Martin has said. "From Bo on down, that's how you keep the culture going. But there wasn't anyone on the staff who was ready. But boy, that would have been so much easier for everyone."

Martin interviewed Carr's two coordinators, Mike DeBord and Ron English, but passed on both. English would become the head coach at Eastern Michigan in 2009, and finish five seasons later with an 11–46 record. Given Eastern's well earned reputation as a graveyard of coaches, English's struggles were predictable. More surprising was DeBord's failure at Central Michigan, a program where Herb Deromedi set the Mid-American Conference record for victories, and Brian Kelly, now at Notre Dame, and Butch Jones, now at Tennessee, both launched their careers. DeBord, however, had a 12–34 overall record and 7–25 in the MAC, and quit after the 2003 season. Martin had to search outside the family. The 2007 search careened left and right. At one point, in a New York hotel room, Martin offered the job to Rutgers' Greg Schiano, subject to negotiating a suitable contract. Schiano accepted that night—then declined the next morning.

Michigan flirted with Les Miles, who had played and coached for Schembechler and would lead Louisiana State to a national title a few weeks later. Miles was clearly interested, but each time the two parties started discussing the possibility, someone leaked the calls to the media, which repeatedly put Miles in hot water down in Baton Rouge. LSU's athletic director finally ended the speculation by locking Miles into a five-year contract worth $3.75 million a year, plus $1,000 each year to ensure he would be the nation's highest-paid college coach, ahead of Nick Saban.

Jim Harbaugh's name often came up, with good reason. His first Stanford team that fall made national news when they faced Pete Carroll's number-one-ranked USC team, favored by 41 points, and riding a 35-game home winning streak. They beat them in Los Angeles, 24–23, which many experts consider the second-biggest upset in college football, behind only the Appalachian State game.

Harbaugh was just getting started, but his comments about the Michigan football team's academics—followed by angry responses and the *Ann Arbor News* investigation—effectively killed any chance he might have had to replace Lloyd Carr, who still had a say about his successor.

At the eleventh hour, Martin seemed to pull a rabbit out of a hat when he hired West Virginia head coach Rich Rodriguez, who had turned down Alabama just one year earlier—prompting Alabama to move on to its second choice, Nick Saban. Just a few weeks earlier, Rodriguez had missed a shot at a national title when his second-ranked Mountaineers, favored by four touchdowns, had to pull their star quarterback in the second quarter, and lost to lowly Pitt, 13–9, in the third-biggest upset of a crazy season.

At the time, it looked like Harbaugh wouldn't get another chance for many years, if ever.

Rodriguez never had a single easy month in Ann Arbor, starting with his first one—and it only seemed to get tougher.

Even today, more than four years after Michigan fired Rich Rodriguez, the autopsy is not a simple matter. It's fair to say people on every side of the equation could have done better to make the transition work. The list of mistakes included the president and athletic director bungling Rodriguez's buyout from West Virginia, which made many fans turn on Rodriguez from the start; Rodriguez not learning the importance of Michigan tradition fast enough; neither side pushing hard enough to get Jeff Casteel, Rodriguez's defensive coordinator from West Virginia, to join his staff; the previous coaching staff not supporting Rodriguez, sometimes actively; and, not least, a historically bad defense.

In the process, everyone discovered a basic truth that separates college football from the pro game: in the NFL, a big-time coach like Bill Parcells can leave New England and go to archrival New York Jets, and it makes no difference. But in college football, installing a powerful coach into a winning program steeped in tradition is not as simple as plugging an appliance into a socket and switching it on, but more akin to performing a heart transplant. For that operation, you need to be sure the new organ is the right size and blood type, the body will accept it, and everyone will do their part to make sure it was not rejected.

At Michigan, none of that happened.

Minutes after Brandon told Rodriguez he was fired, on January 5, 2011, Rodriguez returned to the staff room, where his assistants were waiting. He walked in, sat down, laid a manila folder on the table, and said, "Well, as expected, they fired me."

There was a long pause. No one moved, or made a sound.

"It was a bad fit from the start."

For all the factors that went into Rodriguez's early departure, four-plus years later it is hard to improve on Rodriguez's basic analysis.

In 2008, Harbaugh's second season at Stanford, the Cardinal improved slightly to 5–7, then upset USC in Los Angeles again in 2009, en route to an 8–5 record. Things were looking up in Palo Alto.

In the middle of that 2009 season, Bill Martin announced he would retire as Michigan's athletic director, effective September 4, 2010, the day Michigan would rededicate Michigan's stadium in the season opener against the University of Connecticut. Rodriguez knew his fate—like that of Martin's 226 employees, 800 student-athletes, 500,000 alumni, and 2.9 million fans—would be left to the next athletic director.

But even if the Michigan job didn't open up any time soon, it bothered Harbaugh greatly to be estranged from his alma mater and his hometown. When his friend Todd Anson visited Harbaugh at his Stanford office shortly after Martin announced his retirement, Anson saw that Harbaugh wanted to make things right with Michigan, simply for the sake of making them right.

"So, we decide to write an ice-breaker e-mail to Bill Martin," Anson said.

From: Jim Harbaugh
Sent: Tuesday, November 10, 2009
To: [Bill Martin]
Subject: Best Regards
Mr. Martin,
    Congratulations on your retirement announcement. You've done a great job the last ten years. Don't let the bastards get you down.
Go Blue/Go Stanford
—Jim Harbaugh

To Harbaugh's surprise, Martin replied the same day.

Jim,
    Thanks for your note. Your team is really improving. I talked to Bob [Bowlsby, then Stanford's AD, now the Big 12 commissioner] just last week about Stanford playing in the Big House in '12, '14, or '16. Interested?
    It's time to have you back on campus. You're a part of Michigan's football history. All the "drama" of a couple of years ago is over. I would be honored to host you anytime, even if we can't work out a game.
Regards, Bill

A few minutes later, Harbaugh wrote back:

Bill—
    Thank you for your kind note and offer. Please understand that I love Michigan and never intended to disparage the program in any way. I still have Bo ringing in my head! And for family entertainment my Dad does his Bo, "The Team, the Team, the Team!" impression frequently.
    My comments were only intended to underscore how difficult the recruiting job is at Stanford [but the comments] ignited a small blaze for us both. For that, I have regret and, if there is anything I can ever do to support the [Michigan] program consistent with not igniting a similar firestorm out here at Stanford to the effect that I am either a traitor or distracted, I would be happy to do it.
    As for the idea of bringing the Cardinal into the newly expanded Big House, it sure would be strange to stand on the east sidelines looking back at the Michigan team. Let me give it some thought. My principal concern is

to keep this team bowl-eligible which as you know, in part, requires hold-ing as many homes dates as possible.
Best regards,
Jim

Once again, Martin replied almost immediately:

Jim,
Understand completely on both subjects. It's simply time for healing; you're too much a part of our football legacy not to be recognized for your contributions to Michigan and now to college football.
Let's give some thought as to possible next steps.
Bill.

When Anson was about to leave Harbaugh's office that day, Harbaugh said, "The healing feels good, doesn't it?"

If you are looking for the humble headwaters of the river that would rush Jim Harbaugh to Ann Arbor in the last days of 2014, that simple e-mail exchange was it.

THE BRANDON ERA BEGINS

CHAPTER 10

THE PIZZA KING

Unlike picking a new football coach, picking a new athletic director looked like it would be a simple, straightforward process. Michigan had the luxury of choosing among three candidates who were experienced, successful Division I athletic directors with deep ties to Michigan: University of Buffalo's Warde Manuel, who had played for Schembechler, then worked under Martin; Oregon State's Bob DeCarolis, who had coached softball, then served in Canham's department; and Miami of Ohio's Brad Bates, who had also played for Schembechler, and spent his adult life working in college athletics. The search committee didn't seem to give much thought to candidates without Michigan ties, perhaps because they simply didn't have to. The pond was already stocked.

All three had done strong work both at Michigan and their adopted schools, but Bates seemed to stand out. He had earned a doctorate in education while working at Vanderbilt. After being named the athletic director at Miami (Ohio), the football team earned its first back-to-back bowl games in 30 years, he built a new state-of-the-art hockey arena where the men's team would earn the school's first national number one ranking in any sport, and he graduated 75 percent of the school's athletes at a highly regarded academic institution.

Bates's rise through the ranks was not lost on Schembechler. In 2006, he gave me this quote for his book: "Today Brad Bates is the athletic director at Miami of Ohio—and they love him, there, too. They love him! He's done a marvelous job, and I'm sure you'll be hearing his name whenever a big job opens up. I would not be surprised if he becomes Michigan's athletic director down the road.

"If he doesn't, it'll be our loss."

The careers of Manuel, DeCarolis, and Bates stood as a testament to the program Canham and Schembechler had built. The search committee could have picked any of them, and been confident Michigan athletics would continue to thrive, on and off the field.

But President Coleman asked the committee to interview a fourth, less conventional candidate: Dave Brandon.

To understand any leader, you have to understand his past. For Brandon, of course, that included his stint as a player, his term as a Regent, and his decade spent leading Domino's Pizza.

"Dave was an *outstanding* Regent," says Paul Courant, who has served the university in more important posts than just about anyone, including: provost, dean of libraries, director of the Institute of Public Policy Studies (now the Ford School of Public Policy), director of University of Michigan Press and now a professor of public policy, economics, and information. "I'm not sure if everyone realizes that. But in many organizations, especially nonprofits, there is a tension between the board and management. Often each board member thinks he or she knows how the organization should work in detail, and there can be a tendency to step over the line between setting policy and managing operations. At Michigan, the Regents are supposed to make the big decisions, and let the administration handle implementation and the smaller issues. But there is often a temptation to get into the weeds, I think, which I suppose is human nature.

"When Dave was a Regent you could rely on him to back off from micromanagement, and to encourage his colleagues to do so as well. He would bring the conversation back to helping management perform well. His argument was simple—and I'm paraphrasing here: 'We all say we want excellence at Michigan, in all areas. Well, excellence is costly, so we'll have to pay for it—and then trust our guys to be the experts they are in their fields.'"

Brandon impressed Courant on a personal level, too. "He was always dead straight with me, and even willing to change his mind. For example, on the need to raise tuition, which he initially opposed. But when you sit down with him and make your case, he understands, and can see the value, and make a tough choice. I think that would surprise a lot of people."

When Brandon's eight-year term ended in 2006, he ran for reelection. Regent elections are almost impossible to handicap, because the office isn't big enough to warrant polls, surveys, and the like; the candidates are not as well known as other office seekers on the ballot; and they're voted on statewide.

Despite Brandon's almost universally praised work on the board, 2006 was a Democratic year, and Brandon's reelection bid fell 225,908 votes, or about 14 percent, short from winning the second Regents' seat. More surprising, Brandon also finished behind fellow Republican candidate Susan Brown, a Michigan alumna and interior decorator, who did not have the advantage of being an incumbent.

"I've always thought the [Regental] elections are largely luck," says Larry Deitch, who has been elected Regent three times. "Not Dave. I understand he took losing pretty hard. It's a job that grows on you, and you don't want to give it up—particularly if you love the university as much as we do. I'm sure he was pretty upset."

Although many believed Brandon would use his post on the Board of Regents as a springboard to the governor's office—just as Schembechler had hoped and predicted—after Brandon lost the 2006 election, the same people believe he became turned off by electoral politics. After a long conversation with the state GOP, he ultimately decided not to seek the 2010 Republican nomination for governor. Instead, Brandon set his sights on another prestigious office: athletic director at the University of Michigan.

If Brandon's term on the Board of Regents generated virtually unanimous praise, his record as a CEO is more complicated.

In 1998, Bain Capital—the firm Mitt Romney co-founded, that buys companies, then usually sells them for large profits—bought Domino's Pizza and hired Brandon to succeed the company's founder, Tom Monaghan, as CEO.

Monaghan had enrolled at the University of Michigan in 1959 to study architecture. To pay for it, he and his brother James bought a pizza place in nearby Ypsilanti, Michigan, in 1960, for $900. But the place was losing so much money, Monaghan decided he needed to drop out of school to work on it full time.

He quickly discovered he had a passion for pizza, and it showed. He estimates he's made more than half a million pizzas with his own hands, and he has the burns to show for it. "The worst are the double burns," he says.

"I was tough on the help, but tougher on myself," he told me. "We worked! But just about any time someone got married, they asked me to be their best man. There was a mutual respect between us."

The key to Domino's success was simple: they delivered the pizza to your door in a corrugated cardboard box Monaghan invented to keep the pizza hot, and they did it fast.

"I didn't invent delivery," he says, "but I was the first to make it work. We showed everyone else how to do it."

Once they figured out how to deliver pizzas effectively and consistently, they started growing. For a few years, Monaghan recalls, their first store in Ypsilanti made more pizzas than any store in the country. The chain opened its 1,000th store in 1983, the same year Monaghan bought the Detroit Tigers. The next year, the Tigers won their fourth World Series.

It was a magical decade for Domino's, too, opening its 3,000th store in 1986—tripling the total in just three years—and the 5,000th store before the end of the eighties. Monaghan bought a helicopter to fly his family from Ann Arbor to Tiger Stadium each night, and purchased a lodge with 3,000 acres on Drummond Island in Lake Huron, where he took his family for vacations and Domino's biggest achievers as a reward. He appeared just about everywhere, including *Late Night with David Letterman*, where he made a pizza on stage.

"I thought I could enjoy everything the world had to offer," he said, "including fame, and still be a good Catholic. I learned you can't have two masters." By the early nineties, "I was done with all the pursuit of toys. I wanted a simpler life. I wanted to work to help others, not for myself."

When he finally decided to devote himself to a number of Catholic charities, he put Domino's up for sale, and stepped back from day-to-day operations. But as a result, the company started falling apart, and he couldn't find a buyer.

The problem was simple, he realized. "I lost my focus."

Pizza Hut had passed Domino's, market share was slipping, and the franchise was in trouble. So, Monaghan did what he always did in tough times: he recommitted himself to his brainchild and got back to basics.

In 1991, Domino's various businesses had loans with 32 different banks, so Monaghan hired a man from Goldman Sachs to help consolidate them. In the process, the consultant told Monaghan he'd need to hire a CEO from outside the company, because he believed Monaghan didn't have anyone to run the place—including, apparently, Monaghan himself.

"I think I know this company better than anyone," Monaghan recalls thinking, "and we've made comebacks before. I paid [Goldman Sachs] for their work, five million dollars, then I put the pieces back together, and just started working my tail off. Just like the old days."

He gave his employees an annual pep talk, modeled after Vince Lombardi's famous mantra: "God, Family, and the Green Bay Packers."

"For us, it was God, Family, and Domino's—and the Golden Rule. Simple stuff. It's almost too cliché, and the sharpies will tell you it's too trite—but I did it anyway."

It's worth noting, however, that Monaghan's motivational phrases always came after, not before, a period of intense effort that produced results that confirmed the cliché that followed.

Monaghan was unconventional in other ways, too. "I never cared about profits," he says. "I couldn't even tell you what our revenues were. I've never understood the price of a share. But I could always tell you our store sales, delivery times, and market share, off the top of my head. I wasn't worried about profits. I figured, as long as I was paying the bills and the sales were going up, we would be doing fine. And we always were.

"It was a labor of love. I thought that's how you should run a company: As a labor of love."

By 1996–97, Monaghan remembers, Domino's enjoyed the highest per-store sales increase over the prior year of any restaurant chain in America. "You name it," he says. "McDonald's, Burger King, Denny's, Taco Bell. We beat 'em all."

Domino's had recaptured 31 percent of all pizza delivery in the United States, and was still enjoying rapid growth, while Pizza Hut had slipped behind Domino's, down to 20 percent. When the same consultant from Goldman Sachs consultant came back, Monaghan couldn't resist. "Remember the last time you were here?"

The man had to confess, "This is the most dramatic turnaround I've ever seen on Wall Street."

Having gotten his baby back on its feet, Monaghan turned his attention to starting a Catholic university. But to do that, he would need an abundance of time and money, and that meant one thing: He had to sell Domino's.

In 1998, Morgan Bank lined up five potential suitors, and 14 weeks later Bain Capital bought the franchise for an estimated one billion dollars. Within a few months, Bain's headhunter selected Valassis CEO Dave Brandon to run the company. That surprised Monaghan, because Brandon didn't have any experience in the food industry, but Monaghan became a convert when the company held a worldwide rally in Las Vegas.

"Dave introduced himself to hundreds of franchise owners and other leaders," Monaghan recalls, "and he was just very, very impressive. He's smooth—so much more than me."

Brandon also seemed eager to show his respect to Monaghan. "He was always very cordial with me, both privately and at public events I attended, and continually complimented me on the fine company I had built."

After they returned from Las Vegas, Brandon invited the Domino's board, including Monaghan, to his house for dinner—although calling Brandon's home a house is like calling Niagara Falls a creek.

"His house is mind-boggling," Monaghan says, "and I'm an architecture buff!" Domino's Farms is inspired by Frank Lloyd Wright's "Prairie Home" design, and sits on Frank Lloyd Wright Drive. "Dave's creativity and attention to detail were amazing. His closet alone was a masterpiece. He had clearly planned it out, down to the finest detail.

"Running a company is like building a house. To create a home like that, you have to have some vision. You have to have the courage to do things that may not have been done before. You have to execute it. You have to take the risk and pay for it. As I'm walking around, taking all this in, I'm thinking: This guy might be able to run my company after all."

Monaghan and Brandon met twice after that. The first time, Brandon asked Monaghan to give him a scouting report on all of his vice presidents.

"I thought we had great vice presidents," Monaghan says. "I gave them generally glowing reports, and I believed every word of it. I still believe most of them could have run the company."

The second time, Brandon told Monaghan he was going to get rid of Domino's "no beards" policy, which Monaghan had originally enacted back in the 1970s. Years later, due to an employee lawsuit, they conducted a customer survey and found about a quarter of them had a negative impression of people with beards.

"We're coming into your home at night," Monaghan explained. "Trust is essential. We felt having sharp uniforms and being clean-cut was really important."

Brandon replied that they were losing a lot of good people because of it.

"Well, we've been through that," Monaghan told him, "and we don't agree with that. The *caliber* of help is important too—and so is the image of the company."

"Well," Brandon replied, "if Mark McGwire can have a beard, so can our delivery guys."

Monaghan thought, but didn't say, that Mark McGwire was not likely to come into your home that night to hand you dinner.

Brandon also floated the idea of letting employees wear casual attire, because it would help morale. Monaghan replied, "Only in the short term."

"I told him what I thought," Monaghan recalls, "but he did it anyway. I'm not sure why he asked me."

Because Bain couldn't finance the entire purchase, Monaghan kept about 5.5 percent of the stock, and his family another 2 percent. He also stayed on the board.

"I only went to a few meetings. But I tell you, those meetings were really boring for me. They had all the Bain guys up there, spouting all the buzzwords. They talked a lot about all the room for improvement the company had, and all the things we were doing wrong. I think they thought we had a bungling founder running this place, and they thought they could turn it around. I got the feeling that Bain thought they could make the company work a lot better than I could. Think of what they would have said if I *wasn't* there!

"After four of those meetings, I stopped going. After a while, Dave called me and said, 'If you're not going to come to meetings, maybe you should not be on the board.'"

Monaghan agreed, and stopped coming. Within 18 months, four of the six members of Monaghan's executive team were gone, and the other two soon followed.

"All our vice presidents are gone. They're all gone. And they're all good—very good. It was hard for me to see that happen."

In 2003, however, the trade publication *Pizza Today* named Domino's "Chain of the Year." The next year, Brandon led Domino's to the largest initial public offering (IPO) of a restaurant company. The new CEO looked like a wunderkind.

But the new-CEO shine wore off almost as fast. In 2009, the year Brandon stepped down, Domino's stock price had fallen from the 2004 IPO price of $13.56 per share to $8.38 a share in just five years.

By the most important business metrics, Brandon's stint at Domino's had been a mixed bag. But it wasn't just the dollars and cents that suffered: so did the product. In 2009, a Brand Keys survey of pizza chains had Domino's tied with Chuck E. Cheese's for eleventh place—dead last.

Brandon's successor, Patrick Doyle—whom Monaghan had hired in 1997—started Domino's own focus groups, which confirmed all the bad news. After Brandon left, Domino's spent millions on ads telling customers they were right: their product was bad. In one, a Domino's customer describes the pizza as, "Mass-produced, boring, bland."

In another, Karen Kaiser, Domino's marketing director, says, "Oh ho ho, this one's bad: 'Worst excuse for pizza I've ever had.' . . . We basically had to start over, with a new recipe."

To Domino's credit, they changed everything—and even paid to broadcast the reasons for it. The surveys two years later showed a dramatic improvement, with Domino's ranked in the middle of the pack, and first in Brand Keys ranking of customer loyalty among pizza chains. Under Doyle, Domino's has held the top ranking for customer loyalty every year since.

"This primarily has a lot to do with taste, image, and listening to consumers' wants and needs," Sean Williams wrote in The Motley Fool in 2015. "Domino's Pizza is actually listening to its customers. The company's mea culpa advertising campaign fessed up that its pizza wasn't very good and it completely revamped its recipe and menu. The results from that makeover have thus far been incredible."

Domino's stock rose even faster than its pizza, from a low of $8.38 in 2009 to $115 in 2015—a 13-fold increase in six years.

In 2005, in the middle of Brandon's run as Domino's CEO, he sold 930,844 stock options, at an average price of $21.60 per share, for a total of $20,104,754. When those shares lost over 50-percent of their value by the time he stepped down in 2010, to $8.53 per share, selling them five years earlier appeared to be a good strategy.

But had Brandon kept his shares under Patrick Doyle's regime, and sold them on April 1st of 2015, those shares would have been worth $100,391,525. They also would have earned an additional $17,769,812 in dividend income during 2006–2015—almost as much as he earned for selling the stocks in 2005—for a total take of $118,161,337, or almost six times more than he gained from his 2005 sale.

But the people at Bain Capital who hired Brandon didn't care about taste tests, customer loyalty, or Brandon's personal portfolio. What they cared about is what Brandon delivered: Bain received a 500-percent return on its initial investment.

When Brandon pitched for the athletic director's seat, his chief selling point was his ringing success as the CEO of Domino's Pizza. No one at Michigan seemed to look any deeper than Bain did.

CHAPTER 11

THE IDEAL CANDIDATE

Brandon's unlikely bid to become Michigan's next athletic director went public at the 2009 football reunion weekend, during a series of speeches Saturday afternoon at Cliff Keen Arena.

With a few hundred former players and coaches gathered, and the Wolverines coming off Rodriguez's 3–9 debut season, "Coach Carr got up to make a speech," Jamie Morris recalls, "and told us, 'We all need Dave Brandon to be our next athletic director, so we need to support him.'" The crowd cheered.

If the glaring weakness on Brandon's resume was a lack of experience in athletics, Carr was in the best position to convince university leaders it would not be an issue, and he threw his weight behind Brandon. But the key, always, was President Coleman.

"Dave is an alpha male," Michigan's longtime director of admissions, Ted Spencer, explained. "When he was a Regent, he demonstrated leadership skills that convinced President Coleman that he was the sharpest knife in the drawer. And he agreed with her on some of her most important initiatives, and she needed his help.

"I also like this kind of guy, who thinks he can do anything. I want someone who can go in and fix things to be on my team. For President Coleman, Dave was that guy."

"Over time, she appeared to be completely enamored of him," Regent Larry Deitch confirms, "and he always provided her with staunch support. Her modus operandi as an executive, if you will, entailed being very loyal to her team—*very* loyal. With Dave, her loyalty and connection seemed to go even deeper than with other members of her team. So if, in 2009, Dave wanted the athletic directorship, she would have been likely to think that was a fine idea.

It's even possible that she recruited him to take it, as a way of putting the position in the hands of someone who was very loyal to her, and vice versa."

It still seemed a bit strange for a Fortune 500 CEO, who was making millions and leading 140,000 employees worldwide, to want to trade that in for a few hundred thousand dollars and 260 employees, but Brandon came by it honestly. He'd always wanted to be a teacher and coach, he'd told Deitch, and this was his chance. His love for his alma mater, never in question, was also a great motivator.

Likewise, President Coleman showed no reservation backing Brandon as the top candidate, although it is unusual for one of her former bosses to become one of her top lieutenants. By comparison, when Penn State named a trustee, Dr. Dave Joyner, to become athletic director in 2011, the decision attracted the attention of the Pennsylvania auditor general, who released a report a year later, stating, "This movement gives rise to the reasonable public perceptions of insider influence and conflicting interests, particularly when the movement involves persons at executive levels." Penn State ignored the warning. After a tumultuous tenure, Dr. Joyner stepped down three years later.

President Coleman, however, never expressed concern or hesitation.

"She made it clear to me in the beginning," Deitch recalls, "that she wanted Dave as the next athletic director. It was *so* clear, I asked her, 'Then why don't you just appoint him?'

" 'No, no,' she said. 'I need a search committee.' And so we had one."

The search for a new athletic director marked a rare case where virtually everyone with any knowledge of the Michigan athletic department already knew the top three candidates, and their histories, which usually renders the need for search firms and the like unnecessary. Nonetheless, President Coleman hired recruiter Jed Hughes, then at Spencer Stuart, to run background checks on the candidates, and then assembled a search committee consisting of then-Provost Teresa Sullivan, now the president of the University of Virginia; Liz Barry, a university lawyer and administrator who later became Coleman's chief of staff; Tim Slottow, the university's CFO; Percy Bates, a highly regarded education professor who served as chair of the Faculty Board in Control of Intercollegiate Athletics for 22 years; and men's basketball coach John Beilein.

"We needed someone who could hit the ground running," Bates said, "and not have to learn this business on the job, because we're too far away from Canham. When you bring someone in who understands the culture of intercollegiate athletics, you avoid some major mistakes with ticket prices, student seating, marketing, and the like. You know that alumni are not students, or vice versa. You understand these things better and you don't make those mistakes."

The committee had trouble deciding who the most qualified candidate was, but not the least: Dave Brandon. More than one member of the search committee told more than one Regent that Brandon was the least impressive candidate on the list. Throughout the process, however, "it was clear that was the direction she wanted to go," Bates says, echoing Deitch's observations. "And even with some pushback and discussion, it remained clear that's what she wanted."

With little choice, the committee ultimately told President Coleman what she wanted to hear: Dave Brandon should be Michigan's eleventh athletic director. (President Coleman politely declined my interview request.)

Brandon's appointment, Bates says, "is still is a mystery to me. In organizations where everyone is a specialist, you don't go up to the Medical School if you're not a physician, you do not get to run the law school if you are not a law professor—let alone a lawyer. Except in athletics. Now how did that happen?

"I've asked the questions many times: I wonder if the public image of athletics plays a role in this. We have doctors and lawyers on a pretty high scale, but athletics is a different animal, which allows me to treat it differently. Everyone who's been to school thinks they can do that job."

On January 5, 2010, President Mary Sue Coleman announced Michigan had hired Dave Brandon as the Director of Intercollegiate Athletics. She introduced him as "an ideal candidate for athletic director.

"One of the things that David talked about during his interviews was really quite intriguing—how to enhance our fan experience. I am confident that he will carry on the tradition of excellence in U-M athletics as we enter a new era."

The Associated Press added, "Brandon said his business background will help him manage an athletic department with a budget of more than $90 million, media and licensing agreements, and fundraising efforts under way in a sputtering economy."

"I view [the athletic department] as a selling organization for the entire university," he told the press. "I can't think of many jobs in the world that I would pick up and leave that great company and great brand for," Brandon explained, "but this is one.

"I love the University of Michigan. I loved it when I was here as a student-athlete, [and] I've been connected to it ever since in one way or another. I'll bring my life experiences to this job and I'll work harder than any athletic director has ever worked to be successful."

There would be no bait-and-switch in Brandon's promises. He was not an athletic administrator, but a former Regent with a CEO background—one he didn't hide but promoted. He flatly stated he viewed the athletic department as the "selling organization for the entire university." In his interview with President Coleman, he obviously stressed he wanted to "enhance the fan experience," and he declared his love for the university and his determination to work extremely hard.

It's worth noting in hindsight that Brandon highlighted his own success, not the department's; he vowed to work harder than any previous athletic director had to be successful, instead of making the department a success. That might seem like splitting hairs, but the distinction would become manifest early into his tenure.

While Brandon's introduction might have left a few things out, it was admirably candid, completely accurate, and laid out what the next few years would entail. If Michigan's fans ultimately didn't like what Brandon was offering, it's hard to argue they were misled. But, like almost everybody else, they were initially enthralled with their new leader.

"Don always believed you have to hire coaches to be athletic directors," Peg Canham says, "but everyone was excited about Dave Brandon! I wrote him a note, saying 'Congratulations! I think you're going to do a great job!' Everyone liked him!"

In 2010, shortly into his tenure, Brandon explained his business philosophy. "I don't talk about the past," he said. "I create the future."

He didn't waste any time creating that future, either, drawing up plans for gigantic, pro-style, four-sided scoreboards for the hockey, basketball, and football facilities, for an estimated $20 million.

"Before Dave became the AD," former athletic department CFO Jason Winters says, "we were already planning the new scoreboards for the three big sports. But Dave Brandon embraced it, and it happened faster because of him."

Everyone knew Brandon's biggest decisions, however, were fast approaching. He would have to make tough judgment calls on dicey situations not of his making: the ongoing NCAA investigation into the football team's practice time, and the fate of the football coach himself.

CHAPTER 12

FIRST IMPRESSIONS

The NCAA's initial report, issued in late February 2010, stated that Michigan was being investigated to determine whether Coach Rodriguez promoted "an atmosphere of compliance within the football program," and if the department "adequately monitor[ed] its football program." These issues would be hashed out for months, and not settled until midway through the 2010 football season.

But one issue was settled on Tuesday, February 23, 2010, when the new athletic director held his first press conference: Dave Brandon was in control of the situation. He started by asserting that Michigan takes all allegations seriously, especially given its reputation for clean play. He did, however, hint that "major" is an adjective the NCAA attaches to any and all alleged violations, no matter how serious or trivial. He enjoyed a small chuckle recounting how his old coach, Bo Schembechler, never hesitated to punish players for missing class, no matter what time of year it was—which was one of the violations for which the NCAA was investigating Rodriguez's staff. Brandon then fielded questions from the two dozen or so reporters like a Hall of Fame shortstop playing a friendly game of pepper. The man was not about to break a sweat.

It marked Brandon's first real introduction to the Michigan fan base, and he did not disappoint. Here was someone who stepped confidently in front of the storm: accountable, yes, but direct and strong, with just the right measure of stubborn defiance. He even had the steel to turn the tables, making the subtle suggestion that the fault was not with the program—and certainly not with Michigan's values—but the charges themselves, which most fans and many media members agreed were ridiculous. Brandon not only looked calm, cool, and collected, he had successfully sent a message to the media and fans without quite saying it: This is just a nuisance that will soon be in our rear-view mirror. Michigan is still Michigan.

By the time Brandon left the podium, he had successfully disconnected the gravity of the NCAA's charges from the actual matters at hand, which boiled down to a few extra minutes of stretching per week.

"He was awesome at that," Jason Winters says. "And, playing amateur psychologist, that's where he's at his best, because he's able to be dismissive, and explain why it's so complicated, and translate it all into layman's terms."

No sooner had the cameras turned off than Michigan's fan blogs lit up with hosannas for their new leader.

At one of Brandon's first meetings with some of the employees he inherited, he made a similarly indelible first impression. When Brandon got up to speak, he didn't waste too much time on pleasantries or cheerleading, opting instead to get their attention.

"At Domino's," he told them, "I had six senior staff members, and within six months I had four new ones. The other two were gone within a year."

"And these were the first words out of his mouth," recalled Kurt Gulbrand, one of eight athletic department development officers working under Joe Parker. "The response? Shock and awe. But we didn't believe he'd do the same thing here. Our team had just put in the best decade in the history of the department, so we couldn't imagine why he would."

Thus, when Brandon introduced the department's new mantra, "Relentless striving to be the Leaders and Best in every way," Gulbrand recalls, "That sounded really good! The way we all received it, Dave was going to take the successes we'd already had, and enhance them. Sounds great! He was someone who had done it before, and he was masterful at painting a picture of a perfect department organizational structure, that we all believed in. I think we were all on board."

Brandon held his first meeting in the Champions Conference Room, located on the first floor of Weidenbach Hall, just inside the main double doors on the left. It's a pleasant, unassuming board room with a solid wooden table in the middle, surrounded by comfortable office chairs, and glass walls on two sides: one facing the lobby and the other facing State Street, so you can see who's walking in and who's walking by. Given its location as the gateway to the athletic campus, those people walking by are usually student-athletes on their way to practice, workouts, or the Ross Academic Center. If the University of Michigan athletic department has a war room, this is it; the place where Brandon and his staff held their most important meetings, conducted crisis management, and brought in outsiders to make plans and solve problems.

Brandon's first leadership meeting was not momentous, certainly not compared to the ones that would follow. But what was telling, in hindsight, was the agenda, which included Brandon's proposal to produce a commemorative coin for the upcoming Michigan Stadium Rededication Game, September 4, 2010, against Connecticut.

"It wasn't a lot of money to make the coins, maybe $80,000," recalls Jason Winters, an early backer of Brandon's. "But Dave obviously thought it was a good idea, and wanted other people's reactions.

"When Bill [Martin] asked for our reaction, he expected us to give it to him, and we did. Sometimes that led to a discussion or a debate, but Bill was always in charge. I don't think anyone questioned that.

"So when Dave asked what we thought about the coin, I figured the same rules applied. But I think I was the only one who spoke up and said, 'I think it's a bad idea, because it's a waste of money.'"

At this memory Winters laughed, realizing he could now pinpoint the exact moment when he should have started getting his resume ready. "I believe Dave was just testing who would speak up," Winters said, "because I think he'd already decided he was going ahead with the coin no matter what anyone said."

Winters might have been one of the first, but many other former employees now look back on their time in the department and can identify the beginning of the end of their tenure. What's striking is what tended to precipitate those moments: responding to one of Brandon's proposals, or even a question, with an honest, sensible answer. Sometimes it didn't even take that much. In one meeting, an assistant coach asked a benign question about parking, and two weeks later found herself packing her belongings into a box.

The threshold for perceived disloyalty, or "resistance to change," was so low, many veterans couldn't see the bar until it was too late.

The commemorative coin was not a particularly significant item, but it portended countless other expenses for things that were more symbol than substance. That included the next item on the agenda that same day: a proposal for a gigantic video board on Stadium Boulevard between Crisler and Michigan Stadium.

"He wanted this from the start," Winters recalls. "I did my best to stall that, because why do you need it? Here's what I could never understand—and maybe I'm just jumping to the conclusion that everyone should think like me—but it was such an obvious waste of money, why do it? I just want to put that on the record.

"It's an incredible leap of faith to think there's going to be a return on investment on those—and an even larger leap to think it's worth $2.8 million, not to mention the operating costs. But it's all whiz-bang stuff, 'That's what the pros do,' so by God we should do it, too. How he got that by President Coleman and the Regents is beyond me."

Also on the docket in Brandon's first weeks: alternate jerseys—or, as they're called by fans online, "Uniformz."

"I remember Dave reflecting on the fact that Ohio State wore alternate throw-back uniforms to our game in 2009," Winters recalled, "and he thought that looked funny, because Michigan wore its standard home uniform. His thought was, if one team is wearing alternate jerseys, both teams should.

"My thought was: I don't give a fuck what the other team wears. *This is Michigan.* But I'm not the AD.

"The uniforms were all part of the planning for the 2011 Notre Dame night game, something Dave worked on from the start. He wanted to do something with commemorative uniforms for both schools, because both were Adidas schools. But let the record reflect: the idea for alternate uniforms did not come from the players, or the recruits, or from Adidas, as was often claimed. They came from Dave, from day one."

In the early going, no one other than Winters had the temerity to question Brandon's plans to his face, but a few eyebrows went up when Brandon assigned his employees an organizational culture survey, which asks 30 questions designed to measure an organization for four traits: adaptability, involvement, mission, and consistency. Then the results are tabulated and compared to those of 20,000 other organizations around the world that have already used the survey.

The final product is a circle broken into four quadrants, each with a different color—which is why the employees privately called the survey "the color wheel."

"It has a lot of credibility," Winters said of the Culture Survey. "But it's the first time it's been applied to intercollegiate athletics that I know of—and that's the problem. High performance is easy to quantify for a business—through share price, growth, market share. But in intercollegiate athletics, the wins and losses on the field impact everything—the budget, the mood, and everything else—but only the football coaches can really impact that. If we got a high score on the survey, would we win more games? I think it's irrelevant."

By all accounts, Brandon wasn't too concerned about any statistical anomalies. He had a concrete goal in mind: He wanted Michigan's athletic department to be ranked in the annual publications of the nation's best places to work. But Brandon knew he could only do that with dramatic "before" and "after" snapshots.

He also didn't give much thought to using organizational experts already on campus. A few years ago, Michigan's Ross School of Business created a new discipline called "positive organization scholarship," where professors research not what goes wrong in organizations, but what makes them go right. The most common traits they've found among the best organizations: Trust and gratitude.

Now the rest of the business world is following Michigan's lead in researching positive workplace cultures—but not the athletic director, who probably could have gotten the business school's help for free. That's how universities collaborate at their best, but Brandon viewed collaboration suspiciously.

"Change was the big thing he was measuring," Winters says. "The surveys showed that our organization was resistant to change, and this is where Dave came in with all the mantras about 'Change is good,' and 'If it ain't broke, break it!'"

There is bound to be tension between contemporary business slogans and century-old traditions. An institution steeped in tradition like Michigan tends to resist the idea of change for change's sake. But, as any Michigan player or coach can tell you, tradition doesn't protect them from criticism. Quite the opposite, the most common criticism is that they failed to uphold Michigan's tradition of excellence, on or off the field—whether it was the Wolverines' long history of great offensive lines or a sterling graduation rate—not that they failed to break what wasn't broken.

For some of those working in the department, Brandon's opening meetings provided the first indication that he might not, in fact, be the ideal candidate to lead Michigan's athletic department. But for most of the Michigan faithful, it seemed, Brandon's arrival was received as a breath of fresh air at a place that could use some.

Brandon capitalized on that notion on March 18, 2010, when he announced plans for Michigan to host its first official night game. Brandon's first public break with tradition might have been his best.

"If all goes well, we'd love to have at least one game a year scheduled at night at Michigan Stadium," Brandon said. "It would be a terrific tradition to start."

CHAPTER 13

RESORTS AND RIVALRIES

In May of 2010, Dave and Jan Brandon, Rich and Rita Rodriguez, Joe Parker, and one of his top development officers, Kurt Gulbrand, flew to Phoenix for the "Fiesta Frolic," a three-day gathering of coaches and athletic directors. Gulbrand had organized a side event so Michigan alums could meet the people running their department and their football team. Since the Brandons have a second home in Desert Mountain, a top ten–rated resort community just outside Scottsdale with six Jack Nicklaus courses, they invited the group over for some drinks and conversation a couple hours before the reception.

"It was clear Dave was dying to show Rich and Rita the home—and I can see why," Parker recalls. "The house was amazing. It was elevated, overlooking a championship golf course. The entire backside of the house was a glass wall, which they could move to make those rooms open to the outside, which was pretty cool. The master bath had a tub bigger than any I'd ever seen, surrounded by three huge windows, with dramatic views. Dave quoted how much it weighed, and told us it had to be craned in before the house was enclosed. It was all custom. The home could have been used as the set for a James Bond film."

After giving his guests the grand tour, Brandon eagerly asked them what they thought he had named the house.

After a few people guessed, Parker offered, "Pizza House?" citing the name of a popular campus joint across from Rick's American Café.

"Dave didn't say anything," Parker recalls, "just looked at me kind of funny."

With that, Brandon ended the guessing game, and volunteered the name: "Camp David!"

"He was clearly proud to come up with something pretty clever," Parker says, "and that he could associate something so presidential with himself."

After Brandon divulged the name, he showed his guests the coasters, tumblers, and towels that all had a distinct, custom-designed logo consisting of an open C attached to a bigger D representing "Camp David." The front doorknob was the logo itself.

Gulbrand recalls more about the conversation that followed when they sat down with their cocktails.

"This is when the Big Ten was talking about expansion," Gulbrand says. "We're all sitting down, enjoying our drinks, when Dave says, 'I've got a great idea! Expand the Big Ten to 16 teams, eight a side, and break those down into groups of four, A, B, C, and D, that just play each other. After the third game you reshuffle the deck, and then the top teams play each other, and the second teams play each other, and so on.'"

"I'm sitting there in amazement," Gulbrand said. "Essentially, he wanted to do away with our annual schedule, but it was the most confusing thing you've ever heard of."

Gulbrand felt compelled to speak up. "Wouldn't that be difficult for us to sell season tickets without knowing who we're playing, or when, or where—or even how many home games we'd have?"

"Oh, no, we'll figure that out," Brandon said. "It'll be great. Everyone will love it!"

"I'm looking at Joe [Parker] and Rich [Rodriguez]," Gulbrand recalls, "and we're thinking 'What the hell is this?'"

No one else spoke, however.

The thinking behind the harmless idea, that Michigan's traditional rivalries and seasonal rythms don't count for much, could be easily refuted by anyone who knew about Michigan's failed attempt to create instant rivalries after leaving the Big Ten in 1907, or how hard Don Canham had worked to restore the Notre Dame rivalry in 1978. But no one with any power seemed to possess that knowledge, so the notion that rivalries were disposable persisted, and would resurface to impact Michigan's schedule for years to come. But at the time, no one gave it much thought. Camp David itself was the star of the day.

When their guests reached for the Camp David doorknob, the Brandons gave them chocolates wrapped in foil, all stamped with the Camp David logo.

A few weeks before the Michigan contingent flew out to the desert, Todd Anson suggested Jim Harbaugh write to Brandon to introduce himself. Brandon responded that they should meet during Brandon's trip to Arizona, since

Harbaugh would be at the same conference. When they met, the two had a brief, friendly chat. Afterward, Harbaugh seemed pleased, going out of his way to call Anson and tell him, "I think Dave likes me."

The exchange carried a little weight. For Harbaugh to become Michigan's head coach one day, people at Michigan would have to come to terms with Harbaugh's comments and see the value of his return, while Harbaugh would have to feel sufficiently welcomed to want to make that leap. Their short conversation was a small but vital indication that both outcomes were at least possible.

Unlike Martin, however, Brandon failed to keep in touch. Although mutual friends suggested Brandon could connect with Harbaugh through Todd Anson, Brandon declined, once describing Anson as a "nutty attorney in San Diego."

"He was always polite, but he had no interest in anything I had to say," Anson told me. "He wouldn't even listen, [and] never signaled to me any interest in pursuing Jim at any time."

Of course, in 2010, Rich Rodriguez was still Michigan's coach, and was expected to have a better team that season—perhaps a job-saving season. Brandon's initial diffidence might not have reflected a lack of interest in Harbaugh, but caution.

Brandon's distance later would be harder to explain.

A couple months later, Parker and Gulbrand joined Brandon and several Michigan head coaches—Rich Rodriguez, John Beilein, hockey's Red Berenson, and baseball's Rich Maloney—for Michigan's annual "Summer Caravan" tour of Jackson, Kalamazoo, and Benton Harbor, Michigan. Parker launched the Caravan in 2007 to get Michigan fans excited for the seasons ahead. It's been a hit with the fans and even the coaches, who get a rare chance to enjoy long conversations with peers they admire.

"While we're on the bus," Gulbrand recalls, "Dave asks all of us, 'If you could only keep two games, what would they be?'"

Michigan's biggest rivals are Notre Dame, Michigan State, and Ohio State, so paring that down to two gets tricky. These rivalries not only define each season, but help define Michigan itself, since the three schools represent Michigan's peers and enemies. College football runs on tradition, and a big part of that tradition is the rivalries—and stereotypes—that go back more than a century.

"Okay," Brandon said. "Notre Dame, Michigan State, Ohio State. Which two do you keep?"

Once again, Gulbrand had the audacity to speak up—which would not prove wise with the new administration.

"Well, for me," he said, "it's a no-brainer: Notre Dame and Ohio State."

"Notre Dame? Really?" Brandon asked, genuinely surprised. "Why?"

"That's easy," Gulbrand said. "In development we get more requests for extra tickets for those two games than the rest of our opponents *combined*. Hundreds of requests. We simply could not get enough tickets for Ohio State at home, or for Notre Dame—home *or* away. Michigan fans don't always want to go to the Horseshoe [in Columbus], but they always want to go to South Bend. The South Bend Marriott can charge $400 a night, three night minimum, because they can get it when Michigan comes to town. And they sell it out. It's a big deal."

Not getting much traction, Gulbrand continued. "We actually get more requests to go to Notre Dame than to Ohio State—and we get more request for tickets at either place then we do for the Michigan State game, even when it's at the Big House."

"Why's that?" Brandon asked.

"Because Notre Dame and Ohio State are both national games—*always*," Gulbrand continued, unwisely. "Even when either team is down. But when we play Michigan State, it's a regional game. People don't fly in for that one. They just don't care about Michigan State as much. Notre Dame has a global reach. And academically and athletically, they're on par with Michigan. Our fans know that—and they care about that."

Gulbrand recalls, "I tried to disagree with Dave, respectfully, but he wasn't hearing it. He was *adamant* about dropping Notre Dame. It didn't matter what I said, he thought Michigan State was a bigger game. The coaches stayed quiet. Guess they were smarter than I was!"

Like Winters did with his objection to Brandon's idea for the Rededication Game commemorative coin, Gulbrand circles this moment as the beginning of the end of his time at Michigan.

"One thing was clear," Gulbrand said, "Dave didn't think Notre Dame was that important, no matter what anyone said."

Brandon then turned the conversation to his plan for a 16-team league and some sort of interleague playoff, sorted out week by week. The coaches on the bus didn't follow it any better than Brandon's guests had at Camp David, but they kept it to themselves.

Before Bill Martin announced his retirement, he and Notre Dame athletic director Jack Swarbrick had exchanged e-mails agreeing to lock in the rivalry for 25 years—by far the longest agreement in the history of the rivalry. It helped that Martin and Swarbrick had done business together going back to the 1980s, and had established a respectful, trusting relationship.

"I like Jack!" Martin told me.

Given the effort Don Canham and Notre Dame's Moose Krause spent to overcome the historic distrust between the two schools, it seemed smart to try to secure the rivalry for years to come. The news was very well received by the players, lettermen, and fans of both teams.

Those constituencies, however, would turn out to be silent partners in the decisions to come.

Brandon's first public plans were well received by most fans, from the new scoreboards to Michigan's first night game. But when he went public with one of his private ideas about the Michigan–Ohio State game, it went over like the Maize Halo.

During the spring of 2010, the Big Ten announced Nebraska would start playing football in the league in 2011. That would give the Big Ten twelve teams (go figure), and break the league into two six-team divisions. And that, in turn, would create a title game between the two division champions—all new.

That forced the Big Ten to make some tough decisions about the Michigan–Ohio State game. This was no small thing. The rivals had been playing each other on the last game of every season since 1935, the year after Thanksgiving became a fixed national holiday. Since the two schools have both been in the Big Ten, starting in 1917, their record is 46–46–4—as good as it gets. In 44 of those games, almost half, the winner also won the Big Ten title.

In 2000, ESPN viewers voted the Michigan–Ohio State football rivalry the best in the nation. Not just in college football, or in football itself, but in all sports. Even with Ohio State dominating the rivalry for that decade, "The Game" remained the sport's most popular rivalry. More college football fans have seen this rivalry in person, and on TV, than any other.

Bo Schembechler didn't need any stats to tell him that. "I don't know if there's another one in the country that is as intense and is as great a rivalry as this one," he told *The Wolverine* back in 2003, the year of the 100th game between the two schools. When asked what makes the Michigan–Ohio State game such a great rivalry nationally, he said, "We have historically played this game as the last game of the season. These are the two most dominant teams in the Big Ten Conference. . . . It's a natural. It's just an absolute natural."

To ask why anyone would care about the tradition surrounding this game is to ask why anyone cares about college football.

Given all this, you'd think it would go without saying that the fans of both schools—and of college football itself—did not want to see the game trifled with. In 2003, when Martin's administration merely mentioned the idea of letting SBC Ameritech sponsor the game by calling it the "SBC Michigan–Ohio State Classic," before and after each TV break, based on the fans' reactions, you'd think they'd just sold the White House to Uncle Ed's Oil Change. Martin's people quickly rescinded the idea, and learned their lesson—though the lesson would just as quickly be forgotten.

If the Big Ten decided to keep Michigan and Ohio State in the same division—which made sense geographically—the rivals could never face each other in the title game, reducing The Game to a quasi-semi-final. But if the Big Ten put the two teams in different divisions, and still had them play on the last day of the regular season, if they both won their divisions they would have to play each other again in the title game just one week later, diluting the importance of both contests.

In the middle of this debate, on August 20, 2010, Dave Brandon appeared on WTKA Sportstalk 1050, "The Unofficial Voice of Michigan Athletics," with morning hosts Ira Weintraub and Sam Webb. Brandon covered a lot of ground, but what got the most attention by far was his suggestion that Michigan might not play Ohio State at the end of the season, but in October, and some seasons not at all. He boldly proposed putting the two schools in different divisions, and moving their annual game up to mid-season. Even if they faced each other again in the title game, he reasoned, the rematch would come at least a month later.

As co-host Ira Weintraub recalls, "I remember that day distinctly. It was a typical Dave Brandon trial balloon. Let's throw something out there to the die-hard Michigan fans to see how they react. He did this with alternate jerseys, too, though he didn't listen to some of us [warning] about those. But regarding Michigan-Ohio State, he got exactly what he wanted—a lot of responses. But none were in support of moving the game or even potentially having some years off in the rivalry."

The callers, fans and former players "pretty much reached consensus that moving 'The Game' to October is one of the dumbest ideas in the history of college football," Weintraub says. "Don't let realignment, which already has damaged so many great college football traditions, kill the greatest rivalry in the sport. It must be played at The Big House or The 'Shoe on the last Saturday of the regular season. Period. End of story."

The idea itself upset Michigan fans, but not as much as the fact that it was coming from their new athletic director. Not Ohio State's Gene Smith. Not Big Ten commissioner Jim Delany. But Michigan's own Dave Brandon, who had been in uniform for two of the historic battles between Bo Schembechler and Woody Hayes. Fans of both teams responded with their "usual

level of cool maturity," as Dave Barry would say, "similar to the way Moe re-
acts when he is poked in the eyeballs by Larry and Curly."

Ohio State fans sent so many e-mails to athletic director Gene Smith, he
half-jokingly pleaded with them to stop. The fans were blasting away on the
Web sites serving both teams, and the former players weren't any happier.

Rob Lytle, a stoic Ohio native who became an All-American at Michigan,
spoke for the majority when he said, "Bo would have hated this. I'm glad he
and Woody don't have to go through it. They're probably marching around
[in heaven] throwing tantrums right now."

MGoBlog's Brian Cook described the response to Brandon's trial balloon
as "the first rumblings of discontent from the [Michigan] fan base . . . the first
sign that Brandon's suit was empty. Brandon envisioned a world in which the
loser of the Michigan–OSU game could find redemption. That's not how it
works. That's not how any of this works. You lose the game, you fume for 364
days until you have an opportunity to right the wrongs. This is not a carnival
fun ride. It's college fucking football."

Rejecting Brandon's plan still left the question unanswered: What *should*
the Big Ten do?

That one was easy: absolutely nothing. College football is famous for coming up with elaborate solutions to problems that don't exist, like rearranging
historic conference every few years. But messing with the Michigan–Ohio
State game might have topped every unnecessary bad idea since New Coke.
Of course, that's not entirely fair. No one made you drink New Coke.

The arguments for maintaining one of the greatest traditions of college
football were both obvious and overwhelming. So it left a lingering question:
Why didn't Michigan's athletic director seem to recognize that?

CHAPTER 14

REDEDICATING THE BIG HOUSE

Ben McCready is a portrait artist who's painted George Clooney, Robert Redford, four presidents, more than 100 Fortune 500 CEOs, and countless university leaders. According to the Associated Press, "More leading colleges and medical schools select Benjamin McCready to paint portraits than any artist in the country."

The *New York Times* wrote, "He is neither a bartender nor a therapist, but executives open up to Benjamin McCready anyway, about everything from family quarrels to boardroom clashes."

The McCready's family history with Michigan runs so deep, it's almost genetic. Ben's uncles, aunts, parents, grandparents, and great-grandparents all graduated from Michigan—but that's just the start. McCready's uncle, aunt, father, and grandfathers were all members of Michigan's faculty, and his great-grandfather was elected mayor of Ann Arbor in 1903, while serving as the lawyer for the University of Michigan athletic department. Finally, two of his great uncles played football for Fielding Yost.

McCready's family tree is unusual, but not quite as unusual as you might think. People who work at Michigan receive countless e-mails from alums that start, "My mother, father, grandfather, and great-grandfather all attended Michigan," before launching into their request or complaint.

But that's not quite all. McCready's mother, Sally Wyman, grew up right across State Street from Ferry Field in one of Ann Arbor's most popular neighborhoods, Burns Park. So many professors and deans live there, it's known locally as "The People's Republic of Burns Park." Sally's family happened to live next door to the legendary Bennie Oosterbaan and his wife, Delmas, who treated Sally like their own daughter.

Oosterbaan had been a high-school state-champion runner before enrolling at Michigan in 1924, where he dropped track for baseball and became the Big Ten's batting champion, the Big Ten's scoring leader in basketball and a two-time All-American in the sport, and the Big Ten's touchdown leader in football and Michigan's first three-time football All-American.

In the mid-twenties, quarterback Benny Friedman and Oosterbaan formed Fielding Yost's famed "Benny to Bennie" passing combination, which popularized the forward pass, changing the game forever. The NFL inducted Friedman into its Hall of Fame in 2005, but Oosterbaan—who was also an excellent student—declined NFL offers because they played on Sundays. Nonetheless, in 2003, *Sports Illustrated* ranked Oosterbaan the fourth-best athlete in the state's history, and the best ever at the University of Michigan.

Oosterbaan took over the football team after Fritz Crisler's undefeated 1947 national championship season, and duplicated the feat the next year. But, after winning one more Big Ten title after the 1950 Snow Bowl game against Ohio State, Oosterbaan couldn't win another one, and retired after the 1958 season.

Still, Oosterbaan had made a lasting mark on Michigan—and on the girl next door, Sally Wyman, who named her son after Bennie Oosterbaan, and asked Oosterbaan to be his godfather. He gladly agreed. Because the Oosterbaans' two children had passed away, McCready was the closest thing to family that Dave Brandon could find to ask permission for an idea he'd been nurturing.

Thus, when Brandon asked to meet with Ben McCready on Friday morning, September 3, 2010—the day before Michigan's game against Connecticut and the rededication of the Big House—the first-year athletic director told McCready he was thinking about bringing back Michigan's five retired jerseys, with a ceremony to honor the families and a patch to indicate each number's special status as a "Legends Jersey." Of course, Oosterbaan's number 47 was among them.

"No one knows what the numbers are of any of these people," Brandon told McCready. "What do you know about the Wisterts?"

Whitey, Albert, and Alvin all played tackle at Michigan, all became All-Americans, all were inducted into the College Football Hall of Fame, and they all wore number eleven—but few Michigan fans know that.

"Well," said Ben, who knows more Michigan football history than most, "I think there were three brothers."

"See? What was the number?"

"I don't know."

"That's why we need to bring them back. Because we're in uncharted territory here, I want to know: What would you think about seeing 47 on the field again?"

"I think it would be wonderful."

"There may be some blowback on it," Brandon predicted—accurately, it turned out.

"I'm glad you're asking for our permission," McCready said. "For me this is an easy call. I'd love to see the jerseys on the field again because it would give a whole new generation of fans a chance to learn about these great players. I can't see a problem with it."

Looking back at that meeting, McCready says today, "What made me feel bad afterward is, after Dave made more and more missteps along the way, everything he did was viewed in a negative light. But the 'Legends Uniforms' program was not undertaken as a moneymaker, just to sell jerseys. People have the Legends Jersey thing wrong. I was in on it from ground zero. I was the person who gave him permission to bring the first retired jersey, my godfather's jersey, back on the field. I think Dave had a lot of good intentions when he came in, but then he got a bit carried away."

Near the end of their winding, unhurried, 90-minute conversation, "Dave said something that was so poignant, I've never forgotten it. He knew I'm really close friends with Joe Roberson," Michigan's AD, who stepped down in 1997 after a very hectic four-year run.

"I said to Dave, 'You know, I think you'll do a good job'—and I did. I think we all did. There was so much hope. But he was looking very wistful, very thoughtful. He looks out the window, then he looks at me—one of those moments that stick with you—and he says, verbatim, 'You know, Joe Roberson said being the AD was the worst four years of his life.'

"I just sat there, silent. Must have been 15 or 20 seconds. It was so awkward.

"Then Dave says, almost to himself, 'I hope it doesn't turn out that way for me.'"

McCready didn't say anything.

"I've never forgotten that. That just stuck with me."

The next day, Saturday, September 4, 2010, the weather for Michigan Stadium's Rededication Game against Connecticut was picture-perfect. No one was surprised when they announced a record crowd of 113,090.

Dave Brandon could not have asked for a better opening day to start his career as Michigan's athletic director, including the $226 million stadium renovation. To celebrate, Dave Brandon brought some of the "Wow! Factor" he promised fans after becoming the athletic director, including fancy receptions, game programs, commemorative pins and coins, and not one but two military flyovers, followed by an important game against a serious Connecticut team.

But the show-stealer was a guy walking very slowly, with a cane in each hand.

On Christmas Eve, 2007, the Mealer family's SUV was T-boned by a 90-year-old man running a stop sign. Brock Mealer's father and his brother Elliott's girlfriend were killed instantly. Brock was paralyzed from the waist down.

Doctors gave Brock less than a 1 percent chance of walking again. Even though it was Brock's younger brother, Elliott, who was on the team, Michigan's football strength coaches, Mike Barwis and Parker Whiteman, used their lunch hours three days a week to work with Brock. He had to relearn how to stand, then walk with arm crutches, and, by the spring of 2010, just canes. And that's when Rich Rodriguez told Brock they wanted him to open the renovated stadium.

Amid all the official announcements and the flyovers and the pomp and circumstance, Brock Mealer sat in his wheelchair at the front of the tunnel. The team stood behind him while the two big scoreboards played a video of Brock's story. When it finished, the fans gave Brock Mealer a heartfelt cheer, many of them already in tears.

Then Brock got out of his wheelchair, wearing a blue T-shirt reading "1%" in maize, grabbed his canes, and did something the experts said he never could. He took one step, and then another, and then another, while the record crowd stood and cheered him on.

Since Michigan first raised its "M GO BLUE" banner in 1962, Michigan football players have touched it more than 30,000 times—and every one of them got there faster than Brock Mealer did that Saturday. But until Brock approached the Block M in the center of the field, stopped, and reached up to touch the banner, no one had ever received a sustained standing ovation, bathed in tears not normally associated with the ritual.

Underneath this unforgettable scene were some simple lessons: It wasn't the commemorative coins or flyovers or rock music that moved Michigan fans to tears—but a man who wasn't even on the team, doing something both simple and extraordinary, before their eyes.

You had to be there.

A few minutes later, the Wolverines went out and manhandled Connecticut, 30–10.

It was a good day to be a Michigan fan.

CHAPTER 15

INTERNAL DOUBTS

The honeymoon was just starting on the field, but it was coming to a halt off it—at least inside Weidenbach Hall.

The department's director of development, Joe Parker, came to this conclusion when traveling with Brandon to New York, which in itself was an experience. Where Bill Martin and his staff flew coach, then took cabs or the subway, or walked to their destinations, Brandon would borrow donors' corporate jets—and only those big enough to accommodate his tall frame, standing up, which he also used to travel to games. When he'd arrive in New York, a Lincoln Town Car would be waiting, with a driver—which cost the department more than $1,000 a day, a point of contention with the university's CFO on the Hill. Whenever Brandon's car was a few blocks from his hotel, wherever he traveled, he would call his assistant, who would then call the concierge to be sure he was ready to run out and open Brandon's door, so he wouldn't have to wait.

In fairness, Brandon's traveling tastes were formed before he became the athletic director. A few years earlier, when the president of the Traverse City, Michigan, alumni club, Tom Pezzetti, asked someone from the university to give a talk, the speaker would generally drive four hours up to Traverse City, stay in a mid-range hotel, and be content. When they invited Regent Dave Brandon, however, he insisted on a flight to the local airport, and a driver, which turned out to be Pezzetti and his brother-in-law. When Pezzetti told Brandon's secretary they had reservations for him at the Bay Shore Inn, on Grand Traverse Bay, she called back to let them know they would be putting up Brandon at a suite at the Grand Traverse Resort—home of golf courses by Jack Nicklaus and Gary Player. Pezzetti countered by sending pictures of the suite at the Bay Shore, which the secretary showed to Brandon. He approved, and she informed Pezzetti it would suffice.

"We had such great experiences with Tom Goss and Bill Martin," Pezzetti told me. "They were class acts and very low maintenance. Brandon was a Regent at the time, and he was very demanding and difficult. I actually drove him to some Domino's stores in the area where he had meetings set up."

Brandon's trip to New York made a similar impression on Joe Parker, who realized, "Dave had listened to us as much as he was going to."

This became clear to Parker when they were between appointments, in a conference room at a donor's high-end office in midtown Manhattan. "The room had expensive art on the walls," Parker remembers, "framed photos of buildings they've developed, and a beautiful conference table—a nice slab of rich, shiny wood—one or two walls of windows, with gorgeous views of Midtown.

"I was asking Dave about Domino's Pizza, what it's like to lead a big corporation, and he begins this diatribe about how Domino's was so dysfunctional when he got there, and started beating up on Mr. Monaghan, saying Monaghan had taken his eye off the ball, and he had not been paying attention to the culture—one of Dave's buzzwords.

"I'm listening to this and thinking, 'Give the man some credit. He revolutionized the food delivery industry—he all but created it! And it worked very well for a very long time.'

"Then I realized Dave perceived the athletic department the same way: The previous leadership was incompetent, our culture stunk, people were going through the motions, we didn't care about what was happening."

Of course, if Bain hires you to be a turnaround artist, you tend to see the organization you take over in those terms. But it wasn't long after Parker's epiphany that others in the department came to Parker's conclusion. They soon started seeing Brandon's attitude toward them elevated from thought to action.

Brandon had fired his first Michigan employee a few months earlier, but it was an exceptional case.

Jamie Morris had held Michigan's career rushing record from his senior year, 1987, until Anthony Thomas broke it in his last game in 1999.

Morris had started working in Michigan's athletic department as a development officer in 2002, and was popular with many big donors. He directed the department's car program, getting free loaner cars from area dealerships and distributing them to the coaches. He also served as the unofficial liaison to football lettermen, helping them buy tickets when they returned to campus and letting them know about the annual Lettermen's Chili & Cornbread tailgate and Victors Night, a special reception held at the Chop House after the spring game.

I've been friends with Jamie at least since I started writing the book with Bo Schembechler in 2005, and probably earlier. In 2008, I asked him to cohost my Sunday morning radio show with me on WTKA, until I turned the show over to him in the fall of 2014.

After Bill Martin announced that he'd be stepping down, Morris told me, "If Dave Brandon gets it, I'll be gone in six months." There had never been any conflicts between the two, but for whatever reason, Morris simply believed Brandon didn't like him.

In the spring of 2010, when a football assistant coach asked Morris to help his graduate assistant—who had little money, a wedding coming up, and no car—Morris provided him with a compact car he was not entitled to. Sure enough, a couple weeks later, the young man got in an accident.

When the director of Football Operations asked Morris what happened, Morris panicked and lied, telling him the graduate assistant hadn't gotten in the accident. When Morris met with Brandon, he told him the truth, but it was too late.

"I was trying to take care of someone, and I got caught," Morris told me. "I didn't steal anything. I didn't do it out of self-interest. But it was wrong, and stupid. [Brandon] was within his rights to do what he did, and he wanted me gone anyway, so I gave him the knife to cut my throat."

Another athletic director might well have fired Morris, too, but it was clear when Morris met Brandon to negotiate his departure, Brandon was not in a forgiving mood. Morris declined the buyout to avoid signing the non-disparagement clause. The same day, Brandon sent a press release to Annarbor.com, which put the top story on the front page.

For the remaining staffers, Morris's departure could be rationalized as a good guy making a dumb mistake. They figured: Don't break the rules, don't panic and lie about it, and you'll be fine.

But their false sense of security would not last long.

Marty Bodnar served as the captain of Michigan's 1979–80 basketball team, then graduated from the University of Akron law school, but he couldn't resist coming back to Michigan to run the ticket department. By all accounts, he did very good work, and was happy doing it. He had a sixth sense for striking the subtle balance between commerce and customer care, and knew better than anyone how to treat students—and also how important that was to the Regents. Perhaps the best measure of Bodnar's skill is the fact that Michigan fans probably can't recall a single public controversy with tickets during Bodnar's 12-year reign.

When Michigan's top marketing maven, Mark Riordan, left in 2010, Martin asked Bodnar to take that job over, too, while still running the ticket department. A good soldier, Bodnar agreed. In 2009, the Community Foundation in Bodnar's hometown of Barberton, Ohio, offered him the post of executive director, and a higher salary. Bodnar took it for one day, then realized he'd rather be back at Michigan.

After Brandon had been in office for a few weeks, he gathered all the marketing people to discuss strategy. Bodnar asked Brandon—perhaps to demonstrate his eagerness to learn his new job, or to give his boss a chance to show off—what he thought about the "Four Ps of Marketing," which are product, place, price, and promotion.

"This is Marketing 101 stuff," said Ryan Duey, an Ann Arbor native and Michigan graduate Martin hired in 2005, who rose to director of marketing and events presentation. "Dave just looked at Marty and chuckled. We left that meeting knowing Marty's days were numbered."

It's easy to look at that brief exchange between a subordinate, who had recently added marketing to his job description, and the two-time Fortune 500 CEO, who promised fans that Michigan's marketing would get a big boost under his leadership, and conclude the underling was in way over his head. But it's worth pausing here to consider their divergent approaches to the task at hand, and their models.

Bodnar's mentor was Don Canham, and his bible Arizona State University professor Robert Cialdini's *Influence: The Psychology of Persuasion*, a highly regarded book of serious scholarship "based on his groundbreaking body of research on the ethical business applications of the science of influence." Cialdini's book has held up since it was first published 31 years ago. It is now on its third edition, and is still Amazon.com's top-ranked book in marketing and consumer behavior.

Brandon most often cited Bo Schembechler as his mentor, but as we'll see, however, it's not clear how many of Schembechler's lessons Brandon actually followed. Brandon seemed to take more seriously the advice offered in another book, *If It Ain't Broke . . . BREAK IT! And Other Unconventional Wisdom for a Changing Business World*, by Robert J. Kriegel and Louis Patler, which became a bestseller in 1992:

"In this unique book you learn to . . . break the rules of business—and break away from the pack. Most of all, you will become a 'Break-It' Thinker, applying innovative principles to your own career, and with this book's unique Victory Log, enjoying the adventurous—and profitable—advantages of Break-It Thinking in your life."

If the book quickly faded from the national scene, it left a permanent impression on Dave Brandon. It fit nicely with his philosophy of ignoring the past to focus on the future. The "Break It!" worldview fed Brandon's belief in himself as the "turnaround CEO," which was exactly what Valassis and Bain had hired him to be. If you're paid good money to be a problem solver, you naturally find problems to solve. And if it ain't broke, you break it—even if your underling could tell you, you don't have to.

Not long after Bodnar's failed attempt to engage his boss in a discussion on marketing, on May 24, 2010, Brandon called Bodnar into his office to tell him that he had a year to find a job. Bodnar was still looking when Brandon called him in at the end of September and offered him a severance package. Bodnar accepted. His career at Michigan was over.

The humiliation was not over, however. Bodnar had to return the next day—a cold, gray Saturday—to pack his belongings in a box, with a human resource official escorting him out the door.

"Here's my problem with this," Kurt Gulbrand says. "When Dave let Marty go, the claim was he was not a marketing guy. He was a ticketing guy—and a good one! He agreed to pitch in with marketing to help out. He was asked to do it, as a favor to Michigan. Marty would have done anything for Michigan! Super guy, great colleague. Big loss."

But what Bodnar had contributed to the Michigan community, especially the students, would not be fully appreciated until it was too late. Bodnar would ultimately get the last laugh—but by then, neither man would find it very funny.

If Morris's firing could be dismissed as an aberration, Bodnar's firing cut a little deeper. What had he done wrong, except volunteer to take on more responsibility—marketing—for no extra pay?

Athletic development director Joe Parker didn't have too much time to ponder the issue before Brandon called him into his office, just hours after the department learned of Bodnar's pending release.

"These were Dave's exact words," Parker recalls. " 'This afternoon at our executive team meeting, I'm going to announce my leadership team, and I want to know if I can script you into it.'

"So what am I going to say? I have a family to support, and I've worked hard to build a career in intercollegiate athletics. 'Absolutely, Dave.' "

Brandon pressed for more. "I need a commitment from you."

"Well, tell me what that looks like," Parker said.

"I need you for three years to not consider any other opportunity outside of Michigan. And I need you to narrow your focus on development, only."

Before Brandon arrived, Parker had sought to learn as much as he could about the business to help the department, and to prepare to become an athletic director himself one day. Parker's additional responsibilities included serving as a liaison to football and managing corporate sponsors.

Parker had informed Brandon about his interviews to be the athletic director at San Diego State and Rice, but, he says, "Dave perceived those interviews as indications of my unhappiness, but they were not. Not at all. In intercollegiate athletics, when you get a chance to get up to the plate, you swing the bat," and take the interviews.

"But that's why he asked for me to commit to three years. I said, 'Absolutely. You can count on that. I serve the athletic director at the University of Michigan.'

"If I had told him anything else, I'd be stripped from his leadership team, maybe that minute, and probably let go pretty soon after, when he'd tell me he 'needed to move in another direction.'

"At that instant, I felt I was a hairline from suffering Marty's fate myself. Give the wrong answer, and you'll see an e-mail sent to the entire staff saying you're leaving to pursue other endeavors, and a box to take your stuff home in that Friday."

In Brandon's leadership team meeting that afternoon, Parker saw Brandon's organization chart, and Bodnar was already off it. The people who remained on the chart were at the table—the survivors. Parker felt more rattled than relieved, knowing full well that, whatever commitments he had just made to Brandon, he could not count on them being returned. Even if he could ride the Brandon bull without getting bucked off, he was no longer sure that's what he wanted.

"As soon as I got in my car that afternoon," Parker says, "I called my four mentors, all current or former athletic directors around the country. I gave them all the briefing of what had just happened. I told them all, 'If anything opens up, even a lateral position, I'm available. I'm no longer attached to Michigan,'" which was saying a lot from a former Michigan varsity swimmer, who planned to raise their family in the shadow of the University. "The quicker I get repositioned, the better off I'm going to be.'"

By the fall of 2010, the wheels were turning on another key staff departure.

CHAPTER 16

FIRE 'EM FRIDAYS

To Brandon's credit, he refused to keep someone on staff simply because they'd been there for a long time, or hire only his pals, regardless of their qualifications.

"He *despises* cronyism," says Regent Kathy White, an African-American Princeton graduate, "and I *love* that! Why? Because it's wrong. And also because I have not often been its recipient.

"How is it that someone that tall and good looking didn't get pulled into the cronyism way of working in corporate America? He took cronyism out of the athletic department."

But many of his former employees argued Brandon went too far in the opposite direction, discounting loyalty, too. In Brandon's first two years, he made countless speeches to just about any alumni club or civic group that asked. Early on, he promised his audiences he'd be letting 100 of the department's 261 employees go, and would hire a chief marketing officer. This might not have made much of an impression on his listeners—who probably didn't realize Michigan didn't have a CMO before Brandon was hired, or why the department might need one now—but it accurately reflected Brandon's priorities.

"Under Bill [Martin], we had a great senior team," Gulbrand says. "Bill was the leader, but the people on his senior team could tell him, respectfully, what they thought, and push back when they thought it was necessary. He created a great culture—a checks-and-balances culture. I don't know if they realized what they had under Bill, or realize what they're lacking now. But I do know you couldn't question what Dave did, or at four o'clock the next Friday, you'd see an e-mail saying, 'TEAM: So-and-so's chosen to pursue other opportunities outside the Michigan athletic department, and we wish him well.' Literally a, 'Thank you very much, please give us your keys.'"

"Those e-mail messages were a big topic of conversation within the department," former men's tennis coach Bruce Berque told me. " 'TEAM: So-and-so is no longer employed at the University of Michigan. We wish him best of luck in his future endeavors.' They were pretty short, but I think everyone got the message. When they started coming out [in the fall of 2010] it could be two or three a day—usually on Fridays."

After Morris and Bodnar, the trickle of "Good luck!" e-mails became a flood, with dozens going out week by week, washing away long careers of people dedicated to Michigan, who had often proved it by declining offers elsewhere over the years. In most cases, their firings were framed as resignations, and included a three- to six-month buyout if they signed a "non-disparagement clause"—followed by months of soul-searching that often entailed a bout of depression.

Tellingly, Brandon's approach ran 180 degrees counter to that of his mentors, Bo Schembechler and Don Canham, who were both known for being unusually competitive in already competitive fields.

"I know there are times you've got to bring the ax down, but," Schembechler said, in his last book, "I think letting people go is usually a bad idea. It eats up too much time, energy, and morale. That's why I'd much rather *teach* them than *fire* them.

"You have to do everything you possibly can to develop your middle tier of talent. It's your job, as the leader, to make those people do more than they thought they could—maybe more than *you* thought they could—and put them in the best possible position to help the team."

Brandon's people often left, and then his HR director, whom he retitled his "chief talent officer," would try to find and hire only from what he called "the upper five-percenters" of the talent pool for a particular position. But who, exactly, is in the upper five-percent of any given field? How would you identify them?

Brandon and his chief talent officer often answered that question by hiring people from outside the University of Michigan, and even collegiate athletics itself, frequently from professional teams and corporations. They then paid them significantly more than the person they had just fired had received, even more than market value, and gave them long, convoluted titles.

Brandon had a penchant for paying his people very well. The hiring process usually followed a pattern: the department would offer a candidate a position with a decent bump in the salary they were already making—which is standard operating procedure almost anywhere—but the compensation would often be higher than the income of the person they were replacing, even when the new hire had considerably less experience. The new employee would eagerly accept, then Brandon would inform his surprised lieutenants that they needed to increase the salary even more, and sometimes much more, for no reason anyone could discern.

When the department's director of development left in 2011, for example, he received $154,000 a year. That same year, Brandon replaced him with the university-wide Office of Development's Human Resources Director, who was making $190,000. Brandon offered her $225,000 a year. Before Brandon left three years later, in 2014, he had increased her salary to $260,000—$70,000 more than she was making in Development in 2011, and $106,000 more than her predecessor had made—an increase of almost 70 percent, though he had 8 years experience working in athletic development, and she had none. On the other hand, her staff tripled, and Brandon gave her the added responsibilities of Community Engagment, Alumni Engagement, and, later, Communications. Still, it was clear Brandon was not afraid to spend significantly more money to get the people he wanted.

Compared to the people Brandon let go, the people he hired tended to be younger, often with new families and few or no ties to the campus or community they were joining. They appreciated Brandon's generosity, and were eager to keep the money flowing—even if it meant keeping their questions to themselves.

It wasn't long before Martin's "Team of Rivals" culture was replaced with a "yes-man" culture, with Brandon's hires leading the charge.

The effect of Brandon's purge was often quite dramatic. When Brandon had come on in 2010, Ryan Duey—the Ann Arbor Huron High School graduate who rose to director of marketing and event presentation—was one of seven people in Martin's marketing department. Ten months later, he was the only one left.

CHAPTER 17

A WATERSHED WEEK

After the first five games of the 2010 season, Brandon's first as athletic director, Rodriguez's Wolverines had racked up a 5–0 record heading into three straight marquee contests—Michigan State, Iowa, and Penn State. A win against any of them would have given Michigan its first bowl bid since Carr's 2007 team, and likely would have secured Rich Rodriguez's immediate future at Michigan. But the Wolverines lost all three, leaving him and his staff with a must-win game against Illinois just to keep their jobs.

But the players had not given up on their coaches, or each other—witnessed by a stirring speech by walk-on-turned-captain Mark Moundros at a players-only meeting the Tuesday before the game.

The next day, Wednesday, November 3, Dave Brandon visited practice, and motioned Rodriguez to the sidelines to tell him the NCAA investigation into Michigan's practice time was finally complete, and the news was good: The NCAA had agreed to Michigan's self-imposed sanctions except probation, which they increased from two to three years, but they concluded Rodriguez had not, in fact, been guilty of failing to promote the all-important "atmosphere of compliance," but found him responsible for the far less serious "failure to monitor" those who were in charge of the monitoring. Given the possibilities, the ruling represented just about the best possible outcome.

The next day, Thursday, November 4, 2010, at the Junge Champions Center, Michigan's media staff handed all the assembled reporters a copy of the NCAA's 29-page report, which actually referenced the *Detroit Free Press*'s initial story, noting "that the violations of daily and weekly countable hour rules, though serious, were far less extensive than originally reported and that no student-athletes were substantially harmed." The committee characterized the violations as "relatively technical."

After the NCAA officials finished an innocuous Q&A with the media, Brandon took the podium.

"There were no surprises and there will be no appeal, because there is nothing to appeal," he said, once again in complete control of the situation. "Effective today, this process is over and done and we can focus all of our time and energy on the future."

He mentioned that "a local newspaper did a very high-profile story" that suggested Michigan players were being harmed due to a lack of concern for the players and the rules—two things even his critics would readily acknowledge Brandon took very seriously throughout his tenure. "There was nothing found that even remotely suggested that our players' well-being was at all at risk."

Throughout the 14-month investigation, from the *Free Press* front page in August of 2009 to the NCAA report in October of 2014, Brandon had successfully defended the honor of his alma mater and the reputation of a coach who had been unfairly accused. Brandon had put on a veritable clinic of public relations: taking responsibility for mistakes, explaining how they happened, fixing them immediately, and underscoring how serious Michigan was about doing things the right way. He was clear and confident, direct and appropriately defiant—and gave a full-throated defense of Michigan's values. He seemed to be following Canham's maxim to a tee: Never turn a one-day story into a two-day story.

Brandon closed the press conference with a simple conclusion: "Let's just go play the games."

That, too, was deftly done: shifting the focus from the NCAA and the *Free Press* to the field. The distractions were finally out of the way, putting Rodriguez's fate back in his own hands.

On the first play of this do-or-die game for Rodriguez, on November 6, 2010, Denard Robinson started to run forward, saw all the Illini defenders running toward him—then noticed Roy Roundtree cut straight up the middle, wide open. Robinson stopped cold, as he had been coached, then tossed a simple pitch-and-catch to Roundtree, who took off for a 75-yard touchdown. Michigan kept it up all game, scoring almost at will.

But the Illini returned the favor, possession after possession. Early in the fourth quarter, with the score tied 38–38 and Robinson putting in another incredible performance, a few guys on Michigan's sideline pointed to backup quarterback Tate Forcier, warming up, about 10 feet from where I was standing.

"What's going on?" one player asked. They looked over to see Michigan's team of doctors and trainers talking to Robinson. In *Three and Out*, this is how I described it:

"Denard Robinson told the trainers [and doctors] he was feeling dizzy, and had a headache. They ran some rudimentary tests, huddled, and decided he should not return for the rest of the game.

"They did not consult the coaches, and the coaches did not give their opinions. This is the way it should be, of course—even if the coaches' jobs could very well rest on their best player getting back in."

Robinson had not taken any big hits to the helmet, and even he wasn't sure when he might have suffered the collision that induced the symptoms. He had probably played in that state for a few plays, and maybe more, while exhibiting good judgment and skill. But that didn't matter to the trainers and doctors, either.

They ruled that Robinson was out for the day, and that was that. No debate. No discussion.

And that is exactly what I saw repeatedly during my 37 games on Michigan's sidelines, in Michigan's locker room, and even in Michigan's training rooms, which I visited almost daily for three seasons.

Tate Forcier went in. On his first play, from Michigan's own 35, Forcier dropped back, hitched to throw—then amazingly, inexplicably, lost his grip on the ball. He watched it float in the air, then bounce on the turf, where Illinois's Clay Nurse gobbled it up.

Six plays later, Illinois went ahead, 45–38.

But Forcier stayed in, and eventually found his rhythm, and his receivers, leading the Wolverines to a wild, triple overtime, 67–65 victory.

The Wolverines improved to 6–3 on the year, and the Rodriguez regime was still alive.

On a cold, muddy day in West Lafayette, Indiana, Denard Robinson led a four-minute drive late in the game to secure a 27–16 victory, and a 7–3 record. After the game, in the showers of the visiting team's double-wide, separate standing locker room, the chant went up: "Somewhere warm! Somewhere warm!" The players knew the victory would spare them the dreaded Motor City Bowl and send them south.

The next week, they really believed they were going to knock off Wisconsin, but the Badgers dismissed that notion with a 24–0 halftime lead.

In the locker room, while his teammates slumped in their stalls, center David Molk stood up and marched around the room.

"Hey, Michigan! Are we fucking scared?! Because we're playing like it! We are *not* laying down! We are *not* scared! We will fight! We will *fight!* And we will *get after them!*

Molk got his men moving. Just five minutes into the second half, they managed to cut the lead to 24–14, then 31–21 when the third quarter ended, but they couldn't contain Wisconsin. Despite outscoring the Badgers 28–24 in the second half, they lost 48–28, and the calls for Rodriguez's job grew louder.

CHAPTER 18

STRIKE ONE

That weekend, freshman punter Will Hagerup had invited his high-school friends from Whitewater, Wisconsin, in for the game, which amounted to a celebration of sorts for his choosing Michigan over a dozen other schools.

Hagerup's older brother, Chris, had been an all-conference quarterback who had earned a scholarship punting for Indiana. Will, the nation's top-ranked high-school punter, visited Indiana, but made his last official visit the weekend of September 26, 2009, to Ann Arbor. That day, the Wolverines beat his brother's Hoosiers in a thriller, 36–33, to start Rodriguez's second season 4–0.

Rodriguez and his staff were still feeling the effects of the *Detroit Free Press*'s investigation, which consumed a lot of their time and energy. But the coaches still had to recruit, so the Sunday after the Indiana game, Hagerup had break-fast at Angelo's with Michigan's recruiting coordinator, Chris Singletary. He then returned to Schembechler Hall to say good-bye to the coaches before heading back to the Campus Inn to pack up and drive home with his parents.

"Going back to the Campus Inn, I got butterflies—good butterflies," Hagerup recalls. "The Big Ten, I've always loved. And I love fall, which is hard to beat here. I was really impressed with the classy quality of everything at Michigan—especially the people. And on top of that there are some things you can't explain. I felt like I got the complete picture of Michigan that week-end. It felt like home."

When Hagerup started packing his bags at the Campus Inn, he told his parents he wanted to go to Michigan. They told him they could talk about that on the drive home.

"No," he said, "I want to do it now."

Hagerup's mom broke into a broad smile, shed a few tears, then gave her youngest son a big hug.

Hagerup called Singletary. "Hey, can I come back, and talk to you guys?"

"Sure, whatever you need," he said. "Everything okay?"

"Everything's fine."

When Hagerup saw Singletary back in Schembechler Hall, he didn't waste any words. "I want to commit," he said.

"At that point," Hagerup admits now, "you're so nervous, but in a good way. I imagine that's what proposing will be like. It's because I wanted to be there so badly—and because my parents raised me this way, that once you start something, you finish it—that I knew I was never going to leave."

A year later, after the Wolverines got drubbed by the Badgers, 48–28, Hagerup and his high-school buddies drank and smoked some pot. The next day, Will Hagerup learned he had to take a drug test, which were almost always unannounced.

He didn't bother waiting for the results. He called special teams coach Eric Smith immediately after taking it to confess. "I was so scared," Hagerup told me. "Coach Smith is a good guy. He said, 'I appreciate your honesty. You should go see Coach Rod tomorrow.'"

Hagerup walked into Rodriguez's office Monday morning.

"What's up, Will? What can I do for you?" Hagerup realized Rodriguez had not gotten the news.

"I'm so sorry about this," Hagerup started, struggling to hold his voice. "I had some friends in town, we did some stupid things, and I just took a drug test. I think I failed."

Hagerup told me Rodriguez then "got this really sort of 'upset parent' look on his face."

"I appreciate your honesty," Rodriguez said, "but I'm incredibly disappointed. We'll see what comes back. But you know the policy, nothing I can do about it—and nothing I would do, even if I could. We're not going to hide this. So we'll see what comes back—and you'll have to deal with the consequences."

Hagerup didn't have much to say. "I deserved it," he told me. "Looking back, you can see the pressure everyone was under in Coach Rod's last year. But when you're 18, you're just worried about your own ass. In hindsight, it hurts even more knowing the pressure these coaches were under."

The next weekend, when the Wolverines traveled to Columbus to play 10–1 Ohio State, Hagerup drove home to Whitefish Bay to watch the game at Buffalo Wild Wings with his high-school friends. Michigan's walk-on place kicker, Seth Broekhuizen, had to learn how to punt with a few days' notice.

"And that's your first game?" Hagerup says, sympathetically. "That's asking a lot."

Not surprisingly, Broekhuizen had a tough day punting, which caused Hagerup's Facebook account to "blow up. These are people I don't even know, and they're telling me, 'You're losing the game for us!' 'It's all your fault!' "

When Broekhuizen shanked one in the second quarter, Hagerup recalls, "The announcer said, 'Right now, Michigan could sure use their punter, Will Hagerup, who's out with a suspension because he violated team rules.'

"The lady sitting right next to me asks, 'Do you know why Hagerup's not playing?' "

Hagerup felt compelled to confess. "Yeah, I'm him," he said, sheepishly. "I made a mistake."

"You don't have to tell me!" she said. "I'm so sorry!"

"Well, I didn't steal anything or kill anybody, but I made a mistake."

"We just moved across the street from your parents! We're big Michigan fans!"

Needless to say, Hagerup's friends found the exchange funnier than he did. In hindsight, Hagerup says, "It's not funny, but you had to appreciate it. My friends were cracking up."

The eighth-ranked Buckeyes finished the regular season by notching their seventh straight victory over the Wolverines, 37–7.

After the game, Jay Feely, a former Michigan kicker who went on to a long career in the NFL, tweeted: "Kills me watching Michigan struggle like they have the last three years!! Not even competitive in Big Ten games. Time for a change."

By then, most Michigan fans agreed. The question was, did the one man whose opinion mattered, Dave Brandon?

When Hagerup returned to Ann Arbor, he went to see Greg Harden, Michigan's associate athletic director. "We all like Greg," Hagerup said. "I told him I want to apologize to Dave Brandon."

"Okay," he said, "I think that's probably a good call."

That was a little scarier than it sounded, however. Hagerup barely knew Dave Brandon. In August, Brandon had given the team his no-nonsense lecture on classes, cheating, and drugs. I witnessed his first one, in 2010, and no one had any doubt he meant every word.

"I knew he was a formidable guy, a real presence," Hagerup says. "He had put the fear of God in us from the start."

In fact, Brandon earned uniformly high marks from those inside and outside the department for his commitment to running a clean program, with an unusually strong focus on academic success, and he was against drug use of all kinds. This tenet of the Michigan Man credo—from Yost onward—Brandon followed religiously.

"Let me call him," Harden said, "and see if he can meet now."

"What do I say?" Hagerup asked.

"Tell him the truth," Harden recommended. "Tell him you screwed up."

One of Harden's favorite phrases is "Pay up and shut up," which Hagerup has found to be "really good advice."

Brandon made room for the meeting immediately.

"Any time a student athlete wanted to talk to him," Chrissi Rawak says, "that always took priority. Always."

After a very nervous Hagerup confessed his sins and apologized, Brandon got to the point. "Was the policy not clear to you?"

"No," Hagerup said. "I believe it was."

"You will be tested much more frequently now," Brandon told him. "I don't want to see you in here again for this."

Hagerup nodded. But then, Hagerup recalls, the tone shifted when Brandon asked him, "What does the team think of Coach Rod?"

"We didn't get too in depth," Hagerup recalls, "but I thought it was pretty cool that Dave Brandon was asking his freshman punter a question like that. It showed respect."

CHAPTER 19

HOLIDAY CHEER

Almost a year earlier, Bill Martin had performed one of his last official acts as Michigan's athletic director on January 28, 2010, when he announced Michigan's hockey team would play Michigan State in an outdoor game at the Big House on December 11, 2010—or 12/11/10. It would be called "The Big Chill," in honor of Michigan alumnus Lawrence Kasden, who wrote and directed the famed movie about a group of Michigan graduates. In a nice touch, Michigan flew him back to drop the first puck.

The day couldn't have worked out any better, on and off the ice. Given the smooth operation, you wouldn't know it was the first time Michigan had hosted an outdoor game. Each time Michigan scored, en route to a 5–0 shutout, fireworks flew—a Brandon addition.

But Brandon learned something that day that would impact the seasons to come.

"This was Dave's first real encounter with Michigan Stadium attendance," former CFO Jason Winters recalls. "He wanted to make sure we set the record for the Big Chill hockey game. He thought it would be a good idea to have officials from *Guinness Book of World Records* attend the game. So I had to explain that Guinness would have some problems with our methodology.

"This is where it got a little awkward. We finally had to point out to him, 'Dave, you *do* realize we make up the number?'"

Like many programs, to calculate attendance, Michigan adds up all the sold tickets, comprised mostly of season ticket holders, whether they show up or not; then it adds everyone else in the building, the players, the coaches, the officials, the band, the ushers, the staffers, and even the press; then they look around and say, "How about 106,435?"

And that's how they calculate the attendance at the Big House.

The charade could have continued for years, and no reporter would have called them on it, until they pushed it so far no one could believe them. But that would come later.

Although Michigan announced the attendance as 113,411, the people from Guinness initially calculated Michigan's crowd to be 85,541, still good enough for a world record—but not good enough for Brandon. So Brandon sent photos and other documents to Guinness, which eventually recalculated the attendance to be 104,173—a new world record for hockey.

"There's really no credibility," Winters says, of the attendance figures.

After the game, Brandon gave his director of marketing and events presentation, Ryan Duey, "a huge hug." The same day, Brandon introduced his new chief marketing officer. He picked Hunter Lochmann, the former vice president of marketing for the New York Knicks.

A blond-haired, 40-something who looked ten years younger, Lochmann was an upbeat, naturally likeable guy. His background was just what Brandon was looking for—big city, big team—one Brandon could plausibly claim counted Lochmann among the "upper 5 percent" Brandon was always seeking.

Lochmann and Brandon both viewed Michigan athletics largely as a business, and both approached it with the same strategy, bringing their solutions in search of a problem. Lochmann shared Brandon's vision for marketing the University of Michigan the same way you would the New York Knicks. Of course, that's exactly why Brandon hired him. Like Brandon, therefore, Lochmann delivered just what he promised.

The question was: Did Michigan need what Lochmann offered?

"When you're working for the New York Knicks, you're only working with one team," Ryan Duey says. "When you're working for Michigan, you have two or three dozen varsity teams. But what was really lost [under Lochmann's leadership] was some of the organic appeal. Look at [softball coach] Carol Hutchins, and the blood, sweat, and tears that woman has put into her team, her program, and this community. I'll guarantee that she knows 90 percent of the fans at her stadium. That doesn't happen in New York."

"I enjoyed my time with Hunter," Winters says. "My problems with Hunter were ones that typically come up between a financial guy and a marketing guy: What's the cost-benefit for this idea?"

Winters recalls once asking Lochmann why the department was paying for a Facebook promotion to sell Michigan tickets.

"Dude," replied Lochmann, who named his Twitter handle "Lochdogg." "We had a great return on investment on that!"

"Well, Hunter," Winters explained, "in the past, all we've had to do is send one e-mail blast for free, and we'd sell all the tickets we wanted to. Why should I have to incur a cost for Facebook to do the same thing?"

But anyone listening to Brandon could have answered the question: If it isn't broke, break it.

The next night, December 12, 2010, Dave and Jan Brandon hosted the department's leadership team, coaches, and significant others at their Barton Hills house overlooking the Huron River.

When you turn into the Brandons' driveway, you meet a gate supported by two pillars. The one on the left features a plaque, with the words "Ever After" engraved in calligraphy.

The one on the right, engraved in the same style, explains the one on the left: "Once upon a time a talented group of people came together to dream, and to design and build a place like no other. Ever After is the culmination of the work of those gifted people who spent years creating a place the Brandon's [sic] could live . . . Happily Ever After."

The driveway winds up the hill about 700 feet, then bends to the right behind the home and into a parking circle. Aerial photos of the Brandons' home look more like a regional airport than a house, with a circular center and wings shooting off toward the Huron River, seemingly hanging over the cliff. But the tour is what visitors remember, as Monaghan did.

The Brandons planned for just about everything—even, it turned out, inclement weather. The clear skies from the Big Chill had vanished overnight, replaced by a terrible winter storm, with lots of snow and freezing temperatures.

Despite the storm, the guests were greeted outside by musicians playing holiday songs with hand bells. Numerous visitors, on different evenings, have described the routine the same way: Dave and Jan bring everyone downstairs. Dave stands on a step, with Jan on a lower step, near him. He offers all his guests the opportunity to go through their home, and tells you where you can find food and drink. Guests get the clear sense they are expected to take the tour.

"It has no right angles," Winters recalls. "All the walls are curved. He was obviously proud of the home, and he should be, I guess."

The guests who've taken the tour have mentioned the stunning vistas, the inviting spaces, and the world-class craftsmanship, but everyone agrees with Monaghan that the highlight of the tour is Dave's walk-in closet.

"We have two closets," Brandon says. "Come on in and take a look!"

"Dave's walk-in closet is bigger than some apartments I've lived in," Joe Parker says. "It's very large, and very, *very* well organized."

Brandon owns more tailor-made suits than his guests can count, which hang in the closets on both sides. They are organized by color and fabric, with the wooden doors open for the tour, and lights over each rack.

Brandon's dress shirts are monogrammed, or adorned with his name, in script, in his handwriting on the cuff in dark stitching. His shirts are folded in the drawers below each suit closet, which they pull out for the tour in cantilevered fashion so you can see all of them. In the center of the room, the wooden island is filled with silk ties, again organized by color.

One guest recalls another small detail. "You and I would throw our change in a bowl on the counter. Not Dave. He had a very nice, ornamental bowl located on the island in the center of the walk-in closet. You could tell it was a bowl he had selected for this purpose, a well thought-out plan. 'This is where I'm going to put my change from this point forward. This is what I envisioned when I built this home.'"

The Brandons organized a few games for their guests. For one, they requested all the guests submit childhood pictures of themselves ahead of time, which they displayed at the party on a screen. Then everyone tried to figure out who was whom.

Many of the young people in the photos were hard to match to the adults in the room, but not the host. Brandon's photo was a black-and-white picture of a little boy, probably eight or nine, in his winter jacket, at a Christmas tree farm—with an ax. Whether intended or not, more than a few guests found the symbolism of the photo hard to miss, especially when Dave had just let several longtime staffers go, with dozens more to come, and many of his guests feared they would be next.

Most visitors I've talked with find "Ever After" fascinating, impressive, even spectacular.

"Dave, was hospitable and inviting throughout the night," Bruce Madej said. "Clearly, he gave the tour because he was proud of his house and I believed the house said a lot about him."

But many visitors also come away feeling the house is more than they would choose for themselves, even if they could afford it. Brandon's wealthy neighbors jokingly refer to it as the Barton Hills Convention Center. One guest asked him, after the tour, where he might find the gift shop.

Of course, if a multimillionaire wants to spend a small fortune on a colossal, custom home, that's his decision. But Brandon's preferences became a public issue when he transferred the same values to his vision for the University of Michigan athletic department, where getting the biggest, best, and most expensive of everything was what he wanted for his alma mater—and then seemed to assume everyone else did, too.

When he interviewed with President Coleman, she was impressed by his ideas on how to "enhance our fan experience," even though fans did not seem to be clamoring for that. It's why he constantly pushed the appeal of the "Wow!" experiences his administration was constantly working to create.

But when the fans he was supposed to serve preferred simple pleasures like tailgating, chili and cornbread, singing with the Michigan Marching Band, being together with their old friends in the same section for years and passing their traditions down to their kids, and if the athletic director couldn't fathom why those things would be more important to them than fireworks and Beyonce, that's a public problem.

If visitors to "Camp David" and "Ever After" left impressed and amused, many would not respond as lightly when they started noticing what he was doing to their communal home, the Big House.

HOKE'S HONEYMOON

CHAPTER 20

FIRING AND HIRING

On January 1, 2011, Mississippi State beat Michigan, 52–14, to give the Wolverines their worst bowl loss in Michigan history, and a final record of 7–6.

After that game, if Brandon didn't know he was going to fire Rodriguez, he might have been the only person in the state of Michigan who didn't.

During a team practice in Jacksonsville, a student manager told me, the players "knew before the Gator Bowl, Rich Rod was going to be gone. Even the assistants knew. The day before the Gator Bowl, Coach Frey pulls me aside and says, 'It's been really great having you manage for me. I just want you to know you're the best manager I've had. We should stay in contact.'"

On Tuesday afternoon, January 4, 2011, Brandon asked Rodriguez to come to his house for their review meeting. Most observers assumed Rodriguez would be fired that day, including his two children. Jan Brandon told two people at a charitable event that morning she was feeling "much better today" because "Dave is going to fire Rich Rod. It's been really tough on [Dave], and I'm just glad it's over. A lot of sleepless nights for everyone."

But there would be one more sleepless night, because after the hours-long meeting, Brandon told Rodriguez that he still hadn't made a decision.

That night, the Rodriguezes stayed home and pondered the possibilities. While they held out some hope Brandon might not fire Rich, it wasn't much. "Brandon's Barton Hills," Rodriguez told me that night. "I'm Spaghettio's," he said, enjoying a can of that very product. At the end of the day, that might have been the deciding difference.

The next day, Wednesday, January 5, 2011, Dave Brandon fired Rich Rodriguez.

"I made this decision last night," he told reporters at the press conference. "I'm a disciplined guy. We sat and talked for three and a half hours [the day before]. You don't do that if you have a preconceived idea of how the meeting's going to end. Anyone who suggests differently doesn't know what he's talking about."

That list would apparently include his wife.

No matter how one sifts through the accuracies of a press conference, consequences of greater importance were immediately clear.

After spending four days to fire a coach even the coach in question assumed would be gone, Brandon woke up two days later to discover the San Francisco 49ers had just hired Jim Harbaugh. One option, at least, was off the table.

So why *did* Brandon keep Rodriguez for another month? He might have wanted to give Rodriguez a chance to save his job at the Gator Bowl, or at least the appearance of it, to appease his supporters. By firing Rodriguez after January 1, 2011, Rodriguez's buy-out was reduced to $2.5 million. He also prevented Rodriguez from accepting a mid-December offer from Maryland, which decided not to wait, and hired Randy Edsall instead. This also meant Denard Robinson would not be following Rodriguez out of Ann Arbor.

But many others believe Brandon spent five weeks firing Rodriguez, and another week hiring his next coach, for personal reasons. "Why drag the whole thing out a month?" one employee asked me. "Because you get more time with the spotlight shining on you. The second you name a coach, it's supposed to shift to him. But when Dave dragged it out, everyone was following his jet on Flight Tracker. People were hanging on his every word. The spotlight was on him, and he was drinking it up. 'I'm the owner of the team, the general manager, and the head coach, all rolled into one.' He thought it was a game."

Everyone can see, however, what did not motivate Brandon, including a desire to soften the blow for Rodriguez, and do everything he could to hire Les Miles or Jim Harbaugh—a break from the blueprint Charles Baird, Ralph Aigler and Don Canham followed in identifying their man, and getting him, no matter what.

Two questions resurfaced four years later: Did Jim Harbaugh really want the Michigan job, and did Brandon really want Harbaugh?

These answers are complicated—because both changed.

According to Harbaugh's friend, Todd Anson—a Michigan law school graduate who has occasionally given Harbaugh negotiating advice over the past decade—"Coaching Michigan is all Jim's ever dreamed about. He talks about it all the time."

Brandon was certainly aware of Harbaugh's interest in the position. When

Tom Monaghan ran into Brandon that December, he told Brandon that he had learned from another Harbaugh confidante that, "If offered, Jim would come back to Michigan."

Brandon replied, "Of *course* he would!"

Did Brandon want Harbaugh?

Brandon's boss, President Coleman, was not a Harbaugh supporter, thanks mainly to Harbaugh's comments from 2007. But insiders say President Coleman would not have denied Brandon his wish, if that's what he wanted. Second only to President Coleman, Brandon owed his job to Coach Carr, who had decided not to hire Harbaugh as his quarterback coach in 2002, and responded strongly to Harbaugh's comments in 2007. While Carr might have softened on Harbaugh since, his former assistant coach, Brady Hoke, was clearly his guy.

Despite these obstacles, several people close to the search believe Brandon wanted Harbaugh. Brandon later told Bill Martin, Andrea Fischer Newman, and others that he thought he had Harbaugh lined up, and it was just a question of when to announce the hire.

"I do believe Dave wanted Harbaugh," a member of Brandon's leadership team told me, "but he wanted Jim on his terms." What were Brandon's terms?

Many believe Brandon did not want to hire someone whom he could not control, or outshine, and there is little question that Harbaugh would draw more attention and be more strong-willed than a lesser-known candidate like Hoke.

Brandon, intentionally or not, sent this conditional message to Harbaugh when he did not make a decision on Rodriguez sooner, rarely contacted Harbaugh, and declined to visit Harbaugh in person—sending not Michigan's highly paid search consultant Jed Hughes, either, but Hughes's subordinate, a young man named Philip Murphy, who graduated from Notre Dame in 1999 and the Wharton School of Business in 2006. All this told Harbaugh that Brandon was not dying to bring him back. Coupled with the backlash Harbaugh experienced from his 2007 comments, a fence which only Bill Martin had worked to mend, Harbaugh decided trying to return to Ann Arbor in 2011 was not his best move.

After Harbaugh signed with the 49ers, Todd Anson asked Harbaugh if he really had been interested in the Michigan job. Harbaugh paused, then replied, " I just wasn't feelin' the love."

And that's what it came down to. Not money. Not power. Not fame—but love. And Michigan, under Brandon, wasn't offering it to Harbaugh.

"I will never know what Brandon's motivations were," Anson told me, "but it seems clear to me that Dave was so insecure that he needed to be *the* big deal and could not countenance a strong personality as Michigan's head football coach.

"The 49ers swooped in and grabbed Jim, while Michigan stood on the sidelines. In my mind, Michigan should have had Jim locked down a month before that, and could have. I can only conclude that Dave Brandon is the sole reason Jim did not become our football coach in 2010."

Privately, Brandon seemed genuinely surprised when Harbaugh didn't come back.

"When it was apparent that Dave wasn't going to get Harbaugh," Jason Winters recalls, "he was very self-critical. He'd told me, 'I'd criticized Bill [Martin] for not having the next person in line. And here I don't have the next person in line when I'm ready to pull the trigger.'

"It was one of the few occasions I saw Dave express humility. He thought he had Harbaugh and recognized it wasn't as easy as he thought it was. If that was insincere, he's one hell of an actor. I honestly believe he thought he was getting Harbaugh."

Anson concludes, "I used to think Dave was deceitful. My take now is that he was inept."

Poorly handled or not, ultimately Brandon might have gotten exactly what he wanted. While many Brandon miscues were the product of inexperience or hubris, one constant shines through, and that was Brandon's burning desire to be recognized by the Michigan family and his former teammates as an "All-American athletic director," just as he had proudly told them at Schembechler's first reunion that he was an "All-American in business." To achieve that, he needed control, from the expanding budget to the expanding staff, right down to the quality of the crease in his employees' khakis. If it wasn't sharp enough, he would send them home.

Consciously or not, Brandon had to sense helping Jim Harbaugh make a triumphant return to Ann Arbor would only get Brandon a life sentence in Harbaugh's shadow.

The morning of Tuesday, January 11, 2011, was a busy one, the culmination of what Brandon called "The Process," his objective, data-driven methodology for determining who should be Michigan football's next leader. Brandon kept "The Process" in a thick, three-ring binder, with each section tabbed under a dozen or so subjects. He occasionally gave journalists a peek, without going into it in great detail.

On this morning, presumably for privacy and comfort, Brandon was working out of his spacious home in Barton Hills. Shortly after Joe Parker and Jason Winters got to their offices, Brandon summoned them to join him at his estate. After Winters got the call, he walked down to Parker's office. "Hey, we're making a decision. Boss wants us."

At Brandon's home, they met Jed Hughes, the consultant leading the search, and Brandon, who explained that he had boiled down the process to Brady Hoke and Les Miles.

Miles was well known to any fan of college football. Hoke, much less so. He had grown up in Ohio, graduated from Ball State, and started his coaching career as an assistant at Yorktown High in Indiana. He was a football man, through and through.

In 1995, Hoke was hired by Gary Moeller, who was soon replaced by Lloyd Carr. Hoke's eight-year stint as an assistant on Lloyd Carr's staff included the Wolverines' first national title since 1948. The coaches and players from that era still loved him, and kept in touch after Hoke became the head coach at Ball State, and then San Diego State. His eight-year record of 47–50 was underwhelming, but both teams finished on upswings, and Brandon believed Hoke could duplicate those turnarounds at Michigan.

"I don't know to this day if Dave wanted our opinion," Winters says of the meeting at Brandon's house, "or simply wanted cover to say he'd talked to other people. He told us in the ranking system for 'The Process,' he had Brady higher than everyone else in *every* category," which is a rather remarkable result when Hoke was the one with the 47–50 record and no league titles at second-tier schools, while Miles had mounted a 90–38 career record to that point, reviving traditionally moribund Oklahoma State and leading LSU to four 11-plus-win seasons, two division titles, one SEC title, and a national title.

But, Brandon told Winters and Parker, "I don't want to get ripped on for not including Les, so I feel I have to have a conversation with him."

"That doesn't make any sense," Winters told him, mimicking Larry Deitch's response to President Coleman regarding the AD search. "If Brady's your guy, just hire Brady."

Brandon gave Winters' suggestion little consideration. "So we get Les on the phone," Winters recalls, "and this goes to Dave Brandon's lack of transparency: When Dave talks, it's him talking to Les through the hand piece. When Les talks, Dave clicks back to the speaker phone—so everyone in the room can hear Les, but Les can't tell he's on speaker. He doesn't know we're all listening, and Dave doesn't tell him.

"Dave was really good at it, too. He didn't fumble around with the buttons. You got the feeling he'd done this before.

"Brandon told Les, 'Hey, look, you're a Michigan guy. We want to be on the same page. We don't want to have conflicting stories. Do you want to come, and if so, what's the price tag?'"

Whatever it was, the call ended without Brandon making an offer. Les Miles, for the second time in three years, would not be coaching at the University of Michigan.

Brandon's next call went to Brady Hoke. "But the funny thing is," Winters recalls, "Brady Hoke doesn't want to take Dave's call, and Dave is freaking out. We later found out Brady was not going to make any big decisions without [his wife] Laura, and she's at her workout, so Brady wants to wait for her to come back before they talk about the Michigan job."

When Brandon and Hoke talked again 90 minutes later, Brandon made it clear he wanted Hoke, and Hoke made it just as clear he wanted Michigan—a noted contrast to Brandon's dance with Harbaugh. (Hoke did not reply to my interview request.)

"Just like I don't think it's fair to second-guess Bill for hiring Rich [Rodriguez]," Winters says, "I don't think it's fair to second-guess Dave for deciding on Brady. I think hiring Brady Hoke was the right call at the time.

"But I think Dave Brandon had read too many Bo Schembechler books," referring to the famous scene where Schembechler accepted Don Canham's offer to coach Michigan a day before asking what it paid. "Dave wanted that, so Dave tells Brady, 'I want to be truthful. I want to be able to report at the press conference that you accepted the job without knowing what the salary was. Can you do that?'"

Hoke said, "Sure." And why wouldn't he? His base pay at San Diego State had been bumped the previous year from $675,000, but was still under a million. No other major program was seeking his services at any price, and here was Michigan's athletic director saying the job was his if he wanted it.

"I think it's fair to say most negotiating experts would recommend agreeing on compenstion before someone accepts a job offer," Winters says. "You say, 'This is the offer, salary and all. Do you want the job or not?' Simple. But once Brandon tells Brady the job is yours, without a salary attached, we've lost all leverage. As soon as Brady Hoke says, 'Sure,' now *he* has all the power."

That might seem counterintuitive, when Hoke had just agreed to a deal with no number attached, but in fact Brandon was making the blind bet. Brandon would have to accept almost any price Hoke named, or he would have to admit Brady Hoke had turned down Michigan—an embarrassment that would not play well, locally or nationally.

"As soon as Hoke says, 'Sure,'" Winters recalls, "he tells Brandon, 'Now you can talk to my agent.' Who happens to be Trace Armstrong, an experienced negotiator. And sure enough, Trace is smart enough to counter Brandon's initial offer by a considerable amount more, which Dave has to agree to. And that's why Michigan gave Hoke a six-year deal worth $3.25 million a year.

"So, for the privilege of having an idiotic, dark-ages quote that no one gives a shit about, Brandon probably paid $500,000 a year more of Michigan's money to get Hoke than he ever had to." While Brandon and Hoke's exchange copied the letter of the Canham-Schembechler conversation, it lacked the spirit of the two men who genuinely cared more about Michigan than about money.

In this way, a touchstone story of Michigan tradition—Schembechler accepting the Michigan coaching job without even asking about his salary—became a media talking point for Brandon, and leverage for Hoke.

Later that day, Brandon told the Associated Press he had never offered the job to Harbaugh, Miles, or anyone else but Hoke.

"Dave never wanted that out there, that he went after Harbaugh," Regent Andrea Fischer Newman says, "because he never wanted Brady Hoke to think he was second choice. He was taking one for Hoke. Dave keeps his mouth shut. He's got big shoulders. He takes the accolades, but he also takes the blame. Very smart guy."

CHAPTER 21

"THIS IS MICHIGAN!"

After taking a Michigan donor's private jet across the country that same afternoon, the next morning, Wednesday, January 12, 2011, Hoke, his wife, Laura, and daughter Kelly met the same people at Brandon's home who had talked to him on the phone the day before, including Jed Hughes, Winters, Parker, and Dave Ablauf. The contract settled, it was time to discuss matters that couldn't be addressed before the deal was done, then plan the day's all-important press conference.

"Brady Hoke was keenly interested in Tate Forcier's standing," Winters recalls. "He gave every appearance that he was not sold on Denard Robinson as the starting quarterback—or, at least, he seemed to prefer Tate."

Brandon had to explain that Forcier had already flunked out of school and left campus. Hoke also wanted to hire his brother, Jon Hoke, as Michigan's defensive coordinator, but both Jed Hughes and Dave Brandon persuaded Hoke to look elsewhere. Michigan soon hired Greg Mattison for $750,000 a year, plus bonuses—about three times more than Rodriguez's coordinators received.

"Dave Brandon gets credit for opening the checkbook," Winters says. Mattison would prove to be worth every penny.

They then turned their attention to the press conference they would be leading just a couple hours later, at the Junge Champions Center, attached to Crisler. It would mark a crucial introduction for a candidate who was not at the top of many Michigan fans' lists.

Contrary to popular belief, "Dave Brandon didn't coach Brady on his press conference," Winters says. "He asked Brady, 'How are you going to lead off this press conference?' And Brady didn't know. I never got any sense, or had any confidence that Brady Hoke was going to pull this off."

But Dave Brandon knew how to stage an event, and he was at the top of his game that day. He had invited dozens of prominent Michigan Men, spanning the generations, to demonstrate their full support for the new coach. They happily provided quotes to the full flock of media members before and after the press conference, creating a tapestry of approval across the decades.

Brandon's comments, however, indicated he was well aware Hoke was not a popular choice among the majority of Michigan fans. Brandon seemed to feel a need to explain why he hadn't hired Harbaugh or Miles, while stopping just short of naming names.

"All that glitters is not gold when it comes to some coaches," he told the reporters. "Sometimes the hype or PR does not match the real person."

If Brandon's comments got back to Harbaugh, they might constitute another reason not to listen to Brandon if he ever came calling again. The football team's student managers found Brandon's remarks, "rude," "unnecessary," and "classless." A month later, they would be called in at 6:30 a.m., and warned if they ever spoke to the press, they would be released. Fort Schembechler was back.

Even in praising Hoke, Brandon could not resist taking thinly veiled shots at the previous coach, and the other candidates.

"Unlike some other coaches," Brandon said, "it's not about him, it's about his players and his team . . . Brady understands Michigan and what football means here. He has lived it as a coach and he knows what it takes to be successful. He doesn't have to learn the words to 'The Victors'—he's sang it many times in the locker room. He doesn't need a map to get around Ann Arbor; he was a member of our community for eight years."

When Hoke got up to the podium, he said all the right things, if not quite as eloquently as his boss.

"Our goal is to win the Big Ten Championship—multipally, consecutively. I made that word up, the first one." The reporters laughed. Hoke was charming them in a different way than Brandon might, but he was charming them just the same. The fans' comments on Twitter showed they were warming up to Hoke very quickly—but they were about to fall in love.

When a reporter asked Hoke if Michigan was no longer an elite job, Hoke asked, "Who said that?" He was genuinely agitated. "I'm serious."

"ESPN," the reporter replied.

"This is an elite job," Hoke said, with force, "and will continue to be an elite job. This is Michigan, fer Godsakes."

With that, Hoke had hit the bull's eye that had eluded Rodriguez. Hoke's line resonated deeply with Michigan fans, who refused to believe the Wolverines' glory days were behind them.

Brandon loved it, too—so much so, he saw fit to splatter "This Is Michigan" on T-shirts, posters, and the wall of the rebuilt Michigan football museum in huge letters.

But Brandon missed the point.

He perceived the line as a worthy boast, but this is not how most Michigan people I know think of that statement—a phrase Michigan people say to each other constantly.

From my discussions with faculty, staffers, and even students, a few themes emerge. After you arrive at Michigan, whatever your role, there is inevitably a moment that comes when someone pulls you aside and says, "Look, you're a nice person, and you've got good intentions, but your work just isn't good enough. I'm glad you're a nice person. I'm glad you have good intentions. That's essential. *But this is Michigan.* The standards are higher."

At this point, you have a choice. You either say, "To hell with this," and take your ball and go home—and plenty do. Or you figure it out and rise to the occasion. And that means you meet the culture where it is. You meet the expectations where they are. And you meet those standards while also upholding the solid Midwestern values of teamwork and integrity. The expectation is clear: that you'll be a good person, you'll do things the right way, and you'll do them better than anyone else.

In other words, your mentor is more likely to tell you, "This is Michigan" after you've screwed up, than after you've succeeded.

"This is Michigan" is not a boast, but an expectation.

When I teach at Michigan, on the first day I tell the students, "You will not miss class. You will not be late to class. You will not use a laptop, or a cell phone, or wear a hat. My late-paper policy is simple: There will be no late papers, ever. That is my 'late-paper policy.' Why? *This is Michigan.*"

That marks the end of the explanation. Nothing more need be said. They might not *like* it, but they *understand* it—and those who stay eventually embrace it.

This expectation informs the vast spectrum of activities on campus.

When my friend John Lofy was an MFA student two decades ago, his work earned three prestigious Hopwood Awards, whose previous winners include Arthur Miller, Lawrence Kasden, and Max Apple. He later became the editor of the university's alumni magazine, *Michigan Today,* where he learned there is no escaping Michigan's expectations. "You let even a simple typo get past you," he told me, "you'll hear it from alumni: 'This typo is unacceptable!' They don't care if it's hard to catch every single piece of punctuation—and they shouldn't. *This is Michigan.* They take it personally."

All those expectations can be reduced to three words, "This is Michigan," and everyone on campus understands it—whether they're engineering students pulling all-nighters to get Michigan's solar car ready to defend its national title, or physics doctoral students running experiments in a windowless basement laboratory seven days a week, or the director of Michigan's screenwriting program putting a red pen to a couple thousand pages in one week, when some of the students aren't even enrolled in his class.

Lofy, now the assistant director for the university's $4 billion capital campaign, said, "I've worked harder at Michigan than I ever have anywhere else— harder than I ever thought I could. But that's how you accomplish incredibly gratifying things. That's why other people think we're arrogant. When you've succeeded at Michigan, you know you've accomplished something serious, without cutting ethical corners. And you deserve to be proud of what you've done. Because if you did something good at Michigan, you did something really fucking good.

"Michigan is far from perfect, and sometimes we fall miserably short of our own expectations. But when people say, 'This is Michigan,' that's what we're talking about: two centuries of striving together to carry on a tradition of excellence."

On Hoke's first day on the job, when he spontaneously said, "This is Michigan," he understood what he was saying. It's less clear if Brandon did.

After Hoke finished, in an unorthodox move, Brandon returned to the podium to answer more questions.

He described his itinerary the previous week, interviewing coaches and consultants. "Five cities in six days—going at it pretty aggressively," he said. "Tried not to turn it into a circus, when everyone was turning it into a circus."

When a reporter asked where he went, and which coaches he met, Brandon replied, "You want to know who I talked to, when I talked to?" clearly enjoying the exchange. "It aiiiin't gonna happen!"

That left Brandon's money quote still sitting on the table. He had paid handsomely for it, and he wasn't going to waste it.

"I made the decision that I wanted Brady Hoke and I called him. And he accepted it. And we never talked about what we were going to pay him," Brandon said, answering a question no one had asked. "And the only guy I've ever heard of who took a job without knowing what it paid was a guy named Schembechler.

"Kinda eerie, isn't it?" he said, with a broad grin.

Brandon closed with an impassioned defense of his newly hired coach.

"Those people out there who love this place, and care about this place, and understand this place, they're going to love this football coach and they're going to love the way this team plays.

"And those people out there who like to tear apart and like to criticize and like to, you know, find fault, and you know all that stuff, they're out there. And let 'em be out there. But they're not going to distract me or this coach or our team from getting on the path we all want to be on."

It was less, "We're all in this together," than "Us against the world."

That motif would play again, many times.

CHAPTER 22

THE COLOR WHEEL BLOOMS

Despite Michigan's 42–33 record over the previous five seasons, and a football family that fractured during Rodriguez's three years, one problem Brandon did not inherit was ticket sales.

In 2015, I analyzed Michigan's official attendance records, which every Big Ten team has to submit to the league. During the 2010 season's seven home games, Michigan sold an average of 103,323 tickets and gave away 2,875 tickets per game. Only Michigan's game against the University of Massachusetts fell just shy of drawing 100,000 paying customers, with 99,114. But with 5,883 complimentary tickets, Michigan easily kept the 100,000-plus attendance streak alive.

Michigan's season ticket wait list also remained robust throughout Rodriguez's 15–22 run, proving that losses alone are not enough to scare Michigan fans away. They might have grumbled about Schembechler's offense and bowl record and Carr's 10 seasons with three losses or more, and pulled their hair out over Rodriguez's defenses; they might have endured a civil war during the Rodriguez era; and they might not be happy, as I've often said, unless they're not happy.

But on one subject they still fervently agreed: They loved Michigan football, and wouldn't trade their tickets for anything.

Feeling good about the football team's future, the ticket sales, and his growing staff, Brandon figured it was time to check in on the culture of his department. One year into Brandon's tenure, he was well on his way to fulfilling many of the promises he'd made in his early speeches to alumni groups, like replacing a hundred staffers, and adding dozens more. He had also hired a chief talent officer and a chief marketing officer.

But he also wanted to establish Michigan athletics as one of the "Best Places to Work in America." which he had achieved his last three years at Valassis.

To do so, they took the Organizational Culture Survey again, less than a year after taking it the first time. According to the old guard, the new people Brandon had hired helped the even newer people fill out the survey, by simply telling them how to answer each question.

"He rigged it by picking his own questions the second time," one employee says. "He changed them to be more positively worded, so our score could only go up. Everything increased.

"Why not lie to keep him happy? During that whole stretch, he was shit-canning everyone. The people who were afraid lied on the survey, and the new people thought everything was great."

Sure enough, Brandon got the results he was hoping for.

"Suddenly, miraculously, the next time we filled it out, the wheel was all color," Gulbrand recalls. "It looked like a giant rainbow," indicating a happy, healthy, productive workplace, in noted contrast to the almost colorless wheel from the first survey a year earlier. In 2012, the *Detroit Free Press* awarded Brandon's department "one of the elite companies to work for."

"That would be bullshit," Gulbrand says of the second survey results. "I didn't know anyone who felt that way. But no one dared say anything. By then, everyone feared the Friday e-mail. In just one year, Dave had established a culture, no question about that. But it was a culture of fear, nothing else."

Of course, a certain measure of fear has always been part of Michigan's culture: fear of falling short, of letting down your teammates and your colleagues. That fear has fueled countless all-nighters, champion relay teams, and record-breaking capital campaigns. But when it's just fear, it turns in on itself and implodes.

It wasn't just seeing what the department had become that disappointed Gulbrand, but losing the much happier workplace it had been just a couple years earlier.

"I would have taken half the pay, because I loved working there," he said, "and I think a lot of people would tell you that. Working for Michigan Athletics was a labor of love. It had been a family culture—and that changed overnight. Even though Dave was claiming to create just that, a family atmosphere, it quickly became the opposite."

Brandon also instituted 360-degree evaluations of his leadership team and directors. The results were equally unreliable, but for a different reason: some employees used the evaluations to bash their colleagues, "just to make sure you don't get ahead of me," a veteran employee told me. "And that's the way

Dave Brandon created this culture. There was never a collaborative atmosphere. People were stepping on top of each other to get ahead. They weren't working together, but against each other."

Brandon's "Us against the World" philosophy, outlined at Brady Hoke's introductory press conference, had been internalized.

Brandon's office also sent an e-mail to all his employees, urging them to vote for Michigan's athletic department on *Crain's Detroit Business*'s online survey for the "Best Company to Work for in Southeast Michigan." This time, the department had no way of knowing who filled one out, or what they wrote. But we do know the Michigan athletic department was not a finalist.

Brandon often delivered a few speeches a week in his first couple years, in which he would talk openly about the turnover in his department.

"We've gone through a period of change that certainly results in a completely different organizational structure," he told one audience. "We are much stronger."

The problem with the previous administration, he explained, was the attitude. "We're Michigan. We didn't want to change. We were stuck in 'This is the way we do things at Michigan.' If we didn't like the way things were going, we would just sing the fight song."

When it got a laugh, Brandon repeated it often, but it also got back to those employees who had left, for various reasons. They pointed out to me that their team left Brandon some $400 million in capital improvements—in the form of fourteen state-of-the-art buildings, both new and renovated, including the Big House—plus about $10 million in annual operating surpluses and over $50 million in the reserve fund. Further, they generated the plans and the funds for the renovations to the basketball and hockey venues, which were completed after they left.

"From my perspective," Jason Winters said, "it's hard to appreciate how positive the situation was that Dave inherited. In the history of intercollegiate athletics, has there ever been an AD who received the keys to a department that had all that?"

CHAPTER 23

"PAY UP AND SHUT UP"

Punter Will Hagerup's punishment for his failed drug test started shortly after Brady Hoke had settled in. Hoke made Hagerup work with longtime strength coach Jim Plocki for 30 days straight. Hagerup "shut up and paid up," just like Greg Harden told him to, until his debt was paid.

But by midterms in February, 2011, "I felt like I'd been doing a good job keeping my nose clean," Hagerup told me. "We were in the middle of winter workouts, and they're killing us—6 a.m. stuff, Monday through Friday. I've got class all day, plus midterms, and I had econ and bio left. I'm so tired, when I try to study, it's not clicking. So I think, I'm going to pull an all-nighter."

Hagerup decided to take an Adderall, a drug to help those with ADHD focus—which can be readily found all over campus, from those who've had prescriptions for it and many who didn't, like Hagerup. It's a virtual epidemic on campus, with a majority of students saying they have tried prescription stimulants at some point in their career. Normal students, however, weren't tested for it.

Hagerup studied at the athletic department's Ross Academic Center, located in the middle of Ferry Field, until the custodian kicked him out at 4 a.m. He then walked across the street to a teammate's house, where he studied for two more hours until 5:30 a.m., when his teammates all woke up to do the team run from six to seven.

Hagerup finished the run, showered, then walked up the hill to take his biology midterm at 8:30, and his economics exam at 10 a.m.

"Physically, I felt terrible," he recalls. "But I felt good on the tests—and that was the point."

Hagerup would get an A on the biology exam and a B on the economics midterm, in two highly competitive courses, loaded with future medical school and business school applicants. He would also get a call immediately after his second exam from the football office, telling him he had to take a drug test.

"I was aware they test for Adderall, but I thought it went out of your system pretty fast. Four days later, Hoke calls me into his office again: 'You failed the drug test.'"

Hagerup burst into tears. "I'm so sorry. It was so stupid of me."

"You know I love you," Hoke said, "but there are consequences. So you're going to start your 30 days with [strength coach Aaron] Wellman, and you're going to be out of the lineup the first four games."

"And he made it clear," Hagerup remembers, "if I didn't finish the 30 days, I'm off the team. I walk out, and I'm thinking, 'How did this happen? How did I *let* this happen?' Bad luck? I suppose, but your decisions make your luck. I would have rather failed the two exams than the one drug test."

Hagerup, still a freshman, lived in West Quad. It was a brutal winter, and on February 19, 2011, he woke up at 4 a.m. to a 10-degree morning, got dressed, brushed his teeth, and walked into the dark cold, down to Schembechler Hall. They had told Hagerup that, if he was even one minute late, just once, he'd have to start the 30 days over again, so he always got there well before the required 5 a.m. start time. The strength coaches were always there already, and would let him start his daily punishment early.

"The coaches were nice to me," Hagerup said. "They weren't dicks about it."

"All right," Coach Wellman said, "you know what you did, so get this done. Get a 45-pound plate out of the weight room and come out to Glick [Fieldhouse]. You know what a plate push is?"

"No."

"Push this plate down the field. If you take either hand off at any time, or either knee touches the turf, start over. You have 1,000 yards. Go."

"Maybe that doesn't sound so hard," Hagerup said, "but after the first 100 yards, your legs are shaking, you feel like puking, but you haven't eaten breakfast so you're dry heaving. The 1,000 yards took me 40 minutes."

After Hagerup finished the 1,000 yards of plate pushes, Coach Wellman said, "Okay, now you have 200 yards of log rolls." This requires the player to lie on the turf, keeping his body straight, then roll toward the far endzone. Again, it sounds simple—and again, it's a lot harder than it sounds.

"Taylor [Lewan] can roll 500 yards, fast, and not puke," Hagerup says. "It's amazing, because log rolls make you feel like you have alcohol poisoning. After I do it, I'm sick the whole day. Everyone on the team agrees I'm the worst roller on the squad.

"After 20 yards, I'm puking—water and acid and whatever's left—but I finish. And then Wellman says, 'See ya tomorrow.' But I'm thinking there's no way I can do 29 more of these workouts. That was just an hour of work, and I felt physically worse than I ever have my entire life.

"I could barely walk. I felt sick to my stomach. Then I had a full day of class, and I've got 29 more of these. And that's going to be weekends, too.

"That walk down to Schembechler Hall in 10-degree weather and snow was a lonely one. And when you head home, it's still about 5:30 in the morning, and it's still pitch-black and freezing—and your legs are spent, and you're trying to walk up State Street on the snow and ice.

"When I looked in the mirror, I'm sheet white, I'm sleep deprived, I'm dehydrated.

"Drew Dileo was my roommate. When he sees me, he just said, 'I'm so sorry.'"

Hagerup had a hard time believing he'd survive 29 more mornings like that—but he had a harder time imagining leaving the University of Michigan.

"If I didn't finish my degree, I'd just be running away from my home, Michigan, a place I love so much I could barely talk when I said I was committing—and I can talk! So I cannot imagine what it would be like if I left. It would have been a horrible, horrible decision."

So the next morning, at 4 a.m., Will Hagerup got up again, got dressed, brushed his teeth, opened the dorm door into the frozen, black morning, walked down to Schembechler Hall, and did it all again.

The coaches showed a bit of mercy, however, after he pleaded with them, "Please don't make me roll. It makes me sick the whole day. I'll do anything else." They let him replace the rolls with the crab walk—in which he walked on all fours, face up, but backward—which some players find worse than rolls, but not Hagerup. When he finished his work out, he walked back up the hill.

And the next day, and the next day.

"Fast forward to day five," he said. "If I've already done four of these, I figure, I'm finishing this thing. If I don't finish 30, I've done these first four mornings for nothing, and I'm still kicked off the team. At that point, I knew, I'm going to finish. Even after just four days of this, I would not have forgiven myself for making myself do all that for nothing. That's how hard it was."

Hagerup did get one respite: Spring break. He went to Arizona with his friends, strictly avoiding anything that would trigger another failed drug test, and flew back Sunday night. But their flight was delayed, so they didn't get back into Ann Arbor until 2:30 in the morning. Day 8 of his 30-day punishment would start in two hours.

It didn't matter: Hagerup got up at 4 a.m., got dressed, brushed his teeth, and walked down to Schembechler Hall.

Every day Hagerup finished between 1,000 and 1,200 yards of plate pushes, except three days, when they had him do the Stairmaster at level 12 for 45 minutes. He considered that a welcome break.

After 29 days, therefore, he had done 28,000 yards of plate pushes—or about 16 miles. "So when I show up for Day 30—and there is *no* way I'm going to be late that day, a day I've been imagining for weeks—I'm pretty damn good at this thing. I gained four pounds of leg muscle. My leg muscles are bulging through my shorts.

"So the last morning, I'm there at 4:20, like always. Jim Plocki says, 'Congratulations, you're almost there.' I started with 1,000 yards of plate pushes at 4:20—and I finished at 4:29. It took me 40 minutes the first time. On the last day, I was pretty much sprinting.

"I'm done, man. I'm done! The strength and conditioning guys said, 'We didn't think you could do it. First time in our careers we did it like this, and we made it tough on you, and you did it, and we're proud of you.'

"I walk back to West Quad in the dark—last time! When I get back to the room, Drew's congratulating me. I call my parents. They're proud. All I'm thinking is, I'm done, and that night, I'll be able to sleep in. That's really all I wanted: to not have to wake up at 4 a.m. I was even thinking of skipping my classes that day, and I don't skip. I never got one strike for skipping a class in five years. But I decided I wasn't going to do shit the next day. I'd earned that much.

"That night, I can't wait to go to bed, but at about 10 p.m., Drew starts laughing. 'What's so funny?'

" 'Have you checked your phone?'

" 'No.'

" 'You better.'

"I look at my phone. We'd just gotten a text from the staff, saying one of your teammates got his fourth strike—missing class—and when that happens the whole defense has got to come in. They put the kickers and the punters with whatever side screwed up, offense or defense. Drew's a receiver. He could sleep in.

"Are you fucking kidding me?"

Will Hagerup did not sleep in, but he didn't get up at 4 a.m., either. This time he had company, and got a ride down to Schembechler Hall at 5 a.m. "Guys are complaining, 'Why do we have to be up?' 'I hate this.' I was thinking, 'Man, you guys have no idea!'

"We did the crab walk, 100 yards of rolling—I still puked—buddy carries, and bear walks. After all the leg stuff I'd done for 30 days, this was nothing.

"It only took about a half hour. I went home and slept. But at that point the idea of sleeping in didn't have the same satisfaction. I woke up at eleven, and ended up going to the class I was going to skip. Sleeping in the next day wouldn't be the same either, so I got up and went to class.

"It was back to normal."

Given everything Hagerup had just put himself through, however, that wasn't so bad, either.

CHAPTER 24

BRANDON'S VISION REVEALED

While the fan base started gathering behind Brandon and Hoke in the 2011 off-season, the athletic director started bringing his pet projects out in the open.

In June of 2011, Brandon told *Michigan Today* he wanted to create a mascot for Michigan—something every previous Michigan athletic director had refused. Don Canham went out of his way to ignore a student-created mascot, "Willy the Wolverine" near the end of his reign, for a simple reason: It wasn't Michigan.

Brandon, however, saw all manner of possibilities for a new mascot. "You can't get your picture taken with a Block M," he told the alumni magazine. "Mascots are really embraced by the youth demographic and we want to take advantage of that, for all the reasons that are obvious."

The most obvious reason was money. Michigan State, for example, rents out its popular mascot Sparty for weddings, birthdays, Bar Mitzvahs, and just about anything else you'd like. But Michigan fans sided with Yost, Crisler, and Canham: A mascot isn't Michigan. When they expressed their objections via e-mail, blogs, and talk radio, Brandon shelved the idea.

The list of things Don Canham would not do for money was a surprisingly long one. Brandon's list was getting shorter by the month, but when he had to put aside one of his revenue enhancing marketing concepts, it wasn't his staff or people on the hill telling him to slow down. It was the fans.

A month later, on July 22, 2011, the department announced it would be partnering with StubHub to sell tickets on the secondary market—a form of legalized scalping—something the department had also repeatedly refused to do before the Brandon era.

"We just didn't want to go to StubHub," Marty Bodnar told me. "It just didn't feel right. It goes back to the 'scarcity principle.' With that many tickets on the market, you lose that. Do you want people to know that you're selling Miami Ohio tickets for ten bucks? StubHub made it very efficient—and now you don't buy season tickets."

Brandon didn't see any downside. "We are confident," he said, "that our fans will appreciate the convenience and security this partnership provides when purchasing or selling tickets on the secondary market when our tickets are sold out."

They did—maybe too much. Instead of Michigan just making a buck on legalized scalping through StubHub, which was the plan, the more efficient, transparent marketplace unwittingly showed their customers just how over-priced the product had become—which was exactly why Bodnar thought it was a bad idea.

That same off-season, when Brandon spoke to the U of M Club of Ann Arbor's regular meeting at their home base, Weber's Inn, Bodnar was in the audience.

"He was telling the crowd, 'Feel free to use StubHub!'" Bodnar remembers. "And in the same breath, he says, 'Nebraska's coming to the Big House this year, and they travel well, but don't sell your tickets to Nebraska fans! We want the home field advantage!'

"Well, you can't have it both ways. You put your tickets on StubHub, you have no idea who's buying them. You don't control it! But this goes back to community. Those sections grow and develop over decades—people know each other—and now you split them all up for a few bucks? You lose something important."

In early August, 2011, the department released a "pump-up" song from a group named Pop Evil called, "In the Big House," which came complete with a video Michigan paid for, and ran twice on the scoreboard screens during games. The band members were huge Wolverines fans, and serious musicians. The song was technically proficient, sung in a style combining heavy metal and coun-try, whose first two lines went like this:

"We are the Blue Regime
Ferocious, lean and mean . . ."

It might have gone over very well at another school, or for a pro team. But, "This is Michigan." At first the fans thought it was a prank, but when they realized it wasn't, they turned on it quickly.

In a radio interview with Ann Arbor's own Lucy Ann Lance, Hunter Lochmann said, "Event presentation and how people experience the brand at our events is a big part of building the brand, and we are in the midst of hiring some event presentation folks to really focus on making it a wow experience for our fans who go to basketball, hockey, football, soccer. It's not just a PA announcement."

After fans expressed their displeasure with the song—and more than that, the idea that Michigan needed a rock anthem in the first place—Lochmann doubled down, revealing more than he thought he was. The song, he said, was "gaining traction. We know there are people who love it and some people who hate it, but our core customers—the players—they want to hear it."

It goes without saying that, if any collegiate athletic department does not take care of its student-athletes, it has missed the point of college athletics, and it is merely exploiting them. Everyone in the department, including the old guard, believes no athletic director could surpass Brandon's devotion to the student-athletes.

As Brandon's administrative assistant, Annette Howe, told me, "One of [Dave's] guiding principles was: 'We create positive academic and athletic experiences for student-athletes and prepare them to be successful in Life.' Another was: 'We Demand Integrity.' These were Dave's top priorities. He was there for the love of the student-athlete and he was passionate about it.

"Dave's top priorities, were in this order: 1) Over 900 student-athletes; 2) coaches; 3) athletic department team members."

This is essential, admirable, and not always practiced elsewhere. But if the department really believes its "core customers" are the athletes, and the students, letterman, alumni, faculy and fans don't even rank, then it shouldn't charge money for people to watch the student-athletes, and start running a Division III–style program instead.

This was a consistent, central, and crucial misunderstanding Brandon brought to his position. It explains why so many student-athletes liked him, and why most of the department's other constituencies eventually did not.

"He wants our fans to make decisions like consumers, and he treats them that way," Kurt Gulbrand says. "Example: We have 81 suite holders. He had us send them an invoice in the mail with a due date on it instead of showing up at their door to drop it off, thank them for their support, and have a nice chat, check in on their families, their business, and build a solid relationship. That is development. We have only 81 suite holders. It's not that hard to do.

"After I left [in 2011], and they made that drastic change, I can't tell you how many Michigan suite holders called me every year to tell me, 'We now feel like we're purchasing a product from Michigan, not contributing to something we love.' If you're contributing to something you love, what's the limit? There is no limit. Your love for Michigan is boundless. But if you're just purchasing a product, suddenly the suites are overpriced, and so are the seats and the hot dogs. As a development officer, the last thing I want you to do is vote as a consumer. People who make gifts are not voting as a consumer, they were voting with their hearts. They don't *need* to give a hundred thousand or five hundred thousand dollars to their alma mater. They *want* to. They feel good about it!

"A consumer-driven decision is whether to buy Coke or Pepsi or fly American or United. Does anyone want to *give* those companies a million dollars, because they love them so much?"

On August 25, 2011, Michigan announced it had scheduled the 2014 season opener against Appalachian State. Yes, the same team that pulled off what many Michigan fans to this day call simply, The Horror.

"This was the final straw for me and a legion of like-minded folk," Brian Cook wrote years later, in a retrospective on Brandon's regime. Cook, like most Michigan followers, was initially very impressed by Brandon, and thought he would do a great job. "The original Horror remains the worst feeling any Michigan fan has ever had about a game, and even seven years on it marks the point at which 'This Is Michigan' transitioned from fact to aspiration. To dredge that back up was a breaking point."

Brandon always sought to get a reaction beyond Michigan's fandom—and he did. Scheduling Appalachian State marked the first time Brandon's leadership raised eyebrows nationally.

Spencer Hall, who runs the popular college football Web site Every Day Should Be Saturday, wrote, "No matter what happens, greater glory is paid the lowest point in the history of the Michigan football program in exchange for national television exposure. This is Michigan football becoming a celebrity rehab patient. This is Michigan's amateur sex tape that no one wants to buy. We're beginning to think Dave Brandon is not a very smart person."

Most people who know Dave Brandon think he is a very smart person, but even they had to ask: Why did he do it?

Seen by itself, scheduling Appalachian State again was simply an attention-grabber. But seen in the broader context of his decisions, it was another example of Brandon's apparent desire to remold Michigan tradition—an oxymoron if ever there was one.

Good intentions or not, fans soon resented Brandon's inability to leave a yard of Michigan tradition alone. All of it, it seemed, had to be "rebranded" through Brandon's marketing machine: the Legends Jerseys, the uniforms, the helmets, the buildings—including 23-year-old Schembechler Hall, which he would knock down—and even the Appalachian State game, as if playing the same school seven years later could erase the worst loss in school history. Everything that had been built by Baird, Yost, Crisler, Canham, and Schembechler had to be rebuilt, repainted, and renamed—and all of it in Brandon's image.

Not many were paying attention, a few months earlier, when one possible answer surfaced during an event at the U of M Club of Greater Detroit, held in the classic Detroit Athletic Club. One of Brandon's new lieutenants addressed the crowd in February 2011. Marty Bodnar—recently released by Brandon but still loyal to his alma mater—recalled her saying about the department's latest fund drive: "You know, this is about Dave Brandon's legacy.' "

Bodnar did a double-take. "Did I just hear that?" he remembered thinking. "You're telling me, I have to give because you want to secure Dave Brandon's legacy? It's not about Michigan or the student-athletes or even the fans?

"She was just verbalizing what a lot of people felt: All the things they were doing weren't about Michigan. They were about Dave Brandon."

The lieutenant's statement might be written off as a slip, if Brandon himself hadn't said virtually the same thing in a staff meeting a couple years later, in the fall of 2013. To help the 20 or so gift officers get to know the athletic director, they organized breakfast meetings called "Donuts with Dave" in the Ross Academic Center's main classroom.

They asked the gift officers to submit questions in advance, and Brandon would answer them. But one question came from the athletic director himself.

"He'd clearly planned to do this," one officer told me. "He asked the group, 'What do you think is the most important thing to me in my role as the athletic director at Michigan?' "

His employees raised their hands, offering answers like:

"Big Ten titles."

"The Directors' Cup."

"The welfare of the student-athletes."

"Graduation rates."

"Being fiscally responsible," and

"Being 'leaders and best,' " all of which Brandon clearly cared about a great deal.

"No," he told them. "What is most important to me is my reputation. I have worked very hard to have the reputation that I have."

"And the point we took away was," this former employee told me, "'I'm not going to let anyone or anything destroy that.'"

He would make this point more than once with his staff. It's very clear he meant it.

This set up a fundamental conflict Brandon created for himself: It is difficult to believe simultaneously, "This is Michigan" and "I am Michigan."

Like almost everything Schembechler said, "The Team, the Team, the Team," is pretty clear.

CHAPTER 25

LET'S DO IT THEIR WAY

If selling tickets was a problem Michigan didn't have in 2011, Brady Hoke was another.

"From day one, Coach Hoke was great to the players," says Jordan Kovacs, the two-star walk-on turned defensive starter. "Everyone loved Hoke. Everyone knew that he truly cared about you, and that made it easy to play your ass off for him. It was *fun* to play for him."

Since Kovacs also told me three-quarters of the NFL players he's talked with during his stops in Philadelphia and Miami did *not* like their college coaches, the affection Hoke's players had for him should not be taken for granted. That love was put to the test, though, on the last day of Michigan's 2011 summer workouts. Traditionally, the players have come down to Schembechler Hall, seen the weights and contraptions staged for a big workout—then been told by the strength coaches that they had the night off. They would celebrate by bursting through the doors and running across Stadium Boulevard to the Michigan Golf Course, where everyone would jump into the pond in front of the 18th green.

The players felt good about the work they had done that off-season, and believed they had prepared for a great year. When they came down to the weight room at 10 p.m., they were looking forward to a well-earned night of fun.

"Historically, the last night is always a bullshit workout," Hagerup says. "They always make it look serious, then you go bolt for the pond at the golf course. Everyone jumps in, and sings 'The Victors.' Even when the pond was off limits [due to renovations], we ran to the Diag and sang 'The Victors.'

"We knew [new strength coach Aaron Wellman] was a no-bullshit guy, but we figure he's on board with this. The seniors have got their workout gear on. I'm asking the seniors, 'Wellman's on board, right?'

"The seniors all say, 'No, it's all real. The workout's on.' But David Molk winks at me, and he's a captain, so I figure we're okay.

"We go into the weight room, and Wellman's got the workout written on the white board, and it's the longest fucking workout you've ever seen. Tire pulls, sled pushes, farmers' walk, dummy pulls through the sand, army crawls through the sand—you name it. Okay, it's clearly a joke to scare us, and that'll make it that much more fun when we go jump in the pond. We're still joking with each other, 'Okay, we'll play along.'

"Wellman breaks us up into groups of ten, and we start doing the workout. Then we see the seniors tearing their shirts off, and running out the door. We follow. But we don't see that Wellman is running after us, screaming. He's going *ape shit!*

"We get to the pond, and Molk—who's a wonderful speaker—starts into his speech, when Wellman gets out there, and interrupts him.

"'I don't know what the fuck you think you're doing, but if any of you motherfuckers jump in that pond, you're off the team!'

"I've never seen anyone so mad in my life. Considering he's a strength coach, that's saying something. We don't know what to do.

"Molk says, 'You know what, I like Wellman, but fuck him. This is our team. This is what we do. Freshmen, get your ass in that pond.'"

Kovacs remembered it the same way. "Molk, he's an asshole, but he knows he's an asshole, so you gotta respect it."

After they jumped in, Molk, "gives this amazing speech," Hagerup recalls. "'We've worked so hard for so long. This year's special. When we run back to Oosterbaan, whatever Wellman tells us, we're walking right past him with our heads high. This is us.'"

When they got back, Wellman was waiting for them. "We spent three fucking hours setting up this workout. We've got breakfast set up for you guys. *But no one is touching that fucking food who hasn't completed the workout!*

"Tradition? That's great. How about wining? You guys haven't beaten Ohio State in eight years. Eight years! You seniors have nothing to show for it. Your team last year sucked, your team the year before sucked. We can't possibly take one workout off. If you guys don't stay here and finish your workout, don't come back for camp."

Wellman had a point, of course. All the tradition in the world doesn't count for much if it's just a habit, not a history of character and hard work, and your team keeps losing.

"Then he starts calling out specific guys, Hagerup recalls. "'Molk, you're not a leader. You're a fucking pussy!' Then he walks off."

The players were genuinely unsure what to do next. Some seniors said they should finish the workout. Others said, "Fuck this!"

Molk and fellow senior Mike Martin huddled up, talked it over, then told the rest of the team: "Go to your stations. We're going to finish the workout."

"We already had the pond smell, and sand on us from the sand pit, and everyone stunk," Hagerup says. "But to this day, that was one of the most amazing workouts of my life. Everybody was into it. Wellman came back, and instead of being pissed off, he was pumping us up. We were going nuts on the bench press, the curls, the tire pulls—all of it. After a while there's pond water everywhere and the mirrors are steaming up, with so many wet bodies in the weight room."

When they finished, they were more jacked than they had been all year. Wellman brought them in and said, "When the summer's up, we don't jump in a pond. We work."

It was half past midnight. As promised, the staff had a catered breakfast, large even by football team standards, waiting for them upstairs.

"I remember feeling like that was a turning point," Hagerup recalls. "We sort of surrendered to the coaching, in a good way."

Kovacs agrees. "It's a new regime, a new program. Let's do it the way they want it done."

CHAPTER 26

OH, WHAT A NIGHT

Brandon certainly wasn't afraid to try new things, even if the old guard would not always have approved. Some of his ideas backfired, but others worked out exceedingly well.

In July of 2010, Brandon decided to ban fans bringing water bottles in Michigan Stadium—ostensibly for security, although they never quite spelled out why—and charge $5 for a 12-ounce bottle of water. Beyond a lot of grumbling, fans survived the 2010 season's seven home games without incident.

But for the 2011 home opener against Western Michigan, temperatures soared to 92 degrees, and a reported 120-degrees on the field.

"The humidity was outrageous," Jordan Kovacs recalls. "The game was *so* hot. I was doing a lot of double duty on defense and special teams. By the end of the game, I was cramping up so bad [due to dehydration]. And once you start cramping up, it's hard to stop."

One of the "Absopure Hydration Stations" typically sold 225 gallons of water for an entire game. But for the season opener, its supply of 450 gallons had been sucked down by halftime.

That's when the trouble started, with fans dropping from heat exhaustion and dehydration, plus 10 members of the Western Michigan band. The overwhelmed Huron Valley Ambulance company had to call the Ann Arbor Fire Department for backup. Fortunately, a huge storm broke during the second half, averting a potential disaster, and Hoke walked off with a lightning-shortened 34–10 debut victory.

But once again, the Brandon administration had blithely removed a safeguard, only to discover, much later, that it had been there for a reason.

Perhaps Brandon's best idea was hosting the Big House's first night game, then convincing ABC to subsidize the cost of installing the permanent lights needed to do so. All Brandon needed was a suitable opponent, and Notre Dame eagerly accepted.

As the big day approached, the football lettermen started calling the department to buy tickets for the game, as they'd done for years. The department had always done its best to accommodate them, offering at face value whatever random tickets were left—often two seats in different rows, one behind the other. The lettermen never complained about paying full price.

"They loved 'em!" Martin recalls. "They didn't ask for much, and those seats weren't prime seats anyway. They just wanted to come back and see the game with an old teammate or their son, maybe their grandson. It was their chance to show 'em what the old man used to do! They were always very appreciative. Seemed to me, for what they'd done, that was the least we could do."

The lettermen were still excited to see one of their own rise to athletic director. They not only assumed Brandon would keep Martin's ticket policy, but they expected him to hire a permanent, official letterman liaison, and create an area at the stadium for them to gather before and after games—which other programs had added for their lettermen years before.

But in August of 2011, when the lettermen started calling and writing to the department in the weeks leading up to the Notre Dame game, they discovered their main contact, Jamie Morris, was long gone, and so was the ticket director, Marty Bodnar, whom Schembechler had often praised for taking care of his former players with face-value tickets. The lettermen weren't sure what to do next, and many of them simply dropped it. Those who persisted got through to Brian Townsend, a former linebacker. He passed on the lettermen's requests to Brandon, who instructed Townsend to send an e-mail to all the lettermen, announcing that the policy had changed.

In short, it said, if you wanted season tickets, you were welcome to get on the wait list—which now cost $500 for the privilege of getting in line—just like every other wannabe ticket buyer. If you wanted tickets for a single game, the department suggested you get on StubHub—where the price for the first night game was soaring. Again, just like every other fan who wanted a ticket.

Predictably, the lettermen were livid.

It marked the first time a group of people outside the department had issues with the athletic director. Brandon probably assumed his treatment of the lettermen would never bring any consequences—like banning fans from bringing water into the stadium—but it, too, would come back to hurt him when he needed them most.

———

Another longtime custom Brandon changed was the distribution of sideline passes. Under Martin, the department gave out roughly 200 sideline passes each game to Regents, major donors, lettermen, auto dealers who loaned cars to the coaches, and good friends of the program. If you were walking around the field before a game, you were likely to pass congressmen, senators, governors, CEOs, rock stars, actors, and famous athletes, not to mentions dozens of supporters and former players. Most of the passes were good for only one game, and only until warmups ended. In short, there was no downside for the department, and a ton of upside, though mainly in the tough-to-quantify category of goodwill.

"It was a free benefit that people loved," Kurt Gulbrand said. "They'd take photos of themselves on the sidelines, and put them on their Christmas cards. How do you put a price on that kind of loyalty?"

No one knew this better than Brandon himself.

"Dave would call in often for field passes at Michigan Stadium for him and his sons," Gulbrand says, "and we'd take care of him when he was a very generous donor, and a Regent, and even a former Regent. We had no problem doing it, because people at that level should be taken care of, because they take care of the program.

"He probably took more advantage of that program than anyone else. But when he became the athletic director, one of the first things he did was kill the onfield access program."

Before Michigan's first night game, Bill Martin called Gulbrand to ask for two pregame sideline passes for himself and his friend Stephen Ross, the billionaire New York real estate tycoon who owns the Miami Dolphins. With Martin's coaxing, Ross had given $5 million for the Stephen Ross Academic Center, and $100 million to Michigan's business school, now called the Ross School, with many more millions to come. Because Martin parked on the east side of the stadium, and the suite he shared with Ross in the Stephen M. Ross Tower was on the west side, it was more convenient for them to walk through the stadium, on the sidelines, than around it, especially when so many fans would stop them to chat along the way. For that, they needed sideline passes.

Sounds like a simple request. But, Gulbrand says, "It took three days for me to get approval for this. Late in the week, I went over to see Bill at First Martin 'World Headquarters.'"

After the two caught up for a bit, Gulbrand had to get to the unpleasant business at hand. "Bill, here's the deal," he said, sliding two sideline passes across the table to Martin. "I've been instructed by my boss that you can have the sideline credentials. But I have to personally escort you on and off the field."

Exactly one year after being publicly celebrated for rebuilding the Big House at the rededication game, when he cut the ribbon at midfield, the former athletic director and his billionaire donor friend were being treated like potential vandals.

Martin smiled a sardonic smile, and shook his head in amused disbelief. He was not upset with Gulbrand—whom he'd hired—but Gulbrand's bosses. He picked up the laminated cards, told Gulbrand, "You can tell her to keep her fucking passes," and tossed them back across the table.

"I couldn't blame him," Gulbrand says today. "Hell, I think I would have done the same—and for the same reasons."

When Saturday finally arrived, "Here come Martin and Ross walking right down the tunnel, without any credentials," Gulbrand recalls. "You know why? All the ushers and security guards and cops knew Bill and Steve, and what they'd done for the university. They liked them. And out of respect for them, they let 'em in—very happily, I should add. I gave Bill a giant hug and we had a good laugh about the credentials."

Then Martin and Ross walked around the sidelines, past the north endzone, and up the staircase to their suite.

That part of the night's drama, at least, was done. But once again, Brandon had set a trap for himself—and once again, the upside was hard to see.

When the game everyone had been anticipating for months finally rolled around, at 8 p.m., Saturday, September 10, 2011, the problems Brandon had courted with the lettermen, the former athletic director, and the major donors were known only to them.

To Michigan fans, despite a few bumps in the road that summer, Brandon was still the man with the plan—a reputation reinforced when an NCAA record 114,804 people showed up to see his latest attraction. They also saw one of Brandon's most daring decisions: Tampering with Michigan's staid, traditional uniforms, which have consistently ranked among the best in college football, and remained virtually untouched since Fritz Crisler brought the winged helmet to Ann Arbor in 1938. That changed under the lights against Notre Dame, when the Wolverines ran out onto the field in their new "throwback" jerseys—which went back all the way to September 10, 2011. It was less about tradition than trade.

But what if you invited the entire nation to see your first night game, and your new uniforms—and your team laid an egg?

In the first half, the Wolverines couldn't have looked worse, trailing Notre Dame in first downs, 15–3. The only stat that was even close was the only one that mattered: the score. Notre Dame had completely dominated Michigan, but had only a 17–7 lead to show for it.

If lightning had been sighted near the end of the third quarter—as it had in Hoke's debut against Western Michigan—with Notre Dame ahead, 24–7, you could have made a case for calling that game early, too. When Dave Brandon walked through the press box between quarters, he looked gray and drawn—almost sick—as if he deeply regretted scheduling this game.

Michigan started the fourth quarter with the ball on Notre Dame's one-yard line, but running back Stephen Hopkins dropped the ball. If it had bounced toward the Irish, the fans would have headed for the aisles, and Michigan's first night game would have been declared a failure.

But on this night, the luck of the Irish had switched to the Wolverines. The ball bounced right back up into the sure hands of quarterback Denard Robinson, who did what he usually did: trotted into the endzone for an easy touchdown. The score was 24–14—and all of a sudden, another improbable Michigan comeback against Notre Dame seemed entirely possible.

The 114,804 fans—minus the Irish backers, of course—came alive.

Because Hagerup had to sit out the first four games, he had the chance to take in the entire atmosphere on the sidelines for the Notre Dame game. "Don't tell me it's the acoustics of the Big House that make it not so loud," he said. "When the fans show up, and they're into it, they can make it loud. The place can get *really* loud."

Kovacs agreed. "When you're on the field at the Big House and the fans are behind you 100 percent, it's awesome. You feel it. After Denard scored, and the fans were going nuts, we felt it, we believed it—we just *knew*—we were gonna win the game."

What happened next is hard to believe, even now. The same team that couldn't do anything right for three quarters, suddenly couldn't do anything wrong. The Wolverines caught fire, scoring touchdown after touchdown, taking the lead for the first time, 28–24, with just 1:12 left. The fans stood and cheered the rest of the game.

But Notre Dame finally woke up, responding with its first touchdown of the quarter. That left the Wolverines stuck with a 31–28 deficit, and just 30 seconds left. It seemed like the Wolverines had finally run out of tricks.

When you lose, no matter how heroically you played, people talk about what you did wrong. The critics would have asked what happened to the high-powered offense Hoke had inherited, and why the defense wasn't any better than the disastrous unit from the year before. But when you win, all people talk about is what you did right. And Michigan did a lot right in that fourth quarter.

On second and ten, from Michigan's own 20-yard line, it looked like just about everyone wearing blue was running long, taking Notre Dame's defenders with them. Everyone, that is, except Jeremy Gallon, who found a patch of turf for himself near Michigan's bench that was so large, no Irish defenders appeared on the TV screen. This caused Brent Musberger to scream, "THEY LEFT HIM ALONE!" and Don Criqui to groan, "This is unbelievable."

Robinson saw Gallon and fired. Gallon caught it and dashed downfield, getting to the 16-yard line. With just eight seconds left, probably everyone assumed Hoke would choose to kick a 33-yard field goal, and take the game into overtime. But, instead, Brady Hoke very bravely decided to take one shot at the endzone first—which he knew might be Michigan's last play.

Roy Roundtree hadn't caught a pass all night, but in the huddle, the normally unassuming young man did not suggest but told Robinson, *"Give me the ball."* And that's what Robinson did, sending a pass soaring to the edge of the endzone. The Irish defender was all over Roundtree—but it didn't matter. That ball was his. And when he grabbed it, the game was Michigan's.

It's fashionable to say Michigan Stadium is home to the quietest 100,000 people in the world. But thanks to a full day of partying, the new skybox acoustics, and the almost surreal feeling in the Big House that night, no crowd could have been louder.

"If that game was at Notre Dame, or at home during the daytime, I don't think we'd have won," Kovacs told me. "I really think the atmosphere made the difference."

The fans didn't stop, either. Not when Michigan's players jumped into the student section to sing "The Victors." Not when Denard Robinson actually skipped off the field. Not when he returned to the field for a postgame interview. They finally had to turn the lights out, half an hour after the game ended, just to get the fans to leave.

It didn't stop all week. Days later, fans were *still* buzzing about it.

"I got home in bed by 2:30," Kovacs says, "and I was still so wired, I didn't fall asleep until five. I just couldn't put it away.

"That was just a huge win for the program. And you think, man, if we can keep this going we can have *such* an amazing year."

CHAPTER 27

UNIFORMZ, BUCKEYES, AND BCS BOWLS

Will Hagerup returned as Michigan's starting punter by the fifth game, against Minnesota, but getting the rust off was harder than he'd expected.

"The nonconference games are such an important time," he told me. "The weather is nice, and the stakes aren't as high. Now it's colder, the games matter, it's Big Ten. I was just out of sync with the season.

"Being a punter is more like being a golfer than a football player. I played tight end in high school. You have the butterflies, you hit someone, you catch the pass, you hear the crowd, you're focused.

"But when you're a punter you don't get to play against another guy. You're not lined up against anyone. You might hit a punt in the first three minutes of the game, and not hit another one until the last five minutes. When you're working well, during games you feel like you're just booming punts in practice—no big deal. But when it's not working well, you feel like all those parts are working against each other.

"My first game back, I'm nervous in a way I wasn't my freshman year. The whole season, I never felt like I had 'it.' I never felt like I got in a groove."

Hagerup's team, however, was firing on all cylinders.

The momentum from the Notre Dame game catapulted the 2011 Wolverines past Eastern Michigan, 31–3, Minnesota, 58–0, and Northwestern, 42–24. At 6–0, ranked 11th in the AP poll, it seemed no one could stop this train—and certainly not Michigan State, which had gotten spanked by Notre Dame, 31–13, just one week after Michigan had pulled off its miracle.

After warm-ups in East Lansing the Wolverines returned to Spartan Stadium's visiting locker room—the most cramped in the Big Ten—to see brand-new alternative uniforms hanging in their stalls.

"We had no idea," Kovacs told me. "Nobody knew anything. The locker room is so small, you have 80 guys in the tunnel waiting to get back in. Then you hear everybody yelling, so everyone in the back starts yelling, 'What's everyone yelling about?!' When we finally got inside, some guys were pretty excited about it. It didn't matter to me, as long as they fit right and felt good.

"It was hectic. First, it was 'Oh sweet! We got these new uniforms!' Then it was, 'Oh crap, we've got eight minutes to get them on!' You're helping your lockermate out, trying to get his old jersey off and his new one on."

The players soon discovered the new uniforms were slightly smaller than their old ones. Equipment manager Jon Falk used scissors and knives to slice off David Molk's brand new pair of pants, but Molk still decided he couldn't get his new ones on fast enough, so he started walking down the tunnel to the field wearing only his gray stretch pants. A coach stopped him, made him return to the locker room, and got him into his uniform right before kickoff.

On Michigan's first possession, Denard Robinson led the team to a quick touchdown—but that was just about the last highlight for the Wolverines that day. They seemed out of sorts and unfocused. They lost their first game of the season, 28–14—their fourth straight loss to Michigan State.

"Look, we're Michigan, so we're not going to blame uniforms for a loss," Ryan Van Bergen told me. "We just didn't play our best. They did. But I can't tell you it helped that we didn't have any time to get ready before the game, and we were tugging at our uniforms the whole day. You look at the mistakes we made out there, mistakes we hadn't made all year, and you'd have to say Michigan State was better mentally prepared than we were."

Talk to anyone from that team, and even four years later, you'll find that loss still grates.

After Kurt Gulbrand's friend and mentor, Joe Parker, left to become the deputy athletics director at Texas Tech, Brandon hired Chrissi Rawak to take his place.

Rawak grew up outside Philadelphia, and came to Michigan on a swimming scholarship in 1988—the second year of Michigan's 12 straight Big Ten titles. Rawak earned four Big Ten rings as a swimmer, and six more as an assistant coach.

"I love this place," she told me. "That's why I coached. It wasn't what I planned to do, but it was time to give back, and I did it longer than I thought I was going to."

After marriage, kids, and seven years working in Northwestern University's development office, in 2004 Michigan's Vice President of Development,

Jerry May, called Rawak and her family back to Ann Arbor, where she ran the human-resource office, and created the Office of Development's talent management program, then expanded her duties to include finance, administration and development services, which increased her staff from five employees to more than 60. The people I've talked with in the university Development Office give Rawak good reviews for being smart, innovative and fun to work with. When Joe Parker left, Brandon knew he wanted Rawak to replace him.

Shortly after Rawak said yes, Brandon called Gulbrand into his office to update him on the direction he wanted to take the department.

"He looked me square in the eye," Gulbrand recalls, "and said—'I love you here, I want you here, I need you here, and I am going to compensate you.' What else do you want to hear from your boss?"

Gulbrand responded by saying, "I love Michigan and I will do whatever you want me to do to serve Michigan."

Today, Gulbrand looks back on that conversation differently than he did at the time. "I have never met anyone in my life that would look you square in the eye and flat out lie to you. But internally you knew the organization was becoming quite toxic. Following that conversation, I took the advice of my mentors not to discuss anything with anyone but Joe Parker, Bill Martin, and my wife. After Dave took over, I didn't talk to another soul at Michigan other than them, because you couldn't trust anyone."

Gulbrand didn't have to think too hard when the University of Colorado athletic department offered him the unwieldy title of assistant vice chancellor and associate director for development on Wednesday night, October 19. Still, he knew he would miss a lot about Michigan, including the head football coach.

"Brady Hoke was awesome," Gulbrand said. "I loved working with Brady. Couldn't have been a nicer person. At my going-away party, he delivered a signed football. 'Thanks for all you did for Michigan.' Brady was salt of the earth. Still is."

On one of Ann Arbor's beautiful late October days, chief talent officer Kristen Orlowski asked Gulbrand to meet for an exit interview outside the Ross Academic Center, under the umbrellas.

"Can we talk about your time here?" Orlowski asked, pen and paper at the ready.

"Sure," Gulbrand said, then offered to make it easier for her. "You can put a J over one column, and a C over the other [for Joe Parker and Chrissi Rawak]—and I'll give you an answer for both of them."

She looked up, and Gulbrand continued.

"I think you'll see that during most of that time people felt very favorably toward Joe and his style, and very unfavorably toward Chrissi and her style. The difference was very dramatic.

"One knew what he was doing, working with the Victors Club members, the priority point system, and philanthropic giving, and the other didn't understand one iota of it. I felt as if I had to teach her how to do her job."

Gulbrand says today, "I wasn't trying to do Chrissi in. I was trying to be very fair and honest regarding two completely different leaders during my exit interview, and I think I was."

It's worth noting that Rawak moved to athletics at Brandon's urging, and she was largely doing his bidding. But Gulbrand was gone—and with him, one of the last bridges between Martin's athletic department and the donors went, too.

Some donors, most notably Stephen Ross, admired Brandon very much. Others were less enamored of the change in culture they perceived after Martin's people had left. One of them, Lyle G. Davis, sent me his thoughts.

"I first met Kurt Gulbrand in 2008 and Joe Parker a short time later. They could not have been more welcoming to the Michigan family. We had developed not only a business relationship but a personal friendship that still goes on today. Kurt and Joe were everything that was first class about the Michigan athletic department. Relationships were the driving force behind the engagement. They understood that we had a choice as to where we could spend our money and our football Saturdays. Unfortunately, Joe and Kurt left a short time after the stadium was completed.

"As David Brandon arrived the changes came swiftly and abruptly. Gone were the days that our personal relationship meant something to the athletic department. Everything became about the dollar bill and I believe himself. He committed the cardinal sin if you are a Michigan Wolverine. He tried to make himself bigger than the 'team.'

"All while the product on the field deteriorated. Tickets pricing went up, food pricing went up, the personal relationship that we all once enjoyed went from loyal and appreciative to [dealing with] a new customer representative every year or two. These people were all wonderful people who were trying to do the right thing. They just didn't last in that environment very long."

Another, Bob Elgin, echoed Davis's take on the transformation. "The bad news came in a telephone call when we were informed that Kurt was leaving Michigan," Elgin wrote me. "At that time, I was not concerned about the business part of our relationship, but that a friend of mine was leaving

Michigan . . . My relationship with the University has not been the same. It is not because there have not been good people, but they are not Kurt."

Even in business, relationships matter, and many relationships at Michigan were changing dramatically.

The Wolverines rebounded from their loss against Michigan State with a solid 36–14 win over Purdue, then stumbled at Iowa, 24–16. One loss they might overcome, especially with Ohio State on probation, but two losses effectively knocked them out of the Big Ten title race, their stated goal.

They recovered by beating Illinois, 31–14, and 17th-ranked Nebraska, 45–17, on the Cornhuskers' first visit to the Big House.

"This is a big win—huge—I can't stress that enough," Kovacs said after the game. "I think that this is the best win that we've had since I've been on the team. I don't think that we've ever had a game this late in November that really meant as much as this one."

This set up The Game. Although Ohio State had struggled to a 6–5 record under interim coach Luke Fickell, the Wolverines' seven straight losses to their archrival gave them no reason to take the game lightly. The old cliché, "Throw out the records," applied once again.

Denard Robinson put in one of the best games of his career, passing for 167 yards and 3 touchdowns, and running for 170 yards and 2 more touchdowns, with only 3 incompletions.

"Denard played out of his mind," Kovacs recalls. "He was cold-blooded."

But the Buckeyes, led by freshman quarterback Braxton Miller, stubbornly stuck around. With the Buckeyes trailing 40–34, with the ball on their own 24 and 1:48 remaining, Miller dropped back to pass, and saw receiver DeVier Posey slip past his defender by about 5 yards. Miller cocked his arm to throw—and showed his inexperience by firing a flat rope, instead of an arcing pass Posey could run underneath. The pass fell incomplete, and Michigan had its victory.

"That felt *so* good," Kovacs said. "It was so awesome to be part of it."

The best part, perhaps, was the feeling that 2011 was just the start.

"I can still remember, after the Ohio State win, you just thought this was something special," Hagerup recalled, in 2015. "We felt like we were well coached, we felt like we were being well developed in the weight room, and that the mind-set was there.

"Hoke has 'it,' an unassuming character, but everyone knew he was the leader. I loved Coach Rod and his staff, but a change was made, and I'm thinking this guy is going to be the next Bo."

In the Sugar Bowl, Virginia Tech doubled Michigan's yardage, but the

Wolverines pulled the upset over the 17th-ranked Hokies with a 23–20 overtime victory. The 2011 Wolverines finished with an 11–2 record, and their first BCS bowl victory since a young man named Tom Brady finished the job in the 2000 Orange Bowl over Alabama.

The Associated Press story started with this lead: "Here's another tradition that Brady Hoke has restored at Michigan: Winning."

"Personally, I was disappointed in the season, in my own performance," Hagerup said. "But we won the Sugar Bowl, I got to be a part of a BCS win, and we just thought at that point, we were going up.

"We had a mandatory breakfast the next morning, probably 8 a.m. It just felt like you were talking to a bunch of zombies. Loading the van up was painful. No one had showered, no one can put sentences together.

"On the plane going home, everyone needed a bed. Everyone was tired—to put it lightly—coaches and players alike.

"But man, it felt great."

PART IV: 2012

WELCOME TO 2012

CHAPTER 28

COACHING EXODUS

If Dave Brandon had retired on January 2, 2012, he might have gone down as the James K. Polk of Michigan athletic directors: He came, he saw, he did just about everything he had promised, and he left on his own terms—making him perhaps the best "one term" leader Michigan athletics ever had.

Brandon had restored energy, enthusiasm, and public confidence in the department. He dismissed the *Free Press* story for what it was—an exaggeration of an unintended error—and the NCAA investigation that followed, like a bear swatting away flies. Even on the heels of Bill Martin embarking on the most ambitious facilities upgrade since Yost's building boom in the 1920s, Brandon was developing plans to build more, and remake it all again—while generating more revenue than Michigan ever had before.

The department's operating budget alone—which does not include capital expenditures—would grow from $100 million in the 2010–11 fiscal year to $137.5 million just two years later. Even better, its annual operating surplus soared to $15.3 million in fiscal year 2012, 72 percent higher than the previous year.

Brandon had money pouring in at a record rate—and for a reason. He very clearly stated that Michigan fans wanted titles, and titles cost money—and not just for the big three sports of football, basketball, and hockey, but all of Michigan's then-29 varsity teams.

But it would be a mistake to conclude Brandon simply applied a strictly corporate ethos to the athletic department, despite his statements and decisions that often gave his critics ammunition for that theory. In several fundamental ways, Brandon's approach was the antithesis of the bottom-line mentality.

If he had approached his work the way a turnaround specialist CEO would, the student-athletes would be milked for all they were worth, and at least a dozen teams would be dropped from varsity status. Instead, Brandon considered the student-athletes his primary constituency, and did everything he could to make their lives better within the rules. He also brought a broad vision to the department, providing unbridled support for all Michigan's teams, in terms of facilities, funding, and personal support, even though all but three Michigan teams lose millions of dollars every year, and are expected to. Instead of scaling back the 26 varsity teams he inherited, Brandon would promote five more to varsity status. This included men's and women's lacrosse, which cost five million dollars to set up the first two years, paid by donors. This was a popular move, but the way it was decided—by fiat—upset the Facult Advisory Board members, who were told about the decision after the fact. The Board had already been demoted to Advisory status a decade earlier, and now, it appeared, it was "advisory" in name only. They no longer had the power to so much as object to Brandon's spending, and had to sign confidentiality agreements that kept them from divulging everything but their meetings.

"I know Don [Canham] would be very disturbed that the Faculty Board in Control was dropped," Canham's son-in-law, Don Eaton, told me. "Don valued this group as a necessary resource for intercollegiate athletics and the student-athlete."

Of course, what fans liked most were big wins in the three big sports, and during Brandon's first two years, those teams delivered, too. The 2011 football team, led by the unheralded coach Brandon had boldly hired, knocked off Notre Dame and Ohio State and won its first BCS bowl game in 12 years; the hockey team earned a number-one seed in the 2012 NCAA tournament, and the 2012 men's basketball team won a Big Ten title for the first time since 1986.

It looked as though Brandon was just getting started, and the best was yet to come.

By 2012, Brandon had also fulfilled his promise, delivered in dozens of speeches to let go 100 of the 261 original staffers—and then some. He was well on his way to not only replacing those he'd let go, but adding dozens more staffers to the department, increasing the number of employees from 261 to 342.

Brandon reorganized the department and created the Athletics Leadership Team, consisting of 12 people who reported to Brandon and met regularly to discuss department matters. He added counseling services and human resources, which reinforced his admirable focus on the student-athletes, and got rid of one sub-department, the M-Club, which looked after varsity letter winners from all sports.

Under Brandon, a few departments grew faster than others. Marketing and promotions would increase from three to eight employees, including Hunter Lochmann, with only one holdover, Ryan Duey, who would leave in 2014. Media relations and Creative grew from 16 to 19 employees, with 10 remaining from the original staff, and event management—which coordinated the logistics of putting on sporting events, banquets and the like for the department and donors—more than quadrupled, from two to nine employees, while their budget tripled.

But the biggest winners were development, growing from 12 to 28 staffers, with only one employee still remaining in 2014 from the staff Brandon had inherited, and facilities, which expanded from 21 employees to 57, with each facility gaining its own sub-department.

Just two years into his tenure, one thing was certain: Dave Brandon was not playing small.

If Brandon had one constituency he could count on for support, it was the student-athletes. His capital budgets always included big plans for facilities for non-revenue sports, like rowing and lacrosse. But he not only put his time where his mouth was. He showed up to their games, and even their practices. He made it a point to talk to them whenever he could, and showed a genuine interest in them. If he didn't have them all, he seemed to have most.

Among some of Michigan's most successful and established coaches—ice hockey's Red Berenson, softball's Carol Hutchins, and women's gymnastic's Bev Plocki—Brandon earned very high marks for his business savvy, and dedication to the entire department, not just football and basketball. Plocki recalls Dave and Jan Brandon rushing through LA traffic to get to the 2014 NCAA championships, texting updates the entire way. Then she heard their shoes click as they ran to wish Michigan's team good luck before they marched in to be introduced. Plocki held the team back until Brandon arrived. When he told the team how proud he was of them, "It meant the world to the team," Plocki told me. "It is those little things that make a big difference in the athletes feeling like they really matter." But at least as many, it seemed, would have preferred to receive less attention from the athletic director, not more.

Part of Brandon's intense interest in the Olympic sports was due to his fervent desire to win the Directors' Cup, which has been awarded annually to the athletic program with the best NCAA tournament finishes in all sports, men's and women's, since 1993–94. In the Cup's first 16 years, Michigan finished in the top ten 14 times, best in the Big Ten. During Martin's ten years, Michigan finished sixth or better every year but one.

In 2008–09, Martin's last full season, Michigan finished fifth. The following year, 2009–10, which was split about evenly between Martin and Brandon,

Michigan finished a school-worst 25th place. Brandon was determined to fix that, making the Directors' Cup a top priority. He frequently sent all-department e-mails giving updates on Michigan's standing in the Directors' Cup, stressing its importance, and urging everyone to do everything they could to help Michigan claim the Cup.

As Bill Martin had said in his first speech to the athletic department, winning is in Michigan's DNA, and a Michigan athletic director is expected to build a competitive program in all sports, a philosophy shared by every Michigan athletic director from Charles Baird to the present. But not everyone shared Brandon's belief that the Directors' Cup is the ultimate measure of the department's success, because it requires schools to be good in two- to three-dozen varsity sports, at great expense. It's no accident that Stanford, with 36 varsity teams, has won all but the first Directors' Cup, a total of 21 straight. This is why Don Canham, who cared deeply about non-revenue sports, including his beloved track team, nonetheless called the Directors' Cup "a race to see who can lose the most money."

One veteran employee spoke for many who worked in Martin's administration when he told me, "The greed to win the Directors' Cup was the dumbest thing we ever did. It means nothing. It just means you have a lot of sports."

Still, it would have been a harmless—if expensive—pursuit, were it not for the toll it took on the coaching staff, and by proxy, the athletes. The same employee said, "The coaches, Dave drove them into the ground, with all the demands he placed on them. And all for the Directors' Cup."

When a 66-year-old cross-country coach, Ron Warhurst, officially "resigns" after 36 seasons, it doesn't get much attention. But when a 47-year-old football coach, Rich Rodriguez, who'd been the hottest coaching candidate in the country when Michigan hired him in 2008, gets fired after just three seasons, that gets national news.

No one had any reason to make a connection between such seemingly unrelated dismissals, but the next round of departures would establish a pattern. Brandon inherited 111 varsity coaches, including assistants, but soon started scrutinizing their performances, on and off their fields of play.

After Ron Warhurst and Rich Rodriguez made their exits shortly after Brandon took office in 2010, three more head coaches left in 2011, and three more in 2012. The eight departed head coaches represented almost a third of the total, all gone within two years of Brandon's arrival.

The quality of the coaches who left was as striking as the quantity. In 1989, Steve Burns earned his degree at Michigan in Aerospace Engineering, which has produced eight astronauts. But Burns passed up good money and a secure career to coach soccer, at almost every level. In 1992, he started coaching Michigan's club soccer team for $800 a year, then led them to the national club title in 1997 and 1998—for $6,000 a year. After that season, the Regents announced Michigan would be promoting men's and women's soccer to varsity status. Burns got the job—at $45,000 a year.

His team practiced in the Oosterbaan indoor football facility, which is not big enough to conduct a full soccer scrimmage, forcing the team to run half-field drills. Burns made it work, though, winning the 2010 Big Ten conference tournament, and advancing to the NCAA final four, before losing to eventual champion Akron, 2–1. Michigan finished with a school-best mark of 17–5–3, and Burns's peers named him the NCAA Coach of the Year.

At the team banquet, Brandon addressed the crowd. "Congratulations on making it to the Final Four. Do you know what happens when you make it to the Final Four? We expect you to do it again." The air left the room.

Instead of getting a raise or a guaranteed contract, Burns was told by the department, "Your success only means you get to coach at Michigan for another year." Burns turned down offers from other schools, and returned for his 12th varsity season, minus his five best players and 98 percent of the goal scoring from his Final Four team.

Predictably, after the first 16 games of the 2011 season, the team's record stood at 5–10–1—with every single loss coming by a single goal. Their next-to-last game that season would be against second-ranked Akron, the returning national champions, at the new, $6 million soccer stadium Bill Martin had built.

On a cold, gray day, Dave Brandon watched from the sidelines as Michigan held Akron to 0–0 in the first half. Burns invited Brandon into the locker room to listen to his halftime speech. Whatever Burns said, it worked. His team went out and pulled off the greatest upset in Michigan soccer history, 1–0, a victory Michigan soccer fans still discuss on their blogs.

On November 30, 2011, the department announced Burns's resignation. Brandon then hired Chaka Daley, and paid him $125,000, 60-percent more than Burns's salary, with a guaranteed contract. Coach Daley's teams won 11 games in 2012, then 8, then 6—almost the exact same downward trajectory as Hoke's teams.

Women's basketball coach Kevin Borseth, after assessing the changing environment swirling round him—with five Big Ten champion head coaches already gone—did not wait for Brandon to come after him. After leading

Michigan to its first NCAA berth in 11 years, Borseth announced 19 days later he'd be returning to coach the program he had come from, the University of Wisconsin–Green Bay, a very unusual reversal.

Six weeks after Borseth left, women's swimming coach Jim Richardson retired after 27 years at Michigan. In 14 of those years, he'd led Michigan to a Big Ten title, including a record 12 in a row, while placing 141 swimmers on the Academic All-Big Ten team. But he hadn't won a conference title since 2004, and that was too long for Brandon.

In 2003, baseball coach Rich Maloney arrived from a great run at Ball State to take over a Michigan squad that hadn't had a winning season since 1999, and promptly rattled off eight straight winning seasons, three Big Ten titles, two Big Ten tournament titles, and the NCAA Super Regional title in 2007. In 2010, Maloney's team finished second in the Big Ten, before dropping to tenth the next two seasons, largely due to top players jumping to the pros, and pitcher injuries. But Brandon was not interested in excuses, so one week after Richardson retired, Maloney followed him out the door when Michigan announced on May 23, 2012, that his contract would not be extended. Maloney immediately returned to Ball State, where his teams have finished second and first in the MAC.

"Dave didn't have his finger on the pulse of coaching," one coach told me. "He didn't know how hard it was. Look at all the coaches who left under Brandon. That's not an accident."

Before Brandon arrived, all these coaches had proven records of integrity and success, athletically and academically. But like Burns, almost all of them suffered their worst seasons shortly after Brandon arrived, and left soon thereafter. More would follow.

One coach everyone agreed was safe was softball's Carol Hutchins, who had won 26 Big Ten Regular season and tournament titles, gone to 11 College World Series, won the 2005 NCAA title, and came within a few runs of doing it again in 2015. She once told me the secret: "Even in a bad year, a good program is a good program. And you spend years to get to that point."

Two years into Brandon's tenure, it was no longer clear if Michigan's coaches had that luxury.

CHAPTER 29

LOSING THE LETTERMEN

When Schembechler held his first players' reunion in 1989, it was such a hit, various groups of lettermen began coming up with new ways to stay connected. Schembechler started holding the reunions every five years, and opened it up to lettermen of all eras. He often said, near the end of his life, that Michigan needed to do more for the former players.

One group of lettermen, led by Tim Wadhams, Don Eaton, Mark Elzinga, Mike Leoni, and the Dufek brothers—a group that spanned the seventies— started an informal gathering in 2002 they called Chili & Cornbread, a tailgate for their teammates and families before the Michigan State game. They started hosting it under a tent, on a patch of grass near Crisler Arena.

"This was a grassroots effort all the way," Wadhams recalls. "Literally! You had to tape your ankles to stand up on the hillside, but we made it work."

The group dropped about $10,000 each time for food, beverages, chairs, and tables, and packed it all up into Eaton's truck after the game.

"It was an opportunity for us to bring the group together for some cama-raderie and show some appreciation for what the guys had done," Wadhams said. "To introduce family members to teammates, and reconnect, and show the guys who built Michigan football the respect they deserve. That was well received, really a lot of fun."

The second year, 2003, Marty Bodnar arranged for the group to get on the field before the 100th Ohio State game. More than 600 lettermen lined the pathway to midfield, and held the ropes of the "M GO BLUE" banner. The Wolverines won, 35–21—their only victory over Ohio State that decade.

In 2007, Charles Woodson, Brian Griese, and Steve Hutchinson started a weekend event that included a VIP dinner Friday night, followed by an out-ing the next day on Michigan's golf course and a big banquet Saturday night, all to raise money for the university's new C. S. Mott Children's Hospital. Brandon himself held the VIP dinner at his home the night before, partly in gratitude for the care Mott gave his twin sons at birth.

In 2012, it attracted Steve Everitt Jarrett Irons, and Marlin Jackson, and TV stars Dana Jacobson, Adam Schefter, and more, most of them from the Carr era. They raised $1.3 million—strengthening the already strong bond between the athletic department and the hospital, which has included weekly visits from current athletes, and large donations from former ones, for many years.

The success of these annual events inspired another group to start "Victors Night," a party held a few hours after the spring game in the basement room of the Chop House on Main Street. The lettermen and their spouses moved freely throughout the room, grazing on high-end appetizers and lining up at the open bar. It was all courtesy of James Hall, a former Michigan defensive end who, undrafted, managed to play 12 years in the NFL, from 2000 to 2011. Every year he quietly paid the bill for the evening—which started around $10,000 and grew to about $20,000 by 2012 when they needed both floors to accommodate the growing crowd—without asking anything in return. Each year, they honored one of their own with a short speech about the man of the evening, which included Gary Moeller, Jerry Hanlon, and Vada Murray. It was a true feel-good night, with no downside—provided, of course, you weren't paying the bill.

If the lettermen still didn't have a dedicated liaison to the university, or a place of their own to gather before the games, they had found ways to stay connected throughout the year.

By 2012, Brandon had noticed the success of all these events, and he wanted in.

The football players responded by canceling their Michigan golf outing—a rare case where everybody lost.

That fall, before the 2012 Michigan State game, the lettermen had planned to host their Eleventh Annual Chili & Cornbread get-together, which had moved to Mortenson Plaza, attached to the stadium, but Brandon decided to take over the event and move it to Oosterbaan Fieldhouse, a half mile away, and far from the energy of the tailgate scene.

He set up a team of golf carts to transport the lettermen from the stadium to Oosterbaan, where they had tables set up for a sit-down lunch, and then take them back again when they were done. As anyone who's been to a Michigan game knows, trying to get back and forth anywhere through that crowd is dicey, and eats up the precious minutes before kickoff.

In one fell swoop, Brandon had transformed a decade-old custom that was close and casual to one that was far and formal.

Since becoming the athletic director in 2010, Brandon had tried to gain control of Victors Night, too, and move it from the Chop House on Main Street to Glick Fieldhouse. There, he proposed to have the field filled with white-linen-covered tables for everybody to sit, and a dais at the front with a podium, where they would conduct Michigan's version of the ESPYs, with him serving as emcee. James Hall and company wanted no part of that. They dug their heels in to stay at the Chop House, then killed the event altogether in 2013.

All three events had started organically, through the generosity of former players, in the 2000s. By 2014, all three were gone. No doubt, Brandon had good intentions. He wanted to make all these events bigger and fancier, and was willing to spend the department's money to do it. He just didn't understand that's not what his former teammates wanted.

"Dave lost the Bo Boys after stiffing them on tickets for the first night game against Notre Dame," Jamie Morris explains. "He sealed it when he moved Chili & Cornbread. Then all of sudden, he lost the Carr guys with Victors Night and the golf outing. When you lose the Carr guys—whose coach had promoted Dave for the position—you're in trouble."

CHAPTER 30

BRANDON'S MASTER PLAN

If the lettermen were leaving the Brandon camp in droves by 2012, the fans weren't. Despite a few setbacks, most Michigan fans were still squarely in Brandon's corner. His next announcement would give them reason to stay there.

On May 16, 2012, the department announced a master plan to renovate ten facilities and build seven new ones, including a field hockey project for $10 million, new lacrosse facilities for $12 million, a pool expansion for $20 million, a new combination rowing/strength and conditioning center for $25 million, a new multipurpose gym for $30 million, and a new track facility for $90 million—plus "The Walk of Champions," which would create "one complete, contiguous athletic experience that will be as impressive in its scale as it is in its vision."

The department reported the price tag for the whole thing would come to $250 million, which left most fans more impressed than concerned. It demonstrated Brandon was serious about Michigan being "the leaders and best" in all sports, not just football, basketball, and hockey.

"Man, Dave's Master Plan starts at State and Hoover and goes all the way out to Briarwood!" associate athletic director Greg Harden said. "He's getting donors to commit to building *Michigan athletics*—track and field and volleyball and rowing and lacrosse—not to just give to this or that, but all 31 teams, almost 1,000 athletes! No one had ever talked about upgrading everything for everybody before.

"Brilliant! Absolutely brilliant!"

This translated very well to the donors. "The vision of Dave Brandon," says Chrissi Rawak, Michigan's Executive Associate Athletic Director for External Relations and Strategic Initiatives, "this commitment to all student athletes, was something that people believed in and were inspired by." Michigan's athletic directors have done a remarkable job supporting all the university's teams, going back to Fielding Yost's Fieldhouse—just one reason why Michigan has 373 total Big Ten titles in all sports, dwarfing second-place Illinois's total of 237. But Brandon planned to take it a step farther, with a comprehensive plan for both fund-raising and facilities that earned him still more support among the student-athletes.

It earned him less, however, among those who had been managing the money. Revenue soared under Brandon, partly because he increased the average price of attending a game, including tickets and seat licenses, by about $100 per seat. The Big Ten started paying out record amounts to its member schools from TV rights, which would total $31 million per school in 2014–15, and it's still growing fast, thanks largely to the stunning success of the Big Ten Network.

But Michigan athletics' expenses under Brandon were growing at an even faster rate, from $89.1 million in 2010 to $115.2 million in 2012. In a corporation, this might not raise too many concerns, but in the athletic department of a nonprofit state university, it caused many, including additional pressure on already stressed-out coaches.

If Michigan football, basketball, and hockey continued to win and attract fans, Brandon's projections would be safe. But if they started losing their fans for any reason, Michigan would find itself facing red ink, lots of it, with no easy way out.

Former department CFO Jason Winters saw this coming before he left the department in 2012. "There is no question Dave was aggressive in investing in sports that were not producing any revenue," he told me. But buying racks of powerful lights so field hockey, lacrosse, and other sports can play night games, Winters told me, "represents an enormous wealth transfer from football and basketball families to soccer families. The issue for me was resource allocation, and to what end? Improvements were needed, but who in their right mind spends $12 million on a palatial field hockey stadium where you get 200 people to attend a game on a good day?"

While these figures would be reduced, and donors paid much of it, spending continued to rise.

A month later, when Brandon's department went public with plans for a 48-foot-wide, $2.8 million video board outside of Michigan Stadium, far more people stood up to protest. The City of Ann Arbor allows signs up to 200 square feet, while Brandon's billboard runs 1,296 square feet, but he could get away with it because the university is immune from Ann Arbor's signs and outdoor advertising ordinance. Still, it struck many as another example of Michigan testing town-gown relations, which were already strained with the university buying up so many of Ann Arbor's lots and office buildings, and taking them off the tax rolls.

Few fans cared about the commemorative coin that also came up in one of Brandon's first staff meetings, but many more Michigan fans and Ann Arbor citizens, including the mayor, would care about Brandon's billboard when it went up in mid-2013. It marked the first time the public complained en masse about one of Brandon's ideas.

For most, the billboard failed the tests for good taste and goodwill, but Jason Winters had a different take.

"Here's what I could never understand," he says, "and maybe I'm just jumping to the conclusion that everyone should think like me—but I just want to put it on the record: It was such an obvious waste of money.

"That was Dave's 'Maize Halo.' Big mistake."

Brandon's plans for the electronic billboard aside, the public didn't raise a ruckus on July 23, 2012, when President Coleman announced a three-year contract extension to Brandon's original five-year deal, which would also increase his salary from $600,000 to $800,000 immediately, then run up to $1.05 million in 2017–18. Those figures did not include bonuses, which were not insignificant when Brandon received an additional $300,000 in 2012, 2013, and 2014, which did not come to light until 2014.

Perhaps most surprising—and most overlooked—was the extension's buyout provision. If Michigan terminated Brandon's contract before July 1, 2016, he would get his remaining base salary through the end of the contract in 2018, plus an amount equal to the deferred compensation left on the deal.

If another school sought to hire Brandon, it would need to pay Michigan that amount.

"Nobody at that time could imagine anything like that happening for years, if at all," Regent Larry Deitch says. Because the possibility of Brandon being fired seemed a virtual impossibility at the time, "that made the extension more palatable to the Regents."

The purpose of including a buyout clause is to discourage competitors from poaching your employee, but if any other university athletic department was considering making a pitch for the services of Dave Brandon, it has not been reported. The deal certainly surprised those who had worked for Bill Martin, who had insisted on being paid one dollar his first two years on the job, then a relatively modest $300,000 or so, while declining all performance bonuses—secret or otherwise.

The Regents approved it, but not without misgivings. They were surprised by President Coleman's request, especially coming as it did just two years into Brandon's initial five-year contract. They were even more surprised by how firmly she insisted on doing it. The deal, at the least, was highly unusual for an athletic director.

Just a month earlier, the Regents had given President Coleman a two-year extension, which meant she would be stepping down in 2014, ending an excellent run. In 2010, Coleman was named by *Time* magazine as one of the nation's ten best college presidents, and is still widely considered one of the best in Michigan's history. She made several big, bold decisions, including buying the former Pfizer R&D headquarters and converting it into the North Campus Research Complex, and forging a ground-breaking partnership with Google (co-founded by Michigan alum Larry Page), to digitize Michigan's seven-million-volume library.

But she will likely be best remembered for protecting Michigan from the economic downturn by spearheading a $2.5 billion fund drive, that ultimately produced $3.2 billion—the most ever for a public university at the time—then embarking on another $4 billion capital campaign, which was more than half complete when she retired. She and her team wisely protected a far larger chunk of University's endowment than did most major universities during the market crash of 2008. She also allowed the endowment to build, leaving Michigan in much better financial shape than it was when she arrived in 2002—and indeed, much better than almost any public university except Texas, which is supported by oil money.

"Before she left," Deitch recalls, "she wanted to extend certain contracts for her executive team. We enthusiastically agreed that she would renew the contract of [vice president of development] Jerry May, for example. We'd just started a $4 billion campaign, he knows all the donors, he knows the staff, he's as good at that job as anyone I've ever seen. Locking him up for five years, through the campaign, was a good idea.

"But Dave's contract extension didn't have the same compelling logic behind it. In fact, there were a number of Regents who did not want to approve the extension, but Mary Sue made it clear this was something she really wanted. Ultimately, we supported her on it, out of respect for her long tenure and commitment to the university.

"My rationale for approving it, in the face of her insistence, was that athletics was not broken, the new president [the Regents were due to hire in 2014] would have other fish to fry, and the last thing a new president will want to be dealing with in his or her first year is a search for an athletic director.

"Of course, that's exactly what happened: it all blew up a lot sooner than anyone imagined, and the new president had to hire a new athletic director in his first few months—but no one saw that coming in 2012."

Another factor in the Regents' 8–0 decision was the timing of President Coleman's request.

"Look at the dates," Regent Kathy White says. "She got her two-year extension in June, 2012, and *immediately* after, not a month later, she was pushing for Dave's extension. President Coleman was very popular, and she wasn't stupid. She knew if we had said no, she'd be a complete lame duck—and that's a great burden for a university to have for two years, while running a search for her replacement. If we didn't want to do that, the only real option we had would be to fire her—and that's even worse.

"Of course, we pushed back a bit, but she took every chip of political capital she had and put *all* of them on the table for him—and she didn't put them on anything else: not on the other executive officers, not on the other contracts.

"Hey, it's the president's team, so you can say she has a right to pick her people. And at the time, he was fine. The students weren't even ticked off yet."

CHAPTER 31

THE ENVELOPE

"I always have a crappy off-season," Hagerup told me, "and 2012 was no exception."

A few weeks after the 2012 spring game, it was raining hard one night, so Will Hagerup parked his car in a lot near his house and ran in. Because they tow so often near campus, he knew he had to move his car before he went to bed. At midnight it was still pouring, but he couldn't wait any longer. So he ran out to his car, in the dark, and stepped his kicking foot into a pothole filled with water.

"Man, I *hear* it pop," he recalls. "I ran back to my house, got back into bed, and I already know it's broken. I'm thinking, 'You just came off a crappy season, and now you might not even play this year. What are you gonna do about this?'

"I went to sleep, woke up, got in my car, and drove to the hospital. Yep, it's broken. They say it'll take two months before I can kick again. I miss all the kicking camps. I miss all the summer runs. I'm barely healthy enough to prepare for fall camp.

"I'm not just worried about my foot, but winning back my job for my junior year. I didn't get to practice until August. I told my parents, 'Don't make reservations for [the game against Alabama in] Dallas,' but of course they did. They don't miss any games, home or away. I didn't know until the week before the Alabama game that I was going to be the punter."

Hoke's honeymoon season aside, the eighth-ranked Wolverines faced Alabama as 14-point underdogs. It didn't help Michigan's chances that Brady Hoke announced the day before the game that starting running back Fitzgerald Toussaint would stay at home because of his DUI conviction a month earlier.

"The decision was not easy, but I feel it is in the best interest of this program and for these kids, and those always will be my priorities," Hoke said in a press release. "It's about teaching life lessons, and if this helps these kids or someone else make a right decision later, then we've won. That is ultimately what we are here for, to help them grow and mature to become better sons, fathers, husbands, and members of society."

For Michigan fans, this marked one more reason why they loved Hoke: His values matched Michigan's values, and those values took precedence over mere victories.

But that didn't mean Michigan fans were willing to accept losing. They held out hope that their Wolverines were on the edge of returning to the big time. After all, they still had Denard Robinson at quarterback. An upset victory over the Tide would make Michigan's comeback official.

Hagerup was hoping to make a comeback of his own. "You're named the starter a week before the game, against Alabama, in Cowboy Stadium, with a national audience. You got suspended twice. You broke your foot. Now do this. Against those odds. Do this."

Alabama sought to stop the fleet-footed Denard Robinson with a "containment" defense to prevent Robinson from running wild, while Michigan obliged by setting up Robinson in the pocket, looking downfield for open receivers— exactly what he was least-equipped to do. Those targets included Devin Gardner, who was playing wide-out that game.

On the other side of the ball, Michigan had no answer for Alabama's A. J. McCarron, who led the Tide to a 31–0 lead with 4:31 still left in the first half.

Three years later, Kovacs said, "That was our welcome to the 2012 season."

Hagerup certainly wasn't happy about the loss, but he was relieved to see he could still punt. "I had the best game of my career that day. Everything felt smooth again, for the first time in almost two years, and that catapulted my season."

Despite the shellacking, the Wolverines still had reason to believe this could be their best chance to grab their first Big Ten title in eight seasons.

The Wolverines were coming off Hoke's triumphant 11–2, Sugar Bowl–winning debut season. Denard Robinson was back for his senior year. They had beaten Notre Dame the previous three years. Ohio State had finished 6–7 the year before and would be on probation for the 2012 season. And, with Alabama in the rearview mirror, the rest of the slate seemed to be Michigan's for the taking, starting with Michigan's home opener against Air Force.

Historically, after a bad loss like the one the Wolverines suffered against Alabama, Michigan would invariably come back strong the next week and crush the poor souls who dared to get off the bus.

Not this time. With just 2:45 remaining, and Air Force down 31–25, with the ball, Michigan's defense had to stop the Falcons' drive to avoid adding another historic loss to its list.

"It's always good to win," said Hoke, sticking to his list of non-quote quotes. "Sometimes they're not very pretty, and this would be one."

The bright spot, as usual, was Robinson, who accounted for 426 yards and 4 touchdowns, becoming the first major college football quarterback to have at least 200 yards rushing and 200 yards passing in three games. Texas's Vince Young was the only other player to do it twice. Robinson kept it up the next weekend against Massachusetts, piling up 397 yards of total offense and 4 touchdowns—all in three quarters—to help Michigan put away the Minuteman, 63–13.

"We needed to get a good win before Notre Dame next week," Robinson said. "We knew we needed to get better before that game."

The Fighting Irish were gearing up for the Wolverines, too—and not just the players.

Notre Dame athletic director Jack Swarbrick obviously wasn't sitting on the bus for Michigan's Coaches' Caravan in the spring of 2010, when Brandon made the case to Kurt Gulbrand and others that Notre Dame was the least important of Michigan's three main rivals. But Swarbrick was shrewd enough to pick up Brandon's lack of regard for the rivalry along the way. As a Notre Dame graduate, he already knew enough about the long and rocky history between these two titans to be forever vigilant for signs of yet another schism.

Despite the e-mail between Swarbrick and Bill Martin agreeing to 25 more games—which helped Notre Dame secure another generous deal from NBC—when Swarbrick got down to the nitty-gritty of a binding agreement with Brandon, the two athletic directors were much less ambitious. In a contract dated May 16, 2011, the schools agreed to play the next seven years, through the 2017 season. Swarbrick, however, insisted on a rejoinder to the contract: Either team could end the rivalry with three years' notice.

"Here's what the media has never picked up on," says former CFO Jason

Winters. "Because the Michigan–Notre Dame series resumed in 1978 in South Bend, Swarbrick's escape clause enabled Notre Dame to get one more home game than Michigan."

Since each home game in that series is worth millions, the issue of an extra home game is not merely a competitive one.

"I tried to impress upon Dave," Winter's says, "that the three-year deal could be fine so long as the games balanced out and both teams got an equal number of home games, and Notre Dame does not get an extra home game out of the deal. He understood my concern, but he put his trust in Jack."

Brandon also dismissed Winters's concerns about the contract itself, which was "incredibly convoluted. I told Dave he should listen to Michigan's attorneys, who recommended simplifying the language to make it clear both schools would get an equal number of home games, but Dave said, 'Jack's an attorney and he takes pride in being an attorney. We don't want to insult him by asking for changes in a legal document that he might have written.' He discounted the whole thing, convinced Jack would never screw him."

Brandon often insisted business relationships be conducted "top to top," that is, between him and the leader of the other organization, be it Adidas or Notre Dame, with underlings rarely involved. When he was able to establish such relationships, he readily deferred to kings, but not to minions.

Brandon gave Swarbrick a free pass—thereby removing yet another safeguard of Michigan's traditions.

Not long after Brandon signed Swarbrick's clause, Swarbrick started flirting with the Atlantic Coast Conference, which had been cannibalizing the crumbling Big East. The ACC had always been interested in Notre Dame, like every other conference in the country. If Swarbrick was keeping his eye on Brandon, it's not clear if Brandon was returning the favor. The week before the 2012 rematch, Brandon was apparently surprised to learn, along with the rest of the nation, that Notre Dame had joined the Atlantic Coast Conference in every sport but football. But the ACC didn't need Notre Dame's middling basketball program. It wanted its vaunted football team—and got it, for a guaranteed five games a season.

Whether Brandon failed to recognize how this might threaten Michigan's series with Notre Dame, or didn't care, is an open question. But one of the predictable side effects of Notre Dame's new arrangement soon became clear to everyone.

On September 22, 2012, at 6:41 p.m., a military plane boomed overhead at Notre Dame Stadium. The way Brandon told it, about the same time, Swarbrick approached Brandon on the sideline and handed him an envelope.

"I put the letter in my pocket and didn't bother to read it right away," Brandon told a reporter, "because I was focused on the game we were about to play."

Swarbrick's hand-off would prove to be the most interesting play of the day. The two traditional powerhouses squared off in one of the worst-played games of their century-old rivalry.

The Wolverines' main problem was not Notre Dame's defense, but their own game plan, which seemed designed to use Michigan's race horse, Denard Robinson, to plow the fields, leaving Robinson's feared feet stuck in the grass behind the line, just where opposing defenses wanted them. On Robinson's first four passes, he threw four interceptions, and the Wolverines lost 13–6.

"In the 22 years I've been living," Robinson said, always refusing to blame anyone but himself, "this is the most disappointed I've ever been in myself."

In victory or defeat, Robinson unfailingly said the right thing—and meant it—just another reason his teammates loved him.

"I really admired the way Denard handled himself during the postgame," Kovacs told me in 2015. "He was really upset. Another guy could say, 'I'm not talking,' but he knew he was the face of the program, and he took the questions. I respect the hell out of him for it. Down-to-earth guy, never changed. Everybody in that locker room loved that guy."

Kovacs thought less highly of the reporter who asked Kovacs, "Denard didn't help you out today, did he?"

"Fuck, you kidding me? That kid's in the locker room really upset with himself now. You think I'm going to say that?"

Heading into the Big Ten schedule, the 2012 Wolverines were 2–2.

Three days later, on Tuesday, September 25, 2012, Brandon told the Associated Press about the envelope Swarbrick had handed him right before the game. "I read it on the way home Sunday morning."

Swarbrick's letter was dated September 21, 2012, the day before the game, citing the contract's complicated escape clause that Swarbrick had added the year before: "Because I am providing you with this notice prior to the commencement of this year's football game on September, 22, 2012," Swarbrick wrote, "there is no liability to Notre Dame for canceling those games."

Three more games and the rivalry was done, with no return in sight. By all accounts, Brandon was furious—and not just at Swarbrick's decision to end the rivalry, but the way he did it: with no warning, minutes before kickoff at Notre Dame, guaranteeing the Irish would get an extra home game.

"When I heard that Jack did that," says Jason Winters, who had been replaced by then, "that was the first thing I thought of: Jack screwed us, just like I feared he would. I believe in my heart, that Jack knew three years ago that he was going to screw Dave right before the 2012 game.

"Brandon got snookered like a country bumpkin. Not only did Dave have to find a replacement for Notre Dame—which was clearly going to be an inferior game—but he would have to pay the next team about $1 million more in guarantee money."

The legal fine points aside, the Michigan–Notre Dame rivalry ended for two reasons: a dysfunctional relationship between the two athletic directors, and money.

What neither man seemed to care too much about were the Michigan and Notre Dame players, lettermen, alumni, and fans. If any of them wanted to see one of the best rivalries in sports end, I have not met them.

CHAPTER 32

PLAN B—AND PLAN C

After a welcome bye week, the Wolverines rolled past Purdue, 44–13. Robinson avoided throwing an interception for the first time that season, running the ball 24 times for 235 yards to become the Big Ten's career rushing leader for quarterbacks with 3,905 yards, passing Indiana's Antwaan Randle El, by 10. Randle El started four full seasons to set that mark, while Robinson needed less than two and a half years as a starter to break it.

The next weekend, Homecoming, brought the floundering Illinois squad to town. The Wolverines thrashed their guests, 45–0, in a freezing rain, with Robinson notching 4 touchdowns.

"It's probably as complete as we played," Hoke said. "But it's not nearly good enough."

Why not? Because the next week, the Spartans of Michigan State were returning to Ann Arbor. So were Michigan's lettermen, but their plans to host their Eleventh Annual Chili & Cornbread get-together at Mortenson Plaza, attached to the Stadium, Brandon changed in favor of an armada of golf carts shipping lettermen back and forth to Oosterbaan Field House. The break with their relatively new tradition was not well received.

A win over the Spartans—who were riding a four-game winning streak over the Wolverines for the first time since 1962—would go a long way toward convincing fans Hoke was still the man for the job.

Down 10–9, with 3:07 left, Hagerup had to punt the ball back to the Spartans. Michigan State could have killed most of the clock, if not all of it, simply by running the ball three times. But the Spartans threw two incomplete passes to stop the clock and allow Michigan to mount a final drive with two minutes left. On second and eleven, Denard Robinson threw a 20-yard pass to Drew Dileo to set up a potential game-winning 38-yard field goal—but he couldn't watch when Brendan Gibbons lined up for the kick. Gibbons made it, Michigan won 12–10, the students stormed the field, and the scoreboard flashed "900 WINS!" announcing Michigan as the nation's first team to hit the nine-century mark.

When asked about Denard Robinson, Spartan coach Mark Dantonio grinned and said, "I'm glad he's gone."

In hindsight, Kovacs said, "That game was the highlight of that year."

On October 27, 2012, the 20th-ranked Wolverines—5–2 overall, 3–0 in the Big Ten—traveled to Lincoln, Nebraska, for the first time in 101 years.

Late in the first half, with Nebraska leading, 7–3, Denard Robinson went down hard on his elbow and had to leave the game. It would be his last start as a college quarterback.

Instead of moving Devin Gardner back to quarterback from wide receiver, where the coaches had been playing him that fall, Hoke and Borges decided to bring in Russell Bellomy.

When linebacker Brandin Hawthorne watched Bellomy run into the huddle, he yelled at Gardner: "Devin! Whatchoo doin'?"

"What?"

"Go get your rotator cuff warmed up!"

"I'm not going in!"

Three years later, Gardner grinned at the memory. "Brandin was, like, *mad* at me! Hey man, you know that's not how it works! You can't just put yourself into the game!"

It marked another setback in a career that had started with such promise.

The most-celebrated member of the 2010 recruiting class was not punter Will Hagerup, who was ranked number one nationally at his position, but a quarterback from Detroit named Devin Gardner, who was also ranked number one nationally at his position. He had it all: size, speed, strength, a great arm, athleticism, toughness, and brains—and he didn't even drink.

Even though Coach Rodriguez already had more good quarterbacks than he could play, and not enough defensive stand-outs, he didn't think twice before offering Gardner a scholarship. Just about every team wanted him, but since he was interested in Michigan, many of them told Gardner—and other Michigan recruits—that the NCAA investigation would cost Michigan scholarships, bowl games, TV appearances, and perhaps its head coach, even though most of them knew better. Gardner didn't care. Like Hagerup, he knew he wanted to go to Michigan, and nothing could change his mind—not even two starting quarterbacks just one year ahead of him, Tate Forcier and De-nard Robinson. Gardner was so eager to go to Michigan, he petitioned to graduate early from Inkster High School and enroll at Michigan in January 2010. Michigan approved the decision, but the Inkster school board held up Gardner's application for early graduation until mid-January, when his prin-cipal finally called him into his office.

"You need to get your stuff and go."

Gardner wasn't sure what that meant.

"The school board approved your graduation. You're going to Michigan."

"That," Gardner said on signing day, 2010, "might have been the happiest day of my life."

By 2012, his third season on the team, he still hadn't topped it.

Russell Bellomy was a 3-star quarterback out of Arlington Martin High School, outside Dallas, who accepted Michigan's offer to be a redshirt freshman in 2011. By the fall of 2012, he had been named Scout Team Player of the Week a half-dozen times, and completed 70 percent of his passes during spring ball. This gave the coaches enough confidence in him to move Gardner to wide receiver.

"I was excelling," Bellomy told me. "I built my confidence up really well. I just loved, loved, *loved* playing football that year."

Against Alabama, he took a snap late in the game and threw his first pass a little behind Vincent Smith, got it tipped, and got picked off.

"One and done—one play—in my hometown!" he said three years later, chuckling. "Gosh, that sucked!"

Bellomy played again in the UMass game, pulling a zone-read from the 12-yard line to the goal line, but Justice Hayes finished the job.

"Such a good dude," Bellomy said. "Couldn't be happier for him."

From there, the coaches gave Bellomy only mop-up time, until the Ne-braska game.

"It was a tough situation for Hoke and Borges," Bellomy says. "You have Denard, and then you have *me*—and I'm no Denard."

Bellomy's self-effacing assessment aside, many wondered why the coach-ing staff seemed so unprepared for a situation that was all but inevitable—especially when the nation's former top quarterback prospect was already on the field, at receiver. A case could be made for keeping Gardner at receiver, and putting Bellomy in at quarterback—but the case gets weaker under these circumstances, with no warning, or warm up.

"A lot of people talk about having regrets," Bellomy says today, philosophically. "You wish you could go back and change something. But I'm not making any excuses. I made plenty of bad throws."

His first interception, however, wasn't one of them. After Bellomy was flushed out of the pocket, he threw the ball low and away, right where Vincent Smith could catch it without getting blasted. But when Smith reached down to catch it, the ball somehow popped up in the air. Bellomy was already on his back when the Cornhuskers made the easy interception.

"I hear the crowd go nuts," Bellomy recalled. He knew what that meant, so he got up and chased down the ball carrier at about the 5-yard line. Bellomy dove at his feet, tripped him up—and got a foot in the stomach.

Not that big a deal, of course, but they learned later that week that Bellomy has a rare condition called "horseshoe kidney," in which the two kidneys are connected by a thin strand of the organ, wrapping around Bellomy's abdomen. Thus, when he took the Cornhusker's foot in the gut, it lacerated the band of kidney spanning his stomach.

The team medical staff couldn't possibly have diagnosed such a rare condition at the time, and Bellomy wasn't one to complain, so he stayed in the game. "When the adrenaline's going," he said, "you don't feel anything."

A quarter later, he threw his second interception off a play-action fake, when the center and running back tripped up in the backfield, and the Nebraska noseguard got to Bellomy right as he released the ball. Bellomy finished his day with a good drive, but when he tried to force the ball into Gardner, the Nebraska defender out-jumped him for Bellomy's third interception.

"I clearly remember [Michigan lineman Michael] Schofield putting his arm around me after that pass," Bellomy says, "which was basically at the end of the game. I was in disbelief. It put the icing on the worst game I ever played."

Bellomy's stat line: 3-for-16 with 3 interceptions. It marked Michigan's third game that season without a touchdown—Notre Dame and Michigan State being the other two—with a final score of 23–9. The Wolverines flew home with a 5–3 record, and would drop out of the rankings the next day.

Three years later, Gardner offered nothing but sympathy for Bellomy.

"They put Russell in a situation where he was not able to succeed," Gardner told me. "He had no warm up. I don't think he knew he'd be going in. And they didn't go easy on the playbook, either.

"I don't think people really understand how big that stage is, until you're on it. I learned that early because I was living with Denard. I watched what he went through, on and off the field, and how he handled it. But that stage still looks a little different when *you're* the one running out there, and it's your game, and the lights come on.

"When you're the quarterback, you get the ball to start every play, and there are 100,000 people up there not looking at anything else—except maybe a baby or two!

"Russell's not a bad quarterback, but they didn't prepare him for that situation. That's not on him."

No one could have prepared Bellomy for what came after.

"I received a far amount of grief for that game," Bellomy recalled. "Been the butt end of many jokes. I can't use Twitter anymore. Too much on there."

After he tore his ACL in 2013 spring practice, most fans expressed their disappointment for him, but more than a few "applauded the news," Bellomy recalls, describing an all too common class of people.

"I fired back at a few of them on Twitter, but it is a losing battle, keyboard courage is inevitable and not worth the fight."

Another fan sent a handwritten letter to Bellomy at Schembechler Hall. "You should never be allowed to play for Michigan," he wrote. "You are terrible and you should not even play the game of football: you are better off not doing anything important with your life."

"Then," Bellomy recalls, laughing, "he signed it, 'Sincerely'! What a prick."

It got worse. On Sunday night, in his South Quad dorm room, "I couldn't sleep. It felt like someone was jamming a knife into my stomach, twisting and turning it. On Monday morning, I pissed red and black. Holy shit! I drank a lot of Gatorade, then peed red and black again."

Bellomy went to University Hospital to spend a day getting CAT scans, MRIs, and the "whole nine yards," before the doctors diagnosed his condition: a rupture, due to Bellomy's rare horseshoe kidney. It helped to get the diagnosis, but it didn't prevent him from urinating blood for another two weeks.

That's why, when he dressed for games after that, he was wearing "that big, goofy stomach pad."

The next weekend against Minnesota, November 3, 2012, with Bellomy waylaid, the coaches started Gardner. He delivered drives of 91, 90, 86, and 79 yards in a workmanlike 35–13 win.

"It didn't surprise us," said Michigan coach Brady Hoke on Gardner's success. "Being a receiver, being over there, that's a whole different animal.

I think that helped with some development. I think he did a nice job of managing the team. I think we had four drives over 79 yards."

The Wolverines kept the Brown Jug in Ann Arbor for the 38th time in 41 years.

"It's always important," said Kovacs. "It's one of our rivalry games. That's one of those trophy games that you want to win every year, and it's a trophy that you want to keep at Schembechler Hall year in and year out."

CHAPTER 33

WIN SOME, LOSE SOME

Winning always helps, but Michigan fans had already demonstrated their loyalty went deeper than a few losses. They'd complain, but they wouldn't leave.

But each time the Wolverines didn't just lose, but looked bad doing it, it put more stress on the relationship between the department and the fan base. When the team and the department started wobbling simultaneously, both became more precarious.

In a game the Wolverines had to win to keep their preseason goal of a Big Ten title alive, the coaches put Denard Robinson and his injured elbow in against Northwestern for occasional duty as the running back, and kept Devin Gardner at quarterback.

"Northwestern is a team we respect," Gardner told me. "They're physically tough—very tough—and they're mentally strong, the *real* kind, not just the hoo-rah stuff. That's how they keep up with everyone else, with teams that probably have more talent. They can handle tough situations without breaking. They keep after you.

"That's a hard team to beat. If you're not at your best, they can beat you. Look at us. Look at Ohio State. Almost got us both. And with what? Players I bet neither team recruited."

And that was exactly how Northwestern got ahead of the Wolverines on a gorgeous day in the Big House, 31–28. With 4:46 left, the Wildcats intercepted Gardner's pass and returned it to the 50, seemingly dashing Michigan's hopes.

"One thing I remember from that game," Kovacs told me, "was how fast they moved offensively, how well coached they were."

Gardner is close to the Dumars family, including their famous father Joe, a Detroit Pistons legend, and his son, Jordan, who played basketball for Michigan. After the game, Gardner met them in the parking lot past the tunnel, where Jordan's mom Debbie Dumars had to confess they left the game after that interception.

"I guess a *lot* of people left," Gardner said, grinning. "They left too soon!"

On fourth and one from Michigan's 41-yard line, Northwestern head coach Pat Fitzgerald had the guts to go for it.

"They needed a first down, they got it, and you look at the clock," Kovacs recalls thinking. "Oh shit, is that it? We have no time-outs. Clock's ticking away. You're doing the math. *If* we can stop them, we *might* have 30 seconds."

In fact, the Wolverines did stop them, and got the ball back on their own 38-yard line. But they only had 18 seconds left, and no time-outs. Gardner stepped back, and launched a high-arcing, wobbly pass.

"That thing just hung up there," Kovacs recalls.

It could have been easily knocked down by the Wildcat defender, leaving Michigan just a few seconds for one last Hail Mary.

Instead, the defender tried to intercept the ball and jumped too soon, so he could only tip it. That gave Roy Roundtree a chance to tip the ball up in the air as he fell. Amazingly, the ball came down right to him, as he lay on the turf on the nine-yard line. To complete the play of the day, he secured the ball against his helmet.

"I remember the pass like it was yesterday," Northwestern defensive end Quentin Williams told me. "I saw the ball go up—and I'm like, 'Awesome, we got 'em.' Then I saw him catch it, and I'm like, 'Wow, we're really screwed here.'"

"After that, you just knew," Kovacs said, "it's *our* game now." Even the president of Northwestern University, who attended the game, suspected as much. "To be honest," President Morton Schapiro told me, "after watching Michigan pull off a minor miracle to tie the game, I wasn't that optimistic in overtime."

Kicker Brendan Gibbons converted that 53-yard miracle catch into a game-tying field goal, and Devin Gardner finished Michigan's first overtime possession by running into the right corner of the endzone.

It was the fourth touchdown Gardner accounted for that game—but he had never, his entire life, scored a game-winning touchdown. Michigan's defense stuffed the Wildcats on fourth down, which gave Gardner his first game-winning touchdown. Michigan's hopes for a Big Ten title were still alive.

In the postgame press conference, Hoke smiled and scanned the room, then asked the first question himself. "Who started writing the article before the game was over?" This got a few hands sheepishly raised, and a lot of laughs.

With Devin Gardner accounting for all 6 touchdowns, Michigan took care of a surprisingly bad 4–6 Iowa team, 42–17. That gave the Wolverines an 8–3 record overall, but more importantly, a 6–1 record in the Big Ten. With only Ohio State left, Michigan could win a share of the division title and advance to the second championship game in Big Ten history.

But under first-year head coach Urban Meyer, Ohio State was riding a very unlikely 11–0 winning streak.

Borges started Gardner at quarterback, rotating Denard Robinson in occasionally. But because Borges never called a pass for Robinson, the element of surprise wasn't too surprising. Robinson did rush 10 times, however, helping the Wolverines take a 21–20 lead into halftime with a 67-yard touchdown run. But in the second half, for reasons few could understand, Borges gave Robinson only four carries for minus-2 yards—and the Wolverines failed to score a single point, losing 26–21.

During the four years Brandon and Hoke worked together, Brandon's stock would typically drop a notch or two during each off-season, and Hoke's would follow that fall. But Hoke's drops were never as deep, and the criticism was rarely directed at him personally, but at his team's performance. Still, the conventional wisdom that Hoke was the answer to Michigan's problems after his first season was eroding fast in his second.

Just one year earlier, Brady Hoke was the darling of Michigan football fans. The man could do no wrong. When he referred to injuries as "boo-boos" and Ohio State as "Ohio," fans did not savage him as an ignoramus who knew nothing about the greatest rivalry in sports, but a motivational genius who understood exactly what the duel was all about. When fans saw Hoke working the sidelines without a headset, they decided he was not an out-of-touch, glorified cheerleader, but a master delegator and teacher, trusting the play calling to his assistants while he focused on coaching his players.

When you're winning, it's all good. But when the losses start piling up, the same idiosyncrasies seem less charming. After the Wolverines got smoked by Alabama, then lost to Notre Dame, Nebraska, and Ohio State—three teams they had beaten Hoke's first year—some fans started dusting off their pitchforks and torches.

But Hoke's phenomenal freshman year was just as predictable as his sophomore slump. In 2011, almost all of Michigan's key players had returned, including an exceptional class of senior leaders, and the schedule was much easier than 2010's. Perhaps most important, the defense simply *had* to be better, and all that figured to be worth two more wins, maybe three, and that proved true. Throw in a little luck—Notre Dame or Virginia Tech, anyone?— and you get eleven wins.

In 2012 the same logic applied, just in reverse: the Wolverines lost clutch players—like Molk, Martin, and Van Bergen—their schedule was tougher, and their levels of leadership and luck were bound to dip, and they did. Sure enough, they finished the regular season at 8–4—and just to get there, they needed last-minute comebacks against Michigan State and Northwestern. Because neither Penn State nor Ohio State were eligible to go to bowl games, Michigan would move up in the bowl selection pecking order and have to play a tougher team than they normally would have.

But to Michigan fans, it was not just the losses, but the *way* they were losing that made them search for their pitchforks.

If you're going to let your assistant coaches pick your plays, as Hoke did, you better pick those assistants very carefully. Just as Greg Mattison transformed Michigan's defense from one of the worst to one of the best in 2011, Al Borges took a high-octane offense, led by one-of-a-kind Denard Robinson, and reduced it to a sputtering engine that ran on linseed oil. In the final plays against Ohio State, Borges had Robinson sitting on the bench—which didn't sit well with anyone, even the announcers.

But Robinson didn't sign up to play for these coaches, and these coaches didn't recruit him. Most fans felt it wouldn't be fair to judge Hoke until his highly ranked recruits became his players, and that takes a few years. By then, fans would either find Hoke's coaching style charming or cheesy, depending on one thing: how his teams played.

As General MacArthur once said: There is no substitute for victory—especially over Ohio.

CHAPTER 34

STRIKE THREE

The 2012 Ohio State game, Hagerup said, "was one of those losses that hurt the most, because we really thought we were going to win.

"On the bus ride home, I got a text from my brother. 'I know you lost, I know you're pissed, but you just broke the U-M punting record for the season, with a 46-yard average or something.'

"A few days later, I was sleeping when my phone rang. It was [Michigan football PR man] Justin Dickens. 'What are you doing this weekend?'"

"Nothing," Hagerup said.

"Want to go to Indy?" Dickens asked.

"Why?"

"You just won Big Ten punter of the year."

"That," Hagerup told me, "and hitting a walk-off home run when I was 12 years old, were the best feelings I ever had in sports. Pure excitement and happiness. I yelled at CJ, my roommate—an engineering major from my hometown—'I just won punter of the year!' I was really happy, and really proud."

Hagerup traveled to Indianapolis with offensive tackle Taylor Lewan, who also earned All-Big Ten honors, on December 1. During halftime of the Wisconsin–Nebraska game, they introduced the All-Big Ten players.

"And now I am the best thing since sliced bread," Hagerup says. "I just thought nothing could stop me.

"The next weekend is Friday, December seventh, my 21st birthday. Everything's going right, but I'm back to making stupid, selfish decisions. My birthday was like most birthdays—drinking and everything else [including pot]—but I'm a football player, and I shouldn't be doing any of those things. By then we know we're going to the Outback Bowl. Our first practice is Saturday morning, December 8, at 8 a.m. But when we get to the building, we also have a drug test—it's always a surprise—and this time, I already know before it comes back. And the test came back quickly."

Three days later, Hagerup received a text message from Kelly Vaughn, one of the football secretaries. "Coach Hoke needs to see you immediately."

"I'm telling myself, it's the end of the semester, he's just checking in with us on academics," Hagerup says. "That's it. Just academics. But when he calls me in from the hallway, as soon as I saw his eyes, I knew it wasn't academics."

Hoke was direct. "You failed another drug test."

Hagerup just sat there, "locked up. I couldn't move."

"It breaks my heart," Hoke added.

"To this day," Hagerup told me, "I don't know if it was a two-minute meeting or an hour-long meeting. I know I cried for a while. Coach was comforting, not yelling at me."

Still, there was no spinning the hard facts before them.

"This is your third one now," Hoke said. "You know the rules; you probably won't be back at Michigan. But I'm here for you, whatever you need."

Hagerup finally spoke. "I have a problem with decision-making, and I need help."

"Well, we have whatever resources here you need," Hoke said.

After Hagerup left Hoke's office, devastated, he went directly to Greg Harden's office, unannounced. Harden invited him in, and Hagerup told him the bad news.

"Greg had this, 'Oh shit!' look on his face," Hagerup recalls.

"I've helped you through some stuff," Harden said, "but this might be more than I can help with. We'll need some reinforcements," refering to campus counselors.

Nonetheless, Harden canceled all his meetings that day, and talked with Hagerup in his office for three hours.

A few days later, Hagerup wrote a letter to his teammates. He wrote, in part:

Team 133,

I want to thank all of you for the 3 best years of my life, which I will hold very dearly as long as I live.

The last week, as you might imagine, has been very difficult for my family and me, and I have thought about all the people I have hurt and let down. When you act a certain way, whether it is positive or negative, you are representing every single person who supports you, as well as any man who wore a Michigan jersey the last 132 years. Consider that for a moment.

I failed you guys, and it breaks my heart to know that my opportunity to play for the best program college sports has and will ever know, is over. I am truly sorry and would give anything to practice or play with you all one more time.

I also would like to encourage the younger guys who may have personal issues to talk to the people around you. Trust me when I tell you it is far easier to be proactive with your loved ones than it is to call each and every one of them, telling them you're no longer a Michigan football player.

I will miss all of you and the times we shared, on and off the field, more than I can put into words. I will be cheering for this team New Year's Day louder than I ever have before and will remain a Wolverine for the rest of my life. It was an honor to play with you guys.

Thank you and Go Blue!

–Will Hagerup

A couple days later, Greg Harden read Hagerup's letter to the team.

"The toughest was trying to tell my parents," Hagerup told me. "I went back to my house on campus, and I just felt so numb. I felt like my life path was completely altered. My roommates happened to be in an especially good mood, making chili, and about to go play racquetball.

"I didn't tell them what happened. I just played racquetball. And finally, after the match, I just told them. I knew them before football. They helped a lot. If I lived with someone on the team, I'd feel like I had to ostracize myself.

"I went to bed that week, and would wake up so depressed. I skipped my finals. I didn't know what to do. I waited a couple days to tell my parents. The worst part is them sending me text messages: 'We're bringing our friends down to Tampa! Hope you can get two more tickets!'

"I never want to feel like that again. Such a low feeling.

"I knew I wasn't going to call my parents and tell them. I know it's cowardly but I sent them an e-mail. So that week was terrible."

A week later, however, when Hagerup woke up, he suddenly felt better—for no apparent reason.

"You know what?" he told himself. "If anyone can get themselves into a better place, you can. You don't have football, you don't have Michigan, but you still have your mind, your family, your friends. And you're just going to have to figure a way out of this."

Hagerup went to see Coach Hoke, and told him, "I don't know what's next, but I'm going to make this right. Here or somewhere else."

"You know I love you," Hoke said, "and you know what the rules are. I can't imagine Dave Brandon is going to let you back. Go home with your family, look at some schools you might want to go to—look at their depth charts at punter—bring that back to me, and we'll do everything we can to find you a good fit."

And then Hagerup packed up his car and drove back to his family in Whitewater, Wisconsin. Once he had unpacked, he made it a point to avoid everyone but his family and all but his closest friends. He got online, as Hoke had advised, to see what his options might be playing elsewhere.

"I looked at different teams and punters. Teams with freshmen and sophomore punters, I don't want to go there. Teams with seniors, maybe. I felt like I was being recruited again."

But this time, he was the Big Ten punter of the year—with a past. That made his prospects much better, and much worse.

But a funny thing happened: when he was considering other schools this time, it wasn't much fun. He realized he was right the first time: Michigan was his home, and he didn't want to go anywhere else.

One night, when his dad was away on business, they talked on the phone. Will told his dad that his feelings for Michigan hadn't subsided, and he still couldn't imagine going anywhere else.

His father said, "I think you should try to stay at Michigan."

"Dad, you don't understand," Will answered. "Dave Brandon is not going to budge."

They went back and forth, but Will didn't budge, either.

"My parents didn't understand how severe it was."

CHAPTER 35

FULL STEAM AHEAD

With exquisitely bad timing, two weeks after Michigan's loss to Ohio State sealed the 2012 Wolverines' disappointing 8–4 regular season, and right as the holidays were approaching, the Michigan athletic department sent letters to season-ticket holders announcing that their "Personal Seat Donation" levels were being "adjusted"—upward, it turned out. This marked the first price increase of PSDs since Martin's administration first introduced the seat license in 2004.

People from Martin's regime saw this, and predicted trouble ahead.

"Keep raising the prices, and what happens?" Jamie Morris asked. "You're not bringing the family anymore. You're not bringing your boys and girls. You're bringing business associates. They're trying to write this off now. It's a business expense, not a family event.

"I guess Dave thinks all the fans are all like him: millionaires, who don't care what things cost. They just want the best of everything. He figures, if he likes it, everyone else should like it. But what if he's wrong?

"And let's not forget, we keep raising the ticket prices to get that wait list to go away. Brandon figures, if we've got a wait list, we're not charging enough. You're leaving money on the table! So he charges more, and the wait list shrinks.

"Be careful what you wish for."

Another variable: what if the football team failed to bounce back? The athletic director was eating up the football coach's margin of error, year by year.

But if Brandon wasn't afraid to spend money, he redoubled the department's efforts to raise it, too, first by tripling the development staff from 9 to 28 full-time fund-raisers, to help cover the department's operating budget.

Brandon also raised revenues by creating or increasing "seat licenses" for football, basketball, and hockey and closed off virtually all Michigan facilities to the public. The athletic department started charging for corporate events in the skyboxes ($9,000), for wedding receptions on the 50-yard line ($8,000, or $6,000 for one hour), and even for school tours, which Michigan had provided free for decades.

Until the stadium became a construction site, in 2008, when they started the renovation, Martin continued Michigan's long-held tradition of keeping the building open during the week, letting the fans roam freely in the "people's house." Almost every Michigan fan has a story about visiting the Big House with out-of-town guests when it was empty, running the steps or playing a little pickup game in the snow before going to watch the basketball team next door—just one more generous gesture that connected the fans to their team. Even after the renovations were complete, Martin assumed Michigan would continue to keep the stadium open during the week for fans to tour, with a guide or on their own.

But the day it reopened in 2010 is the day Martin resigned. Under Brandon, the open-door policy ended, and everything had a price.

In 2012, the Michigan football team alone generated $61.6 million in profits, second only to the University of Texas Longhorns, which had the considerable advantage of its exclusive 20-year, $300 million TV deal with ESPN.

If Brandon's departed advisers saw trouble ahead, few others did. In 2012, the department was still going full steam ahead.

When the New Year's Day Outback Bowl pitted Michigan against a very good South Carolina team, coached by Steve Spurrier, the Wolverines were slated to be the home team, and therefore permitted to wear their classic navy-blue jerseys with maize numbers. But Brandon decided he wanted new bowl uniforms, Michigan's eighth different look in two seasons, and had Adidas draw up some designs.

He opted for uniforms with blue shoulders and—most quizzically—highlighter-yellow numbers against a snow-white torso. Fans couldn't see the numbers from the stands, viewers couldn't see them on TV, and the announcers couldn't see them from the booth—a fact they complained about constantly during the telecast.

Once again, however, it would be a mistake to blame Adidas—although Brandon did. In fact, as with all uniform changes, Brandon was involved in the design process. Adidas made few of the final decisions. Brandon did.

But when he got the temperature of the fans and announcers during the Outback Bowl—who were complaining that the numbers were illegible, the jerseys looked ugly, and the whole thing was an affront to Michigan tradition—he started tweeting his displeasure with the uniforms as well, as if he was as shocked and appalled as the fans seeing them for the first time.

"If you want to jazz it up, fine," says former Michigan quarterback turned Adidas representative John Wangler. "You're the client. If you don't, that's fine too. But if you pick your design, don't blame it on the company if people don't like it."

Wangler never got the chance to discuss this with Brandon, however, since Brandon had informed Adidas as soon as he took office that he would only be talking with the president of Adidas North America, in keeping with Brandon's "top-to-top" mode of communication.

The game itself featured the now-famous highlight of Jadaveon Clowney charging in, unblocked, to make his explosive hit on little Vincent Smith. The hit popped the ball from Smith's hands and his helmet from his head.

That iconic play aside, Michigan's offense, led once again by Devin Gardner, played quite well, establishing a 28–27 lead with 3:29 left. But Michigan's usually tough defense gave up six plays of 30 yards or more, plus a 63-yard punt return for a touchdown. With 11 seconds left, from Michigan's 32-yard line, South Carolina's backup quarterback Dylan Thompson threaded the needle to his receiver on the goal line for the game-winning touchdown.

Michigan finished with an 8–5 record, and 3–3 over its last six games. The team's margin of error was shrinking, even as Brandon was raising the stakes.

But for Denard Robinson, there would be no more games. "I know I'm going to remember the downs and ups," he said. "It's always going to be a bittersweet feeling because I'm leaving. [Michigan] was my home for four years."

Over the winter, Brady Hoke appeared at a clinic for high-school coaches in Kalamazoo. When he assessed Michigan's 2012 campaign, he spoke with admirable candor.

"We had a shitty season, to be honest with you," he said. "Proud of the kids, how they kept moving forward, but it wasn't the year Michigan deserves."

Hoke took responsibility, but many have wondered if he deserved all of it. Unlike other athletic directors, Dave Brandon stood on the sidelines with the players, high-fiving and chest-bumping them when they came off the field after a good play. He was a mainstay in the locker room—before, during, and after each game, home or away. After games, he would stand next to Denard

Robinson outside the tunnel, signing autographs for fans—some of whom weren't sure who the taller guy was. After Brady Hoke pulled into Schembechler Hall on Sunday mornings after games at 6:30 a.m. to watch film and start his long day, Brandon pulled up 30 minutes later to watch the film with him.

When other college football coaches I talked with learned of Brandon's close proximity to Michgan's players and coaches during and after games, they were incredulous. It's simply not done elsewhere, and most big-name coaches wouldn't put up with it.

"To what extent did Brandon's presence in Schembechler Hall affect Brady's performance?" Bill Martin asks. "According to several football staff members who confided in me, it just changed the whole culture down there. Everybody was on edge, all the time."

If so, it mirrored the experience of many of Michigan's non-revenue coaches, and would only get worse when the losses started piling up.

All this raised the question: How much pressure could Brady Hoke take? And that raised another: How much losing could Michigan fans take?

That depended, Joe Parker believed, on how the fans were being treated.

"If Michigan is not doing well on the field, the fans will still come if they feel like they're part of the community," he told me. "That's what makes it so beautiful and wonderful—and that's what frustrates me when we move to the 'sports entertainment' model. If they don't feel any more attached to the Wolverines than to the Detroit Lions, when you lose a few games, they'll give up."

But no one could claim losing didn't matter, either. The losses added to the water building behind the dam. As the engineers let the dam fall into disrepair, ignoring protocol after protocol, each loss put more pressure on the dam. Year by year, loss by loss, mistake by mistake, the dam kept crumbling, while the water kept rising—a very dangerous combination.

The Harbaugh brothers enjoyed a much better season. Both Jim's San Francisco 49ers and older brother John's Baltimore Ravens made it to the 2013 Super Bowl in New Orleans. Jim had always been the better athlete, but that gave John a 14-year head start in coaching. He'd used those years well, ultimately pushing the Ravens to the AFC title game three times before finally getting to the Super Bowl in 2013.

In the big game, Jim's 49ers came back from a 28–6 deficit to pull within one play of winning. But Colin Kaepernick's pass fell incomplete, and John's team took home the Lombardi Trophy.

Michigan fans, watching this, wondered why their team hadn't been able to get either hometown hero—who both revered Schembechler, the winged helmet, and all that came with it—to coach the Wolverines before the NFL snapped them up.

Only a fringe of fans believed Michigan would ever get another chance.

2013: JUMPING OFF THE BANDWAGON

CHAPTER 36

HAGERUP MAKES UP HIS MIND

Just a few days into the New Year, Hagerup went to breakfast with his sister, Ingrid, who's six years older than he is.

"She's kind of like my half-mom, half-sister," he says, due to the age gap. "She's very responsible, and morally, she's so sound. She said, 'Listen, if there's anything you're really good at, it's working with people, and getting people to believe what you believe.

"'So, if you believe you should be back at Michigan, that it's the only place for you, you can convince them. What's the worst that can happen? You're already off the team, and out of school. Why not at least try?'"

Hagerup came to the same conclusion Denard Robinson did: Michigan was his home. But unlike Robinson, for whom that statement was an answer, for Hagerup, that was his problem. He decided he had to do something about it.

Hagerup took his sister's advice. He returned to Ann Arbor in mid-January, and bravely went back to Coach Hoke's office.

"Coach, I was looking at other schools," Hagerup told him, "but it felt weird, like I was cheating on my wife. I came here as a freshman, I fell in love with Michigan, and I want to finish at Michigan.

"That's why—after the first, second, and third issues I had—people kept asking me, 'Why don't you transfer?' I had options. But then you're just running away from your problems, which will come with you. They have the Internet at other schools, too. Anyone could look up my past.

"I will do anything you ask of me, and more. I want to stay at Michigan."

Hoke listened, equal parts surprised, impressed, and uncertain. "Well, I don't know what Dave Brandon will do," he said, "but right now, you focus on getting Will better. You need to go to class, get the help that you need, and

I can't promise anything—I don't think they'll let you back—but come in and try it. Go see Dave Brandon and try to make it better."

It was sound advice, and as helpful as Hagerup could have hoped.

But, Hagerup admits, "I was not ready to see Dave Brandon! If I thought Dave Brandon was mad when I screwed up my freshman year, I could only imagine how mad he was now."

To Hagerup's relief, Greg Harden told him there was no point meeting with Brandon until he had something good to tell him. Hagerup could put that off for now.

He returned to campus, enrolled in classes, and settled back into his rental house on Church Street, across the street from campus. He also set up an appointment with Wendy Yallop, a university counselor.

At first, Hagerup told Hoke, he admitted he was going to her solely to check the box. "If I go do this, I can get back on the team." But, he said, "That lasted one session. Next time I went in, I thought, 'Wow, I'm doing this for me.'

"I figured out a lot about what's important. Football's great. And I want to do this. But with or without that, there are places I need to grow, and this woman can really, really help me with this."

It also helped that Hagerup's housemates were not on the team, so he would not be reminded every day what he was missing. The previous semester, when Hagerup was still having a good time, the house's location a block from South University, lined with student bars, proved too convenient. But when he returned in January of 2013, he decided not to even visit South U for a year. It turned out their house proved just as close to the classroom buildings and libraries, and Hagerup took full advantage.

"Location, location, location," he said. "I could wake up 10 minutes before a class. For that semester I was just a college student. It was kind of nice. All my roommates were engineers, including one of my best friends from home. We went to the student gym and played racquetball every day. I worked out with the shitty, dusty workout equipment the other students have to use. I did *homework*. I went to the library for a few hours every night. I no longer had the excuse, 'I'm tired, I've been at practice all day, I just want to sleep.' I kind of took advantage of being just a normal student."

When I was researching *Three and Out*, I often visited Denard Robinson and Devin Gardner in their hotel room before games. When I asked Devin Gardner what he would be if he wasn't a Michigan quarterback, he thought about it, then said, "An A student."

That applies to most of the Michigan football players I've gotten to know, including Hagerup.

"Everybody said if I wasn't a football player, I'd get As," said Hagerup. "That semester, I took a class in sociology, two in poli sci, and a leadership class at the B-School. Well, it was nice to prove that was true. I got all As.

"Being a football player is a dominating identity. There are some college football players who see themselves mainly as that, but that becomes problematic when you're not that any more. When we're waiting in line somewhere, my friends tell me, 'Just say you're a football player!' I always say no. If they don't know I'm one already, they're not going to care if I tell them. It'll just make it worse.

"The identity can help you, but it can work against you. It's a more complicated identity than people think. People assume it makes life easier. In some ways, yes, but not always.

"Running out on the field and touching the banner is a high. Skipping a long line at the bar is a high. People knowing who you are is a high. But when it's over, are you prepared to be Will Hagerup, the person?"

In this, Hagerup was almost echoing the comments Jim Harbaugh had made six years earlier. "Okay, fine," Hagerup continued, "you can go to Skeeps [Scorekeepers], the bartender knows who you are, Greek life knows who you are. Well, enjoy that. But when you come back to Ann Arbor in ten or twenty years, unless you're Tom Brady or Denard, they won't know who you are, or care.

"If I hadn't gotten in trouble that year, I don't think I would have prepared myself for not being a football player as much. I worked out on my own, went to class, went to the library. Some people recognized me, but most didn't.

"What do they call the kids in Harry Potter who don't have magic powers— Muggles?" That's how former teammate Elliott Mealer once described the nonathlete students, or "normies," as the players often call them. "I think that's the funniest thing ever. But that's what I was that semester."

Hagerup adapted surprisingly well to his new status as a Muggle.

"If they're not kicking me out of school, I'm staying for my degree. I realized that's what I wanted more than anything: to get my Michigan degree. No question: I was going to stay. Whether I'm playing or not."

Hagerup's new resolve would be tested.

When Hagerup first asked Greg Harden when he should meet with Dave Brandon, "G says, 'Don't meet with him now.' Finally, after a couple months, when I felt like I had more to say than just, 'I'm so sorry!' I asked Greg again. I had a story to tell now. And G said, 'Yeah, I think it's time.'"

Hagerup walked down the hallway to make an appointment with Brandon's secretary, Annette Howe. "I'd like to meet with Mr. Brandon."

Howe did not know Hagerup was an athlete. She looked at Brandon's calendar, and said, "He's booked for two months."

"Well, Greg [Harden] said I should talk with him."

"Oh, are you an athlete? You should have said so." If being a football player allowed Hagerup to cut in line for bars, it was nothing compared to the star treatment he was about to receive from the athletic director.

"Well, he's actually going to be back soon," she said. "He's in a meeting now, if you want to wait."

This threw Hagerup off. "I was not expecting that," he told me. "My palms started sweating, I was so nervous. Every time I'd hear footsteps, I'm thinking, 'Please don't be him. Please don't be him.' And it wasn't—then the next person, and the next person.

"Finally, it *was* him. It had probably only been 20 minutes, but it felt like 12 hours."

"Hey, Will," Brandon said, walking in, "Let's talk."

Walking inside Brandon's office, Hagerup explained, "First of all, I wanted to talk to you earlier, but I was told it was a good idea to wait."

"Oh, are you kidding?" Brandon said. "I was expecting you to come to me earlier. If you had come to me the first day, I think I'd try to get in a fistfight with you. But I'm glad to see you here, healthy." Brandon had been keeping tabs on Hagerup, checking in with Hoke and Greg Harden weekly.

"I don't know if it sounds sincere or not," Hagerup said, "but I have to say it: how incredibly sorry I am. I wasn't ready to make the right changes, but now I am. Maybe it's too late for Michigan football, but it's not too late for me. I'm willing to do literally whatever it takes to get back on track."

Brandon gave him good advice. "I'm glad you're getting help, that's really important. But I need you to forget about football right now."

Hagerup nodded, then told Brandon he was willing to waive his right of confidentiality with Wendy Yallop, his campus counselor, so she could talk openly with Brandon.

"I'd love to talk with her," Brandon said, and not long after this meeting, he did.

Looking back, Hagerup said, "I think that it was probably important for Dave to hear from her. To get what I wanted, I had no choice—and I had nothing to hide at that point."

The meeting was productive, but Hagerup had no illusions about where he stood—and Brandon wasn't providing any. Hagerup recalls Brandon's mood as "appropriately upset."

"You're literally at square one with me right now," Brandon told him. "I'm not promising you anything," something he repeated often, along with the fact that Hagerup knew the rules.

Brandon then said, to Hagerup's surprise, "Come and see me every week. My schedule will be open to you."

"And it was," Hagerup says. "There was not one time I wanted to meet with him that he couldn't. When you consider how busy he was, to give a guy who's not even on the team, who's already royally pissed him off—to give that guy all the time he wanted, showed me he really cared."

Hagerup left the meeting a little shaken, but mainly relieved. "It was nice to get that out of the way. Not to get back on the team, but just for me, my peace of mind. I'm the kind of guy who would rather talk it out than sweep it under the rug."

Hagerup got into a routine of regular meetings with his counselor, Wendy Yallop, Greg Harden, Brady Hoke, and Dave Brandon. Annette Howe looked forward to his visits.

"Dave has the best secretary," Hagerup says. "Annette was always a cheerleader for me. 'I'm so proud of you! I'm so excited!' she'd always say, referring to my progress.

"The meetings sort of started synchronizing with each other. I'd have a great meeting with Wendy, then a great meeting with Dave. I left each office always feeling better about my situation and the relationships I had been making with each person. I could write an entire book just about those meetings."

The gap between Hagerup's public persona and his private progress grew wider, week by week. He recalls his mind-set at the time very clearly: "I know on paper I shouldn't be happy right now. A lot of people read the blogs, and all my mistakes are on there [posted by the readers], and that's embarrassing, but I felt really happy. Each week, I didn't know what was going to happen, but I know this feels really good. I know I'm going to school, I'm staying in shape, and I could sort of feel the tone changing in my meetings, starting around midterms.

"That's when I thought I could be on the offensive a little bit more with Dave. I could say, 'Here's what I'm doing with Wendy, here's what I'm doing with Greg. I know what the rules say, that I'm done, but I'm working my ass off, going to class, staying clean. So, if nothing else, you'll see me as a more trustworthy person.'

"They'd say, 'We're so happy that you're getting better. Nothing more important than that—not football, not winning or losing games.'

"Well," Hagerup would respond, following his sister's advice, "if you're so proud of me, is there any chance I can come back? This is where I want to be. What, if any, are the chances?"

Brandon continued to promise him nothing, but Hagerup sensed, week by week, that Brandon was starting to entertain the idea.

One day in early April, as final exams approached, Brandon finally told him, "Well, we'll see. We'll consider that."

That was good to hear, but Hagerup knew he could still be kidding himself. The odds of getting back on the team might finally be better than zero, but they were still pretty long.

But even if Hagerup was never allowed back on the team, he reasoned, there were worse things than being a Muggle in good standing.

CHAPTER 37

DISRESPECT

While the 2012 football team suffered through Hoke's self-described "shitty season," the 2012–13 men's basketball team blazed through a glorious 19–1 start, the best in school history. But after Jordan Morgan, a defensive specialist and engineering student, went down with an injury, the team split the last 10 games of the Big Ten regular season. Beilein's bunch bounced back in the NCAA tournament, launching an impressive run through the brackets, drawing lots of positive attention to his program and the school on the biggest stage in college sports.

Much as Brandon had violated unwritten rules by chest-bumping the football players, visiting the locker room, and signing autographs next to Denard Robinson after games, he broke a few more on the basketball court. He could often be seen in the Crisler tunnel high-fiving the players, some of whom had misgivings about his pregame speeches admonishing them not to act "like thugs." At Crisler Center on March 3, after fourth-ranked Michigan beat ninth-ranked Michigan State in a thriller, 58–57, Brandon joined the handshaking line, normally reserved for players and coaches—a breach of long-standing protocol that raised a few eyebrows among athletic directors nationwide.

In the NCAA regional semifinal, with 2:52 remaining, the Wolverines trailed third-ranked Kansas by 10 points—then turned that deficit into an overtime win. When they followed up with a solid victory over 14th-ranked Florida, the Wolverines clinched their first regional title since the Fab Five last did the trick in 1993. It was unalloyed good news for Michigan fans, who occasionally joked, "We're a basketball school now!"

When Michigan's players and coaches started cutting down the net, Brandon started cutting down the other net. This did not garner much attention

among the fans or media, but it did among the close fraternity of athletic directors nationwide, who started calling Brandon's former staffers, who had
since scattered across the country.

"What is this guy all about?" one asked Joe Parker, who had landed at Texas
Tech. "Is he for real? Because there isn't another athletic director in the country who would think high-fiving players in the tunnel or jumping into the
handshaking line or cutting down nets is something that would make a lot of
sense for an AD to be involved with."

"They all said the same thing," Parker recalls. "'I see what you were saying.
This fits the pattern you were talking about.'"

For Adidas, the NCAA title game pitting Michigan against Louisville was
a dream matchup: two Adidas schools in the spotlight, the perfect showcase.
It also presented a great opportunity for Adidas to recoup some of the losses
it had absorbed on the Michigan account.

Adidas signed Michigan to a record deal in 2007, with a contract that
would dole out $4.5 million in cash annually, plus about $3 million in Adidas products of all kinds, from shoes to sweatsuits. The entire package was
more than double what Nike was giving top programs like Ohio State and
Alabama. After giving Michigan the best deal in the nation, Adidas watched
Michigan's football team go 43–33, and 24–24 in the Big Ten—which didn't
inspire Michigan fans to buy enough Adidas shoes and shirts to make the deal
pay off.

The 2013 NCAA Final Four also gave Adidas a chance to give some of its
people a long-awaited reward for a job well done by inviting them to special
events at the Final Four and providing prime tickets to the game. It's a conventional clause in these contracts that teams reaching the Final Four are
required to give the shoe company a number of tickets throughout the building, including eight tickets right behind the teams' benches. Louisville
happily fulfilled its commitment, while Michigan gave only three—with the
balance used by Brandon, his sons, and friends. Michigan compensated by giving Adidas much less appealing tickets, farther from the action—and at the
Georgia Dome, built for football, those can be pretty far away.

This was another in a long series of indignities Adidas had suffered after
Brandon took over. By the 2013 NCAA Final Four, the people at Adidas
were getting tired of being made to feel they were supposed to apologize for
giving Michigan twice as much as any other program got from anyone.
They were getting weary of Michigan never defending the brand when critics said Adidas was costing the football team recruits who preferred Nike.

Hoke's recruiting classes were quite strong, and Beilein's 2013 class ranked seventh.

Yet they acquiesced when Brandon insisted he would only speak with the CEO of Adidas North America. They let Brandon order design after design—which took time and money, of course—and when he finally picked one, and his idea was lampooned by tradition-bound Michigan fans, he blamed it on Adidas.

It was no secret that Adidas paid Michigan twice as much as Nike would have, and many believed Adidas paid far too much. Yet their people were still getting treated like Michigan was doing them the favor.

Adidas is not a $150 million athletic department, but a $20 billion global company, after all, whose partners include Manchester United—the most famous team in the world—and the Premier League, the NBA, NHL, and a hundred other schools. After fielding endless requests and several threats from Michigan, the leaders at Adidas had finally had enough. The Final Four ticket fiasco was the last straw.

The people at Adidas North America headquarters called Brandon's bluff with a short, direct letter, which said, in essence: We work with the most famous athletes, teams, and leagues in the world, and no one has ever treated us this badly. Not even close. So, if you'd like to end this contract, please do so. You'd be doing us a favor.

No one at Michigan apologized to anyone at Adidas, but Michigan got the message, and backed down.

This exchange occurred above Wangler's paygrade, but he had seen the change in Michigan's culture at close range, spanning from his playing days to the present, and he speaks with authority. "When we were at our best, we were confident," he asserts, "but we were never arrogant. Bo wouldn't allow it. Canham wouldn't allow it. So our captains wouldn't allow it, either. None of us."

But the arrogance crept in, and soon permeated the department. But, as Joe Louis said, "If you have to say you is, you ain't." Another Michigan alum, whose company is one of dozens that partners with the athletic department in a different field, told me, "When our guys came in and dealt with Brandon's people, it's amazing the way our guys were treated. They'd come back and tell these stories, and I'm just embarrassed. What can I say to them? 'This is not the way Michigan used to be. I'm just telling you.' But they see what they see."

In other words: This is not Michigan.

Disrespecting an apparel company might not be admirable, but it's not likely to boomerang on the offenders. Disrespecting the lettermen, however, was risking a revolt.

In the late 1980s, as Schembechler's coaching career was winding down, he started raising money for Schembechler Hall. He envisioned creating something he'd never had when he was coaching: a single building to house the football staff, with offices, meeting rooms, a weight room, and a museum showcasing the program's rich history.

He started fund-raising by asking friends, including former players, and kept at it until he had raised the $13 million needed for the state-of-the-art building, designed by famed architect Gunnar Birkerts, who also had designed the spectacular new underground law library and Domino's world headquarters.

After they finished it in 1990, Schembechler kept a small office there, which he used whenever he was in town. He was deeply proud of the building, and all it represented.

Twenty-three years later, Brandon knocked down the front of the building. Admittedly, the blue metal façade didn't fit in very well with the rest of the athletic campus, which consists almost entirely of traditional brick buildings, but it wasn't falling apart. In the endless arms race, however, it was not hard to justify replacing just about anything, and the new design is definitely an improvement, both in appearance and functionality.

However, in the process, "Dave does something that he never should have done," Jamie Morris says. "He takes down the plaques with the names of all the donors, and sends them a letter, 'Would you like your plaque back?' If you didn't respond soon enough, they threw it away. Their contributions to Bo for the first Schembechler Hall are erased."

This angered a lot of former donors and former players, sometimes simultaneously. Once again, it wasn't any one decision that turned people against Brandon, but a series of decisions that established a pattern of disregard for almost everyone except the student-athletes and a select group of coaches. Brandon's observers recognized the pattern at different times, over a two- or three-year period, but once they did, they jumped off the Brandon bandwagon, creating a slow wave of defections.

"In 2011, the players were privately pissed off about Notre Dame tickets, but no one really knows about that outside the lettermen," Morris says. "In 2012, he's trying to control former players by taking over Victors Night, Chili & Cornbread, and the sideline passes—but he's trying to keep the stars happy:

Desmond [Howard], D'Hani Jones. And he's trying to get Tom Brady—but Brady gets wise to him, and keeps him at a distance.

"But I keep trying to tell ya, the stars are not always the leaders. And Brandon doesn't get that. Woodson was a great player, and his teammates love him. But Eric Mayes and Jon Jansen were the leaders of the '97 team. And Brandon's lost them.

"By 2013, once he throws out the Schembechler Hall donor plaques, word gets out, so even if you weren't one of the original donors, some of your teammates might have been, and you're not happy about that, either. So, after that, it's over with the former players. They're done with him.

"From this point on, most of the former players want Brandon gone. Not Hoke—*him!* They start calling other donors, and telling them what's happening. The groundswell starts, and it's no stopping it then. The train has left the station. It's gone."

Though few outside these circles would have noticed, by mid-2013, Brandon had alienated many of the current and former employees, the lettermen, and the donors—and that put still more pressure on the football team.

The dam kept cracking, while the water continued to rise.

CHAPTER 38

THE STUDENTS FIGHT BACK

Michael Proppe was born and raised in Plymouth, Michigan, just 20 miles east of Ann Arbor. A corn-fed Catholic kid, he looks the part: fair-skinned and open-faced with a toothy smile. His parents, Jim and Cathy, are both Michigan graduates. Their son never wanted to go anywhere else.

In October of 2009, Proppe's dream came true when he opened an e-mail from U-M's Admissions Department.

"Michael: CONGRATULATIONS! You're IN! You've been admitted to the University of Michigan College of Literature, Science and the Arts for Fall, 2010!"

Proppe is the prototypical Michigan undergraduate, just the kind of in-state student looking for "an uncommon education for the common man," that the place was created to serve. Proppe became a dual-degree student, earning both a BS in statistics and a BBA from the Ross Business School, with a concentration in accounting—both top ten progams. Like most undergraduates, he was also a huge fan of Michigan's athletic teams.

But he also had an interest in student government—not to pass feckless motions about this country or that, but to pursue more pragmatic improvements in university bus routes, dining hall hours, and the like. He rose through the ranks, becoming speaker of the Student Assembly by his sophomore year. With the elections coming up at the end of March 2013, Proppe decided it was time to throw his hat in the ring and run for president.

But to do that, he needed a running mate—and that's when things got dicey. His fellow youMICH party members suggested Bobby Dishell, who had served as a representative on the assembly and vice president of the Interfraternity Council.

"No," Proppe said. "Not Bobby."

Proppe is a pretty easygoing guy, not quick to argue or object—which made him an effective speaker of the assembly—but as soon as he heard the suggestion, he immediately put his foot down.

To get the story, I met with Proppe and Dishell in 2015 over a few pints at Ashley's Pub, right across State Street from the Diag.

"I was trying to keep order during meetings," Proppe told me, "and Bobby would constantly talk out of turn. He was very forceful and direct in meetings. I thought he was"—here Proppe searched for a word, before settling on—"rude. I thought he was rude—and he knows this! That's one reason I didn't like him. Plus, he was a sophomore, and I wanted to run with a fellow junior—someone with a little more experience and maturity."

"We were not friends before this," Dishell added.

The two don't look or act much alike, and their backgrounds reflect that. Dishell is an olive-skinned guy from a hotshot private school in Brentwood, California, in the shadow of UCLA, the kind of candidate modern Michigan now attracts by the thousands—which helps explain why Michigan's ratio of out-of-state students is pushing 50 percent, up from 35 percent twenty-five years ago. In fact, Michigan now gets more students from L.A. than from Detroit—which would have been unheard of just a generation ago.

Unlike the sports-soaked Proppe, Dishell had seen only one Michigan football game—in person or on TV—when his dad's uncle invited them to the 2007 Rose Bowl. He confessed that he couldn't name the players on his hometown Lakers. A sports nut, he is not.

"I was big in the business school," Proppe said, "and Bobby was big in the Interfraternity Council."

"I was involved in Jewish life," Dishell says. "He's Catholic."

"I didn't like him at first," Proppe says.

"We were not friends before this," Dishell repeated, with a diplomatic grin.

But Proppe's colleagues pushed for Dishell, convincing Proppe to at least sit down with him.

"When I met with him one-on-one, it changed my mind," Proppe said. "He's very smart, with great political instincts—far more than I thought at first. It was basically a blind date, deciding to run together. But after that, I said, 'Okay, we can do this. It's worth a shot.' "

It's fair to say, like just about everyone else in this story, they had no idea what they were in for.

The Proppe-Dishell ticket promised to improve campus safety by adding late-night, off-campus bus routes; to increase networking among student organizations to help each other recruit and raise money; to keep the library cafés open 24 hours a day; and to promote student entrepreneurship—the normal stuff of student government. They campaigned by knocking on doors in the dorms ("dorm-storming"), apartments, and houses, approaching students in the libraries and the Diag, meeting with student groups and the *Michigan Daily*, and plastering fliers all over campus and chalking the sidewalks, for six weeks solid.

On March 27–28, more than 10,000 students, about a quarter of the student body, voted online, the highest recorded voter turnout. The five-way race ended at 2 a.m., March 29, when they learned Proppe's friend, Chris Osborn, had won by some 400 votes.

"I vividly remember when we found out we lost," Dishell said, turning to Proppe, drinking his pint. "You and I took several laps around Sybil Street, racking our brains as to how we could have lost. People reassured us that it was going to be okay, but there's no worse feeling in the moment than losing and not being able to do anything about it."

The next day, however, photos emerged of Osborn standing over fellow students in the libraries, and watching them vote for him online—a clear violation of election rules. Proppe's party submitted the evidence to the student-run University Elections Commission. Although a few members of the board were friends with Osborn, they made a stand for ethics and disqualified Osborn, and declared Proppe and Dishell the winners.

Michigan's student government, at least, had successfully demonstrated its ability to self-correct, based on principle.

By March 30, Proppe and Dishell learned they'd won with 2,928 votes, 390 more than the next runner-up.

They looked forward to being sworn in three weeks later, on April 23, 2013. But on April 22, the day before their inauguration, with no prior notice, the athletic department sent all Michigan students an e-mail informing them that the football tickets they had already purchased for the 2013 season would not entitle them to a reserved seat based on seniority, as they had been promised. Instead, the department had decided to institute a new general-admission seating policy, which meant the students could grab whatever seat was left when they arrived each game day.

The department hoped to end the students' habit of coming late, or not at all—two things that bothered Brandon greatly.

Don Canham sold out the Big House and kept a long wait list. "What's everyone's favorite restaurant? The one with the line out the door. No one wants to walk into an empty restaurant." (*Michiganensian*, Bentley Historical Library, University of Michigan)

"In a crisis, no one was better than Bruce Madej," Bill Martin said. "His counsel was always correct. I mean, always." Madej followed Canham's great advice: "Never turn a one-day story into a two-day story." Michigan could have used Madej in the fall of 2014. (Martin Vloet, Michigan Photography, University of Michigan)

In 2000, Bill Martin took over a department $3 million in debt, and left it a decade later with $400 million worth of capital improvements—fourteen state-of-the-art facilities—plus $60 million saved. Yet he said, "Just because you can charge them more, doesn't mean you should!" (University of Michigan Athletic Department, Bentley Historical Library, University of Michigan)

Former athletic department CFO Jason Winters, hired by Bill Martin, was stunned by Brandon's spending on commemorative coins, video billboards, and a $2.85 million contract for Brady Hoke. A few months after Brandon stepped down, Michigan announced it had a $7.9 million deficit. So many ideas, Winters said, "were such an obvious waste of money, why do them?" (Jason Winters)

As a Michigan basketball player, Marty Bodnar won four games with last second shots, went to law school, and returned to run Michigan's ticket department. He worked well with the students, and mastered the "scarcity principle." "If you're selling anything," he said, "it's community." (Robert Kalmbach, Bentley Historical Library, University of Michigan)

(Steve Kuzma)

Bill Martin had groomed former U-M swimmer Joe Parker to become an athletic director, but when Parker saw the direction Brandon was taking the department, he left for Texas Tech, then Colorado State, where he was named athletic director in 2015. (Jenny Sparks/*Loveland Reporter-Herald*)

Scott Draper, Joe Parker, Kurt Gulbrand, and Bruce Madej (front) at the National Football Foundation banquet, when they all worked for Bill Martin. After Brandon arrived, all left. "Working for Michigan Athletics was a labor of love," Gulbrand says. "It had been a family culture—and that changed overnight." (Kurt Gulbrand)

Getting kicked off Michigan's team for one day, Brandon has said, "was the best thing that ever happened to me. I was the hotshot kid coming out of high school with nine varsity letters, and I learned that didn't count for very much." (University of Michigan Athletic Department, Bentley Historical Library, University of Michigan)

When Brandon asked his staff what was most important to him as Michigan's athletic director, he answered, "My reputation. I have worked very hard to have the reputation that I have." Already a two-time Fortune 500 CEO, his profile rose dramatically as Michigan's athletic director. (Eric Upchurch)

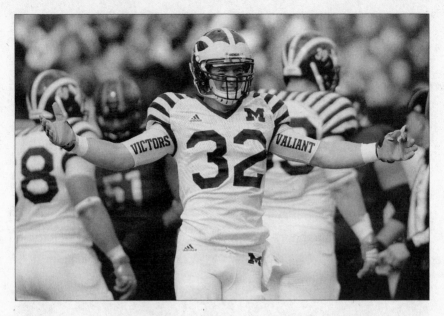

One of Brandon's best ideas was playing Notre Dame "Under the Lights." After Michigan scored twenty-eight fourth quarter points to win on the last play, walk-on-turned-team-MVP Jordan Kovacs, pictured here, admits, "I got home in bed by 2:30, and I was still so wired, I didn't fall asleep until five. I just couldn't put it away." (Marissa McClain/*The Michigan Daily*)

Punter Will Hagerup was as loyal to his alma mater as he was to athletic director Dave Brandon. "Dave has certainly been a mentor to me. All I know is the guy changed my life, made me a better person, and I owe him everything." (Eric Upchurch)

"I defy you," one university leader said, "to find an athletic director, current or former, at any school who got as much ink as Dave, ever. He made it about him." Here Brandon is cutting down the net at the NCAA Regional in 2013. (Albert Pena, Michigan Photography, University of Michigan)

"Everyone loved Hoke," Jordan Kovacs said. "Everyone knew that he truly cared about you, and that made it easy to play your ass off for him. It was fun to play for him." Hoke's habit of not wearing a headset, however, left him at the mercy of his coordinators. (Associated Press)

Devin Gardner was the nation's top-rated high school quarterback. He was so eager to go to Michigan, he petitioned to graduate early. When his high school finally approved the decision, "That might have been the happiest day of my life." (Eric Upchurch)

During spring ball of 2014, Gardner waited "every day for us to pick captains. I saw Molk, Martin, and Denard all do it—good captains! I can't wait for my turn." When Hoke decided not to name captains until after the season, Gardner said, "I thought we were in trouble from the start." (Eric Upchurch)

Michael Proppe and Bobby Dishell were the "Odd Couple" when they teamed up to win the Central Student Government election in 2013, but they became close friends—while winning over the Regents with their reports on why the "General Admission" seating policy for students wasn't popular, and didn't work. (Patrick Barron/ *The Michigan Daily*)

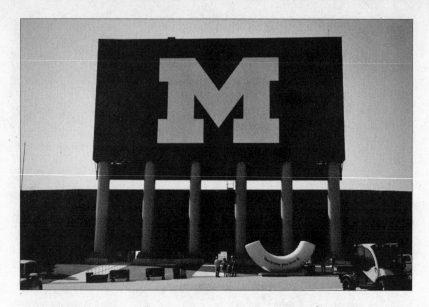

The day before Michigan's 2013 season opener, fans saw a gigantic Kraft macaroni noodle, with "You know you love it" written on it. Predictably, Michigan fans did not love it, any more than they loved the skywriting "GO BLUE" over Spartan Stadium, leasing seat cushions, or other marketing mistakes. The backlash forced the department to remove the noodle. (Haley Goldberg/*The Michigan Daily*)

Michigan's fourteenth president, Mark Schlissel, earned a B.S. from Princeton and an M.D. and Ph.D. from Johns Hopkins School of Medicine. He is world-class brilliant, winning awards for research and teaching. But no one thought he'd be hiring a new A.D. and football coach his first six months on the job. (Eric Bronson, Michigan Photography, University of Michigan)

Regent Andrea Fischer Newman (top, second from left), frequently defended Dave Brandon, while Regents Kathy White (top, far right), Larry Deitch (top, second from right), and Mark Bernstein (bottom, first left), started pushing back. "When I realized this department was completely out of control," Bernstein said, "I was done with the current regime." (Scott Soderberg, Michigan Photography, University of Michigan)

The Hit Seen 'Round the World. After getting hit, quarterback Shane Morris leaned on Ben Braden for support, but the medical staff didn't see it. When Morris stayed in, the fans booed, but the situation was made much worse by ineffective media relations that lasted a week. (Ace Anbender)

The students' "Rally to Fire Dave Brandon" had no focus until senior Craig Kaplan got his bull-horn, stood on the steps of the president's house, and told the crowd, "I love this university! I love this football team. I love our sports. I do not love Dave Brandon." The crowd cheered wildly. (Ace Andbender)

In 2003, Marty Bodnar invited the football lettermen to line the pathway to the M GO BLUE banner, and hold the ropes. Six hundred showed up. Eleven years later, in 2014, some lettermen were un-happy with Brandon's handling of their tickets, their reunions, and their golf outing. Only a fraction showed up. "From this point on," Jamie Morris says, "most of the former players want Brandon gone. Not Hoke—him! They start calling other donors, and telling them what's happening. The ground-swell starts, and it's no stopping it then. The train has left the station. It's gone." (M Club Archives)

Michigan law graduate Todd Anson met Harbaugh when he was coaching at San Diego, and became one of his biggest boosters for the Michigan job. In the summer of 2014, he introduced Harbaugh as "the only man in the history of the University of Michigan's venerated football program whose manifest destiny it is to coach Michigan!" At the time, it seemed crazy. (Todd Anson)

Jim Harbaugh, John Ghindia, and Heisman Trophy winner Charles Woodson. John Ghindia played with Harbaugh. Three decades later, he was making DVDs of Harbaugh's reunion speech for Regents, and getting Michigan lettermen to tell Harbaugh how much they wanted him back. "Man, Ghindia was all over this thing!" (John Ghindia)

John "Flame" Arbeznik, Michigan's 1979 captain, hosted U-M greats Jon Giesler, far right, who played ten years for the Dolphins, and legendary Anthony Carter, center, for the 2014 Ohio State game. At halftime, they took turns talking to Jim Harbaugh for forty-five minutes, trying to convince him to return. (John Arbeznik)

When Harbaugh's friends needed Tom Brady to call Harbaugh, did they call the Patriots, or his publicist? No, they called Jay Flannelly, aka "The Beav," a forty-three-year old dishwasher at Pizza House. Standing here between Drew Henson and Aaron Shea, Flannelly is one of the most trusted men in the Michigan football family. As Ghindia says, "Never underestimate The Beav!" (Jay Flannelly)

No player or coach in Michigan history grew up inside the program like Jim Harbaugh did. While his father Jack coached the defensive backs, Jim and his brother John used the practice field like a playground, and served as ballboys on Saturdays. (University of Michigan Athletic Department, Bentley Historical Library, University of Michigan)

"That's Jim Harbaugh when he was one of our ball boys! I must have kicked him out of a hundred practices."

After Harbaugh beat Ohio State, Schembechler told him, "What it must feel like to have a son play the way you did! I'm proud of you, Jim." Harbaugh recalls, "I felt as loved and appreciated as I have ever felt, like I was one of Bo's sons." (*Michiganensian*, Bentley Historical Library, University of Michigan)

Former player and Steelcase CEO Jim Hackett, here standing between former coaches Lloyd Carr and Gary Moeller, and next to Jim Harbaugh, accepted President Schlissel's offer to serve as interim A.D. Two months later, after many conversations and a scary afternoon with a dead computer, he captured "The Unicorn," his code name for Jim Harbaugh. (Eric Bronson, Michigan Photography, University of Michigan)

Harbaugh's gold-plated Michigan Man pedigree and boundless passion inspired Michigan fans to give him a reception like no coach before him—not even Schembechler himself. Bill Martin's Bank of Ann Arbor plastered six billboards with messages for the new coach. Three of the billboards are shown here. (Bank of Ann Arbor/Perich Advertising + Design)

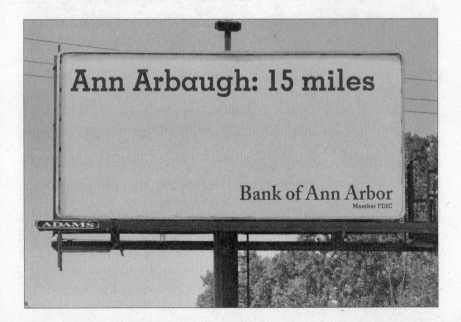

"If Harbaugh had gone to New York, Chicago, or Oakland, he'd still be a great coach—and would likely get fired one day. But if he returned to Michigan, he'd be greeted as a savior." That was an understatement. (Roger Hart, Director of Michigan Photography, University of Michigan)

"I don't get sick. I don't observe major holidays. I'm a jackhammer." Harbaugh's boundless energy won over the students minutes after Hackett announced he was Michigan's new coach. The revolution was over. (Eric Upchurch)

The e-mail told the students, "This change in policy from reserved seating was put in place as the student section is the driving force behind our home field advantage and we need students to get there early and often to create a loud and full student section for kickoff."

All true, but for decades, Michigan had given students reserved seats, based on their class standing. Thus, students considered gradually moving from the high endzone seats their freshman year to the prime midfield seats close to the field their senior year a rite of passage—if not a birthright. With one e-mail from the department, however, the seniors-to-be learned their long-awaited prize had been replaced with first-come, first-served. Thus, any freshman willing to wake up before they did could readily claim the seats the seniors considered theirs.

Even more upsetting to the upperclassmen, the new policy meant they could no longer reserve tickets with their friends in blocks. Because it was nearly impossible to find your friends among 20,000 students on game days, when cell phone service was spotty at best, there was no way to sit together unless you and your friends all entered the stadium at the same time.

That might not sound like a major obstacle, until you understand how Michigan students tailgate. Unlike Michigan State, where Munn Field provides the central gathering spot for student tailgates, Michigan doesn't have a place for students to get together. The stadium parking lot and golf course are dominated by middle-aged fans who can afford the parking. If the Spartans' tailgates are akin to Woodstock, the Wolverines' play more like wedding receptions, complete with maize tablecloths, blue cocktail napkins, and even the occasional candelabra.

That's why Michigan students party closer to campus, at one of Ann Arbor's thousands of hundred-year-old rental homes, where they drink, dance, and play beer pong on the wooden front porches and postage-stamp front lawns. The problem is, these houses are strewn about a two-mile circle from the stadium. That's one reason why the students tend to show up late for kickoff, and why it's very difficult to synchronize the arrival of friends from so many starting points around town.

If the department implemented the general-admission policy, it would require the students to leave their tailgates a couple hours before kickoff—or more—to claim the best seats, or they would take whatever was left, and not sit with their friends, something few Michigan tailgaters of any age would consider doing. The tailgate, after all, was a huge part of the game-day experience—exactly as Don Canham had intended it to be.

As just about anyone who knew more than three Michigan students could have predicted, the department's e-mail would not go over well with the student body.

Historically, the only Michigan students who know who runs their student government are the students who run their student government. They often do important work, from adopting a "medical amnesty" law for underage drinkers who need medical attention, to allocating several hundred thousand dollars a year to student organizations, to amending the student code of conduct on plagiarism and assault. The deans, executive officers, Regents, and presidents generally take them seriously, but their good deeds are typically unknown to the student body.

That was all about to change.

As soon as the athletic department's announcement hit the students' e-mail boxes, hundreds of students looked up who their student government leaders were, and started pounding them with calls, e-mails, and texts.

"They were pretty upset!" Dishell recalls. "I sent out some tweets, asking, 'What do you think about the new policy?' A few supported it, but not many. I got a lot of, 'It sucks!'"

Before they were even sworn in, Proppe and Dishell knew they had to act. That night, another student set up a Central Student Government (CSG) "U-Petition," asking the athletic department merely to "grandfather in" the general-admission policy. By letting the seniors-to-be sit together in their midfield seats, and starting the policy with the freshman class, no one would feel like they had fallen for a bait-and-switch, and the younger students would never know anything different.

That night alone, more than 3,000 students signed the U-Petition. Seeing the overwhelming response, Proppe, Dishell, and graduate student John Lin decided to draft two resolutions that night. The first "condemned the decision to go forward without student input," Proppe says, and the second opposed the new policy itself.

The resolutions said, "The new seating policy no longer rewards students for their time spent at the university; it will make it more difficult for groups of friends to sit together at games . . . and that it will take away from pregame activities that are part of the experience."

For students, those "pregame activities" generally consisted of drinking beer at house parties spanning the "student ghetto." The athletic department was well aware of this—and didn't like it. As Brandon would one day tell Michael Proppe over the phone, "We know students are not studying before the games. If they're willing to put down their beer a little earlier, they'll still get good seats." Brandon also didn't appreciate the specter of students partying on their porches while major donors walked by on their way to the stadium—not good for the brand. Ultimately, Proppe gathered from their conversations, "The [athletic] adminstration simply didn't like Michigan's tailgate culture."

Framed this way, you could argue Brandon was trying to kill Canham's creation, which sold the game-day experience over the score. But if so, Brandon was in for a fight. Canham's culture had a 40-year head start, and it had sunk in quite deeply. The students immediately recognized the threat general admission posed to their time-honored rituals—and they were not going to take it lying down.

The following day, Tuesday, April 23, 2013, Proppe and Dishell were sworn in at the CSG Chambers in the Michigan Union. Before they left, they easily passed their first two resolutions objecting to the general-admission policy, and the athletic department's failure to seek student input.

"We saw an opportunity," Proppe says. "Here we had the rare case where students were reaching out to *us*—a situation where student government could have an impact on issues people actually care about."

The freshly minted officers e-mailed their resolutions to Dave Brandon, PR man Dave Ablauf, and the department's business manager, and invited them to come to a CSG meeting.

"We didn't consider that the chief marketing officer [Hunter Lochmann] would be in charge of seating policies," Proppe admits. "We really didn't know a lot about how the athletic department worked."

When they did not receive a response, Proppe e-mailed Brandon's assistant, Annette Howe, to request a meeting.

A week later, on April 29, 2013, Brandon addressed the Faculty Senate committee meeting to explain the problem, as he saw it, and present his solution. He estimated that at the 2012 Northwestern game—which fell on a gorgeous fall day, and finished with Devin Gardner scoring the game-winning touchdown in overtime—roughly a third of the 22,000 student ticket holders didn't attend, and more than half of those who attended came late.

"It's just a downer for our team to charge out of the tunnel and see the student section half-empty," he said, viewing the situation from the players' perspective. "I'd like to believe that they're all studying but you and I have been up and down State Street enough to know that our students have a lot of choices."

On May 13, Proppe received a call from Brandon, who was in Chicago for Big Ten meetings. In their half-hour conversation, Proppe recalls, "I expressed that seniors were upset, because they were looking forward to great seats, and everyone else was upset that they couldn't form seating groups. And *we* were upset that we weren't consulted on this ahead of time."

Brandon replied, "I'm pretty sure you could arrive at the game 30 minutes early and still find a great seat." Proppe remembers Brandon also expressed his frustration with students showing up late. "Why?" Proppe recalled. "Because, Brandon said, he could sell that ticket to someone who would use it, and cheer for the team."

Undeterred, Proppe asked Brandon if he could grandfather the policy over a four-year period, starting with the freshmen. "We went back and forth on whether that was feasible," Proppe recalls. "But Dave's position was clear enough when he said, 'We're not going to change it, we've already sold it, we already have the policy in place, and logistically it would be difficult to change, even if we wanted to—which we don't.'"

Brandon added that he was not going to grandfather the policy, either. "In a few years no one will care because the upperclassmen will have graduated," he said.

Proppe did gain one potential concession: Brandon did agree to address a CSG meeting in the fall to discuss the policy.

When Proppe e-mailed Annette Howe again, this time to schedule a CSG meeting for Brandon to attend, she asked him to follow up in a few months. Proppe did so on July 18 and August 8, but got no response. When the CSG met again on September 17, Brandon sent Hunter Lochmann to represent the department.

You might recall the extraordinary lengths Martin's leadership team went to before taking any action to expand the transfer policy, and add the Personal Seat Donation, the priority points system, and other changes. They conducted numerous meetings across the state, sent countless letters and e-mails and other communications, to explain why these new policies were needed, how they were going to work, and gain valuable feedback from the people who were going to be affected—all over a two-year period. You might also recall that, as a result, the policies were incredibly well received, with almost no blowback to speak of.

The people now in charge of the general-admission policy, however, did not seem to recall any of those valuable lessons.

On May 16, 2013, three days after Brandon and Proppe talked on the phone, Proppe addressed the Regents at their monthly meeting to make sure they were aware of the new general-admission policy, and the students' anger over it.

This alone marked a break with the decorum Proppe's predecessor, Manish Parikh, had established. "He was always very polite, very gracious to President Coleman and the Regents," Proppe recalls. "I certainly didn't want to come across as rude, but they only give you five minutes, and I had to deliver a message on behalf of the students."

He told the Regents, "The students—who will soon be alumni, who drive the vast majority of football ticket sales, keep in mind—are outraged. The athletic department broke its long-held social contract with the students." Proppe predicted general admission would create chaos and perhaps even stampedes for the games against Notre Dame and "that School Down South," Ohio State.

"But these aren't my objections," he explained. "These are points raised by the hundreds of students who flooded my e-mail, Facebook, and Twitter with complaints. The athletic department might have at least wanted to hear some of these objections before implementing the new policy. But they didn't . . .

"Had they reached out, they might have mitigated the backlash, which included a petition to the Central Student Government to grandfather in assigned seating for upperclassmen signed by 3,569 students."

Brandon did not attend the meeting, and none of the university leaders responded at the time—but many others did, almost all of them initially taking Brandon's side against the students, whom the critics accused of being spoiled, lazy, and apathetic.

"MGoBlog ripped me for it," Proppe says, with a laugh.

MGoBlog's founder, Brian Cook, who had initially praised Brandon's work, had become increasingly anti-Brandon. Nonetheless, after Proppe's presentation to the Regents, Cook wrote a column item titled, "I'm with Dave here though."

"YOU broke the 'long-held social contract,' Michael Proppe," Cook wrote, "by not showing up. You and lots of other people. The deal was: you get cheap tickets, show up, and be loud. You have altered the deal. Pray Dave Brandon doesn't alter it any further."

The Michigan community has a rich tradition of airing its differences—over just about everything, including many issues that wouldn't generate a single e-mail elsewhere. Michigan was the only school in the Big Ten, for example, that had a group organize protests against the skyboxes.

It's important to point out that growing student apathy is not unique to Michigan, nor is the switch to general-admission seating. And not all top programs allow every student who wants season tickets to get them in the first place, as Michigan always has.

Nonetheless, the students' anger was plain, and unusually broad-based. Just three hours after the announcement, CSG received some 3,200 "likes" for their movement on a Facebook page. In an admittedly unscientific poll conducted by the *Michigan Daily,* 85 people said they "love it" while 497 said they "hate it."

Yes, some contemporary students can display a breathtaking sense of entitlement, and they wouldn't get much sympathy from the average fans, who have to pay two or three times more for their tickets, plus a Personal Seat Donation—assuming they can get off the wait list, which Brandon had raised to $500 just to join.

But the department did not pause to ask *why* the students were not showing up. Getting mad at your paying customers for not liking your product as much as you think they should, then punishing them for it, is probably not something they teach at Michigan's Ross School of Business.

"Why didn't the athletic department ask for any student input before implementing this?" Proppe asked. Good question.

The alumni who wagged their fingers at the students probably forgot that their Michigan football habit formed because they knew the game was going to start at 1:05, every Saturday, for years. Now it can be noon, or 3:30, or 8—and sometimes they don't tell you when until a couple weeks before the game.

Why? TV, of course. Which is to say, money.

When the alums were students, they also knew Michigan would be playing a serious opponent—every game. In Bo Schembechler's 21 seasons, Canham scheduled 60 regular-season games against nonconference teams. How many Michigan opponents were not from a major conference? Exactly four: Tulane in 1972, Hawaii in 1986, Long Beach State in 1987, and Navy, seven times. And how many MAC opponents? Exactly zero. Canham scheduled every one of the remaining 50 nonconference games against Power Five conference teams, like Texas A&M (twice), Miami (of Florida, not Ohio—twice), UCLA (4 times), Washington (4 times), and Stanford (4 times), which beat Michigan in the 1972 Rose Bowl, plus Notre Dame, for 10 games.

From 1981 through 1984, the Big Ten played a round-robin nine-game schedule, giving each team only two nonconference games—half as many as they schedule now. If you enrolled at Michigan in 1981, you watched the Wolverines play every Big Ten opponent every year (on TV or at the Big House), plus #1 Notre Dame and Navy in 1981, #20 Notre Dame and #12 UCLA in 1982, Washington State and #16 Washington in 1983, and #1 Miami (Florida) and #16 Washington in 1984.

The whole thing would have cost you $156—*for all four seasons.* Do you think you would need the athletic director to prod you to show up on time?

The students from those years are in their fifties now. They're the ones paying full price, plus a PSD, and sometimes five or six figures for a suite. But their habit started 35 years ago, under very different circumstances. Now Michigan gives the fans a steady diet of junk-food football from lesser conferences, even lesser divisions, and expects them to pay steakhouse prices. Delaware State, anyone?

Everything the alumni could take for granted—the starting time, the schedule, the nonstop fun—the current students cannot.

Habits are hard to develop, but they're easy to break. Instead of bringing back the elements that got students hooked on Michigan football in the first place, Brandon sprung the deeply unpopular general-admission policy on them, while simultaneously increasing the price of student tickets by 23 percent—from $175 to $280 for seven games.

"Even though they want to try," Brandon told MLive.com, "no one can make a claim that we're doing anything here that's financially motivated. [Because] we're not."

So how was a 23 percent price hike not financially motivated? Brandon said it would help pay for Recreational Sports, but it all came from the same pot of money that paid the director of a nonprofit department more than $1 million a year—a sum that would just about cover the price increase for every student who wanted tickets.

After angering these students, did he think they would come back 10 or 20 years later, at four times the price—and bring their kids, to keep the chain going? You probably wouldn't bet the Big House on it.

The students were not leaving Michigan football. Michigan football was leaving the students.

For making their stand, Proppe and Dishell received unprecedented support from their constituents, but initially got grief from just about everyone else.

Privately, however, some knowledgeable people understood exactly where they were coming from.

"I went to the Regents every year to talk about student tickets," former ticket director Marty Bodnar told me, "and Dave [Brandon] was actually sitting there as a Regent most years. I went to present at their meetings because the Regents cared deeply about student tickets.

"The Regents were *adamant* that every student who wanted a ticket get a ticket, so Bill [Martin] and I always made a great effort to get every student into that stadium who wanted to be in that stadium, even if they were late getting their form back to us, because we knew it was a strong, strong desire of the Regents.

"Dave wanted the students to be there early—to support the team, and make the place look good for TV. I don't think he wanted to get rid of them to sell tickets for more money to the alums, as some have accused him. But then he went too far to get the students there on time.

"In my opinion, one of the biggest mistakes Dave made was his handling of the student tickets.

"Once you change to a general-admission policy, without even asking the students or warning them, you just pissed them off, which led to the protest just about anyone who'd been around could have predicted. I was out of the department for a year and a half by then, but once they announced they were going to get rid of the seniority system, just like that—boom!—I *knew*, in my heart and my mind and my soul, that was a mistake. I knew the students would protest, and I knew the Regents would care about this issue.

"What you're selling, if you're selling anything, is community. You threaten that, you're going to hear about it—if you're lucky. Worst-case scenario: they just drop their tickets without saying a word, and you lose them forever."

Regent Kathy White agreed. "The students are not going to get everything they want, and we're not either, but we're all on the same team here. The Michigan Team. So you listen! And you think, 'How can we find common ground?'

"The thing I find so annoying about this situation is that the students are the reason we are here! It's really important not to forget that!"

The students are also the reason Michigan football exists. They invented it, after all. It only remains important because students play the sport and watch the sport.

But instead of asking, "What's best for all of us?" the department framed the situation as an "us versus them" debate—one that was doomed to create serious conflict.

CHAPTER 39

HAGERUP MAKES HIS PITCH

"You have to relate to Coach Hoke and Dave Brandon differently," Hagerup explains. "Brady Hoke will tell you, 'I've done more stupid stuff than all of you. I'm here for you!' He backed me completely.

"Dave Brandon has never done any drugs, he's run Fortune 500 companies. He doesn't drink *coffee!* You can't go into his office and say, 'You know how it is!' Because he doesn't!"

Seeing his friends from the team was also uncomfortable. Hagerup didn't participate in spring ball, or workouts, or see anyone at the Academic Center. "I was still in my own world—intentionally. I'd see those guys in class, and we'd talk, but I wouldn't ask about it. It wasn't my place as much."

In some ways, Hagerup admits, being off the team, out of the public eye, and persona non grata on the fan sites, "was kind of a fun place to be: You can only go up from here. In a twisted way, because everyone thinks you're a screwup, they don't expect anything out of you but failure—and that's not a bad place to be. It gave me a chance to rewrite my story.

"Then in April of 2013, after spring ball, when I really thought 'I *think* I can get back on the team,' I met with Dave Brandon and Brady Hoke on the same day. I basically said, 'Here's what I've done. Here's what I'm going to keep doing. I believe I've proven that I can commit to this, and I've really made an effort to ensure I don't make those mistakes again.'"

Then Hagerup got bold, just like his sister advised, telling them: "This has been enough time for you guys to decide if I should be back on the team or not."

Both Hoke and Brandon said, "Give us a week."

A week later, Hagerup went back to see Hoke, who greeted him, as he always did, with, "Hello, William."

Hoke continued: "Summer workouts start in May. We're letting you join the team. However, you know you broke the rules. This consequence will have some teeth to it. This isn't going to be easy. We'll pay for your school this summer, but not in the fall, and you're going to be suspended for the season. You'll be on the team, but you can't play."

For Hagerup, the news was bittersweet. He knew neither Brandon nor Hoke had much to gain by letting him back on the team—and a lot to lose. "I'm a punter, not a quarterback," he pointed out. There are no game-winning punts, after all. But if he failed again, in just about any way you could name—another drug test, a public incident, flunking out of school—they would be excoriated. It would have been far easier for them to wish him luck than to take him back.

But Hagerup didn't get everything he wanted. He would be back on the team for his senior year, but not on the field.

"I was sort of happy-go-lucky at that point because I knew how much progress I had made. I still felt like I could play a great game the next morning. So the fact that I had to pay the $25,000 out-of-state tuition for a semester sucked, and having to sit out for a whole year sucked, too.

"But overall, when I was walking out of Hoke's office, pride was the dominant emotion. I had done it.

"I was a Wolverine again."

After Hagerup finished spring workouts, Hoke told him he would not be joining the team for August camp, so he packed up and went back to Whitewater, Wisconsin, for the last six weeks of summer.

"I didn't want to sit around Ann Arbor feeling sorry for myself," he says. "I wanted to do something productive. I wanted to work when I was home."

He called a family friend, Joe Gemignani, whose friend Al Scargal is the president of a steel foundry in Jackson, Wisconsin. They make parts for Harley-Davidson, based in Milwaukee.

Scargal answered. "You're Joe's friend," he said. "We'd love to have you come work. Be here at 5:45 a.m. tomorrow."

"This is how dumb I am," Hagerup says today. He asked if he should wear khakis. "I thought I'd be pushing papers."

Scargal laughed. "No, wear Levi's and steel-toed boots."

When Hagerup got to the foundry, he got a culture shock when Scargal assigned a veteran worker, a short, middle-aged Hispanic guy named Jaime, to show him around.

"It's loud as shit," Hagerup recalls, "and Jaime's English isn't great, so he motions me around by hand. He shows me these ovens that run 5,000 degrees, for cooking steel. I follow him to a workstation, no bigger than a booth, with wooden blocks and 100-pound steel pieces that sit over this crate. Jamie takes a hammer out—a 20-pound hammer. He doesn't say anything. He just starts smacking the steel piece to break the cast mold off the steel, a minute straight. I just stand there.

"He hands me the hammer, and a pair of thick gray cloth gloves. He gave me a nod—and walked away. Well, 'Have a good day!' I guess!

"Now, I'm in pretty good shape. I just finished summer workouts. But after a minute of this, I couldn't lift my right hand. So I go to my left hand. Within five minutes of going back and forth, I hit my right hand. It splits the glove, through my fingernail, through the skin. I can see muscle pulsing. I'm screaming—but no one can hear me.

"I'm swearing. I go up to Jaime and start pointing: 'Finger! Finger!'"

Jaime nodded, went to the first-aid station, taped up Hagerup's finger, then motioned back to the station: There you go. Hagerup walked back, picked up the 20-pound hammer, and started swinging—this time focusing on not smashing the same finger.

"Halfway through my second shift," he remembers, "I get a couple texts. 'How was Tom Brady?!?' Apparently, he was in town, talking to the guys in the team room. Everyone ate it up. I was in Jackson, Wisconsin, swinging a 20-pound hammer."

Hagerup went through three pairs of thick gray cloth gloves that day, and every day. He got a break every two hours for five minutes, "in a shitty cafeteria," and he worked every day from 6 a.m. to 2 p.m. When he went home, he was covered in cast dust, and his face was black.

"When I get in the car after my first day, I put both my arms on the wheel to steer. I've been through a lot of hard workouts, but nothing like that. It was the hardest thing I've ever done.

"Football workouts last two hours, not eight. When you're done, you're a football player, in class. That's pretty cool. There was nothing sexy about this job. You're working with a bunch of hard-edged guys. Friendly, but not warm and fuzzy. They work."

One of his coworkers walked up to Hagerup one day, and said, "I've been doing this for 25 years. I have a family, I'm blessed to have a job. You don't want to do this. It's really, really hard work. You know, this should be motivation for you, to get that degree."

It was. Just as Hagerup had completed his 30 days of hell with Coach Wellman, he got himself up every morning at 4 a.m., drove an hour to the foundry, and did his work without talking to anyone, then went home. Every weekday, for six weeks.

After a few weeks, Hagerup had proven himself. His boss told him, "You're a Michigan football player. You don't need to work a job like this, but I respect that you're doing it."

In Hagerup's sixth and final week, they brought a guy in to work with Hagerup, but he quit after the first day.

"That was vindication for me. This was hard—too hard for most people."

On Hagerup's last day, he presented Jaime with a pack of Dunhills. Jaime just smiled and nodded. A few hours later, when Hagerup finished his last shift, they let him keep his hammer. He had earned it, and it still stands on his dresser, a good reminder of what hard work really looks like.

"It was a really nice summer day," Hagerup recalls. "When I was driving home, I was soooo happy."

At the end of August, when Hagerup got back to Schembechler Hall, he could see how much his perspective had changed. For his teammates, it was back to business—just part of the grind. But no one else in that locker room had committed three strikes—nor paid the price for all of them. No one else would likely have been able to convince both Brady Hoke and Dave Brandon to give him an unprecedented fourth chance, simply because they thought he would make the most of it. And it's a certainty no one else had spent six weeks that summer swinging a 20-pound hammer in a dark, hot foundry, instead of hanging out in sunny Ann Arbor.

So when Hagerup walked into the team locker room at Schembechler Hall, and went straight toward his stall, he couldn't help but pause in front of it.

"Seeing my name on my locker again—that was awesome," he says. "It was such an amazing contrast to my summer job, such a change of worlds."

Hagerup was happy to be back in his first world: Michigan football.

CHAPTER 40

MARKETING MISTAKES

On June 28, 2013, the department announced a new "dynamic pricing" program, which would let the market set the price for nonstudent tickets the department had available for any given game.

Here's how it worked: Through a computer program, season-ticket holders could sell their tickets by code, online, back to the department at face value. The department would then put them up for sale on its Web site. Heightened demand for tickets would boost the price for big games like Notre Dame, Nebraska, and Ohio State. The department, however, would not allow the price to drop below face value, even if few fans wanted to buy a ticket for Central Michigan, Akron, or Indiana.

"Dynamic pricing is a practice that has been widely used throughout the travel industry and is quickly becoming the standard across sports and entertainment organizations," Hunter Lochmann said in his press release. "Pricing dynamically will allow us to adjust single-game ticket prices upward or downward based on real-time market conditions with the biggest factor being fan demand and ticket scarcity. We've seen strong demand for tickets and encourage fans to buy early to access the best deals.

"One of our guiding principles is to drive change and innovate and in this case, it's a win-win, creating extra value for our season ticket holders and also creating more revenue to support our 900-plus student-athletes across 31 teams."

While the program would help season-ticket holders make their money back, legally, it would be hard to argue that paying a few hundred dollars more than face value for a Notre Dame ticket created extra value for the fans who wanted them.

Jesse Lawrence, a contributor to *Forbes* and the founder of TiqIQ—"a live-event ticket-pricing aggregator and search engine that provides flexible buying and selling options"—thought it was a good idea. "There's so much money to be made in the whole college football ecosystem that to think that they would not maximize revenue is a bit naïve frankly," he told the *Michigan Daily*. "It is business, even though it's a collegiate program. They're obviously dedicated to making as much profit as possible."

Lawrence estimated Michigan's athletic department could make an addition $5 million a year—every cent of it from fans eager to see their favorite team play. Lawrence was right. Michigan made $4.5 million.

Joe Parker and Marty Bodnar had both been gone for over two years, but they still loved Michigan, and were concerned by the damage Brandon's policies could do.

"Marty and I would always portray that we were sold out," Parker said. "We wouldn't market at all that there were tickets available. He believed in the scarcity principle. But if we had a few available—say the visiting team didn't use up all its tickets—we could make a very discreet gesture by offering a few tickets to the lettermen or the Victors Club or good donors or just loyal alums and fans—always at face value, never trying to get another dollar out of it.

"It felt good to be able to call someone special, who needed a few more tickets when their grandkids came to town, and say, 'Yeah, we can help you.' Part of a special relationship—and it *felt* like a relationship.

"But when the department goes to dynamic pricing, your loyal fans can't call to get a favor. You're just a guy off the street now, and you're going to be charged more than face value—maybe a lot more—for the same tickets you used to get for face value from your friends at the athletic department."

Dynamic pricing would not only diminish the relationship between loyal fans and the department, it would affect the psychology of everyone buying tickets for a Michigan game.

"The key to filling the Big House was always the 'scarcity principle,'" Bodnar explains, "which states that, when people think tickets will be hard to get, they gobble them up, and don't let them go, for fear of not being able to get back in. That's why you keep a wait list. It gives strong incentive for people who have the tickets to keep them.

"And the flip side is also true: When people no longer believe tickets are scarce, they no longer want them as badly.

"It's a proven psychological principle. I lived it for 12 years, and I know it's true. And I knew, once Brandon cranked up the ticket prices, the PSDs,

StubHub and the 'dynamic pricing' and even the $500 to be in the 'interest list,' he didn't understand what he was doing, and he was headed for trouble.

"I wish I was wrong."

On April 13, 2013, Michigan held its spring game in front of an estimated 15,000 fans. For the 13th straight year, it wasn't a game, but more of a glorified practice—a missed marketing opportunity if ever there was one. The department charged a $20 "donation," however, in exchange for an official "University of Michigan Seat Cushion or Kneeling Pad," perfect for games that fall. Because the proceeds went to C. S. Mott Children's Hospital—the department's favorite charity—few complained. People ponied up without complaint.

But in July, the department banned seat cushions—including the "official dual-purpose" model they had sold to the fans for $20 at the spring game three months earlier. Even on the day they banned it, it was still on sale at M-Den, with the same promise that it had been officially sanctioned for stadium use. The department announced that, instead, it would let season-ticket holders "lease" seat cushions permanently attached to the bench for the entire season, directly from the department, at a cost of $35 per season.

To the department's surprise, the fans responded by writing to the blogs, the Regents, and the department itself. It was a small thing, literally and figuratively, but another symbol of the growing divide between the fans and the department.

After a few days weathering the backlash, the department announced that the whole thing had been a big misunderstanding—created by others. The department said it had never intended to ban the spring-game seat cushions, nor force fans to lease cushions from the department.

"Inaccuracies were driven by social media," the statement explained—ignoring the fact that the social media in question was its own official Web site, MGoBlue.com.

Don Canham was a great marketer and judge of coaching talent, but he was philosophically opposed to asking for a raise, or even a contract, soliciting donors, or selling advertising in the stadium, and he couldn't fathom why you'd want to charge elementary school students money for stadium tours. It's remarkable that, 20 years after Canham stepped down, Bill Martin was still opposed to all of those except soliciting donors—which even the least competitive programs were doing in the 21st century.

Martin kept all advertising out of the Big House, then quietly and slowly removed all advertising from Crisler Arena, too. Brandon's administration brought it back to Crisler in every form possible—the brighter and louder, the better, it seemed—and started sneaking advertising into the once-pristine Big House, too: ads for Flagstar Bank and StubHub on the concourse pillars, the All-State "good hands" logo on the field goal netting during a spring game, video promotions to hold your corporate event at the Big House, and placards for Arby's, plus some sort of mascot resembling a bag of fries walking around, during the outdoor hockey games.

When fans objected to each and every one of these marketing attempts, the department usually pulled it—and then went right to the next idea.

Before any home football game, especially the season opener, hundreds of fans in town will walk or drive past the stadium, just to see their old friend again. But on Friday, August 30, 2013—the day before Michigan's opening game against Central Michigan—fans noticed something new: a giant Kraft macaroni noodle, balanced on a stand beneath the north scoreboard, with a message written on the golden noodle in blue letters: "You know you love it."

It turned out Michigan fans didn't love it—at least not near the Big House. Michael Proppe tweeted, "Nothing says umich football tradition like a giant noodle under the scoreboard! I predict many angry donors." His prediction was quickly confirmed, with hundreds of fans tweeting, posting online, and e-mailing their disgust—a now practiced response that seemed to multiply with each misstep.

Whenever Brandon committed another PR gaffe, he would give spokesperson Dave Ablauf the unenviable job of explaining an unpopular policy he usually didn't know about any sooner than the upset fans did. This time, Ablauf gamely said the noodle had been delivered for the inaugural W.O.W. (Welcome Our Wolverines) Friday event—which included $10 stadium tours—that the athletic department would be holding the day before every home football game throughout the season.

"It's actually kinda funny, everyone seems to be fixated on a noodle and not about a football game being played tomorrow," Ablauf told MLive.com. "but it will be moved out of the stadium this evening."

The department got the noodle out of the stadium that evening, posthaste—but that was not the original plan, despite the "W.O.W." explanation. Former employees have since told me Ablauf had been instructed to concoct his story to cover the truth: The noodle was supposed to remain right where it was, to greet fans entering the north gates for the entire season, but when fan outrage grew too loud they decided they had to remove it. Ablauf apparently came up with the idea that this was merely the "initial W.O.W. Friday of the season," which was supposed to explain why they were planning to have the noodle for only one day. The first W.O.W. Friday of the season turned out to also be the last.

Ablauf was right about one thing, though: Such stunts distracted fans from the team itself. The fans' complaints about the department were starting to add up, and they were growing accustomed to objecting in unison.

In 2011, Brandon said on *60 Minutes* that the "business model [of college athletics] is broken," failing to grasp that college athletics was never supposed to be a business, since it doesn't pay shareholders, partners, owners, taxes, or the star attractions, the players and the band.

From its inception under Charles Baird in 1898 to Martin's retirement in 2010, the Michigan athletic department's goal was simply to be self-sufficient. But the Brandon administration's goal seemed to be more for the sake of more—simply because it could—and then find things to spend it on, so revenue didn't show up as profit. In the five years before Brandon took office, Martin had already built or rebuilt 14 facilities, at $400 million. Did it all need to be rebuilt again the next decade?

Bo Schembechler earned $21,000 his first year at Michigan. Brady Hoke's first-year salary was more than 100 times greater. Could anyone argue Hoke was 100 times better? For the first time in Michigan's long history, the athletic director was making more than the president. Was there a compelling reason for breaking that precedent?

The noodle would be gone by game time, but the general-admission policy for student seating would just be starting. On July 22, 2013, CSG President Michael Proppe and Vice President Bobby Dishell did not meet with Brandon, as promised, but they were invited to meet with Hunter Lochmann and Shelly Fabrizio, director of operations and event management, in Lochmann's first-floor office, to discuss the new student seating program. Dishell was out of town, so Proppe went alone.

The always-affable Lochmann invited Proppe to sit down, then gave him a 45-minute PowerPoint presentation explaining the department's byzantine plan to manage the general-admission seating policy, and avoid people rushing to get the best seat possible.

Boiled down, the plan went something like this: First, department officials would gather the students in organized lines on the southwest corner of Hoover and Greene, then move them in waves across the street to the gate. There, Lochmann told Proppe, the students would get in new lines for the section they wanted to sit in, which would no longer be numbered, but identified by the letters: H-O-K-E.

"The funniest part of the meeting was at the end," Proppe said, "when Hunter asked me, 'How do you think we can communicate this to the students?'"

Proppe told him, "I just saw a 45-minute PowerPoint slideshow, and I'm still confused."

"Well," Lochmann said, "we're hoping that after a couple games, people learn it, and get used to it, and we'll make tweaks as we go. We're looking for feedback as we go."

They would get plenty of it.

CHAPTER 41

THE CHICKEN DANCE

After a lifetime of dreaming, and three and a half years of waiting since the day he arrived on campus in January of 2010, Devin Gardner stood in the tunnel of Michigan Stadium that Saturday knowing he was seconds away from running out for the first time as the team's opening-day starting quarterback.

"I was so excited that I kept telling myself not to trip and fall when I was running out to touch the banner," Gardner told me. "I can't even describe what it felt like coming out of that tunnel, knowing that I was the starting quarterback at Michigan."

Gardner passed for 1 touchdown and ran for 2 more, with 2 interceptions, en route to a 59–9 blowout of Central Michigan. It was Michigan's highest-scoring opening game since Fielding Yost's "Point-a-Minute" Wolverines beat Ohio Wesleyan, 65–0, back in 1905.

The day also marked the debut of the general-admission seating program, to mixed reviews.

The good news: "The student section looked really, really good at kickoff," Proppe says. "It looked full, but it was not absolutely full—about 75 percent full at kickoff. When the students don't have assigned seats, they spread out a bit."

Not a problem, by itself—and maybe even a solution to a number of other issues. But the students spreading out created an unforeseen by-product.

"After kickoff," Proppe reports, "some students are still arriving late, and the ushers are telling them that, 'This section is full, and you can't go in. Go to the next section,' as they'd been instructed to do. So now the students can't get into the student section. It *wasn't* full, they were just spread out, so it looked that way."

The students were just as unhappy about the GA policy in practice as they were in theory, but Proppe and Dishell urged patience. They were trying to help the department make it work.

"We learned some important things from the first game," Proppe says. "Under general admission, people will spread out. We communicated this to Hunter during the game. We proposed a solution: Give everyone an assigned seat when they show up."

The next game would be a fine test for the general-admission program: Notre Dame versus Michigan, "Under the Lights II."

The Michigan and Notre Dame fans didn't need any help getting excited for game day. Swarbrick had already taken care of that when he triggered the "three games and out" clause, with a pregame envelope the year before. That meant this would be the last Notre Dame game at the Big House for the foreseeable future.

But if the game needed more fuel, Brady Hoke provided it. At a May 13, 2013, luncheon speech in Grand Rapids, he said Notre Dame was "chickening out" of the series after the 2014 game. Because Notre Dame wasn't interrupting its series with Michigan State or Purdue, the logic went, the Irish must be afraid of the big, bad Wolverines. Like just about all communications between the two schools, this got national attention. The anticipation generated for this game guaranteed the general-admission program would get a severe test.

Ten hours before the 8 p.m. kickoff, thousands of students started gathering in the "veal pens" at the southwest corner of Hoover and Greene, in 90-degree heat. But the students were very well behaved—for which the department should be grateful—and the time passed without incident. By 5 p.m., they were ushered across Greene Street in waves, with the police stopping traffic for them to cross each time.

As Proppe, Dishell, and Lochmann had planned after the Central Michigan game, all students handed the ushers their general-admission tickets when they walked through the gate. The ushers scanned the tickets, then handed each student another ticket, this one with an assigned seat, to avoid having the students spread out too much.

"But, crucially, the ushers would not open up the next row of seats until the previous row was completely filled," Proppe says. "So if you showed up on time with a group of ten of your friends—just like they now required you to, if you wanted to sit together—they'd put five people at the end of one row, then the remaining five at the start of the next row. So after waiting for ten hours in the heat, you're still not sitting together."

It was also a very slow process. The ushers—who were doing exactly what they had been told to do, and were no happier than the students about the new policy and procedures—used ropes to block off the empty rows of seats until each of the lower rows was filled, then pulled the ropes back another row, one by one.

"So you had a *huge* congregation of students on the concourse, waiting to get in," Proppe says. "And they're waiting out there for a while, because the ushers are only taking down one person at a time. As we got closer to kickoff at eight p.m., the students start pushing forward because they knew the game was about to start, and they'd been waiting all year to see it. After the game, we got students saying 'I feared for my life, because I was getting crushed.'"

When Proppe and Dishell sent out a student survey in October, they included a question about safety. Of the survey's respondents, 1,234, or 20 percent, checked the box that said, "felt unsafe/in danger of being trampled while waiting to get to my seat."

This potential tragedy went unnoticed by the rest of the crowd. The second night game at Michigan Stadium came complete with a new set of faux "throwback" uniforms, and another NCAA record crowd, 115,109, breaking the record set two years earlier at Michigan's first Notre Dame night game. Michigan celebrated with a lengthy pregame flyover, and the sixth pregame ceremony for the Legends Jersey program. The family of Tom Harmon—including his son, actor Mark Harmon—presented Tom's famous "Ol' '98" to Devin Gardner.

"It's an amazing feeling to wear that number," Gardner told reporters at the time. "I knew about all the great things that he did on the field, but there are all the other things he did. He played two years of basketball, he fought for his country, and he was a great human being. It's an honor to know that his family felt I deserved to wear that jersey."

Every word was sincere, and Gardner repeated them to me when we talked in 2015. He added, "When they picked me to wear it, as tough as Tom Harmon was, that's pretty amazing.

"But you also want to create your own legacy. What about Jeremy Gallon? He set the record for most yards in a season, and he's wearing Desmond's 21. Again, that's pretty cool, but it kind of overshadows what Jeremy accomplished."

Gardner and Gallon both accomplished a lot that night against the 14th-ranked Fighting Irish. Gardner connected on 21 of his 33 passes, 4 of them for touchdowns, and added 82 yards rushing, for another touchdown. He had one costly interception, making an ill-advised pass out of the endzone, but recovered to close out the game with a final touchdown pass to Drew Dileo with 4:18 left, to seal the 41–30 victory.

But the star of the game was Gallon, who caught the other 3 touchdown passes and marked a career high with 184 yards receiving. "He's like a little bulldog, man," Gardner said of the 5-foot-8 receiver. "Behind the doors, we work so hard. Now we finally got an opportunity to display it in front of the biggest crowd in college football."

Even 18 months later, when I asked Gardner what his favorite game had been over the course of his five-year, 62-game career, he didn't hesitate: Notre Dame, 2013.

"Me and Gallon, man, clicking all night, in front of the biggest crowd in the history of football. We were on fire, unstoppable. That was the most amazing feeling I ever had in my life."

Gardner's performance was as impressive as his response was authentic. It would have marked a fine note to end one of sport's great rivalries at the Big House, but instead of honoring the rivalry, and Michigan's tradition and values, by acting like they'd done it before—which they had, 23 times—Brandon went for the "Wow!" moment, and a cheap shot. Soon after Gardner took the final snap in the "victory formation," the "Chicken Dance" blared over the stadium sound system, echoing Hoke's comments about Notre Dame being "chicken" from his speech that spring.

The fans who stayed to cheer on their heroes got the joke: a musical accusation that Notre Dame was backing out of the rivalry because they were afraid to play Michigan. That theory would get blown to pieces 364 days later.

After the game, Brandon said, "You're a 17-, 18-year-old kid watching the largest crowd in the history of college football with airplanes flying over and Beyoncé introducing your halftime show? That's a pretty powerful message about what Michigan is all about, and that's our job to send that message."

As happy as Michigan fans were that night, not all of them would agree that flyovers, rock music, and Beyoncé are what Michigan is all about. To many, Beyoncé is to Michigan football what Bo Schembechler is to—well, Beyoncé.

But they were all better received than the Kraft macaroni noodle.

CHAPTER 42

STUMBLING ON AND OFF THE FIELD

After two impressive victories, it was tempting to believe the ghosts of Appalachian State and Toledo were gone. The Wolverines had won 16 straight home games, the longest streak among BCS teams, and entered the season's third week ranked 11th in the nation. They seemed bound to move into the top ten with two very weak opponents on the menu.

The aura of invincibility, it seemed, was back.

Next up: the Akron Zips, named for rubber galoshes manufactured in that town, which were all the rage 90 years ago. By 2013, the Zips were living up to their name, finishing their last three seasons with identically miserable marks of 1 win against 11 losses—or 3–33 over that stretch. They had not won a single road game in five years—28 straight.

The challenge ushers faced before the Notre Dame game was simple, as Proppe says: "Everyone wanted to be there, and be there early. Akron was the opposite problem. Nobody wanted to show up on time—or even go."

It was a gorgeous day, with a promising Michigan team to cheer for. But a noon start, an appallingly weak opponent, and Yom Kippur didn't help boost attendance.

"The effect on the student section was 60 rows of completely empty seats," Proppe says. "It looked like a half-empty student section. If the goal of the new policy was to get a good TV shot, Akron was the game that disproved it."

Fellow student Jay Sarkar, who worked the game for the Big Ten Network from the Michigan press box, overheard the producer tell the cameramen to tighten their shots, to show as little of the empty student section as possible. Sarkar shook his head. "The Akron game student attendance makes a mockery of Michigan Football on television."

The game also brought the ghosts back, in full force. On the last play of the game, down 28–24, the Zips had the ball just 4 yards from Michigan's endzone. It wouldn't have made as big a splash as Michigan's loss to Appalachian State, but it might have been a bigger upset. Michigan fans could be seen covering their foreheads, eyes, and ears, fearing it could all come true again—but Akron's pass fell incomplete.

Some pundits quickly named it "The Worst Win Ever"—but the keyword was "win." Unlike upsets, fans forget about ugly victories pretty fast.

The Wolverines were 3–0.

While the Wolverines were busy escaping the Zips in Ann Arbor, just up the road in East Lansing, before Michigan State's game against Youngstown State, skywriters spelled out "GO BLUE" over Spartan Stadium.

It was a sophomoric prank that would have blown away almost as quickly as the letters themselves, until Michigan's athletic department seemed to go out of its way to make it worse. Michigan initially denied having anything to do with the stunt, until MLive.com contacted the skywriting company, Oregon Aero Skydancer, which confirmed "someone from the Michigan athletic department" hired them for "a multi-thousand-dollar job." The department then claimed the skywriting was not intended to target Spartan Stadium, but the "I-96 area."

With this misfire, the pattern was becoming publicly recognizable: the department kept committing gaffe after gaffe—from seat cushions to giant noodles to skywriting—followed by absurd explanations that always placed the blame somewhere else.

People working for Brandon found it difficult to save him from some of these mistakes. Many told me he didn't ask many questions and would rarely listen to their answers.

The department's leaders didn't seem to understand that the people who used to nip such bad ideas in the bud, or minimize them afterward if no one listened the first time, were both powerless to help the department now.

Longtime sports information director Bruce Madej had moved to Crisler to run "special projects" before retiring, while his protégé, Dave Ablauf, who had replaced him, was being kept in the dark on such decisions. A year later, when Ablauf gave a guest lecture for a class at Michigan (not mine), he explained one of the problems the PR people found themselves frequently facing.

"We talked a lot about us being on the front lines, as communicators," Ablauf told them. "Not reactive, but proactive. But how can we do that when we're not in the loop? We never know what they're up to until it blows up, and then we're just doing damage control—and doing it the way they want it done. Ideally, your PR people should be in front of the parade, helping to direct—not in the back, cleaning up the horseshit." Getting in front of the parade, directing traffic, is the best way to follow Canham's Razor: "Never turn a one-day story into a two-day story."

Brandon's department was doing the exact opposite: turning one-day stories into stories that never died, thanks to the Internet. This bad habit, established during small-potato incidents, would prove to be career-killing for several leaders when the stakes got higher.

Three days after Michigan survived Akron, on September 17, 2013, Michigan's ticket office sent out e-mails announcing that students who had purchased Michigan basketball tickets that spring for the upcoming 2013–14 season no longer had guaranteed tickets for every game they'd purchased—although they phrased it differently.

After the basketball team's run to the 2013 NCAA finals, demand for tickets naturally soared. In an e-mail to students that spring, the department had urged students to order now to be sure they would get to see the big games against Arizona, Iowa, Michigan State and Indiana. Although the department had only allotted 3,000 seats for students, it took orders from 4,500 students, with the students paying up front. It's hard to understand why a department that knew it had 3,000 available student seats would sell 4,500 of them, but that would not be the last mystery.

Lochmann introduced something called a "claim pod" system, grouping the 17 home games into four groups, or "pods," of three to four games each. To go to any of the games, each student had to "claim" the ticket he or she had already paid for months ago by going online at least 24 hours before the contest, and promising to attend by clicking a box. If the student didn't confirm, the department would sell their ticket for whatever it could get on StubHub, and keep the money.

But if you confirmed, and you didn't attend—say, for example, on December 7 you realized your time might be better spent studying for your final exams than watching Michigan pound a school called Houston Baptist, 107–53—you'd lose the right to claim tickets for the remaining games in that "pod." They would sell all your remaining tickets in that pod to the highest bidder, again without paying you a cent. If you failed to attend games you had confirmed you would attend three times, you'd lose the right to your tickets for the rest of the season. The department would again sell your remaining tickets to the highest bidder, and again you'd get nothing.

Even attending all the games, on time, would not guarantee that you'd be able to get a ticket you'd already purchased for the big games. Fortunately for all involved, however, the students who attended the most games were ulti-mately able to get those seats "as a reward," Lochmann said.

How a department can take your money for tickets to every game, then change the rules, sell your tickets, and give you nothing in return is a mystery—and perhaps a miracle that someone didn't file a class-action lawsuit.

It not only confused students, it infuriated them. Fifth-year senior Jay Sarkar wrote an editorial on his own personal blog that drew 16,000 clicks in two days, and was picked up by *The Ann Arbor News*. He said, in part, "I can-not wait to get out of Ann Arbor and not donate to this cash-hungry school for a long time. David Brandon and Hunter Lochmann, whether they like it or not, are antagonizing and alienating the student body. Do they expect me to send my kids here in 20–30 years and buy season tickets for them? This is how you make money now and lose money in the long term. Michigan athletics motto may be 'We On' but join me and my fellow students in saying, 'We Out.'"

If the department was trying to get back in the students' good graces, they were doing it the hard way.

Because Brandon's tenure was marked not by any major scandals but a se-ries of paper cuts, those who left the Brandon bandwagon did so when each person had reached his or her personal threshold. Depending on the person, just about anything could serve as the final straw, from scheduling Appala-chian State to the seat cushion to the skywriting to student tickets, and more.

For Regent Mark Bernstein, that moment arrived on September 21, 2013, at a Michigan Stadium event that had nothing to do with football.

"M-Hacks" is a semiannual gathering by one of Michigan's entreprenue-rial student organizations, MPowered Entrepreneurship—a bunch of "insanely bright computer programmers," Bernstein says. They bid to host a "hackathon," which is a meeting of hackers that Google, Yahoo, and other Internet compa-nies sponsor around the country. During a 36-hour marathon session, the hackers develop applications to do just about everything, from automating your daily to-do list to creating a personalized system of workflow to separat-ing your trash into its component recyclables, then show off their work to each other.

When the M-Hacks decided to host a hackathon, naturally they thought the Big House could compete with Palo Alto, California, Cambridge, Mas-sachussetts, and the like to attract the nation's best hackers. When the club asked the athletic department what it would cost to rent the Jack Roth Stadium Club—the common area that serves the luxury suites on the east side—the department came back with its answer: $30,000, plus additional expenses "to be determined," and $10,000 more if they wanted to use Crisler, next door.

"If I had personally seen the 'TBD,'" the M-Hacks' faculty advisor, engineering professor Thomas Zurbuchen, told me, "I would have stopped the entire process right there." But no one, not even an engineering professor, could have anticipated what happened next.

"It's a lot of hidden fees, like the way hotels mark it up," Bernstein says of the athletic department's billing procedures. "It's outrageous. But M-Hacks found the money to rent the space, thanks to Professor Zurbuchen asking their sponsors, who're looking to recruit these talented students, and they paid it."

Michigan's hackers got the word out, and drew a very impressive 2,000 hackers from around the country to the most famous building on their campus. They held their event in East Tower, a big, open, comfortable space overlooking the empty stadium, and it was a huge success.

"I went to see it," Bernstein said, "and I was so amazed by it, I went home and brought my son back and e-mailed every Regent and told them you have to come down and see this. It was great—a tremendous showpiece for what this university can do at its best, and a great example of our range: hundreds of hotshot computer programmers setting up shop at the Big House."

After everyone packed up and went home, the athletic department sent the M-Hack club an additional bill, this one for almost $60,000 more, bringing the total to host the event to almost $100,0000

"I looked at the contract after the fact," Zurbuchen told me, "and I could not believe my eyes. Needless to say, nobody expected that the 'TBD' would be larger than the number ahead of it! I had absolutely no idea it would add up to so much and neither did the students.

"Basically, I think it came from two aspects: First, students were behaving like they normally would at a university event, using university facilities. Since this stuff is never really expensive, students tend to make a lot of changes at the last minute, and everybody expects that. But, second, you had an organization that was operating more like a high-end hotel. Needless to say, the food and service were not to that standard, but the way they charged for it was: every wish from students added up in dollars and cents. Nothing was free. And it was expensive—superexpensive!

"So, after we asked, they gave detailed justifications all related to, for example, specific rooms and actions. But, we only learned the exact cost after the fact. The students did not have the experience to see it coming and I caught the issues too late, when the damage was done. We did not manage to get any relief on this, and basically we [the College of Engineering] had to pay to bail them out. MPowered, the student organization, had to pay back a smaller portion of these funds during the year, which strained its ability to run exciting, engaging programs the rest of the year.

"My first reaction was disappointment, and then anger. I felt the students dealt with athletics like we all thought of it—as part of the university."

But Dave Brandon seemed to recognize very few differences between the corporate world and the University of Michigan, even though the mission of the former is to maximize money, and the latter is to pursue the truth in all its forms. Those differences Brandon did recognize, he resented, and often tried to eliminate.

Another example: filmmakers Buddy Moorehouse, an alum, and Brian Kruger, a U-M father, set out to produce a documentary on Willis Ward, Gerald Ford's best friend on Michigan's 1934 football team, who was ordered to sit out when Michigan played Georgia Tech, simply because he was African-American. The filmmakers sent the athletic department a list of photos they needed. The department sent them back an estimate for $190,000—a figure exceeding their entire budget—and that's before they got into video footage.

When the same filmmakers asked Greg Kinney, the professional archivist for the sports collection at Michigan's Bentley Historical Library on North Campus, he confirmed they had all the photos and video the filmmakers wanted, at a more reasonable price: zero, plus $5 to $10 for reproduction costs. Why? Because that's what state universities are supposed to do: promote research.

"If we were kids starting out," Moorehouse told me, "as soon as we got the athletic department's bill, we would have stopped." Instead, they produced *Black and Blue*, which has been showcased by the Ford School of Public Policy—with Ford's son Steve attending—the Gerald Ford Presidential Library and Museum, and schools throughout the country.

The department's reputation for shunning the rest of Michigan's learning community was spreading.

"Many of us have been trying to host science or academic conferences in the stadium as well," Professor Zurbuchen says. "Consider the scenery—unforgettable and amazing! It would allow us to make U of M more of a national destination. But, most of us cannot afford it.

"I still regret this whole thing today. It was such an amazing idea by MPowered, and such an iconic experience for all participants to see Michigan taking off in a hot tech field, with huge benefits to the entire university. But, due to a vastly different cost model for these facilities—a model I had never experienced anywhere else at the university—this amazing event had a very bitter aftertaste for all of us.

"And it ended in the worst financial debacle of any student team I have mentored during the past 20 years."

Bernstein was even less thrilled. "When I heard about that M-Hacks bill," he told me, "*that* is when I realized this department is completely out of control. After that, I was done with the current regime, and how it was being run."

Another university safety mechanism had been tripped, engaging one more person hoping to save the university from itself.

Later that same day, the Wolverines played on the road at Storrs, Connecticut, to complete the second half of the home-and-home series with UConn. The Huskies had already lost to Towson State and Maryland, so the Wolverines were expected to roll them on their way to Big Ten play the next week. Brandon had pushed hard to hold the game in the Meadowlands, much closer to Michigan's 20,000 New York–based alumni. But UConn AD Warde Manuel, the former Michigan player and associate athletic director who had been a finalist for Brandon's job, turned down the bigger paycheck to honor the wishes of the UConn fans eager to host their biggest home game in the short history of their new stadium, and the the state legislature, which had kicked in a good chunk of the cost. Manuel brought in 2,000 temporary seats to accommodate the overflow crowd, which included former UConn basketball star Ray Allen and Michigan native Derek Jeter.

The Huskies took a 21–14 lead into the fourth quarter, with a good chance to upset 15th-ranked Michigan. The Rentschler Field record crowd of 42,704 went crazy, thinking they were about to witness the biggest win in the stadium's short history. But Brendan Gibbons capped Michigan's two-score comeback with a field goal to secure a 24–21 win.

Brady Hoke was not fooled by Michigan's 4–0 record, however. "We've got a major league problem," he said after the game, "and we've got to fix it because that's not going to win championships."

Many have drawn comparisons between Brandon and Hoke, but they seemed to have less in common than believed. If Brandon didn't recognize the problems he was creating until it was too late, Hoke knew his team wasn't good enough yet. The question, in Hoke's case, was if he could fix it in time.

Despite winning its last two games, Michigan had slid from 11th to 19th in the polls. One reason: Gardner already had 10 turnovers that season, including three interceptions each against Akron and UConn, and at least one interception in each of his previous nine starts.

But after a bye week, the 4–0 Wolverines defended the Brown Jug in their Big Ten opener.

"We were thinking about Minnesota all week," Gardner told me, "and Minnesota was it."

Gardner and company piled on 4 second-half touchdowns to walk away with a 42–13 win, and the Jug. The most impressive number on Gardner's stat line was not his 13-for-17 passing, his 235 yards through the air, or his 2 touchdowns, but zero turnovers.

CHAPTER 43

THE STUDENTS WIN A ROUND

While the elected student government officers wrestled with general-admission seating, the elected Regents had to find a new president.

Mary Sue Coleman's two-year extension would run out in 2014, so the Regents knew they had to start looking for her replacement by the summer of 2013. The first order of business was to assess where they were, and therefore what they needed from the next administration.

"Mary Sue [Coleman] is very well liked by the public," said Regent Kathy White. "She raises a ton of money—no president has done it better—but it's generally for the sexy stuff: the Life Sciences building, the Walgreens Theater, the business school, the law school.

"But she was not focused on raising money for the core mission of the university. I want to raise money for the English department, for the math department. Of course, it's a lot harder to make that sale to donors. We're building a graduate-student dorm for $100 million, but we don't even know if people will want to live there. Maybe they will, but endowing more professorships would likely be more successful; $100 million can get you 40 endowed professorships. That's a department's worth!

"If you look at the core mission of the university—English, sciences, languages—it's in the center of campus. But it's the fancy stuff outside the Diag that gets all the money—law, business, medicine, engineering, athletics. What about history? What about biology?"

When the Regents—who serve as the committee for all presidential searches—sat down in the spring of 2013 to consider the criteria for the next president, they knew the health system, the cost of tuition, and athletics would always be important responsibilities for any Michigan president. They also knew one of their prime candidates, Brown Provost Mark Schlissel, had no experience with big-time college athletics.

"But [in 2013] I wasn't that worried about the finances of the athletic department yet," White said. "It was still okay in 2013, because we had 2012 Fiscal Year data. But we already knew Dave's leadership style was a problem. This was partly because [President Coleman] was not taking an active interest in reining him in. If there had been some 'parental supervision,' it might have been fine, but we didn't have that. The parents were not home. The president's office did not, and was not, going to pull him back in."

The presidential search was well under way, however, when the Regents realized they'd forgotten an essential part of the process: student input. When the Regents announced the people they had picked for their search advisory committee—which had no students on it, unlike previous searches—and did so after graduation, when the students had already gone home, Michael Proppe let his displeasure be known to Royster Harper, the vice president for Student Life, who works closely with the Central Student Government.

"What Royster did that was so great," Regent Kathy White told me, "she *told* me how unhappy they were. We hadn't realized, though we probably should have, but once we knew, we could do something about it. You have to see it from Proppe's point of view. If you are the CSG president, you're elected in March, for one year. You have a platform to serve your fellow students, including having a voice in who the next president is going to be. That's a big deal, because we only search for a president every decade or so.

"Then the Board of Regents announces they're starting the search after all the students are gone for summer vacation. The students are only here eight months a year, for four years. You have to engage them when they are *here*. If you wait until May, you've missed them. If you wait until they're seniors, they're gone. And now they're not students anymore, but ticked-off alumni. Not good.

"What I learned was this: You have to be very sensitive to the students and their schedules, and to make sure they're included when we send out notices about important things. It was an unintentional mistake—truly—but we worked to correct it by reaching out to them immediately, apologizing, and setting up meetings that fall."

The Regents organized six outreach meetings for various stakeholders, including U-M-Dearborn, U-M-Flint, the faculty senate, the medical campus, and the students. White describes the report and survey Proppe and Dishell produced as "brilliant. *Brilliant.*" They were charged with presenting their report to the Regents, the search advisory committee, and a public audience of about 200 people at the Modern Language Building, which lasted about two hours.

"They had three dozen students give brief oral presentations on each point," White recalls, "so it gave life to the data. It was classy. It was on point. Really, it was the best outreach meeting. The best. And we had six."

By October, everyone involved felt much better about the presidential search, because the Regents demonstrated a skill vital to any organization: the ability to self-correct.

If Brandon wasn't meeting with the Central Student Government officers, other campus leaders were—eagerly, and often—including Regents and executive officers. And they had good reason to.

From the start of the season, Proppe told me, "I'm getting a steady flow of e-mails from unhappy students." But because Proppe and Dishell were so busy working on the presidential search, they had never collated them, or quantified the students' reaction to the general-admission policy.

Until, that is, Proppe received an e-mail on Monday, October 7, 2013, from David Potter, a very popular, respected professor of Greek civilization, who also happened to be the chair of the Student Relations Advisory Committee (SRAC). He asked if Proppe or anyone else in the CSG would be interested in attending his committee's next meeting, to address the new seating policy.

Sure, Proppe said. When?

"The next meeting is Friday, October 11, from 11:30 to 1 p.m," just four days away.

It was a tall order.

They had spent long hours working on their presentation for the presidential search, and school was another matter. They were still full-time students, after all, in very demanding majors. But Proppe had prepared for that, too.

"My plan was pretty simple," he said. "I banked a really good GPA my first three years." How good? A 4.0. That, he calculated, would allow him to let his grades slip while spending countless hours working for the students, and still pull off a 3.8. The guy had it down. Whatever Proppe and Dishell were doing for the students, it would be hard to accuse them of acting out of self-interest.

They weren't just sacrificing study time, either. As Dishell told me, "For the record, many a night at the bar was given up to work on this and other issues."

So, when Professor Potter asked if they could talk about the general-admission policy in just four days, they quickly agreed.

Proppe and Dishell knew they needed to survey the student body, so they would have "actual data to present, not just spouting off our own opinions," Proppe recalls. They worked all day Monday, and all night, to get the survey ready to go out Tuesday morning. The education they were receiving at Michigan in statisics, accounting, and politics was paying off, in surprising ways.

Because it typically takes about a week to get an all-student survey approved by the registrar's office and sent out to all students, Proppe and Dishell had to work unusually fast. And they needed help.

On the morning of Tuesday, October 8, just three days before they were to make their presentation to a the SRAC—and a room full of professors and peers—Proppe walked to the Ross Business School to meet with Royster Harper, the vice president for Student Life, who was attending President Coleman's "State of the University" address. Like so many people in this story, Harper worked hard, smart, and unselfishly for people she would likely never meet—most of whom would never know her role in the story.

With the clock ticking, Proppe got to the point. "Royster, we have a survey designed, ready to go, and we have to get it out and back by Friday, October 11." In hindsight, he says, "Now, that's asking a hell of a lot. If we didn't already have a good relationship with her, I don't know if she would have considered it. But she didn't blink.

" 'Okay, let me make a call. This is obviously important.' " Royster Harper got it out within two hours—about four days faster than usual.

Even with the survey completed and sent, they were at the mercy of their fellow students to respond. They needed enough of them to return the survey to get a statistically significant response, then analyze the results and publish a report before the meeting that Friday.

After Harper sent the survey out, they waited. She commended Proppe on his hard work. "But," she said, "I'm concerned you're not going to have enough responses in such a short period."

Proppe was, too. So, he flipped open his MacBook Air and checked. Just 60 minutes after Harper had sent it out, they already had received 2,000 responses. When they closed the survey after 24 hours, 7,305 students had started the survey, and 5,892 had finished it. (They only counted finished surveys.) Proppe heard from many students unhappy that they closed it after 24 hours. He was sympathetic, but, he explained, "We had to begin putting together our report *fast* and we couldn't do that if the data kept changing as people filled it out."

Fortunately, they had plenty to work with already. When they had sent out their survey asking for student input for the presidential search that fall, only 2.6 percent of students had responded. For the general-admission survey, however, 14 percent responded, in only 24 hours. "That," Proppe says, "is a ridiculously high response rate."

You couldn't say the students didn't care.

Proppe didn't waste any time gloating. He closed his laptop, loaded his backpack, and headed home to squeeze in some schoolwork. After they closed the survey, they started working on their report Wednesday night. What had seemed impossible two days ago now seemed likely: They were going to have solid data, thoroughly analyzed, to present to the committee Friday afternoon.

When he sifted through the survey data, Proppe boiled it down to two main points:

1. The students clearly did not like general admission. "This wasn't my opinion. We had the data." Of the survey respondents, 76 percent were opposed to it, and 17 percent supportive.

2. Whether students liked general admission or not, it had not achieved Dave Brandon's stated goal: a full student section.

"Yeah, you could show photos of the empty rows in the student section, but I wanted real data," Proppe says. "And for that I needed attendance figures, so I had to ask Hunter [Lochmann] earlier in the week, 'Can you share this info?' He provided it, no problem, and said, 'We want to be very transparent about this.' But he probably said that because he thought the figures made them look really good."

Lochmann gave Proppe the figures Wednesday morning, two days in advance of the meeting, which showed the overall student attendance rate up slightly from 79 percent in 2011 and 2012, to 81 percent for the first four home games of 2013, and the on-time rate up from about 45 percent in 2011 and 2012 to roughly 65 percent in 2013.

Sure enough, as Proppe had predicted, Lochmann thought the data vindicated the department's decision to switch to general admission. But, crucially, Hunter Lochmann was a former marketing man for the New York Knicks, not a statistics major at the University of Michigan. Proppe had been taught by some of the world's best statistics professors that you can only make analytical conclusions when comparing apples to apples.

Instead of lumping all of 2011's and 2012's games into one pile and all of 2013's into another, as Lochmann had done, Proppe analyzed comparable games from both seasons: noon games to noon games, afternoon games to afternoon games, and night games to night games. He noticed that, in 2011 and 2012, Michigan played a lot of noon games. In 2013, in contrast, Michigan had played one game at noon (Akron), two at 3:30 (Central Michigan and Minnesota), and one at 8 p.m., Notre Dame. Not incidentally, the quality of the opponent went up with the time of day. The distinction was crucial, Proppe knew, because students were far less likely to show up on time for noon games than 3:30 or night games, no matter what the seating policy.

"Look, I don't know how to say this without sounding like a jerk," Proppe told me, "but Hunter and his group were not as sophisticated as we were about analyzing data. When I looked at this data for ten minutes on an Excel spreadsheet, I could figure out what the data really meant. I realized once we segment it out by start time, the attendance for both being on time and showing up overall, was *worse* under the general-admission policy than it had been in 2011 and 2012. When Hunter gave me the data so quickly, and urged me to share it with the public, I don't think he realized that."

Looking at Lochmann's numbers, Proppe quickly recognized something else: The department measured attendance one way in 2011 and 2012, and a different way in 2013. In 2011 and 2012, they used the number of tickets scanned, which is a flawed system because the scanners depend on cellular service, which any fan can tell you is notoriously spotty in Michigan Stadium. "Department employees have told me the electronic scanning system can miss 5,000 to 10,000 tickets a game—or about 5 to 10 percent, a remarkably high margin of error," Proppe told me. "Yet these were the numbers Brandon used to justify switching to general admission.

"As shaky as that was, the department's system for tracking attendance in 2013 was even worse: They measured student attendance by the number of section cards they handed out to students, which the ushers handed to them when they walked into the stadium. But the number of section cards handed out was higher—significantly higher—than the number of tickets scanned. When I saw this, I called Hunter and said, 'We have to use the same measurement, which can only be tickets scanned, since they didn't use section cards before.'"

Lochmann agreed, and gave them the data for the number of tickets electronically scanned in 2013. Looking at data gathered with the same methodology revealed student attendance was actually lower in 2013 than it had been in 2012 and 2011. Instead of the 81 percent attendance rate the department presented, based on section cards handed out, the ticket scanning data showed a 76 percent attendance—which was obviously lower than the 79 percent attendance rate from tickets scanned in 2012 and 2011.

Likewise, the department's claim of an improved on-time rate from 45 percent in 2011 to 65 percent was at least overstated, as Lochmann's ticket-scanning data showed 61 percent of students showed up on time for the 2013 games.

But even at that, Proppe knew, the data would tell an even more dramatic story once it was broken down by game times. And that's a surprise he prepared for the meeting the next day.

To get all this done by the next day, Proppe stuck with his weekly routine that semester, working every night until two or three, then getting up at 6:30 a.m. But when Proppe walked to the Michigan Union that Friday, he had everything he needed in his bag. He was ready—and he knew it.

Proppe walked to the Michigan Union's Welker Room, armed only with his laptop, where he met Dishell and four other members of the Central Student Government. They were surrounded by about 20 other people, mostly faculty members, plus Royster Harper and Hunter Lochmann.

Professor Potter asked Lochmann to start the meeting by explaining the general-admission seating policy.

"Hunter talked about why they started the policy," Proppe recalls. "He explained the changes they'd made to respond to student complaints, and showed how well the policy had worked, based on their original data. He closed by saying, 'We're open to feedback.'"

Lochmann sat down, satisfied. Professor Potter thanked him, then asked Proppe to make his presentation. Before Proppe spoke, however, he noticed one of his former stats professors, Ed Rothman, in the first row. Proppe smiled. "I'm thinking, 'Great! He's on the committee. He's going to love this.'"

When Proppe took to the podium, he left his prepared remarks briefly to tell the committee, "I had a great stats prof, Dr. Rothman, sitting here in the first row. This is the guy who taught me about stratifying variables. When you're analyzing attendance, the stratifying variable is the start time of the game. If you miss that, you'll read the numbers incorrectly."

The trap, Dishell knew, sitting in the audience, had been set.

"You have to use a consistent basis of measurement," Proppe continued, "but the department's conclusions depend on two different bases for measuring attendance."

Proppe glanced at Professor Rothman, who was already nodding his agreement, grinning. From Proppe's introduction alone, Professor Rothman knew what was coming next.

Proppe then got to the two main tenets of his PowerPoint presentation.

"One: 76 percent of the students were opposed to the general-admission policy. The number one reason: it makes it harder to sit with your friends."

That complaint had arisen as soon as the policy was announced, and confirmed with the first four home games, but since then CSG had discovered a serious safety issue before the Notre Dame game. Proppe read a few quotes from the 1,234 students who had responded to his survey that they "felt unsafe/in danger of being trampled while waiting to get to my seat":

—"Going to football games is far less enjoyable now than it was during my 4 years of undergrad. It is much more stressful, been dangerous at times, and makes it hard to enjoy games with friends."

—"I have gotten hurt with people pushing and have felt extremely claustrophobic while waiting in not only one, but TWO different lines to get into my section."

—"I got my head slammed against a pole in a fight waiting in line."

This explained another stat Proppe had uncovered: Of those students who were initially supportive of the general-admission policy when it was announced, 27 percent of them were now opposed to it, compared to just 4 percent who were initially against it and were now for it. Put it all together, Proppe said, and you can safely conclude, "General admission, in practice, was turning people against it who initially liked the idea."

But that's what a claustrophobia-inducing mob will do.

Proppe then pointed out that the football team, despite a few wobbly victories, had a perfect 5–0 mark that season, and was ranked 18th in the AP poll. It would be hard to claim the students' dissatisfaction with the Michigan football experience was due to failure on the field.

"But we can agree," Proppe said, building to his crescendo, "if the students didn't like it, but it achieved the department's goals of better attendance and punctuality, we'd have to debate the cost-benefit analysis of the policy. But once you segment out the attendance data by start times, you can see that it did not achieve the department's stated goal, either."

He then ran through the rest of his PowerPoint presentation, flashing data that compared similar games from 2011 and 2012 to 2013, matching the relative quality of the opponent, the time of year, and most important, the start time.

Proppe started by comparing the data from the games that started at noon, then 3:30, then 8:00 p.m. Once separated by kind, or "stratified variables," as Professor Rothman had taught him, the data was damning. When Proppe clicked to a slide comparing the 2011 Western Michigan game and the 2012 Air Force game to the 2013 Central Michigan game, all of which started at

3:30, the numbers clearly showed that in 2011 and 2012, under the old system, more students showed up, and showed up on time, than in 2013, with fewer no-shows.

When he compared the two Notre Dame night games from 2011 and 2013, the slides showed the 2011 game attracted 727 more students at kickoff and 2,520 more total, with 1,413 fewer no-shows.

By Proppe's last slide, Professor Rothman and Bobby Dishell looked a lot happier than Hunter Lochmann did.

"So, in conclusion," Proppe said, "the students don't *like* the general-admission policy, and it *doesn't work*."

In a nutshell, if you examined the data professionally, there was nothing to debate.

When Proppe finished, the faculty members gave him an ovation. Lochmann sat at the same table, head down, taking notes.

When Professor Potter returned to the front of the room, he opened the floor for questions—and he got them, directed from the faculty to Lochmann, most of them critical.

The faculty wanted to know more about student safety, for example, and how Lochmann believed the GA policy fit in with the mission of the university. Lochmann struggled to answer these questions, but took them with good humor.

When they finished the drubbing, Professor Potter asked Lochmann, "Are you going to reconsider this policy at the end of the year?"

"Yes," he said, which surprised the crowd.

Proppe recalls, "Everyone kind of looked around at each other, kind of shocked, like, 'Did he just say that? Did we just get a win here?'"

A full 10 seconds passed before Laura Blake Jones, dean of students, said, "Hunter, did I just hear you say that getting rid of general admission is on the table at the end of the season?"

"Yes," he said. "It will have to be."

When the meeting adjourned, Dishell recalls, "We were so excited! We weren't sure if we should hug or high-five."

Instead, to make sure they didn't spoil the professional impression they had just made on the faculty members, they contained their excitement until they got out of the meeting room. Then their big smiles gave way to a quick high-five.

"Well, we've got some momentum!" Proppe said. But he didn't have any time to celebrate. He left the meeting at 1:30, ran home, grabbed his already packed bags, hopped in his parents' 2010 Chevy Impala, picked up three friends, then took off for Penn State.

Lochmann, likewise, had to bolt to the airport to catch Brandon's private plane. It's very likely, however, that Proppe's recap of the meeting with his friends in the Impala was more fun than Lochmann's review with his boss on the plane.

The next day, Saturday, Proppe was standing on the balcony of a friend's apartment on Beaver Avenue in State College, enjoying their pregame party, when he looked down to the sidewalk, saw people wearing Michigan shirts, and recognized Lochmann.

He yelled down, "Hunter!"

Lochmann turned, recognized him, and bellowed, "Proppe! What's up?"

These two, at least, had the ability to disagree without being disagreeable.

CHAPTER 44

HOKE'S TIPPING POINT

Michigan had problems getting past lowly Akron and UConn, but they were still 5–0, ranked 18th, and had a full roster of 85 scholarship players, 70 of whom traveled to Penn State. While the Wolverines were still recovering from the transfers and the weak recruiting class that inevitably followed Rich Rodriguez's final year in Ann Arbor, Brady Hoke and his staff were signing blue-chips at levels rarely seen in Ann Arbor. Most of their top recruits were still underclassmen, of course, but Hoke probably wouldn't have swapped his young recruits for the guys on the other side of the field.

Thanks to NCAA sanctions, Penn State had a mere 57 scholarship players in uniform that night. That was not their travel squad. They were playing at home, and that's all they had.

Even the 57 included a dozen glorified walk-ons—Penn State head coach Bill O'Brien called them "run-ons"—who received scholarships that year simply because no one else was going to claim them. The list included their starting long-snapper, Zach Ladonis, who just made the team a few weeks earlier in an all-campus try-out; their starting holder, Adam Geiger, a true freshman playing in his first game; and nine walk-ons on the kick coverage team. In sum, one of their special team units was composed almost entirely of walk-ons.

On paper, the Lions had no business battling the Wolverines. But on paper, the Lions should have folded the year before—twice—after Paterno was fired, then died, and the NCAA sanctions hit. Instead, the 2012 Lions posted a very surprising 8–4 mark. In State College, they had grown accustomed to ignoring the experts.

Against Michigan, the Nittany Lions mounted a 21–10 halftime lead, then helped Michigan jump ahead, 34–24 with 10 minutes left. But Michigan showed no killer instinct—from the coaches to the players—and failed to put Penn State away.

With less than two minutes remaining, holding a 34–27 lead with third-and-nine from the Penn State 27-yard line, the Wolverines needed one more first down to kill the clock, or even just a few more yards to kick a comfortable field goal to establish a 10-point lead. But they failed to snap the ball in time, losing 5 yards for delay of game.

How did this happen? It goes back to Hoke's unorthodox practice of not wearing a headset. If he had, his coaches would have told him to call a time-out before the clock ran out, or he could have simply looked at the play clock himself. Instead, he always relied on a student equipment manager to tell him when the clock was running down. On this particular play, however, according to student equipment managers I've talked with, the student in question was busy trying to find Fitzgerald Toussaint's helmet, and therefore wasn't by Hoke's side to tell him the clock was running down.

Why a $2.85 million-a-year coach would let his job security rest on the shoulders of an unpaid, non-scholarship student equipment manager is a valid question. When Hoke was an assistant coach under Carr, Schembechler was a big fan of his, personally and professionally. Schembechler never saw Hoke as a head coach, of course, but if he had, he might have asked the same question. When we talked in 2005, for his book, he felt compelled to discuss another coach who didn't wear a headset.

"I remember one time we were scouting a high-school player here in Michigan," he said, "but I couldn't take my eyes off of his head coach. The guy was just standing there on the sidelines, his arms folded, with no clipboard, no headset. Nothing! And he'd always stand 20 yards away from everyone else. If their opponents had the ball down by his 10-yard line—which seemed to happen a lot—he'd be standing out by the 50. His poor assistants—and why they worked for this guy is a mystery to me—had to keep running back and forth to him just to let him know what they were doing.

"I couldn't believe it! Honestly, what the hell is that? Why are they paying that guy? Why does he even show up for the games? Needless to say, his team was awful—undisciplined, unfocused, uninspired. But what would you expect, with no leader?"

After the delay-of-game call, the Wolverines lost 3 yards on a run, then punted the ball into the endzone. That was enough for Penn State's true-freshman quarterback Christian Hackenberg to run an impressive 80-yard drive in 33 seconds to tie the score and force overtime.

Michigan followed by blowing three chances to kick walk-off field goals, when the normally reliable Brendan Gibbons missed two and had another blocked.

Down 37–40 in the fourth overtime, and facing fourth-and-one on Michigan's 16, O'Brien had to make his big decision, one that would not have been debated by the coaches across the field. If you were playing not to lose—which seemed to be Michigan's plan—you wouldn't even think about it. You'd kick the field goal, and live to fight another overtime.

But not Bill O'Brien. He had only a few seconds to make his decision, but a lifetime of crunch-time calls to draw on. The ones he regretted most? When they played it safe, and lost. Whatever was going to happen next, he resolved, it wasn't going to be that.

"I looked down at the field," he told me, "and the grass had been all chewed up. We'd run about 180 plays on that field. I looked at the players, and they'd all emptied their tanks—and we don't have as many subs as Michigan does. I figured it was time to take our chances, and win the game. If we didn't, we didn't."

After Penn State tailback Bill Belton cut through Michigan's line for 3 yards and a first down, it seemed inevitable that the Nittany Lions were headed for the endzone—and four plays later, they were, when Belton ran up the middle, bounced to the left, and trotted across the goal line.

Beaver Stadium's ancient press box shook for minutes. It was more than a celebration. It sounded like salvation.

After the loss, Michigan fans were apoplectic, with a critical mass of fans openly wondering for the first time if Hoke was the right man for Michigan.

It was clear after that devastating—and easily avoidable—loss that Hoke would no longer be judged by the happy transition from Rodriguez, but by whatever happened next.

Hoke reached his tipping point with the fans later than Dave Brandon had, but after the Penn State loss, Hoke was now in the same uncomfortable position Brandon was in: having to prove to the faithful that they could do their jobs.

CHAPTER 45

EARLY MORNING E-MAIL

After Michael Proppe spent two nights in State College, PA, on the floor of a friend of a friend's apartment, college-style, then finished the seven-hour drive back in his packed Chevy Impala Sunday night, he was predictably exhausted when he got to his parents' home. Fortunately, the following week was Michigan's fall break, with no classes on Monday or Tuesday.

"That was a real blessing," Proppe said. "I had a lot of work to catch up on. So it was nice to go to my parents' home, and to get away from Ann Arbor for a bit, and all that went with it."

By Monday, Proppe refocused on the CSG work at hand. "We had to take all the data we had gathered and put it into an actual statistics report—something more formal than a PowerPoint, about 15 pages long. I e-mailed the full report to Hunter at 12:45 a.m. Tuesday, the night before I returned to campus.

"I thought we had made a very solid argument in the meeting, and a really solid argument in the report, and I wanted to get this out there sooner than later, and I wanted the students to know we were working on this issue. But I wanted to give Hunter a heads-up that our report was going out, as a courtesy."

Proppe e-mailed Lochmann, "We probably will publish this (or a version of it) on our Web site. Is there anything included in here that you gave us that you want to keep internal (i.e. attendance numbers, broken scanner at CMU game)?"

"In hindsight," Proppe says now, "I was way too nice even to ask the question. But I knew we had the upper hand and, given that Hunter said he wanted to be transparent about attendance numbers, I really didn't think there would be a problem."

On Tuesday morning, October 15, Proppe got himself out of bed after five hours of sleep so he could get to Ann Arbor in time for an 8:30 a.m. meeting to finalize plans with the food service people to open a 24-hour café in the Duderstadt Library on North Campus.

At 6:45 a.m., Proppe was literally out the door, walking toward the Chevy Impala in the driveway, while he checked his e-mail on his phone.

He saw an e-mail from Lochmann, which came in at 5:28 a.m., less than five hours after Proppe had e-mailed him.

"Good morning, Mike," wrote Lochmann, who usually responded to Proppe's e-mails within a day or two, and his requests for a meeting within a few weeks. Not this time. After some pleasantries, Lochmann asked to meet to go over Proppe's report because, he said, he wanted to keep "a bunch of this" private for now, such as the specific scan counts. "Also," Lochman wrote, "we need your help not painting the AD in such a negative light . . . if we aren't careful we will be playing defense and in this case I think unfairly."

Proppe stopped before he got to his car, turned back into his house, and responded before he drove to Ann Arbor.

"I wasn't rattled," he says, "but I was surprised. Lochmann had never been that responsive."

Proppe also noted that the bit of data Lochmann specifically requested be kept "internal right now and potentially forever," the ticket scan numbers, was exactly the datum Lochmann had said they wanted to be completely transparent about the previous week—when they still thought it made them look good. Apparently, Proppe's Friday presentation had changed Lochmann's view of the department's own numbers.

Proppe responded immediately, giving Lochmann the answer he knew he wanted to hear: He would hold back the CSG report on the general admission policy until they met. Proppe's growing political instincts, however, told him something else.

"Lochmann's response also told me I had a bit of power," Proppe says, "because it's clear I have information they don't want out there. I wrote, 'Let's meet to discuss this, and hopefully soon. Here's my schedule.' The way we left it, we wanted the information out there, and they were going to consider it."

The next day, Wednesday, October 16, 2013, Lochmann cleared time on his schedule to meet with Proppe and Dishell in his office.

"When we walked through our report," Proppe recalls, "Hunter had no questions about our methodology or our data, with one exception: He pointed out our survey hadn't asked the students for their class standing—which admittedly was a miss on our part."

But that was a minor matter, one Lochmann didn't bother pressing. Instead, Proppe recalls, "He just said, 'We don't want this published.'"

"We said, 'Okay, the attendance is yours. You do own that data.' Bobby and I thought, if we're going to doing anything for the students on this, we'll need the department down the road. No point losing them now, over something like that. We tried to walk down the middle, because we were playing a long-term game."

A longer term game, perhaps, than the paid professionals running the department seemed to be playing.

"But," Proppe told Lochmann, "the student opinion data are ours. We'll publish our information, but not yours."

Relieved, Lochmann nodded. He then pushed his second objective: "Let's meet in December, after we have a whole season to review the policy, and let's see where things are at."

"Okay, fine," Proppe said, but he was not about to let the department off the hook on its promise, stated before the SRAC faculty, that they would consider scrapping the GA policy. "Let's put out a press release saying you're going to meet with us in December. We want this in the *Daily*, AnnArbor .com, and the Detroit papers. And we're going to publish our data."

"Fair enough," Lochmann said.

After an hour of horse-trading, they ended the meeting amicably. Proppe and Dishell went home to draft a press release and e-mailed it to Lochmann. He replied by e-mail that he wanted to take one part out: that the department was going to reconsider the GA policy. "It sounds like we're going to get rid of general admission, and we don't want to say this, because we don't know if we will."

"Okay," Proppe replied. "What do you want to say?"

"Let's say, 'We're going to evaluate the policy based on student input.'"

"Okay," Proppe said. "As long as we have you on the record saying you're willing to make changes to the policy, that gives us enough leverage to move forward."

Late that night, the CSG released its full report on its Web site and to every media outlet that covers the University of Michigan. They removed the number of scanned tickets from the report, per Lochmann's request, but their report still told quite a story, with 76 percent of students responding that they did not like the general-admission seating policy, and even more saying they preferred the old, seniority-based system. Because this was the first time the students or media saw CSG's survey results, it confirmed for thousands of students that they weren't alone, and weren't being unreasonable.

"That was basically it," Proppe recalls of their exchanges with the department, "for the rest of the season."

Decision after decision revealed the department's leadership to reject opportunities to be collaborative, transparent, and objective—the very pillars of the institution it represented.

The college kids, on the other hand, were willing to collect, compile, and share solid data and analyze the situation impartially.

The students were beating the sharpies at their own game—and in the process, the values the university espoused were enjoying a minor resurgence.

CHAPTER 46

WRONG-WAY WOLVERINES

Against an upstart Indiana team, Devin Gardner broke his former roommate's school records with 584 yards of total offense and 503 yards passing, with 5 touchdowns. Jeremy Gallon set a Big Ten record 369 yards receiving, and the Wolverines set another school record with 751 yards of offense.

But whenever Michigan's offense finally got going, the defense seemed to disappear—and vice versa. Michgan's defense gave up 572 yards to Indiana's offense, second only to the 624 yards the 2007 team yielded to a powerhouse Oregon team, led by Heisman trophy candidate Dennis Dixon.

Add it up, and you get a 63–47 Michigan victory.

"We've got to play better," Hoke said. "You don't win championships without playing defense."

The Wolverines were 6–1, until they rode to East Lansing to play the Spartans. The final score said Michigan State 29, Michigan 6, but the Spartans did a lot more damage than that. They sacked Gardner seven times, and held Michigan to minus-48 yards rushing.

After the Spartans beat their archrival for the fifth time in six years, Michigan State was 8–1 overall, 5–0 in conference, and playing for a Big Ten title. The Wolverines were 6–2, 2–2 in the Big Ten, and were playing to keep their fans from jumping off the bandwagon.

But to the fans' credit, only the fringe was calling for Hoke's head. His two great recruiting classes were just starting to get playing time, and even hinting that the coach was in trouble could scare off the next class of recruits. Further, if Michigan fired two consecutive coaches after giving both only three years each, the program would look like a revolving door that no credible coaching candidate would even consider.

The fans were hanging in there. According to the attendance data, from 2010 to 2013, ticket sales fell only slightly, with an average of 101,023 paying customers per game, and 3,143 freebies. Once again that season, only one nonconference game failed to sell 100,000 tickets: Akron, at 95,978, with an additional 7,017 receiving complimentary tickets. The attendance streak, therefore, was still alive—but it was looking increasingly vulnerable.

Anyone looking ahead would have seen another looming problem: Michigan's 2014 home schedule, arguably the worst in Michigan's long history. Instead of hosting Notre Dame, Michigan State, or Ohio State, Michigan would be bringing Miami of Ohio, Maryland, and yes, Appalachian State. But the prices for those historically unappealing tickets were still highest in the Big Ten.

Michigan's bean counters were worried that thousands of fans, already pushed to the limit, might finally drop their tickets and break Michigan's 38-year streak of 100,000-plus crowds.

A few more losses in 2013 wouldn't help generate much-needed enthusiasm for 2014.

The Wolverines stumbled home from East Lansing with their pride wounded. But because Brady Hoke had still not lost a game in the Big House as head coach, the Wolverines remained 19–0 at home, the longest such streak in the country, with an underwhelming, unranked Nebraska squad coming to town.

None of it mattered. Right from the start, the Cornhuskers' defense manhandled Michigan's offense almost as badly as the Spartans had. After Michigan finished its second drive of the game with two sacks and minus-20 yards, the fans started booing the team—a rarity in Ann Arbor. The Cornhuskers left the Wolverines with minus-21 yards on 36 carries, and a demoralizing 17–13 loss to ponder.

"I have to do a better job coaching this football team," Hoke said.

Devin Gardner was less diplomatic. "Whoever questions our toughness, they can shove it."

The Wolverines traveled to Evanston the next weekend, November 16, to steal one in triple overtime, 27–19, from luckless Northwestern.

Seemingly on a roll, the following game Michigan pulled ahead 21–7 against Iowa at halftime, but the Wolverines' offense could manage only 45 yards and no points in the second half. They had to watch the Hawkeyes put up 17 unanswered points to take a 24–21 lead. The Wolverines were driving, however, with 2:12 left, when Gardner fumbled the ball, effectively ending the game.

"I lost the game by myself," Gardner said.

Michigan had just dropped four of its last six games to fall to a 7–4 overall record, and 3–4 in the Big Ten. They were now playing for a shot at a mediocre bowl game, and the slim chance for salvation with a major upset over undefeated Ohio State. With the 11–0 Buckeyes coming to Ann Arbor to take on the wobbly Wolverines, the criticism of Brady Hoke from fans and media alike was getting loud enough that Brandon felt compelled to address it publicly.

On Wednesday, November 27, 2013, just three days before the Ohio State game, he posted an entry in "Dave's Blog," his weekly outlet on MGoBlue.com, the department's official Web site. Nothing unusual about that. But his subject was: Brady Hoke and his job security.

To no one's surprise, Brandon came out unequivocally in support of his head coach. "The only threat to our continued success in recruiting," Brandon wrote, "is the same old, tired tactic being used by some who wish to see us fail—to try and scare young recruits into believing that our coach 'is on the hot seat'—which simply isn't true. I have seen firsthand what Brady and his coaching staff are doing to make this program better. It takes time and sometimes patience by all of us before we can build the consistent winner that meets our expectations."

Once again, Brandon did not depict Michigan's family as being all in it together, but "Us against the world."

Jamie Morris noticed something else in the letter he calls "The Brandon Doctrine," which he paraphrased: " 'We're going to be fine, because Hoke, Mattison, and I are going to lead this team.' When you see Dave, in writing, mention the top two coaches and not Al Borges, everyone knew Borges was gone."

I've often joked that some Michigan football fans aren't happy unless they're not happy. But after 11 games, even an optimist would have plenty to be unhappy about.

The Wolverines had been surprisingly bad all season, and Michigan fans had reason to fear the worst against the Buckeyes. Urban Meyer had already demonstrated a Woody Hayes–like penchant for burying teams. If Meyer had the chance, it was not hard to imagine him following in Hayes's footsteps, running up the score against That School Up North, and then going for the two-point conversion. Why? "Because they wouldn't let me go for three."

But the Wolverines thought different. "The guys in that room and the guys in this program were the only ones that knew what was going to happen today," Taylor Lewan said afterward. "We were ready to fight. Everyone was fighting for each other. . . . I'm proud of these guys."

With almost everyone in the Big House fearing a blowout, the first quarter ended 14–14. The first half ended 21–21. The Wolverines were in it to win it. The offensive linemen were effective, but the coaching staff finally made it easier for them by giving Devin Gardner quick-developing plays, with the option to pass or run—something resembling the spread option offense.

"A lot of people didn't like Borges," Gardner said, when we talked in 2015. "But I really didn't care about that. I just wanted to do my job. Against Ohio State, Borges mixed it up, allowed me to run first, and gave me a chance.

"Denard [Robinson] was just like a bolt of lightning—a freak of nature. His gaps are five feet. Mine might be five inches, but I can get a first down. Once we ran a few, they had to respect that. After that, when I dropped back I could pass, because they didn't know what I was going to do. 'Oh, he's dropping back? What should I do? Rush!' Too late! I've already completed the pass."

But in a second-quarter scrum, Gardner broke a bone in his left foot. "I knew it immediately," he told me. "I was almost in tears. But I didn't take any shots—nothing. Man, it hurt like hell—but I didn't care. I could have broken a thigh bone and kept playing. Nothing was going to stop me from finishing that game."

But in a season when Michigan could never get both sides of the ball playing their best, the offense was as focused as the defense was lost, giving up 6 touchdowns to the Buckeyes. Finally, in the waning seconds, Gardner threw a 2-yard touchdown pass to Devin Funchess to pull within one, 42–41. But instead of kicking the extra point for the tie and possibly pushing the game to overtime, Hoke asked his players if they wanted to go for the two-point conversion, and the win.

They were unanimous.

"We played the game to win," Hoke said afterward.

Like his teammates—and a majority of the crowd, it seemed, which cheered the decision—Gardner agreed with Hoke's decision to go for it, but not with the play itself, which they had already used that game. The play called for Drew Dileo to run just over the goal line, then turn back to Gardner, who would fire that instant.

When I started to explain to Gardner that I'd since learned the Ohio State coaches and players already knew, after the time-out, what Michigan's coaches had called and were ready for it, he cut me off midsentence by raising a hand.

"I know, I know," he said, with a resigned grin. "They [the Buckeyes] called a time-out, and we come back with the same look, the same play. When you see them set up, you knew they were ready for us.

"I'm pretty sure the only person who didn't know they knew was Al Borges. That's the only way they covered it so well."

Gardner might have been stoic about how it went down, but the resulting loss still stung, more than a year later.

"My least favorite moment of my career had to be the end of that Ohio State game. It's the biggest game of the year, we had just run a perfect two-minute drill, and we're losing by just one point. Everyone was covered and I was about to get tackled. Had to get rid of it. But I beat myself up about that for a long time."

Afterward, many people online opined that Borges called the play partly to avoid Gardner having to run, or even roll out, on his broken foot. Gardner shook his head.

"My foot was broken, but I've come this far. I'd already run on it on a third-and-nine—and made it. Man, give me the ball! I'll run this thing! I'll jump over this pile! I'll make something happen."

Still, the team's effort was so good—and so surprising—it might have been the first time in history Michigan fans felt better about their team after a loss than before it.

The most common reaction that week: Where was *that* team all year? And which team would return next year—the one that got crushed by Michigan State, or the one that almost beat the Buckeyes?

Fans got a hint in the Buffalo Wild Wings Bowl, when the Wolverines had to play Shane Morris in place of the injured Devin Gardner, and lost to Kansas State, 31–14.

CHAPTER 47

CSG SHOWDOWN

While the football fans simmered over Michigan's 7–5 regular-season record, Central Student Government leaders Michael Proppe and Bobby Dishell met with just about everyone who ran the university, including three executive officers, six Regents, and President Coleman herself, all in separate meetings.

Each time, they were met with a respectful listener and, usually, gained a supporter for their cause to end general admission seating, but it was rarely easy. The one exception was Regent Mark Bernstein, who had actually dared to go into the student section before the Notre Dame game to see how general admission was facing its first real test. He saw the veal pens, the ropes, the long waits, and the dangerous pushing and shoving at the top of the gates. His first question for the CSG leaders was a simple one: "How messed up is this GA policy?"

This was in noted contrast to the other Regents' initial questions. "Invariably," Proppe recalled, "the first thing they'd say is, 'Don't you think Dave Brandon has a great point about student attendance and students showing up before kickoff?' "

No one offered this more eagerly than President Coleman herself.

"We were nervous before every meeting with her," Proppe says of their monthly, standing appointment. When they met at her office in November, she led with the predictable opening about Brandon having a great point about student attendance and punctuality. Nervous though they were, they mustered the confidence to say, "No, we don't. In fact, here's the data: General admission has made attendance and tardiness worse."

"Once that argument was cut away," Proppe says, "they were really receptive to the concerns students have about the policy."

Over breakfast with Regent Andrea Fisher Newman, an ardent supporter of Brandon's, she thanked them for the report, and promised to read it. She said, "You guys are up against a very powerful athletic director, but maybe we have to have this next meeting with Dave Brandon."

That was a good idea, one Proppe and Dishell would have been eager to pursue. But the meeting never materialized, which they believe hurt Brandon more than anyone. What's striking is how easy it would have been for Brandon to meet with them, at his convenience. They would have come running, or he could have simply walked down a flight of steps when they were already in his building, meeting with Lochmann and others, often in the Champions Room directly below Brandon'soffice.

"I think he could have conceivably disarmed us to some degree just by meeting with us," Proppe told me. "We still believed in our data, and the policy we made from it. But it's harder to rail against a person you have a relationship with. And I didn't have a relationship with Dave Brandon. He's kind of a bogeyman; he's put in these policies that people hate, and he delegated the fallout for subordinates to face.

"He made it very easy to turn him into a villain in the students' eyes, and I had no reason to push against that narrative. I didn't know him."

Proppe and Dishell gained allies quickly among the university leaders, but progress with the department was much slower. In an e-mail exchange that started on December 2, and went back and forth through December 10, Lochmann started hinting that the department was less willing to consider dropping general admission than he'd stated in the faculty meeting. He wrote, "As for pushing forward with GA, that is the first question we'll ask ourselves . . . but we still think the pros outweigh the cons."

Undeterred, Proppe and Dishell came up with a proposal for a new seating policy—rewarding students who showed up to games on time with better seats, which is what Brandon wanted, and allowing students to form seating groups, which is what the students wanted, and seating them by the group's average number of points earned.

When they pitched it to Lochmann, he praised them. "When we say 'Leaders and Best,' this is what we're talking about." But he quickly added he was not sure their plan was feasible. In response, Proppe went home that afternoon and whipped up an Excel spreadsheet that automatically reassigned seats based on attendance, and e-mailed it to Hunter.

Four days later, on December 10, Lochmann e-mailed Proppe and Dishell, liberally using his trademark elipses. "Thanks for sending this as well as coming up with the idea. . . . Again, while innovative, it's fraught with infrastructure issues as discussed (mostly staffing, technology, etc.) . . . something to look for in the future potentially. In the meantime, we need your feedback and help making the GA experience the best GA experience in college football as this is where we netted out collectively after meeting on Friday."

Leaving the phrase "netted out collectictvely" aside, the duo concluded Lochmann was humoring them. "Nice try with your Plan B," he seemed to be saying. "Now please let's get back to putting your credibility with your constituents behind our Plan A."

All this came to a head on Thursday, December 12. Proppe and Dishell were scheduled to meet with Lochmann in the Champions Room, but this time they would be joined by Shelly Fabrizio, and Rob Rademacher from the department. For support, Proppe and Dishell decided to invite CSG program manager Julio Cardona, who had completed his doctorate in Education in May.

Cardona brought several strengths to the table. Because he knew he was going to be at Michigan only one year before rejoining his wife back at Stanford, he wasn't overly concerned about univesity politics. He was also, Proppe says, "a very smart guy. When we were brainstorming on this or that, we'd throw ideas at him and he'd throw objections back. Great sounding board. And it didn't hurt that he's a big guy, maybe 6-foot-4 and 250. Not easily intimidated."

Before their meeting, Proppe and Dishell—still exhausted from final exams—told Julio, "We don't know how this is going to go, but we do know we want to walk out of this meeting being the moderate voice of reason, just trying to get to a solution. But if *you* want to say something to them, feel free."

They met in the Champions Room, the glass-enclosed meeting space at the entrance of Weidenbach Hall.

As Proppe recalls, "Hunter kicked off the meeting by saying, 'We've reviewed your data, we've reviewed your report, we've reviewed the attendance numbers—and looking at all this, the decision to stick with general admission was pretty easy, so that's what we're going to do.'"

Proppe was flabbergasted.

"At this moment, I'm thinking, 'Are you serious?' Sure, we're emotional, and we're into this, but I think our data is so solid, that there is frankly no way a rational person could take a look at it and disagree with our conclusion.

We were trying to be dispassionate observers, with the facts—but this tested me."

Proppe looked at Bobby, then Julio, and then Hunter. Proppe came armed with even more clear-as-day data—charts and graphs and a copy of their report—and he was prepared to use it.

"Why?" Proppe finally said to Lochmann. "I object to that. You had a lot of 3:30 games this year. That's why you think attendance is up. But if you compare this year's 3:30 games to last year's 3:30 games, attendance is *down*."

Lochmann was ready with a response, though not a very good one. "Well," he said, "this year's 3:30 games are not comparable to last year's 3:30 games."

"I disagree with you," Proppe said, keeping his cool and sticking to the facts. "How are they not comparable?"

Although Lochmann had no good answers—even the opponents, dates, and weather were comparable—he refused to concede the point. As Proppe told me, "You can only argue over 'two plus two equals four' for so long. At some point, if he wanted to keep arguing that the games weren't comparable, with no evidence, there's not a lot you can do."

What was stunning about this exchange—so unlike others on campus—is that they could not even agree on the facts, let alone think creatively about a solution. It was not the give-and-take of a community of academics working together to solve a problem, but the stonewalling of businessmen who've decided not to negotiate.

Lochmann and his staff then started trying to take CSG's plan apart, point by point, with each objection sillier than the last. Lochmann asked how they would reassign seats, when they had just handed everyone a detailed program that actually did exactly that, and worked quite smoothly. Then Lochmann and company argued CSG's plan would require more staffing, until Proppe pointed out it would actually require less—and Michigan's ushers are volunteer, in any case. Then they claimed CSG's plan depended on the scanners working accurately, which no one could guarantee, when Proppe replied that their plan depended on exactly the same scanners general admission did.

As this Kafkaesque exercise continued, Proppe and Dishell were about to burst, but Julio Cardona beat them to the punch.

"Julio had had enough," Proppe told me. "He slapped down his legal pad—which got everyone's attention—and said, 'These guys came in here with a plan that you were supposed to vet, but all I hear from you guys is excuses! "Oh, I have to buy a new scanner!" Those cost $10,000—but you're willing to spend $10 *million* for Wi-Fi service in the stadium that the students have told you, in their survey, they don't care about? You guys have so much money to spend compared to everyone else at this university, how can that be an excuse?"

Lochmann jumped in. "Julio, Julio—we're not a bank here! It's not like we're making unlimited amounts of money. I would love to sit down with you and talk you through athletic-department finances, so you can go up on the hill and evangelize for us, but we don't have the money to implement this plan."

This is where Lochmann unwittingly walked into the plan the trio had established before they'd arrived.

"Now, I get to be the moderator," Proppe recalled. "The calm voice of reason."

"Wait—we all want the same thing here," Proppe told everyone sitting at the table. "We want students to get to the stadium, and get there early, and we want them to be happy."

With that, Lochmann followed Proppe's lead and shifted his tone, too. He tried to give the conversation a positive turn, delivering a prepared list of changes they were willing to make. But it didn't take Proppe and Dishell too long to realize all their concessions were as pointless as their objections, including changing the markers for the student sections from H-O-K-E back to the original section numbers, which no one had complained about. Further, Proppe recalls, all of Lochmann's concessions were either irrelevant, like the section numbers, or would benefit the department, not the students. They weren't concessions at all.

Unfortunately for both Brandon and Lochmann, the people they were talking to—be they Michigan fans, alumni, students, lettermen or CSG's elected leaders—were definitely not stupid. And for that reason, they often concluded the department's ideas were.

"Hunter," Proppe finally said, struggling to stay calm, "what you're proposing is not going to address the issues that we care about. We need to think more creatively about this, and focus on how to solve it."

The meeting ended there, well short of the hour they'd planned to spend together. Proppe doesn't know if Lochmann and Brandon—who remained in his office, directly above the Champions Room, throughout the meeting taking place below—genuinely thought the CSG leaders would be satisfied with Lochmann's flimsy responses and drop their plan, or they simply didn't care what the student leaders thought.

Proppe also didn't know if Brandon and Lochmann knew the Regents had already invited Proppe and Dishell to speak at their monthly meeting in one week about the progress they had made working with the athletic department's leaders on the general-admission policy.

Proppe and Dishell intended to tell the Regents whatever they wanted to know.

Proppe e-mailed Annette Howe to ask if he might be able to meet with her boss before the Regents' meeting. That was not possible, yet again, but she was able to set up a phone call six days after their meeting with Lochmann, on the eve of the Thursday, December 19, Regents meeting.

After a few pleasantries, Proppe told Brandon, "Here's where we are with Hunter." Although Proppe assumed Brandon had already been debriefed by Lochmann days ago, he gave him the rundown of the previous week's meeting. After the review, Proppe said to Brandon, "We need to think more creatively about this. The students are not happy."

"Brandon actually said, 'Well, we might be able to work something out. The students who are being good citizens and showing up on time, maybe they can get assigned seats,'" which was exactly the policy that was making the students unhappy.

"This is not what we're talking about," Proppe said. "We need something that's going to work for *all* students."

Brandon replied, "Michael, you're a smart guy. You're a business student. If students don't use their tickets, I'm going to keep raising the price."

"Wait—*what?*" Proppe asked, thinking he could not possibly have heard Brandon correctly.

"If students don't use their tickets, I'm going to keep raising the price, until it becomes valuable enough for them to use it."

After a long pause, Proppe refrained from replying to that idea, turning the conversation back to CSG's report, and the data. He repeated the thrust of it: "Attendance is not higher under general admission, and students don't like it"—but Brandon wasn't interested.

"Hey," he said, "I think you can make the numbers say whatever you want them to say."

"And that's the thing that really got me," Proppe told me. "Brandon has this reputation for being a data-driven guy, all left brain and logical, and here we are in a fight over data, and he's not paying the slightest attention to what's crystal clear in the numbers. We were not making an emotional argument to him." They were speaking in what they thought was the language of business, numbers—Brandon's language.

But their communication problem ran deeper than that. By Brandon's own stated priorities, he focused on two things: the group he considered his "shareholders," the student-athletes, and his reputation. He did not seem to be worried about the students, or the community they came from. It's not that he couldn't understand Proppe's presentation. He didn't try.

Brandon got the last word. "I think the message you need to give to the Regents tomorrow is, 'We're working on this, and we're trying to get to the solution.' "

Proppe refused to agree, while trying to avoid restarting the same circular arguments.

"I wasn't going to say, 'Oh yes, that's what I'll do!' It obviously wasn't true."

Instead, he once again reached for the diplomatic response: "I hear what you're saying, and I thank you for your time."

On Thursday, December 19, 2013, at 3 p.m., Proppe walked to the podium at the end of the Regents' long table and laid down his papers. He addressed the Regents sitting in front of him, and the observers—staffers, reporters, interested faculty, students, and citizens—sitting along both walls.

"Now that the football season is over," Proppe said, "we have had a chance to review the numbers on the general admission seating policy. Unfortunately, we haven't seen the improved attendance numbers the policy was supposed to generate.

"We spent some time in the last few weeks working with Athletics to design a survey on this as a follow-up to the survey we put out in October. Those results are still rolling in, but the preliminary results are not too surprising. The biggest problem students have with the policy is actually *not* that seniors didn't get their reserved seats in the front. The biggest problem is that it is really hard to sit with your friends. . . . We are working with Dave Brandon and Hunter Lochmann in Athletics to address this problem and help design next year's policy."

After listing the four basic tenets guiding their work, he wrapped up his remarks by saying, "We are already floating some proposed changes for next year and those are in the process of being vetted by the Athletic Department. I'm hopeful they will come back and let us know what will work, what won't work—and *why*."

After Proppe's previous appearances at Regents' meetings, they had no follow-up questions, but this time the Regents had a lot to say.

Regent Denise Ilitch, whose parents own Little Caesar's and the Detroit Red Wings and Tigers, said, "I've heard a lot of complaints about this general admission policy, and I encourage you to be very tenacious in working with the athletic department on this."

Proppe recalls, "So you're thinking, 'All right. They're on our side.'"

Andrea Fisher Newman spoke next. "We are very impressed with the way you've gone about working on this policy, gathering a lot of input from students, doing it in a way that's nice. And we want to help you solve this."

Mark Bernstein echoed his fellow Regents' comments, and added, a bit more explicitly than the others, "We're supportive of your efforts on this, and please keep us updated."

Due to the beefed-up media there to watch Proppe's presentation, word of the meeting, and the Regents' response, got out very quickly. The readers naturally included Hunter Lochmann.

The next day, Friday, December 20, 2013, Proppe returned to his parents' home in Plymouth for winter break, for a much-needed few weeks of rest and relaxation. But he did see an e-mail from Julio Cardona that day, addressed to both Proppe and Dishell. "Hunter called," Cardona wrote, "and sounded really stressed out. He wants to make up."

After the Regents' meeting, Lochmann suddenly wanted to make peace with the same student leaders he had summarily dismissed a week earlier. Proppe and Dishell grasped the significance immediately. They were no longer voices in the wilderness. On December 19, 2013, they had been joined by the people who stood atop the university ladder—people who possessed a power Brandon should have understood only too well.

The tide had officially turned against Brandon—but it was not clear if he recognized the sea change.

PART VI: 2014

THE FALL

CHAPTER 48

PRESIDENT SCHLISSEL'S INTRODUCTION

The presidential search started in the spring of 2013 and lasted about nine months. Amazingly, the Regents kept the process and the list of candidates completely confidential—no small feat in the Internet age. To this day, not one candidate's name has leaked to the public. Virtually no one outside the Regents knew who was even being considered.

Thus, on Friday, January 24, 2014, when Michigan prepared to introduce its new president on the university simulcast, hundreds of employees across Michigan's campus stopped what they were doing and gathered in their conference rooms to find out for the first time who Michigan's next leader would be. Speaking from the Michigan Union's Kuenzel Room, Regent Andrea Fischer Newman announced Michigan's fourteenth president would be the former provost of Brown University, Mark Schlissel, 56, who would assume Michigan's top office on July 1, 2014.

Schlissel's curriculum vitae could hardly be more impressive. A native of New York City, Schlissel graduated summa cum laude from Princeton University with a degree in Biochemical Sciences, then earned both MD and PhD degrees at the Johns Hopkins School of Medicine. He did his postdoctoral research on the developmental biology of the immune system at MIT, then returned to Johns Hopkins as a faculty member, where he won awards for his research.

You get the idea: The man is world-class brilliant.

But Michigan's Regents were just as impressed by Schlissel's commitment to educating others, including undergraduates. At Johns Hopkins, he earned awards for his teaching. He then served as dean of Biological Sciences at Berkeley, where he taught immunology to graduate students, and the gateway course in biology required of all undergraduate life-science majors. It's clear he takes seriously the core mission of the university. Throw in Schlissel's success as an educational leader at Brown, and Michigan had recruited, in the words of Regent Larry Deitch, "simply the best of the best."

And that is exactly how the president-elect came across when he stood up to speak at his first press conference, with hundreds of U-M employees watching.

"We were all in awe," said a friend of mine, who was watching with his university colleagues. "He was answering every question just as we would hope, and he was clearly brilliant and had a great sense of humor. Then a reporter asked him about athletics. He said a lot of the right things—I think everyone loved it when he said that when you google U-M, the top ten results are athletics, and he wanted to get the balance more toward academics—but he also said something like, 'Brown has more varsity sports than Michigan,' and implied the difference was just a matter of degrees."

In fact, Schlissel said, in part, ". . . obviously it's an area that I do have to learn a lot about because at my current institution, you'd be surprised to know, athletics is a big part of campus life, but it doesn't happen on a national stage very often, for example. You might be surprised to know my current institution has 37 intercollegiate athletics teams. That's actually more than this institution, so it's not that sports don't permeate the campus, it's just at a different level."

At that, my friend recalls, "All of us looked at each other and kind went, 'Aww. That's cute.' To his credit, he knew he had a lot to learn. But I think all of us thought, he has *no* idea just how much."

The Ann Arbor News noted Schlissel's responsibilities had grown, literally overnight, from being "second-in-command of an Ivy League institution with 8,620 students, 3,630 full-time employees—including 1,050 faculty—and an $854 million annual operating budget to leading a public university with enrollment nearing 44,000, a workforce of 22,000, and a budget exceeding $6 billion a year. He'll oversee the management of the largest health system in Michigan, as well at U-M's campuses in Flint and Dearborn."

Because President-elect Schlissel had no real experience with big-time college athletics, no one expected the athletic department to be the centerpiece of his presidency—or anyone's, for that matter. Besides, despite a few bumps the previous year, no one expected the athletic department to be in dire need of intense presidential management, either.

"When we hired him," Regent Andrea Fischer Newman recalls, "we told him, 'You won't have to worry about athletics for a while. We've got a great athletic director in place, with a long-term contract.'

"We told him that! Well, there we are."

A mere four days after President Schlissel's introduction, the *Michigan Daily* came out with a bombshell: The football team's starting kicker, Brendan Gibbons, "was permanently separated from the University of Michigan last month for violating the University's Student Sexual Misconduct Policy," effective December 20, 2013.

The expulsion stemmed from an encounter between Gibbons and a female student on November 22, 2009. The four-year delay between the incident and Gibbons's punishment predictably raised suspicions that the department had postponed Gibbons's punishment as long as possible so he could keep kicking field goals for the team.

Even now, very little can be said with absolute certainty. But we do know the woman contacted the Ann Arbor Police that night, then decided not to press charges. In 2009, the university would not investigate such cases unless the alleged victim came forward. But in 2011, the Department of Education told schools to take action if a "preponderance of evidence" indicated sexual harassment or violence, a much lower burden of proof, one that did not require the alleged victim's cooperation.

The new standard also came with a threat to revoke federal funding if the DOE found schools insufficiently aggressive in pursuing complaints, though it's highly doubtful fear of losing federal funding affected Michigan's approach. There is no question, however, that Michigan ruled the new threshold had been reached when officials discovered the alleged victim was giving numerous speeches about the incident on campus.

Thus, in August of 2013, Michigan reopened Gibbons's case. On November 20, 2013, the university concluded that Gibbons "engaged in unwanted or unwelcome conduct of a sexual nature, committed without valid consent, and that conduct was so severe as to create a hostile, offensive, or abusive environment." Gibbons did not appeal the decision, and left Michigan's campus.

I have since spoken privately with people I trust in the athletic department, in student government, and in the Fleming Administration Building—informed people I believe would tell me the truth about the university's conduct, right or wrong. From everything I've seen and heard, the university played the Gibbons case as straight as it could, both before and after the Department of Education changed the rules. Just as important, I have found no evidence, and heard no witnesses suggest, that the athletic department attempted to interfere with the process in any way.

That's the good news.

The bad news is, after the university did the hard part right, the athletic department seemed determined to get the easy part wrong. Hoke played Gibbons three days after the university's ruling, on November 23. Although it is possible Hoke didn't know of the ruling, it didn't look good in hindsight. Then Hoke claimed Gibbons did not dress for the Ohio State game because of a leg injury, and later said Gibbons went home before the bowl game due to a "family matter."

It is entirely possible that Hoke was following instructions, but the various ham-handed responses coming from the department—including flat-out lies—gave the appearance of skullduggery where none had existed. The athletic department once again failed to follow Don Canham's advice: "Never turn a one-day story into a two-day story."

For many Michigan followers, the Gibbons case seemed to push the Brandon administration across a line it it did not have to cross—in a direction that was impossible to reverse.

CHAPTER 49

A QUALIFIED VICTORY

On the heels of their encouraging meeting with the Regents, Central Student Government president Michael Proppe and vice-president Bobby Dishell designed a second survey. They wanted the department's input, too, and got it when Lochmann suggested including a question about how important good cell-phone service was to the students inside the stadium on game days, which Brandon often cited as "the biggest challenge we have."

"Brandon thinks it's Wi-Fi," Proppe says, "and you're about to spend $10 million dollars on it—and you haven't even asked the students the question? Yes, we were happy to put the question on the survey."

When the survey asked the students to rank seven reasons they buy season tickets, however, the students ranked cell-phone service seventh—dead last. What did they rank first? Being able to sit with their friends—which is exactly what general admission had effectively ended, and the main reason the students hated it.

The same week, Lochmann sent Proppe and Dishell a hybrid "General Admission/Reserved Seating" plan that would give reserved seats to students in the first rows of the student section who had attended five of the previous seven games on time, or 3,338 eligible students. The rest of the seats, about 13,000, would be general admission. Proppe and Dishell weren't too pleased with the plan, however, because it still relied too heavily on general admission and didn't allow the majority of the students to sit with their friends—which was the whole point of their objection.

On January 23, Proppe and Dishell met with Hunter Lochmann, Shelly Fabrizio, and Rob Rademacher—the same people who had attended the truncated, unsatisfying meeting a month earlier—plus some members of the ticket office, in the Champions Room.

"We think we have the Regents on our side," Proppe told me, "so we think we can push through what we want: a proposal that puts a general admission section in front, reserved seating in the middle, and freshman general admission in the back. We kept this hybrid system because it was clear that hanging on to general admission in some form was very important to Athletics."

It was less clear why—but CSG was trying to get a solution, not grandstand. But Proppe couldn't resist taking Lochmann's frivolous objections to the CSG plan from the previous meeting, and calculating a cost to each one. He showed everyone at the meeting what it would cost to get a new scanner, and hire an extra person in the department, minus the cost of the pregame entertainment the department had concocted to entice students to arrive earlier, but which had proven so unentertaining no one wanted them to continue with it. The total cost of CSG's plan: $150,000—or 0.1% of Brandon's budget, to solve a problem that had already cost him much, much more.

Lochmann looked at CSG's proposal, the same one he had quickly rejected a month earlier, before the Regents' meeting. He asked the others for their opinions, and everyone quickly approved it. "I think this accomplishes most of our goals," Lochmann said. "We'll look at it internally, and get back to you."

The meeting was adjourned, not long after it had started.

Proppe couldn't help but be amused. "What was impossible a month ago, was all of a sudden quite feasible."

Proppe and Dishell—now good friends—walked up State Street in the cold to the Union. "I think that went well," Proppe said, before adding, "Did that go well?"

Having walked out of several meetings with Lochmann feeling good, only to be disappointed later, they could no longer be sure. They tried to anticipate the next round of objections. Having crushed the cost argument, they looked at the "too difficult" argument.

"I'm a nerd," Proppe says. "I went home that day and wrote an Excel macro sheet that did the reassigning of seats for Lochmann, based on previous attendance and punctuality. If you set it up right, you can just put the data in the spreadsheet, and make a hypothetical section with 20,000 students and 2,000 groups, each between 2 and 20 people. Then you press a button, and it assigns people seats for the following game—just to show them it could be done, and it was not that hard to do.

"Took me two hours."

On January 30, Lochmann sent them a new plan, which was basically the CSG's plan with a few small compromises. Realizing they had achieved their primary objective of ending a strict general admission seating policy, Proppe and Dishell accepted.

"We were very excited," Proppe says. "This was our 'reach' goal."

Two weeks later they met again with Lochmann to finalize details. They planned to announce the new plan on February 25, right before the students left for spring break. Instead of studying for midterms, the two spent February 23 and 24 hammering out the press release with the athletic department staff.

And then, at 4:53 p.m. that same day, Monday, February 24, when they were supposed to send out the triumphant announcement, Lochmann e-mailed all involved to tell them he had just spoken with Brandon, who wanted to discuss the new policy in person with the executive officers before it was announced.

"I know you guys are disappointed," Lochmann wrote, "but Dave needs to run it by them, to get their approval."

That meant they would have to postpone the announcment until after spring break—costing the CSG another "win" with its constituents.

"What the hell kind of chain of communication do the executive officers have where Dave hadn't yet told them?" Proppe asks. "Assuming, of course, he had to in the first place."

Proppe knew the executive officers met on Tuesdays, so the next meeting would be the very next day. They told Royster Harper—who was also an executive officer—they had agreed on a new hybrid policy, and they were prepared to announce it. "So please bring this up in tomorrow's executive officer meeting, in case Dave doesn't."

After the meeting, Harper e-mailed them: Brandon wasn't at the meeting. This prompted Proppe and Dishell to e-mail Lochmann: When will it be announced? Lochmann answered: the next Tuesday meeting. By then the students would be on spring break, so Lochmann suggested March 11 as the best day to announce. They agreed, but that would put the announcement two weeks closer to the next CSG election, when Dishell would be running for president.

Finally, the Tuesday after spring break, everyone said, "All systems go." They put the press release on both Web sites, the department's and CSG's—and the CSG Web site got such a flood of clicks, it started crashing immediately.

"The first hour, we had 200 people every minute on the site, and almost all went straight to the press release," Proppe said. "It received 9,505 page views in the first 12 hours."

MGoBlog's Brian Cook, who had chastised Proppe a year earlier for complaining about general admission seating, had become a convert to their cause—and to Proppe himself. He titled his piece, "War On Students Over: Students Win," and celebrated their work. That summer, he would title another piece "Michael Proppe for Athletic Director," and sort of mean it. The two would even go out for beers a few times, in a fine demonstration of how you win over the press.

In March, Dishell won the election in a landslide by 3,987 to 2,850 for the runner-up. Shortly after, Dishell and Proppe met with Lochmann in his office. By then, the returning students had already sent in their ticket applications, or decided not to.

Shortly after the trio sat down, Lochmann asked them, "How many student tickets do you think we sold?"

"Well," Proppe said, thinking out loud, "I said you had 20,000 last year, a quarter of them graduated, and based on our survey data two-thirds said they'd buy tickets again at the current price, *if* assigned seating returned, which it largely had. So, I'm guessing 10,000."

Proppe recalls Lochmann leaned slowly back, palms on the table, with an air of "I told you so."

"Seven," he said. "Seven thousand."

Proppe recalls, "He didn't say he blamed the new reserved seating policy for that, but you could tell he did."

Dishell, still the more vocal of the two, spoke up. He had the 2014 schedule in his pocket, pulled it out, waved it at Lochmann, and said, "Right here! This is why."

"The schedule is out of our hands," Lochmann said, in a partial truth.

"Right," Dishell conceded, even though it wasn't when they scheduled it. "So lower the price."

"But it's the same price as last year, so it can't be the price," Lochmann said, displaying either disingenuousness or a surprisingly poor grasp of logical reasoning. Brandon would reiterate Lochmann's points in interviews that spring and fall.

True, the price of Michigan student tickets in 2014 would be the same as it had been in 2013. But this left out some salient facts. For the second straight year, Michigan was charging its students far more than other Big Ten teams: a league record $295 for seven games, up from $195 for six games two years earlier, compared to $252 for seven games at Ohio State, and a league median of $109 for seven games—or about a third what Michigan students were being asked to pay.

While Michigan's students were paying by far the most, they were getting the least, or something close to it: Only three Big Ten teams had worse records than Michigan's 2013 mark of 7–6: Northwestern, Illinois, and Purdue. Those three teams charged their students a total of $218 for season tickets, *combined*, or about two-thirds what Michigan alone charged its students.

Finally, Michigan students were not only being asked to pay record prices for a weak team, but a remarkably bad home schedule, consisting of Appalachian State, Miami of Ohio, Utah, Minnesota, Penn State, Indiana, and Maryland.

In short, the department was expecting Michigan students to pay by far the most in the league, again, even as the team and the schedule were demonstrably worse than they were the year before, without complaint. And if they didn't, the department would blame it on CSG's reserved seating plan, which the Web site hits and comments indicated was infinitely more popular than the department's despised general admission policy.

Proppe and Dishell, to their credit, declined to argue with Lochmann—it hadn't gotten them very far in the past—and returned to potential solutions.

"Isn't it worth it to lower the ticket prices now, retroactively, to get more students in?" Proppe asked.

"No, we've already sold the tickets," Lochmann said, not answering the question Proppe asked. "Too late."

"And that was that," Proppe recalls. "But we did not include the freshmen, who bought 5,000 tickets, like they used to, which made a 12,000-student section—or just about two-thirds of the 20,000 they got before introducing general admission in 2013. That was exactly how many said they would buy tickets again if assigned seating returned.

"What the department never considered, was what would have happened if they had pushed through their general admission policy for a second year. We surveyed the students, and they told us only 6,000 of them would have bought tickets."

Someone who believes in carefully collected data and sound logic—these student leaders, for example, and their professors—would reasonably conclude the 12,000 students who signed up for season tickets in 2014 were twice as many as the department would have gotten if they had stuck with their general admission policy. And you'd also have to concede the 12,000 students they got in 2014 were about half as many students that bought tickets in 2012, which the department would have kept if it had never tried the disastrous general admission policy in the first place.

Hindsight is 20/20. But so is foresight, when you do your homework.

CHAPTER 50

O CAPTAIN! MY CAPTAIN!

At Michigan, the role of captain is a serious one, not always given to the best player but the best leader. In fact, some of Michigan's best players, including all three Heisman Trophy winners, were not named captains, whereas some of the captains are better remembered for their leadership than many stars are for their play.

Frank Gusich was not the best player on his '71 team—or even close. The squad lost only one game by one point—the 1972 Rose Bowl—and produced four All-Americans and 21 professional players. Frank Gusich was not among them, starting eight games that season at a position Schembechler called "wolfman." But, clearly, Gusich's teammates, including a sophomore named Dave Brandon, saw something in him they needed, so they elected him captain.

"Frank loved Brandon," says Michigan's 1979 captain, John Arbeznik. Despite the eight years between them, Arbeznik became close to Gusich, the way so many lettermen bridge the age gap. "Frank thought Brandon was one of his closest friends. I told him Brandon only cared about himself. We agreed to disagree."

Gusich married his college sweetheart, Linda, moved to Cincinnati, and had two sons, but came back to Ann Arbor every fall for at least one game. He organized his team reunions for 40 years, and was one of the leaders of the all-team reunions in 1989, 1999, and 2004. He was a popular addition to the Chili & Cornbread tailgates and told great stories, often at his own expense.

"There was no greater Michigan captain or Michigan Man than Frank Gusich," said John Ghindia, who played ten years after Gusich graduated.

Not long after they moved to New Orleans, in 2002, Gusich learned he had multiple myeloma, a form of cancer. He fought it for years, and at times it looked like he was going to beat it. But on April 1, 2014, he lost the battle.

On April 11, dozens of Michigan lettermen traveled to New Orleans for Gusich's funeral. The mourners included Jim Brandstatter, Fritz Seyferth, Paul Seymour, fellow captain Guy Murdock, and teammate Mark Duffy, who served on the Chicago Board of Options Exchange. Brandon did not make it, however.

"Brandon not coming to Frank's funeral changed everything for me," Arbeznik said. While some of the lettermen in New Orleans that weekend were squarely in Brandon's corner, Arbeznik, Paul Seymour, and others started sharing their concerns about Brandon's leadership of the department.

They agreed to stay in touch. After Arbeznik returned to his home in Hobe Sound, Florida, he called fellow captains Don Dufek Jr., Dwight Hicks, and Jerry Meter, and expanded his calling circle as more lettermen expressed similar reservations.

One of those football lettermen, Yale Van Dyne, had played wide receiver for Schembechler's last teams and Moeller's first. He started 15 games, was named All-Big Ten Honorable Mention, and earned a bachelor's degree in General Studies, with a focus on English and sociology. After graduating in 1992, he worked in sales for Adidas, Boston Scientific, and Medtronic before becoming a consultant in Kansas City, Missouri.

Like almost all Michigan's lettermen, Van Dyne stayed in touch with his teammates, and expanded that circle during each reunion, Victors Night celebration, golf outing, and Chili & Cornbread tailgate.

In the spring of 2014, when most pundits expected the Wolverines to compete for the Big Ten title that fall, Van Dyne received an e-mail from John "Hoss" Ghindia, who played offensive line from 1981 to 1984. Ghindia's e-mail included a picture of Dave Brandon cutting down the net after Michigan won its 2013 NCAA regional. A year later, the department was recycling this image of its director as an advertisement for Michigan's success.

This triggered something in the normally easygoing Van Dyne, prompting him to fire off a quick, impassioned response to Ghindia about Brandon's stewardship of something they cared about deeply. Van Dyne's English classes paid off in a powerfully written, full-page missive.

Van Dyne made it clear his beef was not with Brady Hoke, whom he liked and wished the best, but the athletic director. Van Dyne believed Brandon was habitually crossing what the lettermen considered a sacred line between coaches and players on one side, and department officials on the other. The list of trespasses included chest-bumping players on the sidelines, watching game tape with the coaches, shaking hands with opposing basketball players, and cutting down the net after winning an NCAA regional title. What rankled the lettermen more than those public displays, however, was a private one: Brandon singing "The Victors" in the locker room after a win with the team and coaches, an honor historically reserved for the players.

But ultimately, Van Dyne was less concerned with Brandon himself than the direction he was taking Michigan's athletic department. "Our once classy and great school," he wrote to Ghindia, "somehow feels cheap, tacky and frankly, desperate for attention."

The athletic department no longer represented what Michigan meant to these men.

Ghindia was impressed—so impressed that, unbeknownst to Van Dyne, Ghindia forwarded his letter to dozens of former players, including Arbeznik's group of captains, most of whom sent it on to more. Ghindia even forwarded the e-mail to President Coleman and the Regents.

Van Dyne was surprised to learn Ghindia had forwarded his letter, especially to university leaders. As someone who takes his writing seriously, he was a little embarrassed it went out before he had reviewed it and shaped it for a broader audience—but the recipients of his letter didn't seem to mind.

Over the preceding few years, with the Wolverines riding a roller coaster, hundreds of lettermen had written to Michigan's leaders, who were often struck by the high quality of their letters. There wasn't much new about that. But only Van Dyne's letter went viral within Michigan circles, because it crystallized concerns many of them were feeling but hadn't expressed, making it the lettermen's first formal objection to the direction Brandon was taking the athletic department.

"This is the irony of my letter being considered the opening shot across the bow," Van Dyne told me, a bit bemused. "It was just a spontaneous rant I sent to Hoss, who forwarded it on." But it clearly hit a nerve.

The Van Dyne Manifesto became the spark for a loosely organized but deeply devoted group of lettermen and university leaders, who started working behind the scenes to help Michigan's athletic department self-correct.

"Yale's letter laid out the scope of the problem," Ghindia told me. "It was the catalyst for action. It was the opening round, as far as I'm concerned. Things had been percolating behind the scenes for a while, and now it was time for Michigan to move."

The practice of naming captains goes back to Michigan's very first team, in 1879, and a man named David N. DeTar, who guided the original Wolverines to their sterling 1–0 record, thanks to their 1–0 victory over Racine College.

The earnest black-and-white photos of Michigan's team captains run all the way from Captain DeTar to the present, and cover a wall in Schembechler Hall just as big and prominent as the one featuring Michigan's All-Americans. Given the history of Michigan captains, and the respect given them, it's no surprise that the players who walk past these photos every day imagine their own photo added to that wall before their careers end. It gives them something to aspire to.

For years, near the end of spring practice, the players walk over to the Big House in the early evening, gather in the bleachers, talk about their goals and what they need to do to achieve them, then write down the names of the teammates they think should lead them for the upcoming season. You break this tradition at your peril, as Rich Rodriguez discovered when he announced he would not name captains until the end of the 2008 season, and received heavy criticism from lettermen and fans alike, who educated him on the importance of Michigan's captains through the years.

Rodriguez created a hybrid system his last season in Ann Arbor, 2010, with two captains named prior to the season, and two more added after. When Brady Hoke arrived, he stated early and often that Michigan would return to its practice of naming captains before the season, and he was hailed for it. With it, came the return of the players' hopes to be named team captain.

When one of those players, Devin Gardner, was a five-star recruit in high school, he declined even to flirt with other programs before committing 100 percent to Michigan. During his freshman year, I listened while Tate Forcier and Denard Robinson told him about the usual illicit benefits other programs had offered them.

"Man, am I the only one to do it clean?!" Gardner asked, laughing.

"*We* did it clean!" Robinson told him. "I didn't take any of that stuff! But the *schools* didn't do it clean! How many visits did you take?"

"Just one," Gardner said.

"That's why, man! You go visit [other big-name schools], they're gonna offer you money and cars and women."

"Man, Michigan didn't give me *anything!*" Gardner said, keeping up his mock anger. "This place sucks!"

Of course, Gardner devoured almost everything about Michigan, including the classes, but not the bars. Like his mentor, Denard Robinson, Gardner doesn't drink. For our interview, which happened to fall on St. Patrick's Day, 2015, I had to walk past countless drunken students on my way to meet Gardner at the Chop House, where I found him dressed in a button-down plaid shirt, a sharp sport coat, and big round glasses, looking more like Clark Kent than Superman. The contrast with his inebrieted classmates outside was striking.

"During spring ball," he told me, "I'm waiting *every* day for us to head to the stadium, fill out the ballot, and pick captains. I saw Molk, Martin, and Denard all do it—good captains!—and I'm thinking, 'Man, I can't wait for my turn.'"

One night, when the coaches told the team it was time to visit the Big House, Gardner assumed the moment he had been waiting for had finally arrived.

"We walked to the stadium, we talked," he said, "but this time we came back before we'd voted. There would be no vote.

"We're not going to have captains? What? When they said we'd pick captains every week, and 'permanent captains' after the season, a lot of guys didn't like that. *I* didn't like that! [Hoke] didn't talk to me about it. I didn't hear a word about it. Obviously, I'm not going to express it publicly, and challenge his authority. But that is something I was not onboard with—at all. Personally, for me, I was very uspset. I've waited my entire life to be the captain of Michigan.

"Selfishly, obviously, I feel you took that from me. But as a team, whether they would have picked me or someone else, you're saying we don't have any leaders? I think people still looked to me and Jake [Ryan, the team's star linebacker], but you're not the captains. It's not the same. Getting voted after the season was great, but that's an award, not a responsibility.

"Who goes into the season not knowing who your leaders are? Without leaders we don't have a chance.

"I thought we were in trouble from the start."

CHAPTER 51

THE REVOLVING DOOR

Of the 26 head coaches Brandon inherited, 11 resigned, retired, or were fired by Brandon within four years—more than 40 percent, a stunning turnover rate. That number rises to 13—or exactly half—if you include Brandon releasing the second head coaches for diving and men's cross-country. Only one of these 13 head coaches was replaced by an assistant coach inside the program—golf coach Chris Witten—in keeping with Brandon's philosophy of hiring outsiders.

The exodus of coaches started early under Brandon, and never slowed down. After Ron Warhurst made his exit shortly after Brandon took office in 2010, three head coaches left in 2011, three more in 2012, two in 2013, and three more in 2014. They included women's golf coach Cheryl Stacy and men's track and field coach Fred LaPlante, both in 2013, and water polo's Matt Anderson, men's tennis coach Bruce Berque, and Alex Gibby, who had replaced Warhurst, before getting replaced by one of Warhurst's star runners, Kevin Sullivan—all in 2014.

Once again, these coaches had been successful before they got to Michigan, and they were successful at Michigan—"on and off the field," racking up the usual list of Academic All-Big Ten and All-American honors. But things took a downward turn for all of them shortly after Brandon took over.

Cheryl Stacy's golfers qualified for the NCAA Central Regional in 2011 and 2012, then finished tenth in the Big Ten in 2013. She resigned shortly thereafter. In men's track coach Fred LaPlante's second year, 2009, his team finished second in the Big Ten indoor season and third outdoors, but it was downhill from there. His next three seasons, his teams didn't finish higher than eighth in the Big Ten, indoor or outdoor. He resigned shortly after the 2013 outdoor season.

In his 12 years as Michigan's women's water polo coach, Matt Anderson's teams earned 10 division titles, 5 conference titles—the most of any coach in the conference—and 4 bids to the eight-team NCAA tournament, in 2005 and 2008–2010, producing Olympic goalie Betsey Armstrong along the way. But Anderson's teams failed to win the league title in both 2013 and 2014. Days after expressing "uncontrollable excitement for next season" to Brad Whipple of the *Michigan Daily*, Anderson resigned.

In their prepared statements to the press, not one of the coaches who left between 2010 and 2014 mentioned Dave Brandon by name, a pretty good sign they were not resigning on good terms—if they were resigning at all. You don't have to be as smart as Michael Proppe to understand the difference between causation and correlation. It is impossible, with the data we have, to determine if Brandon's arrival had anything to do with the dramatic drop in the performances of all 12 teams during his tenure. But the data clearly show that, no matter the sport or the coach, for some reason almost all of them suffered their worst seasons shortly after Brandon took the job.

We can also conclude, from interviews with many of them, that they felt he interfered unnecessarily with their teams, which they believe had a profoundly negative impact on their performance.

From 1999 to 2004, Bruce Berque served as the associate head tennis coach for the powerhouse Illinois men's team, which won all six Big Ten regular-season titles during Berque's tenure there, and five of the six Big Ten tournaments, plus an NCAA team title in 2003 with a perfect 32–0 mark. They also set an NCAA-record 64 consecutive dual match wins spanning almost two complete seasons, snapped only when the Illini lost in the NCAA 2004 final four.

In July of 2004, Bill Martin hired Berque to take over Michigan's struggling program. Once the pride of the league, with 16 straight Big Ten titles in the '70s and '80s, the Wolverines had not won a conference title since 1996, and had fallen to ninth place two straight years before Berque arrived. Clearly, Michigan tennis was in pretty bad shape.

In Berque's first year, the Wolverines team finished third behind only Illinois and Ohio State—two of the nation's top teams—and stayed after them the rest of Berque's run, beating Illinois four times in dual matches. Although Berque's Michigan teams never won a Big Ten title, they finished second in 2007, 2012, and 2013. After missing the NCAA tournament his first season, the tennis Wolverines earned nine straight NCAA Championship berths, getting to the Sweet 16 in 2008, and rising to number eight in the national ranking in 2008 and 2011. They also broke into the nation's top 25 nationally seven straight years, from 2007 to 2013, and barely missed in 2014, with a 26th ranking.

Berque got along very well with Martin and his staff, but like most of his coaching peers, when President Coleman named Dave Brandon the AD in 2010, Berque thought Brandon would do very well, and looked forward to working for him.

"When Dave first came," Berque told me, "I liked his speeches, I liked what he was saying. He wanted all of us to succeed, and gave us the resources to do so."

In the spring of 2012 and again in 2013, Berque's teams went an impressive 9–2 in the Big Ten, and finished second in the conference both years behind Ohio State, which finished fourth in the nation both years. Berque's star, Evan King, earned Big Ten Player of the Year both years, while Berque himself was named the Midwest Region Coach of the Year in 2012. Through his 10-year run at Michigan, 18 of Berque's 34 players—more than half—earned a combined 30 Academic All-Big Ten nominations.

He had turned the program around, dramatically, and achieved just about everything short of a title.

"Was I satisfied?" he asked me. "Definitely not. We wanted to win championships. It was frustrating that we hadn't gotten that done, but we were getting closer."

Brandon assigned a staffer to supervise Berque's squad, as he did with all his varsity teams. Starting in 2013, former Michigan assistant football coach Mike DeBord occasionally traveled with the team.

"I liked having him there," Berque said. "We got along great."

DeBord seemed to like it, too. A few days after the 2013 season ended, he confided in Berque that after he'd come back from watching Berque's team in the Big Ten tournament, he'd told his supervisors, Bitsy Ritt and Dave Brandon, "I would take you as our tennis coach any day of the week!"

Like almost all Michigan's coaches, for whom Ann Arbor is a destination, not a stepping-stone, Berque loved Michigan and intended to stay as long as they'd have him. But by 2013 he had already watched seven of his fellow Michigan head coaches leave, one way or the other, and he would see two more. Further, some head coaches had been pressured to make changes among their assistants—fire this assistant or that, or you'll be gone. Also, after nine very successful years, Berque was still on a year-to-year contract, while the coaches Brandon hired usually got multiyear deals. So, when Arkansas contacted Berque about coaching there, he would have been foolish not to listen.

After a second phone conversation, he withdrew from consideration, but he still felt honor-bound to tell DeBord about the conversation. "I just want to let you know I was contacted," Berque said. "I'm *not* interested. I want to stay at Michigan. But I am interested in a multiyear contract, which Bill [Martin] and I had talked about."

On the heels of DeBord's praise for his work a few weeks prior, Berque believed it was the right time to ask.

"Okay," DeBord said, "let me check on that."

About an hour later, DeBord called back to tell him they were not going to do it. "We give contracts to coaches who win Big Ten titles," DeBord explained, "and you haven't won one, and we think you should have by now."

This conversation rattled Berque, but he decided to stick with Michigan.

"But," Berque recalled, "in restrospect, it was about that time that the tone of my relationship with the administration changed. I had always felt it to be very positive through my first nine years. From that point on, though, I just never felt the same vibe from the department."

When Berque described his situation a year later to Kurt Gulbrand, Michigan's former athletic development officer, Gulbrand listened quietly until Berque got to the call from Arkansas.

"Stop right there," Gulbrand interrupted. "That's it. That's where you lost them."

"Really?" Berque was skeptical. He told Gulbrand that he had been very clear with DeBord "that I wanted to stay at Michigan, and I didn't want to use Arkansas's interest as leverage."

"Yep," Gulbrand said. "You absolutely lost them right there."

Although employees get outside offers in just about every industry, under Brandon, they were not to be entertained, or even confessed. Just fielding the call was considered a sign of disloyalty, something Brandon would not tolerate.

A few weeks later, the department started giving him negative feedback about his team's lack of a Big Ten championship and their "culture," something Brandon frequently mentioned with his coaches. "We were on a big culture kick," Berque recalls, "and we all agreed that striving for a championship culture was a top priority. But any coach can tell you, it's pretty rare to have your team's culture exactly where you want it to be. It's something you're always working on, always tweaking."

This showed up in Berque's annual program review that fall. Brandon conducted these in a round-table meeting with his lieutenants, and anybody else who worked with a particular program, including trainers, academic advisers, media people, and others.

"You go around the table," Berque recalls, "and Dave asks each person, 'Greg: any feedback for Coach?' Coaches also had the opportunity to give feedback, so it went both ways. And it's good, but it's awkward, because if you really have a problem with someone, you don't want to air that in front of everyone. But it was usually pretty innocuous, pretty much a love fest."

Until, that is, Brandon asked the final question to one of his assistants. "When is the last time they won a Big Ten championship?"

The assistant had been prepped. "1996," he said.

"That's unacceptable," Brandon said. "We need to do everything we can to help Coach Berque win a Big Ten championship."

That included Brandon taking the tennis team out for dinner that fall at Mediterrano, an Italian restaurant near Briarwood Mall, with a nice private room off to the side. This was something Brandon liked to do with all the teams, to get to know the athletes without their coaches present.

While it's admirable for an AD to spend his limited free time taking all the athletes out for dinner—and not just the stars or the football players—the practice has potential downsides, downsides that Canham would have recognized.

"I never talk to players about their coaches," Canham told me in 1999, in an interview for my first book. "I had coached myself, and I know enough not to do that."

With many teams, if not most, Brandon created stronger bonds with the athletes than he did with their coaches, which some coaches found nerve-wracking.

After Brandon's dinner with the tennis players, Berque asked if he could meet with Brandon to review where things stood.

"We met in his office," Berque recalls. "The tone of that meeting was not very good. I asked him for his thoughts. That fall, we had a small team, a young team, a pretty quiet bunch. And they're tennis players, not football players. You could imagine that, for them, having dinner with the AD could be pretty intimidating."

Brandon told him that none of the players said anything negative, but only a few players spoke during the dinner. Brandon concluded it was a high-strung group, due to Berque's coaching style.

Berque started to explain, "Well, it's a young group, kind of quiet—" but Brandon held his hand up, making it immediately clear that he was not interested in any explanations.

"That was the first meeting I ever had with Dave that went poorly," Berque says, "and that shook me a bit, too."

After that meeting, the department's concerns with the culture Berque fostered heated up—something they raised with every coach Brandon eventually fired, and often other employees, too. Many found this hypocritical, because they believed Brandon himself had instilled a culture within the department of fear and intimidation—but they never dared to express that publicly.

Brandon often told his employees, "One of the great things about Michigan is that it's a great place to work!" To that end, he formed something called "The Smile Committee," which planned for flag football games under the lights at the Big House, golf outings, the annual holiday party, and an ice-cream truck to pull up to the building after a staff meeting.

"If you're kicking ass, great," another coach told me. "But if you're not, and you're being ruled by fear, I don't think an ice-cream sandwich is going to make up for it."

It turned out the coaches were not 12 years old. They didn't want an ice-cream sandwich. They wanted to be treated fairly, with respect, and feel supported through the ups and downs that inevitably happen in any coaching career.

Going into the fall of 2013, "For the first time, I think, 'Damn, I'm in trouble.' That fall felt the worst. The weird part is, we were coming off two of our best seasons in the Big Ten, with a combined 18–4 record."

Berque entered the 2014 season fighting for his job, which he figured would require nothing less than winning a Big Ten title, while hoping none of his players complained to DeBord or Brandon—about anything.

"It affected the way I coached that year, for sure. No question. It was that double-edged sword—win championships and make sure your guys are giving us good feedback in our exit interviews. I felt like I knew what it would take to win a title, but I felt powerless to push the guys, for fear of a negative comment."

When I related Berque's story to the department's former CFO, Jason Winters, who had left in the fall of 2011, he was not surprised. He knew it was always a tricky balancing act for any athletic director to support the coaches while watching the budget. But he also knew how important it was to insulate the coaches from any unnecessary pressure.

"Coaches weren't particularly happy that they didn't get all the money and security they wanted from Bill," he recalls, "but they weren't living in constant fear for their jobs, either. Most coaches don't perform well under that kind of constant doubt."

The world of coaching is a surprisingly fragile ecosystem. Those who have done it, at virtually any level, understand intimately the fear, the pressure, the tension, and the occasional helplessness that every coach feels at some point, and sometimes all those things in a single day.

Successful coaches seem so strong and confident, it's hard to believe they are so vulnerable to doubt, to mutiny, to the terror of a losing streak—but they know all those things can start up with no warning. That's why great coaches rarely relax. They all know they're just one bad game, one injury, or even one incident away from losing it all. They also know how little they ultimately control.

The job is hard enough as it is, and that's why autonomy is so important to most coaches. Thus, to add another supervisor, with your subordinates in direct communication with your superiors, can be very unsettling—like trying to raise your kids with Child Protective Services looking over your shoulder, taking notes.

"I didn't feel I had the security to coach the way I can," Berque says of the 2014 season. "I couldn't be tough on them when they needed it. I wasn't as true to myself as I could have been. And that's a lesson learned going forward: You have to stay true to your beliefs."

Despite all the negativity surrounding the team, the 2014 Wolverines finished in the top half of the Big Ten, they made it to the conference semifinals, and earned a bid for the NCAA tournament for the ninth consecutive year. Berque had also signed a great recruiting class, including a player from New Zealand named Cameron Norrie, who was top ten in world juniors.

"When you have a number one stud coming in," Berque says, "it makes all the difference in the world."

At the 2014 NCAA tournament, held at the University of Southern California, Michigan bowed out with a close match to 25th-ranked Oklahoma State.

"After the match," Berque says, "we had a great meeting in the hotel with the returning players, discussing how things were going to be next year, how we were going to support each other and emphasize a great team environment. I was really looking forward to it. There were a lot of things to look forward to."

But after taking the red-eye flight home, the next morning Berque received an e-mail from DeBord: "I need to meet with you at 4 p.m. tomorrow. In my office. Mike."

"I knew, 75 percent, that I was done," Berque says. "I said 'Okay.'"

A severe spring storm delayed the meeting until after hours, so an administrative assistant, Suzy Henderson, met Berque by the door to let him in. They took the elevator up the back way, and she led him into the HR room, where Berque met DeBord and Kristin Orlowski, Brandon's chief talent officer.

As Berque recalls, "Mike just got up and shook my hand and said, 'Thank you for coming in.' He sat down and said, 'We decided to go in a different direction.'"

"Can I ask a reason?"

"You know what," DeBord told him, "we're not going to get into a reason. We already know you're hurting, and we don't want to make it worse."

Berque looked over at Orlowski. She looked back, and finally said, "Failing to meet expectations."

"Well," DeBord said, "Kristin is going to go over the details about how this works from a human-resource perspective."

DeBord got up and left. Orlowski told Berque Michigan was offering three months' severance pay, and explained the process.

"She was very nice," Berque said. He told her he'd think about it, and left. But an hour later, Berque got a call from Dave Ablauf, asking him to approve a statement that announced Berque's resignation. "But I haven't agreed to resign yet," Berque said. "Can't I wait until tomorrow?"

Ablauf told him Brandon "wants it done now so social media doesn't get it wrong." There was a logic to this: Berque's players would be finding out that their head coach would not be back. If they got on line, they would break the story. Far better it come from the department with a comment from Berque.

They agreed on a statement saying Bruce Berque was no longer the coach at Michigan.

The next day, Berque explained to Orlowski that three months' severance was less than he would have made from running Michigan's summer tennis camp alone, and added that no one was accusing him of doing anything wrong.

"No," Orlowski said, "you haven't done anything wrong." With those two facts in mind, they bumped Berque's severence to four months.

"That's a very generous severance pay," she said, and it was clear that would be the final offer. They agreed that Berque would think about it, and get back to her regarding the non-disparagement and severance pay agreements. A few months later, Berque accepted a position as a volunteer coach at the University of Texas.

"It's been a tough thing for me," Berque says today, echoing a comment the vast majority of the other 142 employees who'd left since Brandon started could probably say. "I busted my butt for 25 years to get where I was, and we were respected throughout the country for running a good, clean program.

"In the end—" Berque stopped to collect his thoughts, then went back to his first one. "It's been tough for me—but I realize I'm not the only one. There's a lot of good people who've been hurt.

"The new tennis coaches are great people, and they will do a great job for Michigan. But I never wanted to leave, and I was confident we were about to take the next step.

"I'm hopeful I'll get another chance."

A year after Berque left, Michigan's 2015 tennis team finished at 7–17 overall, and 3–8 in the Big Ten, with half as many conference wins as Berque's worst team won. Berque's teams never finished lower than sixth in the Big Ten, and were in the top four eight of ten years. But in 2015, Michigan finished ninth out of twelve, and missed the NCAA tournament for the first time in ten years.

After Berque left, his star recruit, New Zealand's Cameron Norrie, the top ten world junior player, decided to enroll at Texas Christian. As a freshman in 2015, he made the NCAA quarterfinals, and pushed his team—which had missed the NCAA tournament the previous year—to the national semifinals. Berque was right: That's what a number one stud can do for you.

What was lost is pretty obvious. What was gained is harder to see.

If Berque's experience was isolated, it would be a men's tennis problem, not a Michigan problem. But he was far from alone.

The amount of turnover under Dave Brandon is especially apparent when looking at the entire coaching staffs of all the varsity teams, from head coaches to recruiting coordinators. When Brandon came aboard in 2009–10, Michigan employed 111 coaches. When he departed four years later, only 31 of them remained—or a 28 percent retention rate.

Of the 25 varsity coaching staffs, just one—the two-person women's tennis staff—remained completely intact through Brandon's four-year tenure as athletic director. Brandon cleaned out the entire coaching staffs of seven programs; football would account for the eighth if not for the continued employment of recruiting coordinator Chris Singletary, who would leave in the spring of 2015.

When you include the 80 departed coaches, a grand total of 143 employees left the athletic department during Brandon's tenure, which is more than half the staff he had inherited four years earlier. This remarkable turnover rate—for any organization, in any field—produced a number of by-products, some measurable, some not. Those employees who had been hired before Brandon invariably speak of the unusual camaraderie of the department prior to 2010, and its rapid disappearance soon thereafter. They have given me many examples, big and small, but the experience of Ryan Duey, the Ann Arborite who rose to attain his dream job, director of marketing and event presentation, echoes many of those I heard.

"I think this is the biggest difference between the two regimes," Duey told me. "Just a few years ago, we were all making peanuts compared to what the salaries are now, but at that time we were all in it for more than just the paycheck. We genuinely cared about the coaches, and the student-athletes, and for one another—and you could feel that. We could put the long hours in together, because we were a family. We worked hard, we played hard."

But when the new hires started pouring in, the veterans were charged with bringing them up to speed. "You're feeding all this information to these new people," Duey says, "and you know they're making 50, 60 or $90,000 more than you are, and you're basically training them to take your job.

"When the culture changed, it didn't change because *we* stopped caring, but because the people *above us* stopped caring about the team. When you bring in the new athletic director, making a million dollars a year, and his new leaders are making a quarter million, and you saw what they focused on, you got the feeling they didn't care—and that's not Michigan."

For Duey, all these growing aggravations came to a head one cold afternoon in December of 2013. Duey had just finished working on the Ohio State football game played in Ann Arbor that year, and had to jump right into preparing for the NHL's Winter Classic, an outdoor hockey game between Toronto and Detroit, to be held at the Big House January 1, 2014.

It was late in the day when he grabbed some files and tapes at Weidenbach Hall and delivered them to Michigan's video production team at Crisler. He hopped back in his Explorer at about 5 p.m., rush hour, and started driving off, but he only got as far as Hoover and Greene, near the back entrance of the athletic department's parking lot, when an engine belt slipped off, causing smoke to billow from his engine. He got out, popped the hood, then watched five people in the department see him standing next to his disabled Explorer, hood open—and keep driving right past.

"That's when I thought to myself, this is a whole different beast," he said. "You're dealing with different people now. To me that story sums up the whole change. All the new people who came in for great salaries and fancy job titles, they didn't have that care, or that passion for working at Michigan."

Eventually, one person did stop: the always friendly Brenda Yaklin, a University of Michigan police officer who works many athletic events, but is not employed by the department. Duey thanked her—and soon thereafter left the department.

"I think Dave Brandon's a tremendous business leader," he says today. "I really do. And I have the utmost respect for his professionalism. His demise was the leadership team he put in place. The biggest thing you can take away: Dave Brandon surrounded himself completely with yes men and yes women."

During this period of tremendous turnover, the department had also lost a few centuries' worth of institutional knowledge. So, when Rick Leach, one of the greatest athletes in Michigan history, called the department to buy tickets, the person answering the phone asked him to spell "Leach." When Jon Giesler, one of Schembechler's left tackles who protected Dan Marino for ten years with the Miami Dolphins, called to ask why he was not receiving the lettermen e-mails, the person answering the phone spelled both Jon and Giesler wrong, then said, "You're not in the system."

Michigan tradition is fading fastest among those who should know it best.

Despite all the tumult such a high rate of turnover creates—both in the present and the future—if Michigan was approaching Brandon's stated goal of winning the Directors' Cup, you could have a fair debate over the cost-benefit of his approach.

Under Martin, Michigan finished in the top six nine out of ten years. After Michigan finished 25th for 2009–10 school season, which Martin and Brandon split, the Wolverines climbed to 15th the next year, then 10th, and a sterling fourth place in 2012–13. In 2013–14, however, with Michigan's veteran coaches gone or going, and Brandon's hires taking over, Michigan finished 13th, and in 2014–15, the Wolverines finished 19th, Michigan's third-worst performance. Without exceptional seasons by women's track coach James Henry and softball coach Carol Hutchins—both hired by Don Canham—Michigan would have finished 29th, worst in school history.

Like the general admission policy, Brandon's handling of coaches ultimately seemed to come with a lot of cost, and little benefit.

CHAPTER 52

THE NATIVES GET RESTLESS

By the spring of 2014, the mass of Michigan fans were starting to get glimpses behind the department's curtain, and the view wasn't reassuring.

In May, the Michigan athletic department was forced to admit publicly what Michael Proppe and Bobby Dishell had known for months: Student football ticket sales were down, way down, from about 21,000 in 2012 to a projected 13,000 to 14,000 for the coming season. In fact, the actual number would be 11,569.

The department blamed cell phones, high-definition TV, and student apathy sweeping the nation. All real problems, to be sure, but they didn't explain how Michigan alienated 40 percent of its students in just two years—and many of their parents, too.

The cause was bigger than cell phones or high-definition TVs, and simpler: Michigan was forgetting why its fans love college football.

Michigan's athletic department had always followed basic business practices, but it has never been run strictly as a business. The proof was the wait list, which Canham grew by the thousands. Canham was a multimillionaire businessman in his own right. If he wanted to "maximize revenue," he knew he could increase the price to meet demand, just like hotels do. But he didn't, because he believed that would dispel the magic of Michigan Stadium.

Brandon's predecessor, Bill Martin, introduced Personal Seat Licenses to the Big House, but only after Michigan's peers had done so, and he still kept it relatively moderate, sparing the fans in the endzones. Even after Michigan finished 3–9 in 2008 and 5–7 in 2009, Michigan's wait list remained robust, partly because the fans didn't feel exploited. During the 2008 recession, Martin actually lowered ticket prices, and gave the Big Three automakers free full-page ads in every program because they had supported the department for decades.

"Just because you *can* charge them more," Martin told me, "doesn't mean you *should*. You're not there to ring up the cash to the nth degree. It's a nonprofit model!"

Canham would have agreed. "He respected that fan base so much," his son-in-law, Don Eaton, told me. "I know he struggled when the budget dictated a price increase of a dollar or two. He just didn't want to do that to the fans."

By Brandon's fourth year, he had increased the department's operating budget from $107 million to $147 million. That does not include the building program, estimated at $346.5 million. In Brandon's defense, he generated a $5 million surplus (down from $9 million the previous year) and the buildings would benefit all Michigan's teams, not just football and basketball. But his budget also included his $1.25 million annual compensation, which contributed to the department's stunning 72 percent increase in administrator compensation; not to mention an 80 percent increase in "marketing, promotions and ticketing"; and a 340 percent increase in "hosting, food and special events."

How long could those numbers, fueled by increasingly unhappy fans, continue to skyrocket before they came crashing down to earth?

All that money came from someone, and that someone was the fans—and they were beginning to notice. For decades, Michigan football tickets were underpriced, and the fans knew that when they scalped them for more than they paid. By 2014, the tickets were overpriced, and fans started figuring that out when they tried to sell them through StubHub and got far less.

The fans were learning something else, too: They could drop their season tickets and get virtually the same seats, without paying for a Personal Seat Donation, or for three weak nonconference opponents, just by going on StubHub. One fan wrote to me that he dropped his season tickets when he figured out he could buy his exact same seats from the previous season for less than a third the price he paid—and have the additional convenience of only paying for games he wanted to see, or staying home if the forecast looked bad. Brandon was teaching the fans to see Michigan football tickets not as a golden invitation for a unique experience to be shared with family, friends, and 100,000 of your closest buddies, and passed down through the generations, but as a commodity to be bought and sold on the open market.

The faithful were reluctant to adopt this cold outlook, but by the spring of 2014, they could no longer kid themselves. When they wrote the checks for their tickets every winter, they used to feel like loyal fans, but they were beginning to feel like fools.

The department could no longer conceal the fact that the wait list was long gone. The department spent the spring and summer of 2014 sending wave after wave of e-mails to former ticket holders, retired faculty members, and even rival fans to assure them, "The deadline has been extended!" Beg your former customers to come back five times, and you don't have a deadline, and you don't have a wait list.

Put it all together, and going into the fall of 2014, Michigan was in danger of breaking its string of 251 consecutive games with 100,000-plus paid attendance.

Michigan's problems went deeper than marketing and logistics. The department seemed to forget who their customers were, and what they loved.

Brandon often said, "We all think of every home Michigan football game like a miniature Super Bowl."

I don't know any Michigan fans who think that. Quite the opposite, they think Michigan football games are the antidote for the artificial excess of the Super Bowl—as do most college football fans. For them, Michigan football is all about lifelong fans who've been coming together for decades to leave a bit of the modern world behind—and the incessant marketing that comes with it—and share an authentic experience fueled by the passion of the team, the band, and the students. That's it. In 2005, then-athletic director Bill Martin commissioned a survey that revealed more than 50 percent of Michigan season-ticket holders had been buying them for more than two decades, but only 9 percent of them also bought season tickets to any professional team. The vast majority of Michigan fans are devoted to only one team, the Wolverines.

In his speeches, Brandon often mentioned that he had served as the CEO for two Fortune 500 companies—the apotheosis of a recent trend among major programs such as Oregon, Notre Dame, and Penn State, who've passed over experienced athletic directors to hire outside business gurus. With his deep business background, it was a mystery why he seemed to know so little about the people who had been filling the Big House for decades.

When the late Michigan broadcaster Bob Ufer said, "Michigan football is a religion, and Saturday is the holy day of obligation," he was on to something.

If the people running college football see their universities as just a brand, and the athletic departments merely a business, it seems inevitable they will turn off the very people who've been coming to their temples for decades.

The people who fill the stands year in and year out, rain or shine, are not customers. They're believers. Break faith with your flock, and you will not get them back with fancier wine.

If you treat your fans like customers long enough, they'll start behaving that way, reducing their irrational love for their team to a cool-headed, dollars-and-cents decision to buy tickets or not, with no more emotional investment than buying a lawn mower.

After a friend of mine took his kids to a game, he told me, "Michigan athletics used to feel like something we shared. Now it's something they hoard. Anything of value they put a price tag on. Anything that appeals to anyone is kept locked away—literally, in some cases—and only brought out if you pay for it. And what's been permanently banished is any sense of generosity."

By the spring of 2014, the natives were getting wise—and restless.

CHAPTER 53

FIREWORKS

By the time the Regents met on Thursday, July 17, 2014, Brandon had served as Michigan's athletic director for about four years, depending on when you counted his first day—when President Coleman announced his hiring on January 5, 2010, when he actually took over on March 8, or when he officially took the reins, on September 4. He had immediately stamped his style on the department and established complete control.

After four years, however, many university insiders had come to believe he had also isolated the department from the rest of the university and ruled by intimidation within it, so anyone who disagreed with him was likely already gone by the summer of 2014. That long list included a lot of smart, capable people who cared more about working for Michigan than making more money elsewhere.

Brandon's critics, inside or outside the university, had two common complaints: First, his hunger for the spotlight when things were going well, which seemed far greater than that of his fellow Big Ten athletic directors, who happily worked behind the scenes. As one university leader told me, "I defy you to find an athletic director, current or former, at any school who got as much ink as Dave, *ever.* He made it about him—but it's a job that, if done well, it's done in the background. You have to have the kind of ego and personality that understands that. It's bigger than you, and it will be here after you're gone."

Second, Brandon's tendency to reach for the biggest, loudest, most expensive, and therefore—to him—best of everything, from his house to the Big House, without understanding that everyone does not share his taste.

Brandon's allies and critics alike were struck by his apparent inability to recognize that the retirement of his greatest booster, President Coleman, would

affect him—yet he continued to lead as if he had the administration's uncon-
ditional support.

After President Coleman officially stepped down on July 14, 2014, three
days before the next Regents' meeting, President Mark Schlissel was not likely
to butt into a running debate between the Regents and the athletic department
which had started well before his arrival. But he was just as unlikely to spend
his limited political capital on a man he barely knew.

The Regents typically receive the agenda for their meetings three days in
advance. On Monday, July 14, a few Regents were surprised to see "Game Fireworks" on the list. The athletic department had requested "close-proximity
fireworks" for the late afternoon game against Miami University (Ohio) on
September 13, 2014, and for the night game against Penn State on October 11.
State law required the Regents to approve the fireworks before the state would
issue a permit.

"I was minding my own business, talking to somebody in India," Regent
Larry Deitch recalls, "and that Monday I got an e-mail from a friend about
this fireworks thing, the first I'd really heard of it. I looked in the book and
it's on the agenda. Right away, I decide, I'm opposed to this, I'll vote against
it, and I have to say it publicly. Then [fellow Regent Mark Bernstein] called,
and said, 'Me, too.'"

But beyond that, Deitch maintains, he and Bernstein "did no campaign-
ing. I made no phone calls [to the other Regents] about it. We just figured we
were going to have to say something about our values—what we believed in,
what we believe Michigan is about—so it was easy to do."

Probably no one in the athletic department had more experience with fireworks than Ryan Duey, who had set up fireworks for the rededication game
against Connecticut and the Big Chill hockey game in 2010, the first Notre
Dame night game in 2011, and the NHL's Winter Classic on New Year's Day,
2014—all great successes.

"There are a few keys to getting fireworks right at Michigan," Duey says.
"It's got to be tasteful. It's got to be for the right moment. And before you
even get that far, you better work closely with Michigan's safety officers to create a systematic, organized plan of events. They're very cautious, as you'd expect. Their default answer is 'No.' You have to make sure you don't give them
any reasons to say no, or they will. But we always worked well together, because of our preparation, and the events always worked out."

But Duey had decided to take a job outside the department a few months earlier, which left nobody with any experience to create the plans needed to apply for fireworks permits, and nobody with any relevant relationships.

"Once I heard fireworks were on the agenda for that Regents' meeting," Duey told me, "I knew it was doomed. Dave wanted every Michigan football game to be a Super Bowl—but it can't be. And I feel our Michigan fans didn't want that, anyway."

Regent Andrea Fischer Newman, however, has a different take. "To this day," she says, "I don't understand what happened with that meeting. We'd voted on fireworks four times before, and there had never been an issue raised. I don't know why [the Regents who opposed the idea] didn't pick up the phone and tell Dave, 'It's not going to happen, so you should pull it off the table.' When I show up I see one of my colleagues, Larry [Deitch], had a speech, typed up and ready to deliver."

As Deitch had told me, however, "There was zero coordination in our efforts. We just kind of laid it out there."

Michigan's Regents rarely split their votes or denied Brandon's wishes, which almost always had the backing of President Coleman. But when the Regents looked into the fireworks proposal this time, they were surprised to find Brandon wanted to set off fireworks not just after both games, but during the Penn State game, after touchdowns—replacing the century-old tradition of celebrating a score with the Michigan Marching Band blasting "The Victors."

Once bloggers saw that, they exploded like—well, fireworks.

More telling were the Regents' official remarks. Deitch said, "I have religiously attended [Michigan] football games for 50 years. I have not found that experience wanting for lack of fireworks."

Regent Mark Bernstein termed the fireworks a "huge symbolic issue. . . . We are not Comerica Park, Disney World, or a circus. I love Michigan football for what it is, and for what it is not. It remains and should be intentionally simple. The fireworks should be on the field, not above it."

When the Regents voted against fireworks for the Miami game, 4–3, and the Penn State game, 5–2, it got people's attention. (Regent White, then a lieutenant colonel and now a colonel in the Army Reserve, was at War College, and had to miss the meeting.)

The fans voiced their wholehearted agreement, through social media and the blogs. They might have set a record for quoting Regents. Several noted that Brandon had declined to show up to answer the Regents' questions himself.

The day after President Schlissel's first Regents meeting, he told a reporter that, being new, he had no opinion on the matter. But it was clear he understood the power of Michigan's tradition and community, and what those can lend a university.

He made it a point to tell the faithful he appreciated just how important athletics are to the university. "It's a great part of the culture." But, he added, "As you can tell from yesterday's discussion, [the Regents] have different opinions about . . . what's happening to the culture of athletics, what's happening to the commercialization of athletics, and all the wider issues that are being discussed in the national media as well.

"Ultimately we'll have a community discussion of the direction Athletics is heading and we'll arrive at a consensus, but I'm quite comfortable that it's run professionally, it's run with high integrity, and we'll have to see how the discussion plays out.

"We're an academic institution, so I want to work on the appropriate balance between athletics and academics. . . . The athletic director does have delegated responsibilities, but he works for me."

On Michigan Web sites, this sparked another chorus of "Hallelujah."

But it would be easy to read too much into the comments from the Regents and President Schlissel. When you boiled their quotes down, they represented not a radical departure from the status quo, but a return to it: reinforcing the chain of command, the customs, and the traditions Michigan has relied on to become a leader, academically and athletically, for more than a century.

Taken together, however, their comments suggested the people who ran the university no longer felt compelled to rubber-stamp the athletic director's every request—a shift Brandon should have noted.

The athletic department had bigger things to worry about, in any case. With only six weeks to go until opening kickoff, the panic to unload tickets was on, forcing the department to try increasingly unorthodox means to dump tickets any way it could. It started running ads on its Web site, its electronic billboard, on TV, and even at a street stand during the Ann Arbor Art Fair, urging fans to buy football tickets—all completely unprecedented. If you went to Michigan, lived in Michigan, or could find Michigan on a map, you were likely to have received a pitch from the athletic department offering you free Michigan football tickets.

It was a boon for thousands of fans who had already dropped their tickets, and discovered they could get back in the Big House for a song, if they wanted to. But it was a bust for those loyalists who had already paid full price for theirs. They had clearly overpaid, and if they wanted to sell any, they would take huge losses.

CHAPTER 54

ALL ABOARD THE S.S. *BOIKE*

Despite the setback, even Brandon's toughest critics had little reason to believe he would be leaving Michigan any time soon.

Likewise, with offensive coordinator Al Borges departing during the offseason, and Doug Nussmeier in from Alabama to work with fifth-year senior Devin Gardner, Brady Hoke seemed poised for a solid season, and maybe a great one. With eight or nine wins, Hoke's job would be safe, Brandon would give him an extension to sustain recruiting, and the Brandon-Hoke Era could continue for many years.

On the West Coast, everyone expected Jim Harbaugh's 49ers to make their fourth straight trip to the playoffs, if not the NFC title game. True, his relationships with the team's owner, Jed York, and general manager, Trent Baalke, had become strained. But that could be said of many successful NFL coaches, past and present, from Jimmy Johnson to Bill Parcells to one of Harbaugh's predecessors in San Francisco, Bill Walsh.

In the summer of 2014, the idea that Harbaugh would return to Michigan any time soon seemed absurd. And even if Michigan's head coaching position somehow magically opened, many people weren't sure if Harbaugh would want it. He hadn't seemed to want it in 2011, after all, and Brandon hadn't hesitated to take some thinly veiled jabs at Harbaugh during Hoke's first press conference.

But one of these impediments, at least, was not what it appeared.

The day after the Regents voted down Brandon's fireworks request, Jim and Sarah Harbaugh traveled to Michigan for the wedding of Garrett Celek, the 49ers tight end. In four years at Michigan State, Celek only had 12 starts, 14 catches, and 3 receiving touchdowns, which explains why no NFL team drafted him. But Harbaugh saw something he liked, asked general manager Trent Baalke to pick Celek up as a free agent, and helped him become a regular.

During college, Celek met Sarah Hinton, a native Michigander. They decided to have their wedding in the Leelanau Peninsula, the "pinkie" of Michigan's mitten. And that's how the Harbaughs happened to be in Michigan that weekend.

They flew in Friday afternoon and spent the evening with Todd Anson—the San Diego attorney—his wife, Terri, and a dozen or so of Anson's friends, including yours truly. I had gotten to know Todd while researching my previous two books. That weekend, I happened to be attending a reunion at Camp Hayo-Went-Ha on Torch Lake, not far away, so it was easy to visit.

The Ansons' cottage is less cabin than castle, built in a rustic, northwoods style, with plenty of room for entertaining. The Ansons' neighbors—most of them Michigan alums—had already arrived at the Ansons' when the Harbaughs walked up the driveway about six. After some appetizers and cocktails, the entire party boarded the S.S. *Boike*, a pontoon boat with ample bench seating and a couple of coolers.

The boat's owner, Bill Boike, a Michigan-trained neurologist, donned his captain's hat and guided the boat through some narrows in a no-wake zone near the Ironton Ferry. Boike just happened to have a recording of "The Victors" handy, and couldn't resist blaring it through the speakers, "just to welcome Jim to our little piece of heaven," Boike told me later. "Jim's response was awesome. With no hesitation and unabashed enthusiasm he joined in, fist pumping in the air, singing at the top of his lungs. He was obviously one of us—an ardent supporter of our great university with a deep affection for the maize and blue."

The passengers hadn't gotten too far into Michigan's fight song when Boike's boat encountered another boat with a few Spartans on it, and their green flag flying high. It turned out they just happened to have their own fight song ready to blast in response to "The Victors," while the two boats raced down the lake. But the S.S. *Boike* had more volume and more passengers, and eventually won the battle of the bands.

"No one enjoyed the exchange more than Jim," Boike said, "who told us that's what he *loved* about college rivalries. 'This stuff just doesn't happen in the NFL.'" Sarah later recalled, "Jim told me, 'You've got to learn this song!'"

"Our Spartan friends turned their boat around," Boike recalls, "and a young lady stood up and proudly mooned us as they took off."

When the passengers on Boike's boat that night later heard and read various experts say there was no way the Harbaughs would ever leave California and the NFL for Michigan, they knew better. They had seen it firsthand.

They also saw how quickly Harbaugh would engage just about anyone in conversation, and how much Sarah enjoyed that. Harbaugh can be intense, impatient, and occasionally combative, but he is no snob. Jim's status, Boike told me, was quickly forgotten by everyone on board—just the way Harbaugh likes it. "He and Sarah were simply fellow Michigan fans and supporters."

After the first playing of "The Victors," Boike slowed down so Anson could stand in the center of the boat, raise his drink, and welcome Jim and Sarah to Lake Charlevoix. "Then he said something that stood out," Boike recalls. "'Ladies and gentlemen, I give to you the only man in the history of the University of Michigan's venerated football program whose *manifest destiny* it is to coach Michigan!'"

Everyone cheered and laughed. Harbaugh responded in kind, throwing both arms in the air to make the "touchdown" signal, and cracking, "He's talking about me!"

"Jim was *sooo* happy," Sarah told me later. "It was easy to see he still felt very much connected, and excited!"

Even the notoriously unpredictable Michigan weather, which turned chilly and gray that evening, couldn't dampen Harbaugh's enthusiasm. When he told Sarah he loved this type of weather, and hated the way the sun always beat down on you in California, she smiled and nodded.

"We had read that Jim would never consider coming to Michigan to coach and that Sarah would never leave the West Coast," another passenger, Sherri Stephens, recalled. "I was prepared to find Jim intimidating and standoffish, and Sarah detached and disinterested. [But] both were extremely gracious, clearly having a good time with people they had never met before. By the end of the evening I concluded that Todd's insight was 100 percent accurate: Harbaugh had a manifest destiny to come back to lead his alma mater!"

But Anson himself wasn't sure he was right at that point, just optimistic.

Most of the guests left about 10, but Todd, Jim, and I stayed up until 2 a.m., catching up and talking about mutual friends, Ann Arbor, and Michigan football.

In the middle of our conversation, Harbaugh said, "I think it's great to grow up in a college town, don't you?"

"That," Anson said later, "was the first sign I had that I might be right about Jim's 'manifest destiny.'"

"He's said that many times to me," Sarah later told me. "'Wouldn't it be great to raise our kids in a college town?' Palo Alto is great, but it's not really a college town like Columbia [Missouri, home of her alma mater], like Ann Arbor. That's always been in the back of his mind."

When the Harbaughs headed to the Celek wedding the next day, there was still a mountain of obstacles between Harbaugh and the Michigan coaching job. Only a lunatic would have made that bet.

But that night, two bits of conventional wisdom—that the Harbaughs were unwilling to leave California and the NFL, and had no interest in Michigan— were revealed as illusions. They did not exist.

In fact, the opposite was true. Harbaugh had never lost his feeling for Michigan, and his desire to coach there was as strong as ever.

That meant only the mountain of obstacles remained.

CHAPTER 55

TRACK TOUR

On August 2, 2014, Brandon put on another world-class showcase. The Big House hosted a "friendly" exhibition game between Real Madrid and Manchester United, two of the most popular franchises of any sport in the world. Brandon's department pulled in 109,318 people, enough to break the record for an American soccer crowd, set three decades earlier at the 1984 Los Angeles Olympics final when 101,799 watched France beat Brazil at the Rose Bowl, 2–0.

This fit a pattern: Big, splashy spectacles, like the Notre Dame night games, the NHL's Winter Classic, and big-time soccer in the Big House, Brandon knocked out of the park. But it was not clear if he recognized that those were fundamentally different events, with different fans and different expectations, than what Michigan fans generally wanted when they went to a Wolverines' game.

He catered to the top echelon, and the student-athletes. What he did considerably less was what the university was created to do: serve the public. During Brandon's tenure, many of the messages coming from the department to the fans about tickets, luxury suites, and the like were seasoned with adjectives like "elite," "exclusive," and "privileged."

If nothing else, Brandon came by it honestly. He owned lavish, custom-designed homes in exclusive neighborhoods, with memberships in world-class country clubs. He understood these people; he knew what they wanted and how to package it. In his new role as athletic director, this trait served him well—except when it didn't.

On August 3, 2014, hoping to generate support for his building program, Brandon gave a tour of the facilities for Regents Shauna Diggs, Denise Ilitch,

Andrea Fischer Newman, and Kathy White. Brandon wanted to show them what needed remodeling or replacing, and why, while Regents like Andrea Fischer Newman wanted to make sure they were doing all they could to ensure the safety of the student-athletes, including building a sidewalk to allow them to get to all the venues without having to cross busy streets.

Within reason, the Regents wanted the new facilities to be made available to all students, not just the athletes. Under the Regents' plan, the varsity athletes would still get to use the weight rooms, the track, and other facilities during practice and team workouts, but the facilities would be open to the rest of the student body at other times—much the way the Ferry Field track is used now.

It's no ordinary track, either. Yost's "Point-a-Minute" teams played on the infield, and at the 1935 Big Ten track-and-field meet, Ohio State track star Jesse Owens put in the single greatest hour in the history of athletics, setting four world records in 45 minutes. For this, Canham commissioned a plaque commemorating his feat on Michigan soil, just off the track—surely the only Buckeye to be so honored in Ann Arbor.

While Brandon was explaining to his tour guests why this track had to be pulled up and paved to create more parking spaces, and a state-of-the-art track facility built up the road, a random collection of faculty, students, and Ann Arbor residents ran by on the track.

"You could tell he was kind of irritated by that," White recalls. Brandon commented that the athletic department had closed the gate to the track, but people kept jumping over it and using the track anyway. White couldn't resist responding to Brandon's annoyance at the random professors, staffers, students, and even townies running on his track.

"Why do you care if people from the community are using it?" White asked.

"Liability," he said, perhaps forgetting he was talking to a Princeton graduate and professor of law at Wayne State University in Detroit.

"Liability?" she asked. "What kind of liability?"

"Heart attacks," he said, citing perhaps the most unlikely of all the lawsuits Michigan might have to defend.

White couldn't resist. "What about 100,000 people walking up and down the stairs at the Big House seven or eight days a year?" she asked. "And we didn't have handrails for years. What about people running through the Diag, or the Arb? Of all the people in our community, the least likely to have a heart attack are probably the people running on Michigan's track."

White explained to me why this was important. "The Regents weren't interested in spending $350 million for his Master Plan just for the 900 varsity athletes," says White, who earned varsity letters at Princeton in both track and volleyball. For them to sign off on the plan, "There would need to be access for all students. He wasn't going to shut down the track on my watch.

"Frankly, it puts pressure on the student-athletes when they're treated so differently from the rest of the student body. The more we can do for all students, the better for everyone."

After this exchange, White concluded, "We had to get an agreement signed, outlining how the athletic facilities were going to be used, before Brandon broke ground on the project, or we were never going to get it."

They did.

CHAPTER 56

GETTING READY FOR SOME FOOTBALL

To start Michigan's 2014 fall football camp, Coach Hoke instituted a new rule: Every time players walked into Schembechler Hall, they had to stick their cell phones into a big box near his office with 125 little slots, each with a jersey number, as if they were "clocking in" for their shift. Once all the phones were in the box, they locked the box.

"The idea was was, 'We're from Michigan,' a blue-collar state, lots of factory workers," Hagerup says. "But as you can imagine, the cell phone box did not go over well with most of the guys, especially in the first few days. There were a lot of complaints.

"But as camp went on, we started noticing we're having real conversations, getting to know each other—and not just looking up between texts. By the end of camp, it felt like we were so close. And that led into this really wonderful night."

Another team tradition: At the end of summer camp, the players walk over to the stadium and gather in the stands. The newly minted seniors talk to their charges about what's expected of Michigan Men, then they jog over to the Michigan golf course, where the freshmen jump into the pond.

"Having the seniors up there talking to the team at the Big House," Hagerup says, "and the younger guys looking and listening was really empowering. When you're an underclassman, you always wonder what the responsibility of being a senior is like. That night, I really got to feel that. It was special. From the freshmen to fifth-year guys like me and Devin, we felt so together, like we weren't going to lose a game.

"I hadn't felt that chemistry since high-school ball with my friends. And you grow up with those guys, and you're in class with the same people every single day—so that says something to feel that again on a college team. We had *such* chemistry on that team!

"But it really comes down to executing. All the chemistry in the world can't save you if you can't execute."

Before the season started, more serious problems surfaced. Hagerup knew that one of his friends on the team, whom we'll call Mike Burger, had a history of binge-drinking, drugs, depression, and mental-health issues.

"He was sort of a ticking time bomb," Hagerup says, "and we were really worried about him. Because I'd gone through the wringer of counseling, and dedicated a year of my life to learn about decision-making and that type of thing, I could see trouble coming.

"Jake Ryan, Joe Kerridge, and I were really worried about him. I'd had experiences with him before when I was the designated driver, and he was blowing coke in the backseat of the car. I kicked him out of the car."

Burger had stopped drinking during camp, when the players stayed at a local hotel. But when camp ended, Hagerup recalled, "He comes back to his house 20 minutes later with a 30-pack of beers, and just starts pounding them at an incredible rate. That was an eye-opener for me. Jake and Joe had warned me—but seeing that was a 'Wow!' Such desperation.

"The Sunday night before our last week of practice, we had to get in Burger's room, in the attic, because one of our friends forgot his backpack up there. Our friend comes down and says, 'Burger must not be here.'

" 'Why?'

" 'Door's locked.'

"So we go up and pick the lock—and it reeks of cigarette smoke and old beer, and he's in his bed passed out. And it's eight o'clock. It's a big room, but you couldn't see the floor. If you asked, what color is Burger's floor? You couldn't answer. Cigarette cases, butts, pizza boxes, beer cans—the most vile mess.

"I thought, this is so far beyond the point of 'Ha ha! Burger is drunk.' We've got to do something."

Hagerup texted Hoke immediately: "Burger needs help. This is really bad." After Hoke told them to come talk to him, and they described the situation, he said, "You're right. We need to bring him in."

Hoke set up a meeting two days before the season opener, with Hagerup, Kerridge, Jake Butt, director of athletic counseling Greg Harden, and Burger, who did not know the others would be there.

"When Burger walked into Hoke's office," Hagerup recalls, "he was startled. He didn't know we were going to be there. Hoke said, 'You have some really concerned teammates here who love you a lot and care about you, and they want to say a few words.'

"I went through my own stuff," Hagerup told Burger, "and I don't want to see you go through all that. Your room is disturbing and saddening. You're feeling a little cornered right now, but this could be the most important day of your life."

Butt, Kerridge, and Harden also added their thoughts, which initially put Burger on the defensive. Soon enough, though, "he got emotional and said, 'I don't like being sober. The only thing I want to do is get fucked up. I don't know what to do.'"

Hagerup said, "I'll take you to see someone. I'll take you there.'"

Burger agreed to that.

"That's Thursday," Hagerup says. "Okay, we made progress."

The morning of August 29, 2014, the Friday before the season opener, portrait artist Ben McCready once again met Dave Brandon in his office. The world looked a lot different than it had when they first met four years earlier, the day before the 2010 Big House rededication game against Connecticut.

Brandon had fired Rodriguez, hired Hoke, watched the team slide to 7–6 in 2013, and saw support for himself slide much farther.

"It had all gotten to be too much," McCready told me. "I supported the Legends program, and the flyovers were fun. But, sadly, it had all become too much about Dave—what was Michigan's past, present, and future. It seemed like he was always trying to outdo himself.

"He had the power and the glory of being the AD at the most storied athletic department in the nation. But I think all the attention and notoriety, and then the criticism—which he didn't handle very well—it all just became too much for him. Instead of opening up more to people and letting them in, which I encouraged him to do, he became more closed off and gave the appearance more and more that he knew better than anyone else what needed to be done.

"That story always seems to have the same ending, and it isn't a happy one.

"I've painted more than 100 Fortune 500 CEOs. I know these guys. A lot of times the arrogance people saw in Dave, this 'my way or the highway' approach he often took with people—well, it doesn't take a very accomplished psychologist to figure out that that's often driven by a real need to prove something to others, and it became sad to watch.

"What always struck me was my feeling of empathy for him—my sense that he was struggling to prove to people that he was more than people thought he was, that he was better and smarter than they might think he was.

"I don't think he really understood how successful he had been. I saw this person who, for no reason, seemed very insecure about what he had done, so he always needed to show people how successful he was.

"When I interacted with him, I enjoyed our chats—always. But I never *understood* him and I think it would be very hard to *be* him."

"He is not an open book," one employee told me. "Sometimes he could be so generous, and other times you couldn't get anywhere. You never know what you're to get from him on a given day."

This kept the people working in the department off-balance, which gave Brandon an advantage, even when he was not always aware of how he was coming across.

"He had a deep-seated need to be perfect, and it drove everything he did, and it was never enough."

When Brandon welcomed McCready into his office that morning, "I was taken aback at how tired and beaten Dave looked. He'd lost weight—and not in a good way. He looked 20 years older than he looked when I first met him four years earlier.

"I think Dave knew that things might be coming to an end with the mounting criticism all around him. He had always been pretty upbeat and optimistic when I had seen him before, but this time his mood and demeanor were very different."

McCready shook Brandon's hand, sat down, and asked, sincerely, "How are you doing?"

"Ah, I'm doing okay," Brandon said, then proceeded to talk about all the criticism he was getting. "I guess that goes with the job. But it does wear on you."

McCready had already seen a few sides of Brandon, but never this one.

"He could be very thoughtful and generous and considerate, when he didn't need to be, when no one saw it," he says. "He shows up at funerals of families when nobody knows about it, he helps people through crises when there's nothing in it for him. There is that side of him that not many people ever saw.

"But there was also this side that was completely tone-deaf to people. He pushed so many people around, without a thought. He never thought people would compare notes, that they would decide to push back. And when they did, I think he was utterly surprised.

"Looking at Dave that day, the man who had become for so many people the poster child for the 'Donald Trump-ism' of intercollegiate athletics, all I could see sitting across from me was a man who cared so deeply about his alma mater and really had this incredible vision and who now looked so tired, so alone, and lost in his own thoughts and dreams, which were slowly slipping away.

"I never thought Dave understood people at all."

By 2014, thousands of people had an opinion on Dave Brandon, and almost as many liked to boil down his problems to a single blind spot or another. But with that simple sentence, Ben McCready might have found the central issue, from which all Brandon's other problems arose.

McCready knew that a few people, including a friend of his, had suggested to Brandon that he invite MGoBlog founder Brian Cook—who had gone from one of Brandon's biggest backers to one of his biggest bashers—to his office for a personal meeting.

"I can't do that," Brandon told McCready's friend.

"Why not?" McCready's friend asked.

"Because," Brandon said, "it would be like negotiating with a terrorist."

When I mentioned this to Brian Cook, he didn't need much time to ponder the proposal, either. "Funny thing about that Brandon quote is that if anyone had tried to set up a face-to-face, I would have refused—and for the same reason."

At this point, Brandon did not feel he could reach his hand out for help, nor would most of his critics consider helping him. He had dug a very deep hole, and it was taking a toll.

McCready couldn't help but be struck by the exhausted figure he saw before him, and the contrast from the vibrant, vital man he'd met four years earlier. "And not just physically," he says. "Dave's extreme confidence, his bravado—it was still there, but nothing like it was. He looked more like someone who'd been battered, but had one more round in him."

McCready felt compelled to try to help. He told Brandon he thought he was at his best when he explained to people what he wanted to do, and why. Brandon "just kind of shook his head in resignation and said, 'I hope you're right, but I'm not so sure anymore.'"

This sad scene reminded McCready what Brandon had told him exactly four years earlier, the day before Brandon's first football game as Michigan's athletic director in 2010: "You know, Joe Roberson said being the AD was the worst four years of his life. I hope it doesn't turn out that way for me."

Looking at Brandon that morning, four years later, McCready realized if he had reminded Brandon of Roberson's line, even Brandon might have had to admit that, yes, despite all his efforts—and often because of them—it had turned out that way for him, too.

CHAPTER 57

POSTGAME DRAMA

Michigan football's rich tradition raised an obvious question: With all that history, all those records, and the countless great games and players to choose from, why would anyone associated with Michigan want to pay money to relive the worst day in Michigan football history?

The vast majority, it seemed, did not. But when the athletic director scheduled Appalachian State for the 2014 season opener on August 14, no one had much choice. The players, the lettermen, and the fans would all have to go through it one more time.

The Wolverines responded the only way they could, by doing to a weak Mountaineer team what their predecessors had failed to do against a much better one. After Gardner threw 3 touchdown passes to Devin Funchess in the first half, the Wolverines were well on their way to a ho-hum, 52–14 drubbing of the Mountaineers.

Hagerup gave the Appalachian State performance about as many words as it deserved: "We did what we were supposed to do." But that's all you heard of the actual outcome. Just about everything else about the matchup that you could read, hear, or see on TV revolved around what had happened in 2007, not 2014—just as many fans had feared.

That night, Hagerup got a text from his housemate, Jake Butt, that their troubled teammate, whom we're calling Mike Burger, was very upset that he hadn't played more, and could be in "bad form" that night.

"So we're watching for that," Hagerup recalls, "when I'm sitting in Burger's house with some other people around eight o'clock. It's pouring outside— but then Burger storms in the the door, soaking wet. He is *so* drunk, I don't know how much alcohol or drugs he consumed to get that fucked up. He can barely talk.

"He starts confessing that he's on all kinds of drugs, and finished a fifth of vodka. From the language that he's using, I'm thinking he was suicidal."

After a while, Hagerup got Burger to sit down in the living room, when Ryan and Kerridge walked in. Then Burger announced, out of nowhere, that he was going to a party at the baseball house, two blocks away.

"He goes out the door and starts walking to the baseball players' house," Hagerup remembers, "but then I think, 'Wait a second: His car is at Schembechler Hall, same direction as the baseball house. He's not going to the party.'"

After Burger had left the house, his teammates got in Butt's car and drove to Schembechler Hall. They stopped in the parking lot and turned the lights off, watching for Burger. They waited, until they saw him walking across State Street, headed for Schembechler Hall and his truck. When Burger pulled his keys out of his pocket, his three teammates jumped out of their car.

"Burger!" Hagerup yelled. "Get the fuck out of the car, you're not driving!"

As Hagerup recalls, Burger had a bottle of Jack Daniel's in his hand. He was very belligerent, while the others tried to restrain him. "Quit trying to fucking run my life and save me! Just let me do this! If you don't let me do this, I'll go up to my room and put a bullet in my head."

"He was hoping to kill himself, one way or the other," Hagerup says. "He was so fucked up, if he had gotten in his car, he or someone else would have been killed that night."

While Jake Ryan tried to calm Burger down, Hagerup snuck off to call Coach Hoke. It was 10:30, pitch dark, and pouring rain. When Hoke picked up, Hagerup said, "Coach, I don't know what else to do. I don't want to call the police, but I feel helpless, and I need you to come over to our house."

Hoke was hosting family and friends over at his house for a postgame party. "Most coaches," Hagerup says, "would say, 'Take him to his house, put him in his bedroom, and I'll see you tomorrow.'"

But Hoke didn't hesitate. "I need to tell my guests I'm leaving, then I'll be right over."

When Hoke arrived at the house, with his wife and daughter, he wasn't rattled, or upset, just ready to handle the situation.

"The amazing thing was," Hagerup said, "Hoke was in control the entire time. Burger got in his face—and Hoke got right back in his face, and pushed him down in a chair. He was in control. 'You need to be a fucking teammate.

You got three guys down there who care more about you than you care about yourself.' "

Burger's parents, who were staying at a hotel, soon arrived. His mother was understandably distraught, and started cleaning up his room. Hoke and the other players decided it was best for Burger's parents to take it from there.

The next day, Sunday, the Burgers visited Hoke's office. Together, they came up with a plan: Mike would get the help he needed—provided free by the university.

Behind the scenes, with only a few players watching, Hoke showed how much he cared for his players. But in Hoke's fourth season, his players had come to expect that.

It was Hagerup's fifth year on campus, and the maturity the punter displayed that night, that was something new. He had learned to take responsibility for himself, he had become strong enough to take responsibility for someone else, and he was wise enough to give the help Burger needed.

Hoke might have been the hero that night, but without Hagerup's intervention, the head coach might not have gotten the chance.

"We're on the cutting edge at Michigan, with one of the nation's first and best depression centers," Hagerup told me. "One of our old teammates, Will Heiniger, has become a spokesman there. It's not flashy stuff, but it's really, really important stuff. It's important that your university cares about that stuff.

"I'm proud to say I'm from a place that does care."

CHAPTER 58

THE FLAME GETS HOT

Notre Dame athletic director Jack Swarbrick once again added a little spice to a rivalry that was already running pretty hot when he announced the day before the Michigan game that Notre Dame had just signed a deal to play Ohio State in 2022 and 2023—dates that would have been saved for Michigan in years past.

It was the best possible response to Hoke calling Notre Dame chicken, and Brandon playing the "Chicken Dance" after Michigan's 2013 victory. Replacing Michigan on Notre Dame's schedule with the Wolverines' archrival, the same team that had beaten Michigan 9 of their last 10 meetings, dismissed the "chicken" claim quite efficiently.

But on the slim chance anyone didn't get the point—underscored by the timing of the announcement, 24 hours prior to the last Notre Dame-Michigan game—Swarbrick added, "Football games between Notre Dame and Ohio State make great sense from a strength-of-schedule standpoint."

Swarbrick's message: Notre Dame's not chicken. Notre Dame is dropping Michigan for stiffer competition.

Notre Dame was a five-point favorite, but that didn't mean much in this rivalry, which almost always delivered down-to-the-wire excitement. Everyone expected another classic on September 16, 2014—but they didn't get one.

The revved up Irish, led by quarterback Everett Golson, scored 1 touchdown in the first quarter, 2 in the second, and 1 in the third, then added a fourth-quarter field goal to shut out the stunned Wolverines, 31–0. After the game, Notre Dame did not bother playing the "Chicken Dance." They didn't have to. The scoreboard said plenty.

"Those guys played an incredible game," Hagerup says of the Irish. "Golson was lights out, so smooth. Every pass he wanted, he completed.

"Thirty-one to zero? Jesus. Yeah, that one hurt.

"As Coach Hoke said in the locker room afterward, 'That's a classic ass-whooping. You take your shower and you get the fuck out of the locker room.' And that's what we did."

The whitewash was Notre Dame's first shutout of the Wolverines since they played their first game in 1887. It also snapped Michigan's NCAA-record streak of games without being shut out at 365. That string went back to October 20, 1984, when Schembechler's team lost to Iowa, 26–0—a team that had lost its starting quarterback, a young man named Jim Harbaugh, in the fifth game of the season.

Despite being picked to finish 9–3 or 10–2 that season, after only the second game, the last of Michigan's century-old rivalry with Notre Dame, the Wolverines had already fallen off the national radar.

"Michigan had lost games before," Regent Larry Deitch said, looking back on the 2014 season, "but not like this. We didn't appear to be competitive."

In Hobe Sound, Florida, former captain John Arbeznik watched the game at his home, and had a reaction similar to Deitch's: "I could not believe what I was seeing," Arbeznik said.

The next day, still despondent from the drubbing, even a round at the Lost Lake Golf Club didn't cheer him up. He found himself sitting in his car in the parking lot, wondering what to do. Arbeznik decided to call John Ghindia, Jim Harbaugh's old teammate and friend, who gave Arbeznik Harbaugh's cell number.

"I was miserable after the blowout and felt semi-helpless," Arbeznik told me. "I knew Les Miles, among others, wanted the job. I was feeling better about Dave Brandon's impending demise but knew we needed to act in order to identify the next coaching regime. It became strongly apparent to me that Hoke and Brandon's fates were aligned.

"I was reaching out to Jim for two reasons: to fill him in on our efforts to fix Michigan football, and second, to see if he would support our candidates." They did not believe Harbaugh himself might be a candidate for the job. Harbaugh didn't answer, so Arbeznik left a message.

"I was almost crying," Arbeznik admits. "I was still distressed by the effort the previous night. I told Jim, 'We need help. You're Michigan.' I wasn't expecting to pitch the job to him, but get his help getting Les back. But I even said on the message that I would cut off my right hand if *he* would be our next coach."

That's how big a long shot it seemed, and how desperate Arbeznik and his friends were to see Jim Harbaugh return.

"Thank God he didn't take me up on that!"

Jim Harbaugh gets a lot of messages, especially during the season. Why would he return Arbeznik's?

The answer goes back a few decades.

Arbeznik had been a somewhat sheltered student at St. Ignatius in Cleveland, a school that produced countless stars for Ohio State, Michigan, and Notre Dame. By his senior year in high school, winter of 1975, Arbeznik had had a few beers, but nothing stronger. In the mid-seventies, that set him apart as a veritable Boy Scout.

That changed during his recruiting weekend with the Wolverines. Schembechler paired him with a freshman lineman, Bill Dufek, son of Michigan great Don Dufek Sr., and younger brother of All-American Don Dufek Jr. Bill Dufek took his understudy to the West Quad dorm room of fellow freshman lineman Mike Kenn, who would go on to start 251 games for the Atlanta Falcons.

"We're lighting shots of Bacardi 151, then slamming them," Dufek recalls. "So I handed one to Arbeznik."

Arbeznik recalls that he didn't want to drink the shot, so he threw it over his shoulder. He thought he had gotten away with it, but he hadn't realized the shot was lit.

Here's where the stories diverge. Arbeznik remembers the shot lighting his sweater on fire, then Mike Kenn throwing him on the bed and smothering his face with a rug to put the fire out. Dufek recalls the flames igniting not Arbeznik's sweater but his face, and another roommate slapping him to put it out.

Either way, both were grateful Arbeznik didn't suffer any burns. They were also relieved nothing else started burning, either, or they would have received a visit from the Ann Arbor Fire Department, and an unwelcome call from one Bo Schembechler.

And that is how John Arbeznik got his nickname: The Flame.

A year later, when Dufek brought Arbeznik home for Thanksgiving, Dufek's mom Pat asked Arbeznik why everyone called him "The Flame." Dufek smelled trouble, and tried to cut it off at the pass. "Oh, that's because of his red hair," he said, interrupting. "You know, carrot top—Flame!"

But the still innocent Arbeznik, not getting the hint, said, "Oh, no no no, Mrs. Dufek. It's because we were doing shots last year and lighting them on fire, and the flames got on my face."

Dufek bowed his head, defeated, while his mom shot him a familiar look, shaking her head. "She didn't say anything," Dufek recalls. "She was used to it by then."

Arbeznik's teammates named him captain in 1979, Michigan's 100th season. He graduated the next spring and got a cup of coffee with the New Orleans Saints and New York Jets before entering Proctor & Gamble's management training program.

A couple years later, during the winter of 1982, Arbeznik and former Michigan All-American tight end Paul Seymour—who had blocked for O. J. Simpson in Buffalo—walked into a popular campus club, Rick's American Café. There they saw Jim Harbaugh, sitting by himself at the bar, in town from California for his official recruiting visit. Arbeznik recognized Harbaugh as the 18-year-old version of the kid he remembered when Jim and his older brother John would "use the practice field and locker room as their personal playground."

Harbaugh immediately recognized Arbeznik as one of the players he'd idolized growing up. After they caught up for a bit, Arbeznik asked Harbaugh, "Where are the players who are taking you around campus?"

"I ditched them," Harbaugh said.

Arbeznik laughed. "Meet Paul Seymour."

The two lettermen gave Harbaugh about the same treatment Dufek and Mike Kenn had given the Flame seven years earlier. They started drinking, and didn't stop until Rick's closed. The next morning, Flame and Seymour slept in, while Harbaugh had to face Bo Schembechler at 8 a.m.

"Needless to say," Arbeznik says, "Jim committed the next morning!"

The two had a bond, forged through Michigan football. So when Arbeznik left a message for Harbaugh the day after the Notre Dame debacle, Harbaugh called him back and left his own message. After a couple rounds of phone tag, they finally connected on October 3.

"We told him what we were up to regarding Dave Brandon," Arbeznik recalls, of their first 20-minute conversation. Near the end of their second conversation, Jim told Arbeznik, "I'm not having any discussions about jobs." He was still focused on coaching the 49ers, and he had nothing but respect for Brady Hoke. He gave Arbeznik his father's phone number, and asked him to keep his father in the loop. "It all goes through my dad," he said.

Arbeznik did as instructed, which made him one of the first persons from Michigan to reach out to any of the Harbaughs. When Arbeznik called Jack Harbaugh, "Jack thought the possibility of Jim coming to Ann Arbor, though remote, would be a 'good fit' for Jim."

At the time, no one could imagine the 49ers' front office imploding, the 49ers missing the playoffs, Brandon resigning, and Michigan staying home during bowl season.

But a connection had been made, and a conversation begun.

Encouraged by the mere fact that Jim Harbaugh hadn't instantly killed the idea of one day coaching at Michigan, Harbaugh's unofficial ambassadors went to work. The effort was led by Todd Anson in California, John Arbeznik in Florida, and John Ghindia in Michigan, who was in constant communication with the other two, and just about everyone else. They all knew, before Michigan and Harbaugh could even consider teaming up, they faced three major obstacles, obstacles that grew from Harbaugh's comments in 2007, the backlash that followed, and the 2011 coaching search.

First, they had to "rehabilitate" Harbaugh in the eyes of Michigan's leaders. They planned to do this by showing them how much Harbaugh loved his alma mater, in the hopes of increasing his supporters, and decreasing the number of people who might try to blackball Harbaugh's candidacy before it even started. Second, they would also have to convince Harbaugh he'd be welcomed back with open arms by the Michigan family, including the lettermen, the former coaches—especially Lloyd Carr—and the university leadership. They needed to show Harbaugh how much Michigan wanted him to return, so he would feel comfortable putting his heart above his head, and bypassing the big lights and big bucks of the NFL to come home.

If they somehow managed to accomplish those two sizable diplomatic missions, however, they knew the third obstacle—Brandon—would likely render their efforts moot. After the bad taste the 2010 search left in Harbaugh's mouth, his supporters didn't believe Brandon could recruit Harbaugh, even if he wanted to—and that wasn't entirely clear, either.

But if they wanted to see Michigan football return to its former glory, it's a chance they were willing to take—a chance they felt they *had* to take. If the opportunity for Harbaugh to return somehow, magically popped up, and they hadn't completed rebuilding the bridge in time to make it possible, they would not forgive themselves. "Not an option," Anson said.

If Hoke pulled through, problem solved. No one wanted to see him fail. But if Hoke didn't succeed, and Brandon was out of the picture by December, they figured they had to be ready. If Harbaugh was simply another candidate, they could afford to wait until after Michigan's season, and let the athletic director make the call on Hoke's future. But given the extra work that had to be done to rebuild the bridge between Harbaugh and his alma mater, they felt they couldn't afford to wait until late December to get started.

In this, they had two great advantages. First, the NFL teams were strictly forbidden from talking to any NFL coach under contract, and would have to wait until after Harbaugh's last game on December 28 just to ask permission from the club to talk to their coach. But there were no rules preventing people at Michigan, especially lettermen, from recruiting an NFL coach whenever they liked.

This was a break they had to have. If they didn't feel they could wait until the Michigan-Ohio State game on November 29, waiting until December 28 would be impossible.

Second, they had something no NFL team had: lettermen—players who had *chosen* to play at Michigan, and remained loyal to it the rest of their lives. NFL players, on the other hand, are literally drafted into service, and usually by the team and town they least want to play for. Then they get traded, too, and cut. Talk to just about any NFL player, and he will almost always tell you he preferred playing for his alma mater than any pro team. Harbaugh's ambassadors had an army of loyal soldiers, and they had a couple months to deploy them—two things no NFL team could match. They started creating lists of people to call, e-mail, and meet throughout the fall, and they got busy.

Unlike during the 2010–11 search, Todd Anson told me, "This last time around I did not waste one minute on Brandon. I was prepared to allow him to fail all on his own because I knew he wouldn't listen anyway, but I could also sense that he was not long for the job. In my opinion, that was our only hope for landing Harbaugh. Brandon had to be gone, because either he didn't want Jim, or he was not up to the task of getting him."

On September 10, 2014, four days after the Notre Dame shutout, Todd Anson sent an introductory e-mail, out of the blue, to Regent Larry Deitch, asking to talk on the phone. Deitch responded promptly.

"My first talk with Larry Deitch was *amazing!*" Anson recalls. "He told me, 'I've had dreams of getting Jim Harbaugh back to Michigan for six, seven, eight years.'"

After Deitch's son had received his MBA from Stanford, he settled in the Bay Area, and Larry visited often. In fact, he told Anson, he was headed out to San Francisco that weekend, so he asked if he might set up a casual meeting with Harbaugh.

Anson would have loved to play middle man, but he told Deitch there wasn't much point. "Jim is so focused and disciplined during the season, there is no way he would meet with anyone about another job, so I never even asked

Jim. But I knew right away that Larry Deitch was a guy who was serious, and could get things done."

As the fall unfolded, the conversations between the two increased—a noted contrast to Anson's experience with Michigan's athletic director.

"Brandon never got it," Anson says. "He was not big enough to get the job done and he embarrassed his university with either his feeble effort or his bungling ineffectiveness. Yes, you can quote me. I said many times to the people involved, 'It takes a village to hire a superstar football coach.'"

Therefore, it takes a leader strong enough to seek the help of the village. The growing village of ambassadors trying to get Jim Harbaugh back to Michigan seemed to be guided by a few basic principles. Their plan, boiled down, was simply this: Whatever Brandon had done in 2010, they would do the exact opposite.

Don't play games. Be direct.

Don't hold back. Show the love.

Don't do it yourself. Get help.

Don't worry about who gets the credit. Harbaugh's return would be credit enough for everybody.

"You know there's an old saying," Deitch told me: "'It's kind of amazing what you can accomplish when no one cares who gets the credit.' And that's what happened here. It was *teamwork!*

"Flame and Ghindia, I met them years ago through my good friend Dan Horning [a former Regent]. Those guys were *completely sincere.* They were *completely credible.* They just wanted Michigan to be good so they could be proud of it, and they wanted respect for the people who worked very hard to build the Michigan football tradition."

A grassroots effort had begun. No one in the loosely organized group was in it for money, fame, power, or even credit. The proof is simple: You've probably never heard of most of these people, or what they did, until now. They simply wanted to see Michigan football return to its former heights, and they believed Jim Harbaugh was the man to get them back there.

"All we wanted to do was create the marketplace where both sides wanted to buy," Ghindia told me, "so all Michigan had to do was get in front of Harbaugh, and make their pitch."

They still had far more work in front of them than behind them, and even if they completed their mission, the odds were still long. But they had made two vital decisions: to take action, and to work together—two elements that were crucially missing in 2011.

CHAPTER 59

GETTING NOWHERE, SLOWLY

With the nation ready to write off the 2014 Wolverines after getting hammered by Notre Dame, they didn't help their cause by coming out flat against Miami, Ohio. In the second quarter, the Redhawks tied Michigan, 10–10, before Derrick Green ran for a touchdown to give Michigan a 17–10 lead.

With less than a minute left in the half, the Wolverines had the ball on Miami's 32-yard line. After a time-out, they somehow managed to get called for delay of game, then punted from Miami's 37-yard line. Neither the penalty nor the coaches' decision pleased the fans. When the players ran to the tunnel, they were surrounded by the loud boos of the home crowd.

"First time I'd ever been on a team that got booed by its own fans," Hagerup said. "I don't think they wonder if it will help the team or not!" But, he had to admit, "That game was, like, a touchdown away from turning into a total disaster."

After Michigan scored 17 second-half points to put away Miami, 34–10, Hoke handled the inevitable question about the first-half boos with aplomb: "We have great fans. They have high expectations, like we do."

In other words, it's still Michigan.

The following week, an unranked but decent Utah team came to Ann Arbor and put up a 26–10 fourth-quarter lead. That included the first touchdown Hagerup had ever given up on a punt—although it didn't help that Michigan had only 10 players on the field. It was not the first time that season, and it wouldn't be the last. Right before halftime, after Michigan suffered a 5-yard penalty for sideline interference, the TV cameras seemed to pick up Hoke barking a profanity at defensive coordinator Greg Mattison, who responded in kind. When asked about it after the game, Hoke played it off beautifully, insisting it was nothing. "You ought to see us play euchre," he quipped, getting a laugh.

But it was hard to imagine the growing pressure and occasional boos weren't beginning to get to the coaching staff, too.

With a little under eight minutes left in the contest, lightning sent the fans headed for the exits, and the teams to the locker room. The break would last two and a half hours.

"Oh God, that was weird," Hagerup says. "We went back into the locker room after that break. And guys at first were like, 'Can we just go?' Then we're like, 'No, we're gonna play football!' Then we got guys really, really rallied to play—more than any game we've ever played—yelling in the locker room, in the tunnel.

"If we're going to go out and play, let's play! No one's going to be there. It's going to be weird—but it's going to be awesome!"

When the teams returned, the field glistened with rain and reflected the overhead lights. A few hundred fans returned, most of them wearing Utah red.

"We heard so much about the Big House," Utah receiver Dres Anderson said. "It was the Ute House at the end."

Neither team scored after the long delay, sending the Wolverines back to the tunnel with a 26–10 loss, and a 2–2 record.

Once again, after the game Hoke had to answer a question about being booed.

"I don't like that with 18- to 22-year-old kids," Hoke said, taking a stronger stance than he had the previous week. "I know the fans pay their money and they have the right to do that, but I don't like it.

"If the boos are for me, that's fine."

Gardner hit 14 of 26 passes for 148 yards, but threw 2 more interceptions. Michigan's defense scored the Wolverines' only touchdown, off an interception return. It was little noted, due to the thunder and rain, but Hoke had benched Gardner in favor of Shane Morris right before the rain delay.

"There's not going to be any answers to that tonight," Hoke said, when asked about it at the press conference. "We will compete and challenge like we have every day. And then we will have a starting quarterback against Minnesota."

Looking back on it, Gardner told me, "Coach Hoke kinda threw me under the bus after that game. 'Hey, Devin's the problem!'"

Likewise, some fans and bloggers started to interpret Hoke's trademark answer after losses—"We practiced really well this week, but we just didn't execute"—a little differently. Translated, Hoke was really saying he and his staff recruited the right players, trained them well, ran great practices, and concocted brilliant game plans, but these players kept screwing it up on game days.

When I mentioned this to Gardner, he asked me, "If you can hear that, what do you think the players hear?"

At the end of the Wolverines' four-game nonconference schedule, they had played two teams from the newly nicknamed "Power Five" conferences. They had failed to score an offensive touchdown against either one, and lost to Notre Dame and Utah by a combined 47 points.

"So that sucked, and now we're an ugly 2–2," Hagerup said, months later. "That's probably when some disbelief started creeping in. Four weeks before, we were singing in the pond at the golf course, and we thought we had talent and chemistry. And now you have to reframe things. Okay, that's nonconference. We can still go win the Big Ten."

Hoke stressed exactly that point. "Our goals are all out there."

They were, but the 2014 squad was also vulnerable in ways Hoke's first team hadn't been. If Brandon believed his primary constituents were the student-athletes, and he sought to give them everything he possibly could, then the pressure for them to deliver was that much greater.

Brandon was also more exposed. When you go out of your way to ignore tradition and "create the future," and the future turns out to be less utopian than advertised, you have few places to hide. It's harder to fall back on tradition in tough times if you didn't take care of it when the livin' was easy.

CHAPTER 60

FROM SELLOUTS TO HANDOUTS

The department's problems had started internally and grown outward, circle by circle, from unhappy employees to lettermen to students to fans to Regents, but the team usually felt these ripples only as reverberations, the aftershocks of someone else's mistakes. The wall separating the players' locker room from the outside world had started to shake, and then leak a little, but it was still standing.

It was about to come crashing down.

The Monday night after the Utah game, September 22, 2014, Michigan senior Alejandro Zúñiga was working at the *Michigan Daily* when he heard rumors of a Coke-for-tickets deal at the small convenience store in the Michigan Union basement. He decided to go see for himself, and sure enough, there it was. The white plastic sign advertised two free tickets to that weekend's Minnesota–Michigan game if you bought two bottles of Coke, Coke Zero, Diet Coke, or Sprite—limit two tickets per person.

"I still couldn't believe it was real," Zúñiga told me. "So I bought two Cokes, and got two tickets. I sold one ticket for $5, kept the other—and made a profit!"

He took a picture of the sign and tweeted it with this caption: "Michigan sold some football tickets Monday evening. At a 98 percent discount." Within hours, it received 795 retweets and countless mentions by national media.

This caused the department's PR people to kick into crisis-management mode yet again, always from their vantage point at the back of the parade. The department quickly fired out a press release : "Coke as a partner of ours . . . purchased a limited block of tickets for the Minnesota game for a Coke retail activation aimed at Michigan students. Due to a miscommunication in the approval process, this promotion should not have run as is. As a result, it is being pulled immediately. However, all purchases to date will be honored by Coke."

Predictably, the already bruised Michigan "brand" got battered some more by the national media. MGoBlog teed it up on its front page: "The program was 'pulled immediately' after the Union had already run out [of tickets], i.e., not pulled. There's the silver lining: Michigan tickets are still worth more than two dollars."

After yet another "unforced error," followed by another ridiculous explanation, this one featuring the phrase "retail activation," the department had all the credibility of *Pravda*, and half the charm.

"A lot of people are putting a lot of pressure on our coaches," wide receiver Dennis Norfleet said to the media on Tuesday. "It's not really about our coaches. Our coaches do a great job coaching us, telling us what we need to do. It's up to us, to the players, to execute and play on the field. We know what we need to do and right now we're not doing it, it's our fault."

Publicly, at least, the players were buying the idea that execution was the only issue.

How did this once-proud program sink so low, so fast?

It's worth remembering Hoke's worst record to that point, 7–6, matched Rodriguez's best mark in Ann Arbor, back in 2010, a year after the economy had bottomed out—but the wait list was still long. But in 2014, the department had to resort to desperate measures to keep the streak going, selling deeply discounted tickets on Groupon, LivingSocial, and Amazon, and dumping thousands of free tickets on local schools, churches, camps, the ushers, Michigan golf club members, and the student-athletes—and yes, through TV ads, the electronic billboard, and a Coca-Cola giveaway—urging them all to come to the games to make it look good.

The department had been blessed with gorgeous weather for all three home tailgates. Even the Utah game started out with clear skies and balmy temperatures. By unloading tickets just about every way imaginable, Michigan had managed to draw enough fans for each game to claim with a straight face that the attendance streak was still intact. Sure, they were covering the foundation's cracks with wallpaper—but that was load-bearing wallpaper. It was best not to pull on it.

The department even sent out e-mails to the student-athletes of its other varsity sports, imploring them to support their classmates and show their school spirit by coming to the football games, and to bring their friends—creating the unseemly situation in which amateur athletes were being asked to forego rest or study to help the millionaire athletic director save face. These were the same athletes, it should be noted, to whom the department would not give free tickets a couple years earlier when the volleyball team, or wrestlers, or softball squad was being honored in the endzone during a TV time-out for winning a Big Ten or NCAA title. Then they would be ushered out of the stadium, just as fast.

There was a significant upside to the department's predicament: Thousands of people, especially kids, who couldn't afford the soaring ticket prices were getting a chance to visit the Big House for the first time, potentially starting a lifetime habit as the previous generation had. But that's not why the department was doing it.

Season-ticket holders had skin in the game, lots of it, and they generally showed up rain or shine. But anyone receiving a free ticket was, truly, a fair-weather fan. The department appeared to be just one cold, rainy day from having to admit, once and for all, that the hallowed streak was over.

It didn't help that the Wolverines had lost both their games against Power Five opponents—despite outgaining all their opponents—and dropped 8 of their last 12 games overall. No fans are more passionate than college football fans—or more myopic. If their school wins a few games, they believe they'll never lose again. And if they lose a couple, the situation is hopeless. A win against Minnesota, therefore, might have been enough to get Hoke's team on a roll, giving people good reason to hope for more in 2015, and justify keeping Hoke for at least another year.

But even if the Wolverines won that Saturday against a mediocre Minnesota team, as they were expected to, and enough fans showed up to allow the department to continue to claim the attendance streak was alive, something had already changed. Most Michigan fans were unhappy, as you'd expect, but this time I noticed many were upset that they were not that upset. They were alarmed by their lack of alarm. They were afflicted by something I had never seen before: indifference.

But the department's biggest problem went largely undiagnosed. To prop up its Potemkin Village, it was mortgaging the future.

When they discounted and then dumped thousands of tickets, did they expect the people who paid full price not to notice? When you paid a few thousand bucks for your four tickets, and the guy sitting next to you got in for a couple of Diet Cokes, did the department's leaders really think you would pony up for the same sky-high prices the next year?

As longtime fan Peggy Collins Totin told me, "I feel betrayed for being loyal."

Michigan had somehow created a world where loyalty was punished with price hikes, and disloyalty was rewarded with freebies.

Michigan fans may be irrational about their love for the Wolverines, but they're not stupid. Their Saturday habit developed over a lifetime, but once they felt they had been pushed too far, they had shown they could break it in a week.

I heard constantly from fans of other programs that their favorite teams were heading in the same direction. Would other schools learn from Michigan's mistakes in time to avoid Michigan's troubles?

If things had continued on this path, Michigan's ticket prices would have to come down, or thousands of fans would quit coming. Either way, the department's burgeoning budget would have to be cut back, or the department would be going into debt, and soon.

But what stood out was how easy all these problems were to predict, and how easily they could have been avoided. When faced with a decision, the Brandon regime consistently opted for style over substance—the exact opposite philosophy that Baird, Yost, Crisler, and Canham had followed to make Michigan football great for well over a century.

Early in his tenure, Brandon famously said, "I don't talk about the past. I create the future."

It's hard to believe this was the future he had in mind.

College sports eventually boil down to relationships, the heartfelt connections that link the athletes with the students, the alums, the lettermen, and the fans—and all the cross-pollination that happens among them. These are the ties that bind the university with those who love it, far more deeply than a trade school ever could. These relationships can be assessed statistically in a number of ways, but every measurement falls short of complete comprehension. As Einstein said, *"Not everything that counts can be counted. And not everything that can be counted, counts."*

Ultimately, these relationships have to be felt to be understood. On this, painter Ben McCready was spot on: Brandon simply was unable to do so.

He had "Us versus Them" down cold, but he couldn't seem to get his mind around "We."

CHAPTER 61

A BAD WEEK

The day after the "retail activation" gone bad, Brandon called two people into his office, separately: the department's associate director of communication, Peter Skorich, and his executive associate athletic director, Chrissi Rawak.

Since Brandon had become athletic director, the seasoned pro Bruce Madej had left media relations to run special projects, and moved his office across the grounds to the Crisler Center. Dave Ablauf had taken his mentor's place as director of media relations, until Brandon moved him aside in 2013 when Brandon hired Pete Skorich from the Detroit Pistons.

Underneath this level, Brandon had hired Justin Dickens from the Indianapolis Colts to become football's director of media relations in 2010. But in the spring of 2014, Brady Hoke had requested Justin Dickens leave his post working with the media to become Hoke's director of football operations—where Dickens's brusque personality would fit better in a position that requires saying no many times a day. To replace him, they hired Dickens' former intern with the Indianapolis Colts, Derek Satterfield, whose twitter bio read, "Mediocre people don't like high achievers, and high achievers don't like mediocre people." (As MGoBlog's Ace Anbender said to me, "I don't think he intended that to come off the way it does.") In case you weren't sure where Satterfield placed himself in that dichotomy, he later changed his twitter bio to, "Confidence is earned." After Brandon changed his director of media relations more times in his first four years than Michigan had in the previous 45 years—a chain that that ran from Will Perry to Bruce Madej to Dave Ablauf—Brandon called in Skorich, and when he left, he added his name to the long list of resignations. Then he asked Rawak, who had already taken over Joe Parker's development division, to take over Skorich's job, too.

Rawak had never previously worked in the media, or with the media. She thought about his offer for two days, before accepting.

On Thursday, as they always did, the crew that would be doing the game for ABC/ESPN visited Schembechler Hall, but then they split up, with producers, directors, and field personnel going with the experienced Dave Ablauf to Michigan Stadium for a walk-through, and the broadcasters going with the brand-new Derek Satterfield to practice.

While many of the veteran journalists weren't terribly fond of Dickens—who returned their disregard—almost everyone could work with him. But I have yet to find a single media member who enjoyed working with Derek Satterfield. As one former colleague in the department told me, "He was as abrasive as 50-grit sandpaper."

That view was soon shared by the TV broadcasters, who got fed up with Satterfield constantly telling them they can't visit this place, they can't mention that, and they can't talk to this guy for their Saturday broadcast. From Canham's day on, TV crews had looked forward to coming to Ann Arbor, where they were treated as trusted allies. So the cold reception came as a culture shock. When the broadcasters got to practice that afternoon, they had reached their limit with Satterfield, and finally got into an argument over freedom of speech, laced with profanity, and stormed off.

What normally served as a feel-good tour for the home team, setting up some nice puff pieces for the broadcast that weekend, had exactly the opposite effect: Satterfield had so turned off the crew, they would arrive to the TV booth on Saturday in a foul mood, not afraid to criticize Michigan for anything that might go wrong.

They would have no reason to hold back.

Michigan had long benefited from another public-relations safeguard in veteran athletic trainer Paul Schmidt, whom the department had always allowed to talk with sideline reporters during games. Watching Schmidt handle the players and media for three dozen games on the sideline, I noticed he rarely told them anything very definitive—most injuries took some time to diagnose, after all—but he always gave them something they could use, trained as he was by Don Canham to "never say, 'No comment.' It looks bad."

Simply telling a sideline reporter, "We're looking at his knee, and he'll be out for the rest of the half," kept the reporters happy, Michigan's media relations strong, and everyone out of trouble. But the year before, Justin Dickens had ended that policy, instructing Schmidt to speak only to an assigned Michigan PR staffer, who would relay the message to the press box. This practice increased delays, which angered the TV crews, and the odds of mistakes, which didn't please the medical staff. It also severed relationships with several solid reporters, and left Michigan on the outside of whatever conversation they were having in the booth.

This, too, would haunt Michigan when it mattered most.

CHAPTER 62

THE FLAME SPREADS

The drama continued to build the next day, Friday, September 26, but this time in public.

A couple months after Yale Van Dyne's letter started circulating, John "Flame" Arbeznik wrote his own manifesto, which become known among his fellow lettermen as "Flame's 25-point Grievance Letter." The complaints are now familiar—from Brandon visiting the locker room to the increase in prices to the decrease in ticket sales to the firing of stalwart employees—which he ended with, "This is just the beginning. I have lots more."

Arbeznik sent this to several Regents, including Larry Deitch, and other university leaders. It also spread among the lettermen. That week, it reached Gregg Henson, a former Detroit sports talk-show host now working in Pittsburgh, who still followed Michigan football closely, and often reported on it. He discussed it on his blog, which was soon linked by Michigan football blogs.

By Friday afternoon, September 26, Arbeznik found himself on ESPN's Detroit Sports 105.1, talking with popular afternoon hosts Drew Lane and Marc Fellhauer about his grievance letter, and the lettermen's views of Dave Brandon.

On Saturday morning, a few hours before kickoff, MLive.com's Nick Baumgardner published a piece titled "Ex-Michigan captain says some Bo Schembechler players frustrated with Dave Brandon."

"Former players are unhappy," Baumgardner wrote, "not just with the way the team is playing on the field, but with the way the department in general is being run by its athletic director.

"Speaking with Detroit Sports 105.1-FM this week, former Michigan football captain John Arbeznik said there are 'about 35' former players who have gotten together and constructed a letter filled with grievances over the way Michigan football is currently run. . . . The ultimate plan is to present it to Michigan president Mark Schlissel."

Arbeznik told Baumgardner the lettermen involved "just think Michigan is better than what we are today. They remember the great Bo Schembechler and the Don Canhams and the Ron Kramers. The Bo teams are dissatisfied. That, for sure, you can understand and you can understand why.

"When you don't have a captain there's no one responsible for anyone. So when they lost 31–0 to Notre Dame, I thought to myself, 'Well, no one has to put their name on that one.'

"Those little things drive us crazy."

"I can promise you this," Arbeznik told Baumgardner, "there was never a day I saw athletic director Canham. Ever. In a weight room, in a film session, inside a locker room. Ever."

On Sunday, ESPN's College Football Insider Joe Schad made one of his many trips to Ann Arbor to monitor a story he had been covering closely, and talk again with John Arbeznik. "The Flame" was spreading nationally, and so was his cause.

Baumgardner added, however, "There is one notable person who remains supportive, billionaire Michigan alum Stephen Ross."

Ross, a New York real estate mogul who also owns the Miami Dolphins, and has already given some $300 million to Michigan, mainly to athletics and the eponymous Ross School of Business, told *Crain's Business Detroit* that week that Brandon was "probably the most qualified athletic director in the country. I think he's terrific. I wouldn't have given my gift to the athletic department if I didn't believe in Dave.

"No one has a bigger vision for Michigan athletics, all sports. He really cares about the whole department, all the student-athletes. Now is the time to be supportive of him. He will do the right thing."

If the direction of the athletic department came down to a tug-of-war between the lettermen and the major donors, it was not clear who would win.

CHAPTER 63

A GALLON OF GASOLINE

Hoke's message never wavered: The Wolverines' goal was a Big Ten title, and that goal was still in front of them. With games against division rivals Michigan State and Ohio State on the road, however, Michigan didn't have much margin for error against—well, just about everyone else on the schedule.

But the Wolverines still had a decent shot, because all but the Spartans and the Buckeyes would enter their game against Michigan unranked. That included the Minnesota Golden Gophers, who came to Ann Arbor on a beautiful fall Saturday with three wins over nobodies, and a 30–7 loss to Texas Christian. The Gophers were, therefore, the kind of team Michigan should beat—just as it had the previous year, 42–13.

"Everyone knows from our past two games against them that Devin kicks *ass* against Minnesota," Russell Bellomy told me. "He *kills* against Minnesota."

That was just one more reason why, when Hoke started Shane Morris, Gardner's teammates were surprised. So was every coach and commentator I knew in the Big Ten. They spent four seasons shaking their heads over how Al Borges and then Doug Nussmeier were wasting the talent of Robinson and Gardner, if not screwing them up. Their game plans ignored their strength—spread-offense-style decision-making for short, quick passes on the run—and emphasized drop-back passing, which exposed the very weakness of both quarterbacks, and the shockingly porous offensive line they put in front of them.

Lou Holtz, watching his beloved Fighting Irish beat Michigan in 2012, felt compelled to defend Robinson, and question what Michigan's coaching staff was doing with him. After Michigan announced Morris would be starting over Gardner, one opposing coach told me, "What they're doing to [Gardner] is criminal. They don't think Gardner can play? Give him to us, and we'll show you what he can do."

Gardner is a confident young man, but this got to him. "I felt like every-one turned on me," Gardner told me. "I've been through the fire with this team—five years—and then the coaches just give it to someone who hadn't played before.

"I defended Hoke as hard as I can. I had seven [opposing] guys on me—all the time, every play. It's hard to play quarterback under those circumstances. I'm in there at Schembechler Hall every single day at 7 a.m. to 9 at night. I'm trying to find solutions.

"There's no way Hoke's that messed up, to change his mind that fast."

If true, that left two candidates: offensive coordinator Doug Nussmeier or Dave Brandon, and both had been rumored.

"Devin is a very, very competitive player—always striving to be success-ful," Bellomy says. "He got so frustrated. Coach Nuss was always shaking at the opportunity to throw Shane in there. He was very partial to him."

"It was a bizarre day from the start," Hagerup says. "I think guys were a little bit questioning why Devin wasn't starting, but at the same time you trusted that Shane would come in and do the job."

The crowd cheered Morris's introduction—but as former tailback Jamie Morris says, "The most popular guy in the stadium is always the backup quar-terback. Everyone always thinks he's the answer."

Nobody knew that better than Gardner himself. Even while Robinson was setting records, the crowd often cheered for Gardner to step in. But then, as Gardner had said watching Bellomy get thrown in against Nebraska two years earlier, "I don't think people really understand how big that stage is—until you're on it."

With Morris going 6-for-10 for only 41 yards in the first half, the Gophers took a 10–7 lead into the locker room, then broke the game open in the third quarter with a 48-yard field goal, a 30-yard interception return, and a 1-yard touchdown pass to take a 27–7 lead. Morris injured his left ankle in the third quarter, but, after the trainers and team physician checked it out, he stayed in the game.

In the fourth quarter, Michigan announced the attendance was 102,926, enough to maintain Michigan's 39-year streak of 100,000-plus crowds. But with swaths of empty seats throughout the stadium, the home crowd booed its disbelief, then resumed its increasingly popular chant, "Fi-re Bran-don!"

The day wasn't going very well—and that's when it took a turn for the worse.

On a nondescript play, Shane Morris hurt the same ankle. Whe he got up, he limped on it, but gave a hand signal to the bench that he was not coming out, and just wanted the next play.

"He wants to keep playing on the ankle," head trainer Paul Schmidt told me, "and we felt it was acceptable for him to continue. Still do."

The next play provided the day's lasting image: not of the empty seats or the Gophers triumphantly hoisting the Brown Jug over their heads after beating Michigan 30–14, but of Minnesota defensive lineman Theiren Cockran knocking Morris to the ground, followed by Morris wobbling around, his hand on lineman Ben Braden's shoulder.

The cameraman zoomed in for a closeup, while commentator Ed Cunningham urged Michigan's coaches to take Morris out, calling it "appalling" that they were leaving him in.

"We can't see the hit," Schmidt told me. "It's on the far side of the field, behind the [offensive] line, and the ball is already in the air when Shane gets hit. The opposing sideline can see it perfectly, but we can't see it at all."

Watching the replay, Cunningham said Cockran should be ejected from the game for targeting. The official, who was in good position, threw a flag on Cockran for roughing the passer. After Morris popped back up with a push-up, the same official concluded Morris was okay to stay in the game. But when Morris looked to the sidelines for the next play, he started limping, then went into a shaky gait. He quickly stabilzed, while waving off people on the sidelines, his signal that he wasn't coming off, but asking for the next play.

The sequence played very badly on TV, with ESPN2 running Morris's woozy wobble on an endless loop while Cunningham expressed his outrage. TV commentators usually err on the side of diminishing the seriousness of a hit, dismissing even severe collisions as "getting your bell rung," with a chuckle. Cunningham would not be counted among them.

Morris stayed in for the next play, to a chorus of boos from the remaining fans. The student section was particularly loud. Michigan fans are competitive, and expect their Wolverines to win. But they don't like seeing their players being endangered, which is how it looked from the stands, and on TV.

The play had exposed a literal blind spot—the far side of the field—denying the medical staff all the data available, in real time. If Hoke had been in the habit of wearing a headset, his coaches in the press box could have told him how it looked from above, and on TV, and advised him to pull Morris as a precaution. Likewise, if the medical staff had put one of their people in the booth, the doctors and trainers on the sideline could be debriefed on the plays they can't see—a safeguard the staff would introduce the next weekend.

But this marked the confluence of several elements feeding into one narrative: an injured ankle, a nation suddenly obsessed with concussions, fans who were already unhappy, a TV crew unafraid to announce Michigan's missteps, and a hard hit to Morris's chin, serious enough to warrant a flag for targeting. To borrow the cliché: It was the perfect storm.

"We never saw the play," Schmidt told me, "until we ran the replays on TV after the game. But when you see it live—not as a still shot, and not in slow motion—Shane's on the ground for a second, then he does a quick push-up, propels himself right up, and gets up on both feet and walks away. He is looking to the sideline for the play—and *then* he stumbles on his ankle.

"The Big Ten head official checked him out, he assessed him, and felt it was okay for him to continue. I felt comfortable allowing him to continue, too."

After the next play, with the fans booing loudly, and Cunningham criticizing Michigan for leaving Morris in, Michigan pulled Morris from the game.

When Morris came off the field, however, he told everyone within earshot—about two dozen players, coaches, and staffers—the injury was his ankle.

"I was punting in the net, warming up," Hagerup recalls, "when the whole sideline goes 'OOOHHH!' Which means someone got hurt. But when he came off, all I heard was what everyone else heard: 'Ankle! Ankle! Ankle!' from Shane, and from the other guys who saw it, and were helping him off. The 'concussion' word was never said that day, by anyone I heard."

When Morris got to the bench, head trainer Paul Schmidt and Dr. Bruce Miller were waiting for him. "It's my ankle!" he told them, with others overhearing. "My leg—it's killing me! I think I broke my fucking ankle!"

He hadn't, of course. The staff would soon determine he had suffered a moderate sprain.

While the staff went to work, Gardner replaced Morris. But on Gardner's third play, his helmet popped off. The new rules require any player who loses his helmet to go to the sideline for one play to get his helmet back on right—and get examined, if need be—for the player's safety.

Third-string quarterback Russell Bellomy had quickly become the second-string quarterback, but he couldn't find his helmet. Jon Falk's practice of having one of his student managers stand next to the backup quarterback with his helmet left when Falk did. So Bellomy screamed for Morris to go back in.

Hoke asked the ref standing nearest the Michigan sideline for an injury time-out for Gardner. The ref refused, and added that even if Hoke called a time-out, he couldn't put Gardner back in the game. This is incorrect.

"But now the world thinks Hoke is a boob," one Michigan insider told me, "who doesn't want to call a time-out when we're down 30–7, and doesn't care about his players."

Neither was true. Every person I've talked with, including graduated players, underscored the genuine concern the coaching and medical staffs exhibited for the players. This was the same medical staff, it's worth noting, that did not hesitate to take Denard Robinson out of the 2010 Illinois game for a concussion on a hit no one saw, and keep him out.

With the play clock running down, and the referee unwilling to let Gardner back in the game with an official time-out or a team time-out, Bellomy kept yelling at Morris, who jumped up from the bench, ran past the doctors and trainers examining him, and ran another play.

The home fans launched into their third chorus of boos, louder than the rest, their disgust now plain. Cunningham called Michigan coaches' handling of Morris, "Atrocious. Atrocious. Atrocious."

Morris handed the ball off to Justice Hayes, came back to the bench, and was done for the day. The medical staff resumed their examinations.

But the story was just getting started.

But it would be told by everyone except the people involved.

Dave Brandon had pushed aside Bruce Madej, who had since retired, and Dave Ablauf, and Pete Skorich had been replaced that week by Chrissi Rawak.

Thus, for the first time in 241 games, spanning Dave Ablauf's 19-year career at Michigan, he was not working in the press box as a public-relations official. Instead, he spent the day learning what chief marketing officer Hunter Lochmann's job entailed, by following him from his pregame duties at tailgates to visiting an IMG "retail activation" to watching the game with the athletic department's digital team.

Before the game, however, Ablauf visited the press box to tell the staff there, and his many friends in the media—people he'd known for almost two decades—that he would be working in a different capacity the rest of the season.

That also meant Ablauf, for the first time since 1995, would not be listening to the TV feed through an earpiece, as he always did, wherever he went. He had made this a habit because, like Madej, he knew the power of TV to magnify everything—good or bad, on or off the field—and he wanted to be able to respond quickly if, say, Michigan's coach barked at the halftime interviewer, or a player took a bad penalty that got the announcers' attention, or someone suffered an injury that required more information.

Of course, if Ablauf's replacement, Justin Dickens, hadn't ended head trainer Paul Schmidt's practice of talking to the sideline reporter directly during games, the story would likely have ended there, too. If the reporter had been allowed to ask Schmidt what had happened, Schmidt would have told him, "We're looking at Shane's left ankle." If the reporter had expressed surprise that they were not considering the possibility of a concussion, Schmidt would have asked why, the reporter would have told him how it looked on TV, and what Cunningham was saying, and Schmidt would have kept Morris on the bench as a precaution. End of story.

Immediately following every game, Madej or Ablauf would make it a point to stop in the trainer's room to get the status of any injured player the media might ask about. If the evaluation was still inconclusive, the coach would simply say that.

But not on this day.

Four days before, Dave Brandon had asked his development director, Chrissi Rawak, to take over public relations, despite her reluctance and lack of experience in the field. Two days later, after Rawak agreed, Brandon failed to provide her any training, guidance, or help from the more experienced PR people still on the payroll.

When Morris took his hit, Rawak was not in the press box but in the Regents' Box talking with Regent Andrea Fischer Newman, yours truly, and my wife. Rawak was trying to get to know the press—which certainly made sense—but during our conversation all of us missed the play, and the crowd's response, which was replaying endlessly on the TVs a floor above in the press box.

That evening, while Shane Morris dined with his parents, nursing a sore ankle, Rawak called Diane Dietz, who played basketball from 1979 to 1982, being named both captain and MVP by her teammates every single year—a remarkable achievement. She has since been inducted into the Academic All-America Hall of Fame, and is now the chief communications officer for the Big Ten—the perfect person for Rawak to consult.

No one thought they would still be dealing with the Shane Morris story on Monday. But this is how disasters go: an unexpected event, even a minor one, exposes all the safeguards that have been pulled away by leaders convinced nothing bad could happen on their watch.

By September 27, 2014, the rest of Michigan athletics' infrastructural safety nets had been removed, and many of the allies that might have come to the program's aid had become indifferent at best, and hostile at worst. This was the moment of crisis Brandon had never anticipated. Most of the people who could have helped him had turned against him—the lettermen, the students, and even many of Michigan's major donors—or had been removed, from equipment managers to ticket managers to media professionals, and were no longer in a position to help him.

"In a crisis, no one was better than Bruce Madej," Bill Martin told me. "He knew how to identify the underlying issues that came up during a crisis, and he knew how to address them, one by one, and how to make certain that you stuck to the facts, and gave them as immediately as possible. His counsel was always correct. I mean, *always*. He knew how to deal with all kinds of problems, but I think crisis management was his specialty."

Example: In 1993, in the waning seconds of the NCAA title game, Chris Webber called his infamous time-out—one Michigan didn't have to give—which effectively ended the game. Afterward, as ESPN's *Fab Five* documentary makes so clear, Webber was emotionally crushed. When Madej came in to ask him to attend the press conference, both Webber and his coach, Steve Fisher, refused. But Madej insisted, reminding them that Chris was one of the players the media had selected before the game for the postgame interviews. Madej and assistant coach Perry Watson sat down next to Webber, explaining to him that it would be best to answer the questions immediately, and that Madej would get him off the stand quickly. If Webber didn't address the press, Madej knew, the story would haunt him the rest of his life.

Webber reluctantly complied. He got through the painful press conference with a few tears, Madej pulled him off the stage as promised, and that was it.

Webber had also been invited to the Wooden Award ceremony in Los Angeles, to crown the nation's best player. But after the team returned to Ann Arbor the next day, Fisher told Madej that Webber would be skipping the event, to avoid the commotion surrounding Webber's time-out call. Besides, the coaches already knew Webber had not won the award.

But Madej once again insisted, telling Webber it was in his best interest to attend, and everyone there would be supportive if he simply showed his face. Webber again trusted Madej—and the response was even better than they could have imagined. When Webber walked into the room that night, the crowd gave him a standing ovation, a bigger response than that year's winner, Calbert Cheaney, received. A few weeks later, at Michigan's graduation ceremony speech, Hillary Clinton lauded Chris Webber's character.

And that's how you handle a PR crisis.

"Before the Shane Morris incident," Bodnar notes, "Brandon lost 53 years of PR experience. Bruce had 34 years, and Ablauf 19—and that experience wasn't there, at a very crucial time. For that matter, Falk wasn't there on the sidelines, and he always had a student manager holding the backup quarterback's helmet. That would have ended it right there."

A few weeks later, Madej visited my class to discuss public relations. When one of my students asked him how he would have handled the Shane Morris situation, Madej gave the usual qualifications about hindsight and the like. Then he said, in the old days, Ablauf would have heard the TV feed, and told Madej they had a problem. Madej would have dashed down to the sidelines before the game ended, told Hoke he needed Shane Morris and Ben Braden immediately after the game, and had them explain the situation at the postgame press conference, while Madej would have statements ready from the medical staff.

The story would have been over by dusk.

Instead, video of Morris wobbling on the field played across the Internet, on *ABC Nightly News*, *Good Morning America*, and even on Al Jazeera America, amid scenes of ISIS and the Ebola epidemic, the kind of company that wasn't going to help the Michigan "brand."

"In the heat of the moment," Bodnar said, "stuff happens, man. But for the next 54 hours, it was all happening without any proper communication coming from Michigan."

CHAPTER 64

SUNDAY

For medical professionals who work with concussions, the intense media interest the past few years has been a double-edged sword: They benefit from the heightened interest in their work, and the need for safety, but they have to combat a lot more misinformation and hysteria.

"People with less information and training than we have," Paul Schmidt told me, with a shrug, "are quicker to pass judgment. It's now part of the job."

The medical staff could fairly be charged with two mistakes: not seeing the play live, and consquently, failing to keep Morris on the bench immediately after, to be examined. These boil down to logistics—something the staff fixed the next week, then created a national conference for 120 medical staffers that spring to eradicate this blindspot nationwide.

But to accuse them of more, you would have to believe the medical staff members were either incompetent or unethical.

I have no medical expertise, but I have watched the staff work at close range on the sidelines, in the locker room, and in the training room many times. I have also talked to other doctors, and numerous coaches and players over the years, too. We all agree these doctors and trainers are first-rate professionals, who have consistently put the well-being of the players ahead of any strategic considerations—witness the Illinois game in 2010.

In addition to Schmidt's training staff, which has worked together for more than a decade, Michigan's medical team includes the head physician Dan Hendrickson, trained at Penn State, in his 17th season on Michigan's sidelines; Harvard-educated Bruce Miller; Cornell's Dr. James Carpenter; Wayne State's Amy Miller; and neurologist Jeffrey Kutcher, who went to Michigan for his bachelors, Tulane for his M.D., and back to Michigan for his residency—all of whom make Michigan's medical team one of the most qualified in sports.

All have appointments at the University of Michigan Hospital or University Health Services, which runs against the national trend, in which more team medical staffs work for the team itself, which raises obvious conflicts of interest. While the trainers are employed by the athletic department—working long days in Schembechler Hall's training room—none of Michigan's physicians answer to the athletic department, and most get paid only travel expenses.

As one of them told me, "Our focus is on the science, not the sport."

Michigan is also one of the few athletic programs to have a neurologist on the sidelines. Dr. Jeff Kutcher is one of the world's foremost experts on brain injuries. He worked at the Sochi Olympics and is the neurological consultant for the players' associations of the NFL and NHL, monitoring policies and procedures, and seeing patients, to make sure the players' health comes before profits.

At Michigan, Dr. Kutcher spends most of his time seeing patients, from nine-year-olds on up, and supervising his program, Michigan Neurosport, a part of the University of Michigan Health System. During his frequent public speeches on the subject of concussions, he always tries to get two points across: One, concussions can take time to diagnose; and two, there is a spectrum of diagnosis certainty.

"How long does it take to diagnose concussions?" he asks rhetorically. "Either five seconds or 48 hours—somewhere in there." Obviously, it depends on the nature of the injury, but it's rarely as simple as the public would like to believe. As he tells audiences, "The old saying goes, 'If you've seen one concussion—you've seen one concussion.'"

And yes, contrary to popular belief, concussions actually do come in shades of gray, not all or nothing. "We have a spectrum," Dr. Kutcher explains. "Possible, probable, or definite concussion."

None of this sounds very satisfying to the 50,000 fans who watched Morris wobble, or fits very neatly into a media sound bite.

After Morris came out the second time, Dr. Kutcher examined his head for a possible head injury. Based on Morris's initial history, and Dr. Kutcher's examination, he determined Morris had a "possible concussion," the least severe of the spectrum's three levels. On Sunday morning, Dr. Kutcher raised his diagnosis certainty to "probable," which meant there was still the potential that Morris wasn't concussed, but more likely than not, he was.

At 11 a.m. Sunday, after every football game, the medical staff completes its routine postgame interactions with the coaching staff, including Hoke, to apprise them of the status of all the players—something I've witnessed dozens of times. In addition, Paul Schmidt talked with Brady Hoke once on

Saturday, three times on Sunday, and once on Monday, giving him the complete information Dr. Kutcher and the staff had gathered at each stage.

In short, there was no lack of communication between the medical staff and the coaching staff—nor within the medical staff itself, a group that I've seen exhibit mutual respect, personally and professionally.

The Big Ten also called Michigan Sunday morning to let the coaching staff know the referee who had told Hoke that calling a time-out would not allow him to put Gardner back on the field after his helmet came off was, in fact, incorrect, and Hoke was right.

It's not that often the Big Ten office admits it was wrong, but they told the staff, not the media, so no one outside Schembechler Hall knew about it.

Finally sensing that a national story was rising around them, the department sent out a press release from Brady Hoke Sunday evening. It said, in part, ". . . Shane Morris was removed from yesterday's game against Minnesota after further aggravating an injury to his leg that he sustained earlier in the contest . . . The University of Michigan has a distinguished group of Certified Athletic Trainers and team physicians who are responsible for determining whether or not a player is physically able to play. Our coaches have no influence or authority to make determinations if or when an injured player returns to competition . . ."

The release addressed some important points—that Morris had been pulled for his ankle, and that the coaches have no authority over the medical staff—but failed to answer the most pressing question: Did Morris have a concussion or not? If he did, why did he go back in the game?

Needless to say, instead of bringing closure to the story, this half-baked attempt would only raise more questions.

CHAPTER 65

MARATHON MONDAY

To withstand these slings and arrows, Brandon needed the Michigan family to band together like never before. But when he looked up, he found the family had already scattered. They had resigned, they'd been fired, they'd been angered, they'd been estranged. Some had simply become fed up with the whole thing, and walked away from something they thought they would love their whole lives.

Brandon would be on his own.

When the athletic director, his leadership team, his coaches, and the players woke up Monday morning, they found a pile of bad news on their doorstep. The football team was off to a disastrous 2–3 start. The department was still getting lambasted for the Cokes-for-tickets "retail activation," and the stadium was showing large bands of empty seats—and that wasn't the worst news. Then they saw this op-ed headline in the *Michigan Daily*: "Brady Hoke Must Be Fired."

"As [Morris] stumbled on the field," the editorial board wrote, "it was clear that Morris exhibited concussion-like symptoms. Despite that fact, we watched Hoke make a move that jeopardized Morris' health. Even 24 hours later, Hoke didn't acknowledge the possibility of a head injury, referring only to Morris 'further aggravating an injury to his leg' in a statement to reporters. He added he is 'confident proper medical decisions were made.' They very clearly were not."

Given what the *Daily* reporters had seen and heard in the previous 48 hours, they had good reason to make this judgment, and little evidence to counter it. Their view was quickly becoming the consensus, locally and nationally.

Brandon's leadership team's regularly scheduled meeting happened to fall that Monday morning, at 8 a.m. When they met in the Champions Room, they wisely got the more mundane matters quickly out of the way, to get to the bigger issues at hand. They also brought in people outside their team to figure out what to do next.

It turned out this would take them some 17 hours, all spent in the Champions Room. Dave Brandon, Chrissi Rawak, Mike DeBord, and a half dozen others were there most of the time, but before the long day was done, the Champions Room would also be visited by compliance officers, medical staffers, a lawyer, media-relations experts, and more.

The obstacle they faced was large, but clear: What could they possibly say at this stage of the news cycle that anyone would believe?

When the medical team met that same day, in Schembechler Hall, they didn't have to wring their hands over this question: Report the truth, based on the science, and let the public react however it will.

The department's leadership team did not feel they had the luxury to be so direct, without explanation. After sending out helpless PR people to defend the department again and again—after the fiascos over seat cushions, noodles, and skywriters, to name a few—Michigan fans and media could not be counted on to believe department officials, even when they were telling the truth. The credibility bank had long since been emptied. When the department needed the fans and media to give it the benefit of the doubt, and trust that the medical staff was telling the truth, no one was willing to play along.

Over his four years, Brandon's troubles had grown from private to public—but that was, literally, his problem. But now his lack of credibility and good will were metastasizing, spreading from his office to Hoke's and the training room. By the end of this long day, the cancer would reach the hospital and the president's office.

Dave Brandon was everybody's problem now.

After everyone had gathered in the Champions Room, it was not clear who was in charge of the meeting. It also was not clear what their mission was: to find the truth, or shift the blame?

They started out by trying to find the truth—and even that would be hard enough.

"Everybody just wanted to make sure the facts were the facts," Paul Schmidt told me. "Start there. But as we found out, multiple people have facts, and those facts can differ. Doesn't mean anyone's lying or trying to make anything up. Especially under times of duress, your own memory of what you saw and heard and thought is not always completely reliable—even if everyone is doing their best to find the truth."

As another staffer told me, "Chrissi's there, running point, trying to put together a response. But she has no experience at this—zero. You've got a lawyer, you've got compliance, you've got medical staff. The lawyer is worried about saying anything about the medical facts, because if they're contradicted, that's a legal problem.

"So now they're parsing every single word—and I mean *every single word*. 'You can't say this. You can't say that.' So we're making no progress, because these guys are fighting over every if, and, or but.

"How much better can we make it with each draft, with each change? This is diminishing returns. We spend another hour, then another, changing a few words, and changing them back? We're not getting anywhere—and the clock is ticking."

While they dithered, Brady Hoke drove to Crisler Center for his weekly press conference, which was coming up at noon.

Brandon called Hoke right before the press conference to tell him they hadn't finished their statement yet but would have one soon. Brandon advised him to say that, and nothing more about the situation.

But if Brandon and Hoke thought the press had packed the media room to discuss the 2-and-3 Wolverines' upcoming game at Rutgers, they had another thing coming. Repeated questions forced Hoke to repeat just as often that a statement would be coming soon, but his unprepared, and necessarily evasive responses to the reporters' very predictable questions tested the patience of the media and even the most loyal Michigan fans, who had seen Morris wobbling before Hoke had.

Hoke was also in the bad habit, when asked an honest question, of not answering it. This was especially true when it came to injuries, which he called "boo boos." It was considered cute when they were winning, but when he finally needed credibility on the subject, it wasn't there to draw on.

In order to re-establish some trust, Hoke needed to answer three basic questions: Why was Morris put back in the game? When was he examined for a concussion? And what were the results? Simple, straightforward questions, for which Hoke should have been given simple, straightforward answers. Get those right, and the rest was dust.

Hoke whiffed on all three, instead droning on about Rutgers, and how tough his players are. When candor and clarity were called for, Hoke failed to provide either, as instructed.

Hoke did everything but answer the questions asked, admit any mistakes, or take responsibility for anything. He told reporters Morris hadn't suffered a concussion, and he hadn't spoken to his boss, the department, or anyone else. The one thing Hoke said that he was supposed to say—repeating endlessly that the department would be issuing a press release on all of the above, including statements from the medical staff, as soon as Hoke finished the press conference—the department itself was hours away from finishing, making even that statement look like a lie.

The sad part, for the many players who loved Hoke and believed in his basic goodness, was watching the public wonder aloud if Hoke was even an honest man, who cared about his players. Why did it take him several plays to pull Morris? Why did he put him back in the game instead of using a worthless time-out?

Hoke had good answers to these questions—but he didn't deliver them.

Michigan's problems were mounting, on and off the field. The season was already looking lost. The fans were leaving by the thousands. But until Monday people could still believe in the basic decency of Michigan's head coach, and the values he represented.

Now, thanks to woefully poor public relations, that had become an open question—and Brandon's role in it did not sit well with some of the hard-core Michigan Men.

"The whole thing with Shane was terrible," John Wangler said. "It was hubris, the CEO mentality. 'I can spin this.' Well, sometimes you can't, and it catches up to you.

"To let your coach go out there with no information and look bad for you—man, what can I say? That was flat-out wrong.

"That's not Michigan."

Back in the Champions Room, the debate over the press release raged on, while one hour passed, then another. Brandon realized it had to be finished quickly. He said if he catered a decent lunch, they would stay longer, so he didn't feed them. It was not intended to be a staff retreat.

Late in the afternoon and into the evening, a few folks tossed bags of cookies and chips in the middle of the table, and someone scared up some bagels and fruit.

Hoke's press conference reopened the debate over the medical facts, and how much they should share, if anything. True, that night Morris would sign the HIPAA release form, allowing Michigan to share the relevant medical information. But since Morris would do so in the presence of the athletic director and two lawyers Brandon had brought in, without his father, his coaches, or the team doctors present, they had misgivings.

"What's he going to do," one asked me, "not sign it, with his coach's boss, and two lawyers, telling him he should?"

When the medical staff members met that day at Schembechler Hall, they considered sending out their own press release. They decided they should either say nothing about the case, because it's a medical issue, and that's that; or they should share *exactly* what happened, down to the minute, with nothing but the truth, all science.

"From my point of view," one told me, echoing the comments of the others, "one of those two things had to happen. None of the physicians on the sidelines work under athletics. We all have appointments at the hospital and the medical school. So there was a bunch of that going on—doctors digging in their heels on the science."

They ultimately were unanimous, as usual: They would say nothing. The last of the medical staffers who had visited the Champions Room left about 7:30 that night, with the press release still far from finished.

"We didn't sign off on any press release—not one of us," one medical staffer said. "The press release was just kind of done behind our back."

Morris visited Dr. Kutcher and Paul Schmidt again that evening.

After Morris finished his visit, he was summoned to Dave Brandon's office. Before Morris left the trainers' room, however, Schmidt pulled Morris aside. Given the threshold for firings under Brandon—especially when the boss didn't look good—nobody in that building, including the trainers, could have any illusion that jobs were not at stake. Nonetheless, the team's medical professionals felt strongly then, and still do now, that they had gotten it right, throughout.

But, Schmidt advised Morris, "Don't you get yourself into trouble over this. All we ask is that you tell the truth. Let them deal with the rest—including us."

It would be naïve to think finding the truth and communicating it to the public was the top priority of everyone involved in this story. But among more than a few vital figures, it was still all that ultimately mattered.

In the midst of a crisis President Schlissel never asked for, and everyone promised him would never happen at a very stable athletic department, he carried himself with admirable calm. He did not act swiftly, but he was secure enough to resist the temptation to make things worse by overreacting, grandstanding, or hiding. He monitored the situation, waiting for a draft to come up the hill for his approval before it went out.

With the sun going down, and water bottles, pop cans, and potato chip bags strewn about the big table, with stressed-out, haggard people surrounding the mess and the press release still not finished, the remaining team members called for Michigan's vice president of communications, Kallie Michels, and much later, former sports information director Dave Ablauf.

The central difficulty they now faced was not the media, or Morris's injury, but the conflicting objectives of the people in that room, and the interests they represented. As one person in the room told me, "They're trying to get it right—re-enacting it all, bit by bit—but it's all CYA stuff. You got the feeling some of them weren't trying to spare the university. They're trying to save their jobs, because they all think their jobs are on the line—and they probably are. You can see, with different versions of their story, they're going to try to take out the trainer with one version, or a doctor with another version, or this guy or that guy. But it's never anyone in the room—so it took some guts for [the medical staffers] to leave.

"They're asking all kinds of questions. 'What's a "probable minor concussion"?' I'm not a doctor, but I can tell you: It's a fucking headache."

At one point, as one person in the room recalled, they showed Dave Ablauf their draft, and asked him if they should send it out.

"I will not forget his answer," this person says. "'At this point, it doesn't matter. You guys put a coach out there at noon, and you told him to keep telling them you were going to have a statement from Michigan officials as soon as he was done. That was seven hours ago. The media's been waiting for this.

"'So it doesn't matter what you put out or when you do it. We're going to get roasted on this. The media and fans won't stop until they get a head on a platter. But given all that, you might as well tell the truth.

"'Not that it will help much.'"

Hunger, fatigue, and Ablauf's apparent ability to cut through the fog helped those still in the room to finish their draft by 9 p.m., 12 hours after they started working on the one-page statement that morning. Brandon sent it to President Schlissel, who gave it a few small tweaks, then sent it on to the Regents by 10 p.m. They also made some small adjustments, then sent it back to Brandon's group by midnight.

Now the people who remained in the Champions Room had another tough decision: Do they send the statement out in the wee hours, or wait until the next morning? If they sent it immediately, they knew they'd be accused of trying to "take the trash out" under cover of darkness. But, they reasoned, if they didn't send it out, someone would call at 4 a.m. and ask for more changes. And then they're back at the table working over another draft.

Regent Andrea Fischer Newman is a vice president at Delta who has seen plenty of crisis management. She kept close tabs on the process as it unfolded. "It was an insularity problem," she told me. "There were all sitting in the athletic department, not understanding what's swirling around them. No one was in charge of the message.

"The statement didn't go out until 1 a.m., because they hadn't gotten Mark Schlissel to approve it. Mark [Schlissel] had only been here a month.

"It wasn't Dave [Brandon] that held it up. He was told to put it out ASAP. The Regents got in the middle of the statement, which is why it took until Tuesday at 1 a.m."

At 12:52 Tuesday morning, Dave Brandon sent out a press release stating that Shane Morris had suffered a "probable mild concussion." The release asserted that Brandon had been in constant communication with his head coach and everyone else involved, including the team's medical staff, which contradicted what Coach Hoke had told the press just 12 hours earlier.

The response to the 1 a.m. press release was exactly as Ablauf had told them it would be: "We're going to get roasted on this."

The Internet didn't wait until Tuesday morning to weigh in. Just about every regional and national media outlet that covered sports ran the press release, immediately, and picked it apart.

The students at the *Michigan Daily* literally stopped the presses. "We were in frequent communications with our printer to push back our deadline as much as possible," Alejandro Zúñiga told me. "The football beat quickly wrote a response column. We gave the column and statement a full page. Got a lot of national praise for that as well."

The *Daily* column closed with this: "Brandon's press release explained there was a lack of communication on the field Saturday. The contradictions between the coaching staff and athletic director demonstrate institutional dysfunction within the Athletic Department."

Hoke would get hammered, too, of course, yet I've since learned his version of events was closer to the truth than Brandon's: the athletic director's conversations with the central figures were not nearly as many or as deep as the release depicted.

As you can imagine, when Michigan football's medical staffers saw the press release the next morning, they were not terribly pleased—and that's putting it mildly.

"I saw it and shook my head," one of them told me. "It did exactly what I hoped it wouldn't: It didn't tell everything, and it told too much. Once you make the decision to share a patient's medical history, you might as well tell everything, to clear the air.

"The statement made it appear that we were incompetent, or lying, or both. We love Brady [Hoke], but if he had tried to overrule us [during the game], none of us were going to lie for him."

Tuesday afternoon, they met again in Paul Schmidt's office, to vent their frustration and decide whether they should let the athletic department speak for them, or release their own press release. To help decide, they were communicating with the officials at U-M Hospital and the central administrators.

Ultimately, however, the medical staff again decided not to respond. "We didn't want to stoop to that," one told me. "We're physicians. We practice medicine, not public relations. We wanted to stay above the fray. Anything we released would be misinterpreted, and it was not in our patient's best interest."

Regent Larry Deitch happened to be in California that weekend, playing golf with his son. But, naturally, they found time to watch the game—and it wasn't hard to find a TV that had it on. "Who would have predicted Minnesota–Michigan would be a nationally televised game?" he asks.

What should have been a welcome spotlight for the program quickly became a microscope. Like many viewers that day, Deitch couldn't shake the memory of Ed Cunningham calling it, "Atrocious."

That was one problem, of course, but Deitch took the long view. "The way that was handled was poor," he says, referring to the aftermath. "When you have a problem—whether it's at the university or my law firm—you come out quickly, acknowledge that this is a screwup, say we're sorry, this won't happen again, and here's what we're doing to guarantee that. It's not complicated—but I don't think they got any of those steps right.

"Then, to let Brady Hoke go out there on Monday for his weekly press conference and look like a fool—a dishonest fool—when he's not either of those things, was shameful. Simply shameful.

"For someone who seemed to like the spotlight as much as Dave [Brandon] did, to be nowhere to be seen when the heat was on, was highly problematic, and disappointing for me.

"A lot of the case against Dave stemmed from that weekend. I think it was the tipping point."

CHAPTER 66

THE BRANDON RALLY

Five hours after the press release, on Tuesday morning, September 30, Sam Webb and Ira Weintraub started fielding calls on WTKA-Sportstalk 1050—and the lines lit up like a Christmas tree.

Marty Bodnar was listening. "I heard so much anger, so much frustration. I thought, 'What's going on here? *This is Michigan!*'"

Among the many posts on the many Web sites, one on MGoBlog's message board would get national attention: A student announced a "Fire Dave Brandon" rally on the Diag at 6 p.m. that night, and urged readers to attend.

In the meantime, Central Student Government president Bobby Dishell found himself in the middle of another maelstrom he had not created. Two years earlier, probably no one would have expected the CSG to weigh in on athletic issues, but after the pioneering work done by Proppe and Dishell on the general-admission policy, the student body looked to them for a response. They had truly become the leaders of the student body.

After debating whether to respond or not, and then what to say, Dishell wrote, in part, "Saturday's loss was not routine. It was not the result of any particular deficiency of the team. Saturday's loss revealed, instead, a major fault within the athletic administration: a lack of respect for both its students and student-athletes.

"CSG shares the frustrations of the student body, and looks to the athletic administration for an appropriate response."

By the end of the week, just about every branch of Michigan's family tree—from students to Regents and everyone in between—would feel compelled to weigh in with its own judgments on Brandon and his department. They sounded off privately and publicly, leaving Brandon out on a limb. Michigan no longer had a unified voice.

The most dramatic speech of the week, however, might have been the least expected. On that Tuesday, at 6 p.m., a few hundred people showed up for the rally announced just hours earlier. But without a leader, or an agenda, they drifted about the Diag. Seeing the disarray, Craig Kaplan, a senior in Michigan's Gerald Ford School of Public Policy, went back to his home and returned a few minutes later with a bullhorn—and with it, the rally was on. The crowd grew to an estimated 1,000 students, alums, and fans, and marched to the front steps of the president's house.

Kaplan mounted the steps of the president's front porch and turned to face the crowd, which had no idea who he was, or what he was about to say. Perhaps he didn't, either.

But with no script, no focus groups, no lawyers, no PR professionals, and armed only with his Michigan education, his passion for the university, and a bullhorn, Kaplan started yelling.

"I love this university!" he told them. "I love this football team. I love our sports.

"I do not love Dave Brandon.

"I am proud of Michigan's history. I am proud of Bo Schembechler. I am proud of all the Michigan football players, basketball players, athletic directors, and the people that came before us. I am proud of our history.

"I am not proud of Dave Brandon being part of that history."

The crowd cheered wildly at Kaplan's spontaneous speech. The revolution had found its leader—at least for a night. But the crowd had rediscovered something more important, and lasting: an authentic voice, reminding them of the collective identity they still believed in.

A graduate student, Zeid El-Kilani, who had been involved in CSG as an undergraduate, used the same vehicle Proppe and Dishell had to create an online petition, this one for students and alumni who wanted Dave Brandon to be fired. It quickly gathered more than 13,000 signatures—a noted contrast to the petition the students circulated back in 1903, to keep Michigan's first athletic director, Charles Baird, from leaving.

In the following weeks, the "Fi-re Bran-don!" chant would be heard at home football, basketball, and hockey games.

The week was not yet half over.

CHAPTER 67

THE "SAVE DAVE" COMMITTEE

If Brandon had one base of support he could rely on, it was the student-athletes, whom he had consistently treated with respect and generosity.

Hours after the "Rally to Fire Dave Brandon" was over, a diver named Kevin Bain, who also served on the Student-Athlete Advisory Committee, sent out the following e-mail to his fellow student-athletes, urging them all to show solidarity for Dave Brandon and the department by wearing team-issued apparel the next day, and making only positive comments in social media:

> *Let's unite as a community and demonstrate to everyone that we fully and wholeheartedly support our entire athletic community, the athletic department, and every single team and student-athlete.*

Bain then included a quote from Bo Schembechler, which is never a bad move in Ann Arbor:

> *"We're going to believe in each other. We're not going to criticize each other. We're not going to talk about each other. We're going to encourage each other! And when we play as a team, when the season is over, you and I know it's going to be Michigan again. Michigan!"*
>
> *Please tell your teammates to only speak positively about Michigan Athletics. Below are some suggested talking points if anyone wants to address the community:*
>
> *[One example:] "We support the entire Michigan Athletic Department, all 31 teams."*
> *Thank you, and FOREVER GO BLUE!!!*
> *Kevin Bain*

There is no reason to doubt the sincerity of Bain's message, or the organic roots of his mission. Most student-athletes followed his lead and wore their maize-and-blue the next day—though, as a nonathlete pointed out, "they pretty much wear their sweats every day, so it wasn't that dramatic."

In my two classes that day, we debated whether to open the room for discussion on these issues. I finally concluded if we couldn't discuss these matters in classes covering college athletics, where could we? I set ground rules about respect, openness, and the like. I was confident my students would come through, and they did.

But I was struck by the divide between the students and the student-athletes. Many of the latter spoke up for Brandon, pointing out that he cared about all athletes, not just the football and basketball players, and proved it by attending games and even practices.

But the other students were just as passionate, in the opposite direction. While the student-athletes appreciated Brandon's genuine interest and concern, the nonathletes resented him for the lack of those very same qualities, manifest in his unilateral decision to change the student basketball ticketing policy, to enforce general admission at football games, raising the student ticket prices, and other policies that seemed to reveal his underlying attitude toward the students.

When Pete Nichols, a loyal alum and booster, met Brandon in his office in 2012, Brandon was amazed that the students were upset by his first price hike for student tickets. When Nichols responded that, actually, he could understand their displeasure, Brandon replied, "C'mon, Pete! After all, it's mommy and daddy's money!"

This is the bridge that Brandon failed to build: between the need to raise money for the student-athletes, and taking care of the people providing it: the students, the parents, the lettermen, the alums, and the fans. Of course, lowering administrative salaries would have helped him accomplish both.

There were good reasons why most student-athletes appreciated Brandon, and there were good reasons most people in the other groups did not: he treated them very differently. Because of that, he failed in a central mission of any university leader: to build a sense of community among all groups, something you could see was missing even in a single lecture hall.

The "Fire Brandon" rally added to the Regents' sense that the athletic department was something they needed to watch closely.

That week, Regent Mark Bernstein recalls, "I told [Brandon] that some of the Regents have real problems with his leadership. Real problems. From that, you'd think he'd conclude that he does not have the full support of the board."

Regents Deitch, White, and Bernstein were weighing a few options, including a public vote of no confidence, a letter asking Brandon to resign, or simply firing him. But all their options were limited by the checks and balances of university governance, and the politics of the situation. Regents do not hire or fire athletic directors, and they had just hired a president they obviously wanted to see succeed. To take this decision away from President Schlissel, even unofficially through the bully pulpit, would undercut him in a public forum.

For the time being, they decided to sit tight.

Brandon's staff could no longer kid themselves about the trouble their leader was in, either.

They sprung to action, forming a group some employees called the "Save Dave committee," consisting of members of the athletic department and university public relations teams, athletic development staff members, and a Detroit public relations firm, to brainstorm ideas and act on them as quickly as possible. They decided Brandon should go on a media tour, inviting a dozen journalists into the Champions Room—one at a time—to conduct a series of 20-minute, one-on-one interviews with the athletic director.

Hindsight is always perfect, of course, but it was not hard to see flaws in this plan. "That's not how you do it," one PR person told me. "You do *one* interview with all 10 reporters, at once, and you get it over within 30 minutes, max. That way you can start with a statement, then answer every question *once*."

By hosting just one session for all, speakers appear more prepared and positive. They are more likely to stay on message, and avoid the contradictions that inevitably arise when trying to explain the same situation 10 times. As the PR pro told me, "It makes it look like you're changing your story, when you're not."

When all your critics need is one or two statements that miss the mark, they'll run those on an endless loop. And that, of course, is exactly what happened.

Sure enough, Brandon failed to stay consistently on message, losing his one-man game of "telephone," round by round. With the media smelling blood, they focused on statements that seemed inconsistent, defensive, or self-serving. Brandon dug in deeper.

Brandon, to his credit, started the day by visiting the *Michigan Daily* in person—a first, during his tenure. When they asked about the press release being issued at 12:52 a.m., he said, "The appropriate person in athletics—and I judged that to be me—needed to make it very clear that a mistake was made. We own it, we recognize and we acknowledge that a mistake was made, we apologize for it—and I did—and we immediately committed that we would learn from it and make changes to ensure that it wouldn't happen again."

But in the same breath, he said, "That was just another example of the failure of communication that took place among the doctors, all of the trainers—in this case, the head coach—to try to piece together what happened." That comment pleased neither the medical nor coaching staffs, costing Brandon more support.

Near the end of his first interview, Brandon was already struggling to make sense, delivering this line: "I felt very badly. My job and my personality is to the best of my ability, I have to fix that." In the days to follow, that sentence played constantly, and still pops up on fan sites.

Like almost everyone else that day, WXYZ-TV's Tom Leyden also asked Brandon about the 12:52 a.m. press release. "That just seems like one of the worst things you can possibly do," Leyden said. "It just smacks of a news dump."

"We're a little smarter than to think in today's world there's any such thing as a news dump," Brandon said, starting to get a little snippy. "That's almost a little offensive that we'd be that naïve."

Then why the delay?

"I've been busy doing things that I think are frankly more important. And that's probably not what you want to hear."

It also wasn't true, since Brandon was monitoring the Champions Room all day.

Later in the day, Brandon answered a question about the Rally to Fire Dave Brandon: "That's very hurtful," Brandon said. "Anybody who thinks that they want groups to gather with the topic being criticism and sometimes very personal attacks on the work and the job. It's hurtful. It's hurtful to me, it's hurtful to my family."

That, too, would be repeated often, by reporters, bloggers, and some of the 143 employees who had left the department.

"I'm not tone-deaf," he added. He also maintained he had an "excellent" relationship with the students, hundreds of whom had just held a rally to get him fired, and thousands had just signed a petition for the same purpose. He also claimed he had the support of the Regents, three-quarters of whom had already told him privately they had serious concerns about his leadership.

By that night, Dave Brandon knew he had a problem, and the University of Michigan knew it had a problem, too. Dave Brandon's problem, he believed, was public relations. Michigan's problem was Dave Brandon.

They both searched for solutions, but on diverging paths. The university hired a PR firm from Washington, DC, to make sure the athletic department's problem didn't contaminate the rest of the university, while the athletic department hired a PR firm from Detroit to try to save Dave Brandon's job. Whether a university department should be spending its budget to save its director is a fair question, but there was little doubt they were no longer trying to solve the same problem.

The fan reaction clearly indicated that they understood the issues, starting with the readers on MGoBlog, and their 150 comments.

Their leader, Brian Cook, summed it up thusly: "Dave Brandon turned a one-day story about the incompetence of the man who he hired to coach the team into a five-day story about the incompetence of the entire university."

The department's troubles were becoming the university's troubles.

If the fans weren't happy, some of the Regents were downright upset.

"I'm watching Dave Brandon talk to [WXYZ-TV's] Tom Leyden," Bernstein told me. "And Leyden asks him, 'Do you have the support of the board?' and Dave says, 'Yes, I do.'

"That was inaccurate, and I'd say *very* inaccurate—and he *knew* that. That was telling, because Dave, the ultimate corporate insider—and a former Regent—knew exactly what was happening on the board. I was then comfortable that my anger was justified. When the Shane Morris incident blew up, Dave did not have many deposits in the goodwill bank, and when he wanted to write a big check, it just bounced."

When Shauna Diggs, an alumna, doctor, and fellow Regent, who is not quick to anger, saw the same interview, she became so upset she called President Schlissel directly. Regents Diggs, Bernstein, and others felt a renewed sense of urgency.

"After we all saw the media tour," Bernstein recalls, "we decided we were not going to sit around and get played."

CHAPTER 68

SEEKING REDEMPTION AT RUTGERS

Later that day, Dave Brandon attended Michigan's football practice. After their last drill, Hoke blew his whistle, gathered them together, and asked them to take a knee.

"This was one of those times," punter Will Hagerup remembers, "where you just don't know what's going on, or what's going to happen. But Dave walked up, and gave this awesome speech."

Brandon's message made an impression. So much so, a few months later, Hagerup could recall whole sentences from memory.

"When I took this job," Hagerup remembers Brandon saying, "I never imagined they'd be protesting to get me fired in the Diag, and helicopters would be flying over my house.

"But you know what? That's why we're Michigan Men. We know how to be tough, what it takes to get through hard times.

"You all need to know, people are saying I'm going to fire Hoke.

"That's bullshit.

"That guy right there," he said, pointing to Hoke standing off to the side, "is a great friend of mine. We hang out outside of football. He's doing a great job, and not only will I not fire him, I'm sticking by him. If he goes, I go.

"He's taken bullet after bullet for you guys. So, you guys need to be patient. We'll get there.

"You know what would help? I need you guys to go beat Rutgers!"

The players were "definitely into it," Hagerup recalls. "They were leaning forward, nodding.

"You can tell when someone is bullshitting. And Dave was not bullshitting. He even got a little choked up—I never saw him vulnerable like that—in a way you knew he cared."

But the speech, as good as it was, also revealed something else: When Brandon said, "I need you guys to beat Rutgers!" it was lighthearted, but it was also true. And in saying that to the players, the firewall separating Brandon's problems from the players had officially been removed.

On Friday morning, October 4, when the players walked through Glick Fieldhouse to get on the buses for the airport, every team on campus—and many of their coaches, including John Beilein—showed up cheer them on, and show their support.

"That was awesome," Hagerup said. "We loved it." With everything to prove, the Wolverines boarded the buses and started their journey to New Jersey.

They would play one of the world's two original football programs. Rutgers had beaten Princeton, 6–4, on November 6, 1869. In 2014, 145 years later, the Scarlet Knights had already won four games, and lost just one, 13–10, to Penn State.

Hoke started Gardner, who hit 13 of 22 for 178 yards, with 1 interception, and ran for 2 touchdowns. The second one, a 19-yard scamper, pulled Michigan within 2 points, 26–24, with 9:17 left to play.

When Michigan's defense got the ball back, Gardner moved his offense to Rutgers' 38-yard line. On third-and-eight, Gardner dropped back, found Amara Darboh on the sideline, and threw a strike.

Seen live, it looked as though Darboh had caught the ball before going out of bounds. Seen on countless replays, it *definitely* looked like Darboh caught the ball before going out of bounds. But, incredibly, the replay official ruled Darboh did not have possession before stepping out, so it was ruled incomplete.

That required Michigan to attempt a 56-yard field goal, with 3:01 to go. After Rutgers' Kemoko Turay blocked the attempt, the Scarlet Knights managed to kill the rest of the game to secure the world's oldest football program's first win in the world's oldest football league.

The Wolverines had to trudge off the field with a 2–4 record, and an 0–2 mark in the Big Ten for the first time since 1967.

In the locker room, receiver Amara Darboh kept telling his teammates, "I'm sorry! I'm sorry!"

"I'm a pretty calm guy," Gardner says, "but I couldn't take it anymore. I stood up and said, 'One more motherfucker in this locker room apologies for giving it all you got, I'm going to take out every motherfucker in this locker room.

"You lose sometimes! That's what happens. But that doesn't make it anyone's fault."

A wise perspective from a 22-year-old.

But outside that locker room, the fault-finding was already in full swing. Dave Brandon had made that game about his job—and others did, too. The coffin had already been built—with many of the materials supplied by Brandon himself, including the nails—and now a line of people awaited their turn with the hammer. By October 5, 2014, there was no shortage of carpenters willing to help.

The *Michigan Daily* reporters did not see the normally conspicuous Dave Brandon in New Jersey that weekend. The players also noticed Brandon's absence from the sidelines and locker room, his usual posts. What did the players think about Brandon on the sidelines during games?

"It was cool seeing Brandon on the sidelines when we were doing well," Gardner told me. "But he kind of quit doing that when we stopped winning. All of a sudden, you couldn't find him.

"Consistency is the biggest thing for young people—and we notice. We see you when it's going well, but when we're losing you're not there. Then when we're losing and they're starting to blame you more, you think, 'Now I should come around and show my support.'

"The kitchen gets hot, and you look for our sympathy. What do you expect us to feel about you?

"It's the mask. When we're winning, you're wearing it. Whether they tear it off, or you take it off, that's when we see what's really there."

On this point, at least, another player, who asked to remain anonymous, had similar feelings about Coach Hoke.

"When we were kicking ass his first year, he was the stern, tough guy. When we went 11–2, Hoke almost downplayed the success we had. 'The season was a failure because we didn't win a Big Ten title.' He pushed that way too much.

"We did just win a BCS bowl game, didn't we? I'm not even sure we should have been there. That was an accomplishment.

"But when we start losing, we saw a gradual change, from the hard-nosed tough guy, to the guy saying he loves us. By the Rutgers game, he's not a tough guy anymore. It's all, 'I love you guys, I love the team!' Like he was trying to get our sympathy. But he was never really like that when we were winning. Well, who are you?!

"Genuineness, you can't fake it."

The next day, Sunday, October 5, a reader on MGoBlog—who already had a picture of Jim Harbaugh in a Michigan hat for his avatar—put out a call for a "student boycott" of the kickoff for the Penn State game that weekend, Michigan's only night game of the year.

He titled his post, "STUDENTS: BRANDON IS NOT MICHIGAN, WE ARE. BOYCOTT PENN STATE KICKOFF."

If anyone in the department was hoping for an easier week, it didn't look to be coming any time soon.

The next day, Sunday, October 5, Harbaugh's San Francisco 49ers won their second game in a row, beating Kansas City, 22–17, to improve to 3–2 on the season. They would beat the St. Louis Rams the next weekend, which seemed to put them right on course for another playoff season, and perhaps their fourth consecutive trip to the NFC title game.

But all was not well in the Bay. The tensions building between Harbaugh and General Manager Trent Baalke over personnel, contract extensions, and more were becoming personal, leaving *San Jose Mercury News* columnist Tim Kawakami to wonder if the relationship could be repaired. If so, he wrote, it would probably require the intervention of owner Jed York, the 34-year-old son of Denise DeBartolo York and nephew of the team's previous owner, Edward DeBartolo Jr.

For another run at a Super Bowl, Kawakami believed, York and Baalke would probably need to put aside their personal differences with Harbaugh, and perhaps offer him an extension on his contract, which would run out after the 2015–16 season. But if the 49ers started to stumble, the trio that had been so effective in Harbaugh's first three seasons could break up.

Even then, however, Harbaugh would not lack for interest from just about any NFL franchise that had an opening—and some might create one, for the chance at the hottest coach around.

CHAPTER 69

MAKING A STAND

Due to their leadership during the general-admission ordeal, Central Student Government no longer had the option of sitting back and watching it play out. After CSG President Bobby Dishell made his statement on the CSG Web site the Friday before the Rutgers game, Brandon called Dishell to discuss his position. They only talked for two minutes, but Brandon thanked Dishell for voicing his opinion, and invited him to meet in person, telling him Annette Howe would follow up with him to set up a time—and she did, quite quickly.

Even though Michael Proppe no longer had any official role in CSG, and had enrolled in the Ross Business School's Master's of Accounting (MAcc) program, he stayed involved, helping Dishell whenever he could. The former Odd Couple, who started out with seemingly nothing in common, had spent well over a thousand hours working together in the past year, meeting with the people who ran the university, taking on the all-powerful athletic department, and trying to make a real difference.

"It was a lot of long days and late nights," Proppe recalls, during our long conversation at Ashley's Pub. "The new football seating policy was designed over a beer."

"And No Thai," Dishell added, citing a popular campus restaurant. "I'd now say we're good friends."

Proppe nodded and raised his glass.

I asked Dishell, "Would you say Michael is now one of your best friends?"

He took the question seriously, then nodded. "Yes," he said.

"Definitely yes," Proppe added.

The Sunday after the Rutgers game, Dishell and Proppe got together to discuss conducting another student survey. Given Proppe's training in statistics and surveys, Dishell didn't want to move forward without his help. They decided they needed to do it soon, as usual.

The next day, Monday, October 6, 2014, Proppe and Dishell got to work on the survey, while trying to get their schoolwork done, too.

Dishell set up shop in the back left corner of the graduate library's big, beautiful reading room, trying to do too many things at once: finish writing the survey, prepare for his first real experience with the press, talk to his parents and friends by text and phone, and flip through his books. At 5:20 p.m., he sent Dave Brandon a text about the survey.

"Hi Mr. Brandon—this is Bobby Dishell. I apologize for sending this over text, however I could not find your e-mail. We are sending out a student survey this week to get the pulse of the community around seating policies, prices, sentiment on Michigan Football, and potential constructive changes. Are there any questions you would like me to include?"

Twelve minutes later, Brandon called Dishell's cell phone. Dishell once again dashed out to the library's lobby to take the call. They spoke for seven minutes about the survey and its purpose. Brandon told Dishell he was grateful for his reaching out, and asked him to talk to Hunter Lochmann for input. When Dishell asked Lochmann if he had any questions he wanted included, Lochmann offered 23.

Proppe and Dishell couldn't help but notice how much more eager Brandon and Lochmann were to work together than they were a year earlier. Proppe and Dishell incorporated as many of Lochmann's questions as they could, then submitted a final survey of 21 questions to Royster Harper's office for approval.

That same week, Mark Schlissel hosted a "fireside chat" at the Michigan Union for some 300 students. Most of their time together was consumed by students complaining about the athletic department.

On Saturday, October 10, the CSG survey went out to the student body. The students responded with the same passion as they had before, with 5,208 filling out the survey in the first 72 hours.

During this tense time, many student-athletes sent e-mails of support directly to Brandon's e-mail address, which he surely welcomed, "though that doesn't necessarily help Dave," Andrea Fischer Newman says. "It's the Regents and the executives that needed to see those."

Most student-athletes continued to show their support by wearing their maize-and-blue garb, too, saying positive things on social media and, a few days after the Rutgers game, signing a letter in support of Brandon.

Inspired by the student-athletes' gesture, a separate group led by the athletic development brought together staff members from across the department to circulate a petition supporting Brandon, which they would send to Schlissel. Almost all of those working on Brandon's behalf had been hired by Brandon. Almost none of those who had been hired before Brandon's arrival were enthusiastic about the group's efforts. As one veteran told me, "The signed letter that went out [from the staff] was complete bullshit."

One staff member called Bill Martin to meet at her car in the parking lot, after his workout at the Intramural Building. Martin recalls that his former employee, sitting in her car, "was an emotional wreck, in tears. 'I'm being asked to sign this, and I don't believe it, but if I don't, I'm afraid I'll get fired!' She felt tremendous pressure."

At least one employee called up to the hill to let the top administrators know that people were feeling strong-armed to sign the letter. Michigan's General Counsel office soon advised the group to drop the petitions.

They did as instructed, but the Save Dave committee's efforts made a bigger point: When Brandon and his staffers had said, shortly after his appointment, that they were working for Dave Brandon's legacy, they meant it—and this proved it.

The letters weren't about saving the Michigan family, or even the department. Their efforts were intended to save Dave Brandon.

While the people working in athletics were well aware of the discontent with the athletic department, most employees can go weeks without venturing up the hill.

Not so the student athletes, who live in the dorms, the apartments, and the houses up the hill, and attend classes every day. They don't merely read about the unrest on campus. They live in the middle of it.

"The Monday after the Rutgers game," Hagerup recalls, "our professors talked about the football team in *three* different classes. Discussions, all that. When that happens, you never say anything. You just sort of sink in your seat."

The mood wasn't any better Monday afternoon when the players walked down to the Schembechler Hall team meeting room. "Another loss—and we got screwed by that call," Hagerup recalls. "The team was down."

Knowing this, Hoke pulled out one of his favorite stunts, where he runs in from the back of the team meeting room, screaming and smiling.

"Don't you just love this fucking game?!?" Everyone laughed.

Hagerup recalls, "We're hearing all this talk around campus and in the media, but what Coach said was perfect, and he said it a few times: 'You know what that says? That says we're relevant. People care about how we do. At other schools, professors don't talk about their teams. And that's what you sign up for here, so you take the good with the bad.'"

Hagerup thought, "'If that guy isn't giving in, we aren't either. Let's go to practice!' We put a great week of practice in. I can't recall a week we didn't. We certainly didn't give up."

The next day in class, Hagerup's thoughts bounced back and forth—from the unhappy current events to Hoke's speech the day before. His mind wandered: What can we do to make it better?

"So I start writing in my notebook, and I keep writing, and before you know it, I've got a lot on paper. Enough to share with my teammates. I figured, what kind of leader has things to say and doesn't say them? However it was received by my teammates, I wanted to get it off my chest, and I would have felt bad not saying them."

Hagerup typed his notes into his laptop, printed out enough copies for everyone on the team, and taped one in every player's locker. When his teammates arrived at their stalls that day, they were met with Hagerup's letter.

Team 135,

Think back to when you were ten years old. If someone had told you that you would get the opportunity to play six Big Ten Games—three at the Big House—you'd be so excited you wouldn't know what to do with yourself. You'd call your friends and brag, you'd tell your teachers, your family, your girlfriend—you'd tell everybody. Somewhere along the way, we've gotten too complacent with the opportunity we are so fortunate to have. I have made some dumb and selfish decisions in my five years here, but, if nothing else, I have gained a new and deep lasting appreciation for what it means to play FOR (not at) The University of Michigan. It is special for reasons bigger than football.

When you come back to Ann Arbor in ten or twenty years for an alumni visit, inevitably you'll represent this team. Do you want to look down at your feet and mutter, "I played for Team 135, the team that gave up halfway through the season"? OR do you want to say with pride, "I was on the team that had a rough six game stretch, but we fought and clawed our way to win every game there on out"? I've heard so many guys who graduated a year, five years, or twenty years ago say, "Man, I wish I could just get one

*more game. Even just one snap!" Well we have an opportunity to play at
least SIX games this fall.*

    *Effort is between you and you. It can be faked. Buy why fake it? Let's
make these next two months of Big Ten play the most memorable we can.
That starts with practice today and it ends in Columbus when we'll take
back our pride. Michigan is 2–0 under the lights. Let's put a complete game
together on Saturday, let's remind people that we are MICHIGAN, and
let's make Penn State's flight home miserable.*

Win!

—Hagerup

"I think it was well received," Hagerup told me.

That is a considerable understatement. No sooner had his teammates started
reading his letter, than they started coming up to thank him, from seniors to
freshmen. At some point that week, every coach told Hagerup he'd delivered
a great message, and showed real leadership.

A few days later, a teammate's father texted him: "Hey, great letter!"

"What?" Hagerup didn't understand how he'd known about it.

"I saw it online!"

One of Hagerup's teammates had given Hagerup's letter to a friend,
who posted it on TheWolverine.com. MLive.com picked it up, followed
by just about everyone else who covers Michigan football. The response
was overwhelming—and overwhelmingly positive, a rarity that fall.

A couple days before the Penn State game, "I heard a few things on campus about my letter," Hagerup says, "and that was nice, but I really wanted it
to be a thing for the team only."

But it was Hagerup's very intent that the letter be private that made it resonate so deeply with the players' parents, then the students and fans: it was
authentic, the quality fans most appreciate about college athletics, the quality
that can salvage traditions—and, perhaps, even a season.

A student boycott of the kickoff had been proposed to send the administration a message, and ruin the TV shot, but not discourage the players. It
had been supported, debated, criticized, and ultimately dropped. The students
showed up en masse on October 11, 2014, and went right to their sections.
The boycott had been averted.

It was a beautiful night for a football game, the third night game in Michigan's history. It didn't produce beautiful football, though perhaps that was in
the eye of the beholder. The two teams combined for 8 penalties and fewer
than 500 yards offense, but made up for it in intensity.

Penn State took a 13–10 halftime lead—thanks partly to a Gardner interception, which set up a short field for Penn State's touchdown—but Michigan's defense didn't let the Lions score again, notching an impressive 6 sacks. The Wolverines kicked 2 field goals in the second half to take a 16–13 lead.

Late in the game, Penn State intentionally took a safety by snapping the ball out of the endzone. On the ensuing onside kick, the Lions appeared to recover the ball, giving the Lions a chance for a game-winning drive, like they had pulled off the year before in State College. But a dubious offside call gave Michigan the ball, and the game.

If the officials cost Michigan a chance against Rutgers, they gave it back a week later.

Michigan's players didn't care about the details. They had stopped their three-game losing streak to get their first win in a month.

"The guys could have bagged it," Hagerup says, "but we had a great week of practice, and everyone wanted to win that game. The fans were into it, too. This is what the whole season should have felt like it."

In the fourth quarter, a hearty "Let's Go Blue!" chant started in the student section, and spread. Most seasons, that was routine, but this one, it stood out for its uncomplicated, unalloyed show of support.

The win gave the Wolverines a 3–4 record, and 1–2 in the league. A Big Ten division title was already a long shot, with Michigan State and Ohio State on the same side, but it was a much-needed step in the right direction.

"It turned out to be a wonderful game," Hagerup recalls. "I was really proud of that one. I got teary-eyed near the end. If this was the only game we ever played again, this was a fun way to end it."

CHAPTER 70

THE STUDENTS SPEAK, AND EVERYONE LISTENS

The Wolverines would be able to savor their victory during a bye week, but with a Regents meeting coming up Thursday, October 16, CSG president Bobby Dishell didn't have that luxury.

Bobby Dishell had been working on his report, while also practicing his speech to the Regents in the CSG Executive Office in the Union, overlooking the fountain, and in the attic room of his 100-year-old campus rental. At one o'clock that morning, Dishell finished his survey report to President Schlissel, the Regents, the executive officers, and Dave Brandon. When they opened Dishell's survey, they found the results told quite a story—one CSG President Dishell would be telling at the next day's Regents meeting at U-M-Flint.

The fans smelled blood in the water, with some reporters predicting that Brandon would be fired by President Schlissel at the meeting. That was extremely unlikely, but that so many were willing to believe it suggested how eagerly the Michigan community anticipated this meeting.

Dishell and his vice president got caught in traffic heading up to Flint, and "ran frantically" across the Flint campus. "It was the most packed meeting I have ever been to," he told me. They had about 100 seats, all filled, and just about every place you could stand was occupied, too, with a half-dozen TV cameras set up in the mix. The 21-year-old had entered the big leagues.

When he got up to speak, wearing a full suit and tie, he admits, "I have never been more nervous. It was all a bit of a whirlwind."

But once he cleared his throat, his preparation quickly paid off. Dishell started by displaying his recently developed diplomacy. "Thank you President

Schlissel, Members of the Board of Regents, and Executive Officers for the opportunity to address you today.

"These past few weeks have been a troubling time for Michigan students. Difficulties in regard to the football program, focused primarily within the Athletic Department's administration, have made many students wary of the very thing that has united them with alumni, family, and city residents for over a century: Michigan football. Our frustration is evidenced in the recent slew of angry *Michigan Daily* articles, in the student protests, petitions, rallies, boycotts, and on social media."

Though the number of troubles had grown, Dishell said, "the main problem behind them has not." He then closed his introduction with a callback to Michael Proppe's ringing line when he addressed the Regents a year earlier: "The Athletic Department has broken its trust with the student body."

Dishell backed up his thesis statement with the 5,208 student season-ticket holders who completed the 21-question survey, in which they weighed in on general-admission seating, ticket prices, what they cared about, and what they didn't.

During Brandon's media blitz a few days after the Minnesota game, he occasionally claimed the severe drop in student season-ticket sales in 2014 was because they ended the pure general-admission system from 2013—a claim that bothered Michael Proppe greatly. But now they had data.

Bobby Dishell told the Regents that, if the Athletic Department had not changed its 2013 general-admission seating policy, only 65 percent of 2014 student season-ticket holders said they would have bought tickets. As for Brandon's theory that the students who dropped their tickets in 2014 would have kept them with the general-admission policy, the CSG survey results discovered only 13 percent of those who bought tickets in 2013 and dropped them in 2014 would have bought tickets again. Brandon's theory did not test well.

This went to Michael Proppe's central point. Months after this meeting he told me, "Had general admission been in place in 2014, according to the survey, less than 9,000 students would have bought season tickets. We helped Brandon sell about 3,000 more tickets than he otherwise would have, and he was publicly blaming our policy for the low ticket sales. That really upset me."

Through his new friend Bobby Dishell, however, Proppe was getting the last word where it mattered most: in front of the President, the Regents, and the Executive Officers—a learned group that had little difficulty digesting the students' data. Dishell remembers scanning the faces in the crowd, a few looking skeptical, others deadpan, but many trying to hide their excitement as he hit point after point.

The survey's first question asked respondents to rank the importance of a list of factors in their decision to buy season tickets: strength of home schedule; price; team performance; seating policy; love of the sport; and tradition. The clear winner was "tradition," the very quality that had been drawing fans to the Big House for decades—and the element Brandon seemed to care about least. Distant runner ups were "price" and "strength of home schedule."

Dishell said, "Many of these students would be willing to purchase season tickets in the future if the price were to significantly drop or the schedule were to significantly improve." Although Brandon did not attend the meeting, Dishell assumed everyone present would get the hint.

The survey also called into question Brandon's comment that "it's all mommy and daddy's money." It was usually the students' money, and that's why only 10 percent said they would purchase tickets next season at the current rate of $299.

"I am a firm believer," Dishell added, in one of his speech's rare personal opinions, "that no student should be priced out of being able to experience Michigan football."

When they asked students to describe the current program in one word, the most common responses, in order, were "disappointing," "corporate," "bad," and "embarrassing."

In their report, though not in Dishell's speech, Dishell and Proppe included the responses to their request for general comments. When Proppe sent me these responses, he told me, "I'm not just picking out angry rants. Most of the comments were this long and angry." A representative sample:

"Dave Brandon has corporatized Michigan football and left the traditional values of Michigan behind. Make sure Dave Brandon is not around when we pick a new coach because he is toxic to this program. He's a micromanager and doesn't respect the values of the game."

"It's not our Michigan anymore, it's Dave Brandon's. And it sucks just as much as his cheese bread did at Dominos."

"Please stop BLARING MUSIC IN THE STADIUM!!!!!! Please stop trying to supplement the game with gimmicks!!!!!! The Michigan brand is 135 years old, you do not need to expand it or upgrade it. Just because you can make more money does not mean that you should."

" 'Frankly, I've come to the conclusion there are more important things in this world than money.' - Bo Schembechler 1982."

It was remarkable to see that these students, born in the mid-1990s, several years after Canham and Schembechler had retired, display such a firm grasp of Michigan tradition, which they seemed to value more than the people running the department.

Further, Dishell said, according to the respondents, "an 'us versus them' environment had been created [between the department and the students]. Respondents indicated that it is unclear whether the Athletic Director's relationship with the student body is repairable at this point. Drastic changes need to be made to demonstrate that the Athletic Department values students."

In answers to various questions, Dishell added, "The name 'Dave Brandon' was mentioned a total of 1,208 times, almost all of them negative and disapproving."

Given these results, which refuted just about every theory the Athletic Department espoused during Brandon's four years, it might not be so surprising that the department seemed to be in a newly cooperative mood. Dishell told the university leaders assembled, "We had a productive meeting with Athletics yesterday and this afternoon and came to the following verbal agreements."

Dishell listed eight items, including: "Significant price decrease" for student football tickets in 2016; eliminating fees for charitable student groups renting Athletic Department buildings; and a dramatic increase in communication between the students and the department, through the creation of a student advisory board, monthly open meetings with Brandon for all students, and a standing monthly meeting between Brandon and the CSG president.

Those concessions might not look like much, unless you remembered how the department had functioned the previous four years: Exactly the opposite, with two significant student ticket price hikes, outrageous bills for students renting Athletic Department buildings, and a department completely isolated, by design, from the students they were supposed to serve, which even included the CSG president.

In just a few minutes, Dishell had very efficiently laid out the questions on everyone's mind, the survey data that answered them, and the potential solutions they pointed to. The audience had no trouble following Dishell's argument. As he built to his conclusion, they were with him.

"I believe these are a big step in the right direction," he said, "but are not the final solution. Students remain supportive of the *team*. We remain supportive of the time-honored tradition, the sense of camaraderie and fellowship that's so unique to Michigan.

"When students were asked what Michigan football would look like in an ideal world, respondents stated that we hope to be able to afford tickets, enjoy the games with friends, feel a sense of respect on behalf of the Athletic Department, and most of all, students remain optimistic about feeling a sense of unity within the Michigan community.

"While the survey provides many valuable insights about the student body's negative view of the AD, it also reveals one major positive: students, however disgruntled, stand by blue."

When Dishell finished, the assembled crowd cheered, then quickly quieted when the Regents took over. "It felt like I had just begun speaking, and the next thing I know it's all over and I'm answering questions and talking to the press."

His phone started blowing up the second he turned it back on, with text messages of support and media requests. One of his quotes would run in a major story on ESPN.com. His mind was racing, relieved, excited, and anxious at the same time, wondering if he had done enough, or said too much, or if he had endangered his relationship with the department.

But one thing was clear to everyone in that room: Bobby Dishell had given voice to those who had not been heard before.

"He captured the mood of the student body," said Proppe, who watched at home with his roommates, who normally didn't care about student government but fist-bumped Dishell's every point. "I couldn't have been prouder to have worked with him at that moment. Bobby walked a very narrow political tightrope, and did so magnificently. When the spotlight was on, he delivered."

Dishell's diplomatic approach stood in contrast to the more direct tack taken by the next speaker, U-M public policy graduate student and alumnus Zeid El-Kilani, who said, "We are nauseated by the doublespeak, public relations gaffes, and contempt that many see in the Athletic Department. It is clear that change is necessary. That is why I and 11,000 other students and alumni respectfully request the university relieve Mr. Brandon of his duties as athletic director."

After a Regents meeting is adjourned, it is very rare for Regents to speak to the press, but Bernstein told his colleagues prior to the meeting, "I am not running from the press on this. I am not. I'm not going to say anything that will damage the university, but I think someone needs to speak with an authentic personal voice about this situation."

To the press, Bernstein said, "The Shane Morris incident, the poor performance of the football team, is like a spark in a very, very dry forest, and there's not a lot of water around right now."

But Andrea Fischer Newman countered Bernstein's take to the same media members. "You've got to look at the whole Athletic Department. You've

got to look at the addition of sports, you've got to look at the addition of facilities. You've got to look at what we've done with women's sports. You've got
to look at the money that's been raised, you've got to look at the budget.
There's a lot of good things being done on campus right now in athletics."

This was not the majority view of any of the department's constituent
groups, outside the student-athletes, but it did show that Brandon still had
strong backers. The fight wasn't over. It also showed, for that very reason, that
the athletic director was no longer just a distraction, but a cause for division
within the university community, from the students all the way to the Regents.

That afternoon, Brandon told Bobby Dishell what he would tell the *Michigan Daily* a few days later: he would lower student ticket prices for the 2015
season, down from $280 for seven games to $175 for the same number—even
lower than it had been before Brandon arrived in 2010.

"We listen," Brandon said. "We've been listening. . . . We really learned
that two really important components to re-engaging with our students in trying to create a more robust, more enthusiastic and larger student section for
next year's football season was price and strength of schedule. . . . A nearly
40 percent reduction in ticket prices is, I think it's fair to say, unprecedented."

These were big steps for Brandon to make, running counter to his approach
the previous four years. But even at the top of his game, he didn't hear what the
students just told them: the biggest factor for them buying tickets was not
the schedule or the price, but celebrating Michigan tradition. Brandon was
also still inclined to blame the new hybrid seating policy, which actually
spared him. And, of course, he elided the students' biggest complaint, mentioned by more than 1,000 of the respondents: the athletic director himself.

Still, his response indicated a willingness to consider taking the department in a dramatically different direction.

"I always wonder how different things would be," Dishell told me, "if there
was more feedback with the Athletic Department. If Dave had worked with
us from the day he was hired in the same way that he did in the end, I think
Michigan Athletics would look very different and students would be a lot
happier—athlete and non-athlete alike.

"I think we have seen time and time again, that when students have a voice
and give their input, we make change for the better."

CHAPTER 71

REVENGE OF THE OLD FARTS

Right when Brandon seemed to be sincerely working to get the students back, he seemed to lose another group, the "old guard," Michigan's older fans and former departmental leaders. They had kept quiet during Brandon's tenure, but by October of 2014, they were speaking to the press.

One of the most prominent was Peg Canham-Keeley, the widow and long-time assistant of Don Canham, Michigan's athletic director from 1968 to 1988, who started the attendance streak. On October 6, shortly after the Rutgers loss, and before the Penn State game, journalist Ben Freed ran his interview on MLive.com, in which Ms. Canham-Keeley pulled no punches.

"I'm just devastated that his lifetime at the school—he was there for 50 years as a student, a coach, and an athletic director—to see that his legacy is going down the drain, that's what I'm angry about," she said.

"The fine line that he [Canham] walked was that there was the marketing side of him, but he also had the ability to think of the people in the seats. He sold a lot of the tickets to former players and they all supported him for years and years and years.

"I just think it's gone way overboard with the crazy music and Beyonce and Eminem and that sort of thing. I guess he's trying to cater to the students but it's obviously not working. For me the pageantry of the football game is the band coming out on the field and the tradition of the drum major."

Don Canham used to host holiday parties at his company office, School-Tech, long after he had retired from Michigan. After he died in 2005, Peg kept up the tradition with her "Old Farts" party, inviting the former coaches, athletes, administrators, and friends of the department—people like former football coaches Jerry Hanlon, Tirrel Burton, and Gary Moeller; hockey's Al Renfrew, baseball's Don Lund, and diving's Dick Kimbell; and former star athletes like Don Dufek Sr., George Pomey, and Ron Kramer. It was Michigan's "Greatest Generation," if you will.

They first gathered at the Junge Center, between Crisler and the football tunnel, until Brandon moved them to the golf course clubhouse—and then did away with their party altogether.

When I called her, she said, "The parties were about the family of Michigan Athletics, and I think that feeling has been lost. It's all becoming so expensive. There's a lot of frustration."

That frustration, she said, had spread to the games themselves. She still has tickets and attends, but, she said, the experience is completely different from what it used to be.

"To me it's become a circus, and that's not what it should be. I'm born and raised in Ann Arbor. I grew up with Michigan football. That's not—to me—Michigan football."

When the former athletic director's widow's complaints are virtually verbatim what the undergrads said in their survey, it's worth noting. Perhaps it's just as remarkable that, given such a strong consensus of what Michigan football is and isn't, the athletic director was so eager to change what generations of fans agreed on.

If you don't have the lettermen, the students, and the old guard, who's left? The student-athletes, for sure, some of the coaches, and Stephen Ross.

On Saturday, September 27, the morning of the infamous Minnesota game, and just days after the Coke-for-tickets promotion blew up, *Crain's Business Detroit* published an interview with Ross, who came to Brandon's defense. "He's probably the most qualified athletic director in the country," Ross said. "I think he's terrific. You don't go around giving $100 million if you don't feel there is going to be bang for the buck."

In this, Ross underestimated his generosity. You also don't go around giving $100 million to any schools other than your alma mater. His donation was not merely an investment, but truly, a gift, one offered without the expectation of a return.

But his quote raised a lot of questions, and some concerns. Did Ross understand what was happening on campus? Did the other donors share his views? And if so, did they have the power to save Brandon's job, when an apparent majority of Michigan constituents seemed to want a change?

To the first question, someone who knows Ross quite well told me, "Stephen was impressed by Dave's marketing pizzazz. That's really it. Dave makes such a good first impression. Everybody drank that Kool-Aid. But Stephen's not a reader. He didn't keep up to speed on what was happening on the ground in Ann Arbor. He loves Michigan—obviously—but he spends his time on business and his NFL team. He just didn't have all the facts—and he still doesn't have all the facts."

If Michigan wants to remain "Leaders and Best," Michigan needs the Stephen Rosses. But if Michigan wants to stay Michigan, it also needs to preserve a level of autonomy unsurpassed among public universities, a freedom cemented in its founding, which predates the state's, and has been essential to Michigan's becoming arguably the greatest public university in the world.

It's clear the vast majority of donors understand this, and care more about their alma mater than their ability to control it. But it's not the donors' job to protect the autonomy of the university. It's the university's job.

The immediate, smaller question of Ross's support for Brandon became moot after President Mark Schlissel held a private meeting the Friday before October 11, the Penn State game, at the Ross School itself. In an open forum, facilitated by Ross, many major donors expressed their displeasure with Brandon. Before handing over the microphone to President Schlissel, Ross announced to the group that President Schlissel had his blessing to do whatever he needed to do.

This received a hearty ovation.

And with that, Brandon lost another potentially potent power base, and his detractors eliminated another obstacle to his removal.

CHAPTER 72

A COMMITTEE OF ONE

On October 25, 2014, Michigan's football team traveled to Michigan State to renew their century-old sibling rivalry. It was a big game for both teams—but for very different reasons.

The eighth-ranked Spartans had lost only one game, at Oregon, and had their sights set squarely on another Big Ten title. At the time, they seemed like the Big Ten's best chance for a national title, too—something State had not claimed since 1966. Michigan State was favored by 2 touchdowns against the struggling Wolverines, whose dreams were more modest, but more urgent.

Going into the contest, the Wolverines had lost 10 of their last 15 games. College football had changed a lot over the past few decades, but blocking hadn't, and the Wolverines weren't very good at it. They looked poorly coached, especially when they put only 10 players on the field, which they had already done three times that season.

But they had plenty to fight for, including pride, an outside shot at a bowl game, and their coaches' and athletic director's jobs.

It was all still in the balance.

Minutes before kickoff, Michigan linebacker Joe Bolden walked out to midfield with a couple dozen teammates and threw down a two-foot tent stake into the grass field, amid a lot of shouting. It was intended as a tribal challenge, a band of gladiators throwing down the gauntlet, but it came off as a sophomoric stunt. Hoke was not aware of the gesture, but the players clearly did not fear his reaction.

Dantonio and the Spartans felt disrespected. Of course, that was the point. After the game, Dantonio said, "I just felt like we needed to put a stake in them at that point."

They did, easily covering the spread, 35–11. The Spartans kept the Wolverines to zero yards rushing in the first half, and at the end of the game had outgained their foes, 446–186. For Michigan, incredibly, the effort represented a nominal improvement over the previous season, when the Wolverines finished with minus-48 yards rushing.

The Spartans kept the Paul Bunyan trophy for the sixth time in seven years, establishing unquestioned dominance over the state for the first time since LBJ ruled the White House. It also altered the dialogue between the two schools. After all, calling your little brother "Little Brother" gets a bit awkward when he keeps kicking your butt.

After the game, the Wolverines jogged up the tunnel into Spartan Stadium's famously small visiting locker room. When one of the players smashed a towel dispenser, Hagerup wasn't afraid to call him out: "We had three hours to play good and pissed off," he told him, "and now you're going to take it out on their locker room?"

The player stopped, but Hagerup understood his frustration.

"I have never felt worse after a loss than that one," he told me. "Losses never hurt more than when you're a senior. Things are ending soon. There's going to be no off-season, no more chances to play them. This is the last time I will *ever* play Michigan State, and that hurts. From now on, watching that game, I'll be a football alumnus. Most games you get over, but not that one."

Michigan State head coach Mark Dantonio's warning to the Wolverines, back in 2007, now seemed prophetic: "Pride comes before the fall." The tide had turned.

It was now conventional wisdom among Michigans fans that the 3–5 Wolverines would soon be searching for their third new coach in seven years. But if conventional wisdom was correct, who would do the searching?

Michigan fans didn't get to vote on Brandon's fate. Nor did the donors, deans, or even the Regents. Only one person was charged with that decision: Michigan's newly named president, Mark Schlissel. The scouting reports I received on him were consistent: He is brilliant, he is honest, and he "gets it." Michigan could surely do worse.

But if there was one problem President Schlissel would rather not have faced in his first year—as the Regents promised him he wouldn't—the athletic director was it.

If Schlissel decided to fire Brandon, he'd have to negotiate Brandon's exit—and his $3 million buyout, thanks to the contract extension Brandon signed in 2012—then form a search committee, select a new AD, and oversee the hiring of a new football coach. All these things consume time and energy, which Schlissel would have preferred spending on the university's real missions: research and teaching.

But doing nothing might have been worse, resulting in lame-duck coaches, falling ticket sales, dwindling donations, and slipping school spirit, not to mention growing deficits, distractions, and dissension.

With two years left on Hoke's six-year contract, he and his staff would have a hard time recruiting the best prospects, or even keeping the commitments they had, unless Michigan gave him and his staff long extensions—something few were advocating. With optimism at a low ebb, season-ticket sales would likely fall again in 2015, and perhaps fall precipitously, led by a growing student revolt.

But Michigan's problems ran deeper than that. In 2010, Michigan opened 81 skyboxes, costing from $55,000 to $85,000, plus whatever donations you needed to "outbid" the others to get the best suites. Michigan already had a half-dozen empty suites for the 2014 season—a loss of somewhere between $330,000 and $510,000, plus donations—and could have ended up with a lot more empty suites when a third of them came up for renewal during the 2015 off-season. The timing couldn't have been worse, and could have cost the department a good chunk of the $15 million or so the skyboxes brought in every year, plus the $5 million in additional gifts.

If Brandon's reputation for marketing savvy had taken a hit, his equally lofty status as a financial wizard seemed ready to crumble next.

In Brandon's fourth year, department revenues were still breaking records. Continuing to grow at about 7 percent a year, the department was poised to break $150 million for the first time in history—and just four years after breaking $100 million, which seemed impressive at the time. The exponential revenue growth was partly due to the dramatic increase in conference TV payouts to Big Ten members, which had more than doubled from 2010 to 2014, to $44.5 million for each school—a gift the Big Ten bestows equally on all its members.

But Brandon's operating expenses also continued to expand—and expand even faster than revenues, at nearly 9 percent a year, to total $145 million. They were catching up, and fast. As a result, the department's operating margin had declined steadily since Brandon took over, falling from the 15 to 20 percent annual operating surpluses routinely generated by Bill Martin, to a mere 3.4 percent in 2014. It doesn't take a genius to realize a dip in revenues for the

2015 season—for any number of reasons—could put Michigan's annual operating budget in the red.

When I reviewed these figures with a financial analyst, he said, "If Michigan football was a stock on Wall Street, it would get creamed, and the CEO would get hammered." Then, more likely than not, fired.

So, if Michigan needed to make a coaching change to keep the wins coming, and avoid going into debt, would Dave Brandon make that call? Since the best candidate Brandon was willing or able to get four years earlier was Brady Hoke, did anyone expect Brandon would do better the next time around?

It was extremely unlikely that Michigan's native sons—Les Miles and Jim Harbaugh—would be willing to work for Dave Brandon. Of course, Brandon's job security could make it hard for him to attract any A-List coaches, who try to avoid working for bosses who might not be there in a year. Thus, even if Michigan failed to make a bowl game in 2014, if Brandon was still the athletic director, Hoke would probably get another season. If Michigan wanted to change the coaching staff, it would likely have to change the athletic director first.

The danger of waiting to change the athletic director and head coach was not simply that Michigan could suffer through another disappointing season, on and off the field, but that it could lose a group of fans forever. With more fans discovering the joys of staying at home, and not getting gouged on ticket prices, seat licenses, parking, hot dogs, and water, it's fair to wonder how many of them would come back to the Big House after a year or two watching games from their couch.

Yes, the Athletic Department's $150 million was a rounding error at a university with an $8 billion annual budget. Even considering the worst-case scenario—Michigan football stayed in the doldrums through another season, ticket sales plummeted, and fans continued to call for Brandon's head—Michigan would still be a premier public university, even if it missed out on some of the reflected glory from its dazzling front porch. You could even argue a few down years could help reinforce the proper priorities of the university, placing academics ahead of athletics.

But get it *really* wrong, where the losses went deeper than games and dollars, and damage could be done to the university itself, and it could tarnish a presidency before it even started. That's not hyperbole, as more than a few departed university presidents could tell Schlissel.

President Schlissel's dilemma could have gotten dicier after the Regents election, November 4, 2014. Unlike those of most state universities, Michigan's trustees are openly partisan. You have to win your party's nomination before you can be on the fall ballot.

Before the November 4 election, Michigan's board was composed of six Democrats, who wanted Brandon out, and two Republicans, who wanted him to stay. I spoke with a majority of the Regents, all of whom maintained politics played no role in their approach to the Athletic Department, and all seemed to come by it honestly. In fact, a former Regent named Dan Horning ran again for the Republican Party's nomination in 2014, on a platform that included ousting Dave Brandon, but lost his bid by a mere 200 votes. He still talked often to current Regents, however, including his good friend, Democrat Larry Deitch.

But if two candidates who supported Brandon had won in November, when the new board convened in January, it could have split, 4–4, on Brandon's fate. If President Schlissel did not act on Brandon before then, the six Regents who wanted him gone would be upset. If Schlissel tried to act after the election, but before the new Regents took office in January, the two who supported him would howl.

Only one thing was certain: if either happened in November, President Schlissel would pine for the problems he had in October.

Ultimately, the most important issue at stake was not wins and losses, ticket prices or revenues, but the values upon which the University of Michigan was built, including cooperation and compromise, transparency and truthfulness. Under Brandon, until his recent overtures to the students, the Athletic Department had been notably lacking in all four. Each time the department tripped over itself, it sounded less like a part of a world-class university, and more like the troubled subsidiary of an embattled corporation.

It was this tension between what the university stood for, and how the Athletic Department acted, that would persist until someone dealt with it directly. It was possible that that someone could be Brandon himself, if he continued to work with the students and other stakeholders to restore the community to what it had been before he'd arrived.

But more likely, that someone would be President Schlissel.

CHAPTER 73

I SUGGEST YOU FIND
A NEW TEAM

The football team entered the week following the Michigan State game hobbled, and looking for a break. Dave Brandon entered the same week in about the same state. Even his most loyal lieutenants could no longer count on him being in office indefinitely.

Although Chrissi Rawak had been one of Brandon's most trusted aides, she was hedging her bets—perhaps necessarily.

The Sunday after the Michigan State defeat, October 26, 2014, she met with Bobby Dishell and Cooper Charlton, the president of the Student-Athlete Advisory Council (SAAC), to discuss their new ideas of creating a student advisory board and hosting open meetings with the athletic director. In their discussions, Dishell recalls Rawak often framing the topics on their agenda by saying, "Let's talk about how this would look for any AD, not just Dave." In other words, their plans could not depend on Brandon continuing to serve as Michigan's athletic director.

That same day, the *Michigan Daily*'s Alejandro Zúñiga reported that Craig Kaplan, the student who had found a bullhorn to address the crowd from the president's front steps during the "Fire Brandon" rally, was helping to distribute 2,000 custom-made T-shirts purchased by a "very giving" donor who chose to remain anonymous, for Michigan's homecoming game the next weekend against Indiana. The T-shirts were white, to stand out in a maize-and-blue crowd, with "#FIREDAVEBRANDON" printed in big block letters.

"We support the team. That's the crucial part," Kaplan told Zúñiga. "We want to see the best for them. Dave Brandon is not the best for them. That's the message we're trying to get across."

The idea caught on quickly. A few hours later, a group of students announced a "White Out–Dave Out" demonstration for the rest of the student section, with all the students who wanted Brandon fired to wear white shirts at the game, printed or not. After a posting on MGoBlog, many fans sitting outside the student section picked up on the protest, too, and promised to wear white that weekend.

Bruised and battered though Brandon was, he still had a few things going for him—the most important, perhaps, being President Schlissel's reluctance to make a quick decision on his fate. Though no one was working with a lot of data, those who had watched the new president closely described him as a calm, deliberate decision-maker.

President Schlissel was not blind to the problems emanating from the department and its director, but he was inclined to give Brandon a chance to fix what needed fixing, and would not feel rushed to move faster than he thought fair or wise. He would follow the academic calendar, not the athletic one, giving Brandon until graduation to right his ship.

Then, one insider told me, "Schlissel would have needed to see monumental change, showing that [Brandon] knows how to work within a university."

If Brandon could show real change, and give President Schlissel reason to believe he had learned some lessons, the community was coming back together, the finances had been straightened out, and the future was bright, President Schlissel could very well have kept him. If Brandon did not meet these expectations, President Schlissel could move on, knowing he'd given the athletic director a fair chance.

Brandon seemed to be getting the message, witness the many reforms he had agreed to that week, including a number of measures to improve communication with the students—Schlissel's first concern. Brandon had even planned to meet with the *Daily* on a regular basis.

At the suggestion of his greatest champion, President Coleman, Brandon also set up a meeting with four highly respected leaders from different corners of the university for Wednesday morning, October 29; and he agreed to appear at another meeting that same night with the Alumni Association board of directors.

It is impossible for us to know if Brandon's about-face on so many fronts was motivated by a sincere desire to change, or merely survive, but the effort was clear to friends and foes alike. Brandon had a lot of work to do to turn his approval ratings around, if that was still possible. But it was far from a fait accompli, as many fans, bloggers, and reporters believed, that he was a dead man walking. Whether Brandon successfully completed his "probationary period" or not by May of 2015, Hoke would probably still be the head coach, and would get another season to prove himself.

But before Brandon's new approach had time to kick in, and his advisors could offer any meaningful help, Brandon's problems exploded, rendering any attempt at rehabilitation pointless.

On Tuesday, October 28, at 11:15 a.m., Brian Cook published the biggest bombshell in the 10-year history of MGoBlog, with the headline: "Dave Brandon: 'I Suggest You Find a New Team.'"

During the Brandon era, a number of media people, including me, would occasionally receive e-mails from Michigan fans who had corresponded with Brandon. These fans had written Brandon with mild concerns about this or that, but they were generally respectful, and usually expressed their optimism about Brandon's tenure. Brandon often responded to these e-mails with ridicule, scorn, and sarcasm.

When fans forwarded these e-mails to me, I declined to mention them publicly for a number of reasons. But even if I had decided the e-mails were fair game and germane to my coverage of Michigan athletics, I would have had to verify the e-mails' authenticity, which requires a very specific expertise few of us have.

Brian Cook had also received many such e-mails—more than I had. But he had a catalyst others didn't: A couple weeks earlier, one of his avid readers, who goes by "Wolverine Devotee," posted one of Brandon's e-mail responses. One of MGoBlog's moderators deleted it as unverified, but Cook put it back up.

To everyone's surprise, the quote got picked up by ESPN's Keith Olbermann for his nightly "Worst Person in the World" segment. This forced Cook's hand, prompting him to ascertain the veracity of that e-mail—and, while he was at it, the others he'd received.

After the initial post, Cook received a second, near-identical e-mail from a reader. His second-in-command, Ace Anbender, tracked down the esoteric e-mail headers from the first Brandon response. Cook asked his Twitter followers for help verifying their authenticity, and soon heard from encryption experts, one in the military and one at Google, eager to assist. The e-mails checked out. They were authentic, and Brandon never denied them.

But it must be said, if Brandon had done great work as Michigan's athletic director to that point—hiring successful coaches and keeping prices reasonable, the faithful happy, the Big House full, and Michigan tradition alive and well—Cook probably wouldn't have felt compelled to expose Brandon's private personality, as revealed in these e-mails, and readers would have been less inclined to care.

If the Shane Morris situation was a spark in a very dry forest, Brandon's e-mails were a flame thrower.

Thus, on Tuesday, October 28, Brian Cook opened his top story by explaining to his readers that, a couple of weeks ago, one of MGoBlog's readers posted a copy of an e-mail that they claimed was from Dave Brandon's University of Michigan account, in response to a fan's e-mail. Though the picture was a little fuzzy, the words were clearly visible, and quite surprising:

"'I suggest you find a new team to support," Brandon apparently wrote. "We will be fine without you."

Any doubts about the e-mail's intended tone were cleared up in the last line: "Have a happy life."

Brian Cook explained to his readers that they were "already trying to confirm or dis-confirm the authenticity of this when Keith Olbermann's show presented it as a fact we're reporting. At that point we *had* to either confirm it or repudiate it. We've done our best to do so.

"We are now reporting this is authentic."

Cook later added that, about the same time the fan above received Brandon's response, Brandon had "shot off another after receiving a short rant about how Al Borges was bad and should feel bad:

"'I suggest you find a new team to support.

"'I really don't care about your opinions.

"'Have a happy life.'"

Cook continued. "This woman's husband forwarded a much longer exchange with Brandon he had afterward. Brandon closed this one by asserting that 'You may need more luck than our football team' to deal with his wife," a sentiment which did not go over well with women working at Michigan, among others.

Many of these phrases, such as, "Get another team. We'll be fine with out you," and "Have a happy life," recurred in Brandon's responses, suggesting a strong pattern. Another he ended by saying, "Quit drinking and go to bed," which was so comically out of line it was printed on a popular T-shirt, in the same format as the trendy "Keep Calm and Carry On" T-shirt.

To say the e-mails attracted attention is to understate the case considerably. The site received 183,983 unique visits that day, and 433,522 page views—both records—suggesting that people who read it once felt compelled to go back and read it again. It was that stunning, a building accidentally blowing up, in the middle of town. The story reached just about every American media site that covers sports.

"The e-mails did him in," Regent Kathy White acknowledges, "but I still can't explain why he wrote them. There's no explanation. If any other executive officer had written e-mails even remotely like that, they'd be gone too."

Regent Larry Deitch agreed. "It's possible that if the e-mails had not come out, that there could have been a different result. It was still headed in that direction, but he might have been able to save himself. When the e-mails came out, however, Mark [Schlissel] knew what he had to do. I honestly don't know what choice he had."

President Schlissel might have been inclined to give Brandon a chance to turn things around the day before, but by noon Tuesday, that generous opportunity had evaporated.

The e-mails didn't just reveal Brandon's lofty self-regard, and contempt for his constituents. They pointed to the central problem: at a glance, the entire community knew, "This is not Michigan."

And that's why the e-mails were such a watershed. A lot of Michigan backers had bailed on Brandon beforehand, at various stages and for various reasons, but the e-mails made it virtually impossible for even the most stubborn Brandon supporters to believe he was still the right man to lead the department, and should continue.

This was especially jarring on the heels of Brandon's recent attempts to remake his department and himself, which seemed sincere enough. But the very next week, we learned, late at night, in the quiet of his expansive home, Brandon had been sending off these grenades to harmless inquisitors, and been doing so for years. Then, just as he seemed to receive the epiphany he needed to redeem himself, all those little bombs were tossed back at him, hitting their target at exactly the same time: Tuesday, October 28, at 11:15 a.m., their power multiplied to a meteor.

Of course, just about any organization—including Domino's, one assumes—would require any leader who sent such e-mails to their customers to pack his office, but Brandon's e-mails went beyond just crossing a line. Those midnight e-mails brought his true personality to light, and it wasn't pretty.

The e-mails were arrogant, insulting, and demeaning to the very people who initially supported Brandon, the people who should have comprised his fan base in good times, and his safety net in bad ones. But Brandon lumped the people who dared to question him with Monaghan's executives, Martin's administrators, the lettermen who wanted to eat chili and cornbread with their teammates, the students who wanted to sit together, and the critics who didn't appreciate his marketing wizardry: they were all hopeless idiots who weren't smart enough to realize they should want what he wanted.

The e-mails did not represent some unfortunate but understandable faux pas, an all-too-human off-the-cuff remark gone awry. Dave Brandon had written exactly what he had intended to write, and done so repeatedly. The e-mails were not the product of a heated moment. They revealed the man for exactly who he was, by his own hand.

With the publication of the e-mails, the very people Brandon had perceived as his enemies now controlled his fate. But they would be far more compassionate toward him than he would have been toward them, if they had done the same thing.

"I never wanted Dave drawn and quartered in the public square," Larry Deitch said. "Some sort of gracious resignation was fine by me. I think he had earned a soft landing through his service as a Regent, the many good things he had done as athletic director, and his generosity as a donor."

Brandon, however, was not ready to surrender.

CHAPTER 74

LAST WORDS

We don't know how much sleep Brandon got that Tuesday night, but he showed up for work the next morning, Wednesday, October 29, right on time, dressed to the nines.

At 9 a.m., he welcomed his quartet of campus advisors to the Champions Room.

"I'd like to make a remark about the University of Michigan here," Paul Courant told me, over breakfast in downtown Ann Arbor.

Courant was one of the four university all-stars President Coleman had recommended Brandon seek out, along with Dr. Valerie Castle, the chair of Pediatrics; Nicholas Delbanco, the esteemed author of 29 works of fiction and nonfiction, who built Michigan's MFA program into one of the nation's very best; James Jackson, the director of the internationally recognized Institute for Social Research; and Courant himself, who covered—well, just about everything else, as the former director of the University of Michigan Press, provost of the university, dean of libraries, and now a professor at the Ford School of Public Policy. They were as impressive as they were diverse, in just about every manner imaginable, and eager to provide whatever help they could.

"I think it says something about this place," Courant said, "that although it was President Coleman who suggested that Dave talk to us, he already knew all four of us. He was on a first-name basis with all of us, so if he saw any of us on the street, he'd stop and chat. And that was true of Bill Martin, too. I do not think it is true of most large universities that the athletic director knows such a diverse group of senior faculty in that way."

Even on a campus of very smart people, it was a particularly smart bunch—and it was smart of Brandon to ask for their counsel.

"He was, on some level, doing what I think was the right thing," Courant adds. "He had four very senior, well-known, respected campus leaders—or at least three! If he had engaged that kind of brain trust from the start, we might have been able to improve mutual understanding between Dave and others on campus, so that he would have had potential allies and advisors *before* he needed them."

Still, all four were uncertain why, exactly, they had been summoned. When Brandon had called Delbanco three or four days earlier to join this small, high-powered group for the meeting, Delbanco felt it only right to make clear that, while he had become a loyal fan of Michigan athletics, he was no expert on its administration. Further, after three full decades at Michigan, he was about to retire, so he would not be able to return for a longer commitment if needed.

"Dave said very clearly it wasn't a long-term proposition, but a one-off—just a chance to talk," Delbanco recalls. "So, I agreed to come, then I called Paul Courant and asked, 'What the hell is this about?' He didn't have any idea either. I went there with no particular sense of what the meeting would entail."

Although not everyone in that room was fully aware of the e-mail bombshell published on MGoBlog the previous morning, they all knew Brandon was taking a lot of crticism on the Internet. But none of them mentioned it, nor its potential impact on Brandon's job security.

"I don't think in that morning meeting Dave knew that evening that he wouldn't have a job," Delbanco maintains. "If he had known that, he would have simply canceled. I don't think he would have held the meeting if he didn't think there would be something that could be learned from it. This was his chance—ultimately his final chance, it would prove—to work his way out of this mess."

Brandon's guests soon found out the business at hand was as simple as it was urgent: Brandon wanted to know where the problems lay, and what he could do to improve his situation.

"He did have an agenda," Delbanco says. "He wanted to talk about the reality of the football team, the perception of the problems swirling around the department, and what his next steps might be.

"He wanted to know how he could convey to the university community that they are in fact supporting all these other sports—field hockey, crew, gymnastics—that are not even intended to make money. He also told us that Brady Hoke had graduated an astronomically high portion of the players.

What he was saying in effect was that, outside the Athletic Department, no one knows about that. So, how does he change the public narrative?

"It wasn't a structured meeting, a list with problem A, that's solved, so now let's look at problem B. I think it was a genuine moment to figure out what next to do and how best to do it."

Courant came away with similar impressions. "I had felt that what Dave had had, for years, most easily could be described as a tin ear," he says. "He wasn't hearing what people were saying—the fans, the students, the many constituents of the Athletic Department.

"In that meeting, he *listened!*

"I was struck by how aware he seemed to be of what his problems were. Given his public persona, it was even a little surprising. You got the impression that he knew all along. I couldn't help but think, 'Gee, if he had been that way from the start, and been more closely engaged with the broader university, maybe things would have been different.'

"It was sad."

Delbanco also noted Brandon's willingness—even eagerness—to take responsibility for the mistakes he'd made, and those of the department. As subjects came up, Brandon would say almost reflexively, "That's my bad," and, "That's on me."

"His personal affect was far better than I would have suspected," Delbanco said. "He wasn't pontificating. He was talking to us as to a group of more or less respected peers. He wanted to learn from us, 'What can I do to make what's wrong right?' I, at least, saw a man who had looked at the mirror and saw something that needed to be addressed, perhaps even corrected.

"He was not the bully I remembered when he was a Regent and we were searching for our next president, nor the man of considerable self-regard I had been seeing in the newspaper and on TV. If I had gone into the meeting expecting that to be the case, I was, I must say, pleased, and surprised, to a degree, by the—well, humility is not the right word, it would never attach to him—but the candor, the almost-modesty, by the sense of genuine interest in what we had to say. He didn't feel impregnable or self-satisfied or imperious. He seemed genuinely to be after our opinion, and more importantly our sympathy."

That last objective made for a somewhat awkward impasse.

"He kept asking us in one sense or another to agree with the idea that the job had been well done," Delbanco says. "Everyone was very civil, but I don't think there was anyone who even so much as suggested the troubles he was experiencing were all engendered by others, and not of his own making.

Effectively, the four of us did not give him a whole lot of room to maneuver on the idea that it was a job well done.

"In the morning, I believe he thought he would be holding that position: That it was external forces doing him in, while he himself was doing the right things. In that regard, it wasn't a particularly fruitful meeting. If we were something of a last resort, we failed to provide him the life raft to safety he had hoped for—simply because we didn't think any such easy escape then existed. His detractors might have said we added one nail to the coffin.

"That afternoon, he might have had to conclude, this will not be easy to fix, if it could be fixed at all.

"All four of us, from our separate vantages and our separate degrees of intimacy with the program, had a shared perspective. None of us in the room denied that there was trouble, and none of us could offer an easy or obvious solution. I like to think it was not due to any dimwittedness on the part of those present, any lack of imagination or insight.

"The easy and obvious solutions were well in the rear-view mirror by this time.

"Only the hard choices remained."

At 7 p.m. that same day, October 29, Brandon walked halfway up State Street to the Ford School to meet with the University of Michigan Alumni Association Board of Directors. The 23 members included Ann Marie Lipinski, the former editor of the *Chicago Tribune* and now curator of the Nieman Foundation for Journalism at Harvard; Dr. Stephen Papadopolous, the executive vice president and chief medical officer of the Barrow Neurological Institute in Arizona; and Mark Silverman, president of the Big Ten Network.

Many in this high-powered group had flown in from around the country, and they arrived with plenty on their minds. As one told me, "I cannot believe Dave showed up that night."

Brandon started the meeting not by defending himself or attacking his critics, but by telling the story about the chicken farmer's son from South Lyon who could never have gone to the University of Michigan without a football scholarship. He shared how much he had learned from Bo Schembechler. He talked about Mott Children's Hospital saving his twin sons, who were born prematurely, and how, when he learned he had prostate cancer, he called around the country to find the best treatment center, only to discover it was at the University of Michigan Hospital the whole time.

He was recounting the origin story of a Michigan Man, which would have played very well four years earlier. For most of the board members, however, Brandon's actions had eclipsed his words that night.

The board members heard him out, and many were impressed by his sincerity, but that didn't stop them from asking pointed questions about everything from Brendan Gibbons to Shane Morris to the nasty e-mails that had just come out the day before. To Brandon's credit, and probably to the board's surprise, he heard them out, acknowledged the mistakes he'd made, and promised to do better.

"He took bullets, lots of them, from these people like you wouldn't believe," another person present told me. "He got the shit kicked out of him—and he just took it, responding with things like, 'We need to be better,' 'We want to be better partners with you,' 'I'll come back as often as you'll have me, whenever you want me.'

"He was so vulnerable—and when he was vulnerable he was at his best."

Brandon often seemed to confuse his strengths for his weaknesses, and his weaknesses for his strengths. He reverted back to his best self only as a last resort—when it was too late.

The way Brandon had performed his dream job had strained the community, forcing almost everyone he touched to make increasingly tough decisions under less-than-ideal circumstances.

At the end, the one gesture that remained that could help reknit the whole was Brandon nobly falling on his sword. And to his great credit, that's what he did.

That night, Dave Brandon called President Schlissel and offered his resignation.

Nicholas Delbanco was not surprised.

"He did so, I believe, because he wanted to have the honor of resignation," Delbanco told me, "and not be fired, and he negotiated that with the Regents. I do think that in that sense he did the honorable thing, perhaps a bit reminscent of that line in *Macbeth*, 'Nothing in his life became him like the leaving it.'

"So, perhaps, the same could be said of Dave's resignation."

President Schlissel accepted it.

The Dave Brandon era was over.

PART VII: 2014

THE RETURN

CHAPTER 75

A CALL FOR HELP

After President Schlissel got off the phone with Dave Brandon Wednesday night, he called Jim Hackett, who had retired in February of 2014 as the CEO of Steelcase furniture—a job he'd held for 20 years, starting when he was just 39.

The two leaders—one recently hired, one recently retired—barely knew each other, having had just one previous conversation on the phone. But during that conversation they clicked immediately, quickly establishing a mutual respect and trust.

"The context was simple," President Schlissel told me, about their first phone call at the end of September. "Throughout the fall I realized I was going to have to accelerate my learning about athletics around here, given the events that unfolded. One way I did that was to reach out to university leaders—people who knew the university, cared about it deeply, and had insights on how it worked, at its best.

"In athletics, what we saw was a program drifting away from its core constituencies: the students, the alumni, the fans.

"I then assembled a lengthy list of people who might be willing to help. Jim was on that list. He has advised multiple Michigan presidents, and been an adviser to deans and other university leaders. He's been generous with his time, on the advisory board of the Ford School, and on the board of the Life Sciences Institute, almost since its founding in 1999. He's a wise, experienced alumnus—and that was pointed out to me by many others."

President Schlissel first connected with Hackett by phone, shortly after the Shane Morris drama, and well before Brandon resigned.

"I was *not* calling in the context of scouting candidates for athletic director," Schlissel said. "We thought we were far from that at the time."

Instead, Schlissel wanted to get Hackett's general sense of what athletics mean at the University of Michigan, "and how things have evolved through time. We had a long and wonderful conversation."

Hackett remembers their first conversation the same way. Schlissel asked him, "Have you been following this story?"

"I was honest and said, 'Not that much.' I'm in the Bo–Lloyd camp. I didn't think a concussion, and that reaction, made sense to me.

"Then Mark says—and I've still not met him in person yet—'If you thought someone needed to help me get control of this, do you have any recommendations?'

"I said, 'Wow. I would go back and see if we can fix the Dave thing first, because I know him to be a really capable guy.'

"He said, 'I'm working on that. But I'm also asking, who else can help?'"

A couple weeks later, Schlissel recalls, "I had to ask myself the question: What would I do if we needed to make a change? It occurred to me Jim might be somebody who would be wonderful on an interim basis, if we needed him, and if we did, I hoped he would agree."

After President Schlissel accepted Brandon's resignation that night, Wednesday, October 29, he picked up the phone to start the second conversation between himself and Jim Hackett.

"I was retired," Hackett recalls, "sitting at our home on Spring Lake, convalescing from my hip replacement on my right side. Already had the left one done. And the idleness hit me—and I realized something that I didn't realize before: I don't like to be idle. I'm wired to be busy. Serving on boards is good, but they only meet once a quarter. I have a lot of energy, and particularly like solving problems," a central part of the CEO mindset.

Schlissel refrained from telling Hackett that Brandon had just resigned. Instead, Hackett recalls Schlissel saying, "I don't know what's going to happen next. I just need to know if you're interested. And I need to know tonight."

"Gee, I've got to ask Kathy," Hackett said. "So I hung up, and talked it over with her. It was really difficult because she had already lived through the CEO life for two decades, and we had this promise of leisure time with the grandkids. But she knew I wanted to do this, she knew what Michigan meant to me, so she supported the decision, if that's what I wanted to do."

And that was the next question: Did Hackett want to do this? Before committing to such a position, he needed to be sure.

"I called one more guy before I called Mark back," he recalls. "Dale Jones.

He works for Heidrick & Struggles, one of the top CEO recruiting firms. He helped President Obama recruit his cabinet, which often entails convincing very rich and powerful people to take a gigantic cut in pay to work incredible hours, under immense pressure and scrutiny. He can recruit! He often overcame their objections by simply saying, 'Some jobs are for God and country.' It usually worked.

"Over the years, he's been a muse for me. So I said, 'Dale, I've got this interesting thing that just came up, but you can't talk about it.' As a headhunter, he's used to this, and I trusted him. I asked him, 'What happens to people in my situation, after being CEO? Do they go into the abyss? Do they take another position? Is taking a new position a bad idea?'"

Jones replied with the obvious: It all depends on what the next position is. After Hackett told him about President Schlissel's offer, and what the University of Michigan meant to him, Jones had his answer.

"Jim," he said, "some jobs are for God and country. For you, this is it."

"That's what I needed to hear," Hackett said.

Jim Hackett hung up the phone, and sent President Schlissel a text: "I'm in."

There were a few things, however, that President Schlissel couldn't discuss with Hackett in that second conversation. He couldn't mention, for example, that Brandon had already resigned that night, or that the university had scheduled a press conference for Monday to introduce the next athletic director. They did not know where Hackett would live, or how much he would get paid. They still had many more questions than answers.

It was a bit reminiscent of how Hackett's mentor, Bo Schembechler, had taken the job at Michigan, and returned to his home in Oxford, Ohio, before his wife Millie asked what he would be getting paid—and he realized he and Canham hadn't discussed it. But, unlike the staged conversation between Brandon and Hoke, this was organic.

Like Schembechler, Hackett wasn't worried. "I did enough of that at Steelcase," Hackett says. "I needed more than a contract. I needed a bond."

It just so happened that Hackett already had plans to be at the Ford School in Ann Arbor Thursday and Friday, so he texted Schlissel to let him know. Schlissel responded with a surprise: "We're having the press conference on Friday now."

Their entire relationship had consisted of two phone calls. They had not yet met in person. But they had just committed to teaming up to tackle one of the toughest issues on campus, and the first major challenge of Schlissel's young presidency.

"I didn't even know what he looks like," Hackett recalls. "I was so anxious in the car, driving to Ann Arbor Thursday. I just learned I have to make a speech at a press conference the next day. I have nothing written, and really, no idea what I'm going to say at the press conference yet.

"We prepped for the press conference in the Regents meeting room. I saw a president in a setting I had been in before. But then I saw him working so hard, practicing at the podium, with his people in front of him coaching. And that just gave me a lot of confidence, watching him, and I knew we could fix this.

"And that press conference ended up being one of Mark's finest moments."

On Friday, October 31, President Schlissel walked up to the podium, with the press in front of him. He announced he had accepted Dave Brandon's resignation. He said a lot of nice things about him in the process, but added it was "in the best interest of student-athletes, the Athletic Department, and the university community."

He then announced that he had named former Steelcase furniture CEO Jim Hackett as the interim athletic director, who got up and said a few words. Both men seemed calm and in control, well aware of the challenge ahead of them, but not afraid to take it on. Given the never-ending drama of Brandon's final months, it was probably the least agitating news coming out of the Athletic Department in months.

The terms of Brandon's contract would give him a $3 million buyout—or a full 2 percent of the department's budget—plus the use of two university cars through the end of 2014. The university also agreed to pay his family's COBRA health care through June 30, 2015, or until he took another job with benefits.

"The buyout occurred if he was fired, but he resigned," Bill Martin said. "But he got to say he resigned, and he got the buyout. Everyone wonders why."

Given a golden opportunity to make a grand and generous gesture on his way out, Brandon didn't decline a dollar.

On Monday, November 3, President Schlissel welcomed Alejandro Zúñiga of the *Michigan Daily* for an interview. When Zúñiga asked him about Brandon's infamous e-mails, Schlissel declined to make a direct comment. "One thing I will say is I expect everybody who works at this public university to treat the public with respect. That's a sort of condition of working at this university. Everybody should be respectful to the public we serve."

Looking ahead, Zúñiga asked President Schlissel about hiring a "Michigan

Man" as permanent AD: "I'm always open to the idea that someone from the outside might help us be even better," Schlissel said. "I just want to get the best person."

But with the unlikely timing of Dave Brandon's resignation, the biggest obstacle to getting the best person—be it Les Miles, Jim Harbaugh, or another top coach—had been removed.

The odds of Michigan pulling off a miracle had just gone up exponentially.

Like any former player, to find out who Jim Hackett is, all you have to do is ask his teammates.

One of them was John Wangler. In the fall of 1977, Hackett was a fifth-year center playing on the demonstration team, and Wangler was a freshman quarterback playing on the same unit. It was their job to imitate the offense of Michigan's next opponent, giving them a good look at what they'd see that Saturday.

That meant, every day, they were going against Michigan's top defense, which might have been the best in the country that year, the key to Michigan being ranked number one four weeks during that season.

"They had Calvin O'Neal, John Anderson, Dwight Hicks, Jerry Meter, Ron Simpkins," Wangler recalls, easily rattling off five defenders still in the record books. "Are you kidding me? It was wild, getting our tails whipped every day.

"And there were no red jerseys back then for the quarterbacks. I got pounded every day. Tuesday and Wednesday—full-hit practices—those were *wars* back then. Wednesday night was the best night, because you knew you'd gotten through the week alive.

"But Jimmy Hackett kept us together. He'd been taking all that for how many years? And he wasn't afraid of any of those guys.

"He'd always tell us, 'C'mon guys, let's go! We gotta give them a good look so they'll be ready Saturday.' That's how the process worked. We were making those other guys better!

"He was one of those guys in that senior class with [Rob] Lytle and the rest—a great class—that formed my image of what a Michigan Man really is. They had a quiet confidence.

"You just knew Jimmy was going to be a success."

Wangler was right, of course. When President Schlissel called Hackett on October 29, 2014, Jim Hackett had already been a great success. But almost everyone who'd taken up the job of athletic director at Michigan had already been a great success, too—but not all of them had succeeded as Michigan's AD.

Before Hackett even settled into his new office, he had to answer the most fundamental question: Should his first task be hiring a permanent replacement for himself, or a new football coach? Schlissel assumed Hackett would be finding his replacement, but as the season wore on, and the losses piled up, Hoke's status was increasingly insecure.

Hackett said to Schlissel, "You let me stay a little longer, and assess the coach. If he's staying, we know what we need to do next: Get a new AD. If he's not, we also know what we need to do: Get a new football coach."

Brady Hoke is an unusually likeable guy, and his players hadn't given up on him. As Hagerup told me, "I never once heard a player say we're not winning because the coaches suck."

But Hoke's teams were in the bad habit of getting worse every year, and in his second and third seasons, worse as the season wore on. If his 2014 squad swooned again in November, it would not bode well for his future at Michigan.

The dirty secret among a growing mass of Michigan fans was their private hope that their favorite team would fail to make a bowl game. That would force Schlissel and Hackett to find a new coach, and afford them the time to do so, without the distraction of a bowl game—which Brandon had waited for in 2010, much to the chagrin of many fans, and perhaps even the sitting coach, Rich Rodriguez.

If the program went in that direction, as most fans expected, the all-too-familiar specter of yet another coaching search loomed ahead, with a familiar name topping the list: Jim Harbaugh.

Even after making these big decisions, whoever was running the department six months later would have a lot of work to do mending fences with fans, selling season tickets, filling empty skyboxes, and bringing in enough money to meet payroll for an administrative staff that had grown from 261 employees under Martin to 341 under Brandon—and usually at top dollar.

But, one way or the other, the big decisions would be settled in the next few months. How those played out would likely determine what the next decade of Michigan football would look like—and if the Wolverines would reclaim their place among the big boys, or continue riding with the also-rans.

CHAPTER 76

TEAM HARBAUGH GEARS UP

The morning after Brandon's resignation and Hackett's hiring were announced, Saturday, November 1, Todd Anson woke up at 5 a.m. in San Diego and got to work on a "white paper" to promote the merits of pursuing Jim Harbaugh.

"A lot of people had heard a lot of garbage over the years about Jim," Anson told me, "and I wanted to clear that up, once and for all."

Anson's report looks just the way you'd think a $950-per-hour corporate lawyer would make one, even though he was working pro bono for a friend.

"I'd been thinking about this for years," he told me. "It didn't require much thought. I was so ready to unleash something positive about Jim, that might actually reach an audience for the first time, it just poured out of me. Passion moved my fingers."

Titled, "What Jim Harbaugh Brings to Michigan," it includes a "Brief Summary," then the body of the piece, presented in three sections: Football, Academics, and Economics.

On the football front, Anson's report argues, hiring Harbaugh would create a "Race to the BCS," since Harbaugh had already built a BCS-winning team at Stanford in four years, "starting from way behind where Michigan is today."

Academically, Anson writes, Harbaugh would do for Michigan what he did for Stanford: raise the bar in the classroom, while remaining competitive on the field—exactly as Harbaugh had said Michigan should when he made his comments back in 2007. This would be his chance to put his money where his mouth was.

On the financial front, "Hiring Harbaugh results in an epic press conference," Anson wrote. That excitement would mean, "our Season Ticket lists will again be maxed out, our Sky Boxes will be 100% sold out, we will have

100,000 at every 2015 game and, most importantly, our alumni and bases will be re-engaged with greater than ever enthusiasm." That would even give the $4 billion "Victors for Michigan" capital campaign a boost.

No one could accuse Anson of holding back.

In greater detail, Anson listed 37 reasons to hire Harbaugh. Under Football, for example, his 17 reasons included:

- He is one of our own, a Michigan Man of great national stature.
- He took the 1–11 Stanford team to 12–1 and a BCS bowl in 4 years
- Every quarterback he has coached at San Diego or Stanford went pro.

He also pointed out that Harbaugh and Peyton Manning get more "face time" on NFL broadcasts than anyone else, which naturally translates to recruiting, which converts into wins.

Under Academics, Anson pointed out that Harbaugh landed high-school valedictorian Andrew Luck because Harbaugh *encouraged* him to major in Engineering at Stanford, while Texas and Oklahoma took the opposite approach. Anson could have added that Harbaugh had a half dozen engineering majors, and two dozen more in science and engineering, on a Stanford team that finished 12–1 with a BCS bowl win.

And finally, under Economics, Anson listed nine points, including the fact that 60 to 70 percent of Michigan's donor gifts come in during football season—or about $305 million in 2014. "The campus will be alive, vibrant and teeming with optimism unlike anything seen in years," he wrote, which could only help generate more of those fall gifts.

But Anson's boldest claim was this: "We *will* generate over $1 billion a year the next few years with Harbaugh coaching our football program. There is zero doubt about this. We *may* do it otherwise."

Of course, Anson's "$1 billion a year" estimate was only a guess, and even if Michigan hit that mark, it would be impossible to prove Harbaugh's hiring caused it. But Anson had a way of getting people's attention, and that sound bite would get a lot of buzz.

Anson's white paper might not impress a dissertation committee, but it made a good argument that the people in charge should consider not only each candidate's likely success on the field, but also what impact he could have on the entire university. Anson's white paper was also the first public, full-throated case for Harbaugh to come back—something Brandon would not have allowed in 2010.

Later that day, Anson hunkered down with his family to watch the Wolverines. Sitting at 3–5, Michigan had to win at least three of its last four games just to qualify for the Motor City/Little Caesar's/Quick Lane Bowl, and none of those games would be freebies. Indiana, historically a pushover, had given Michigan good scares in their last three meetings. Against Northwestern, Michigan had to come from behind the previous two seasons just to get to overtime, before pulling out victories. Maryland, new to the Big Ten, was largely unknown, while Ohio State was known all too well.

But with Brandon gone the day before, the "Dave Out–White Out" demonstration was cancelled, and the #FIREDAVEBRANDON shirts went with it. There would be no boycotting the kickoff, or chanting "Fi-re Bran-don!" in the student section. The stadium that day seemed to emit a collective sigh, relieving some of the tension in the stands, and on the sidelines.

The Wolverines played like the heat was off, jumping out to a 17–0 half-time lead, and didn't look back. Gardner threw 1 interception, but connected on 22 of his 29 passes, with 2 touchdowns. Drake Johnson, son of Michigan cheerleading coach Pam St. John, replaced Derrick Green, and looked great running for 2 touchdowns. It didn't hurt the Wolverines that the Hoosiers' first two signal callers were injured, and their third-stringer, Zander Diamont, managed just 24 yards passing.

A peaceful student section, coupled with Michigan's 19th straight victory over Indiana, 34–10, made the old stadium feel like the old stadium again, at least for a few hours.

After the game, a half-dozen lettermen joined a couple dozen friends in the upstairs room of Pizza House, right across the street from Rick's American Café. There, they were catered to by an old friend, Jay Flannelly, who worked as a dishwasher at the restaurant, but took the night off to take care of his old buddies.

An unassuming guy who stands about 5-foot-9 and usually wears Michigan or Patriots hats, jackets, and hoodies, Flannelly grew up in Andover, Massachusetts. It was there he got his nickname from a summer playground counselor, who called him "The Beav" because he looked like *Leave it to Beaver*'s Jerry Mathers, adding, "He's always getting into everything."

How did Flannelly become a Michigan fan? Easy: "They weren't Notre Dame. Back then you'd see the Fightin' Irish on the National Game of the Week every weekend. I got sick of them—and Michigan played 'em every year."

He moved to Michigan in 1993, and enrolled in 1995, working as a volunteer student assistant on the football team until 1999, Tom Brady's last season.

"I worked with a lot of good people," Flannelly says, "like Ty Wheatley, who went out of his way to be great to me. Todd Collins was great. Buster Stanley, Steve Morrison, and Walter Smith." He takes a breath. "Jay Riemersma, Jarrett Irons, Jason Horn. The list goes on."

At that point, you believe him.

"They all could have said, 'This guy's an idiot, get him out of there!' But they were great to me."

Of his hundred best friends, however, one stands out: Tom Brady.

"The minute Tom got here, we hit it off," Flannelly says. Flannelly worked late nights at Mr. Spot's, a popular student restaurant on State Street, between the two campus barbershops where most of the coaches and players go. "Tom loved Mr. Spot's, one of his favorite places. He was always either studying or going to watch a film.

"We were already bonded by '98 when Drew Henson came here, also a friend of mine. I'll never forget 'Media Day' that year. Drew hasn't played a single down yet, but he was standing under the goal posts, and there was a line out to midfield of fans who wanted him to sign things.

"Tom's standing by the tunnel, without a soul anywhere near him, except me and my niece, for an hour. I don't think he signed five things. It was sad, embarrassing—and unbelievable."

When the 1998 season started, Carr platooned junior Tom Brady and freshman Drew Henson. "Tom was afraid to make a mistake, or he'd get pulled—and it got to him," Flannelly says. "When [Syracuse quarterback] Donovan McNabb came in and killed us, fans were booing Tom and cheering Drew. They wanted Tom benched and Drew in the game. It was tough, and I gained a lot of respect for Tom.

"The next year, '99, still splitting time, Tom leads comeback victories against Notre Dame, Penn State, Ohio State, and 'Bama [in the Orange Bowl]—and damn near Michigan State," which was coached by Nick Saban.

But Brady never engaged in bravado or boasting—one of the hallmarks of the Michigan Man, as John Wangler said, at his best.

In 1997–98, when Brady was a sophomore backing up Brian Griese, he lived in an apartment building off Packard, near Ferry Field, where a fellow student named Jeff Viscomi lived. The building had a small basement laundry room with a single washer and dryer. Viscomi had left a load of undershirts and boxers in the dryer, he recalls. "I went down to retrieve them and Tom, whom I recognized only as one of several football players living in the building, was standing at the dryer folding my laundry and leaving it in a neat stack on the dryer. It was notable at the time only because most people, myself included, would have left the clothes in a pile on top of the dryer, but Tom had taken the time to fold them."

An entitled jock, he was not. Brady never forgot his friends, either, including "The Beav."

Some of the football players—against the specific orders of the coaching staff—formed an intramural basketball team, naturally sponsored by Mr. Spot's. "We had Jon Jansen, Tai Streets, and Tom—those guys are all really good," Flannelly recalls. "I was the 17th man on the team. At the end of blowouts, Tom would say, 'Beav, just stand under the bucket, and we'll feed you.' I'd play two minutes and get 6 points, on 15 shots."

An hour after Brady got drafted in the sixth round of the 2000 NFL draft, with the 199th overall pick, Flannelly called Brady, and they've kept it up ever since. Every week, Flannelly still sends Brady an e-mail with a pep talk and a scouting report of that week's opponent, and they talk.

But by Saturday night, November 1, 2014, even after a sound Big Ten victory, those happy days of All-Americans on both sides of the ball and BCS bowl victories seemed like distant memories. The athletic director was gone, but the Wolverines were 4–5, and the lettermen were beginning to feel it was time for a change—yet again.

Flannelly has worked for eight years at Pizza House, officially as a dishwasher, but "One of my unofficial roles is to take care of the old football players," Flannelly says. "They think I run the place—which I don't. The guys had two huge tables, filling a third of the upper room. We had Ghindia. Jon Giesler was there. Eric Kattus, Al Sincich."

They were having a good time eating pizza and drinking beer, like the old days, but these guys had won two, three, and sometimes four Big Ten rings in their careers, and could not kid themselves about where the program stood. The question inevitably floated up: "What are we going to do about this?"

"I was a big fan of Coach Hoke's," Flannelly says. "I didn't want to get involved in anything until it was over."

But the consensus at the table was that the critical point seemed to have been reached. The assembled lettermen believed Hoke was clearly in trouble, and the only way he could survive was to win Michigan's remaining three games to finish 7–5—and that hardly portended a return to glory.

"So that's when they started talking," Flannelly recalls. Les Miles's name naturally came up, and Jim Harbaugh's. They knew there were plenty of obstacles, including the players from the 2007 team who publicly objected to

Harbaugh's comments on academics. They weren't sure how those players would react to Harbaugh being a candidate, or their coach, Lloyd Carr, for that matter.

"I was afraid we could have another seven years of Civil War," Flannelly told me. "Think we needed more of that? Nothing was decided at those tables, but it's pretty clear we had to do something.

"Two upshots: This isn't working, and getting Jim Harbaugh is not impossible. Ghindia, Kattus, Geisler, Al Sincich—all those guys—they got organized that day.

"That's when the seed was planted. It was the first time I started to think we might have a chance at Jim Harbaugh."

Before they split up that night, Ghindia gathered the names and numbers of anyone who could help, including Todd Anson and John "Flame" Arbeznik, down in Florida. They shared them with everyone at the table, then started cross-pollinating conversations among Regents, university executives, donors, movers, shakers, lettermen, and captains, to make sure no one who might be able to help would be operating with dated or false information.

That night, Arbeznik's phone started ringing.

"My former teammates never went to the media," Arbeznik told me, "but they worked behind the scenes to rally each other for Les or Jim."

Schembechler was gone. They had sat and watched too long, they'd decided. They had no idea what they could do, or what might happen next, but they decided then and there they were not simply going to sit back and watch it happen.

CHAPTER 77

ALL HANDS ON DECK

Since Jim Hackett had replaced Dave Brandon as Michigan's athletic director four days earlier, the stakes for the Regents' election on Tuesday, November 4, were suddenly lower—at least for Michigan athletics, anyway. But because Kathy White had been unafraid to help curtail the excesses of the Brandon regime, and was willing to listen to the Ghindia guys, the lettermen who'd gathered at Pizza House were pulling for her to win.

White had served with distinction for two eight-year terms, but she knew that didn't guarantee much on election day. She would be running with fellow Democrat Mike Behm, and against Dr. Rob Steele and Ron Weiser, a Michigan business school graduate who had amassed many millions through his real estate company, McKinley Associates. He had also served on several corporate and nonprofit boards, was deeply involved in the University of Michigan—giving more than $50 million over the years—and, in 2001, George W. Bush named him the ambassador to Slovakia.

Ambassador Weiser was playing to win, spending some $2 million of his own money on his campaign. Conventional wisdom, for what it was worth, seemed to favor Weiser to win one of the two Regents' seats up for grabs, and perhaps Regent White would retain hers. But it was anyone's guess—and if two candidates gained office who were pro-Hoke and anti-Harbaugh, the future of Michigan football, at least, might look very different.

The race was far too close to call all day, and all night. At 4 a.m. Wednesday morning, it looked as though Dr. Steele and Ambassador Weiser would both be winning seats on the Board of Regents. But after the counties that covered Ann Arbor, Detroit, and Flint submitted their votes, Regent White and Mike Behm pulled out ahead. White got the most votes, 1,352,347—ahead of the rest by almost 100,000, while Behm slipped past Weiser by just 4,835 votes—or about 0.09 percent of the 5.5 million votes cast.

Whether a Weiser victory would have presented an obstacle to the lettermen or not is impossible to say. In his campaign appearances, Ambassador Weiser was notably noncommittal on both Brandon's and Hoke's fate. He argued that such decisions were the president's alone, and he would respect whatever President Schlissel decided—an unassailable position. But White was the known quantity, which pleased the Pizza House gang.

Weiser handled the disappointing news graciously, and vowed he would continue his generosity to the university he loved. "I always knew it would be a very close race, but I knew I had lost by about 3:30 a.m. This is a state where you have a lot of straight ticket voting and when you have a state that's plus-five Democrat, it's tough to win.

"It's difficult to get that close. If you lose by 25,000 or 30,000 votes that's one thing, but if you lose by 5,000 votes or so, you tend to wonder what you did wrong or what you could've done differently."

Ghindia and his buddies were convinced that White's victory was vital to their efforts.

That Friday night, November 7, John Ghindia drove to Ann Arbor to pay his respects at Kathy White's victory party at Conor O'Neill's Irish pub on Main Street. He brought her a gift he had started working on the day before: a DVD of Harbaugh's speech to the 2004 football reunion. The event marked the 125th anniversary of Michigan football and drew more than 700 former coaches, players, and staffers, from seven decades of Michigan football. The DVD featured speeches by Bo Schembechler and, by video, President Ford.

In the course of Harbaugh's five-minute speech, he said, "What defines people's lives are brushes with greatness. What is Michigan greatness? It's tradition. It's a bar that is raised so high, *so* high, that some people choose not to even attend the University of Michigan. For all of us former players, we share a common experience, tremendous academics, the finest coaching, and we played against the best competition.

"The Michigan experience changes you. You feel you might have a chance. It provides a unique opportunity to find and develop self confidence to go against the very best! Because of the great men who came before us at Michigan, we had the opportunity to find out whether there was greatness in us."

It would be hard for virtually any sentient being to listen to Harbaugh's speech and not conclude his love for Michigan ran very deep. Knowing this,

Ghindia took a day off to work on the DVD, post it on YouTube—where it has received 112,000 views—and make 10 copies, titled, "Jim Harbaugh Loves Michigan."

"There were guys trying to slander Jim before he had a chance to say yes or no to Michigan," Ghindia told me. "All I wanted was for *Jim* to have the chance to say yes or no."

When Ghindia saw White at her victory party that Friday night, "I gave her a big hug, and said, 'Congratulations! You're three for three. You're unbelievable!' "

Then he shifted gears. "I know we're going to be making a change for the coach. Jim Harbaugh wants to be the coach at Michigan. If you're interested in talking with Jim's reps, I can give you the numbers of his representatives." That was a little fancy talk for Jim's dad, Jack Harbaugh.

"All the stuff you heard about Jim not liking Michigan was just not true," Ghindia told White. "The opposite is true—and after you see the video, you'll know he should be our next coach."

Ghindia then walked across the room to Andrew Richner, another Regent, and gave him a DVD, too. "Harbaugh could coach the team by himself," Ghindia said, in a boast reminiscent of the Mike Ditka groupies on *Saturday Night Live*. "No coordinators."

But Ghindia was largely bluffing. He had never heard Harbaugh say he wanted to be Michigan's coach, to him or anyone else—not even to Todd Anson, who was always very careful not to claim Harbaugh wanted the position, or would accept it if offered.

"I was extremely careful to never represent *to anyone* that Jim *wanted* to come to Michigan," Anson told me, "but *only* that it was my judgment that we had a chance and that I had a plan to accomplish it. I was equally careful about never once discussing this with Jim. We both needed to be able to deny everything or else he risked losing his Niners team from underneath him.

"And this is a vital point: Winning out in San Francisco was more important to Jim than getting the Michigan job. That's what kind of a professional he is. Bo had taught him well."

All they had was a hunch—and a lot of hope.

"How did I know Jimmy Harbaugh wanted to be the coach?" Ghindia asked, restating my question. "No one told me anything, but I know how much Jim Harbaugh loves Michigan. I gave Flame Jim's phone number, and Flame called Jimmy after the Notre Dame game, crying. 'We need help. You're Michigan.' And a few days later, Jim called him back."

With their alma mater stuck at 4–5, it was enough for them to go on.

The afterglow of Michigan's nostalgic victory was quickly erased the next weekend, November 8, 2014, at Northwestern, which felt far too much like the rest of the fall for Michigan fans. The Wolverines converted just one of 12 third downs, and committed three turnovers—more than Michigan State and Ohio State had lost *combined*, playing against each other on the same night. Perhaps most embarrassing: Michigan's 256 yards of total offense against Northwestern would be doubled by both Michigan State and Ohio State, playing against each other—just another indication of how far Michigan had fallen behind its archrivals.

Midway through the third quarter, Michigan and Northwestern had still not managed to score any points. The on-screen scoreboard read: M-0 0-N. Thus, this ugly contest will forever be remembered as "the MOON game."

"MOON?" Hagerup said, when I told him about it. "That's pretty clever. But we weren't calling it that on the sideline."

Those guys were too worried about getting another victory.

With Northwestern down 10–3, the Wildcats scored their only touchdown with 3 seconds to play. Pat Fitzgerald decided to go for 2 points and the win. Michigan defensive end Frank Clark broke through the line to break up the play in the backfield, while Northwestern quarterback Trevor Siemian slipped before he could throw.

It might have been the Wolverines' weakest Big Ten win of all time. But when they hopped on the bus, they were 5–5, needing only a win over a mediocre Maryland team at home, on Senior Day, to get back to a bowl game, and possibly save their coaches' jobs.

John Ghindia wasn't about to stop with a few DVDs for a few Regents.

That weekend, he called a Michigan alum named David Katz, who is not famous, but very well known in Michigan political circles. He has served as the campaign manager for Detroit Mayor Mike Duggan, U.S. Senator Debbie Stabenow, and Governor Jennifer Granholm, among others. Since 2006, he has worked as an executive of the Detroit Medical Center.

John Arbeznik, down in Florida, somehow got wind that that Katz was someone they needed to pull in, and gave Ghindia the assignment. Ghindia got on LinkedIn, saw he and Katz had a mutual friend, and got his number.

When Ghindia called him, Katz agreed that everyone liked Brady Hoke, but few thought he would be back in 2015. "If we've got a chance at Harbaugh, we need to get him," Katz said. He was in.

The following Monday, November 10, Ghindia dropped off four DVDs of Harbaugh's speech at Katz's office for him to hand out to Mayor Duggan, another proud Michigan alum, and Regents Mark Bernstein and Denise Ilitch—both friends of Katz's. After Ghindia's visit, Katz promised to do everything he could to help land Harbaugh—including getting the mayor and governor to call Harbaugh and urge him to "come home."

"Now you've got the Regents, the mayor, and the governor," Ghindia said. "And that's what Anson can't believe!"

Anson was thrilled to hear of Ghindia's networking, but he had already gotten Governor Rick Snyder, a longtime friend, on the Harbaugh recruitment team. They were working every angle so hard, their efforts occasionally overlapped.

Through Ghindia, Anson started distributing his "white paper" to the Regents, powerful alums, and even the blogs, where the "Billion Dollar Bonus" idea seemed to stick.

This started two months of three-way conference calls among Ghindia, Anson, and Katz. When Katz asked what it would take to get Harbaugh, Anson replied, "Let's show the Harbaughs that Ann Arbor is the place for them to coach football and raise a family! No effort was made the last time, so we have to do things differently to land Jim now.

"Let's recruit Jim and Sarah like five-star recruits!"

Anson played baseball at Central Michigan and earned his law degree from Michigan. He never played or coached college football, but he knew something about recruiting. As a managing partner at California's most profitable law firm, Brobeck, Phleger & Harrison, he has often been given the task of recruiting the best lawyers in the country.

"I understand how personal it has to be," he says. "You don't just offer the money. You tell them, 'Here's how we'll treat you. You'll have these clients—Cisco, Apple, Google, and more. You'll have this support staff. You'll have face to faces with general counsels, board chairmen, CEOs. We do all these great things socially, too.

"But the main thing is, the more they have, the harder it is to impress them with that stuff. What you need to do is build a *relationship* with them, and you let them know—you let them *feel*—how much you want them there. You let them imagine it.

"It's never just a business. *Never!* You don't just say, 'Remembering the guy's birthday is worth half a million dollars.' In some ways, it might be more than that, and may be impossible to measure."

In other words: Relationships matter, even at the highest levels—and therefore, so do emotions. If these were foreign concepts to Dave Brandon, they were understood intimately by Anson, Ghindia, and Arbeznik.

In fact, Anson had already produced a three-page "playbook" to recruit Jim Harbaugh back to Michigan—in 2007. Anson titled it, *Comeback, Captain Comeback!* and put Fielding Yost's rediscovered quote on the cover: "The Spirit of Michigan is based on a deathless loyalty to Michigan and all her ways, an enthusiasm that makes it second nature for Michigan Men to spread the gospel of their University to the world's distant outposts, and a conviction that nowhere is there a better university, in any way, than this Michigan of ours."

The cover of Anson's playbook made clear his motivation, and the contents spelled out exactly what needed to be done, why, and when, if Michigan wanted Harbaugh to return.

In 2007, after Harbaugh's comments, however, it was very unlikely Lloyd Carr, or anyone else at Michigan, was going to greenlight Harbaugh's hiring. In 2010–11, Anson offered his help to Brandon, but Brandon declined. In 2014, however, Anson was not going to ask for permission. He would ask forgiveness if need be, but he was going to put his playbook into action. And this time, he had help—lots of it.

"I've said it a thousand times," Anson told me, "it takes a village to hire a great football coach. It takes all of us, working together.

"And I'll be danged if we didn't start making progress! I don't take credit. I have come to learn, there are probably a million guys who were doing what I was doing to get Jim to come back to Michigan. There were so many different layers to this, from the brilliant to the mundane, from the economic to the personal. You need to be touching on the right notes personally, historically, emotionally, economically, touching the right notes from student support, alumni support, the lettermen and the Regents. And they all played a huge role in this."

To Anson, the contrast between their "recruiting team" strategy in 2014 and Brandon's approach in 2010 could not be greater.

"To this day, we can't even tell if Dave Brandon was talking to our guy [Harbaugh] or not. And if he was, if he was earnest.

"Two big things made it different this time: when Bill Martin communicated with me that he thought Jim was the right choice if we needed a new coach. That showed me, the previous issues over Jim's comments were no longer show-stoppers.

"And two, Hackett *not* saying, 'Don't do those things to appeal to Jim.'

Hackett never said, 'Yes, go do those things.' But when I'm saying to Hackett, 'I can't get in your way. Let us know if we are,' and he said, 'You're fine,' that's all we needed to hear! And that was the difference.

"If he told us to stand down, I would have done so immediately. So Hackett letting us do our thing was a very important *non*-message! Huge for us. It allowed us to keep going, to keep showing Jim the love, giving him the bear hug.

"I knew we were earnest this time. I knew that from the Regents, even before President Schlissel hired Hackett.

"When you love someone, how can you identify any one thing about them you love the most? Her face, her brains, her heart? It's all of it. And we wanted Jim to fall in love with the idea of coming back. So we gave him all of it, from everyone we could think of.

"What worked? All of it."

CHAPTER 78

PLENTY OF SEATS STILL AVAILABLE

On November 22, 2014, Maryland stood just one game ahead of Michigan, coming to Ann Arbor with a 6–4 record. But the Terrapins had already qualified to go to a bowl game, and they were not fighting for the jobs of their AD or coaches.

The two mediocre teams engaged in a mediocre game, with the score tied at half, 9–9. Michigan pulled ahead in the third quarter, 16–9, and looked to take a dominating 23-9 lead when Dennis Norfleet scored on a punt return. But a Michigan player nowhere near Norfleet took a lazy penalty, and the touchdown was called back.

If the player hadn't succumbed to a dumb penalty, Michigan's 23-9 lead would likely have held up. Michigan would have qualified for a bowl game, and at the very least, any timetable for a coaching transition would have been badly compromised. Heading into 2015, the Wolverines would have been more likely to have Hoke at the helm than Harbaugh—or anyone else.

But given new life, the Terrapins soon took the lead, 23–16, with 5:59 left. The Wolverines couldn't score again. Game over.

"That hurts," Hagerup said. "After your last home game, you want to run up into the stands and sing the fight song."

The joy was all Maryland's, which left the Big House with a 7–4 overall record and 4–3 mark in their inaugural Big Ten season.

"I told our guys we needed to come out here and make some memories so that we could have a reunion 30 years from now and reminisce about the good things," Maryland coach Randy Edsall said. "To beat Penn State on the road, and beat Michigan on the road, and go 4–1 on the road in our first year in the league is special."

The Wolverines, on the other hand, had only one game to look forward to, if that was the right phrase: the 10–1 Ohio State Buckeyes, who still harbored hopes—however narrow—of getting into the first four-team BCS playoff. Ranked seventh, however, they had no margin of error, they needed some help, and they had to notch impressive wins.

The Wolverines promised they were not giving up, and against Ohio State the next weekend, they would prove it.

But the media and fans had already checked out. Many did not believe even a win over the Buckeyes at the Horseshoe, which would probably rank as the greatest upset in Michigan history, would be enough to save Hoke's job.

It wasn't just the team that was suffering. It was the program.

The damage Brandon had done early on could be seen only by the people within the department. But wave after wave, the effects of the earthquake he'd started—quite intentionally—were felt next by the lettermen, then the students, then the Regents and all the fans, until finally, on that dank Saturday in late November, the sad state of the program was on display for everyone to see, starting with the empty seats.

I obtained Michigan's official attendance data Big Ten teams have to send into the league office, for 2010, 2013, and 2014. The pattern was pretty obvious. In 2010, and again in 2013, Michigan fans were quite resilient, refusing to give up their long-held tickets despite disappointing seasons the year before, so long as the experience still "felt like Michigan," as one told me.

But in 2014, Michigan failed to attract 100,000 paying customers every single game. Even the marquee home game of the season, "Under the Lights III" against Penn State, fell just short, with 99,548 paying for seats. Over seven home games, Michigan averaged 90,426 tickets sold—down dramatically from 103,323 in 2010 and 101,023 in 2013.

To cover that gap, keep the streak alive, and save face, the Athletic Department gave away record numbers of complimentary tickets in 2014, an average of almost 9,000 per game. In the season opener against Appalachian State, when the Wolverines were still expected to have a big year, Michigan had to give away almost 13,000 free tickets. Obviously, the Appalachian State game didn't generate the excitement Brandon had anticipated when he announced the rematch in 2011.

After that shockingly poor turnout, the department had to get aggressive with handouts, dumping thousands of free tickets all over town, and get creative with addition, too, to claim the attendance for the remaining games was above 100,000.

How creative? For Michigan's second game against Miami of Ohio, the department sold 87,608 tickets—which they counted, whether the buyers showed up or not—and gave away 10,143 tickets, for a very soft total of 97,751. Yet they made the announcer claim attendance for that game was 102,824—or 5,000 more than even the highest possible estimate.

Behind the scenes, that's how the 2014 season went, week after week.

But the low point of the season would come on Senior Day against Maryland. The thick bands of empty seats throughout the stadium didn't lie—even if the department did. Only 83,268 fans paid for that game—and they probably set a record for no-shows—while the department handed out 16,923 complimentary tickets to anyone who would take one. That number exceeds the total of free tickets given out for the entire 2010 season, when Michigan went 7–6 after going 5–7 the year before.

So what caused attendance to fall off a cliff in 2014? Only a small portion of the change can be accounted for by public season-ticket sales, which fell by less than a thousand during Brady Hoke's tenure, and the vacating of six of Michigan Stadium's 81 luxury suites, which had sold out each of the previous three seasons. Even as increased prices, weak schedules, the 'WOW!' experience, and underwhelming performances caused thousands of season-ticket holders to bail, there were still enough people on the rapidly diminishing waiting list to replace them, and keep the number of season-ticket holders stable.

No, Michigan's attendance fell off because of one group: the students, the group Brandon failed to consult prior to his ill-fated decision to make the student section general admission. In 2012, the final year of assigned seating, 21,763 students bought season tickets. That number dropped to 19,851 in the first season of general admission. In 2014, the student section shrunk to 11,569. In just two years, nearly half of the students disappeared from Michigan Stadium. Notably, poor team performance played a small role in driving them away, but if that were the most important factor, they would have bailed in far greater numbers in 2009, but they did not.

No, the Athletic Department forcing an unnecessary change on the students, without seeking their input, proved far more damaging than any on-field issue.

Brandon often quoted his father, Phil, by all accounts a warm, sincere person. After Dave got his first promotion at Procter & Gamble, he called his dad for advice on how to handle his new staff.

"He said, 'Dave, you know I didn't go to business school or college. I never wrote any books and I've never been in the situation that you're in, but my experience in life has taught me that if you simply find out how people want to be treated and treat them that way, you are probably going to do all right.'"

Phil Brandon gave very good advice.

CHAPTER 79

THE LONGEST SEASON

The Wolverines entered Thanksgiving weekend with a 5–6 record, and only a long-shot game against 11–1 Ohio State remaining. If they lost, as expected, their season was over. Still, it already felt like the longest season in Michigan history.

Harbaugh's very unofficial recruiters decided they would kick their recruitment into high gear over Thanksgiving weekend.

Their reasoning was simple: Michigan didn't just need to show that they wanted Jim Harbaugh. By Thanksgiving, 2014, who didn't? They needed to show that they wanted him more than anyone could ever want anyone, to help him make the somewhat irrational decision to bypass the big bucks and bright lights of the NFL to return to their happy little college town.

The process usually worked like this: Anson would call Ghindia with a list of tasks to complete and people to call. Ghindia would do as much as he could himself, then delegate the rest to Arbeznik, the captains, the lettermen, and others. Then Ghindia would call Anson back and ask, "What's next?"

As Thanksgiving approached, Anson gave Ghindia a list of people he wanted to call Harbaugh, and tell him how much they wanted him back in Ann Arbor. The wish list included Michigan legends: Dan Dierdorf, the Dufek brothers, Anthony Carter, Jon Jansen, Desmond Howard, Charles Woodson, and Tom Brady, among others. Anson didn't stop there, adding Michigan celebrities to their wish list.

"The blueprint we came up with was perfectly planned and amazingly executed," Anson says. "While I was working with Ghindy to take well-timed rifle shots, Flame could not contain his enthusiasm, which was 'unknown to mankind.' I was acting strategically with Ghindy knowing how to get this stuff done. Flame was acting on pure emotion—reaching out with love every chance he could. Ghindy and I were rifle shooting. Flame was machine gunning. It was very effective.

"The only guy who turned us down was Jeff Daniels—and he has two kids who are Spartans, so that wasn't going to work. I don't hold it against him!"

They would add many more names, from celebrities Harbaugh had never met to lesser-known lettermen he probably admired more.

"What's the best way to make the list?" Ghindia said. "Start with any guys Jack Harbaugh coached—because those are the guys Jimmy grew up idolizing: Dwight Hicks, James Bolden, Jerry Meter, George Lilja, Dale Keitz, Jon Giesler, Mark Braman, Mike Leoni, and Tony Leoni. And keep going." A few of those lettermen had already been contacted through Arbeznik's list of captains, but they didn't care. They did it again.

"We made that list," Anson recalls. "We called them up, and had them call Jim. Those guys all love Jack, and they all love Michigan. They didn't hesitate."

Next step? "We really thought the guys who are most like Jim—the former captains, the NFL stars, the guys who were over 40 with families—would hit home with Harbaugh," said Jay Flannelly, a Hoke loyalist who didn't start making calls until Hoke's fate was clear after the Maryland game. "I'm just a yahoo, Jim and I have little in common, but peers reach peers. Ghindia was huge here."

Then the group broadened their scope a bit, recognizing if they were going to "recruit" Jim Harbaugh, they would also need to recruit his parents, Jack and Jackie Harbaugh, and his wife, Sarah. They knew how close Jim was to his parents—Jim still called home every week, often asking his dad for coaching advice—and how much Sarah had changed his life. They put Flame in charge of calling Jack, and Anson in charge of talking to Sarah.

"Then we got anyone we thought could make a difference," Ghindia recalls.

How do you get Billy Taylor, Jon Jansen, and Tom Brady? Through their agents? Their PR men? Their teams?

No, through the 43-year-old dishwasher at Pizza House, Jay Flannelly, better known as "The Beav"—one of the most connected, and trusted, people in the Michigan football family.

"When we wanted to get in touch with all those guys," Ghindia said, "we knew we had to call The Beav."

Flannelly jumped on the idea. "I said to Ghindy, 'Look, we need to go all in and get Jim here. Why don't we have some guys from my era call him? Brady, Jon Jansen, Jarrett Irons,'" three of the most respected names in the Michigan family. "He says, 'Good idea.'"

"I like Jansen," Ghindia said. "He's for Michigan. All he cares about is Michigan. All he says is, 'How can I help?' That's a Michigan Man."

Jansen, originally from Clawson, Michigan, played 10 years for the Washington Redskins and another for Detroit, then moved with his family up to Petoskey, Michigan, in the northern outreaches of Michigan's Lower Peninsula.

Anson had already connected with Jansen after the Michigan–Michigan State game, inviting him for lunch that week with Anson's friend Dick Enberg, the Hall of Fame sportscaster. "I like Jon," Anson said. "Everyone does! But I admit I arranged the meeting solely to start talking about getting Harbaugh to Michigan. I invited big Jon under our tent and gave him Jim's cell number."

Now it was time to activate the plan. Ghindia called Jansen, and told him, "You've got to call Jimmy up. Jimmy wants to buy a place up in Northern Michigan just like you've got. He wants his family in Ann Arbor. So Jon says, 'Got it.' He calls Harbaugh and says all that. And when Jansen says all that, Jimmy listens.

"I wanted Jimmy to hear from guys he didn't expect to hear from. I told Anson that Tom Brady would be calling Jimmy after a 49ers game—and Anson says, 'How the hell did you do that?' I said, 'Easy, brother! Jay from Pizza House. Never underestimate The Beav!'"

Because Anson had graduated from Michigan's law school in 1980, before Pizza House opened, he didn't know about the place—and he certainly had never heard of "The Beav." It took Ghindia a while to convince Anson, a skilled middleman, that Flannelly was the key.

"More than once," Anson told me, "we reflected on the fact that the pipeline to Tom Brady was a dishwasher [at Pizza House] called 'The Beav.' But Ghindy was right! When I came to town in December, I made it a *point* to take Ghindy to Pizza House—where they held the coaches' weekly radio show—and meet the notorious Jay Flannelly!"

Flannelly accepted the assignment, but it would not be as simple as Ghindia had portrayed it to Anson. Flannelly knew he had to execute it carefully. "Tom [Brady] is the kind of guy, if I ask him for five bucks for a charity, he sends $10,000," Flannelly says. "But this is the week the Pats were playing at San Diego. If the Pats lost, I didn't want to ask Tom to call Harbaugh. Tom Brady is the worst loser in the world—outside of myself! He still holds the unofficial record for breaking Sega controllers when he lost games. So, I had to be strategic."

The Anson playbook had been opened, and The Beav was on board.

All players, no matter how badly they lost their last game or how great their next opponent is, always claim that they've put it all behind them, and they're completely committed to beating the favorite next time out.

But the Wolverines, rather amazingly, really believed it.

"I can tell you that last Thursday before Ohio State this year, we were entirely ready," Hagerup told me. "There wasn't a single guy traveling not willing to give everything he had. You can tell when guys are not all in. 'The coaches are probably going to get fired anyway.' No, there was not any of that. We were saying this game can define this team. And I think that showed on the field."

In Hoke's Friday night speech at the team hotel in Ohio, Hagerup recalls, "Hoke said, 'My dad would have loved this moment, the chance to do something great.' It was very emotional, and he was having trouble getting some lines out. At that point, he had every guy on board. Why not leave everything out there?"

On Saturday, November 29, "Right before kickoff, Devin went up in front of the entire team. 'I'm vowing to all of you right now I'll leave everything I have on this field. Whether it's taking a hit, or getting taken out of the game, I'll do that.'

"And he meant it, man. You watch that game, he took some *hits*.

"It was one of those, 'Crazy enough to work!' kind of things. We all thought, 'Why *can't* we win this game? We have great players. Our will to win can be as much as theirs. We can execute. So why not do it?'"

When the Buckeyes scored on their first possession for a 7–0 lead just 3:26 into the contest, probably 90 percent of the people in Ohio State's Horseshoe that day figured the steamrolling was just starting.

"Everyone watches the game, but not the sidelines," Hagerup says. "If you looked over there, you'd see we were jumping around, and we felt hope for the first time all season."

Gardner hit Jake Butt for a 12-yard touchdown pass, then Drake Johnson finished an impressive 95-yard, 15-play drive with a 2-yard touchdown run to give Michigan a surprising 14–7 lead. Beat the Buckeyes at their best, and it was still possible Hoke could return the next year.

"When we took the lead in the first half, everybody was going nuts on the sidelines," Hagerup told me. "Nothing fake about it. 'We could really do this! We could be in the history books!' It was fun!"

The Buckeyes' quarterback, J. T. Barrett—who became their starter after Braxton Miller went in for surgery in the off-season—had to pull off a 25-yard run to the endzone with seven seconds left in the half just to tie the game, 14–14, going into the locker room.

While the players were in the midst of battle, fighting to save their coach's job, the lettermen had to be sure the safety net was ready, in case they didn't. Arbeznik hosted a half dozen friends at his house to watch the game, including a couple Ohio State friends, and fellow lettermen Tony Leoni, whose brother Mike helped start the Chili & Cornbread tailgates, Jon Giesler, who protected the Dolphins' Dan Marino for ten years, and Anthony Carter, one of Michigan's two three-time All-Americans, along with Bennie Oosterbaan.

Arbeznik knew an opportunity when he saw one, and as usual, he didn't waste it. "At halftime, I dialed Jim [Harbaugh] to get his take on the first half, but more importantly, to get him on the phone with Jon Giesler, Tony and AC." They took turns taking the phone into Arbeznik's office, "because I didn't want the Buckeyes in attendance to hear our conversation. After about 45 minutes, I ended the call with, 'You know we open up in Salt Lake City next year, right?' His comment back was 'Utah, huh?'"

After they hung up, they took a group photo out on Arbeznik's driveway, with Arbeznik and Giesler wearing bright yellow t-shirts with "HARBAUGH NOW" in big letters. Giesler texted the photo to Harbaugh, "who got a kick out of it."

The Flame was on his game.

Barrett started the third quarter where he'd ended the second: driving to the endzone, to cap a 5-play, 72-yard drive and give the Buckeyes a 21–14 lead. But the Wolverines came right back with their own 75-yard drive, with Drake Johnson scoring his second touchdown of the day.

21–21. Could they do it, and save Hoke's job?

On Ohio State's next possession, Barrett went down—hard.

"I heard him yell and I ran over to help him up," tight end Jeff Heuerman said. "When I went over I saw his ankle and it wasn't pretty. I just told him, 'Stay down, stay down.' It kind of hit me, 'Oh man.'"

If the lasting image of the Minnesota game was Shane Morris wobbling after being hit, his arm on Ben Braden's shoulder, the lasting imagine of the Ohio State game would be Devin Gardner, on one knee at midfield, seeing if his quarterback counterpart was okay. The image would shoot around the country, prompting hundreds of e-mails and even hand-written letters to Gardner, many from Buckeye fans, to let him know how impressed they were with his show of sportsmanship.

Gardner had received hundreds of nasty e-mails, some of them racial, during the season, so this was a welcome change, but Gardner told me anyone else would have done the same. "What has the world come to when that is such a big deal? That's something anyone would have done. That's the least courageous thing *I've* done! That's just being a human."

It was also authentic and sincere, and that's why people picked up on it immediately. Seeing this, more than a few lettermen called and texted each other, "That is Michigan."

After Urban Meyer had to replace Barrett with Cardale Jones—who was their third-string quarterback a year earlier—"you think maybe they're getting the bad breaks we've been getting," Hagerup says. "But in the second half their team played better. They're obviously an incredibly good team and incredibly well coached, and our magic just ran out."

Gardner completed 22 of 32 attempts, for 233 yards and 2 touchdowns, with 1 interception. The Wolverines went down anyway, 42–28—but they would find themselves in very good company, very soon.

"When you take your shoulder pads off, you *know* that's the last time you'll ever take that jersey off," Hagerup said. "So you do it slowly. And guys are giving you hugs. I'm not a crier, but I cried then. Even though it's a sad moment, you don't want to let it go. That was tough.

"I wish this story had a happier ending."

CHAPTER 80

MOVING IN A DIFFERENT DIRECTION

In the postgame press conference, Hoke had to address the inevitable questions about his job. "What I know is I'm going to be the football coach at Michigan," he said. "That's what I know right now.'"

"Everybody faces this point sometime in their lives," Gardner said. "It's like, you do everything you're supposed to do, you work hard, and what do you do once it doesn't work out the way we thought it would? The answer to that is to continue to do the things you do, work hard, be a good guy."

On November 30, the Sunday after the Ohio State game, Hackett drove back to his house on Spring Lake. His wife Kathy was there, but he sat in the living room by himself, with plenty to think about.

"The sun is setting on the lake," he recalled. "We haven't turned on the lights yet, so it's getting darker in the living room. I remember this kind of quiet, still moment.

"And that's when I start doing this analysis, in my head. This thought comes up. 'You know what the issue is: We can't experiment anymore. We can't extend the Hoke experiment another year. You hire another "experiment," you're in for three, four, five more years before you know how it turns out. We don't have that luxury anymore. The fans have been patient enough. Michigan has given up its option to hire the next Bo, the unknown guy who could become great.'

"It was really clear in my head that I have to get the right guy, an experienced guy we know can do the job. After this moment, when the approach we needed seemed clear, I called the president and said, 'I've come to a point of view.'

"He said, 'Okay,' and we talked it through. It was time to make a change, and get a proven winner into Schembechler Hall."

The next morning, Monday, December 1, Hackett drove back to Ann Arbor to set up meetings the next day with Hoke, the team, and a press conference.

On Tuesday, Hackett told Hoke it was over. It marked the end of a four-year run that started with great promise, and ended in great disappointment. It's hard to feel too sorry for a guy walking away with $17 million, almost a million per Big Ten win. But it's also hard to watch the dream of a decent man turn into a nightmare.

Hackett then met with the players and Hoke in the team room, just 10 minutes before the press conference.

"It was one of the first times Hackett addressed us," Russell Bellomy recalls. "And you have to fire a man we held in high regard."

Hackett didn't drag it out. "We're not going to be inviting Coach Hoke to be coaching next year."

"A lot of guys lost it when Hackett announced it to the team," Bellomy says. "There were no questions, just a moment of silence. Then Justice Hayes stood up, and just went up to Coach Hoke and gave him a big bear hug, and then, boom, we all did. Every single person in that room gave him a hug.

"He took it like a man. He was strong. He did not want to make us feel sorry for him, because that's just who he was: one of the best examples of a man with genuine integrity. A really great guy. We all hated to see him go."

On Twitter, Hoke's players filled pages with well wishes for their former coach. "Never will I appreciate someone more than Coach Hoke," Joe Kerridge wrote. "Taught me how to be a man."

As legacies go, you could do a lot worse.

Hackett left Hoke with his players, then dashed to the press conference at Crisler Center—a full house, with a full complement of cameramen. The word was already buzzing among media members that the Pac-12 had just announced Arizona's Rich Rodriguez was the 2014 Coach of the Year.

Hackett was, once again, to the point. He praised Hoke for not cutting corners, for graduating almost all his players, and for caring about every one of them. But Hackett was refreshingly free of corporate jargon when he explained why he'd made his decision.

"I met with Coach Hoke today and informed him of my decision to make a change in the leadership of our football program," Hackett said, reading his statement. "This was not an easy decision given the level of respect that I have for Brady. He has done a great job of molding these young men, making them accountable to their teammates, focusing them on success in the classroom and in the community.

"I wanted to make sure that Brady received adequate time to exhibit the results that would come from his effort and I believe that Brady and our coaching staff had enough time to produce those results and unfortunately they are not there. In the end, I feel that moving in a different direction is the right decision. I wish Brady and his family all the best in the future."

Hackett then fielded questions for about 10 minutes. He said the biggest issue when considering Hoke's future was how to reconcile what Hackett believed were Hoke's strong values with his team's weak record.

"We should be writing about what kind of program he built based on the values, but we didn't have the results on the field."

How much Brandon's hands-on approach affected Hoke's coaching style—as it did other coaches at Michigan—won't be clear until he coaches somewhere else. But we do know Hoke's teams didn't get better during each of his four seasons, and most of his players didn't get better during their careers. That's a coaching problem.

"When you make the decision to change someone's life," Hackett said, "you'd better take the time think about it. And, in this case, I did take the time. I was very deliberate about it."

Because Hackett let Hoke go before December 31, Hoke would receive a buyout of $3 million, instead of $2 million after the New Year. The way Hackett handled this difficult situation—directly, honestly, and as mercifully fast as possible, always demonstrating great respect for Hoke, personally and professionally—stood in marked contrast to the manner Brandon had dismissed Rodriguez. Hackett's approach was not only the right thing to do, it also let potential candidates like Harbaugh—whose family is very close with the Hokes—know that Michigan treats its coaches the right way, win or lose.

In a statement released to the press, Hoke returned Hackett's civility and responded in kind. "I feel very fortunate to have been an assistant and head coach at the University of Michigan. I will always support the University and this football program."

That left Hackett, who'd worked in an athletic department for all of one month, with one of the most important decisions in the history of Michigan football: Hire a coach who could bring Michigan back, and keep it from going into the red. When Hackett announced he would put off picking a permanent replacement for himself while he ran the search for Michigan's next coach—his first hire of any employee in the department—Michigan fans were feeling more angst than optimism.

It wasn't what Mark Schlissel had signed up for, but he and Hackett had to get to work finding Brady Hoke's replacement, and they had to get it right.

"When we were considering how to conduct the search," Schlissel told me, "we started analyzing not this person or that person, but the ideal characteristics of a football coach.

"First, we wanted someone who was technically proficient at coaching—obviously—but we also wanted someone who understands the role of football in the context of a university in general, and the University of Michigan in particular.

"We wanted someone who understood the challenges student-athletes face—someone committed to making sure they got the most out of their experience, on and off the field, someone who could help them strike the right balance. Most of these athletes will not earn their living playing football. So we were looking for a coach who had that value system, who appreciated football's role in holding our campus together.

"We also wanted someone who had already run a major program. We wanted someone who was proven. We did not want to hire someone who was on his way up. We felt we didn't want to take a chance with this, especially given the past several years."

Then President Schlissel told me exactly what Jim Hackett had, verbatim: "We had to get the right guy."

The president and the athletic director had to think long and hard before making any decisions. The guys following Todd Anson's playbook didn't have that burden. They had made up their mind a while ago—seven years, in Anson's case—so they could focus on execution.

As soon as Hackett announced Hoke's departure, they could work more openly, but so could Harbaugh's detractors. When the rumor mill kicked into overdrive, they did, too.

"After Michigan fired Coach Hoke," Jay Flannelly recalls, "someone was leaking to the media that Jim could not leave California due to custody issues from his first marriage. I called Ghindia and someone else who knows these types of things—and all of it came back the same: It was *all untrue!* But again, people were trying to sabotage our program with nonsense and jealousy. We all felt we couldn't let that happen again."

Another popular rumor held that Sarah Harbaugh wouldn't leave California. Anyone who had talked to her, including her shipmates on the S.S. Boike that summer, would know that was also completely false. Contrary to the rumor mill, which often depicted Sarah Harbaugh as some kind of Las Vegas model attracted to Jim's money and fame, who refused to leave California for Michigan, the former Sarah Feuerborn (pronounced "Fear-Born") is not from Las Vegas, but Kansas City, the youngest of 11 children, whose father was an accountant at General Motors. She earned her degree in education from the University of Missouri, then moved to Las Vegas because teaching jobs were easier to get there.

After a few years teaching, a friend approached her about working in real estate. When her first deal earned her more money than she had earned in an entire year of teaching, she made a career change. By the time she met Jim, in 2006, she was already earning twice his salary at the University of San Diego, where he lived in a cramped, low-rent home near the water. In short, she didn't marry him for his money, and she didn't know who he was until her brother John told her.

She had only been to Michigan twice—once for Schembechler's funeral, and once for Harbaugh's player's wedding—but she loved it both times. She was not about to stop her husband from taking a job in Ann Arbor.

The Anson playbook dictated that they pounce on any false rumors, then immediately go back on offense. Passivity was not part of the plan.

After doing their best to squash those rumors—and not for the last time—John Ghindia gave Chris Balas, from the *Wolverine*, some information to write a story about their recruitment of Jim Harbaugh. On December 3, 2014, Balas's readers were treated to a piece titled, "Mama's calling Jim Harbaugh," which started with an epigraph from Paul "Bear" Bryant, explaining why he had to leave Texas A&M after just four years to return to Alabama, his alma mater: "Momma called, and when Momma calls, you just have to come running."

"Five-plus decades later," Balas wrote, "Momma's on the line again—this time though, she's calling from her cell, not a rotary, and from Ann Arbor. She's ringing San Francisco and Jim Harbaugh, former U-M quarterback and current 49ers head coach for the second time in four years, and while he didn't answer last time, the timing might not be better."

Just a few months earlier, when Anson had introduced Harbaugh on the SS *Boike* as "the only man in the history of the University of Michigan's venerated football program whose *manifest destiny* it is to coach Michigan," you probably couldn't find enough people in America who believed it could happen to fill that boat. Even Anson thought it was a pipe dream, until his talk with Harbaugh that night.

True, a lot of people did a lot of work behind the scenes to increase the odds, and crucially, Lloyd Carr publicly and privately encouraged Harbaugh's return, and urged his former players to do the same. But they still needed a lot of breaks just to make it possible.

In Ann Arbor, the departures of Brandon and Hoke were essential, of course. But in San Francisco, Michigan fans had some unlikely, unwitting, allies.

Michigan would have been wise to consider Jim's older brother John, too, but John had far less incentive to consider Michigan. He had the same pedigree Jim did, of course. Although he played defense for Miami of Ohio, not quarterback for Michigan, he still relied on Schembechler's book as "his bible." But John Harbaugh enjoyed an almost ideal setup in Baltimore, which John Ghindia and his old high-school friend Steve Gagalis discovered when they talked with him in the visiting coaches' room after Baltimore lost to Cincinnati.

"John loved Baltimore's management team, players, and fans," Ghindia recalls. "He's got a great situation. He says he wants to be like Tom Landry at Baltimore, spending his whole career with one team. There was no better place for him and his family."

Jim Harbaugh could not claim the same. His tenure in San Francisco started with a bang—taking a team that had missed the playoffs in 2010 to the Super Bowl in 2011—and his honeymoon with general manager Trent Baalke and 34-year-old owner Jed York was as good as any, but the relations quickly started wearing thin, even as the team kept winning.

Tim Kawakami, a sports columnist at the *San Jose Mercury News* since 2000, initially thought Harbaugh was too brash and bristly to make a good fit with the 49ers. But over the years he came to the conclusion that the problems lay more with the team's management. Sure, Harbaugh could be difficult at times, but it would be hard to name a successful NFL coach who wasn't—with the possible exception of his brother.

Harbaugh frequently found himself at odds with Baalke over scouting, personnel decisions, and even contracts. Harbaugh is a naturally impatient leader—which is how you get to the Super Bowl in your first year—but that requires your boss to tolerate some minor mania in exchange for the success.

As Kawakami wrote in December of 2014, "There is nobody in the front office capable of buffering the two men. . . . That could've been York's role but he chose Baalke very clearly as his long-term guy. (Baalke was given an extension in February 2012 that took his deal through 2016, very pointedly one year longer than Harbaugh's deal.)"

Given this backdrop, neither the general manager nor the owner was willing to bend over backwards to sign Harbaugh to an extension.

"For the last two off-seasons," Kawakami wrote, "York and Harbaugh held brief discussions about a contract extension beyond the 2015 season, but nothing has ever come close to a deal.

"The closer a big-name coach comes to the end of his deal, the more pressure builds about his future. And with Harbaugh—the face of the franchise—that turned 2014 into a virtual lame-duck year."

"No one," Anson told me, "could have orchestrated the perfect storm of bad management with the 49ers, and then at Michigan, too. Those both played right into our hands."

The lucky breaks didn't stop there.

Jay Flannelly knew he could ask Tom Brady for almost anything—except after a loss. The Sunday after the Michigan–Ohio State game, November 30, the Patriots suffered only their third defeat of the season at Green Bay. Flannelly wasn't going to bother asking a favor after that one.

But on December 7, the Patriots got back to their winning ways in San Diego, beating the Chargers, 23–14, to go 10–3 on the season.

The Beav sprang into action.

"The Pats won, and Tom played great," Flannelly told me. "So after the game's over, I'm e-mailing Tom. I congratulate him on the win. He replies, 'Hey, we won, we played great.' Then I ask him to call Harbaugh, and give Tom his number. Tom says, 'Coach Harbaugh is the kind of guy we need.'

"Next day, Ghindy tells me Tom called Jim and talked for two hours. Okay, that's really cool."

"Tom Brady," Ghindia says, "has as much to do with Harbaugh coming back as any player on our list. It showed Jimmy just how deep it went."

"The next week," Flannelly says, "I'm working at Pizza House, and I see a guy at the elevator who looks really familiar, with a nice woman. I went over there, and realized it was Billy Taylor."

Taylor had been an All-American from the Schembechler era, a tailback who inspired the famous Bob Ufer call against Ohio State in 1971: "Touchdown Billy Taylor! Touchdown Billy Taylor!" He is still known by Michigan fans as "Touchdown Billy Taylor."

During the first half of 1972, Taylor lost his mother, his uncle murdered his aunt and took his own life, and his girlfriend was stabbed to death in Detroit. Taylor lost his way, robbed a bank, got caught, served time, became a drug addict, got clean, and got his Ph.D. He is now Dr. Reverend William Taylor, who runs a rehab clinic, and was the subject of a popular documentary, *Perseverance*.

At the elevator, Flannelly asked him, "Mr. Taylor, can you do me a favor? I'm working with some Michigan football alumni guys, and we're really trying to get Harbaugh here."

The second Flannely finished his sentence, he recalls, "Taylor lit up and said, 'Jay, what can I do?'"

The next week, Flannelly read in the paper that Dr. Taylor and Coach Harbaugh had exchanged texts and calls, on a three-way feed that included Anthony Carter.

Despite everyone's eagerness to help, and the flood of calls to Harbaugh that followed, Flannelly still wasn't convinced it would be enough.

"I'm still thinking, there's still no way this is going to happen," he admits. "But Ghindy says, 'Keep it up! Keep it up! Keep it up! You're doing a great job, and it's working!'

"So, I kept it up. We *all* did!"

In fact, Ghindia was right: It *was* working.

"I was aware of all the calls coming in," Sarah Harbaugh told me. "It was really neat—neat to see a whole group of people coming together and really pushing for him. It was a little overwhelming in a sense, but that made it that much harder to say no—not that there was ever a question."

"Everyone's calling Jim," Anson says. "Ghindy would call me every day, sometimes 20 times. And it was always, 'Okay, who's next? Okay, what's next?'

"Man, Ghindia was *all over* this thing!

"'Who's next?!'"

CHAPTER 81

HAGERUP'S FAREWELL

The 94th annual Michigan Football Bust on December 8, 2014, was a little unusual—but about half the previous 10 or so had also been a little unusual. "A little unusual" was becoming the new normal.

"Coach Hoke was incredibly brave to be there," Hagerup says. "We weren't shocked, because that's him. He will not leave something unfinished."

Hoke not only showed up, he introduced each of his seniors. He was well prepared, dignified, and gracious, not once talking about himself or his situation. He was particularly generous introducing Devin Gardner, which Gardner naturally appreciated.

Some fans had been sending Gardner hate mail, but at the banquet, Hoke announced that Gardner had finished in Michigan's all-time Top Ten in every quarterback category, and the top four in most categories. "Until he said that," Gardner told me, "in front of all those people, I had no idea."

In fact, the top 11 games of total offense for any player at any position in Michigan history are all held by either Denard Robinson or Devin Gardner—best friends who lived together for three years.

"I think we represented 1428 Brookfield Drive pretty well!" Later that night, Devin Gardner would be named captain of the 2014 team.

The highlight of the evening, however, was Will Hagerup's senior speech.

"Team 135 won 5 games this year," he told the audience of about 1,000 strong, in part:

We lost 7. We failed to execute in 7 games—or for roughly 25 hours. But what about the other 8,000-plus hours in the year?

Well. We went to class every day, and endured stiff consequences when we didn't, in hopes that we will become graduates of the greatest university in this country.

We woke up at 5 a.m. and lifted heavy things, or sprinted to this line and back, all while getting yelled at for "MORE EFFORT!"

We learned, often the hard way, how to handle the big stage of being a college athlete, and all that that entails. We're put under a constant microscope here, and we have stayed unified throughout.

While our friends got internships and traveled to Europe, we spent our summers in Ann Arbor training, sweating, and fighting so that Michigan could once again be great. We occasionally slept, as well.

Now compare all of that with 25 hours of losing, or "not executing" on a few Saturdays.

Is losing significant? Yes. Should it define who we are? No.

I am so incredibly proud to have been a senior on team 135. We have endured and learned more in one season of football than many people might in a lifetime. The majority of these experiences and lessons learned won't get reported.

It's simply not entertaining to read about a football player who worked really hard on a paper or an exam, and got an A, despite having much less time in his schedule for studying than the average student.

So, being a "champion" as Bo put it, encompasses far more than winning on Saturday. I believe that we are all champions, and that will be evident when you hire one of us for a job.

Do you know how to wake up early and be highly productive?

Do you value teamwork?

Do you know how to persevere through losses?

Do you understand how to deal with pressure situations?

Are you good with time management?

Did you drop a punt snap against Ohio State your sophomore year, but then your team still won the game?

You get the idea.

Hagerup thanked Brady Hoke and Greg Harden profusely, but he was not finished.

I want to thank Dave Brandon, a guy who has my lifelong respect and allegiance. He stuck his neck out for me multiple times and believed in me. I have no doubt that he will be highly successful in whatever he decides to do going forward.

And finally, I want to be very clear, so listen up. Brady Hoke, Greg Harden, and Michigan football saved my life.

They. Saved. My. Life.

This place and these people not only saved me, they transformed and empowered me.

Hagerup then brought his speech full circle, not just with his own story, but Michigan's.

Finally, I'd like to close with something from a guy named Fielding Yost. . . . At his retirement banquet, Yost said, "My heart is so full at this moment, I fear I could say little else. But do let me reiterate the spirit of Michigan. It is based on a deathless loyalty to Michigan and all her ways. An enthusiasm that makes it second nature for Michigan Men to spread the gospel of their university to the world's distant outposts. And a conviction that nowhere, is there a better university, in any way, than this Michigan of ours."

The crowd stood up and cheered. They knew exactly what Yost, and Hagerup, were talking about. The people standing and clapping seemed thrilled to see it was still very much alive.

At the end of the banquet, the seniors gathered in a backroom. Hagerup's teammates had asked him to give Coach Hoke a big, framed picture of the team, with thank-you notes from all of them written on it. When Hagerup handed it to him, he said, "Coach, this can't possibly repay for what all of us owe you in our own way, but we hope you can put this up somewhere and think about us in the future. We thank you for all you've done."

Hoke had been studiously stoic the entire evening, but he couldn't help but get choked up at that.

In February of 2015, Hagerup and I sat down for our first of several long interviews. As I had when Hagerup was in my classroom, as a sophomore and a fifth-year senior, learning about Fielding Yost and others, I always found him thoughtful and honest.

"I would say I had more time with Dave Brandon than most student-athletes," he told me over breakfast. "Maybe more than most people in the department. I really got to know him.

"I played golf with him in January, when I went out to Arizona for a punting camp and he invited me to stay at his place. The guy can play. He made me look bad! He talked about playing golf with Coach Hoke and Coach Mattison in January.

"If he's as evil as everyone he says he was, why was he still in touch with Coach Hoke? They'll probably never be working together again. Hoke can't help him."

I asked Hagerup if he thought Brandon would have kept Hoke for another season.

"I happen to know that's the case, straight from Dave. He would have kept him. He believed in him."

He also believed in Hagerup, of course, and showed it.

"What's big for me is this," Hagerup told me. "If you're a cynic, you could have argued when I was let back on the team that Dave Brandon had some evil plan to hoist up Will Hagerup as the golden boy of his drug program, and this is how it helps you—just to make himself look good.

"But if that was true, then why are Dave and I talking more now than we ever have? What is he getting out of it now? I can't help him.

"Dave has certainly been a mentor to me. When you hear bad things about a mentor and you have sat with this guy for hours and hours, you think, 'What are they talking about?'

"I wasn't there for that other stuff. I didn't see it. All I know is the guy changed my life, made me a better person, and I owe him everything. And that's my point of view."

When I asked Hagerup about his senior speech, he said, "I probably had an experience at the University of Michigan unlike anybody else's. But again, I think that's what college is for, and specifically what the University of Michigan is for.

"And I'd like to think that those indescribable feelings about this place that I got right before I committed to coming here, when I was a senior in high school, that those feelings were signs that the powers-that-be knew I was going to go through all kinds of ups and downs—but I was going to emerge a better person, and love my university more today than I ever have.

"If so, they were right."

CHAPTER 82

SEARCHING FOR SIGNS

On December 10, 2014, one of the all-time great Michigan Men, Don Dufek Sr., passed away, at age 85.

His eldest son, Don Jr., was an All-American football player at Michigan, and a varsity hockey player—the last man to pull off that biathlon. The Detroit Red Wings drafted him in the sixth round, and the Seattle Seahawks in the fifth. He played nine years in Seattle, where he was named captain of the special teams.

His younger brother, Bill, was a preseason All-American his senior year at Michigan, 1978, before he broke his ankle and missed the entire year. He came back as a fifth-year senior, and started the home opener against Illinois, when the Illinois defender John Arbeznik was blocking fell on Dufek's left foot and broke it, ending another season before it started. Bill was drafted by the New York Jets, but injuries cut his athletic career short, so he started a successful career as a State Farm Insurance agent.

Another son, Joe, played quarterback for Yale, and signed with the Buffalo Bills. Joe's son, Mike, walked on the Michigan baseball team, rising to captain as a senior.

As steeped in Michigan lore as they are, Don Sr.'s children did not even know he had played football until they were in the attic one day, opened up an old trunk, and found his 1950 Rose Bowl MVP trophy.

"He kept that stuff to himself," Bill told me. "It wasn't a big deal."

And that's how a Michigan Man handles his business. You can talk about being a Michigan Man, or you can be one—but you can't do both. Don Dufek Sr., clearly chose the latter.

Not surprisingly, the funeral home was packed to overflowing, including a large number of Michigan football royalty, guys like Paul Seymour, John Wangler, Jerry Hanlon, and many others.

A few days after the service, Bill Dufek received a call from Jim Harbaugh, who wanted to express his condolences. After a few minutes, Harbaugh also thanked Dufek for being a good landlord years ago when Harbaugh lived in one of Bill's rental homes on campus. Harbaugh then admitted that he feared he might still owe Dufek some back rent.

Dufek chuckled at that. "Jimmy," he said, "too much time has passed. The statute of limitations is over. In fact, I'll give *you* ten times what you owed me if you just get your ass back to Ann Arbor!"

Dufek says, "We both laughed our asses off at that. But that's when I started feeling strongly that Jimmy was coming back."

A few days later, Mrs. Dufek received a bouquet of roses from the head coach of the San Francisco 49ers.

Of course, the decision was not just Harbaugh's, but Michigan's.

After Hackett put the decision through a rigorous, systematic evaluation process that measured five candidates on 10 criteria, which resulted in all manner of data plastered on three walls of his "War Room," in an empty suite at the stadium, Hackett kept coming up with the same name every time: Jim Harbaugh.

Trusting his results, Hackett decided to do what Michigan had failed to do in the past: Go all in, with no hesitation, and make sure Harbaugh knew it. From the start, Hackett determined to bypass the minnows to go after the great white that had eluded Brandon.

It wasn't as simple as it sounded, however, because Harbaugh was still under contract with the 49ers, which meant Harbaugh would give his current team every ounce of his boundless energy until he was coaching somewhere else. As Anson said, Harbaugh would rather have won in San Francisco than seek a job elsewhere. That meant Hackett had to spend the first two weeks of December communicating through Harbaugh's associates, friends, and family, including Jim's father Jack.

The day after San Francisco lost to Seattle the second time, on Sunday, December 14, with two games left on San Francisco's schedule, Harbaugh and 49ers owner Jed York agreed that Harbaugh would not be coming back the next season. York gave him permission to talk with Michigan, but not other NFL teams—a huge advantage for Hackett, who got a two-week head start on the competition.

Thus, he finally got the chance to talk directly with Harbaugh on Tuesday, December 16—but their first call could have gone better. After a few pleasantries, Harbaugh asked three important questions.

How would Michigan handle his buyout? Harbaugh's contract dictated $5 million would be paid by the team to Harbaugh if they fired him, or $5 million by Harbaugh to the team if he left, in what amounted to a game of high-stakes chicken. Hackett wasn't sure Michigan could swallow $5 million, or even if it should.

Next question: Did Michigan know who can help their kids get into St. Francis Elementary School, where Jim had attended? That was also tricky, because virtually any contact from the Michigan athletic department to the school would leak, and potentially kill the deal.

Finally, who's Harbaugh's boss going to be? Hackett and Schlissel hadn't discussed that yet, so Hackett couldn't give Harbaugh an answer.

If Michigan were an NFL team that couldn't immediately provide good answers to those questions, Harbaugh might have stood up, left the room, and never come back. But this was his alma mater, so before Harbaugh hung up, he said, "Okay, let's talk again tomorrow."

With 24 hours to prepare, Hackett's team had much better answers. Regarding Harbaugh's $5 million buy out, Michigan eventually worked it out with the 49ers that neither side would pay the other—a wash—which solved the problem for all three parties.

With St. Francis Elementary, Hackett's staff worked through intermediaries to find the answers without tipping off who was asking the questions. And as to who would be Harbaugh's boss, Hackett admitted he wasn't sure if he was going to be a long-term athletic director, but he assured Harbaugh, "I won't be leaving quickly."

Satisfied, Harbaugh kept listening, and a direct discussion between Hackett and Harbaugh had begun in earnest.

Just because a formal conversation had finally commenced, Anson and company were not about to slack off.

Anson knew Harbaugh's 51st birthday was coming up the next week, on Tuesday, December 23. In fact, the first page of his 2007 playbook started with these words: "Remember his birthday—December 23—right in the recruitment sweetspot for us."

Needless to say, seven years later, Anson was not going to forget.

"Can't miss that!" he said. Just about everyone Anson, Ghindia, Arbeznik, and Flannelly had already gotten to call Harbaugh that fall, they asked to call or text again. And once again, almost all of them did, including Bill Martin, Regent Larry Deitch, Governor Snyder (who told Harbaugh, "The Comeback State needs the Comeback Kid to come back!"), and the long list of lettermen in their Rolodex: the guys on Jack Harbaugh's teams, Jim Harbaugh's old teammates, plus the stars from the nineties, Desmond Howard, Charles Woodson, Jon Jansen, and many more. Perhaps most important, at this stage, the two men who were charged with making the decision, President Schlissel and Jim Hackett, also sent their birthday greetings.

Anson didn't stop there, either. "We'd been remembering for years to send Jim a DVD collection of the TV series *24*, so he could catch up on the 'Jack Bauer Power Hour' he always missed during football seasons." And that's what Jim Harbaugh got on his 51st birthday from his friends at Michigan.

John Ghindia texted both Jim and Sarah, "Happy Birthday, Jim! It's a great day to be a Michigan Wolverine! Most Valuable M players & recruits in 2015: Jim and Sarah Harbaugh! Look forward to seeing you next week! Go Blue!"

It was a fairly presumptuous message, since Jim had not tipped his hand to Hackett or anyone else. But Ghindia thought they might be getting warmer when Sarah replied, "Ha ha! Thanks, John! Feels nice to be wanted. Looking forward to it!"

Christmas falling two days after Harbaugh's birthday meant more of everything heading Harbaugh's way: calls, texts, e-mails, even presents.

When Harbaugh took the Stanford job, in 2007, Anson picked out two Cardinal-red, Robert Talbot ties for Jim and his father Jack. Seven years later, based solely on private reports of vaguely defined "good discussions" between Hackett and Harbaugh, Anson decided to play the odds and send Jim and Jack two maize-and-blue college rep ties. He called Ann Arbor's iconic men's clothing store, Van Boven's, which had been outfitting students, faculty, and townies right on State Street since former Michigan baseball captain Peter Van Boven opened the doors in 1921.

Calling it a "super secret" mission, Anson asked to speak to the manager, Hank Schoch. He told Schoch he wanted to buy a couple ties, but it had to be kept secret. "I am extremely careful to say to everyone with whom I speak that I know nothing," Anson said, "and they cannot draw any conclusions from this order. I am merely a friend of Jim's who is 'hopeful.'"

Schoch understood, and took a cell phone photo of their rack of Michigan ties, and sent it to Anson, who picked two identical rep ties for Jim and

Jack, and an extra blue one with gold stripes and little Block M's for Jim. Anson added a little message for Jim, "Happy Birthday, Merry Christmas, I hope you'll be needing these soon! Go Blue!"

Three hours later, at a restaurant in Coronado, California, Anson's phone started blowing up with people calling to confirm an order for some ties. Anson told them, "I am merely a friend and I know nothing."

But, the next morning, "I awake to unsympathetic texts from my sons, Chris and Ryan, telling me, 'You really blew it, Dad!'"

"Tie-gate" had reached MGoBlog. Founder Brian Cook had received several e-mails with a picture of the same order form, and posted it on the front page of the site. Titled, "The Tieluminati," the bit made fun of fans' obsession with all things Harbaugh—even things that didn't necessarily mean anything.

"I had no idea what had gone wrong," Anson told me, "until I called Van Boven's. They'd just fired a kid who saw the order form and took a cell phone picture of it, sent it to his friends, and before long someone sent it to MGoBlog."

The little mix up demonstrated just how hungry three million Michigan fans were for any sign that Harbaugh might be coming home, all part of a surreal daily drama. While most NFL reporters still maintained there was virtually no chance of Harbaugh returning to Michigan, those closer to Michigan and Harbaugh himself insisted otherwise. In the middle were desperate Michigan fans, trying to discern why Harbaugh did not wear his college T-shirt at a practice when his 49ers players did, the meaning of Michigan ties being sent to California, and every tea leaf in between.

Jay Flannelly had been in the center of it all, but he admits he still thought Harbaugh's return was a long shot. "At this point, I still didn't think Jim was going to come. I just felt bad for Jim, dealing with the 49ers, so I sent him a Merry Christmas text message. And at 1 a.m. our time, and 10 p.m., California time, Christmas day, I get a text back: 'Thank you, Jay. Happy Holidays to you and yours, and our friend John Ghindia. Thanks for the kind words and sentiment. Jim H.'

"I can't believe he replied," Flannelly told me. "Now I'm thinking, *maybe?!?*"

CHAPTER 83

LANDING HARBAUGH

The good vibrations Team Harbaugh generated over Harbaugh's birthday and Christmas were helpful, but all the texts and neckties in the world couldn't be confused with a contract.

That was Hackett's job. Even as the national press kept saying Michigan had no chance at Harbaugh, the wheels were coming off Hackett's search, and Michigan didn't have a clue, Hackett showed considerable restraint and confidence in ignoring all of it, and keeping his eye on the prize.

Over the next two weeks, Hackett and Harbaugh had long talks on Saturday nights, and occasionally other times, developing a good rapport. (To avoid anything leaking to the media, Hackett always referred to Harbaugh internally as "Unicorn," another indication of where Hackett placed Jim on their list: the one-of-a-kind dream candidate.)

"The interesting thing is," Hackett told me, "we never talked specifically about Jim being head coach. We talked about what Michigan needed. After a few weeks of this, we're going back and forth and getting really excited about the possibilities, and Jim says, 'We're getting excited about this, aren't we?'

"Yes we are," Hackett said.

"You didn't offer me the job, did you?" Harbaugh asked.

"No, I haven't."

"I didn't accept, did I?"

"No, you didn't."

It wasn't an agreement, by design, Hackett says, "But that gave me the confidence, no matter what pressure the media was putting on me, I could stick to my guns."

At one point in their conversations, "I shared with him my time line," Hackett says. "'Here's my walk away date: Saturday, December 27, 2014.'"

Day by day, it became clearer to Hackett that Harbaugh was sincerely interested in leading Michigan's program, and Harbaugh certainly didn't have to wonder if Hackett, or just about anyone else who mattered, wanted him to do so.

But by Saturday, December 27, 2014, the day before Harbaugh's last game as the coach of the 49ers—who were not going to make the playoffs for the first time since Harbaugh took over in 2011—Hackett still didn't have a contract, or any ironclad assurance from Harbaugh that he'd be signing one. That date also happened to be Hackett's self-declared "walk-away day," when he promised himself he'd stop pursuing Harbaugh and move on to his next candidate.

"I figured the minute Jim's season was done," Hackett told me, "he'd be open season for the NFL teams, and he'd get flooded with offers that night. So I wanted to make Saturday my day."

Hackett dialed up Harbaugh for their weekly phone call. It was no longer about relationship building. Hackett needed an answer—a firm one.

"I need to trust you Jim, and I need to know if you're going to come back to Michigan."

"I need to finish my commitment here," Harbaugh said, "so I can't sign anything until we finish here. You understand that, yes?"

"Yes, I do," Hackett said.

"So I can't sign yet," Harbaugh repeated. But then he said the words Hackett—and three million Michigan fans—longed to hear: "But I want to come."

"We need the agreement signed," Hackett said. Then, he recalls, "There followed a long pause. Long pause. Long pause. Finally, Jim says, 'Yes.'"

"That's enough for me," Hackett said.

Looking back on it, Hackett says, "I don't know in business if I would have done that, just accepted a verbal commitment. If I have the commitment with no contract, I'd be facing a lot of heat from the Regents and others—but I would explain: 'Look, this is Michigan, and two guys who played for Bo. If we get to the point where we both get excited, and this is for God and country, I have to trust that.'

"But with this system—Michigan football—I knew I could, because it was a system we'd both been raised in. We know what it means. We know how we're to conduct ourselves. I had faith that he learned what I learned—that your word has to be good. There is a currency we could call on as Michigan Men."

Anson has given Harbaugh some legal advice over the years, but Harbaugh's lawyer in this negotiation was John Denniston, a high-powered venture capital attorney. He was also a Michigan alum Anson had met years earlier when they were playing basketball at the Intramural Building. Anson remembers a short guy who could drain 20 footers. A few years later, Anson recruited Denniston for his law firm.

The next day, Sunday, December 28, 2014, Denniston sent Hackett the term sheet—a "Cliff's Notes" contract that commits both parties until the full contract can be executed. Hackett received it on his tablet computer. He needed to sign it, then send it back to Denniston for Harbaugh to sign. He planned to handle all that on his flight back from California to Michigan, "but the damn thing won't work, and I can't get an e-mail out either!"

Getting anxious over his four-hour flight, unable to communicate and concerned that Denniston might be thinking he'd gotten cold feet, as soon as Hackett got off his plane, he bolted straight for the airport Westin Hotel. By that time, Denniston was waiting for Hackett's signature while standing in the 49ers locker room at halftime.

"You won't believe it," Hackett texted him. "My computer died!"

After Hackett put his trust in Harbaugh Saturday night, it was Denniston's turn to return the favor.

Hackett then tried the Westin business office, but they couldn't handle PDF software. He couldn't fax it from the hotel, because he knew that would get out and hit the internet almost instantly. He decided to take a picture of the agreement with his iPhone—but then the battery died.

"After all this work," he thought, "the Unicorn is slipping from my fingers!"

He asked the bartender if she had a charger. She didn't, but a patron did. Hackett charged his phone at the bar, while watching the 49ers game. One of the customers recognized him, and said, "I bet you're excited Harbaugh's not going to be in the playoffs!"

"And I'm saying, 'Oh, yeah. That must be awful.' No way I'm going to tell them I'm trying to sign Harbaugh to come to Michigan at this bar!"

Hackett's phone came back to life. He signed the deal, and hit send.

"I was eight hours late, with one excuse after another," Hackett said. "If Denniston didn't trust me, they might have wondered if I'd changed my mind, and walked. But it was the same thing with Jim Harbaugh: Denniston was a Michigan guy, so we trusted each other."

Proving the early rumors false, Sarah was on board, with both feet. When Anson's army of friends, former teammates, and childhood idols started calling Jim, and even saying on TV how much they wanted him back in Ann

Arbor, "That's when I said, 'Wow, they really want you!'" Sarah recalls telling her husband. "'Very few people can do that in a lifetime, be that person that everyone wants. You gotta go!'

"A lot of people say, 'You made it to the top, you've got to stay at the top,'" she told me. "Not that he's taking a step down by coming to Michigan, but he's pursuing something that he always he felt was his destiny.

"It happened so fast, I was in shock. But not for one minute did I not see the good in coming to Ann Arbor. We were in a great place, but I'm coming back home in a sense. I'm Midwestern, and I always will be.

"Say you have this guy pursuing you and he's in love with you, but he hasn't come out and said it yet, he's just admiring you from afar. But you're dating this big macho guy who gets all the ladies, but he doesn't treat you right. And you finally come out and say it, and decide to give the other guy a chance, this nice guy just waiting, and that's when you realize it's a match made in heaven.

"And you ask yourself, 'Why didn't I go out with this person ten years ago?' Well, maybe it wasn't the right time yet.

"Michigan was that guy, who loved you the whole time. So you finally say yes, and you can't believe you didn't say yes years ago.

"It was such a fragile process for everyone. If it had not been handled just that way—if you had someone who was pushing you, not letting you make the decision, not giving you your space—I don't think it would have happened.

"Feeling the love. That's what it came down to."

On Monday, December 29, 2014, just minutes before Harbaugh got on the plane that would take him, Sarah and three of their kids from California to Michigan, he signed the long contract.

The same reporters who said Harbaugh would never return to Michigan were now convinced Hackett must have offered Harbaugh a record contract. Harbaugh repeatedly told his friends, however, that "It's not about the money."

It turns out he meant it: Harbaugh's Michigan contract is roughly the same as his deal with the 49ers—about $5 million a year, plus incentives, including a $2 million signing bonus. It didn't exactly qualify as a vow of poverty, but it was undoubtedly less than several NFL teams would have been eager to pay. Harbaugh didn't even try, immediately letting them know he had committed to Michigan, ending the dance before it started..

The morning of Harbaugh's introductory press conference, Hackett told me, "Jim *insisted* that he not be the highest paid coach in college football, or even the Big Ten. I think that tells you something about his values."

When I asked Harbaugh about this, he said, "Let's not make this sound more noble than it is. I'm not on the same dance floor as Mother Teresa. I like a buck as much as the next guy. I wouldn't kill for it, I wouldn't marry for it, I wouldn't cheat for it, I wouldn't steal for it. But I'm open to *earning* it.

"But," he added, "I would say that I didn't pick Michigan because I thought they were going to pay me the most. We didn't wait around for teams to start some bidding war, or even make offers."

The decision was simpler than that, he said.

"Earlier that week, I was talking to my dad on the phone, and I finally cut to the chase. 'Well, whatya think, Dad?'"

"Well, Jim," his dad said, "you make great decisions; you always have. I'm not going to tell you what to do. Follow your heart."

"And that," Jim Harbaugh said, "is what I did."

Some jobs are for God and country.

This was one of them.

Michigan had its man.

EPILOGUE

After Jim Hackett introduced him, Jim Harbaugh stood up, walked toward the podium, and tripped over a TV camera cable. But he regained his balance quickly, chuckled, then said into the microphone, "Anybody see that? A lesser athlete would have gone down."

Harbaugh was quoting Bo Schembechler. Everybody got the joke.

Michigan's disappointing decade had fueled the fans' hunger for Harbaugh's old-school toughness. Just six months into his tenure at Michigan, Harbaugh already had more than a quarter million twitter followers, the most of any coach in the country. Harbaugh seemed to pop up across the nation like Forrest Gump, coaching first base for the Oakland A's one day and conducting football clinics coast to coast the next. Harbaugh's childlike enthusiasm was contagious, because it was authentic.

His Michigan Man credentials and boundless passion inspired Michigan fans to give him a reception like no coach before him—not Yost, Crisler, or Schembechler himself.

"The people here are just grateful," Sarah Harbaugh told me, "and it feels good. I don't feel like anywhere else he could have gone, would we get a reception like this.

"This was meant to be."

Michigan scheduled its 2015 spring game for Saturday, April 4. Early that morning, long before anyone else had shown up, Jim Harbaugh stood on a ladder in the locker room, underneath the big letters that spelled out Schembechler's famous mantra: "Those Who Stay Will Be Champions."

Harbaugh was adding his own phrase above Schembechler's: "Those Who Work Hard Will Stay."

The Spring Game attracted a record crowd, estimated at 60,000, about four times more fans than had been going in recent years.

They cheered Harbaugh's introduction. They cheered the coin toss. They cheered every run, pass, and tackle. And when the Blue squad beat the Maize squad, to earn their steaks—like old times—the fans stood up and cheered that, too.

In Harbaugh's post-scrimmage press conference, he said, "It's happening. The process is well under way."

More than 300 lettermen showed up the night before for a reunion dinner. That included 1971 All-American lineman Reggie McKenzie, who used to block for O.J. Simpson in Buffalo. Inspired by the previous night's celebration, Saturday morning McKenzie pulled out his letterman's jacket. It looked all of its four-plus decades, with the old-school blue buttons and button holes—no snaps—and leather arms that had faded to a pale yellow.

I ran into McKenzie in the parking lot after the game, hanging out with his fellow letterman. When I commented on his jacket, he said, "You know, I was walking down the tunnel today, before the game, and I called my old friend Mike Taylor," another All-American from 1971. "I said, 'Man, I haven't worn this old letter jacket in God knows how long. Maybe since I got it. But I wore it today. It still fits!'

"After the game, when I walked back up that tunnel, I felt proud—*proud*—to be a *Michigan Man*.

"It feels good!"

As of this writing, Will Hagerup had not yet signed with an NFL team. Gardner went undrafted, but the Pittsburgh Steelers picked him up. When I asked Gardner if he had any regrets about going to Michigan, without so much as visiting another school, he said, "Are you kidding? Best decision of my life. I will always be a Michigan Man."

In June, Toys R Us announced it had hired Dave Brandon as its CEO.

In the same month, the Michigan Athletic Department announced it had run a $7.9 million deficit, the worst in Michigan history, partly due to the many buy-outs Michigan had paid out that fall.

But that spring Jim Hackett could also announce that Michigan's season tickets had sold out again, and the wait list was back—a bellwether of the program's health.

It is still not clear if Hackett wants to remain as Michigan's athletic director, and if he doesn't, who would take his place. But the position of head football coach seems to be occupied for the foreseeable future.

It would be a mistake to reduce this story to a simple saga of Dave Brandon leaving, and Jim Harbaugh arriving. It was much bigger than two men, and went much deeper.

After more than a century of sound stewardship, Michigan lost its way. It ignored established safeguards, and forgot the values that had made it great. The resulting downfall was swift and stunning.

But if Michigan's wounds were of its own hand, so were its remedies.

Bit by bit, level by level, the people who understood the values the program was built on stood up, and fought back: The employees, who cared about Michigan more than money; the lettermen, who were more attached to their alma mater than any pro team; the students, who came to Michigan anticipating a thriving community, and insisted that it be rebuilt; the Regents who listened, and took action; and the new athletic director and coach, who returned to the place they loved most.

Tradition reached from the past—from Baird and Yost, Crisler, Canham, and Schembechler—to a new generation of leaders, and they answered.

Michigan wasn't broken for over a century. But when it finally cracked, from the inside out, the people who knew its history rose to fix it, and restore the meaning of a simple, timeless saying: This is Michigan.

AFTERWORD

During Michigan's two previous head coaching searches, fans were split on the best candidate.

Not this time.

When Jim Hackett started looking for Brady Hoke's replacement, Jim Harbaugh was the Michigan family's Great Hope—the native son they dreamed would come back to return their team to glory. If you asked fans for their top three choices, you would have heard Jim Harbaugh, Jim Harbaugh—and probably Jim Harbaugh.

When Hackett did the seemingly impossible, and actually landed Harbaugh, the response was something beyond euphoria. MGoBlog changed its banner to "IT'S HAPPENING!"

From the day Harbaugh took the job on December 30, 2014, the incredible hype and irrational expectations have only increased. A few minutes after his introductory press conference, Harbaugh first addressed the Michigan fans at halftime of a basketball game, for which hundreds of students wore khakis in his honor.

"Oh, we *have* been surprised by the reception," Jim's father, Jack, told me. "But the thing that sticks out is coming home. Seeing him at the airport, the smile that came on his face. Being home. Being happy."

His mom, Jackie Harbaugh, saw the difference as soon as her son's plane landed in Michigan on December 29, 2014.

"It was a happy moment for us, because I could *see* the happiness on his face, the *joy* in his eyes."

"We moved 17 different times in our career," Jack said. "Each time you move, you catch faces, and you're always trying to catch a name, and connect the two. But when Jim stood up to the podium that day [for his first press conference], he looked out and saw Jerry Hanlon, Gary Moeller, Lloyd Carr, Elliot Uzelac, John Kolesar, Paul Jokisch. You're not walking into a room full of strangers. You're walking into a room in your home. You know everyone, and everyone knows you. You belong. Whenever Jim would see one of these old friends, old mentors, both faces would light up, and then they'd embrace.

"I remember saying, 'Wow, this is as happy as we've seen him in many, many months. He's home, and he's happy. As parents, that's what we all look for.'"

Years ago, when Jack Harbaugh packed his kids' lunches, he famously told them to "attack this day with an enthusiasm unknown to mankind!" Four decades later, Jim practices what his father preached.

"Now that we're into prepping for spring ball," Harbaugh told me, a couple months after taking the job, "we've been bunkered down at the hotel. Everyone's wife is shopping for homes, because we don't have time to look.

"At 5:45 each morning, we meet in the lobby, and eat breakfast there—oatmeal, whatever they've got. Then we carpool in to Schembechler Hall—I still don't have a car—and we go until midnight, carpool back to the hotel, get up, and do it again.

"It's been a fun way to get to know each other."

Not many would describe days that run 19 hours, and end alone in a midrange hotel, as fun, but Harbaugh actually meant it. That's part of his charm, similar to his biggest mentor's. When Bo Schembechler was coaching, he liked to gather his players on Labor Day and say, "Men, today is Labor Day, and in its honor, we are going to *labor!*" When Schembechler got plowed over by a player who hadn't seen where his coach was standing, Schembechler would pop right back up and say, "Hot damn! That would have killed a lesser man!"

In the same spirit, Harbaugh was redefining what fun looked like, and doing it largely by example. MGoBlog took one of Harbaugh's quotes as its subhead: "I don't get sick. I don't observe major holidays. I'm a jackhammer."

Weapons-grade intensity was back in town.

Michigan fans recognized the classic dish Harbaugh was serving, and they were eating it up.

"Everyone's showed him so much love here," his wife, Sarah, told me, in the spring of 2015, "I had to put him back in his place at dinner last night, and say, 'You're not the king, Jim.'"

"Trust me, I know," he said—something he's had to address since a reporter at his first press conference asked him about being "the messiah."

But no sooner had Harbaugh assured Sarah than a college kid walked up to their table to show Jim bracelets he and his friends had made.

"And the bracelets say, 'Hail Harbaugh,'" Sarah recalled. "I'm thinking, 'Kid, you're not helping!'"

Then Harbaugh pulled a Schembechler, and started pumping the kid for his name, his major, and his career plans, and launched into his favorite role: assessing someone's strengths, and how to expand them; their weaknesses, and how to minimize them; and how to help someone get where they want to go. In other words, *coach him*.

"He was so into this guy," Sarah said, "you'd think he was his career counselor."

History is replete with the dangers facing anyone declared the messiah. As Michigan State coach Mark Dantonio said, "Pride comes before the fall." But the praise is only dangerous if the recipient believes it. Harbaugh seems too busy to give the hype much attention.

"We're here, in Schembechler Hall, all day," he told me in his first spring. "But I remember telling recruits there's a lot of excitement and hunger for Michigan football right now."

He paused just a bit before adding, "Hungry dogs hunt best."

That Harbaugh, the biggest catch in the coaching sea, seemed to be hungrier than the rabid fans and determined insiders who helped bring him back to Ann Arbor only made them love the guy even more.

But would Harbaugh returning to Ann Arbor work? Rich Rodriguez had been hired with great expectations, after all, and Hoke generated similar optimism after his first season. This time, the stakes were even higher: If Harbaugh didn't work, for whatever reason, where could Michigan turn next, after three strikes? What would be different this time?

Even if Harbaugh succeeded, that would set up another question, almost as big as the first: Would he stay?

Eighteen months in Ann Arbor could not answer either question conclusively, but they went a surprisingly long way toward putting both questions to rest.

Could Harbaugh do the job? Given the scope of the task, it wasn't a rhetorical question. Harbaugh had to restore a program that had fallen into almost unrecognizable disrepair. He had to fill the Big House, and help get the department out of debt, while adhering to Michigan's values of fair play. And he had to reunite the Michigan family, which had been fractured for a decade.

Harbaugh, consciously or not, started doing all these things the day he arrived, but in reverse order. The moment the tires on Harbaugh's plane touched the tarmac, Michigan's fan base was united, in a way it hadn't been since at least 1997.

Likewise, after thousands of Michigan fans stubbornly held onto their ticket applications until Hackett named the next coach, the instant Harbaugh took the podium, the fans' forms started flooding the department to ensure they could keep their seats, including the all-important skyboxes, which quickly sold out. The Nike contract soon followed, ultimately worth a record $173.8 million, which prompted MGoBlog's Ace Anbender to write this headline: "Nike Will Pay Michigan All of the Money." It's safe to assume Nike didn't back up the Brink's truck based on Michigan's 5–7 record, but the man in khakis.

The stunning change of fortune could only be sustained, however, with success on the field, and that would be harder to achieve.

If Harbaugh and the fans were hungry, so were the players. The Wolverines got their five Big Ten losses in 2014 the old-fashioned way: They'd earned them.

One trait throughout history that all successful generals have shared is an uncommon ability to analyze their troops' strengths and weaknesses with cool detachment. Those leaders in the habit of kidding themselves do not last long. Harbaugh demonstrated this vital quality when he started evaluating the game film of Michigan's returning players in his office, which he calls his "football bunker." Despite Hoke's top seven recruiting classes from 2012 and 2013, who were now sophomores and juniors, according to several witnesses, not only did Harbaugh grade most players as average or lower, he was alarmed by what he termed an "intensity deficit." They simply weren't tough enough, physically or mentally. As a direct result, they were prone to wear down and fall apart by the fourth quarter, a tendency Michigan demonstrated in numerous games the previous seasons.

The clear-eyed assessment presented only three solutions: recruit better, coach better, and play better. In typical fashion, Harbaugh didn't waste any time getting to work on all three.

"The biggest change," tight end Jake Butt told me, "and a lot of people noticed it, was this: My first two years [under Brady Hoke] we heard constant talk of challenging each other in practice, and competing to win a Big Ten title, but the level of work did not compare to what we did when Coach Harbaugh first got here. We'd always worked hard before, but we were not as smart, or as efficient.

"He made it crystal clear: The only way to win is to put the work in. Because of the environment he created, we were forced to prepare to compete against the best, every day."

This sea change started on the first day of spring practice. While most college coaches use the NCAA's daily allotted 4 hours with their team by meeting for 90 minutes or more, then practicing for 2.5 hours or less, Harbaugh decided to spend all 4 hours practicing, which was unheard of.

"Very first day, he got our attention," Butt said. "I'd never done a four-hour practice. No one had. It kind of just smacked you in the mouth. By the second hour, because of the pace, it started to hurt. By the third hour, Coach Harbaugh gathered us around him, and told us, 'This is where you guys lost games last year. You ran out of gas. You started making mistakes. And you started turning on each other.

" 'These practices are not *supposed* to be easy. We're not focusing on winning this or winning that. Not now. We're just going to be the hardest-working team in the country. And we're going to embrace that.

" 'We're turning our weakness into our strength. And that's why, this season, we're going to win games in the fourth quarter.' "

With that, Harbaugh blew his whistle, and sent them back to their stations to complete their fourth hour of practice, at full speed.

The visitors to that first spring practice included Jack and Jackie Harbaugh, who've seen several thousand practices between them. But they'd never seen this.

"Four-hour practices?" Jack told me. "I'd not experienced that in my entire career. Golly, is this thing ever going to *end?*

"After practice, Jimmy ran by me and said, 'Class on the grass.' And just like that, it all made sense to me," he said. Yes, Jack is Jim's father, but impressing Jack Harbaugh isn't easy, even for his children—and perhaps especially for his children. But this impressed him. "I've been in so many of those team meetings, which you spend three hours just preparing to run. When you finally got up there, you always had a handful of players that are grasping it, but others who had no interest in it at all. And that was about the best you could do. You get two-thirds, you think you've hit a home run.

"What Jim did is take the meeting out of the classroom, and onto the field, where you don't have much choice but to pay attention! In his class, they're looking at an *actual* 4–3 front, or they're looking at a blitz, they talk about it—and then it comes after them! Yes, they were paying attention!

"My goodness! All those years I was coaching, there wasn't anyone who could come up with that idea? Not me, I'm not smart enough. Glad Jim is!"

Ultimately, the only opinions that mattered were the players'—and Harbaugh had them.

"Coach was right—about all of it," Butt continued. "Last year, when just *one* thing went wrong, we were so shocked we had no ability to adjust, to come back. And we didn't have enough strength left to do it, anyway.

"Coach talked to us about the 'football callous,' the soreness, and the pain, you feel at the end of the day after a good practice. So you just toughen your skin a bit, and you go another week, you get a stronger callous, and by the fourth or fifth week, a four-hour practice is nothing. And everything he told us was true."

By the end of spring ball, Harbaugh had his team.

"The 20-year-olds know when the coaches are sincere," Jackie Harbaugh told me. "I just marveled at the way the players reacted to the practices. They were all quick tempo, but I didn't see one player coming off the field dragging or complaining. They had *smiles* on their faces when they came off the field, because they *knew* they were getting better! 'I feel better! I understand what I'm supposed to be doing in this situation.' And you'd see them in the hallway after, they were all so happy, so polite, so very nice. You could just see the players wanted to compete! They wanted to be the BEST!

"It was just fun for me to watch all of that, to see it develop."

What Harbaugh's players were doing on that practice field, when almost no one was watching, was more important to the future of the program than all the things happening outside it. But what was happening outside it was still pretty fascinating, too.

That same spring, Harbaugh unwittingly threatened to elevate his status to sainthood, in the fans' eyes, when he and his right-hand man, Colonel Jim Minick (Ret.), witnessed a high-speed accident on I-94, then jumped out to help two older women out of their car, and draped their own coats around them. Their quick response kept the women from going into shock. The women later admitted they had no idea they were being helped by Harbaugh, but reportedly stopped short of asking, "Who was that masked man?"

A few days later, when his players were on spring break, Harbaugh popped up like Forrest Gump again, this time coaching first base for the Oakland A's. Every time Harbaugh did, well, just about anything, it attracted national attention. Not since the Fab Five had Michigan captured the country's imagination like this—and this time, it was all about one man. To Harbaugh's credit, he made sure the distractions were his, not his players.

Harbaughmania started at his first press conference, and it never stopped.

When the Big Ten held its annual Media Days at the end of July 2015, a few hundred reporters got to hear fourteen coaches swear that their team chemistry had never been better, their senior leadership was outstanding, and they couldn't wait to get back on the field. Once you recorded the first such batch of comments, you needed only to change the name at the top to cover the rest.

But one man stood out from the crowd. Harbaugh charmed the reporters with spontaneous stories about everything from his daily commute to the office, recounting it street by street, from Bo's house to Schembechler Hall, to his lifelong respect for Woody Hayes—yes, Ohio State's Woody Hayes, Michigan's sworn enemy.

When Harbaugh left the podium for the next coach, an unfortunate guy named Kyle Flood of Rutgers, half the assembled media left the room to follow Harbaugh into the hallway, to ask him still more questions. He happily obliged.

Michigan State head coach Mark Dantonio had to field plenty of questions, too—but his were about Michigan, and Harbaugh. Privately, Dantonio had to wonder what a fella has to do to get out of the shadow of a man who had just arrived, and hadn't even coached a Big Ten game yet.

Going into the 2015 season, Dantonio's teams had won ten games in four of the last five seasons, three division titles, one Big Ten title, and two BCS bowl victories. Only one team in college football had been ranked in the top five the previous two years. You could win a lot of bar bets if you knew the answer wasn't Alabama, Florida State, or Ohio State, but Michigan State.

Yet *Rolling Stone* had just come out with a story stating that Ohio State's Urban Meyer and Harbaugh were the two top coaches in the Big Ten. On ESPN, one of the interviewers kept calling Mark Dantonio "Mike Dantonio."

From coaching high-school hockey, I learned nothing motivates like disrespect. If that held true in college football, no one had more motivation entering 2015 than Mark Dantonio and his Spartans.

Harbaugh was also getting more attention than Urban Meyer, who had already won two national titles at Florida before taking over Ohio State in 2012. His first year, he took a 6–7 team that was on probation and ran the table with a perfect 12–0 record. The next year, the Buckeyes were also 12–0 until Michigan State upset them in the Big Ten title game.

In 2014, after losing starting quarterback Braxton Miller to an injury in the off-season, the Buckeyes stumbled in their second game to Virginia Tech, then rattled off ten straight victories to claim another division title. Problem was, that eleventh victory cost them another quarterback, J. T. Barrett. So what'd they do? Urban Meyer rode his third-string quarterback, Cardale Jones, to a stunning 59–0 whitewash of Wisconsin to slip into the sport's first four-team playoff. Then the heavy underdogs pulled off victories over Alabama and Oregon, in one of the greatest coaching jobs I have ever seen.

What was Urban Meyer's reward for all this? More questions about Jim Harbaugh—who, as I might have mentioned, had yet to win a Big Ten game.

When Dantonio and Meyer got asked questions about the new guy, they handled it with aplomb. Perhaps they knew Harbaugh's return brought much-needed positive attention to the Big Ten, and that was ultimately good for everyone. For the first time in more than a decade, the Big Ten was the conference everyone was talking about. They also knew responding with some sharp comebacks at a press conference was no substitute for settling scores on the field.

After nine months of hype, the Harbaugh era finally hit the grass when the Michigan Wolverines traveled to Utah for the season opener on September 3, 2015. Fox Sports decked out a bus in Harbaugh's trademark khaki—yes, a bus, fitted top to bottom in actual cloth—and drove it across the country before Michigan's first game in Salt Lake City.

Utah had beaten Rich Rodriguez in his debut game in 2008, and Brady Hoke in his last season. The Utes were a well-coached team, and were favored to beat Michigan yet again.

But what Michigan fans saw that Thursday evening was a team that was clearly improving. One that still had to learn how to create holes in the defensive line for their running backs, but had gotten much better at protecting the quarterback, and the ball. No fumbles.

Their quarterback, however, a fifth-year senior who transferred from Iowa named Jake Rudock, missed a few wide-open receivers for potential touchdowns, and threw three interceptions. One of them occurred in the middle of the fourth quarter, when a freshman ran the wrong route, which the Utes returned for a touchdown, helping to seal Michigan's 24–17 loss.

What Michigan fans couldn't see would probably have pleased them more.

After the game, a couple dozen members of the press collected in a glorified broom closet off the visiting locker room, to engage in a half hour of public sweating. The players they brought out—including Rudock and Butt—weren't thrilled that they had lost, but seemed more resolute than resigned.

Ten months later, Jake Butt told me why.

"It was the opening night of college football nationwide, and our first game with Coach Harbaugh—and we *lost*. In years past, when we lost, people would go out of their way to act more upset and angry than they really were. I mean, guys truly were mad that we'd lost, but part of it was to convince your friends, your teammates, your coaches.

"But when we lost to Utah, a lot of us really *were* crushed, because we really thought we were going to win. But in the locker room after, the first thing [Harbaugh] said to us is, 'I'm proud of you. That was a good effort, and we win as a team and we lose as a team. This does not define us. This will put steel in our spines. We are going to bounce back. We're going to get the next one.'

"When you get punched in the face like that, and especially in the first game, he really got to show what he was made of—and what we were going to be made of."

So, when Butt, Rudock, and others said versions of those things to the media, that's where they got it. They say a team is a reflection of its coach after three years. The role modeling at Michigan seemed to take one game.

When it was Harbaugh's turn to face the media, he delivered some of the same lines. When someone predictably asked him about Rudock's status, Harbaugh jumped on any speculation with both feet: "He's the starter, and it's not even close."

The contrast between Harbaugh's approach to Rudock and the previous staff's treatment of Gardner, a proven starter they let twist in the wind, could not have been greater. The players picked up on it, starting with Rudock.

"Whenever you have a coach who backs you," he told me, "that feels good, and makes a big difference. You don't need to look over your shoulder."

"When he said that about Jake, that was great," Butt said. "Who wants to wonder who the starting quarterback is? That doesn't help anyone.

"The leadership Harbaugh has brought is exactly the leadership we needed. And it's *all* true, about him as a person and a leader. Harbaugh is always looking to build the next guy up, and create an environment that makes guys want to succeed. Like he said, it's never one man's success when you get the win, and never one man's fault when you lose."

That basic philosophy would prove vital a few weeks later.

Of course, thinking like a winner and talking like a winner don't count for much if you don't start winning. That was Michigan's job the following week.

Harbaugh's old coach, Bo Schembechler, often said teams improved the most from the first game to the second—and that was a good thing for the Wolverines. They had Oregon State coming to town the next weekend, followed by UNLV and Brigham Young, which had just beaten Nebraska with a Hail Mary pass.

In Harbaugh's first official return to the Big House since playing his last home game in 1986, the crowd let him know how happy they were to see him back with a standing ovation.

"The *enthusiasm* was out of sight!" his mom, Jackie, recalled. "It was like nothing I had ever seen. It doesn't even compare to the years we were there—and those were good years! The students were so good. And at the end of the halftime show, the band did this little thing at the end, and it suddenly spelled out 'HARBAUGH'! And that's when it hit me: He's home! He's where he should be.

"I just thought, 'Gosh, to be able to sing that fight song again, one of the greatest fight songs in college football, feels so good!' Seeing all this, I just thought this is the way college football should be."

With 109,651 in the seats and millions watching, the Wolverines paid the crowd and the band back by blowing out Oregon State, 35–7, then knocked off UNLV the following week, 28–7.

Good wins, but against mediocre teams. In Michigan's previous ten games against ranked teams, they had beaten only one. So, when 22nd-ranked BYU came to Ann Arbor, they had their chance.

"We prepared *so* hard that week in practice," Butt recalled. "Oregon doesn't even wear *pads* in their practices, and we're out there grinding in the heat, Tuesday-Wednesday-Thursday—hitting in full pads.

"Yeah, we questioned it at first, but when we start buying in, we started winning, and then we started blowing good teams out. It was just a beautiful, beautiful thing. And the confidence kept building throughout the season.

"And this time it was a *true* confidence. Sometimes you can have a false confidence, when you convince yourself you're better than you are. I think that happened my freshman year [in 2013, when Michigan scraped past weak Akron and UConn teams], when we started out 5–0, but we weren't really that good.

"This time, we *knew* the team we were playing against could not have prepared harder than we had. From spring ball to game week, it just was not possible. The only thing they could have done is *match* our level of preparation. That's it. And if they did, then we'd have a game. But we'd be ready for that, too."

Michigan's offense ripped through BYU for 31 points in the first half alone. When the game was over, Michigan had outgained BYU 448–105, and notched its first shutout in nearly three years.

Against Maryland the next weekend, Michigan's defense held the Terrapins to a mere seven first downs, one-for-18 on third downs, and 105 yards total. The 28–0 final score marked Michigan's first consecutive shutouts since 2000.

After each victory, three generations of Harbaughs, plus uncles, cousins, brothers, friends from California, a few recruits, and their parents, would fill Jim and Sarah's house. (And, no, it is not an NCAA violation—until the NCAA reads this and concludes maybe it should be.)

"A little different than it was in my day," Jack Harbaugh told me, when the coaches went home to subdued celebrations. "But it wasn't like they were on stage when the recruits came over. It was all unscripted. Everybody would come in, somebody would put the tape of the game on, and everybody would ooh and ahh, and when we saw a play we found funny, we'd run it back and we'd run it back, and everyone would laugh and high-five each other. This fall, we went back to football. We were just having fun.

"In the Harbaugh household, no one—let me say that again, *no one*—enjoys a Saturday evening after a win as much as we do!"

After years of the Big Ten playing in the shadows of the Southeastern Conference, 2015 was already proving to be a heady time for the nation's oldest athletic league, with five teams ranked in the top 25.

Ohio State, the returning national champion, was the top-ranked team in the land. The Spartans were ranked second, until a sloppy win over Purdue dropped them two spots. But they were still undefeated, and would remain so after rolling over Rutgers the next weekend to set up another clash with their in-state rivals the following week.

The Big Ten's good news didn't stop there. The previous year, both North-western and Michigan had finished with 5–7 records. These days, failing to qualify for a bowl game is about as pathetic as not getting a birthday card from your mom. The lowlight for both teams was the game between them, when neither team could score in the first half, creating a TV scoreboard that seemed to spell "M-0-0-N." But going into their 2015 contest, Northwestern could claim a 5–0 mark, and a number 13 national ranking, while Michigan was 4–1 and ranked 18th.

The Wildcats were so bad for so long, they were everyone's favorite home-coming opponent. But since 1995, the Wildcats had won three Big Ten titles, behind only Ohio State, Michigan, and Wisconsin. So when Michigan invited Northwestern for—you got it—Homecoming, nobody thought it would be a cakewalk. In the previous three seasons, Northwestern had Michigan beat, then somehow found new and creative ways each time to lose in the waning seconds.

"They had a really good team, again," Butt said. "One of my best friends [Godwin Igwebuike] is their safety. They *always* play us tough. But this year, it was kind of like the BYU game: They came ready to battle, but we just stepped on their necks from the opening kickoff."

Jehu Chesson returned that opening kickoff 96 yards for a touchdown, the first time a Wolverine had done so since Darryl Stonum against Notre Dame in 2009. Michigan put up a 28–0 halftime score, and won 38–0, marking the first time Michigan had scored three consecutive shutouts since 1980.

After the game, Harbaugh told the press, "The fellas really came out bal-lin', right from the start."

After ten months of unprecedented buildup, it had finally arrived: the Mother of all Michigan–Michigan State games.

The rivalry had too often been dismissed as a regional affair, not a national showpiece, largely because the two teams had almost never been ranked at the same time. When one was up, the other was down.

The Spartans dominated the fifties and sixties, winning six national titles over those two decades. Bo Schembechler's teams ruled the state for the next two decades. In the nineties, Michigan State won four times, but always as the underdog, upsetting a top ten Michigan team each time.

But over the previous seven seasons, it had been almost all Michigan State. The Spartans spanked Michigan so badly the previous two years, whenever a Michigan fan said, "Good game" to a State fan, the State fan would complain that, sure, they'd won, but you know, they just didn't *play that well*. It was no longer enough merely to beat Michigan. Style points suddenly mattered to the Spartans. You got the feeling they were getting a little bored with the whole thing. The credit goes to Dantonio, who's done more with less than just about any coach in the country, beating up Michigan with a lot of players Michigan didn't want.

The previous year, one caller into WTKA, "the unofficial voice of Michigan sports," said waiting for the Michigan State game was like waiting for your dad to come home to punish you. A year later, Michigan fans were the ones looking forward to the annual backyard brawl.

Now, finally, both teams were ranked, and the nation was watching. Both teams had been ranked this highly only once before, back in 1999—when Nick Saban coached Michigan State, and Tom Brady quarterbacked the Wolverines.

It was hard to recall any Michigan–Michigan State game that seemed to mean so much to both sides. Spartan fans wanted to prove their success wasn't just a matter of embarrassing the overmatched Brady Hoke, while Michigan fans wanted to prove they really had returned, long before anyone thought they would.

This game was unusually hard to predict, because Michigan State, despite its perfect record, hadn't played its best football yet, while Michigan kept exceeding expectations every weekend. But a few things were certain: Whoever won this game would be ranked in the top ten the following week, and have a great shot at the four-team national playoff. And their fans would be insufferable for a year—almost as bad as the fans of the losing team.

And that's what a real rivalry looks like.

With ESPN's *College GameDay* on campus, the stage was set for a heavyweight title fight, one in which Michigan was favored by a surprising 7.5 points.

"It was just a different atmosphere around campus," Jake Butt recalled. "For the first time in a while, we felt like we had a really good chance. They were a really good team, but we *knew* we were going to win it. And it was a great game."

The Wolverines opened the scoring with a touchdown, and the Spartans countered six minutes later. The rest of the game, Michigan would land a shot, and Michigan State would follow—always keeping it close, but never quite catching up. It was less a game of mistakes than of great plays, on both sides of the ball.

When Michigan was on defense, Butt couldn't resist following the duel between Michigan defensive back Jourdan Lewis and Michigan State receiver Aaron Burbridge. "Man, that was a matchup for the ages! I don't know how much fans appreciate the technique Jourdan Lewis used, and Burbridge's catches. And [MSU quarterback Connor] Cook was dropping the ball the only place he could for a catch. All three of them, at the top of their game. They were going right after Jourdan, and he didn't back off."

In fact, Cook threw to Burbridge 19 times, to complete nine passes. Lewis prevented almost all of the ten incompletes, a performance that led Pro Football Focus to call him "the top shutdown cornerback in the country."

The Spartans outgained the Wolverines, 386 yards to 230, but trailed Michigan until the last play of the game. How was that possible? By relying on great special teams play, especially from Michigan's fantastic punter, Blake O'Neill.

O'Neill grew up in Melbourne playing Australian rules football, a game that requires unusual strength, stamina, and coordination. He decided to jump the ocean to play American college football, starting at Weber State in Ogden, Utah, where he earned a degree in communications.

"I liked it there," he told me. "Had a great coach, and it's a beautiful part of the country. But I wanted that big American college experience, and that big football experience—and for those two things, you can't get much bigger than Michigan."

When Harbaugh first met him during the 2015 off-season, he asked O'Neill to kick the ball. O'Neill replied, "Which way?"

The question was foreign to Harbaugh, who had never recruited an Aussie before. "We have a few more arrows in the quiver" than American kickers, O'Neill notes. He can deliver the ball high or low, left or right, or with a sidewinder motion. O'Neill also offered a choice of rotation: "Spin, backwards, rugby-style?"

Curious, Harbaugh wanted to see them all, and O'Neill obliged.

"He loved it," O'Neill recalls.

Harbaugh didn't need to think too long to make O'Neill the team's starting punter. In the first half of the 2015 season, O'Neill had been nothing short of spectacular, sticking half his 33 punts inside the opponents' 20-yard line, with only two touchbacks. Opponents had been able to return O'Neill's punts an average of less than two yards. In other words, they hadn't been able to return them at all—one key to Michigan's string of shutouts.

On O'Neill's first punt against Michigan State, Michigan had the ball on the 18-yard line. "I knew I didn't have a lot of time," O'Neill told me months later, "because they would be coming. But I knew the returner, who was quite good, was pretty close, and the flags told me I had the wind at my back, so I made the split-second decision to get it off quick and line it over his head. After that, it bounced and started rolling downfield.

"It wasn't 'til I had already run halfway downfield toward the ball that I realized I'd kicked it the length of the field. The crowd's roar kept growing, and when we downed it on the two-yard line, they were on their feet. I jumped and threw my fists in the air. My reaction was primal, overjoyed. To feel you've elicited that reaction from the 110,000 people, that you're all on the same page—well, that's about as good as it gets, especially for a punter, because you don't often have that much control over a game. That's not a moment many people get in their lives."

The punt went 80 yards, the longest in Michigan Stadium's 89-year history. O'Neill followed it up with two more punts inside the Spartans' ten-yard line. It was all the more impressive because Dantonio's teams are rarely content to sit back on punts, preferring to attack the kicker. When the game was winding down, Michigan's most valuable player of the game was probably the punter.

"I still think that's one of the best games I ever had," O'Neill told me.

As fellow fifth-year transfers, O'Neill and Rudock had already bonded, and became mutual admirers, on and off the field. "Blake's punts kept us in the game," Rudock told me. "He kept giving them a long field, and our defense kept giving us a shorter one. A battle like that, it makes a huge difference."

With 1:47 left, and Michigan holding a 23–21 lead, the Spartans faced fourth-and-19 from Michigan's 45. Connor Cook looked downfield, and, despite good coverage, tried to throw the ball into Macgarrett Kings Jr. When

Dymonte Thomas broke up the pass, the Wolverines joined the crowd's celebration.

"Everyone's going nuts on the sidelines," Butt recalls. " 'We won! We won!' But we had the ball on our own 45. There was, like, a minute and a half left. It wasn't done. I turned to them and yelled, 'The game's not fuckin' over!' "

Needing only a first down to run out the clock, but desperate to avoid a turnover, Michigan ran De'Veon Smith three times, for five, two, and one yards, to give them fourth down and two.

With ten seconds left, and the ball on Michigan State's 47-yard line, Michigan just had to punt the ball downfield to secure the win—arguably the Wolverines' biggest in this century-old rivalry.

And that set up one of the strangest plays in the history of college football.

In hindsight, Michigan might have done a few things differently, including lining up ten men to protect O'Neill, instead of putting two out on the left wing, against one Spartan. A few of Michigan's linemen brush-blocked, as if they were in a hurry to get downfield to tackle the returner, even though the Spartans hadn't put a returner on the field. Unlike most punts, on this one, they had only one job: protect the punter.

"State is known for coming after the punt," said Butt, who was on the line for that play, "even under normal conditions. We knew they were definitely coming this time. We could have used more protection. But regardless, we should have been fine."

I also wondered if perhaps O'Neill had set up farther back than normal, to give himself more time and space against an onslaught of Spartans, or if the snap had come in lower than normal.

"You keep trying to say that," he told me, refusing, with good cheer, to bite on the alibis I was offering, "but I set up where I normally did, and it wasn't a low snap."

Both true. Still, if O'Neill had caught it cleanly, he almost certainly would have gotten a quick kickoff, and the game would have been over. Even if he hadn't caught it cleanly, and simply smothered the ball, the Spartans would be left with one shot at a Hail Mary from midfield. But when O'Neill reached down to catch the ball, it bounced off his hands, and onto the turf. Instead of falling on it, he scooped it up, and tried to kick it.

During these crucial seconds, a few Spartans broke through Michigan's line, and were coming right at O'Neill. Until O'Neill saw the replay, "I thought I'd kicked it to the guy [Michigan State's Jalen Watts-Jackson, who caught the ball]. But when I saw the replay, you could see one guy grabbed my arm, hyperextending my right elbow, causing my wrist to hit the ball, and—in a miraculous act—the ball went right into [Jalen Watts-Jackson's] arms, like I'd pitched it to him. All kinds of places it could go, but that's where it went."

If the ball had landed just about anywhere else, it would have almost certainly resulted in a scrum, with Wolverines and Spartans fighting for possession, making it very unlikely anyone wearing green could have run the length of the field for a touchdown.

But the ball magically landed right in the belly of Watts-Jackson, who was already running full speed, surrounded by a handful of protectors forming a perfect escort down the field.

Jake Rudock had just left the field seconds before the snap. He'd been walking toward the sideline phone that goes directly to Jedd Fisch, the passing game coordinator, when he heard a ruckus. "The play was already going when I turned around. People were running the wrong way, toward our endzone, and I was trying to figure out what the hell just happened."

Jake Butt's perspective was a little closer. "I block my guy, but I didn't hear the punt, and I think, 'Oh shit.' I look back, and I see the ball bouncing around, from Blake to their guy."

Once Watts-Jackson secured it, and started running downfield, the closest Wolverines gave chase, with Butt leading the charge. "When I was running him down," Butt said, "I could *feel* the air coming out of the stadium."

As Watts-Jackson approached Michigan's goal line, with Michigan's defenders forcing him to the sidelines, he had to pick one of three options, and do so in a split-second: run out of bounds, around the 15-yard line, to give the Spartans a good chance at a game-winning field goal; cut hard right to get behind the charging Wolverines, and run for the far side of the goal line; or split the difference by making a slight cut inside to stay in bounds, stay in front of the defenders, and make a mad dash for the endzone. If he got caught, the clock would have expired, and the game would be over.

Watts-Jackson picked the third option, which put him right in Butt's sights. "I knew I would meet him near the goal line," Butt told me. "I just wound up [my right arm] to put my fist on the ball, trying to bust it loose." Butt executed his plan to perfection, delivering full force directly on the football. "I could feel it move a little, but he had the death grip on it. He was ready for it."

O'Neill, running downfield, saw the whole thing. "Hell of an effort by Jake to try and get there. I've got a lot of love for Jake, for running it down the whole way."

Butt was so close to catching Watts-Jackson that the two tumbled into the endzone together, which resulted in a dislocated hip for Watts-Jackson. And a touchdown.

"At that moment, lying in the endzone, I truly thought this could be a dream," Butt told me. "Just a bad, bad dream. This could not have happened."

Michigan fans had the same reaction: too shocked to be upset, standing still, their hands on their heads, in stunned silence.

In the press box, anyone who managed to say anything at all muttered the same thing: "I cannot believe what I just saw."

Afterward, Dantonio admitted, "You go from 10 seconds, a guy punting the ball [and] you're thinking, 'Okay, this is done.' And then all of a sudden, life gets flipped upside down."

But there were no flags, and there would be no replay. Michigan State's touchdown was good. The score was 27–23. The game was over.

That night, Will Hagerup posted this message on Facebook: "You just saw firsthand that punting is really hard. I challenge anyone to go catch a snap in 30-degree weather with 100,000 people watching. He had a terrific game and put our defense in great field position multiple times."

Six months later, from his home in Australia, O'Neill told me, "It's still a raw memory. I think I can remember just about every second. After the play, I grabbed some water on the bench, and headed for the tunnel, when someone shoved a [TV] camera in my face. Even then, I was aware I was in a moment that doesn't happen very often, to anyone—my second [such moment] of the day. I really experienced the tippy-top highs of elation, and the complete valley of devastation—all in one game.

"I just took a couple deep breaths. I didn't respond to the TV people, but I didn't stop, either. Just kept heading to the tunnel.

"When I walked into the locker room, I wasn't concerned about myself. I knew I'd be okay. But I felt I'd let the other guys down. I just wanted them to know, I tried my best, and it didn't work out. I didn't speak to the whole team, but I said that to a few guys, around the room, and a few guys came up to me. [Kicker] Kenny [Allen] was a big one for that."

Jack Harbaugh explained something few people who have not coached would think of. "From a standpoint of a coach, the most trying time is not preparing for practice or the press during the week, or what you're going to say to the team at the hotel on Friday night, or in the last five minutes in the locker room before you take the field. You can prepare for all those situations, and you should be prepared. That's your job.

"No, the most trying time is right after the game ends, because the one moment you can never be ready for is immediately *after* the game, because of how the game went. You can't predict it.

"And if you lost, the first thing is, you're mad! And you want to respond—and you can't do that! You blow up in front of the press, or your team, and you've just made everything much worse. You need a cooling-down period—and you have to do that in a few seconds."

Just seconds away from the biggest victory of Jim Harbaugh's first season at Michigan, he suddenly had to respond to the most heartbreaking loss Michigan had suffered in years. Just a minute after the game ended, there he was, in the middle of the locker room, to address his team. There could be no script for what he had to say next.

As the players remember it, he dispatched with any analysis in a few sentences. "He said, 'It's kind of a fluke, honestly,'" Rudock recalled. "'But that's football. These things happen, and that's why you play the full sixty minutes.'"

Harbaugh quickly pivoted to the future. "He said, 'This will put steel in our spines,'" Butt remembered, months later. "Almost chokes me up, thinking about the way he looked in our eyes when he said it. You could tell he was hurting, too. You know how badly he wanted it. We all did, every game, but this was a statement game."

In college football, unlike every other sport, you get exactly one chance each year to beat your rival. Then you have to think about it for a year, before you get another chance to wipe the blemish off your soul.

Despite the blow, as Butt recalls, "Coach stood there as a true leader, a champion and a winner, and showed us the way. Just like after the Utah game, he didn't blame anyone, and he shouldn't have. We dropped passes [against Michigan State], we had chances to stop their third downs, we could have converted more of our third downs. Shoot, we had three chances to get a first down, right there at the end, and we didn't get that done. It's never one man's fault, like coach said after the Utah game."

Probably no one was more impressed than O'Neill. "I like the fact that Coach's immediate response was to make sure this game 'Put steel in your spine,'" O'Neill told me. "It's easy to go, 'Woe is me, this is horrific, what'll we do?' Better way is to accept it and move onto the next week. And that's what he did. So that's what *we* did."

Months later, Harbaugh told me, "After the really unfortunate circumstances to lose that game, it was our team goal to come back and handle that better than any team had handled that before. That became our focus."

After Harbaugh finished talking to his team, he recalled, "I was looking to find [O'Neill], to make sure he was okay. When I got to him, he seemed okay. He asked me, in his Aussie accent, 'Do you think I'll take some flak for this?'"

Harbaugh couldn't help but grin, and reply with his own Australian accent. "My exact words were, 'Yeah, mate, I think you're gonna take some flak for this. But you'll be okay. Don't listen to it. All will be well.'"

O'Neill remembered the exchange the same way, and chuckled over it. "He found me, because he wanted to make sure I wasn't going to go the other way. We knew each other pretty well by then, but we'd never been through anything like that, so he couldn't be 100 percent sure how I'd take it. I appreciated him going out of his way to find me. I told him, 'You don't need to worry about me. I'm just sorry it worked out that way, and thankful of the opportunity to play.'

"When I asked him if I'd catch a little flak, his reaction was nice to hear! If we could joke about it, I figured, it couldn't be *that* bad, right? For a guy who hates to lose, he was a hell of a sport. Throughout the entire thing, he was a great support and resource for me."

If Harbaugh's reaction earned additional respect from the guys in that room, O'Neill's did, too. "If there's a way to handle a situation like that," Butt told me, "I don't think you can handle it any better than [O'Neill] did. That helped us, too. Something like that would have *crushed* us last year. But after that game, we had twenty or thirty guys come up to Blake and give him a pat and a hug. To see all the guys stand behind Blake, and the coaches, and to see him handle it the way he did—well, it's never good to lose, but it was cool to be part of something like that."

Arguably the two most impressive things Harbaugh's first team did both happened off the field: acclimating to his unconventional four-hour practices, and emerging from the Michigan State game more unified and determined than they had entered it. Their "football callous" was already thick enough to handle it, and getting tougher.

But, even with additional steel in their spine, getting back on the winning track would be no small trick. Historically, Backyard Brawl gives the winner a big boost, and takes the wind out of the loser's sails. After the previous ten Michigan–Michigan State games, the winners went on to win 48 of their remaining games, and lose only 24, while the losers went 21–40 the rest of the way.

Among college football coaches, the old saw goes, "Never let 'em beat you twice." In other words, don't spend so much time agonizing over a loss that you fail to prepare for the next game, and get beaten again. That was Michigan's next challenge, made harder because they had a bye week coming up. Instead of basking in a long-awaited win over their rival, a 6–1 record, a likely top ten ranking, and a shot at a national title, they had to spend the week trying *not* to think of the last game, while waiting an interminable two weeks for the next one.

"We didn't dwell on it," Butt said, "but we all wanted to get out there! We wanted to make someone pay!"

For Harbaugh, it wasn't that difficult.

"The next day," he told me, "I was thinking, if this season goes the way we want it to from here on out, than this could be the greatest season in the history of Michigan football. We couldn't win a national title—we had two losses—but we could win a Big Ten title, creating one of the greatest comebacks, and one of the greatest stories, in our history. And we have a pretty good history!

"Now, if we didn't do all that, it'd be just another season. But that would take one heck of the conclusion to the season, to win 'em all, wouldn't it? That was my motivation."

When they returned for their first practice that week, Harbaugh told them, "Losing always leaves a bad taste in your mouth. The only mouthwash for a loss is making someone else pay for it. One win is not going to do it, but we have to start with one. So that's our focus this week."

Harbaugh was very pleased with their response. "We came out and had some *very* focused practices, very crisp," he told me. "And the next week, game week for Minnesota, we were *laser*-focused."

Two weeks after the Michigan State loss, Michigan traveled to Minnesota to face a resurgent Gophers team, which had thrashed the Wolverines in the infamous "Shane Morris game" the previous season. The Gophers had more motivation in 2015, after head coach Jerry Kill announced he was stepping down due to epileptic seizures.

The Wolverines had plenty of motivation of their own, including a share of the East Division title if they won out. After suffering a historic setback, would the Wolverines fold the tents, as they had in recent years, or would they take the punch and come out fighting, as Harbaugh had been training them to do since their first four-hour practice?

The teams swapped the lead in the first half, with Michigan taking a 21–16 lead early in the third quarter.

"In the first six games," Rudock told me, "I'd felt my confidence and rhythm gradually improving, but it was on and off. It wasn't until the Minnesota game that I really got in a groove, and knew the light was staying on."

But late in the third quarter, Rudock tried to scramble for a few yards. "But the way the geometry and physics of the situation played out, I could see the play was not setting up well for me, so I just tried to get down."

He did, but not before two Gopher defenders got to him. "When my helmet came off, I'm thinking, 'That's usually not a good sign.' It was one of those hits that just hurt—hurt real bad—and I felt it in my neck and ribs. It hurt to move, and I wasn't breathing."

Once he was out of the game, he told backup quarterback Wilton Speight, "Just relax. Just play. Don't worry about the coach, or anything else. If there's a play you don't want to run, tell him now! Trust me, Fisch would rather *not* call it than have you in the huddle saying, 'Shit, what is this?' "

It didn't take immediately. Speight's first three passes were incomplete, resulting in three punts, while the Gophers took a 26–21 lead with 11:43 remaining. But with Harbaugh and Fisch giving Speight the plays he wanted, Speight found his own rhythm. On third and ten from Minnesota's 12-yard line, and about five minutes left, Speight threw a perfectly placed pass to Chesson in traffic, for a touchdown, and followed up with a pass to Amara Darboh for the two-point conversion, and a crucial three-point lead.

Down 29–26, Minnesota drove the ball to Michigan's one-yard line with two seconds left. Interim coach Tracy Claeys bypassed the field goal to force overtime, to try for the touchdown, and the win. In one of Michigan's most dramatic goal-line stands, the Wolverines broke through the line, stuffed the runner, and held their ground, for a gritty victory.

Harbaugh had promised them that, if they stuck with it, they'd be winning games in the fourth quarter, and here was proof.

"To be able to win a tough one, it's a great learning experience because it reinforces everything you tell them about never giving up, fighting to the end," Harbaugh said after the game. "That's the thing I'm most excited about. Our team has learned a very important lesson."

Six months later, the lesson seemed just as big.

"Against Minnesota, we battled back," Harbaugh told me. "The big thing, to me, was this: No one gave up. That's why I don't think anyone on our side was surprised we had a chance to win it at the end. And when we stuffed them at the goal line—man, that was *great*. A *thrilling* victory. The wonderful feeling of winning. Wonderful. Wonderful."

Against Rutgers the following week, Michigan's offensive line prevented Rudock from taking any big hits, paving his way to a career-high 337 yards passing, and a 49–16 shellacking.

The good news for Michigan obscured some serious bad news: Nose tackle Ryan Glasgow injured his left pectoral muscle, which would sideline him for the rest of the season. This, coupled with Mario Ojemudia's season-ending Achilles' heel injury against Maryland, Matt Godin missing a couple games in the middle, and Maurice Hurst getting banged up against Rutgers (not to mention Bryan Mone suffering a season-ending injury in August practices), reduced Michigan's greatest defensive asset, its front line, to a weakness. Unlike Ohio State, Michigan didn't yet have the depth to cover that many injuries.

Like Northwestern, Indiana had played Michigan tough the past few meetings, with nothing but close losses to show for it. The Hoosiers started the 2015 season with four straight wins, followed by five straight losses, with close calls against Ohio State, Rutgers, and Iowa. The Wolverines expected a game, and Indiana gave them one.

"The defense was working their asses off," Rudock said, "and that's a hard offense to defend. They go so fast and get so many plays off. The D already had three straight shutouts, but you knew that wasn't going to happen in this game. We knew we had to score points. So we put that on ourselves."

They did, jumping out to a 21–9 advantage before swapping the lead eight times. With about three minutes left, Michigan trailed Indiana 34–27, but no one in maize and blue doubted the outcome.

"It was everyone, collectively deciding, 'We're not going to lose this game,'" Rudock told me. "When we got into the huddle, I told them, 'We've got to do this. We've got to go down there and score, so that's what we're going to do.' We weren't frantic or panicked. We were focused and determined."

Butt confirms this. "Northwestern and Minnesota and Indiana always seem to play us tough," he said. "Beating us is always a big thing, so you're going to get their best. But this year, we *always* felt we were going to win. You compare that to our mindset last year against Nebraska. It got down a two-minute drill, and we just didn't succeed. But I don't know how many of us really believed we were going to, no matter what everyone was saying on the sidelines. Even games we did win last year, like Northwestern [10–9], I was nervous in the huddle.

"But this year, against Minnesota and Indiana, man, *no one* was nervous, no one was scared. We *knew* we were going to score. We *knew* we were going to win."

Facing fourth-and-goal from the five, with five seconds left, Michigan called a time-out to set up their do-or-die play.

"I could see the stands were emptying," Harbaugh recalled. "Their students were coming right down to the part of the stands where they could enter the field. You could see they were poised to rush the field, and tear down the goal posts. They were ready."

In these situations under Hoke, offensive coordinators Al Borges or Doug Nussmeier would give Gardner the play, and that was it, often setting him up for failure—à la the last play of the 2013 Ohio State game, when even the Buckeyes knew what was coming. In contrast, according to Rudock, Harbaugh and Fisch liked to give their field general two or three options, then ask him, "What do you want?"

Rudock turned down the first play, a quick throw over the line, for the second option, a pass to the endzone. "I just felt more comfortable with the second play. I'd run the same thing at Iowa."

"Okay," Harbaugh said. "We're going to do that."

"It was a basic out-pattern," Rudock recalled. "Jehu [Chesson] made a quick double-move off the line, then cut left. He had isolation.

"They brought a blitz, but we expected that, so we had guys back to protect me. They were still coming full-go, though, so I knew I had to get it off—no time to mess around—and I had to get it to him high, based on the route. But you're not thinking too much, just reacting, like you've been coached to do. You've done this before.

"When it left my fingers, I thought, 'He'll get that. Got it? Good. Cool. Now let's get the extra point.'"

Six months later, Harbaugh recalled the aftermath of that play. With the Indiana students ready to storm the field, "Jake hits Jehu, and even though that just meant we're going to overtime, and we hadn't won the game yet, the students alllll went back up to their seats. That was good to see!"

Despite a wobbly snap on the all-important point-after attempt, Blake

O'Neill caught the ball, and settled it down in time for Kenny Allen to punch it through the uprights. That tied the game at 34–34.

Rudock, hitting on all cylinders now, needed only two plays to score a touchdown in the first overtime, and one play in the second, to put Michigan ahead 48–41, which gave Rudock a stat line worth laminating: 33-for-46, just one behind Tom Brady's Michigan record of 34 completions, for 440 yards, with only one interception against six touchdown passes, breaking the Michigan record of four. He also became the second Big Ten player in the last 20 years to pass for six touchdowns and 400 yards. In the process, Chesson's four touchdown catches tied Derrick Alexander's Michigan mark, set back in 1992.

But the game wasn't over. The Hoosiers' offense battled back to Michigan's two-yard line, to set up the game's final play.

"Then on their fourth down," Jack Harbaugh told me, "the way [Michigan safety] Delano Hill played that was perfect. He kept the receiver in front of him, and when he saw him reach for the ball, he reached, too, and knocked the ball away. Well, that warmed this old defensive-back coach's heart! What a great play, perfectly executed."

After the game, Jim Harbaugh said, "If Jake [Rudock] doesn't play the way he does, we don't have a chance. All those attributes—talk about his accuracy; talk about his arm strength; talk about his durability, his toughness, he's intelligent—but I still go back to that one, he is just unflappable. It does not matter what the situation is."

From the day Harbaugh returned, Michigan fans openly hoped for a rerun of Schembechler's first season, 1969, when he took over a talented but soft team, toughened them up, and dropped a couple games along the way before beating an undefeated Ohio State squad that had won the national title the year before.

Amazingly, the almost exact same scenario seemed to be recreating itself, week by week. If both Michigan and Ohio State won their next games, the table would be set.

At Penn State, Michigan jumped out to a 21–10 lead before the Lions closed the gap to 21–16, with four minutes left. That's when Michigan's Jourdan Lewis responded with a wild, weaving 55-yard kickoff return. Six plays later, De'Veon Smith punched it in from the one-yard line, to secure a 28–16 victory. Great performances all, but Rudock was again the key, hitting 25 of 38 passes for 256 yards and two touchdowns, against one interception.

"In terms of respect and appreciation, [Rudock] left a deep, indelible warmth in our heart for him," Harbaugh said two days later, at his weekly press conference. "He is so tough. This past game, I mean, the toughness was on display. I know I've said it, and maybe saying tough as a two-dollar steak doesn't even give it real justice. This guy is tough as nails, hard as hen's teeth. He's been a godsend for our team."

By beating Penn State, Michigan held up its end of the deal. Undefeated Ohio State was already favored over visiting Michigan State, but when the Spartans announced, shortly before game time, that quarterback Connor Cook, who would be named to his third straight All-Big Ten team after the season, would not play, even Spartan fans thought the game would be a blowout.

Jack and Jackie Harbaugh couldn't make the Penn State game. That week, the wife of the late Doyt Perry—the Hall of Fame coach at Bowling Green (whose stadium is named after him), who mentored both Bo Schembechler and Jack Harbaugh—had passed away at 98. Their son asked Jack to eulogize his mother, and he accepted the honor eagerly.

After the reception, the Harbaughs planned to drive back to Jim and Sarah's house to watch the second half of the Michigan State–Ohio State game, but an icy storm kicked up, so they got a hotel room in Toledo, and went down to the hotel bar.

"Well, guess who's playing?" Jack recalled. "Michigan State–Ohio State! We were watching the game, having a few beers. The table next to us was all rooting for Michigan State.

"So finally I ask one of them, 'You're a Michigan State fan?'"

"No, hell no!" the man said. "I'm a Michigan fan!"

"Well, then you might be rooting for the wrong team," Jack said, knowing that Michigan needed Ohio State to win for a chance at the East Division title.

"I'll never root for Ohio State!" the man said. "And who the hell are you?" The question indicated he might not have been quite as big a Michigan fan as advertised.

Jack's eyebrows went up, in mild surprise, "but Jackie just looked at me, and said, 'Sit down.' So that's what I did."

Amazingly, the Spartans kept an overly cautious Ohio State offense to just 14 points, while their second- and third-string quarterbacks managed to put up 17 points for the upset.

After the game, Jack told his new friends, "We're Michigan fans as well, and it's always nice to see someone rooting against Ohio State. Go Blue!"

They returned to their room unrecognized.

Some speculated that, after squandering a golden opportunity against Michigan State, the Buckeyes would be in disarray for The Game.

When reporters asked Jake Butt, a native of Pickerington, Ohio, just outside Columbus, about that possibility, he quickly dismissed it. "I *guarantee* they will be ready to play. You don't take a day off for this rivalry."

During halftime, Ohio State's coaches did what they had failed to do against Michigan State: identify their opponent's weakness, and exploit it. Thanks to Michigan's weakened defensive line, its linebackers finally were exposed. Ohio State's coaches recognized this, and went after them to great effect, turning a 14–10 halftime lead into a 42–13 thrashing.

"The only time all season that you knew the other team exploited our roster was the second half of the Ohio State game," Michigan PR man Dave Ablauf said. "Every other game, our staff out-schemed and out-coached the other guys. But not that day."

"Ohio State won the game, fair and square," Butt said. "They played a great game, but we had awful timing on injuries. Down the stretch, our deepest position group, defensive line, became our thinnest, and against Ohio State, you need your best players. They had a great, great team."

"How can you possibly have twelve players go in the NFL draft," O'Neill said of the Buckeyes, "and not win every single game? They had incredible talent, and depth, and they finally showed it, against us."

Harbaugh's mid-season vision of winning Michigan's five remaining games to finish one of Michigan's greatest seasons vanished with the loss to Ohio State, but the Wolverines had plenty to play for in their Citrus Bowl matchup against SEC East champion Florida.

"I was just enjoying the team so much," Harbaugh told me in 2016, "and the way they had worked, and the way they were really gelling as a team—we had a bunch of guys you wanted to be around, and the coaches and staff were the same way—that I felt just as good about this season. I wanted them to go out with a win. They deserved it. I didn't want to spoil it all with a loss, and make that the last thing they'd remember about this season."

How do you increase your chances of securing a great season with a final victory? By working harder, of course.

"Oh my gosh," Butt said. "I know I sound repetitive, but after a long season, during the 15 bowl practices, a lot of teams back off. They know they're beat up—but not us. Coach Harbaugh put us through another spring ball. We were smart about it, not just knocking each other's blocks off, but it was every bit as hard as spring ball—and that's saying something. But this time, we knew it was coming. We knew how to handle it, we knew we *could* handle it, and we *would* handle it. And we did. We even laughed about it, calling it 'Christmas Camp.'"

Their "football callous" was fully developed.

Meanwhile, Michigan's players couldn't help but notice their opponent, the Florida Gators, "had guys dropping like flies," Butt recalls. "How many were arrested before that game? I guess you'd have to say they were not as focused as we were.

"In our practices, we were prepared for *everything*. And when we got to the game, *nothing* surprised us."

A few months later, Harbaugh told me, "I knew the morale was good when we were down there the first couple days for bowl prep practices. Man, it was hot, it was focused, it was tough, it was old school. We had hard practices. I knew we had the right attitude when the guys christened it 'Christmas Camp,' like spring ball or training camp—their third go-round of torturous training. It was that hard. Spring ball all over again, when nobody's having any fun—but you know you're getting better. You know when your muscles are sore, your face and your mouth and your tongue and your eyes are tired, you sweated and you ached, and when you laid your head on your pillow at night, you go *right* to sleep.

"So when they were calling it 'Christmas Camp,' in the spirit of good-natured bitching, they were joking about how tough it was, but they knew they could handle it, and they were having fun doing it. That warmed my heart like you can't believe.

"The night before the game, my head is hitting the pillow, and I'm thinking, *'We are ready to play!'*"

He was right about that. Despite being billed as a battle between two of the best defenses in the country, only one of them showed up.

In the game's first possession, Michigan's defense finally stopped Florida at Michigan's 20. When the Gators attempted a fake field goal, Michigan's defenders broke it up quickly, forcing place-kick holder Johnny Townsend into an ill-advised pass, which Michigan's Channing Stribling intercepted. The Wolverines scored nine plays later, and dismantled the Gators en route to a 41–7 stomping.

"It was a case of getting your rump kicked in," Florida coach Jim McElwain said. "That's what it was. They really took it to us on both sides of the ball."

"You could tell in their eyes—you could see they didn't want to play anymore," Michigan's Chris Wormley said. "They were down probably three scores by then, and it's just a good feeling, especially for a defense, to stomp on their throats."

"I would say this was the best game we've played all year," Harbaugh said after the game. "I don't think I've ever seen our offense play better. Our defense was magnificent."

In the third quarter, Michigan outgained Florida 160–2, and did not allow the Gators a single completed pass the entire second half.

"That was the first game I thought I could breathe this entire season, almost right off the bat," Sarah Harbaugh said, months later. "Not having to worry about every play was a relief! That was a fun game."

Rudock was named the game's MVP. He also became the first Michigan quarterback to throw for more than 250 yards in five consecutive games, and only the second, after John Navarre in 2003, to crack 3,000 yards for the season. If there was a better billboard for how Harbaugh and his staff could develop quarterbacks, it was hard to imagine.

The win marked Michigan's second 10-win season in a decade, and its first bowl victory in four years.

"That felt good," Butt said. "That felt really, really good! Oh my gosh! People were tired, we'd celebrated and we hadn't gotten much sleep. But after that long season, we got a chance to breathe a little bit. It was one of the best flights home ever! Not a thing to worry about—and a lot to think about."

For Butt, one thought eclipsed all the others: "Everything coach told us was true. He'd proved it."

Looking back, Harbaugh told me, "We did what we said we were going to do: Let everyone know Michigan was Michigan: tough, hardworking, competitive. When we won this game, I considered this season personally the most fun I've ever had as a player or as a coach. It just felt great to be a part of it."

But just minutes after the game, in the post-game press conference, he said, "Onward, 2016. This was the beginning of that year."

As usual, Harbaugh meant it. After the Citrus Bowl, everyone in the Michigan football program took approximately no time off, for anything. By the time the team plane landed, Michigan had already lost defensive coordinator D. J. Durkin, who was named Maryland's next head coach. Like his mentor, Bo Schembechler—who pushed 11 of his 36 assistant coaches to become head coaches—Harbaugh has not been afraid to hire very strong assistants, and help them become head coaches themselves.

Harbaugh replaced Durkin with Don Brown, who turned Boston College's defense, filled with two- and three-star players who were saddled with an anemic offense, into the nation's fourth-best in scoring defense, and first in yards allowed.

"Love him, love him, love him," Harbaugh said, during spring practice. "Had a meeting last night and had a nice partition in between the offense and the defense and the paint peeled off the walls. He is an intense man, a ball of fire."

Harbaugh focused next on the never-ending task of recruiting, hitting the road like no Michigan coach had before him. He not only logged record miles, but also climbed trees in recruits' yards and slept over at their homes. Harbaugh's rivals accused him of—well, just about everything. But none of it stuck, for two reasons: His conduct was well within the rules, and he was authentic. Harbaugh brings a child-like enthusiasm to everything he does, and if other coaches don't like it, Harbaugh is not likely to lose sleep over it. (You can, however, expect a new NCAA rule disallowing coaches from climbing trees higher than five feet.)

Beyond the tree climbing, Michigan got the most attention for recruiting a top five class, capped by the nation's most coveted prospect, Rashan Gary; for not recruiting Erik Swenson; and for tying it all up with another innovation: the Signing of the Stars event at Hill Auditorium.

Gary is the kind of prospect who might be able to star in the NFL—*now*. His work-out stats are already better than those of the average defensive lineman at the 2015 NFL combine. As Scout's Scott Kennedy put it, "He out-jumped a wide receiver, he out-shuttled a defensive back, and he out-40'ed a BCS safety commit. At 287 pounds, that's insane."

The competition for Gary was intense, with Clemson, Alabama, and other top programs in the hunt. But Gary would not commit until signing day.

Meanwhile, Harbaugh took some flak when he rescinded Michigan's scholarship offer for Erik Swenson, a lineman from Illinois. Nationally, the story played like this: Swenson had been offered a scholarship from Michigan, his dream school, when he was a high-school sophomore. He committed, and never looked anywhere else, until Harbaugh pulled the offer shortly before National Signing Day. The story was driven entirely by Swenson and his high-school coach, who were free to speak to reporters, while Michigan's coaching staff could not comment, by NCAA rules.

Most of what Swenson said was accurate: Michigan made him an offer during his sophomore season, he accepted, then Michigan decided not to save a scholarship for him. That narrative, however, leaves out some salient points, provided by interim AD Jim Hackett after the 2016 signing day had passed, when the NCAA's rule prohibiting schools from discussing recruits in public no longer applies.

When Harbaugh came on board in 2015, Hackett explained, he and his staff initially honored Hoke's offer to Swenson, but on three conditions: Swenson had to keep his grades up, he needed to come to Michigan's summer camp, and he needed to keep improving. By mid-season of Swenson's senior year, it was clear he would be fulfilling none of those conditions: His grades were not good enough to get into Michigan, he had refused to attend Michigan's summer camp, and his play was fading.

Hackett told me Harbaugh and his staff communicated these concerns to Swenson in the fall, when he had plenty of time to change course without losing face. But Swenson decided to wait it out, only to be disappointed—then publicly blast Harbaugh and his staff.

In the media froth that followed, the bigger point was largely missed: Harbaugh had once again exposed the silliness of the system. In this case, a world where coaches and players "verbally commit" to each other two, three, or more years in advance of the one day that commitment actually means anything, on either side: National Signing Day.

Not surprisingly, that far in advance, it's a difficult promise to keep for either side. That explains why more than 300 top recruits for 2016 flipped from one school to another before signing, and why every Big Ten school, including Northwestern, made more than 100 commitments that year, when teams generally have just 25 scholarships to give out.

Within that system, about the only sane way to approach it is the way Harbaugh did: by giving a conditional offer.

As Hackett told me, "We are committed to the authenticity and transparency of the process. We aren't certain [about you], because you're not certain [about us]."

In other words, Harbaugh had made explicit what had always been implicit in the system: If you keep up your end of the deal, we'll keep up ours.

There is only one feasible solution to this conundrum, which Harbaugh spelled out after he completed his next innovation: "Signing of the Stars," a two-hour gala on Wednesday, February 3, at a packed Hill Auditorium, where celebrities like Derek Jeter, Lou Holtz, John Harbaugh, and Michigan's own Desmond Howard and Tom Brady introduced Michigan's 2016 recruiting class. The event was fueled by the suspense of Rashan Gary's decision, who had still not indicated by the time the show started where he'd be going to school the following fall. Finally, near the end of the show, a cheer went up in the auditorium, when word spread that Gary had just picked Michigan on ESPN. Due to some NCAA rule or other, Harbaugh could not announce that, so the day's biggest news went uncelebrated on stage.

Afterward, Harbaugh met with the press in the downstairs lobby of the 103-year-old building. When asked about the nature of commitments, he cut to the chase: The early commitments, he said, require players to "keep getting better, to perform in the classroom, perform on the field, and perform as a good citizen. Also, part of that process is [us] letting them know that they need to get a grade-point up or retake a test or play better on the field. It certainly never includes somebody that's injured, that's something that's out of their control. But that is definitely part of it. We will continue to do a good job of letting them know where they're at, being honest.

"We want to be better today than we were yesterday, better tomorrow than we were today. I can say this: We did our best. There were mistakes made and I take full accountability for them. But I don't apologize [for them]."

The only solution to both sides offering commitments that were nonbinding—and therefore, not worth much—was to expand "signing day" to any day either side chose, to give both sides the option of making their commitment real whenever they liked. And if either side declined to do so, you're not married, you're just dating, and everyone knows it.

But the powers that be—including the NCAA, the SEC, and dominant programs like Alabama, which has recruited the top class the past six years, including 2016—like it the way it is.

Shortly after signing day, Jim Hackett stepped down. He had received a compensation package worth about half of Brandon's $1.2 million, and decided to give half of that, on his way out, to the Michigan Depression Center, the nation's first. The contrast to Brandon's departure, in which he accepted a $3 million buyout, was not lost on the public.

Not long after, Harbaugh shook up the old-world order again when he took his team to Florida over spring break for three days of training camp. As usual, the SEC commissioner and coaches created much ado about not much. It was hard to imagine how spending three of the NCAA-allowed 15 spring practices in Florida would affect anyone, but the SEC's paranoia over Harbaugh seems to know no bounds.

During the Brandon era, Michigan was adept at repeatedly and gloriously violating the simple, sage advice of Don Canham: "Never turn a one-day story into a two-day story." But this time, in a refreshing twist for Michigan fans, the people unwittingly stretching a nothing story into a weeks-long saga were Michigan's rivals, who were inadvertently placing a team that had won exactly one BCS bowl game in the new century on the same plane as a conference that had been dominating the sport for a decade. Harbaugh had managed to get the all-powerful SEC to do his promotional work for him, at no cost to the University of Michigan.

When Hackett, in the final weeks of his tenure, sent Harbaugh a photo of Michigan's practice field that week, buried in snow, he added the following caption: "Dear Jim, You're brilliant."

When the normally diplomatic Ohio State athletic director Gene Smith was asked if Ohio State might follow Michigan's lead, and conduct a few spring practices in Florida, he replied, "If we were jump-starting our program, I'd probably try that, too."

"It felt like one got shot over our bow," Harbaugh told reporters. "It wasn't a knee-jerk reaction. I waited a good eight, nine hours and figured they might consider that it could be construed a certain way toward our program. Actually, some of the scribes and pundits were [already] construing it that way. So when no explanation came, I thought it was time to fire one over their bow."

And so he did, in the following tweet: "Good to see Director Smith being relevant again after the tattoo fiasco. Welcome back!"

The tweet, like so many of Harbaughs, quickly generated tens of thousands of "likes" and "retweets."

Afterward, Harbaugh told reporters, "Consider things even right now."

Apparently, Smith concurred, as he apologized soon thereafter, and the issue died.

The exchange, like so many of Harbaugh's, attracted a ton of attention, and thrilled the Michigan faithful. "For seven years," one department official told me, "people were constantly taking shots at Michigan, and we never responded. It's not the 'Michigan Way.' We also didn't have much to say, because we hadn't been successful, so we just took it."

Not anymore.

Brandon and Hoke had reduced the spring game to a glorified practice, while charging fans a $20 "donation," for an official "University of Michigan seat cushion or kneeling pad." A few months later, the department disallowed the same cushion for stadium use, before caving into another backlash and allowing it, while blaming "inaccuracies . . . driven by social media"—in this case, its official Web site.

Hackett, Harbaugh, and Manuel restored the spirit of the spring game by making it an actual game, with two teams, two offenses, two defenses, plays, refs, and a scoreboard with a football score. They offered this to their fans as a gift, with no strings, or Allstate "Good Hands" netting behind the goal posts, providing one of the few times younger fans could get into the stadium. When the game came down to the last play, a stalwart goal-line stand reminiscent of the Minnesota game, the entire crowd and half the players jumped for joy. Just like in Schembechler's day, the winners got steak, and the losers ate hot dogs.

The striking conclusion was this: Brandon talked incessantly about marketing, and hired an expensive chief marketing officer from the New York Knicks, yet by the time he stepped down, it would be difficult to imagine any of Michigan's foes doing a better job of besmirching the "Michigan brand," on or off the field, than Brandon and his staff had done. There were a number of reasons for this, but the main ones are these: Brandon's ideas were artificial, out of sync with the culture, and insincere attempts to fool his fans for a few more bucks. When the fans objected, the department would backpedal furiously, which demonstrated time and again the department's habitual underestimation of the people it was supposed to be serving.

Harbaugh, who has taken no courses in marketing, held no jobs in the field, and does not even use the term "marketing," has proven to be one of the best marketers Michigan football has ever had. He has been generating enthusiasm almost every week, making it cool again to shout "Go Blue!" to the world's distant outposts. What's the difference? Harbaugh's ideas are organic, heartfelt, and designed to stir the souls of Michigan's faithful first and foremost. Some ideas make money, some cost money, but it all seems incidental to Harbaugh's mission of promoting football in general, and Michigan football in particular. His relentless authenticity is what Michigan fans are attracted to—and it works.

If you want a case study in marketing, there it is: Sincerity sells.

A year earlier, shortly after the 2015 spring game, Todd Anson was sitting with Jim and Jack Harbaugh in Jim's office, discussing some of Harbaugh's ideas, and the pushback he would inevitably face. Anson observed, "Agents of change are never the most popular people in the room."

"I like that!" Harbaugh said.

While Harbaugh was writing that down, Jack added, "Nor should they be." Jim wrote that down, too, in capital letters.

More than a year later, the phrase, "Agents of change are never the most popular people in the room, nor should they be," is still scrawled on Harbaugh's white board.

And that brings us to satellite camps. After running nine such off-site camps in 2015, Harbaugh began planning a greatly expanded tour of 30 or more in 2016—from Nick Saban's backyard in Alabama to Blake O'Neill's hometown in Australia.

"For every person who wants to make change," Hackett said, "there are a thousand people guarding the past."

Harbaugh was about to meet them—and in the process, inspire the NCAA to embarrass itself badly.

Mens sana in corpore sano.

Sound mind, sound body. A simple philosophy, which means exercise is good for the brain. In the late 1800s, when the Wolverines were just getting started, Michigan president James B. Angell hated big-time football, and just about everything that went with it. But the one argument he couldn't counter was "Sound mind, sound body." On that basis, he allowed the Wolverines to play. It's still a good reason, of course, so good Americans have expanded it to include women, thanks to Title IX.

True, the massive money big-time football and basketball programs now generate can easily eclipse the original motives for starting college sports. But for the vast majority of college athletes, that's why you play. A close second is the chance to go to college, something a lot of these athletes wouldn't have if not for sports.

Blue-chip recruits will get plenty of attention from the best coaches, no matter what the NCAA's latest rules are. But average players often can't afford to make trips to every school that might be interested in them, and the mid-level programs that might be interested can't afford to find them, either. Satellite camps can bring all the region's players and coaches together for a day or two, creating a convenient, cheap, and massive matchmaking service. In this way, it is meritocratic, a means of broadening options for student-athletes, and giving more of them access to higher education.

Obviously, the teams that conduct satellite camps are trying to get the best players to play for them. That's kind of the point, just like admissions departments have been sending their representatives to high schools across the nation for decades to drum up interest, find the best students, and help the best students find them.

Critics of satellite camps, led by SEC commissioner Greg Sankey, whispered this as if they were uncovering a sinister secret. Their critique carried about the same moral weight as accusing an admissions officer of trying to attract better students by meeting them. If Harbaugh, who quickly became the most visible proponent of satellite camps in the spring of 2016, was trying to hide his goal of getting good players, he probably shouldn't have invited rival coaches, reporters, and even the NCAA to watch.

With or without the satellite camps, programs like Michigan and Ohio State would get a lot of top players anyway. In 2015, Harbaugh's "Summer Swarm" of nine satellite camps drew 6,500 players, of whom only four signed with Michigan. The people who really benefit from satellite camps are the mid-major, Division II and III schools in the area, and the mid-level players they're recruiting.

Sound Mind Sound Body, started in Detroit in 2004, is one of the leading camps, hosting hundreds of mostly underprivileged high-school players, many of whom receive their first pair of cleats from the camp. They also work out for a dozen or so college coaches, from Grand Valley State to Kent State, and spend half their time in classrooms, learning life skills they'd need to succeed in school, and beyond.

For 2016, Sound Mind Sound Body had scheduled camps in six cities, from Los Angeles to Washington, DC. But after Harbaugh took his show on the road in 2015, the coaches down South took exception to it. The Southeastern Conference had a virtual monopoly on their talent-rich states. They didn't need a Big Ten coach coming down to tamper with a good thing—even if that meant limiting the options for the players themselves. Actually, limiting players' options was not a by-product of the Southern strategy. It seemed to be the whole point.

The SEC voted for an NCAA proposal to ban satellite camps, and the ACC joined in, which was not surprising. But it came as a shock to many of the coaches when their conference representatives at the Pac-12 and Big 12 voted for the ban, too, which seemed to run counter to their self-interest, not to mention the recruits'.

Washington State's Mike Leach told SiriusXM College Sports he believed all Pac-12 teams but UCLA and Stanford were against the ban, but the conference voted for it anyway. "I can't fathom how it's possible we voted to eliminate it," he said. "Whether it's smart, dumb, or in the middle, it's wrong. It's wrong. If we're even remotely close to what we say we are, that needs to be overturned immediately."

A few days later, Leach, who earned a law degree from Pepperdine, texted the *Seattle Times* with more. "The mission of universities and athletic programs should be to provide future student-athletes with exposure to opportunities, not to limit them. It appears to me that some universities and conferences are willing to sacrifice the interests of potential student-athletes for no better reasons than to selfishly monopolize their recruiting bases.

"I will be fascinated to hear any legitimate reasoning behind this ruling."

Of course, there wasn't any. It turned out that UCLA athletic director Dan Guerrero, who had been designated by the conference commissioner to represent the Pac-12, was the only conference AD against the satellite camps. Nonetheless, he ignored the stated wishes of the other 13 member ADs, and voted for the ban. When this discrepancy surfaced, he had some explaining to do.

With the Pac-12 and Big 12 initially voting for the ban, the morally challenged NCAA ended satellite camps, because of—well, they didn't give a reason.

Tommy Tuberville, who coached Ole Miss, Auburn, and Texas Tech before taking his current post at Cincinnati, made the same point. He told

ESPN, "I think you'd have a small amount of coaches in some of the Power Five conferences say, 'Let's don't have them,' but there's more than just the Power Five here that's being affected. You've got all the smaller conferences, [and] you have the thousands of student-athletes that are really being cheated out of the opportunity to be evaluated by more college coaches.

"I just can't imagine, of all the rules in my 35 years of coaching college football, that this was even voted on, because it just doesn't make any sense for the players. Surely we've got more sense than this."

You'd think so—unless you'd actually studied the modern history of the NCAA. The same week the NCAA announced the ban on football satellite camps, off-season satellite camps were already well underway in virtually every sport but football. It seemed to have become an organization that no longer adhered to any principle more substantial than the direction the wind was blowing—except perhaps self-preservation, which matters here because the NCAA is terrified of the SEC splitting off, and taking the ACC and other Power Five conferences with it.

"Sound Mind Sound Body" is not only the name of the do-gooder camp the NCAA just banned, but the foundation on which the NCAA was built back in 1905. Whether that basic principle still matters to the people running college athletics remains to be seen.

Naturally, in the wake of the NCAA's decision, Harbaugh himself became the favorite topic for sports talk nationwide. Within Michigan, he was probably the most popular first-year coach in school history since Fielding Yost, back in 1901. But outside the state, much of it was negative.

"I don't listen to sports talk, or read the papers, but you can't avoid all of it," Sarah Harbaugh said, in a two-hour conversation with her husband in his office. "I get upset when people on the radio are talking like they know him, and they've never met him. People are quick to judge. The good thing about him is, he doesn't worry about almost anything: the pressure, the media, the public reaction. You have to be a certain type of person to stand all that pressure, and not consider it pressure. The good thing is, it doesn't bother him at all."

When she said this, Harbaugh grinned and shrugged.

"What wears most people out is the pressure to perform, and I always really liked it," he said. "The competition, embracing the pressure of it. Man, there's nothing better. Ever since I was a little kid, I always wanted to be the pitcher, the point guard, the quarterback. Give me the ball! I want the pressure! It's life-giving energy."

Sarah continued, "So when I run across something I know is not right, I'll say, 'Did you see this?' And it's not even a concern for him. If he did get congested with all that, he'd never be able to work. His mind expands to come up with all these ideas—all day, every day—that if he was worried about what people said about him, he couldn't do what he does."

That includes his wife, who often plays devil's advocate when a story breaks.

"Initially, I tend to take the other side," she said. "So when the NCAA banned the satellite camps, I asked him, 'What did you do wrong? Why are you doing these camps that are illegal?'

"He said, 'They're not. No one's done it before—not like this. That's the problem.'"

"People think they know you," Jim explained, "but they don't really know you. So, when people don't know you, you can't really worry about what they think about you. I've always been from the school that says, 'Sticks and stones will break my bones, but words can never hurt me.' That school still works for me!"

After the NCAA announced its ruling, Harbaugh didn't say much about it, because he didn't have to. The backlash against the NCAA's hypocrisy was deafening. The leaders took such a beating that, within a month, they decided to reconsider the ban—and elected to drop it, altogether, providing no more reasons than they had in banning it. Harbaugh wasted no time gloating, because he was too busy resurrecting his tour.

If the NCAA had stuck to the ban, Harbaugh would have had a dozen other ideas ready to go. The man is a veritable idea machine. During a two-hour interview in the spring of 2016, at least a half-dozen times he excused himself to walk out to the desk of his administrative assistant, Zach Eisendrath, to have him record another idea that had just popped into his head. Eisendrath wrote these down in a legal pad designated for that purpose, in which he had already filled three pages with his boss's ideas.

In May of 2016, when Jim and Sarah Harbaugh served as the honorary chairs of the University Musical Society's "Ovation" gala, surrounded by world-class musicians, donors, and university leaders, Harbaugh was asked to say a few words. After thanking UMS president Ken Fischer, Harbaugh said, "We believe, as parents and as a coach, in the development of the whole person.

Students should be exposed to everything U-M has to offer, and UMS and the arts are a vital element of the Michigan experience."

It wasn't lip service. Harbaugh went on to brainstorm on the spot, deciding at that moment that some of his satellite camps would include other Michigan teams and groups. Then he followed through just a couple weeks later, bringing the lacrosse, volleyball, and cheerleading teams to Indianapolis; lacrosse and cheer to Baltimore; and the band to Paramus High School in New Jersey. He was in perfect sync with Ken Fischer's maxim, "Everybody in, nobody out"—a noted contrast to Brandon's approach, which usually promised exclusivity for the elite.

No, Harbaugh was not a messiah, a savior, or a king. He was a coach, and clearly a very good one, but something more: an agent of change. Of all the traits he brought to Michigan, that one would attract the most attention, and make the biggest difference. Harbaugh was stirring the pot, and having a good time doing it. He seemed to be enjoying it just a little more, too, because he was doing it all in his old backyard.

On Friday, March 11, 2016, Ann Arbor Pioneer High School held a banquet to honor its native sons, John and Jim Harbaugh, and induct them into the Hall of Fame. The gym wasn't just packed. It was packed with seemingly everyone the two brothers knew from the time they moved to Ann Arbor in 1973, to that day: former teachers and coaches, teammates and rivals, and hundreds of friends—a modern version of the old TV show *This Is Your Life*.

While the program called for WTKA hosts Sam Webb and Ira Weintraub to emcee the show, and the two brothers to take a few minutes of questions, both were asked to speak, on the spot, with no preparation. John was his typically poised, composed self, and did an excellent job. But Jim stole the show by giving perhaps his best speech. He looked out into the room, and started addressing all the tables near the front, calling out his former coaches and teammates, and telling stories about them. He got laughs for each one— and always at his own expense—but he wasn't playing it just for laughs. It was unforced, sincere, and self-effacing, with the revered coach confessing his imagined sins in front of a thousand pastors, generating warmth and appreciation.

"Mr. Nordlinger, you were one of my first coaches, and one of my best. You were always on my side, and you always seemed to like me—back when no one seemed to like me! It was a great gift, and I have never forgotten that."

This confirmed Jack Harbaugh's observations from Jim's introductory press conference: "When Jim's in Ann Arbor, when he walks into a room, he doesn't see a face he's trying to place, he sees an old friend. He sees a story. [At Pioneer's Hall of Fame banquet] he'd pan the room, and he'd see John Nordlinger, and he had a story. That could have never happened in any venue but that one."

Turns out, Dorothy was right: There's no place like home.

By the summer of 2016, the first question had been answered: Jim Harbaugh's return to Michigan was working very well, indeed, better than just about any Michigan fan could have hoped. The team had notched its second ten-win season in ten years, and finished ranked ninth. While many fans were taking 2015's 10–3 record as a baseline expectation for 2016, it's worth remembering Michigan's 2015 team had to pull off last-minute comebacks against Minnesota and Indiana to hit that mark. Further, the 2016 team would face Wisconsin at home, and Iowa, Michigan State, and Ohio State on the road. The Wolverines would be led by another new quarterback, most likely John O'Korn.

Still, Harbaugh's fifth-ranked recruiting class boded well for the future, and he showed no signs of letting up on the recruiting trail in 2016. Academically, his players set Michigan records for the highest APR score, which earned them national recognition for excellence.

If anyone doubted Harbaugh would lead Michigan back to the promised land, on and off the field, they weren't talking.

That brings us back to the second question: How many years will Harbaugh remain in Ann Arbor? On the book tour, that question was by far the most popular. Fans asked out of both fear and hope: fear that Harbaugh would leave after a few years, and hope that he would finish his career in Ann Arbor.

The fear is real enough. Harbaugh gave his previous three teams a solid four years, but no more, leaving for a bigger position each time. Further, the more emphatically Harbaugh answers the first question—"Can he succeed at Michigan?"—the more likely NFL teams will try to lure him back.

Michigan fans will likely have to get used to the idea that, every time Michigan wins on Saturday, and any NFL team loses Sunday, the Monday sports talk shows will start rumors that Harbaugh will be going to one of those NFL teams. Just a few games into Harbaugh's first season at Michigan, established reporters in Indianapolis were already doing just that. But if Harbaugh didn't return to Michigan for the money in the first place, why would he leave for it?

Beyond the temptation to see if he could win a Super Bowl, like his brother, the next likely reason to leave Michigan would be an unnecessarily difficult work environment. NFL coaches face ungodly pressure to win games that usually pivot on just a few plays, but they don't deal with recruiting, academic eligibility, NCAA compliance, or the many competing demands that college coaches must balance on their campus, including faculty, lettermen, alumni, donors, and the like.

None of that seemed to bother Harbaugh in his first year at Michigan, and some of it he actually liked. As one of Harbaugh's closest associates, attorney John Denniston, told me, "Jim doesn't like to recruit. He *loves* to recruit." If that sounds like hyperbole, you might consider the 22-state, 38-stop satellite tour, which Harbaugh described as "more fun than you can possibly imagine, like a pig in slop."

The only issue on that list that would seem to present a compelling reason for Harbaugh to leave is the health of Michigan's athletic department. When people on the book tour asked me to predict how long Harbaugh would coach Michigan, my answer was simple: It depends on his relationship with the next athletic director.

On January 29, 2016, when President Schlissel introduced Warde Manuel as Michigan's next AD, he was giving Michigan probably the best chance to retain Harbaugh long into the future. Unlike the bizarre process that ignored the search committee's input to select Dave Brandon in 2010, or the more common emergency calls that resulted in Michigan presidents naming Bill Martin, Jim Hackett, and others to the post, the process in 2016 was unhurried, thorough, professional, and rational, from the selection of the highly regarded Turnkey Search firm, the sincere inclusion of a search committee, the complete lack of leaks, and the vetting of an impressive raft of candidates, including Boston College's Brad Bates, Colorado State's Joe Parker, and Connecticut's Warde Manuel, all experienced athletic directors with strong Michigan ties.

The selection of Manuel marked the first time Michigan had selected an AD who had worked in an athletic department before since U-M named Bo Schembechler to the post, in 1988—with six ADs in between. It also marked the first time Michigan had hired a sitting athletic director . . . ever. As with the hiring of Harbaugh, when hiring the next athletic director, Michigan's leaders decided they no longer had the luxury to experiment. They had to get a proven success. Manuel had it all: a former teammate of Harbaugh's who is steeped in Michigan tradition (with three degrees, including an MBA), with tenures at two Division I schools, and the backbone to provide private counsel to his coaches and staffers when needed.

He also brought Harbaugh's passion for his alma mater. At Manuel's introductory press conference, he recounted the first phone call he had received from Michigan about the position, asking if he might be interested. He answered, "Oh, *hell* yes!" The negotiations sounded very similar to those Michigan conducted with both Hackett and Harbaugh, appealing to heart over mind.

But in the same way the celebration over Harbaugh's arrival papered over problems Hoke had left behind, Manuel's hiring obscured many issues Brandon had created, chief among them the loss of loyal, experienced employees, and the hiring of more than 200 new employees, many of them inexperienced, with no ties to Michigan, and often overpaid. The result: a department in dire need of restructuring (or, perhaps, reverse structuring), and a severely bloated budget.

With 143 employees leaving the department during Brandon's four years, updating their stories alone would fill several chapters. But a few representatives can suggest the whole. The vast majority of those who left found decent positions elsewhere, usually after a year or so of job searching and soul-searching. They were often forced to leave the University of Michigan, college athletics, or both. The list includes Jamie Morris, who now cohosts an afternoon radio show called *The M-Zone* on WTKA; former department CFO Jason Winters, who is now a principal with Plante Moran's management consulting practice; and former ticket manager Marty Bodnar, who has returned to practicing law at Pear Sperling Eggan & Daniels, one of Ann Arbor's oldest firms, while volunteering to help U-M's student-athletes prepare for the real world. But no one who left has forgotten what they went through, even if they've worked to see the bright side.

"I just felt sad that the University of Michigan community had to endure the Brandon era," Bodnar told me. But, he said, through the rocky process, "we learned that we truly value community and teamwork [at Michigan]. Warde Manuel and Jim Harbaugh are returning us to these past values."

Some former employees have stayed in college athletics elsewhere, including Kurt Gulbrand, who is now associate athletic director at the University of

Colorado, and Joe Parker, who was named the new athletic director at Colorado State, where they are building a new $220 million football stadium, currently on time and on budget.

Others found positions elsewhere at the university, including Mary Walker, who is now the campaign director at the University Musical Society, and former men's soccer coach Steve Burns, who, after working for Northwestern Mutual financial services for three-plus years, found a good fit as the director of global engagement at U-M's Alumni Association.

"I love it," he said. "Many describe this as the perfect job for me, a guy who is loyal to Michigan, bleeds blue, and has it indelibly stamped onto my DNA. Being hired by the Alumni Association showed me and my family that one man's opinion can never measure up to the greatness of an institution like ours."

If leaving Michigan was hard, especially just a year removed from being named National Coach of the Year and turning down head coaching jobs elsewhere to stay at Michigan, Burns's career spent building Michigan's men's soccer program has not gone unappreciated by his former players, at least. Last year, while he was attending a leadership seminar at the Aspen Institute, he was dashing to the program's final lecture when he received a call from one of his former players, Tom Gritter, the captain and offensive MVP of Michigan's first varsity team in 2000, who now sits on the board of the Letterwinners M Club. Seeing Gritter's name, Burns took the call, and was surprised to learn the board had voted to award him an honorary letter jacket, one of the very few they award each year.

"The emotions and gratitude just poured out of me," Burns said. "I never ever considered receiving a letter jacket. From all my time on campus as a student, when I was fiercely proud of representing Michigan as a club soccer player, and during my time coaching, awarding almost 100 jackets to our players, I had letter-jacket envy. And here was an act by a select group that wanted to recognize me for my contributions to soccer on our campus. What an honor! It allowed me to continue to hold my head high about an institution that gets it. And it brought me to tears."

A year after Brandon let former men's tennis coach Bruce Berque go in 2014, Berque took a position as an unpaid assistant at the University of Texas. In 2015, Texas promoted him to associate head coach, a paid post, one notch below head coach.

"Having a job that I enjoy again has made it a lot easier for me to move on mentally and emotionally," he told me. "While my experience at Michigan has no doubt left a scar, it has faded with time, and has been a good reminder for me of the importance for coaches to model the behaviors we preach to our athletes about focusing on what we can control, and on the responses we take toward the obstacles that come in our path. Of course, this is easier said than done, and I still feel bad for the many great coaches and people who had their careers cut short, and were not as fortunate as I was to be in position to take some time off until the right opportunity became available." He's happy at Texas, but hopes to become a head coach again.

After Brandon pushed aside longtime communication leaders Bruce Madej and Dave Ablauf, and fired Pete Skorich after one year on the job, Brandon himself resigned a month later. In his absence, the department soon hired Stanford's Kurt Svoboda to become the associate athletic director in charge of "external communications and public relations," before the 2015 season. Madej became a consultant to the department, while his protégé, Dave Ablauf, had returned to lead communications for the football program, at Harbaugh's request.

Longtime equipment manager Jon Falk had little choice but to accept a buyout in the summer of 2014, but when Harbaugh invited him to come to Minnesota for the battle of the Brown Jug, which Falk has taken special care of for decades, he eagerly accepted. When Michigan's defense made the dramatic stop on the goal line for the victory, "I cried," Falk told Angelique Chengelis, of the *Detroit News*. "I'm 66 years old, and I cried. The players who knew me before I left put their arms around me and said, 'Big Jon, we got that jug back for you.' I said, 'No, you didn't. You won that for Michigan.'"

A few months later, in early 2016, Falk visited Harbaugh in his office. Harbaugh told him, after Brandon's equipment manager, Brad Berlin, left, "You know, Jon, we have an equipment problem. What are you doing?"

"My wife [Cheri] and I are going to Corpus Christi with our dog," Falk told him. "Jimmy, I promised her a trip."

"She's going on a trip," Harbaugh replied. "It's just going to be to Florida."

Before the team traveled to Florida for the practices at IMG Academy, Chengelis reported, Harbaugh asked Falk speak to the team.

"Men, let me tell you one thing," Falk told them. "When Michigan football calls for help, you come back no matter what. That's why I'm here. That's what I was taught in 1974, when Bo said he wanted me in the locker room talking about the passion, desire, and dedication needed to play for Michigan."

Falk considers Harbaugh a breath of fresh air. "That's the thing I've noticed with Jim," Falk said. "He's made football fun here at Michigan. The players love it. They love to be together and play football."

While most who left the department found new positions, and often new careers, many were not as fortunate. Charlie Green worked at Michigan for 52 years, his last post as the general manager of the golf course. When Brandon pushed him out in 2012, Green was heartbroken. Shortly after he left, he was diagnosed with pancreatic cancer. In May of 2016, Green's many friends launched a GoFundMe campaign to help defray the costs of hospice care. As of this writing, three weeks after the fund started, 198 people donated almost $20,000. "Thank you," the Web site said, "for supporting one of Michigan's all-time great ambassadors and friends at a time of true need."

After taking the 2015 season off, Brady Hoke accepted the University of Oregon's offer to become the Ducks' defensive coordinator.

Shortly after stepping down as Michigan's interim athletic director, Jim Hackett announced he had accepted a new position at Ford Motor Company, on whose board he has served since 2013, to be the chairman of a subsidiary called Ford Smart Mobility LLC. Annette Howe, who had served as Brandon's administrative assistant at both Domino's and Michigan, accepted Hackett's offer to join him at Ford.

In the spring of 2016, the University of Delaware hired former associate athletic director Chrissi Rawak, who served as the "right-hand man" for both Brandon and Hackett, to become their next athletic director, the first woman to hold the post.

Shortly after being installed by Bain Capital to become the next CEO of Toys"R"Us, Dave Brandon made headlines by deciding to sell the chain's flagship store in Manhattan, then hiring office workers from India to replace the Americans who had been doing those jobs for years. He did so under a temporary work visa program that had been designed to bring in foreigners with specialized skills. At Brandon's Toys"R"Us, however, it was being used to help move jobs overseas.

Christine Brigagliano, a lawyer with extensive experience advising American companies on obtaining visas, told Julia Preston of the *New York Times*, "At the very least, those are violations of the spirit of the law."

"At the Toys"R"Us headquarters on a leafy campus by a reservoir here in New Jersey," Preston wrote, "someone dressed as Geoffrey the Giraffe, the retailer's mascot, often wanders around greeting employees to bolster company spirit. But the mood was hardly playful on the morning of March 3, [2015,] when a company vice president summoned nearly 70 employees to a conference room and told them their positions would be transferred by the end of June to workers from TCS," an outsourcing company.

"'We were asked to cooperate and show them respect and train them to do our individual job functions,' said a former accountant, 36, who had worked for the toy seller for almost 12 years. But, she recalled, 'If you didn't cooperate, you would be asked to leave.

"'I felt like, "Why am I sitting here showing this man how to do my job when they are taking it away from me and sending it to India?"'"

Many former Michigan athletic department employees readily sympathized with the plight of the veteran Toys"R"Us employees. While there were certainly strong parallels, there were two important differences: The replacements at Michigan were fellow Americans, and they were often paid much more than the people they were replacing.

Brandon's hiring by Toys"R"Us stopped his $3 million buyout at $1 million, which allowed the department to break even in the fiscal year 2015–16. In fact, increased payroll is the biggest reason Warde Manuel inherited a bloated budget, one that expanded from $108 million in expenses in 2011, Brandon's first, to $161 million for 2017. The largest chunk of the $53 million increase is payroll, which has now almost doubled from $33 million to $62 million during that same span. (While Hackett and Manuel have both started trimming it back, contracts and employees are not typically easy things to reduce, and stand as Brandon's legacy.) True, some of the increase is due to the new football coaching staff, which costs Michigan millions more than Hoke's staff, which costs millions more than Rodriguez's. But the lion's share of the budget increase is due to the department increasing from 261 employees to 341, usually at substantially higher salaries than those they replaced.

According to the department's latest budget, the $10 million annual operating surpluses Martin's group regularly produced have been reduced to a break-even operating budget for 2015–16—and that's with the considerable bonus of Harbaugh filling the stands and the skyboxes, which were in danger of emptying without him. The picture is no prettier for the 2016–17 budget. Although the department expects to come out $800,000 in the black, that's due largely to eight home games on the schedule (typically worth $4–6 million each) and the new Nike contract. The following season, 2017, Michigan will have only six home games, with Michigan's game against Florida in Dallas. That schedule will create more financial difficulties, unless something is done about the increase in staff and payroll Hackett and Manuel inherited.

The timing of this top-heavy budget is particularly unfortunate due to three additional major expenses that are hitting all college athletic programs this year: 1) Schools being required to pay more of the total costs for the athletes to attend, not just room, board, books, and tuition; 2) unlimited meals for student-athletes; 3) increase in travel costs, due partly to conference expansion. However, if Michigan was still turning out annual surpluses of $10 million and more, with a far more digestible budget of $108 million, these new costs could be readily absorbed.

Two more takeaways: The 2014 season was an even bigger financial debacle than first imagined. Although both Michigan's 2014 and 2015 football schedules had seven home games, ticket revenue alone in 2014 fell $8 million short of 2015's. One reason: reducing student ticket prices, which reduced revenue but was clearly the right thing to do. But most of the ticket-revenue drop was the result of empty seats, thousands of them. While Brandon's administration maintained they continued the streak of 100,000 crowds in 2014, it did so by giving away millions in tickets, or leaving them unclaimed. (If you want to find the simplest justification for paying the new coaching staff more, there it is.) It's worth noting here that in 2009, when Michigan went 5–7, the department built a surplus of $10.6 million, and in 2010, when the Wolverines went 7–6, a $17.7 million surplus. Thus, Michigan's current fiscal problems cannot all be put at Brady Hoke's feet, but if he and Brandon had remained in their posts through the 2015 season, with growing unhappiness among the fans, the department would be drowning in red ink, and perhaps losing a generation of fans in the process. That, of course, provides another strong justification for reducing student ticket prices, and even scaling that for students on financial aid. Better to make it affordable now, and keep them for life.

When I presented these budgets and bullet points to a financial expert who has a working knowledge of Michigan's finances, he confirmed my findings, and added, "Upon reflection, if Dave [Brandon] had tried to sabotage the budget, he couldn't have done a better job."

Of course, Michigan's financial problems are no longer Brandon's. After accepting the Toys"R"Us position, he and Jan moved to midtown Manhattan, where they live in a $45,000-a-month apartment. At Brandon's request, the company bought a private jet, one large enough for Brandon to stand up in. In the spring of 2016, his real estate agents announced that both "Ever After," their Ann Arbor home, and "Camp David," their Arizona estate, were on sale, at $6.95 and $8.375 million, respectively.

One of Brandon's greatest desires as athletic director was winning the Directors' Cup, which goes to the school with the best NCAA tournament finishes in all sports in a given year. He spent unprecedented millions on the "Olympic sports," and, according to one employee, "The coaches, Dave drove them into the ground, with all the demands he placed on them. And all for the Directors' Cup."

After finishing a sterling fourth place in 2012–13, one of Michigan's seven best finishes, the department slipped to 15th the next year, and 19th the next, in 2014–15. In 2015–16, under Hackett and Manuel, Michigan finished third. Some of the 12 Michigan's teams that finished in the top ten had been hired by Brandon, including water polo and women's swimming and diving, but most had been hired by Brandon's predecessors, including Red Berenson, Carol Hutchins, and wrestling's Joe McFarland, all of whom had exceptional years.

After a tumultuous senior year, in which Hoke's staff used Devin Gardner as the starting quarterback, the backup quarterback, and a wide receiver, Gardner went undrafted in the 2015 NFL draft. He was invited to New England's camp, then Pittsburgh's, but was released by both teams. As of this writing, the two-time Michigan graduate was a free agent, while coaching for former teammate James Rogers on the Madison Heights, Michigan, high-school football team staff. Given Rudock's progress under Harbaugh and his staff, it is not hard to imagine what Gardner might have achieved under the new administration.

Russell Bellomy, the quarterback from Texas who saw action for three years at Michigan, transferred in 2015 to the University of Texas at San Antonio, where he played a few games at quarterback. He is currently pursuing his MBA at UTSA, and spent the summer of 2016 as an MBA intern at American Airlines headquarters in Dallas with the capital planning group.

After graduating, he wrote me, "the pride I take in representing my degree from the University of Michigan has more than quintupled. It is a tremendous honor to carry on the unrivaled legacy that is Michigan football, and even a bigger honor to be permanently tied to the most prestigious public university in the country. Always and forever, Go Blue."

Will Hagerup graduated in 2015, and took a position on the business side of Fox Sports in Chicago. In October of 2015, he shadowed Dave Brandon for a day at Toys"R"Us headquarters in New Jersey. "We continue to stay connected," he told me, "and I am as grateful today for his mentorship as ever."

Years ago, Hagerup said that committing to Michigan was probably what it would feel like when he proposed. In 2015, he found out when he asked his longtime girlfriend, Claire McCarthy, to marry him. She said yes, and they planned their wedding for August 2016. When I asked Hagerup if he had been right, years earlier, that the two experiences would be similar, he replied, "Yes! Nervous beforehand. Elated and relieved afterward.

"Truthfully, I don't miss the day-to-day aspects of football at all. It was a grind on all fronts. What I *do* miss is punting on a regular basis, warming up before games in the Big House, celebrating wins and being with all my peers on campus.

"The camaraderie of being a college athlete is unparalleled. Ann Arbor was and is a special place, and in hindsight, the perfect challenge for me."

While Hagerup is sad that so few coaches and staffers from his time at Michigan are still there, "I'm very proud of how the team played last year. They looked hungry and inspired.

"You realize that the wheel keeps spinning after you and your teammates have left. The team runs out of the tunnel like always, and they still punt the football on fourth downs."

Jake Butt recognizes how lucky his timing is. The 2014 season, he told me, "was a low you couldn't even have imagined when you committed to play at Michigan. It wasn't fun. It was really, really bad. So bad, it didn't feel like football.

"I really thought I loved football, but Coach Harbaugh taught me how to love football even more. Especially at a historic school like this, you feel good, because you're doing it the right way in the classroom, you're playing by the rules on the field, and you're winning."

In the spring of 2016, Jake Butt had the option of returning for his senior year, or jumping to the NFL, where he was projected to be a third-round draft pick. "It was probably the biggest decision of my life. It wasn't an easy one, but I just thought about it, and weighed my two options: Getting to the NFL is a lifelong dream, and the money is big, but it's such a business. You're on a team now with 30-year-old guys with wives and kids.

"But if I came back, I could get my Michigan degree, and learn one more

year of football under these coaches, which will make me so much better prepared physically and mentally for the NFL. And of course I want to hit some
of those team goals. Beating Michigan State and Ohio State are definitely at
the top. That was a huge factor in coming back. I *have* to experience what
that's like. I need those! There are rivalries in the NFL, but there is no rivalry
like Michigan–Ohio State. If we can do that, it would be the biggest win of
my life—no question. Any sport. Any level."

When the people who had shared their part of the story with me read the book,
they frequently told me how surprising they found the rest of it, seeing what
everyone else was doing while they were drawing their own conclusions. They
were often struck that many others saw the situation the way they did, despite
very different vantage points, and had the courage to take action.

Two young men who made a big impression on the others in this story
didn't expect to play a role at all: Central Student Government leaders Michael Proppe and Bobby Dishell.

After Proppe earned his master's degree in accounting at Michigan, he took
the CPA exam, scoring so high he received the Elijah Watts Sells Award, given
to the top 75 exam performers out of the 93,742 people who took it. He now
works at PricewaterhouseCoopers in Detroit, performing due diligence on
mergers and acquisitions. "As accounting goes," he said, "it's as exciting as it
gets!"

After Proppe's term as CSG president ended, "I actually had time to date!
I've been dating my girlfriend almost two years."

The further Proppe gets from his experience at Michigan, the larger it
looms. "It is crazy to look at how much has changed in the three years since
we were elected. A few things that make me really, really happy about Michigan: Harbaugh has, singlehandedly, united the entire Michigan community
that was so broken a year and a half ago. It doesn't hurt that we had a pretty
good season last year, but it's so much more than that. He has been so visible
in student life—showing up in the lines of students waiting to get into the
Big House for graduation, eating at restaurants around town, giving recruits
tours of campus himself, showing up at random club sports practices. He's
creating opportunities for kids while marketing the Michigan brand in a far
more effective manner than any corporate advertising gimmick ever could."

Proppe and his former running mate, Bobby Dishell, the odd couple of
campus politics, have remained close. Dishell is starting his second year of his
Teach For America commitment, teaching seventh-grade English to 60

"amazing young minds who challenge me and my patience every day, without fail. Teaching is, without a doubt, one of the most difficult jobs. It tries you emotionally and intellectually."

In 2017, he will finish his master's in education at Johns Hopkins, then hopes to enter Michigan's joint JD/MBA program. Soon thereafter, he says, "I'll be chasing my long-held dream of running for political office, starting with the Michigan state legislature in 2020 or 2021. After vowing that I wouldn't settle in the Midwest like the rest of my family, it's seeming like the Michigan roots keep pulling me back home."

While Proppe admits he doesn't "have Bobby's itch to get back into politics, at least not yet, I'd consider running for Regent someday, and focus on designing ways for students to have a bigger voice in the governance of the university."

Dishell is as thrilled as his running mate at Michigan's turnaround. "I couldn't be happier with what [the University of] Michigan has become. I often get asked how it all happened, and my answer is that when you truly believe in something, you work collaboratively, you put your all into it, and you don't take no for an answer, you'll get there."

Against all odds, they did.

At the other end of the spectrum, the Regents seem equally pleased with Michigan's current direction, even if some might disagree on how they got here.

While Regent Andrea Fischer Newman remains friendly with Dave Brandon, she says, "Clearly, fans, supporters, students, faculty, and staff are happier now and we have an Athletic Director that people respect. We have ended up in a good place, and that's what people expect. I hope we can stay there.

"Great universities are rarely, if ever, without challenges, and I am proud of the University of Michigan and all the people who rose to the task of meeting this challenge."

The nature of that challenge was neatly captured in a comment from Regent Larry Deitch. "I am delighted with the hiring of Warde Manuel," he told me. "I know that the athletic department is in very capable hands. As you know, I strongly believed that the hiring of Coach Harbaugh was the right thing to do. His tenure to date has been even better than I thought it would be, and I thought that it would be pretty darn great. As we lawyers say, he is *sui generis*. That is, one of a kind. I knew that he was a good coach and that he will win championships. For me, the bonus is that Coach has made Michigan football fun again while at the same time giving off the vibe that he knows that Michigan is an academic institution and that is our core mission.

"President Schlissel, the Board of Regents, Director Manuel, and Coach Harbaugh are in complete alignment. That feels really, really good." '

That some of the leaders of the student government and the Board of Regents felt it necessary to confront the athletic department was unprecedented, but well within their jurisdiction. One of the most powerful components in this equation, however, wasn't organized until their concerns about Michigan athletics compelled them to band together and take action. This loosely defined group included lettermen, alumni, fans, and friends of Jim Harbaugh's. It had no official name, meeting times, publications, or protocols, but without the efforts of this collection of activists, the university officials above would not likely have had the support they needed to hire a new athletic director and football coach—and certainly not Harbaugh.

This group made up in passion what it lacked in authority. It included former Michigan football players John "Flame" Arbeznik, captain of the 1979 squad, based in Florida; John Ghindia, a teammate of Harbaugh's living in Michigan; and Todd Anson, Harbaugh's friend and occasional legal advisor, who lives in San Diego. These three worked hard to connect a surprising cross section of people, from three-term Regent Larry Deitch; to Rob Pollock, a friend of Harbaugh's dating back to junior high; to Jay Flannelly, the 43-year old Pizza House dishwasher better known as "The Beav."

"Something smelled rotten," Arbeznik told me, "and the call for redemption hit a fevered pitch amongst the alumni, students, and former players."

Looking back on their madcap mission, they are not surprised that Harbaugh returned to Ann Arbor, or that he's been so successful, although some are surprised by just how quickly he's accomplished so much.

"I thought he was a perfect fit and would make an immediate, enormous impact if we could land him," Anson said. "I gave him three to five years to restore Michigan football. It turns out that I *underestimated* him. He got us there in one."

They are also surprised by how quickly people forget how dire the situation was just two years ago. It is now taken as common knowledge that Michigan always wanted Harbaugh to return, and Harbaugh always would, though few believed either theory at the time.

"It's so easy now for everyone who wasn't so closely involved over the years to just say, 'Oh yeah, how hard was it to hire Harbaugh?'" says Harbaugh's longtime friend Rob Pollock. "'That was a no-brainer.' People forget two years ago everyone was making up reasons why Harbaugh *wouldn't* come home to Ann Arbor. Those who knew him, especially Ghindia, were ruthless in dispelling those falsehoods and making sure those who mattered knew the truth: Jim was interested and wanted to come back. Thank God!"

Anson concurs. "What looks like the biggest no-brainer ever today was unfathomable in early 2014. Convincing Harbaugh ended up being the lesser challenge we faced. Michigan itself was the enemy!"

In working to help make the Harbaugh-Michigan marriage possible, they have gained a little additional fame in the bargain. Dr. Bill Boike, owner of the pontoon boat Jim and Sarah Harbaugh boarded in July of 2014, has made up T-shirts and hats with S.S. *Boike* emblazoned on them, and enjoys giving them "to anyone who will wear them!" He's been hearing from friends he hasn't seen in years.

Jay Flannelly has since been mentioned in and interviewed for numerous radio, TV, and print stories. Booking representatives from the Howard Stern radio show and the popular TV talk show *Ellen* have contacted him. Business people frequently offer him money or jobs to connect them to Jim Harbaugh or Tom Brady, but he always declines. At a gathering recently, Flannelly found himself in a reception line behind U.S. Congresswoman Debbie Dingell. When she heard him talking, she turned around to ask, "Wait—are you 'The Beav'?"

But this loose band of brothers all have the same jobs they had before, and the same friends. No one to my knowledge has profited from their efforts, or tried to. No one better reflects this spirit of noblesse oblige than Flannelly. When "Flame" Arbeznik was in Ann Arbor for the homecoming game against Northwestern, he went to Pizza House, took the elevator to the second floor, right outside Flannelly's kitchen sinks, saw him working, and exclaimed, "You really *are* a dishwasher!" And he still is.

They had dinner at Pizza House that night with John Ghindia, toasting their unlikely success in helping restore Michigan football. Harbaugh himself always seeks out Flannelly during his weekly radio show at Pizza House, and often mentions him on the air.

Personal gain is not what inspired them to do what they did. Quite the opposite, their actions often came at considerable cost to their professional and personal lives. They shook it off, and kept grinding.

But what they received in the bargain was what exactly they wanted: new leadership, to fix what had been broken, and return Michigan to the place they knew and loved.

After the book came out, a retired athletic director at another Big Ten school called me to share his views of the book. Like almost everyone else, he was amazed by just how crazy things had gotten at Michigan, and how fast. But he was just as struck by how quickly the various groups mobilized to reclaim Michigan's identity. He then asked, "Those guys really believe in all that 'Michigan Man' stuff, don't they?"

"I believe they do," I said.

"We don't have that here," he said. "If we ended up in the same place, I'm not sure we could get out of it the way Michigan did."

Which, I have come to realize, is what makes Michigan Michigan.

The various stakeholders did an amazingly good job removing the many obstacles that would have prevented Harbaugh's return. But as John Ghindia himself said, the best they could do was simply give Harbaugh the chance to say yes or no. After that, it would be entirely up to him.

Once Jim Hackett finally popped Harbaugh the question, on Saturday night, December 27, Harbaugh decided to take his father's advice: "Follow your heart." More than a year later, I wanted to find out if he felt he'd made the right decision.

When I asked Harbaugh in the spring of 2016 what struck him about returning to his hometown, he'd clearly given it some thought, and had a few answers ready, from a few angles.

"What surprised me at first was how healthy people were, and young looking," he said. "Guys I went to grade school with and played with, they looked good. And the people in general seem more grounded, more rational, more centered. They're not in a hurry to be somewhere else. They like it where they are. It's a healthy, productive, happy place, more so than other places we lived."

Harbaugh's assessment was certainly flattering for Ann Arborites. While Ann Arbor consistently appears on the top ten places to live for everyone from students to small-business owners to senior citizens, it's a safe bet many of them would swap all those rankings for Harbaugh's praise, and for a simple reason: His appraisal indicates he has not just returned to his hometown, but found his home—perhaps his final one.

"What I've noticed is that people in Ann Arbor are very community oriented," Sarah added. "People here care about the town. They're connected to it. It's a very good place to raise a family," which is a very good thing for Michigan fans to hear from a woman who happens to be raising a family.

This jogged Jim's thinking. "I've noticed that it's less negative," he added. "People are less negative about where they live, and the people they meet. There's not as much gossip, not as much talking about people behind their backs. The people just feel like they're more trustworthy here."

Unlike Carr, Rodriguez, and Hoke, who all moved to Saline, a former farm town which has become something of an Ann Arbor suburb, the Harbaughs moved into one of Ann Arbor's oldest neighborhoods, a few doors up from Bo Schembechler's home—where Jim used to babysit Bo's son Shemy—and the same neighborhood where Fielding Yost, Fritz Crisler, and Don Canham lived.

The Harbaughs' kids go to Jim's former elementary school. His parents recently moved to the same street, when they could just as easily have relocated near John in Baltimore; or Joanie in Bloomington, Indiana; or stayed in Wisconsin. These decisions are not accidents.

Shifting to football, Sarah said, "Stanford has good fans, the 49ers have great fans, but Michigan football is a way of life here. They've been doing it for years, and they get it from their grandfathers, and their great-grandfathers. They have these memories that stretch back generations. It's great, but to be honest, it makes me sad that I don't have that past with it."

"Our kids will," Jim said.

Sarah turned serious for a moment, relating how some friends of hers actually hated playing college basketball, because it was such a grind. She then asked her husband, "Did you actually *enjoy* playing football here?"

"I didn't like playing football here," he said.

"Okay," Sarah replied, sympathetically.

"I *loved* playing football here!"

Just as the players Harbaugh recruits have their choice of teams, Harbaugh could coach damn near anywhere he wants. He chose to return to Michigan, though the process wasn't easy or obvious, for the most compelling reason of all: It makes him happy.

The morning before my interview with Jim and Sarah, they discovered a baby deer in the woods just off their driveway. They called Animal Control, who told them if the baby deer wasn't gone by the time they got home, to call them back, and they'd come over to help. But if she was gone, that would mean their mom had come back for her. In the meantime, the Harbaugh's children were captivated by the adorable animal.

"They had never seen a deer before," Sarah said, "let alone a baby deer. They were mesmerized."

When they returned that afternoon, the baby deer was gone, indicating its mother had come back to bring her home. The children missed their new friend, but were relieved that all was well.

Taking it all into account, from his new boss to his old pals to his children making friends with woodland creatures, did Harbaugh feel he had made the right decision in bypassing the bright lights and bigger bucks of the NFL for his old hometown?

"When people ask, 'How am I doing?'" he replied, "I tell them, 'Never better. *Never better.*'"

"When we saw that deer," Sarah added, "that's what we said: 'Who's got it better than us?'"

"I know the answer to that one!" Jim chimed in, beaming his famously broad smile. "Noooooobody!"

ACKNOWLEDGMENTS

"Every time, I think my next book won't be as difficult as the last one—and every time I'm wrong."

I wrote that in my previous book, *Fourth and Long*, and once again, I'm wrong, but this one started innocently enough. In October of 2014, a savvy editor named Ben Adams asked my friend David Larabell, now an agent for CAA, if I planned to write a book about Michigan football. Because Michigan was 2–4 at the time, I didn't think that would work. No, Adams said, about Michigan's athletic department, which I'd been writing about for *The Wall Street Journal*, Yahoosports.com's Postgame page, Michigan Radio commentaries, and my blog. After some consideration, I realized Adams was on to something.

With the help of John Lofy, Jim Tobin, Pete Uher and my wife, Christie, and two fantastic agents at William Morris Endeavors, Jay Mandel and Eric Lupfer, and their assistants, Lauren Shonkoff and Kitty Dulin, I put together a proposal, and got a contract with St. Martin's Press. In the bargain, I landed editor Marc Resnick, who had a clear vision for this book, and an unwavering commitment to making that a reality. The entire group at St. Martin's has backed this project to the hilt, including Laura Clark, Jaime Coyne, Karlyn Hixson, Amelie Littell, Joseph Rinaldi, the Associate Director of Publicity, a great bulldog to have on your side, and production editor Ken Silver, who handled many last-minute changes like a pro.

I researched and wrote this book in six months. If you're going to try that, you need help—and I got it, in spades, from Michigan's players to the president, and a lot of folks in between. That includes my parents, George and Grace, who once again provided emotional support and good cheer throughout, and John Lofy, who helped keep me going during the dog days.

I interviewed more than a hundred people for this book, filling a thousand pages of single-spaced notes. These people didn't have much to gain by telling their stories, and often much to lose, including their jobs. I've never covered a story so fraught with fear, yet they showed courage, a commitment to the truth, and ultimately, I believe, a great devotion to the University of Michigan at its best, in putting their thoughts on the record.

Among the players, Russell Bellomy, Devin Gardner, Jordan Kovacs, and Ryan Van Bergen were particularly helpful. Will Hagerup deserves extra credit for sharing his remarkable story. Michigan fans can take justifiable pride in the caliber of young men the football program is producing. Likewise, recent graduate Jay Sarkar, and Central Student Government presidents Michael Proppe and Bobby Dishell were generous with their time, help, and observations.

Michigan's football lettermen gave the reader scenes they would never see otherwise. These included John "Flame" Arbeznik, Bill and Don Dufek, Jr., Don Eaton, Jon Giesler, John Ghindia, Rick Leach, Yale Van Dyne, Tim Wadhams, and John Wangler.

The list of alumni is just as long, and were just as accommodating, including Todd Anson, Bill Boike, Lyle G. Davis, Bob Elgin, Jay "The Beav" Flannelly, Frank Legacki and Alicia Torres, Buddy Moorehouse and Brian Kruger, Pete Nichols, Sherri Stephens, and Jeff Viscomi, who shared the story of Tom Brady folding his laundry in the apartment laundry room, instead of dumping it in a pile on the machines, like everyone else. Thanks to Marek Krzyzowski and his mom, Ruth, for tipping me off. I also received vital help from many people with a deep interest in the university, including Peg Canham, Ben and Anne McCready, Tom Monaghan, and Tom Ufer.

Many current and former employees of the athletic department agreed to talk with me, including Bruce Berque, Marty Bodnar, Steve Burns, Ryan Duey, Kurt Gulbrand, Greg Harden, Annette Howe—one of the nicest people you could meet—Bruce Madej, Jamie Morris, Joe Parker, John Paul, Chrissi Rawak, Jason Winters, and Michigan football's medical staff, including Paul Schmidt. Former athletic directors Tom Goss and Bill Martin and current A.D. Jim Hackett also helped with multiple interviews. Some of my subjects I'm thanking most by thanking least, but you know who you are.

This book also gave me a plausible excuse to seek out some of my favorite campus leaders, including Percy Bates, Kim Clarke, Paul Courant, Nicholas Delbanco, Edie Goldenberg, Terry McDonald, Ted Spencer, and Thomas Zurbuchen, who showed me how this amazing machine of a university functions. I benefitted once again from talking with former Michigan president

James Duderstadt, current Northwestern president Morton Schapiro, and Michigan's new president, Mark Schlissel, thanks to Christine Grant, Alan Cubbage, and Lisa Rudgers, respectively. All were a pleasure, and proved once again it's possible to walk with kings and maintain the common touch.

Michigan's Regents keep a low profile, by design. While they didn't come running at my invitation, they were willing to share their perspectives which added greatly to our understanding of what happened and why—and really, how this university works. I also believe voters will be reassured the university is being led by smart, fair-minded people whose love for Michigan runs deep. When you spend your own money to campaign for a job that doesn't pay a dime, for the honor of being criticized by people who don't even sign their names, all to ensure the University of Michigan continues to go in the right direction—well, I'd say that's a pretty fair litmus test for being true to your school. Thank you, Mark Bernstein, Larry Deitch, Andrea Fischer Newman, and Kathy White.

This is my first book to have photos since *Bo's Lasting Lessons*. Like the interviews, the photos for this book were much harder to collect, due to the range of people we were trying to capture. A lot of people pitched in, including the good folks at the Bank of Ann Arbor, Greg Kinney at the Bentley Historical Library—who also happens to be the best in the business—Roger Hart at Michigan Photography, Beth Moceri, Allison Farrand, and Mark Bealafeld at the *Michigan Daily*, Perich Advertising + Design, Jenny Sparks at the Loveland, *Colorado Reporter-Herald*, and Eric Upchurch at MGoBlog, not to mention many of the people thanked above.

I have followed Michigan football closely for years, but that does not spare you from hundreds of hours of research. This one would have been impossible to complete without the help of Ace Anbender and Alejandro Zuniga. They are former students of mine, who've become great journalists; Ace for MGoBlog, where he's now Brian Cook's trusted lieutenant, and Alejandro for the *Michigan Daily*, where he's won several awards. These two went far above and beyond, organizing the long and often scattered interview transcripts, the timelines for the many different story lines, and original research into everything from the Coke "retail activation," to the attendance figures to the turnover data. They were smart, funny, and cheerful throughout. They also read drafts and made both factual corrections and valued editorial suggestions.

I also received help from three well-known college football historians: Greg Dooley of MVictors.com; the *Toronto Sun's* John Kryk, author of *Natural Enemies*, and the Big Ten Network's star anchor, Dave Revsine, who produced a popular book of serious scholarship, *Opening Kickoff*.

If you look at just about any page of this book, you can probably circle three dozen dates, names, titles and numbers. Multiply that by 460 pages, and you get some 16,000 facts to look up, spell correctly, fix and confirm are accurate. It's a virtually impossible task, but the good folks above helped considerably, as did my small army of expert readers, who caught corrections, and gave great advice on the tone, structure and balance of the book. Thank you, Jim Carty, Brian Cook, Vince Duffy, Thomas Lebien, John Lofy, Jim Russ, Nathan Sandals, Peter Uher, Ira Weintraub, and my wife, Christie.

Speaking of whom, Christie never complained about my six months "in the writer's cave," even when I failed to take a day off in Mexico, Paris, Florida, New York, and Northern Michigan. I'm sure I was not the most interesting traveling companion, but Christie provided not only patience and understanding, she also put the photo section together, and gave me more help of all kinds—e-mailing, fact-checking, proofreading, editing, and advising—than anyone else, all while running our home, and moving us into a new one.

Thank you.